Baseball's Business
The WINTER MEETINGS

VOLUME 1
1901-1957

Edited by Steve Weingarden and Bill Nowlin

Associate editors Marshall Adesman and Len Levin

Foreword by Roland Hemond

Introduction by Steve Weingarden

Society for American Baseball Research, Inc.
Phoenix, AZ

Baseball's Business: The Winter Meetings
Volume 1 - 1901-1957
Edited by Steve Weingarden and Bill Nowlin
Associate editors Marshall Adesman and Len Levin

Copyright © 2016 Society for American Baseball Research, Inc.
All rights reserved. Reproduction in whole or in part without permission is prohibited.

ISBN 978-1-943816-37-8
Ebook ISBN 978-1-943816-36-1

Cover and book design: Gilly Rosenthol

Cover photo courtesy of the National Baseball Hall of Fame.

Society for American Baseball Research
Cronkite School at ASU
555 N. Central Ave. #416
Phoenix, AZ 85004
Phone: (602) 496-1460
Web: www.sabr.org
Facebook: Society for American Baseball Research
Twitter: @SABR

Baseball's Business: The Winter Meetings
Volume 1 - 1901-1957

Foreword by Roland Hemond 1
Introduction by Steve Weingarden 3
1901 FIRSTS, FOIBLES, AND FAILURES — Jeremy Green 6
1902 A PEACE ACCORD — Abigail Miskowiec 12
1903 MARRIED LIFE BEGINS — Marshall Adesman 16
1904 POWER PLAY — Steve Weingarden and Eric Frost 27
1905 CONTROVERSY OVER LEAGUE PRESIDENTS TAKES CENTER STAGE AT MEETINGS — Dennis Pajot 32
1906 GRADUAL DÉTENTE, GROWING PAINS — Christopher Matthews 37
1907 THE NEW COOPERATION — "THE MANIFEST DESIRE TO ELEVATE THE GAME" — Bill Nowlin 40
1908 MAJOR ISSUES IN THE MINORS, BRIBERY CHARGES, AND WORLD SER ES TICKET SCANDAL — Dennis Pajot 45
1909 IF IT TAKES ALL WINTER — Marshall Adesman 57
1910 HO-HUM AFFAIRS — Dennis Pajot 71
1911 SCANDAL? WHAT SCANDAL? — R. J. Lesch 76
1912 DISCUSSING INTERLEAGUE PLAY AND THE SLOW PACE OF THE GAME — Andy Bokser 81
1913 PREPARING FOR THE FIGHTS AHEAD — Travis Stern 85
1914 WARS AT HOME AND ABROAD — Travis Stern 93
1915 PEACETIME FOR THE NATIONAL PASTIME — Rich Bogovich 101
1916 THE MINORS AND PLAYERS ARE RESTLESS — Rich Bogovich 106
1917 WAR? WHAT WAR? — Paul Hensler 112
1918 BASEBALL RETURNS FROM THE GREAT WAR — Jacob Pomrenke 118
1919 THE END OF THE DEADBALL ERA — Jacob Pomrenke 123
1920 THE YEAR THAT ROCKED BASEBALL AND CHANGED IT FOREVER — Marshall Adesman 128
1921 FIRST WITH LANDIS — Joe Marren 140
1922 TO MEET OR NOT TO MEET? — Chris Jones 147
1923 THE BATTLE OF AVALON — Mike Lynch 154
THE NEGRO LEAGUES COME EAST: THE EASTERN COLORED LEAGUE AND THE AMERICAN NEGRO LEAGUE — Jim Overmyer 158
1924 BIG DRAMA IN THE BIG APPLE — Aimee Gonzalez 166
1925 DIFFERENT SCRIPT, SAME CLASS — Aimee Gonzalez 171
1926 CHANGING OF THE GUARD — Abigail Miskowiec 176

1927	A LITTLE ON THE DRAFTY SIDE — Marshall Adesman	180
1928	THE DRAFT MESS AND GLIMPSES INTO THE FUTURE — Silvio Sansano and Marshall Adesman	191
1929	LET'S ALL PLAY BY THE SAME RULES — Frederick C. Bush	203
1930	THE JUDGE AND THE MAHATMA DEBATE THE CHAIN STORE SYSTEM — Gary Levy	209
1931	BASEBALL GETS A TASTE OF THE DEPRESSION — Ted Leavengood	216
1932	WEALTH OF CHANGES REVITALIZES BASEBALL IN POOR TIMES — Ely Sussman	221
1933	THE SELL-OFF — Jason C. Long	225
1934	THE REDS GO UNDER THE LIGHTS WHILE THE BRAVES GO TO THE DOGS — Bob LeMoine	232
1935	INSPIRATIONAL DELEGATES CHURN CREAM INTO BUTTER — Ely Sussman	240
1936	HOME PLATE AND HURLERS — Stephen R. Keeney	244
1937	MORE BUSINESS THAN BASEBALL — Zak Schmoll	252
1938	OUT OF THE HAT — Jason C. Long	255
1939	THE TIE GOES TO THE COMMISSIONER — Jason C. Long	264
1940	LANDIS'S FINAL REIGN — Nick Waddell and Bill Nowlin	271
1941	WAR AND UNCERTAINTY — Jeremy Green	277
1942	GREEN LIGHT: MATTERS OF MANPOWER AND THE MILITARY — Frederick C. Bush	288
1943	WAR ON THE HOME FRONT — Nick Klopsis	294
1944	A NEW ERA WITHOUT LANDIS — Joe Marren	299
1945	RESUMING PEACETIME BASEBALL — Andy Bokser	305
1946	TRANQUILITY AND TURBULENCE — Jerry Nechal	309
1947	LATIN AMERICA, LEO THE LIP, AND HIGH SCHOOL HIJINKS — Gary Levy	314
1948	CONCERNS AND CONFLICTS REGARDING TELEVISED BALL GROW STRONGER — Gary Levy	322
1949	BONUSES, BARGAINS, AND BROADCASTS — Jeremy Green	329
1950	THE HAPPY DAGGER — Nick Klopsis	337
1951	OPEN CLASSIFICATION — Steven Bryant	342
1952	CHANGING DEMOGRAPHICS AND BROADCAST CHALLENGES — Gregory H. Wolf	347
1953	PENSION COLLISION — Abigail Miskowiec	356
1954	LOOKING WEST — Bill Felber	361
1955	MAJORS AND MINORS CLASH OVER MONEY — Dale Voiss	370
1956	A LOVE-FEST — Jim Wohlenhaus	374
1957	SUNDAY NIGHT FIGHT — Mike Lynch	378
	CONTRIBUTORS	383

FOREWORD

By Roland Hemond

THE FIRST WINTER MEETINGS I ATtended was in 1952. I was with the Boston Braves, and we traveled by train from Boston to Phoenix—2 1/2 days it took. I haven't missed many of the Winter Meetings through the years. I know I went to at least 50 in a row, for sure.

I started in baseball working for the Hartford Chiefs. I used to unlock the ballpark in the morning and help Harvey Stone, the trainer, to sweep out the park. Clean it up and get the concession stands ready. Sell tickets in the afternoon and do some p.a. announcing sometimes. Then I would check in the ticket takers and the concessions people at the end of the night, and then lock up the park at 11, 11:30 at night. You wear all sorts of hats, but you're getting your start.

1952 was my first full year with the Boston Braves. I joined them late in September '51. I was typing up scouting reports and stuff like that. John Quinn was the general manager then. He was on that train. We picked up Bob Coleman, the manager, at Evansville. We picked up certain people as we would go along. There was about 8 or 10 people in the Braves party. My boss was John Mullen, the farm and scouting director.

We didn't have computers then, so we had big boxes with all of our scouting reports. It was quite an adventure. I enjoyed the conversation. I did a lot of listening. I was a youngster, breaking in. I figured the best way to learn was to keep quiet and listen to these baseball people.

It's strange today. When I drive to the office here in Phoenix, I see that building—the Westward Ho Hotel. It brings back the memories every time I drive by. Ted McGrew was a great old scout, and when we checked in, he called downstairs and said, "I want a tub of beer." She said, "What do you mean, a tub of beer?" "Well, I'm going to fill the bathtub full of water. I need some ice and bring some cases of beer." People would go to the bathroom and pick up a beer out of the bathtub.

I was always so deeply involved. We had to be well prepared for the Rule 5 draft, and then we had appointments with people for interviews, people who had applied for jobs. I tried to give people attention. Frank Robinson used to say, "I hate going to the winter meetings with Roland because we would never get back to our room." People looking for jobs would be trailing me and they sort of knew how I got into the game.... Frank would say, "I'll see you later." He would give up on me because I'd be interrupted all the time.

They used to have two meetings. They'd have the minor-league meetings first. I'd go to both. The year with the Angels, we were flying back and as we were going to be landing in Los Angeles, the flight attendant came by and she had a great big plastic bag. She said, "You're going to have to remove your shoes. We can't get the landing gear down and if we do a belly-flat landing, your feet may go in different directions and the heels might strike somebody's head and you might fracture somebody's skull." We were all kidding around. We had traded Dean Chance to the Minnesota Twins for Jimmie Hall and Don Mincher. Bill Rigney had been fooling with a lineup card and he said, "I'll bat Hall third and Mincher fourth." When that stewardess came by, I said, "Hey, Bill, you might as well tear up that lineup card. We're not going to make it." Sense of humor. We'd been drinking a little bit, I think. Then Bob Reynolds, the president, said, "Hey, Roland, go forward where Gene Autry is sitting and help him take his boots off." I was on the floor, pulling his boots off and he said, "Isn't it a shame? A cowboy can't die with his boots on."

Fortunately, the finally got the landing gear down and we made a good landing. We were looking out there and they already had been putting foam on the runway.

BASEBALL'S BUSINESS: THE WINTER MEETINGS

Bill Veeck came to the White Sox and in '77 we gave it a real good run again. We came back after a dismal '76 season and made a good run that year against Kansas City. Working with Bill was a tremendous experience that I greatly treasure and will forever relish. It was a fantastic experience to be with him. In all facets of life. He was just an incredible man. He used to say, "Don't bother preparing a budget, Roland. We don't have any money. We'll think of something." We had a lot of fun and competed as best we could.

As a brand-new owner, he told me, "Let your imagination run rampant." We were at the Diplomat in Hollywood, Florida and I asked him, "What if we grab a table, and put up a sign that says, ‹Open for Business?'" He said, "What are you waiting for? Do it."

John Mullen was with Atlanta or Houston then, I don't remember. He said, "Gee, it looks like you're running a meat market. I'm embarrassed for you." I said, "I'm not embarrassed. We just got a trade offer." I called Bill upstairs and I said, "Hey Bill, we've got a trade proposal already." He said, "I'll be right down." We were there the rest of the day.

Bill had our PR man, Buck Peden, call on the phone every half an hour. Bill would answer and pretend another GM was calling: "Hey, Buzzie, how you doing?"—to make other clubs think we were doing business. About 10:15 that night, Bill told me, "We're going to make four deals by midnight." And we did. I went there on a coach ticket, and I came back first class with Bill.

As a GM or executive vice president of baseball operations for the Angels, the Orioles, the White Sox, and the Diamondbacks, yes, I was in charge of the whole operation at the Winter Meetings, but I had some good people working with me. You're only as good as the people who are working with you. The scouts, your assistants…you don't do it by yourself by any means. It's a people game, to me. You have to show recognition and praise to those who are helping you. Bill made it easy to make recommendations to him. Birdie Tebbetts was a good mentor, too. I had a multitude of people who helped me. John Mullen was perfect as a mentor. He had the knowledge and patience to teach various subjects, and was imaginative with even the basics.

Jerome Holtzman, when he was leaving Chicago, told me something, He said, "Roland, I really admire you. You never told me something I didn't already know." He never got any scoops. I respected those who would not want me to break confidentiality.

The last few years, it's changed dramatically, with computers. People talk a different language. And actually a lot of times they don't talk to one another. They just email. I don't think you get the personal touch. The laughs, the sense of humor that guys have. You have a good time and you close a trade.

I treasured going to the Winter Meetings. You don't see people for a whole year and then here you are, face to face, and trying to make a deal.

INTRODUCTION

THIS BOOK—ABOUT MEETings—should never have been written. Meetings tend to be boring. Yet the eventual development of this book was inevitable. Whether it was the 14 meetings of the National Association of Base Ball Players—with the final meeting in November of 1870 at the Grand Central Hotel in New York—or the 1871 formation of the National Association of Professional Base-ball Players at Collier's Rooms on Broadway, or the February 1876 meeting (back at the Grand Central Hotel), baseball has always liked its meetings. Most businesses do, and once an organization grows to a certain level, meetings are an outcome of formal infrastructure. The meetings are where and how important decisions get made.

Indeed, the first chapter of this book—Jeremy Green's winter meetings installment—begins with, "Professional baseball was mired in conflict in 1901." He goes on to share stories about violations of agreements, external threats, internal disunity, and defense of self-interests. Nearly every year of winter meetings has similar stories and hidden treasures that help resolve moments of wonder that have periodically crossed your mind as a baseball fan, and possibly as a scholar. So much of baseball history happened at the winter meetings. This book provides you with a historical answer to the business of baseball over many of the early years of the minor leagues, the American League, and the youthful National League. Important philosophies regarding chosen identity, reactions to societal trends, agreements on how to operate, approval of new members, and player transactions emerged from the discussions and decisions made at the winter meetings. Not so boring.

Thus, there is a book—an exciting book—about meetings. When I transitioned to co-chair of the SABR Business of Baseball Committee, my generous predecessor Gary Gillette and equally generous co-chair John Ruoff spent much time answering my many questions, before I agreed to take on the co-chair responsibility. What emerged most from those discussions was that the committee would greatly benefit from a project that rallied its members together. I took Gary's and John's experiences with the committee to heart, and reflected on what might be a good fit for this particular committee. On November 20, 2010, the following note—edited for this publication—went out to SABR Business of Baseball committee members.

Hello Business of Baseball committee member.

As we have entered the "Hot Stove" time of the year, there are opportunities to share with you.

We seek your interest and willingness to write a book about the History of the Winter Meetings. The concept is to write a three-to-five-page summary of each particular winter meeting—which would be deemed a book chapter. We plan to "match" authors to the city where each Winter Meeting was held, and so for a number of different cities, we will be looking for authors who live in, have lived in, or have an interest in a particular city. The Winter Meetings (including, MLB, MiLB, and Negro Leagues) have been held for more than 100 years. There will be plenty of opportunities, and we can find a role for anyone who wishes to be involved as an author, editor/reader, researcher, etc. Can we count on your interest in getting involved with this project as a potential author, editor/reader, researcher, or in some other role? If so, please contact Steve Weingarden. Depending on the flow of responses, we will most likely kickoff in January with a project team meeting, where we further define the parameters.

I was hoping that the History of the Winter Meetings project would be the tent-pole project that rallied committee members. It wasn't.

Before sending that recruiting email—as well as several follow-ups, through various SABR outlets—I had a ballpark figure for how many interested responses I would require to go forward with the project. I really wanted 40 to 50 interested SABR members in order to proceed. I would continue anyway as long as I was at 25 or more interested SABR members. I ended up with approximately 20 at the end of January 2011. The project, according to my own parameters, should have ended at that point. It didn't.

Many of those original 20 SABR members have remarkably lasted through the course of the development of this book, and I feel as though I have grown to know them well. One of those members was Jason Long, who wrote an email to me expressing his hopes that the project would advance, and also his excitement over the idea. I had developed the same feeling. I conducted preliminary research for a few of the years, and felt compelled by what I found. I wanted to know about the hidden and previously unpublished knowledge from each winter meeting; I wanted to read the book!

So I redoubled my author-recruitment strategies, continuing to reach out to SABR members, and reaching outside of SABR. By March 17, 2011, there were 65 authors committed and I began the project. I remember several potential authors who chose not to participate but wished me luck and let me know that they believed the book would take possibly five years to complete. It was huge in scope, would require difficult research, and necessitated diligent oversight of authors throughout the project.

The issue of scope required me to alter the initial vision of the book. It became clear fairly early on that the baseball winter meetings could not be covered in one volume. Additionally, coverage dating back to the 1850s would have stalled the book indefinitely. The same was true for coverage beyond the primary leagues typically associated with the winter meetings. So I placed the starting line as 1901—the year the National Association of Professional Baseball Leagues (NAPBL, the minor leagues umbrella organization) was formed. Considering how much of this book is devoted to the minor leagues, the 1901 date made logical sense, especially considering the interactions between the NAPBL and the major leagues from the start. Also, January 1901 marked the reorganization of the American League, transitioning from minor to major. So the end of the year represented one of the earliest winter meetings of the newly organized league.

Indeed, the book required difficult research. Many of the authors didn't have access to the needed databases, and some authors were less familiar with the specific search terms that would result in success. I pulled together research "care packages" for many of the authors to use as anchors for their own additional research and for the composition of their chapters. However, research is much more than locating the facts. The interpretation of that research and its insertion into chapters had to be as correct as possible. Our team delved into uncharted territory, and we insisted on accuracy as a guiding principle. There were no previous books on the topic to reference, and triangulation, with the inclusion of firsthand accounts would be impossible for many of the past years. I relied on our team's capabilities to recognize fallacies in the research and the writing. For this, I am thankful for the efforts of Marshall Adesman and Len Levin. This book is unquestionably better to read and more accurate because of their immense contributions.

I would be remiss to not call special attention to Marshall. He is one of the 20 SABR members who originally expressed interest in this book. Marshall has stayed with this book from start to finish, and he has read every chapter, and most chapters through several drafts. He has painstakingly questioned potentially misrepresented information, and suggested additions that are designed to make this book more enjoyable for our audience—for you. When author attrition became an issue that almost dissolved this book, Marshall volunteered to step forward and write a few chapters. Through conversations, Marshall has always been my compass to ensure that the proper attention is given to the minor leagues. He is not only an excellent editor and a former minor-league executive, but he is also a sounding board for me, and he has become a close friend.

As for the diligent management of authors, I built spreadsheets, sent group updates to authors, and followed up on an individual basis with each author to encourage and guide their progress. I was honored when Don Frank (who will be featured in Volume 2) let me know how much he appreciated my editing approach. Yet, five years of author management is a long time — and, in reality this book took nearly six years to produce. Let me be blunt in saying that this book might not have been completed if not for the emergence of Bill Nowlin. Bill became involved in the book somewhere around the beginning of 2012, but in 2015, after he checked in on its status, I asked (maybe pleaded) with him to help solve the author attrition challenge and also to consider taking over the author management. Thankfully, after much discussion, Bill agreed. Almost immediately, a "Bill Nowlin" effect occurred; SABR members, many within Bill's broad SABR network of relationships, eagerly volunteered to write chapters. Bill's access to SABR process information also proved invaluable, as did his diligence in keeping authors on track. Bill also brought Len Levin aboard as an editor. I enjoyed the collegial manner in which Bill and I were able to interact, and we had fun with the choices around final book design. I have no doubt that this book is ready for publication in 2016 thanks to Bill.

These are the stories behind how the book came to completion, but it's the details of the stories at the winter meetings that make this book so rich and interesting. It's the stories like the ones that Roland Hemond shares in the foreword that make me want to read more. What good fortune to have Roland write the foreword for a book about the winter meetings. When I — and several other individuals – imagined the book foreword in 2011, one name stood out as an aspiration to write the foreword — it was Roland Hemond. Roland's impact on baseball is profound. According to his National Baseball Hall of Fame description in the list of recipients of the Buck O'Neil Award (he was the second recipient, preceded only by Buck O'Neil),

"Hemond revolutionized front-office management and strategy during a seven-decade career in baseball, while spending his post-general manager days assisting baseball family members in need." Roland, his work as a baseball executive, and his accomplishments for the game embody the individuals that our authors write about in this book. I and many others are grateful to have Roland as part of these pages.

Absolutely this book was inevitable. I want to know the stories of the baseball winter meetings. Others who worked on this book want to know the stories of the baseball winter meetings. I hope that you want to know the stories of the baseball winter meetings.

I speak for our team in saying that we hope you find this book to be a rewarding read, whether you read it straight through, or pick out the years most desirable to you. Both approaches are appropriate for this material. Reading in sequence opened my eyes to how trends in baseball evolved from year to year. Reading a particular year allowed to me to seek out answers to specific questions.

Each chapter is designed to begin with a high-level overview of that year's winter meetings. More detail regarding the plans and decisions of the minor leagues and the major leagues follows. Finally, player transactions are recounted. An individual chapter also reflects the methods each author applied in order to tell the needed story in the manner most appropriate to the year and to his or her own writing style. As available and appropriate, sidebars are also included with chapters.

As an exciting supplement to the book, you will find Jim Overmyer's article on the Eastern Colored League Winter Meetings.

I know that our team has exhausted our efforts to pull together this book for you. Perhaps this book will be karma for painful meetings you may have endured over the years. In the following pages, our team is at your service, and we thank you and are honored by your sharing in these stories with us.

Enjoy.

Steve Weingarden

— 1901 —
FIRSTS, FOIBLES, AND FAILURES

By Jeremy Green

Introduction and Context

PROFESSIONAL BASEBALL WAS mired in conflict throughout 1901. The American League abandoned the National Agreement of 1892 and announced its intention to compete on equal terms with the National League. The National League faced not only an external threat from the self-proclaimed new major league, but internal disunity revolving around organization and leadership. With the National Agreement having been abrogated and the big leagues at war, the minor leagues circled the wagons and set about defending their own interests. This strife set the stage at all three professional baseball meetings in 1901.

The first meeting, that of the National Association of Professional Baseball Leagues, was held at the Fifth Avenue Hotel in New York City on October 25. This was the second meeting of the year for the National Association, which represented all of the minor leagues except the California League.[1] The leagues had previously met in Chicago at the Leland Hotel on September 6 to draft an agreement that would form a new organization for their mutual protection.[2] The minor leagues were meeting in New York to ratify the agreement.

The American League met in Chicago at the Grand Pacific Hotel on December 2.[3] The new major league had proved to be a potent and viable force in baseball and a serious challenger to the National League. It had acquired four teams from the National when that league contracted, and also inserted itself into Chicago.[4] The AL was meeting for the first time as a major league.

The National League gathered in New York at the Fifth Avenue Hotel on December 10 for the last and most contentious of the three meetings. Casting a shadow over this one was the new contender, the American League. The threat of this strong newcomer, concerns about the league's structure and leadership, and the election of a new president were already causing rifts within the organization. .

Player Movement

Little player movement or trades highlighted any of the three meetings. Business affairs and arguments left scant room for player trades in the National League, and while affairs were much more harmonious during the American League meeting, no trades were listed as having taken place in Chicago. The main form of player movement that winter was the removal of a number of players from the blacklist. The blacklist had been adopted by professional baseball starting with the adoption of the reserve clause by the National League in 1879, and was used primarily to prevent players from jumping to other teams for better salaries. The blacklist barred other teams in the league and their affiliates from hiring a player who had abandoned his contract.[5]

In the American League, pitcher Bill Dinneen was removed from the blacklist and allowed to return to play for the 1902 season.[6] (Dinneen had jumped a contract with Boston's National League club to play for the city's American League team.[7]) Charles Comiskey announced that he had acquired a third baseman for the season, but declined to say who it was. The AL continued to urge players to abandon the National League. One, Brooklyn outfielder-first baseman Joe Kelley, was lured to Baltimore for the 1902 season.[8]

Despite conflicts over the presidency and the future of the league, some trading and player movement took place during the National League meeting. One major deal saw new Chicago manager Frank Selee signing first baseman Hal O'Hagan from the Rochester team.[9] The Giants reportedly signed L. Quinlan, a shortstop with Montreal, and Matt McIntyre, an outfielder with Philadelphia's AL club, although the deal was denied by Connie Mack—and, indeed, McIntyre did remain with the A's.[10] There were attempts made to move manager Ned Hanlon to the New York Giants, but Hanlon remained loyal to Brooklyn. There were reports that the Giants and Detroit had tried to sign Joe Kelley, but as we have seen, he wound up in Baltimore.[11]

The Business Side

The National Association:

Business affairs dominated each of the three meetings. Foremost on the agenda at the National Association meeting was the ratification of a new National Agreement, which protected the minors from the effects of the conflict in the National League and American League; in particular, having their players plundered by the major clubs.[12] The agreement was binding for 10 years and covered salary limits, transfer of players, and rules regulating contract-jumping.[13] National Association President Pat T. Powers had gotten agreements from the American and National League presidents, who were by and large willing to respect existing contracts, though the Brooklyn and Boston clubs in the National League deferred responding until the matter could be taken up with the rest of the league. The minor leagues agreed on a sliding scale, illustrated in Table 1, below, for salary caps and fines for contract-jumping. The meeting set draft periods for each classification of the minors, with Class-A teams getting the most generous allotment of time to sign new talent, nearly the entire autumn.[14]

Clubs that signed the agreement were bound to the salary caps, and those that exceeded the caps would first receive a warning, followed by the withdrawal of benefits and protections of the Association. Similar penalties existed for players who violated contracts by leaving without consent to play for other clubs. Not only would the player draw a fine, but he would be disqualified from playing with any Association club until the Association rescinded the ban.[15] The minors agreed to use a contract form similar to the one employed by the National League.

The minor-league magnates further agreed on a new classification system for the leagues that ran from Class A down to Class D. Table 2 illustrates which leagues were placed under which classification. Though there were no Class-D teams in the minors at this time, there was already talk about creating a Class-E circuit as well. Three leagues petitioned the Association for membership, the Ohio State League and two nascent leagues in Texas and in the "Northwest."[16]

Table 1: Minor League Caps and Fines

League Classification	Salary Cap	Fines for Contract Jumping	Draft Period
A	$2000	$1000	Oct 1-Dec 1
B	$1200	$600	Dec 1-Jan 1
C	$1000	$400	Jan 1-Feb 1
D	$900	$300	N/A

Table 2: League Classification Scheme

League Classification	Leagues Within Category
A	Eastern League, Western League
B	Southern Association, Western Association, New York State League, New England League, I-I-I League
C	Pacific National League, Connecticut State League
D	None at this time

In addition to business relating to the new National Agreement, the minors addressed the issue of protection fees paid to the majors under the old National Agreement. Since the old agreement had expired, President Powers took the position that that the minor teams were due a refund.[17]

Finally, the minors held elections for various offices, which included James O'Rourke to the National Board of Arbitration and Henry Chadwick unanimously elected to honorary membership in the new organization. The Board of Arbitration conducted brisk business on player transgressions. Among its decisions were the denial of Michael F. Hickey's request for release from reservation by Lowell of the New

England League, and the investigation of several instances of contract violation including the case of an umpire/player, George Prentiss, who was charged by the Waterbury club with playing for another club under an assumed name.[18] The National Arbitration Board resolved the case Waterbury's favor in 1902 and ordered Prentiss to return to Waterbury, though by then Prentiss had jumped to the Boston American League club.[19] Prentiss died that same year, however, rendering the decision moot.[20]

American League

In contrast to the National League, the American League meeting was reported as being fairly harmonious. As reported in the *Chicago Tribune*:

"There is a strong contrast between the two big leagues this winter. While the National has so many important matters to attend to, the American has its plans for next year all laid out and well under way toward accomplishment. The only way they could be seriously upset would be a wholesale kidnapping of American League players by the old league or tempting them away by outbidding the already high salaries offered. Many players would stand by their contract at that."[21]

With all clubs represented, Byron Bancroft "Ban" Johnson was reelected president, with Charles W. Somers again winning the vice presidency.[22] One of the first orders of business was the selection of committees, including a committee on playing rules made up of Detroit manager Frank Dwyer (a former umpire), A's owner Connie Mack, and Cleveland owner Jack Kilfoyle; a committee to discuss the transfer of the Milwaukee club to St. Louis, consisting of owners Ben Shibe (Athletics), Fred Postal (Senators), and Charles Comiskey (White Sox); and a new board of directors.[23] Among the committee rulings was a decision to limit teams to a total of 15 players.

One of the main orders of business, and a point of contention at the American League meeting, was the transfer of the Milwaukee franchise to St. Louis. Milwaukee's co-owners, brothers Henry and Matt Killilea, were divided on the question of moving the team. Henry told the meeting he felt the team should remain in Milwaukee and that Matt should join him in retirement, but Matt held with the other magnates and the league approved the transfer. Matt Killilea would move to St. Louis as owner, sharing control of the club with Fred C. Gross after Henry Killilea disposed of his stock in the club.[24] In addition, the league announced a roster of teams and dates for the 1902 playing season, which was to run from April 23 to October 15, starting a week later than the previous season. The Chicago franchise was awarded the pennant for the 1901 season at the Board of Directors meeting.[25]

Changes in ownership of both the Detroit and Washington clubs were announced at the meeting. The Tigers switched hands from owners James Burns and George Stallings to a stock company headed by S.A. Angus. The Senators' Fred Postal exchanged co-ownership with Jim Manning for co-ownership with Thomas Loftus.[26]

Ban Johnson ended the meeting with the proclamation that the AL would move to oppose wagering at league ballparks, including expelling spectators caught gambling on park grounds.[27] Johnson had made a point of upholding the American League as being committed to both fair and clean play, and was thus firmly against betting on baseball.[28]

National League

The National League meeting was the most contentious of the three winter meetings in 1901. The main arguments among magnates concerned the election of a new president and the proposal from some of the magnates to alter the organizational structure of the league into a trust. There is some conflict in the record as to who first sought to create a trust. There are some indications that Albert Spalding and Jim Hart sought to organize the league in this fashion in the late 1890s, but were unable to secure enough options on individual clubs to enact this plan. John T. Brush, owner of the Cincinnati team, proposed a new scheme for a baseball trust in 1901 and acquired the backing of Giants owner Andrew Freedman. In a meeting at Freedman's Red Bank, New Jersey, estate, two other magnates, Frank De Haas Robison of St. Louis and Arthur Soden of Boston, agreed to back Freedman and

Brush's trust. The Brush plan would have eliminated the office of president and turned executive duties for the league over to a four-man board of regents. Profits would be split between shareholders in the trust, with the lion's share (30 percent) going to Freedman, and 12 percent each to Brush, Soden, and Robison. The rest was to be divided among the other NL owners.[29] Management of each team, down to the supplies they used, would be handled by the trust.[30]

Freedman, an enthusiastic supporter of Brush's plan, had long attributed the waning fortunes of the National League to a lack of competitiveness among teams, the league being dominated by three clubs. By redistributing players between franchises, the trust could make seasons far more competitive and standings and championships far less lopsided from year to year.[31] Though the pro-trust faction endeavored to keep the details of their meeting a secret, the information was leaked to the press before they could present their ideas to the other magnates at the winter meeting.[32]

As chronicled in *Sporting Life*, which published the stenographic minutes of the National League meeting in its February 8, 1902, issue, conflict arose on the first day. The meeting wasn't very old when Barney Dreyfuss of the Pittsburgh club, seconded by Charley Ebbets of Brooklyn, nominated Spalding as league president. President Nicholas Young, whose term had expired and who was not eligible to run for re-election,[33] had excused himself from the meeting so that the owners would be able to discuss their candidate freely. Colonel John Rogers of Philadelphia joined Dreyfuss and Ebbets in backing Spalding, citing what he termed Young's unsuitability for president as well as the need for strong, singular leadership that the league could rally behind to face the American League threat.[34]

At this point Robison raised a point of order, calling into question whether the National League still existed, stating that the agreement the League signed in Indianapolis in 1892 was no longer valid and that the organization's charter had expired. Brush and Freedman spoke in support of Robison, but Rogers took the stance that the league was perpetual, that the 10-year dates Robison and the other Red Bank magnates referred to dealt only with procedural matters, as a sort of sunset clause for rules, not as a date on which the league was meant to expire.[35]

After much debate, primarily between Rogers and Freedman, and a personal appeal by Spalding that the owners not let the league expire, the matter was called to a vote on December 11, and the magnates decided in favor of perpetuity, 5 to 1, with Freedman and Brush abstaining and Robison ultimately the only vote in favor of syndicate ball.[36] The league would continue, but the question was: What form would it take?

There were several allusions to the trust mentioned by Freedman during the meeting, as well as criticism of Spalding, who Freedman felt would not fully devote himself to the task of leading the league on a "wartime" footing. The vote on the perpetuity of the league having been decided, it was time to determine if Spalding would lead the league or if it would take a new shape. The vote on Spalding's presidency, the first of 26 such votes, was divided 4 to 4, with the Red Bank faction voting unanimously against Spalding's election.[37]

In an attempt to win over the other magnates, Freedman distributed a copy of the trust plan to each owner, with the caveat that several points would need additional verbal explanation. Rogers objected to the plan immediately. He asserted that none of the other owners would want to trade their property for stocks, that forming a trust would make the National League more liable to lawsuits, and that a single executive was far less cumbersome than a committee.[38]

The vote remained deadlocked, with no sign of compromise. Voting went well into the early hours of Saturday morning, December 14, with no resolution. Multiple votes to postpone the vote until the following month also failed—the matter was to be decided right then and there. Finally, the Red Bank faction walked out of the meeting, ceding the chair back to Nicholas Young. At this point, the other four magnates attempted to vote on Spalding but Young, noting that there was no quorum, refused to hold the vote. However, Hart mentioned that roll call had not been taken and that proxies might be present, allowing the meeting to continue in session. Once Young retired for the evening, the magnates elected

Rogers as temporary chair and voted in Spalding 4 to 0.[39] The Spalding faction claimed that since the Red Bank members vacated without leave, they should be seen as present and abstaining. After the conclusion of the meeting, Spalding went to Young's room at the hotel and demanded access to minutes and records.[40] Spalding claimed he would not withdraw his name but would accept only on condition that Freedman leave baseball. Spalding said, "On (Freedman's) record in baseball, and I speak only of his baseball record, I openly and publicly charge Andrew Freedman with being a traitor and a marplot. He has done more to ruin baseball than any other four forces that ever existed in the history of the game."[41]

The election of Spalding was problematic, to say the least. Freedman immediately initiated legal action against the league,[42] which remained divided, possibly leaderless, and certainly no more unified in the eyes of the press and the public.

Summary and Close

Baseball remained locked in conflict as the winter meetings ended and 1902 began. The National Association had a new set of rules and protocols under which to operate, a major change from the previous year. The American League started 1902 in a much stronger position, unified, growing, and presenting a serious challenge to the National. The National League remained beleaguered as 1902 commenced, divided, no closer to peace, and not even clear as to who was running the league. Freedman and other magnates continued to challenge the legality of Spalding's election until Spalding relinquished his claim to the presidency in April. An executive committee would rule the league until Harry Pulliam rose to the presidency later in the year. During that time, the American League was able to consolidate its gains and set the stage for the peace agreement negotiated by the two leagues in January of 1903.

NOTES

1 Not to be confused with the National League, the National Association of Professional Baseball Leagues (NAPBL) was the corporate name of the minor leagues until 1999, when it renamed itself Minor League Baseball (MiLB).

2 "Minor Leagues in Union," *Chicago Tribune*, September 6, 1901: 6.

3 "Session of the Baseball Men," *Chicago Tribune*, December 3, 1901: 6.

4 Benjamin G. Rader, *Baseball: A History of America's Game* (Urbana-Champaign: University of Illinois Press, 2002).

5 Robert F. Burk, *Never Just a Game: Players, Owners, and American Baseball to 1920* (Chapel Hill, North Carolina: University of North Carolina Press, 1994), 62-63.

6 "Bars Those Who Bet," *Washington Post*, December 4, 1901: 8.

7 Francis C. Richter, "The American League Is Bravely Holding Its Own in Every Direction," *Sporting Life*, Volume 37, Number 4, April 13, 1901: 4.

8 "Approve Changes," *The Sporting News*, December 7, 1901: 1.

9 "Two for Uncle Nick," *Washington Post*, December 10, 1901: 8.

10 "Spalding Acts as League President," *New York Times*, December 15, 1901: 13.

11 Jimmy Keenan, "Joe Kelley," *The Baseball Biography Project*, January 25, 2011. Accessed August 11, 2011. bioproj.sabr.org/bioproj.cfm?a=v&v=l&bid=3632&pid=7362.

12 T.H. Murnane, "Hold the Power," *Boston Globe*, November 3, 1901: 40.

13 "Baseball Meeting," *Hartford Courant*, October 26, 1901: 1.

14 "Banded Together," *The Sporting News*, November 2, 1901: 3.

15 Ibid.

16 Ibid.

17 Ibid.

18 Ibid. Prentiss was misspelled as Prentice in this issue. For more on Prentiss, see David Forrester's biography of him on BioProject at sabr.org/bioproj/person/a3bd6618.

19 "The Prentiss Case," *Sporting Life*, Volume 39, Number 1, March 22, 1902: 7.

20 "George Prentiss," *SABR Encyclopedia*, n.d., accessed May 20, 2012.

21 "Problem for the Old League," *Chicago Tribune*, December 8, 1901: 19.

22 "Baseball Club Owners Assembling," *New York Times*, December 2, 1901: 2.

23 "All Satisfied," *Chicago Tribune*, December 14, 1901: 6.

24 "Approve Changes"; "Bars Those Who Bet."

25 "Approve Changes"; "Session of the Baseball Men."

26 "Make-Up of the Clubs," *Washington Post*, December 3, 1901: 8.

27 "Bars Those Who Bet."

28 Rader, *Baseball*, 80.

29 Burk, *Never Just a Game*, 152.

30 Bill Lamb, "Andrew Freedman," *The Baseball Biography Project*. n.d. Accessed August 11, 2011. bioproj.sabr.org/bioproj.cfm?a=v&v=l&bid=2870&pid=17415; John Saccoman, "John Brush," *The Baseball Biography Project*. n.d. Accessed August 11, 2011. bioproj.sabr.org/bioproj.cfm?a=v&v=l&bid=3632&pid=7362.

31 Rader, *Baseball*, 85.

32 Rader, *Baseball*, 90.

33 "National League Meeting," *New York Times*, December 9, 1901: 10.

34 "Official Stenographic League Minutes," *Sporting Life*, Volume 38, Number 21, February 8, 1902: 10. (Hereafter Minutes).

35 Minutes, 10-13.

36 Minutes, 15; "No Trust in Baseball," *New York Times*, December 12, 1901: 10.

37 Minutes, 15.

38 Minutes, 21.

39 Minutes, 23.

40 "League's Peril," *Boston Globe*, December 15, 1901: 4.

41 "A.G. Spalding Is Made President," *Chicago Tribune*, December 14, 1901: 6.

42 "Freedman Gets Writ," *Washington Post*, December 17, 1901: 8.

1902
A PEACE ACCORD

By Abigail Miskowiec

Preemptive Measures by the Senior League

BEFORE THE 1902 SEASON ENDED, the National League presidents met to strategize their approach to the burgeoning American League. The year-old AL already had four teams in National League cities (Philadelphia, St. Louis, Boston, and Chicago) and was threatening a move to the NL stronghold of New York.

For two days at the St. James Building in New York, John T. Brush presided over a meeting of six of the eight NL presidents. The presidents called the meeting to address what was called a "very disastrous year" by Philadelphia president A.J. Reach. To better address these issues, the NL presidents opted to reconvene a week later on September 26.

While all eight National League presidents sat in a highly secret meeting at the St. James, the American League opted for a more public approach. AL spokesman James C. Kennedy announced to the press that the AL would be placing a team in New York for the 1903 season. However the location of the AL grounds remained tightly under wraps.

National Association of Professional Baseball Leagues

The feud between the National League and the American League was heating up when the National Association of Professional Baseball Leagues gathered for their second annual conference in New York. The meetings, held from October 23-25, resolved only a few concerns facing the young association. However, some of the major-league managers used the meetings as a venue for discussion about several issues.

The NAPBL held elections of officers. President Patrick T. Powers and secretary John H. Farrell were reelected to their respective positions. Farrell's only proposal at the meetings suggested that the organization adopt a more stringent drunk and disorderly policy. The rule changes were submitted for adoption in February.

ST. VRAIN BARRED FROM THE BALLPARK

The Jim St. Vrain incident led to interesting developments during the 1902 season:

August 9 doubleheader: Both games were forfeited by Memphis to Shreveport, because St. Vrain appeared at the gate, and was denied admission. Memphis refused to play.

August 10: Again, St. Vrain was refused admittance, and Memphis forfeited to Shreveport.

August 11: Memphis players took the field, but didn't even remove their coats. St. Vrain was refused admission and Memphis forfeited to Little Rock.

Reportedly, at some point in August, St. Vrain began serving as a ticket collector for the team, instead of as a pitcher.

"At Little Rock," *The Tennessean*, August 12, 1902: 6.
"St. Vrain is Barred Again," *Atlanta Constitution*, August 10, 1902.

Jim St. Vrain, Contract Jumper

Like the major leagues, the NAPBL had to deal with players and managers who jumped from league to league, chasing bigger salaries. Although officials were unable to come to a consensus on the matter of a new minor-league salary scale that might discourage league jumpers, the NAPBL chose to inflict severe penalties against perpetrators, starting with pitcher Jim St. Vrain.

The Tacoma Tigers signed St. Vrain to a contract after he led the Pacific Northwest League with 299 strikeouts. The numbers caught the attention of Chicago Orphans owner Jim Hart, who offered St. Vrain $300 a month to make the jump to the National League.

St. Vrain failed at the big-league level and was sent down to the Memphis Egyptians of the Southern League. Manager Charley Frank played St. Vrain in spite of the Tacoma contract. A legal battle exploded between the two leagues. Pacific Northwest League president W.H. Lucas said, "I wish I had Mr. Charles Frank managing a club in the Pacific League. I'd teach him a base ball lesson he'd not soon forget."

The NAPBL resolved the matter at the winter meetings. Frank was expelled, and St. Vrain was suspended until he paid a $100 fine. John McCloskey, who managed St. Vrain and the 1901 Tacoma team, was censured for his part in the case.

National League

The baseball world remained relatively quiet between the close of the NAPBL meeting and the start of the National League conference on December 9. In the meetings, the road toward peace with the burgeoning American League began to be paved. Like the minor-league talks, the NL meetings were held at the Fifth Avenue Hotel in New York.

The NL presidents passed some minor scheduling and rules changes over the course of the three-day meeting. The Philadelphia Phillies and Boston Beaneaters both agreed to play Sunday games for the first time in franchise history. After frontrunner John M. Ward withdrew from the race for league president, a unanimous vote raised Pittsburgh president Harry Pulliam to the head of the league. In place of an executive board, Pulliam would serve as president, secretary, and treasurer.

The threat of an AL team in New York loomed at the meetings. August Herrmann, president of the NL Cincinnati Reds, sent a letter to Ban Johnson proposing a meeting between the two leagues. The conference closed with a meeting between committees from both the NL and the AL to discuss peace accords.

Rampant Player Movement Between Leagues

Among other things, the frequent defection of players from the NL to the young American League was a major point of contention between the two. The NL faced the decision of what to do with such players. A certain precedent had been set when the senior league banned Nap Lajoie, William Bernhard, and Elmer Flick at the start of the 1902 season.

Lajoie, Bernhard, and Flick played together on the 1900 Philadelphia Phillies team in the National League. In 1901, Lajoie and Bernhard transferred to

HARRY PULLIAM ON THE PRESIDENCY

"I did not seek the presidency of the National League, but I appreciate the compliment and the responsibilities that come with the office. I have been identified with Mr. Dreyfuss for the past eight years and our relations have been most pleasant. I did not want to leave him. Furthermore, my duties as president will be much more exciting than those of the secretary of the Pittsburg club because I propose to make them so. Of one thing you can be assured, I will give everyone a square deal and there will be no pulling of wires with me. The affairs of the league will be conducted open and above board, so far as I am concerned. I shall make an effort to run the league on a business basis."

"Pulliam on Record," *Pittsburgh Weekly Gazette*, December 15, 1902: 10.

the cross-town rival Philadelphia Athletics of the American League. Lajoie led the team, batting .426, and Bernhard finished with a 17-10 record. Flick joined his former teammates in 1902.

The NL obtained an injunction that banned the three from playing in the state of Pennsylvania. Athletics manager Connie Mack allowed them to play for the Cleveland Bronchos, another AL team.

Another member of the 1900 Phillies squad, "Big Ed" Delahanty also caused an uproar at the winter meetings. The defending batting champ, Delahanty had allegedly signed contracts with both the NL New York Giants and the AL Washington Senators. Delahanty had played the 1902 season with the Senators. Delahanty's case served as a major playing piece in the peace talks between leagues. AL representatives stated that Delahanty "would have to fulfill his contract with the Washington club or the war would be continued."[1] The NL hoped that lifting the ban on Lajoie, Flick, and Bernhard would give them leverage in the Delahanty case. Eventually Delahanty was granted to Washington.

Peace Committee Elected

The senior league had already won two "baseball wars" since its inception in 1876. The NL defeated the American Association, its first rival, in 1891 and the Players' League, which folded after one season, in 1890.

Now, the NL faced the task of appointing a committee to face off against Ban Johnson's American League. New NL president Harry Pulliam suggested a mutual respecting of contracts and extended an invitation to the AL for a meeting on December 12. They met at the Criterion Hotel in New York. The two sides agreed to cease hostilities until they could meet again in January.

Not all of the NL moves were peaceful, though. For the first time, the NL released the coming season's schedule before their rival league. Many saw it as a declaration of war because the AL would have to plan its own schedule around cross-town NL games in order to draw better crowds.

American League

Just a few weeks later on December 22, the American League presidents met for a six-hour meeting. The conference, held at the Pacific Hotel in Chicago, was the shortest yet held in AL history. The AL executives gathered to name the three-man committee to negotiate peace accords with the NL in January. Additional player movements and business issues were deferred until another time.

Much of the winter was filled with wild speculation on the location of the New York American League stadium. Ban Johnson insisted that the team play on the island of Manhattan, but several hurdles postponed an official announcement for months. The Interborough Rapid Transit Company refused to lease the land for the original site, situated between 141st and 145th Streets, Lenox Avenue, and the Harlem River. Finally in mid-March 1903, Johnson announced that the New York Baseball Club grounds at 165th Street and 11th Avenue would host the AL New York team.

Elections and Attacks

The primary issue at the meeting was the restoration of peace between the two leagues. The AL chose Johnson, vice president Charles Somers, Cleveland president John Kilfoyle as representatives, and Henry Killilea as the league's legal representation. They were to meet with NL presidents August Herrmann of Cincinnati, Jim Hart of Chicago, and Frank Robison of St. Louis. While on one hand the AL offered peace, they also discussed moving teams from Baltimore and Washington to New York and Pittsburgh, respectively. This would have created a direct conflict with existing NL franchises.

Joint Meetings

In late February, representatives of the NL, AL, and NAPBL convened in Chicago to discuss the state of the game as a whole. In this one-day meeting, officials regulated the slope of the field, ruling that the pitcher's mound could be no more than 15 inches higher than the base lines and that the base lines must be level with home plate. The AL and NAPBL adopted the foul ball-strike rule as written in the NL rulebook.

Initially, the American League representatives were fundamentally opposed to the foul-strike rule, but the alliance between the NL and NAPBL reps swayed the AL in favor of the rule. Finally, the three leagues agreed on a uniform balk rule, stating "a balk shall constitute any delivery of the ball to the batsman by the pitcher while either foot of the pitcher is back of the plate."[2]

Conclusion

The ensuing peace meetings would create a temporary accord between the leagues. They agreed to honor each other's contracts, in line with the ruling on Delahanty. The goodwill continued throughout the 1903 season and resulted in the first World Series behind held in October 1903.

SOURCES

In addition to the sources cited in the notes, the author was also informed by:

"Baseball War Declared," *New York Times*, September 26, 1902: 10.

"For Peace in Baseball," *New York Times*, December 11, 1902: 6.

"Baseball War at an End," *New York Times*, December 12, 1902: 10.

"New Baseball Setback," *New York Times*, January 8, 1903: 6.

"Agreement in Baseball," *New York Times*, January 11, 1903: 10.

"Sweeping Peace Pact is Signed," *Chicago Daily Tribune*, January 11, 1903: 9.

"Grabbing of Ball-Players," *Los Angeles Times*, August 2, 1903: 8.

"Baseball Suits Dismissed," *New York Times*, January 22, 1903: 10.

"More Baseball Troubles," *New York Times*, January 30, 1903: 10.

"Baseball Meetings Called," *New York Times*, February 19, 1903: 10.

"Baseball Season Near," *New York Times*, March 1, 1903: 16.

NOTES

1 "Baseball Legislation," *New York Times*, December 22, 1902: 8.

2 "Changes in Baseball Rules," *New York Times*, February 24, 1903: 2.

— 1903 —
MARRIED LIFE BEGINS

By Marshall Adesman

IT COULD BE COMPARED, IN A WAY, TO a romance novel—first they hate each other, then they start to learn more about each other to where they like each other, and finally they fall in love and get married. Unlike the two protagonists in this popular style of fiction, though, the National and American Leagues actually went to war before they agreed, somewhat grudgingly, to their shotgun wedding.

The ceremony took place in 1903, which has proven to be an early watershed season for baseball. After two years of battling, the established National League and fledgling American League signed a peace agreement in January and proceeded to play their games under a wary and uneasy cloud. Much like a marriage in its first year, the two leagues were learning how to live together, so by the time the last pitch had been thrown and the owners met again for their Winter Meetings, certain things had been learned, certain accommodations had been made, and some things still needed to be sorted out.

The War and What It Meant

In the very early years of baseball, it was common for leagues to come and go. Owners realized that their economic success was tied to bringing people to their ballparks, and people came out to see star players, so there were often fierce battles for these athletes, even those already under contract to another club. The 19th century ballplayer, in fact, rarely gave a second thought to jumping from one team to another, choosing a lucrative salary over legal obligation. Realizing this could undermine the public's respect for the game and thus keep people away, three leagues—the National League, the American Association, and the Northwestern League—got together in February of 1883 and signed the "Tripartite Agreement," which recognized the validity of the signed contract and prohibited all teams from pirating players. This accord shortly became better known as the National Agreement,[1] and by the turn of the 20th century it covered 13 minor leagues, plus the National League.

When the original agreement was signed, the American Association was considered the "other" major league. While it offered fans such amenities as lower admission prices, Sunday baseball, and beer, the league struggled throughout its 10-year history, and after the 1891 season four clubs—Baltimore, Louisville, St. Louis, and Washington—defected to the National League. The owners in Boston, Columbus, Milwaukee, and Philadelphia were subsequently bought out, ending the American Association as a major league, and turning the NL into a 12-team major-league monopoly.[2]

But in the 1890s, such a large circuit proved to be unwieldy, due to poor roads (no interstate highways then) and no air travel whatsoever. Many years later, when both majors expanded and became 12-team leagues (after the 1968 season), they wisely split into divisions to help with travel costs. Their Gay Nineties great-grandparents, however, did not do that, however, and for several years the NL struggled along until they contracted, ousting Baltimore, Cleveland, Louisville, and Washington after the 1899 season.

One man's trash is another man's treasure, and that other man was Byron Bancroft "Ban" Johnson. He was President-Secretary-Treasurer of the Western League, one of the minor leagues that was a part of the National Agreement. Despite its success primarily in the Midwest, Johnson had higher aspirations, and for the 1900 season he moved into the newly-opened Cleveland market, transferred his St. Paul franchise to Chicago, and re-named his circuit the American League.[3] Despite the name change it was still a minor league, but in the offseason Johnson grabbed for the brass ring, announcing his intention to operate the AL as a major league and, when the Senior Circuit scoffed, he renounced the National Agreement and declared war, moving into the open territories of Baltimore and Washington, as well as NL strongholds of Boston and Philadelphia.

All bets were off. The National League had the reserve clause and a salary cap of $2,400 per player in effect, but Johnson said there would be no such thing in his league, and 111 players jumped into the new circuit, including such marquee names as Cy Young, Napoleon Lajoie, John McGraw, and Joe McGinnity.[4] After the 1901 season, Johnson moved the Milwaukee franchise into St. Louis and saw more players make the move, including Ed Delahanty, Jesse Burkett, and Elmer Flick. (You may note that all the jumpers named here would eventually wind up in the Hall of Fame.) The new American League outdrew its more-established rival by more than half a million fans in 1902, which emboldened Johnson even further—he announced the Baltimore team would be moving into New York.[5]

The Big Apple would prove to be the catalyst for bringing the war to an end. John J. McGraw had become a part owner of the Baltimore franchise, and he also became the team's manager and third baseman. The pugnacious McGraw, however, quarreled regularly with umpires, and when Johnson, as AL President, regularly backed his arbiters, it incited the enmity of the Little Napoleon. After another tempestuous on-field dispute, Johnson suspended the Orioles skipper indefinitely, whereby McGraw jumped back to the NL, taking over as manager (and occasional infielder) of the New York Giants, a pitiful aggregation that, at the time of McGraw's arrival, had only won 23 of its 73 games and had already gone through two other managers.[6] It went through some players, too—McGraw brought a half-dozen men with him from Baltimore, including McGinnity and Roger Bresnahan, and he released people he felt were not producing.[7] This soap opera proved to be the impetus for Johnson's decision to invade New York and, when the newly-elected mayor, Seth Low, offered Johnson a site for a ballpark,[8] the National League realized it was time to sue for peace.

On January 9 and 10, 1903, the two leagues met at the St. Nicholas Hotel in Cincinnati to negotiate terms. Both league presidents brought three owners,[9] and the eight men hammered out the "Cincinnati Peace Agreement," which would govern baseball for almost 18 years. Better known as the National Agreement, it established the National Commission, the game's version of the Supreme Court, which would be made up of both league presidents and, as Chair, a neutral third party, which became Reds owner Garry Herrmann, an NL owner but close friend of Ban Johnson. It allowed the Baltimore franchise to move to New York and also established that each league would be comprised of eight clubs, a configuration that would remain in effect until 1961! It mandated that each team respect everyone else's roster, which was a nice way of saying "don't steal my players!" It required the two leagues to coordinate their schedules and to use the foul-strike rule.[10] It prohibited "farming," which meant signing a player to a major-league contract but then assigning him to a minor-league team. (By the 1930s, of course, that clause would become obsolete.) It gave the minors the "absolute" right to their players, except during a six-week period from September 1 through October 15, when a major-league team could draft players and pay the minor-league club a set fee.[11] And, most importantly, it established a standard player contract that included the reserve clause, which essentially bound players to their teams for life unless they were traded, sold or released. Until it was overturned in the 1970s, the reserve clause made the players little more than property.

The National Association of Professional Minor Leagues (now known as the National Association of Professional Baseball Leagues, or NAPBL) also signed this agreement, making it the law of the baseball land. A special ruling was made on several players who were claimed by two clubs; for instance, Sam Crawford and George Mullin were awarded to Detroit, Wee Willie Keeler went to the Highlanders, Tommy Leach headed to Pittsburgh, Nap Lajoie was assigned to Cleveland, Ed Delahanty went to Washington, and Christy Mathewson wound up with the Giants. Despite gaining Leach, the Pirates lost several players to the Highlanders but gained in the long-run when the Agreement prevented Ban Johnson from moving a team into the Steel City.[12] The Pirates, in fact, won the National League pennant in 1903, though they lost the first World Series to the Boston team known at that time as the Americans, led by Cy Young.

The Minors Meet

The minor leagues gathered for their Winter Meetings on October 22 in St. Louis, just nine days after Boston's Bill Dinneen had thrown the final pitch of the inaugural World Series. The Mound City was a happening place at that time, as they were preparing to host the Louisiana Purchase Exposition, and those members of the National Association who gathered for the three-day event at the Southern Hotel were treated to a visit to the grounds of what would be commonly known as the 1904 World's Fair.[13]

John Farrell, the Secretary of the National Association, gave the delegates what was more or less a State of the Minor Leagues address. At that point in time, the Secretary was more like a Chief Operating Officer, responsible for day-to-day dealings, which made him, and not the President, the right person to speak to the gathering. He was very proud to report that, even amidst the tumult of the first season played under the new National Agreement, 19 leagues began the season and 19 completed their schedules.[14] This did not count the independent Pacific Coast League which, because of the nice weather in California, was actually still in the midst of their 200-plus game season.[15]

The Association was hoping that, for at least this year only, the majors would issue an exemption to the National Agreement clause that allowed for minor-league players to be drafted during that six-week period in September and October. They were specifically seeking an exemption for players signed before September 11, but the new three-man National Commission disagreed and ruled that the draft had been held legitimately. The Commission also ruled on the fate of numerous players who were being claimed by two teams or leagues, with the most notable one being Ed Walsh, the big right-hander who had been drafted by the White Sox. Walsh would go on to win 195 games in the majors, all with Chicago, including 40 in 1908, on his way to the Hall of Fame.[16] The White Sox (also known as the White Stockings at that time) had another right-handed hurler bring his case before the Commission. Drafted off the Birmingham roster, Frank Smith balked, saying he preferred to go to the Boston Beaneaters (later known, at various times, as the Doves, Rustlers, Bees, and ultimately, Braves). Smith consulted with an attorney, who told him he could ply his trade wherever he chose because "the reserve clause was stricken out."[17] The new governing body, however, ruled against him, and since the record book shows that he did, indeed, pitch in the same rotation as Ed Walsh in 1904, one assumes he and his lawyer chose not to fight the decision in court.[18]

The Commission expected to have a very serious matter brought before it, the charge of fixed ballgames. Bill Phyle, a pitcher and third baseman who had played parts of three seasons in the majors — 1898 and 1899 with the Orphans, now known as the Cubs and 1901 with the Giants — had played with Memphis of the Southern Association in 1903 and claimed to have information about games that had not been on the up-and-up. He was asked to come to St. Louis and tell the Commission all he knew, but he failed to appear, whereupon he was banned from baseball for life.[19] He appealed the decision and was actually reinstated and played through 1909, mostly in the minors but also 22 games with the St. Louis Cardinals in 1906.

The various leagues were busy on numerous fronts. The American Association (Class A, the highest level of the minor leagues at that time), lost their president when Thomas Hickey resigned. Several people were rumored to be candidates to replace him, but ultimately the post went, for one year, to a writer and editor, J. Ed. Grillo, who was based in Cincinnati and was also a contributor to *The Sporting News*.[20] The Milwaukee Brewers chose New Orleans to be their spring training site, and they also announced a series of exhibition games against (Class-B) Southern Association teams such as Memphis and Nashville on their way north for Opening Day.[21] Brewers manager Joe Cantillon announced he had purchased the contract of third baseman John Hankey from Decatur of the (Class-B) Three-I League. Hankey, however, had already marketed himself and signed to play with Atlanta in the Southern Association. The dispute was resolved by sending Hankey back to the Three-I (which stood for Iowa, Illinois, and Indiana), but not to Decatur; he played instead for Springfield, Illinois,[22] and would, ultimately, never advance beyond Class B. Also in the American Association, long-time minor-league shortstop Bill Clymer signed on to be the player-manager of Columbus.[23] He stayed in the Ohio capital for several years and was a mainstay in minor-league dugouts through the 1932 season. Meanwhile, in an interview with *The Sporting News*, Indianapolis president William Watkins said of the meetings that the "most important things accomplished...were the regulations governing the drafting of players, the acquiring of territory and the fixing of a salary limit," which he said was $2,100 per month.[24]

Patrick Powers, the ceremonial President of the National Association, was also head of the (Class-A) Eastern League and wanted to remain in that position. Some league officials, however, hoped to unseat him with Buffalo owner Harry Taylor.[25] Powers would fight off the challenge and remain in control for two more years, when he resigned after purchasing the Providence club, and at that time was succeeded by Taylor.[26]

You'll recall that the American League had been born when Ban Johnson renamed his Western League and declared it a major, precipitating the battle for big-league talent. In the shadow of this conflict, the Western League re-formed as a Class-A circuit, with cities such as Denver and Des Moines. By 1903 they found themselves facing a challenge—the American Association had been formed and was competing with the Western, not only at the Class-A level, but also head-to-head in both Kansas City and Milwaukee. Obviously, while these were two of the premier urban centers in the Midwest, neither could support more than one club, and the two leagues hoped to settle the matter in St. Louis. While there was some talk about the Western dropping down to Class B, it was eventually decided to allow a "committee of three" to settle the matter via binding arbitration where, as predicted by former-pitcher-turned-sportswriter Tim Murnane, the American Association was victorious.[27] Milwaukee would remain in the AA through 1952, when the Braves left Boston and appropriated the territory for the National League, while Kansas City would be a league member through 1954, when the AL's venerable Philadelphia Athletics were sold and moved to the "Paris of the Plains." The Western League, meanwhile, had to scramble when George Tebeau, the manager of the Louisville club, made an effort to get Omaha to also bolt for the American Association.[28] His effort would not be successful—in fact, Omaha would remain in the Western through 1936—but the league did lose Peoria and operated as a six-team circuit in 1904.[29]

The Southern Association (Class B) seemed poised to lose its leader, Judge William Kavanaugh, who said he would not stand for re-election. No matter, the league's leaders chose him again and he would, in fact, remain as president until his death just prior to the 1915 season. The Southern did, however, lose an umpire, W.B. Carpenter, who moved to the American League.[30] Montgomery hired Bill Stickney to be its manager but, despite being "thoroughly familiar with Montgomery and its people,"[31] he would not complete the season in the Alabama capital.

News was made in other Class-B circuits. Two cities in the State of Washington, Vancouver and Whitcomb, expressed interest in joining the Pacific National League but had travel concerns, especially those long trips to both Salt Lake City and to Butte.[32] Vancouver eventually joined the Oregon State League (Class D), while Whitcomb would never field a team in Organized Ball. The Central League was looking to add Zanesville (Ohio), but did not because of objections to the league policy of playing lay Sunday games.[33] Erie, Youngstown, Peoria, and Anderson, Indiana were also considered, but only the last joined the circuit. The Three-I League decreed that all umpires would work the same number of games in each city, and that a sum of $2,000 was to be set aside to help strengthen any weak franchises, with the aim of raising that figure to $5,000 over time. They also determined that their policy of requiring each team to pay 10 percent of each night's gate receipts to the league for operating expenses was too steep and they made an adjustment, though the new percentage was not reported in the press.[34]

The Hudson River League had an interesting winter. Elevated in status to Class C, they voted not to play any doubleheaders prior to July 1 or after September 23, and replaced Ossining, New York (home of the famous Sing Sing Correctional Facility) with Paterson, New Jersey. Having already expanded to Saugerties, New York, this gave them seven franchises and necessitated adding one more. Three candidates emerged, including two Massachusetts towns — Pittsfield and North Adams — plus Yonkers, New York.[35] The best-laid plans, however: none of the three prospects panned out and, when Peekskill dropped out before Opening Day, the Hudson River once again operated as a six-team circuit.

The Texas League was already thinking bigger — it assigned J.W. Gardner of Dallas to meet with members of the South Texas League to gauge interest in a "consolidation" of the two Class-C circuits.[36] The idea did not go over well and the South Texas wound up operating for three more seasons; the Texas League, of course, is still functioning today at the Double-A level. Another Dallas-based executive, Ted Sullivan, announced he was attempting to convince the White Sox to hold their spring training in the town of Marlin, Texas (also known at times as Marlin Springs or Marlin Wells).[37] Known even to this day for its mineral water, they did play host to Charles Comiskey's club. Meanwhile, things were looking up for the Missouri Valley League. After completing just its second season and watching two clubs go under during the summer, they were promoted to the Class-C level for 1904 after most of the surviving clubs made money, "not a bucketful, but a good profit on the investment," according to the *Sporting News* correspondent.[38] Topeka would become a new member and Leavenworth would re-join after having disbanded in July.

At that time, the lowest rung of the National Association was Class D,[39] and three associations proved to be active. After re-electing George Wheatley as their president, the Cotton States League discussed adding the Mississippi towns of Jackson and Meridian to the fold.[40] Both municipalities did become members, but not until 1905. The K-I-T League (Kentucky-Illinois-Tennessee, also known as the Kitty),[41] was expecting to lose Jackson (Tennessee, not Mississippi), but was poised to replace it with Bowling Green, and was also receiving inquiries from Evansville and Cape Girardeau.[42] Jackson did drop out, as did Owensboro (Kentucky), and when none of the potential suitors followed through, the Kitty operated as a six-team circuit for the next three seasons. Over in the Hawkeye State, a group of businessmen were gauging interest in forming an Eastern Iowa League that would have a salary limit of $700 and travel limits of no more than 300 miles north-to-south and 125 miles east-to-west.[43] Burlington, Keokuk, Marshalltown, Ottumwa, and Waterloo followed through and were soon joined by Boone, Fort Dodge, and Oskaloosa in what officially became known as the Iowa State League.

A couple of other minor-league notes of interest: Waterbury had been one of the founding members of the (Class-D) Connecticut League in 1899, but dropped out after the 1902 season. Perhaps people in the Brass City missed their baseball, or perhaps businesses complained about the loss of collateral income, but for whatever reason they sought to return and did, though not They did, however, have to wait until 1906, when the league moved up to Class B.[44].

Another group of businessmen, this time on New York's Long Island, had a similar intent. Interests from Flushing, Bayside (now both part of the Borough of Queens), College Point, Manhasset, and Port Washington formed the North Side League of Baseball Clubs. They intended to add a sixth franchise, with Corona, Hyde Park, or Roslyn mentioned as the strongest candidates,[45] but the league never got off the ground. Probably the lack of good roads — neither the Long Island Expressway nor the Grand Central Parkway were built for many years — contributed to their failure to launch.

And then there was the Pacific Coast League. As mentioned earlier, it had been operating as an independent/"outlaw" circuit, completely outside the purview of the National Association, and Organized Ball was hoping to bring them into the fold. According to the *Los Angeles Times*, however, there was no great league-wide interest in joining up, and after the Eastern League and American Association attempted to "control matters," the PCL delegates "bolted the convention," which then "proceeded without them."[46] However, the *Washington Post* reported that James A. Hart, owner of the Chicago Cubs, was assigned the task of making the group a part of the National Association and "it is said the outlaws are not only willing, but anxious, to get under the wing of the major body."[47] The *Post* reporter got it right as the PCL joined as a Class-A league, the equal to the Eastern, Western, and American Association, with such cities as Los Angeles, San Francisco, Seattle, and Oakland. Not everyone was pleased—former catcher Daniel Dugdale, who had made a fortune in real estate during the Klondike gold rush, had been operating the Seattle Siwashes in the Pacific National League.[48] Despite having announced plans for a brand-new downtown ballpark,[49] Dugdale saw the loop downgraded to Class B in the wake of the Coast League's admission, and he sold the team and moved to Portland, though he returned to Seattle later in the decade to run the city's Northwestern League franchise until the end of World War I.[50]

The Older Brother Takes Charge

After more than a decade of being the only major league, the NL was not used to sharing, much like an only child who suddenly has to make room for a new sibling. A peace agreement may have been signed, but the National League still felt like this was their game and they should be running things. It didn't help matters when Boston's American League champions defeated Honus Wagner and his Pittsburgh Pirates in the very first World Series. Something needed to be done to restore order, at least as defined by the owners in the Senior Circuit.

The National League formally met at the Hotel Victoria in New York City on December 8 and 9. Several routine matters were taken care of, including the ceremonial ratification of the terms of the peace agreement, which also meant that the league's constitution needed to be amended so it would conform to the new National Agreement.[51] Harry Pulliam was re-elected as league president and his power to maintain discipline on the playing field, including the ability to fine or suspend any player for disorderly conduct, was re-affirmed and written into the by-laws.[52] They also gave him the power to rule that any player who "jumped" his contract was immediately ineligible to play anywhere.[53]

But perhaps the most important news to come out of these meetings was the lengthening of the schedule. A 140-game season had been played for the previous three years, ever since the NL had dropped down to an eight-team league, but now the owners agreed to a 154-game schedule, beginning on April 15 and ending on October 15.[54] Surprisingly, money was not behind this move—the real reason was to kill off the World Series and any other postseason games.[55] The *Boston Globe* reported that "Oct. 15 is too late to start the games," the *Chicago Tribune* remarked that the "American league clubs made such a good showing against the National league this fall…that the effect on the public was not relished" by the NL, while *The Sporting News* opined that starting a series in mid-October would "make it too late in the year to play a world's series with financial profit."[56] The *Washington Post* really railed against the move because it believed "the seasons always have been too long" and that "long before those 154 games are played both leagues will find that the public has tired of the contests."[57] It advocated for the season to begin in mid-May and run through mid-September, and even came out in favor of limited interleague play, all within the framework of a shorter schedule, because a 154-game slate "has been tried before and proved a lamentable failure, just as it will the coming season."[58]

This was just one way the senior circuit tried to "stick it" to the younger league. National League owners also passed a rule that prohibited any player from being traded over to the AL without unanimous consent from the rest of the league.[59] Rumors persisted that the NL would eventually do what it had done in the case of the American Association—absorb four AL teams, let the other four die off, and become a 12-team circuit once more.[60] The scuttlebutt was universally denied, though the influential J. Ed. Grillo wrote that "the two leagues can not continue…change will have to come sooner or later…either…another 12-club league …or one major and a secondary league."[61] There was also talk that the leagues might trade franchises, with Pittsburgh and Cincinnati moving over to the American League while Detroit and Washington joined the NL lodge,[62] a tacit admission that there were a couple of profitable franchises in the junior loop. And the foul-strike rule was another way the NL tried to re-establish its dominance. Its owners voted to continue using the rule, knowing full well that their American League counterparts were against it, and they instructed their Committee on Rules to stand firm on keeping it in place.[63]

The NL also made sure of their dominance over the minor leagues by establishing their "absolute right" to draft players from the minors between September 1 and October 15 of each year.[64]

The meetings weren't only about carrying the biggest stick. Several teams announced spring training sites—Boston would be in Thomasville, Georgia; Chicago would be in Los Angeles; and New York would be in Birmingham.[65] Frank De Hass Robison, owner of the Cardinals, was busy fending off reports that he was trying to find a buyer for his team. The *Chicago Tribune* speculated that this simply meant a "purchaser has yet to be found,"[66] and in fact Robison did hold onto the team for three more years before selling to his brother.

As always, rumors abounded. Cincinnati first baseman Jake Beckley, who would be inducted into the Hall of Fame more than 50 years after his death, was rumored to be coveted by the Cardinals and the Phillies; the *Chicago Tribune* stated with certainty that he "will play with the Philadelphia Nationals next season."[67] It took two months for Beckley to move, but when he did it was to St. Louis. *The Sporting News*, meanwhile, reported that Chicago right-hander Jack Taylor, who won 20 games in both 1902 and 1903, would be shipped to Cincinnati.[68] The Cubs did move him but to the Cardinals, along with catcher/first-baseman Larry McLean. In exchange they received a catcher named Jack O'Neill and a young right-handed pitcher named Mordecai Brown, nicknamed "Three Finger" because of a childhood farming injury that took most of his right index finger.[69] Brown's erstwhile malady gave his pitches great movement and he won 188 games for the Cubs (second only to Charley Root in the team's history), and a spot in Cooperstown.

The Reds were part of one more rumor, which had pitcher-turned-outfielder James "Cy" Seymour heading to the Giants in a straight swap for catcher Roger Bresnahan. According to a Grillo piece in *The Sporting News*, "McGraw can not get along with Bresnahan and Seymour doesn't want to play another year in Cincinnati."[70] Everyone must have learned accommodation, however, because Seymour stayed in Ohio until July of 1906 (when he was purchased by the Giants!), while Bresnahan and McGraw tolerated each other for another five seasons.

Brooklyn surprised baseball fans everywhere by sending shortstop Bill Dahlen to the Giants for infielder Charlie Babb, right-hander Jack Cronin, and cash. The *Washington Post* said that "it looks like McGraw got very much the better end of the deal,"[71] and they were right, as it turned out. Babb had a fair season in 1904, a terrible one in 1905, and then went back to the minors, while Cronin lost 23 games in 1904 and spent the rest of his baseball life in the Eastern League. Dahlen, meanwhile, continued his stellar career throughout the decade, even leading the league in RBIs in 1904.

Cleveland announced that it had signed outfielder Will O'Hara, but this proved to be another case where a player inked more than one contract. Toledo of the American Association also had a deal with O'Hara and that is where he wound up in 1904, not surfacing in the majors until 1909.[72] A conflict that included Detroit, Pittsburgh and Buffalo of the Eastern League was resolved when right-hander Charles "Rube" Kisinger, infielder/outfielder Ernie Courtney, utilityman Lewis

"Sport" McAllister and third baseman Joe Yeager were sent from the Tigers to the Bisons for right-hander Alfred "Cy" Ferry and outfielder Matthew McIntyre.[73]

Two future Hall of Famers made some news. Hugh Duffy had not played in the majors since 1901 and had, in fact, been the president and manager of Milwaukee in the Western League. The lure of the big leagues was strong, however, and he agreed to become player-manager of the Phillies, posts he held for the next three seasons. The Reds, meanwhile, found themselves in need of a second baseman and were willing to give a shot to a young man who had impressed people at St. Paul in the American Association. It was speculated that this rookie would prove to be the best Cincinnati had seen at the keystone since Bid McPhee.[74] Miller Huggins would, indeed, become one of the game's premier second basemen, first for the Reds and then for the Cardinals, but he would cement his Cooperstown credentials by managing the Yankees to six pennants and three World Series titles in the 1920s.

And the Younger Brother Fusses and Whines But Eventually Goes Along

Well, that peace agreement may have been signed, but the National League still seemed to be lobbing grenades towards the Junior Circuit. So when American League executives convened for their Winter Meetings on December 17 at the Auditorium Annex in Chicago, there was some confusion as to what direction they ought to take, especially with the playing schedule. President Ban Johnson told the *New York Times* that he expected their schedule to remain at 140 games (though he personally favored a 126-game slate), and was disappointed by the NL's expanding to 154 games, but admitted that there was a division of opinion among his owners.[75] No doubt there was considerable debate on this topic, but in the end the AL felt they had to follow along. Charles Comiskey of the White Sox called the 154-game schedule "one of the biggest mistakes ever made in baseball,"[76] while I.E. Sanborn, writing in *The Sporting News*, said that "(t)wo wrongs never made a right…" and predicted it would only be a "makeshift" schedule.[77] But the American League felt their hands had been tied and, as Comiskey stated, "… there was nothing left for us to do but follow suit."[78] It is rather ironic, then, that the 154-game season, so publicly maligned at the outset, became one of baseball's most cherished foundations for almost six decades.

The same could be said for the foul-strike rule. The AL formally voted against it, deadlocking the two leagues and forcing the establishment of a conference committee to try and resolve the difference. National League President Pulliam had stated that if the AL declined to endorse the foul-strike rule, it would be a violation of the National Agreement and could renew the war,[79] and perhaps this helped shape the feelings of the conference committee when they eventually met to discuss the issue. The foul-strike rule was upheld for both major leagues (and the minor leagues as well), and has been in full force for more than a century.[80]

Ban Johnson also had to deal with financial instability with his franchise in Washington, DC. Shortly before the AL meetings began, the *Chicago Tribune* reported that the league needed to "bolster the affairs" of its team in the District, and suggested that the current Brooklyn manager (and former Orioles skipper) Edward "Ned" Hanlon was being viewed as a good candidate to own and operate the team.[81] At the same time the *Washington Post* was reporting that Philadelphia Athletics co-owner Ben Shibe was being "importuned" to take over in D.C.[82] All the while a local attorney, Wilton J. Lambert, was doing his best to land the ballclub, which was purportedly $6,000 in debt.

What Lambert found, however, was that things weren't quite on the up-and-up in Washington (imagine that!). He was initially negotiating with a Detroit hotelier, Fred Postal, who claimed to own one-third of the team, but Lambert eventually learned that Postal was just a front man — the club was actually owned entirely by the American League itself![83] He also discovered that the debts were $15,000, more than twice what he had been given to believe. Undaunted, though, Lambert continued to try making a deal, even after the Winter Meetings ended, but ultimately he was unsuccessful. New owners for the Senators would not be found until March.[84]

Other matters were dealt with, of course. Following the NL lead, the National Agreement and uniform players contract were both formally ratified,[85] and a committee was appointed to revise the league constitution so it, too, would conform to the wording of the National Agreement. Rosters were capped at a maximum of 16 players after June 1. Ban Johnson was given a raise of $2,500, bringing his salary to $10,000 a year (the equivalent of about $265,000 today). An attempt was made to also give him a one-time bonus of $5,000, but he objected so strongly that the offer was withdrawn.[86] The St. Louis Browns were confident that they could conclude a spring training deal with the city of Corsicana, Texas (which they did), while Cleveland was also looking for a Lone Star State location. Their manager, Bill Armour, had been hoping to travel to San Antonio and perhaps strike a spring training deal with them, but the city was under a yellow fever quarantine, making a visit impossible.[87] (He must have made it down eventually, because the team did train there in 1904).

Player movement seemed to be restricted to the committee that was arbitrating disputes between the two major leagues, fallout from the Late Unpleasantness. Only one deal of note was discussed, at least publicly — the Highlanders (today's Yankees) were looking to move Jesse Tannehill, a noted outfielder and left-handed pitcher, and found a partner up in Boston, who sent right-hander Tom Hughes to New York in a straight swap.[88] The Red Sox got much the better of this deal, as Hughes was swapped to Washington in July (where he spent the next eight-plus seasons), while Tannehill had great success in Boston, winning 20 games each of the next two years.

Summary

The Winter Meetings of 1903 took place in three different venues, no doubt reflecting the status of a game trying to recover from a harsh two-year war, with its three entities — the National Association of Professional Minor Leagues, the American League, and the National League — still being cautious, not sure whether or not to trust one another, not even certain that the peace would hold. The NL, probably viewing itself as "first among equals," took the initiative and virtually dictated certain terms, especially in the case of the foul-strike rule and the increase of the schedule to 154 games. Their ulterior motive, however, in approving a longer season was to eliminate the possibility of a World Series and prevent being "embarrassed" again, but in this they obviously failed, as the Fall Classic quickly became one of the premier events in American sports.

Yet, while there would be other battles over the years — three attempts to form a third major league, antitrust issues with Congress, and numerous labor disputes with both players and umpires — the peace agreement hammered out in 1903 between the American and National Leagues and ratified at their respective Winter Meetings, has remained intact. Presumably, then, after more than a century of matrimony, we can call this union a success.

SOURCES

In addition to the sources cited in the notes, the author also consulted Baseball-Reference.com and Don Jepsen's biography of John McGraw, part of SABR's BioProject and found at http://sabr.org/bioproj/person/fef5035f, undated, accessed October 9, 2013.

NOTES

1. "The Commissionership: A Historical Perspective." http://mlb.mlb.com/mlb/history/mlb_history_people.jsp?story=com, accessed October 5, 2013.
2. John Thorn, Pete Palmer, Michael Gershman and David Pietrusza, editors. *Total Baseball: The Official Encyclopedia of Major League Baseball, Fifth Edition* (New York: Viking Penguin, 1997), 1858.
3. Joe Santry and Cindy Thomson, "Ban Johnson," SABR Baseball Biography Project (http://sabr.org/bioproj/person/dabf79f8), undated, accessed October 5, 2013.
4. Ibid.
5. Robert L. Finch, L.H. Addington and Ben H. Morgan, editors. *The Story of Minor League Baseball* (Columbus, Ohio: The Stoneman Press, 1952), 15.
6. "The Shaky Peace of 1903," (http://baseballhistoryblog.com/1590/the-shaky-peace-of-1903/), accessed September 13 and October 9, 2013.
7. Ibid.
8. This would become Hilltop Park, in the Washington Heights section of upper Manhattan; it would be the home of the Highlanders for 10 years, from 1903 through 1912. See Philip

J. Lowry, *Green Cathedrals* (New York: Walker Publishing Company, 2006), 151.

9   The National League was represented by President Harry Pulliam, Frank DeHass Robison of the St. Louis Cardinals, James Hart of the Chicago Cubs, and Garry Herrmann of the Cincinnati Reds. The American League was represented by President Ban Johnson and Charles Comiskey of the Chicago White Sox, Henry Killilea of the Boston Americans, and Charles Somers of the Cleveland Naps. "The Shaky Peace of 1903," (http://baseballhistoryblog.com/1590/the-shaky-peace-of-1903/), accessed October 9, 2013.

10 The foul-strike rule is, simply, the rule that we have all grown up with—a foul ball hit with no strikes or one strike on the batter is called a strike, but once the batter has two strikes on him, subsequent foul balls will not count against him. The NL had adopted this rule in 1901 but the AL, in its first two seasons, did not have this rule in effect, which may have led to more offense in the Junior Circuit. Having both leagues play by the same rules was a key aspect of the negotiations. http://www.baseball-reference.com/bullpen/Foul_strike_rule, accessed September 13 and October 9, 2013. Interestingly, with the adoption of the designated hitter rule for the 1973 season, the two leagues have now played for better than 40 years under slightly different parameters.

11 *Reach Guide, 1904*, 115-123; accessed online October 9, 2013.

12 "The Shaky Peace of 1903," op. cit.

13 Judy Garland fans will recall that the 1904 World's Fair was the backdrop for the 1944 musical *Meet Me in St. Louis*, one of her best films. It was also where she met director Vincent Minnelli, whom she later married.

14 "Farrell's Report," *The Sporting News*, October 31, 1903, Vol. 36. No. 8: 2.

15 "Late News: Minor Leagues in Session," *The Sporting News*, October 24, 1903: 1.

16 J. Ed. Grillo, "Subject to Draft," *The Sporting News*, October 31, 1903: 1.

17 "Late News: Minor Leagues in Session," op. cit.

18 Smith had a decent major-league career. He won 120 games in nine major-league seasons, plus another 19 in his two years with the Federal League, the World War I-era group that lured many players in an attempt to become a third major league. Smith eventually did pitch, very briefly, in Boston, but ironically it was for the Red Sox.

19 "Gossip of the Players," *The Sporting News*, October 31, 1903: 2.

20 "Boosted Prices," *The Sporting News*, October 24, 1903:

21 Arthur B. Marsh, "Only Outlaw Body; Cantillon's Spring Plans," *The Sporting News*, October 31, 1903: 2.

22 Earl Obenshain, "Late News: American League Meeting; Needs Three Players," *The Sporting News*, December 19, 1903: 1.

23 Marsh, op. cit.

24 "Not Yet Decided; Advanced Their Interests," *The Sporting News*, October 31, 1903: 1.

25 "Late News: No Prospects for War; Opposition to Powers," *The Sporting News*, December 26, 1903: 1.

26 Charles Bevis, "Patrick Powers," SABR Baseball Biography Project (http://sabr.org/bioproj/person/e95ef025), undated, accessed October 29, 2013.

27 T. H. Murnane, "Disputes to Settle," *Boston Globe*, October 26, 1903: 5.

28 P. H. Saunders, "Late News: No Prospects for War; Tebeau is Scheming," *The Sporting News*, December 26, 1903: 1.

29 "Late News: American League Meeting; Western's Annual Postponed," *The Sporting News*, December 19, 1903: 1.

30 "Late News: No '04 Post-Season Games," *The Sporting News*, December 12, 1903: 1.

31 "Late News: Cases Decided By Herrmann; May Manage Montgomery Club," *The Sporting News*, October 31, 1903: 1.

32 Walter H. Murphy, "Make Them Equal: May Lose Freeman," *The Sporting News*, December 12, 1903: 1.

33 R. H. Archer, "Ignored Patrons; Central League Circuit," *The Sporting News*, December 19, 1903: 1.

34 "Fans Displeased; Reserve Fund of $5,000," *The Sporting News*, October 24, 1903: 1.

35 Skye S. Colt, "Late News: American League Meeting; Hudson River League," *The Sporting News*, December 19, 1903: 1.

36 "Ignored Patrons; Belongs to the Browns," *The Sporting News*, December 19, 1903: 1.

37 Ibid.

38 "Not Yet Decided; Advanced Their Interests," *The Sporting News*, October 31, 1903: 1.

39 Though minor-league baseball had been played for years, official classifications had begun in 1902, ranging from A down to D. The Double-A level was added in 1912, Triple-A in 1946. With the decline of attendance and the corresponding number of leagues in the 1950s and early 1960s, the major leagues affected a reorganization of the minors following the 1962 season, eliminating the B, C, and D levels and, later in the decade, adding the short-season and complex leagues. W. Lloyd Johnson and Miles Wolff, editors. *The Encyclopedia of Minor League Baseball, 2nd edition*. (Durham, North Carolina: Baseball America, Inc., 1997), 479.

40 "Only Outlaw Body; Cotton States League," *The Sporting News*, October 31, 1903: 2.

41 The K-I-T, or Kitty, League was made up of teams from towns in Kentucky, Illinois, and Tennessee, and occasionally Indiana as well. To quote its website, it brought baseball to "fans in Western and Central Kentucky, Southern Illinois and Indiana, Southeast Missouri, and West and Middle Tennessee for thirty years

42 "Late News: Cases Decided By Herrmann; K-I-T's 1904 Circuit," *The Sporting News*, October 31, 1903: 1.

43 "Late News: No Prospects for War; Proposed Iowa League," *The Sporting News*, December 26, 1903: 1.

44 "Late News: No Prospects for War; Wants League Ball," *The Sporting News*, December 26, 1903: 1.

45 "Foul Strike Rule Out," *New York Times*, December 18, 1903: 7.

46 "No Peace for the Magnates," *Los Angeles Times*, October 25, 1903: B3.

47 "Baseball Gossip," *Washington Post*, December 20, 1903: A2.

48 Eskenazi, Daniel and Walt Crowley, "Dugdale, Daniel E. (1864-1934), Baseball Pioneer." HistoryLink.org/index.cfm?DisplayPage=output.cfm&file_id=3431, published July 5, 2001, accessed September 26, 2013.

49 Walter H. Murphy, "Lengthened Race; Dugdale's New Park," *The Sporting News*, December 26, 1903: 1.

50 Eskenazi and Crowley, op. cit.

51 "Meeting of Magnates," *Washington Post*, December 9, 1903: 8.

52 Ibid.

53 "Longer Season on Ball Field," *Chicago Tribune*, December 10, 1903: 8.

54 "More Games," *Boston Globe*, December 10, 1903.

55 A postseason exhibition series between two teams, such as the Cubs and White Sox, was common at this time as a way for both players and owners to make extra money.

56 "More Games," *Boston Globe*, December 10, 1903; "Longer Season on Ball Field," op. cit.; "Late News: No '04 Post-Season Games," op. cit.

57 "Baseball Gossip," op. cit.

58 Ibid.

59 "Late News: No '04 Post-Season Games," op. cit.

60 "No Baseball Combine," *New York Times*, December 9, 1903: 10.

61 J. Ed. Grillo, "Fair Deal To All," *The Sporting News*, December 19, 1903: 1.

62 I. E. Sanborn, "Almost the Limit," *The Sporting News*, December 12, 1903, Vol. 36, No. 14: 1. This wasn't the only buzz about the soon-to-be Motor City, by the way. Reportedly a group out of Milwaukee was hoping to buy the team and move it to Wisconsin, but the AL, however, was not inclined to approve such a deal because, according to the *Washington Post*, it is "a good beer town, but a poor baseball drawing card." "Baseball Gossip," op. cit.

63 "Meeting of Magnates," op. cit.

64 "Baseball Rules Defined," *New York Times*, October 27, 1903: 10; and *Reach Guide, 1904*, accessed online October 9, 2013.

65 T. H. Murnane, "Gets to Work," op. cit.; "Late News: No '04 Post-Season Games," op. cit.

66 "Problem for Old League," *Chicago Tribune*, December 6, 1903: 10.

67 "Longer Season on Ball Field," op. cit.

68 J. Ed. Grillo, "Not Sensational," *The Sporting News*, December 12, 1903: 1.

69 Not long after suffering this injury, he fell while chasing a rabbit and broke his other fingers, which left him with a bent middle finger, a paralyzed little finger, and a stump where the index finger used to be. Cindy Thomson, "Mordecai Brown," SABR Baseball Biography Project, (http://sabr.org/bioproj/person/b0508a3c), undated, accessed November 11, 2013.

70 J. Edward Grillo, "Boosted Prices," *The Sporting News*, October 24, 1903: 1.

71 "Baseball Gossip," op. cit.

72 Sanborn, "Almost the Limit," op. cit.

73 "Late News: Cases Decided By Herrmann," *The Sporting News*, October 31, 1903: 1.

74 J. Edward Grillo, "Cut in Salaries," *The Sporting News*, December 26, 1903: 1.

75 "American League Plans," *New York Times*, December 16, 1903: 7.

76 "Long Schedule," *Boston Globe*, December 18, 1903: 5.

77 Sanborn, I.E., "Lengthened Race," *The Sporting News*, December 26, 1903: 1.

78 "Long Schedule," *Boston Globe*, December 18, 1903: 5.

79 Sanborn, "Lengthened Race," op. cit.

80 Interesting to note that, when the American League voted to implement the designated hitter rule for the 1973 season, it did so alone—the National League refused to add it, and to this day the two leagues play with this slightly different set of rules. There is never any mention of an abrogation of the National Agreement, or of the two leagues going to war.

81 "Magnates to Hold Meeting," *Chicago Tribune*, December 8, 1903: 8.

82 "Baseball Deal Hangs Fire," *Washington Post*, December 9, 1903: 8.

83 Bruce Goldberg, unpublished paper on the history of the Washington Senators, accessed September 28, 2013.

84 Ibid.

85 "Long Schedule," op. cit.

86 "Washington in Deal," *Washington Post*, December 19, 1903: 8.

87 "Tips By The Managers," *The Sporting News*, October 31, 1903: 2; H. P. Edwards, "Not Yet Decided," *The Sporting News*, October 31, 1903: 1.

88 "Long Schedules," *The Sporting News*, December 26, 1903: 1.

1904
POWER PLAY

By Steve Weingarden and Eric Frost

Introduction

AT THE 1904 WINTER MEETINGS, power was the common theme, as the National League, American League, and minor leagues continued to fight for their positions within Organized Baseball. Topics receiving ample attention and dissension included the reserve clause, the foul-strike rule, the length of the schedule, postseason play, syndicate ownership, and unpopular ownership. Most notably, though, a plan for a consistent World Series emerged from these sessions.

The 1904 season had been notable for a few reasons. Future Hall of Famers Ed Walsh and Miller Huggins made their playing debuts, as did Phillies star Sherry Magee. Dan Brouthers and Jim O'Rourke, both also later bound for the Hall of Fame, played their final games. Most conspicuous, however, was the absence of a World Series. After the first modern World Series had been played in 1903, one of the pennant winners was unwilling to play in 1904. Discussions and agreements at the 1904 winter meetings ensured that future World Series would be run by the National Commission rather than being left to the whims of the qualifying teams.

Once these issues were solved, there were even a few notable trades. In addition, a struggling major-league team was purchased, ensuring its survival as a franchise.

The Minor League Meetings

The National Association of Professional Baseball Leagues, the minor-league organization, held its fourth annual convention at the Victoria Hotel in New York City. The first high-stakes dispute involved a minor-league pitcher named Skel Roach. Roach posted a 22-9 record for the Butte Miners of the Pacific National League in 1903. He moved to the Portland Browns of the Pacific Coast League in 1904, claiming that he had a written agreement releasing him from Butte's control. During the season, however, Butte reclaimed Roach even while he was pitching for Portland. The National Association, through its Board of Arbitration, turned down Roach's request to be freed from Butte. On appeal, the National Commission, Organized Baseball's highest court, decided Roach did not belong to Butte. At the New York meeting, the issue reached a head on October 25, when the Minor League Board rejected the National Commission's decision. In fact, the decision was made by the minor-league magnates as a group.[1] A slight modification was made, and plans were instituted to have the Board of Arbitration reopen the situation through a conference with the National Commission in Cincinnati on January 2.

Perhaps the partial reversal stemmed from the implications associated with the case. Roach reached out to American League President Ban Johnson, who sharply criticized the National Association for its action. Johnson declared that the minors were in violation of the National Agreement regarding the Roach case as well as in other instances involving fiduciary claims. Johnson noted that the National League was especially upset with the minors, but he kept his comments focused on the importance of the minors adhering to the National Agreement and the potential consequences of continuing violations. "The National Commission and the Major Leagues have no interest in this player aside from a desire to see that he gets the justice due him under the National Agreement," Johnson said. "It is a matter of indifference to both Major Leagues whether the minors keep this agreement or break it. For the two years of its operation it has worked all in favor of the minors, and if they want to go it alone that will suit the American and National League."[2]

The January 2 conference was later moved to January 9. National League President Harry Pulliam, a member of the National Commission, was ill on the day of the rescheduled meeting and was ordered to stay in bed, but the matter was still resolved as scheduled. Johnson and Garry Herrmann, the other two members of the National Commission, strong-armed the minor leagues into accepting its decision on Roach and rulings on other players, including Pat Flaherty, Lee Tannehill, and Dave Brain. The Commission said that it would not allow minor-league officials to appear before it unless they accepted the validity of all National Commission rulings.[3]

Johnson and major-league officials may have been angered by comments made at the National Association banquet, when P.T. Powers, the president of the association, suggested that the National Association was really more national in scope than either of the major leagues. Major-league representatives, including Frank Farrell, John I. Taylor, and Clark Griffith, were among the approximately 150 guests at the banquet.[4]

The minor leagues' most significant action may have been the creation of a new classification, AA. Previously, minor leagues were classified as A, B, C, and D. The argument in favor of the new classification centered on the contention that too many good players were being drafted by the major leagues from high-level minor-league clubs.[5] A new, higher classification allowed for the introduction of higher posting fees. For about a week, there was apprehension about the potential major-league response to these increased costs.

The Major Leagues

Since the last offseason, ownership of American League clubs in Detroit and Washington had changed, leaving only Philadelphia, Cleveland, and Chicago with their founding owners from four years earlier.[6] Actually, ownership in Washington remained an unsettled issue, although it was considerably improved from the previous season, when the league financed the team. It became a topic of discussion at the major-league meetings on December 7 at the Auditorium Annex in Chicago. The Washington club, it was felt, had too many stockholders, preventing it from making decisions. Ben Minor, who was both American League attorney and secretary of the Washington club, wanted to take over the franchise. Minor noted that the club had incurred expenses exceeding $22,000 in 1904 through relocating its "plant" and ending its old lease, but he said the team had managed to cut those expenses significantly, leaving room for optimism.[7] "I can't say definitely that the present deal will go through, but I feel confident it will, and if so the club will be in the right kind of hands next year, with every prospect of better success," Minor said.[8] He was hoping to complete the sale soon after the winter meetings, and even left the meetings early in hopes of closing the deal.

Other topics occupied day one of the meetings. The American League opposed the increased draft prices proposed by the National Association.[9] The magnates unanimously opposed Garry Hermann's proposal for a round-robin series involving all clubs of both leagues, an early suggestion of interleague play. American League owners favored a 140-game schedule followed by a postseason series between the two pennant winners. National Commission secretary Bruce suggested that scheduling be left to the two league executives instead of two committees. Pulliam expressed hope that by letting the league executives work through the schedule, some of the friction from playing-date conflicts could be avoided.[10]

Discussions also started the first day on the possibility of eliminating the foul-strike rule. The *Chicago Tribune* had recently advocated for its repeal. Its article said the original intent of the foul-strike rule had been to shorten the length of games, which had been growing. The rule succeeded at this, but also had markedly decreased offensive production, the *Tribune* said, while it had made games almost too short to satisfy fans.[11] The deliberations on the fate of the rule carried over to the following day. The underlying issue involved creating enough offense and rhythm to keep fans engaged. Charles Comiskey opposed a rule change, saying, "I didn't see any indication at my gates or in the returns from other cities where my club played that the public was sore on the rules of the game.... My public didn't show me it was aching for a change."[12] Others, including Joe Cantillon and Nap Lajoie, offered possible alternative ways to increase offense.

In a final vote, American League owners deadlocked, 4 to 4, over whether to change the foul-strike rule. They did agree on another change: the size of the strike zone. While the previous strike zone spanned the area between the knee and shoulder, the new rule cut it in half, dictating that a "pitched ball must pass between the hip and shoulder in order to make it a strike." The magnates also created a new waiver rule designed to prevent major-league teams from waiving a newly drafted player. Up to then, clubs could draft a player simply to prevent other clubs from selecting him, and could waive the player right after the draft.

The American League magnates voted by acclamation to raise Johnson's salary to $10,000 a year. The vote reportedly turned into more of a college yell, setting the stage for a toast at 6:00 P.M. to league success.[13] Johnson had been elected president in 1900 for the 10-year life of the American League agreement. Granted a raise to $10,000 in 1903 with a $5,000 bonus, he refused the bonus and accepted the $10,000 salary only for 1903 because he believed the league might not remain prosperous enough to maintain the salary. The 1904 vote established the $10,000 salary for the remaining six years of Johnson's contract. These events may have highlighted one distinction between Johnson and his minor-league counterpart: Powers received no salary for his role as the National Association president. National League President Pulliam may also have benefited from Johnson's raise; his salary was also raised to $10,000.

Controversy also surrounded actions by the New York Giants and by John Hart, owner of the Chicago Cubs, over actions involving the still-infant World Series. The first modern World Series in 1903 had been arranged between the champions of the two major leagues, the Pittsburgh Pirates and the Boston Americans. In 1904 the manager of the National League champion New York Giants, John McGraw, who disliked Ban Johnson, refused to play Boston, which had repeated as American League champion. Though the refusal violated the National Agreement, McGraw asserted that the Giants should be considered the world champions because the National League was, in his view, the only authentic major league. In July Johnson released a scathing statement denouncing McGraw and Giants owner John T. Brush for their reluctance to participate in a world championship series. The statement also denounced Hart, saying, "At a meeting of the joint schedule committee of the American and National leagues last spring, a motion that a world series be played this fall was put by President Hart of the Chicago National Club, and was carried unanimously. Recently, however, Mr. Hart and his associates have shown little inclination to live up to this agreement."[14]

Hart may have compounded the controversy that surrounded him by making some controversial statements about a player just before the winter meetings. He alleged that pitcher Jack Taylor had thrown some games while pitching for Chicago. Comiskey encouraged the National Commission to investigate the charges. Taylor had been traded to St. Louis before the 1904 season. The pitcher said that before the trade, Hart had confronted him with accusations of dishonesty based on some misunderstood comments he had made after the 1903 season. Taylor was offended at the suggestion of impropriety and refused to play for Hart anymore, prompting the St. Louis trade. The National Commission later found insufficient evidence to support the allegations against Taylor.

By the time of the winter meetings, the American League was united and hopeful of a world's series being played once more, but the response of the National League remained uncertain.

The National League meeting began at 3:00 P.M. on December 13 at the Victoria Hotel in New York. The late start time occurred because the whereabouts of St. Louis owner Frank Robison were unclear; it turned out that Robison would miss the meetings because his wife had become ill. On a more positive note, the National League reported that it had overcome its

$125,000 debt, assumed when the league reduced to eight clubs in 1891. Much credit went to former league President Young for managing the debt. Current president Pulliam was re-elected.

In what might have been perceived as a savvy public relations move, the National League invited the minor leagues' attorney, Howard Griffiths, to come to the sessions and explain the minors' position on their proposed changes in drafting fees. These were the same changes the American League had rejected earlier in the month. When Griffiths appeared, the National League decided to champion the cause of the minors. No one knows how much of the support represented a belief in the cause, but that was a moot point. To change drafting fees, and the National Agreement, approval was required by the National Association, American League, and National League. A few days after the meeting, Johnson suggested that compromise might be reached on the minor-league draft rule.

On December 14 the National League voted unanimously to play postseason games with the American League for a world's championship:

> *Resolved, That the National league hereby declares in favor of having post-season contests annually between the champion teams of the National and American leagues for the championship of the world, and,*
>
> *Resolved, That in order that such contests, as well as those that may be arranged from time to time between the National and American league clubs, may be conducted under proper rules and regulations, the national commission hereby be delegated with the authority to arrange all details of said contests in regard to the preparation, rules, regulations, and government of the same, such detail to be submitted to the National and American leagues for their approval.*[15]

The devil, of course, could well be in those details. That resolved, the National League disagreed with the American League over the 140-game schedule, deciding instead on a 154-game schedule. Johnson protested that after the players finished the lengthier schedule, a world championship might be unrealistic. To have the regular season run as late as October 10 and then play a series of postseason games, a world's championship and/or intercity or intracity championships could extend baseball to rather late in the year.

In the National League, the Philadelphia club had fallen on financial difficulties by the end of the 1904 season and there was uncertainty over whether the franchise would continue.[16] Because the Phillies did not have enough money to pay their players, the National League had assumed control of the team and had issued the paychecks. During the winter meetings, ownership of the team was transferred to the Philadelphia Ball Company, led by Bill Shettsline, a former Phillies manager. The team then became active in the trade mart, swapping utilityman Del Howard to Pittsburgh and receiving in exchange first baseman Kitty Bransfield, utility player Otto Krueger, and outfielder Harry "Moose" McCormick. Pittsburgh reportedly was motivated to move Bransfield because he had taken a swing at Honus Wagner in the Pirates dressing room. Philadelphia also made a trade with its bottom-dwelling companion, the Boston Beaneaters. Right-hander Charles "Chick" Fraser and third baseman Harry Wolverton went to Boston, while right-hander Charles "Togie" Pittinger came to Philadelphia. Pittsburgh made a second deal as well, sending catcher Eddie Phelps to Cincinnati for utilityman Henry "Heinie" Peitz.

Summary

The 1904 meetings exemplified the politics that surrounded the early years of professional baseball. The minor leagues and both major leagues fought with one another and among themselves for survival within the national pastime. Baseball executives also showed early concern for topics like the strike zone, offensive production, and the World Series, all of which would become more important to baseball's success in later years.

NOTES

1 "Major and Minor Leagues May War," *Chicago Tribune*, October 27, 1904.

2 Ibid.

VOLUME 1 - 1901-1957

3 "Baseball Men Before National Commission," *New York Times*, January 10, 1905.

4 "Baseballists' Convention," *Los Angeles Times,* October 27, 1904.

5 "New Class for Minors," *Chicago Tribune*, October 28, 1904.

6 "Murnane's Baseball," *Boston Globe*, December 4, 1904.

7 "Baseball Men In Session," *Chicago Tribune*, December 8, 1904.

8 Ibid.

9 "Two Sessions," *Boston Globe*, December 8, 1904.

10 "League Owners Meet," *Washington Post*, December 8, 1904.

11 "Batting Is Too Light," *Chicago Tribune*, November 6, 1904.

12 "Johnson Voted a $10,000 Salary," *Chicago Tribune*, December 9, 1904.

13 Ibid.

14 "Scores M'Graw and Brush," *Washington Post,* August 1, 1904: 8.

15 "Long Baseball Season Planned," *Chicago Tribune*, December 15, 1904: 10.

16 "Philadelphia Baseball Club in distress." *New York Times*, October 7, 1904.

1905
CONTROVERSY OVER LEAGUE PRESIDENTS TAKE CENTER STAGE AT MEETINGS

By Dennis Pajot

Introduction

BASEBALL HAD JUST COMPLETED perhaps its most profitable season ever, with every club in both leagues reportedly showing a profit. There was concern about the decline in hitting as well as questions about the length of the season. Even with these issues, the winter meetings of 1905 were expected to be routine affairs. However, both leagues experienced fireworks that centered on their respective presidents.

American League Meeting

The American League held its 1905 winter meeting at the Auditorium Annex in Chicago on November 22 and 23. However, the day before the meeting began, Chicago White Sox owner Charles Comiskey accused AL President Ban Johnson of conspiring with Cincinnati Reds owner and National Commission Chairman Garry Herrmann in a plan to consolidate the AL and NL into one league. Rumors speculating how this would come about had been circulating in the press for some weeks. Reports varied, but the one most favored was consolidating the teams in Boston, Philadelphia, and St. Louis into one National League team in each city, and relegating the American League teams in Chicago and New York to a new Class-A minor American League. Another version of the story had Johnson at the head of this new National League. Whatever plan came about, Comiskey and Frank Farrell in New York would be on the losing end.[1]

Comiskey felt Johnson had been too cozy with Herrmann and had been too influenced by him. Comiskey made his feeling toward the senior circuit very clear: "I always have fought the National League and always will. It has no real desire to be at peace with the American League and never had. It has only been waiting the opportunity to crush us. This opportunity is now coming in this proposed amalgamation of the two leagues. When this amalgamation is attempted I shall immediately attempt to organize a new league if the American League falls into the National's hands. I will fight the National League to a finish.»[2]

Comiskey and Johnson had been on bad terms for many months over Johnson's handling of two cases in which the AL president backed his umpires, suspending a White Sox player in one case.[3] According to Chicago sportswriter William A. Phelon, it was comical to see how the two behaved at the meeting: "Ban kept at the north end of the hotel, surrounded by his cohorts, and Commy seemed to limit himself to the south end, with a few friends. Between them the crowd of magnates gravitated, going first to one and then the other. On the sofas sat crowds of players and managers, telling good stories and keeping their eyes open for any rows or reconciliations. When the secret meetings were called, so I was told, Ban and Charlie kept far apart, debated every question with punctilious attention and never spoke to each other."[4]

Johnson's reply to the Comiskey charge was simple and to the point: "As far as any amalgamation of the two big leagues is concerned the man who even thinks of such a thing is either a fool or a knave."[5] He pointed out that the AL had just completed the most prosperous year in its short existence, every club in the league making money. "Money came in plentifully, public interest was at a fever point, [and] the quality of ball was superb." There was no reason for a consolidation, and Johnson said he knew of no American Leaguer who entertained the idea.[6]

As could be expected, Comiskey told a *Chicago Tribune* reporter that he had been misquoted: He did not think the AL was in any danger of dissolution, only that he was against anything that was not in the best interest of the league.[7]

Before the meeting opened, the board of directors met, approved Johnson's accounts, and formally awarded the 1905 pennant to the Philadelphia Athletics. When the meeting got under way, the first order of business was the re-election of Charles W. Somers of Cleveland as the AL vice president. After the new board of directors was set, the prime order of business was brought up. There was a strong feeling that changes in the rules were needed to improve hitting in the league. Proposals to this end included giving the batter first base on three called balls; another was to narrow home plate; and a third was to collapse the strike zone to balls crossing the plate between the batter's waist and shoulder. Few thought much of these proposals.[8] In the ensuing weeks more ideas were brought forward, but in the end nothing was done to change the rules.[9]

The league constitution was changed to provide that a game postponed on a team's first trip to any city would be made up on the team's second visit to the city. There was discussion about shortening the season from 154 to 140 games. Six clubs favored the shorter schedule, and it was decided to send the matter to the joint committee of the two major leagues in the spring. The shorter schedule had little chance, though, as most National League owners were against such a move.[10]

On the second day, the AL magnates publicly came out in support of their president. Benjamin S. Minor of the Washington club proposed a resolution saying Johnson "had consistently worked and fought for the maintenance of two independent but friendly major league organizations" and was offered the league's "very sincere congratulations and … its earnest thanks" for his work in managing the affairs of the AL. Comiskey endorsed this resolution, saying, "I always have held the best interest of the American League close to my heart. There never has been any question of my honesty in base ball, nor has there been any question in my mind of the honesty of Ban Johnson, or any of my associates in the league." Even with this, it was considered doubtful that the former intimate relationship between the AL president and the White Sox owner could ever be restored.[11]

Next on the agenda were the minor leagues. The minors wanted the draft rules changed so that no team in a Class-A minor league could lose more than one player in the draft in any year. The minors also wished sales of players barred until after the draft. The AL owners listened but were not disposed to grant these concessions, so they decided to let Johnson talk directly to the minors at their meeting the next month.[12]

Player Movement and Stories

Trade rumors filled the air, but there was very little in actual player movement at this meeting. The biggest player transaction of the session was the sale of first baseman Charlie Carr by the Cleveland Blues to the Cincinnati Reds. The trade puzzled Cincinnati writer Ren Mulford Jr. a bit, as Carr had hit only .235 in 1905 while the Reds' first sacker, Shad Barry, hit a nifty .324 after being acquired from the Cubs in May, and also played nicely in the field, even though he "fell down once or twice in the pinches." It was believed Barry would either go to the outfield or sit on the pines.[13] He was, in fact, traded by the Reds to the St. Louis Cardinals in July. There was also speculation that Carr would manage the Reds in 1906. However, the manager's job would go to Ned Hanlon in December, and Carr wound up spending most of the 1906 season in Indianapolis of the Class-A American Association.[14]

Cleveland sent infielder Nick Kahl to Columbus of the American Association. It was reported the Detroit Tigers traded right-handed pitcher Frank Kitson to the St. Louis Browns for another righty, Willie "Demon" Sudhoff, but the deal did not materialize and Sudhoff was instead sent to Washington a week later for left-handed pitcher Al "Beany" Jacobson.[15]

Perhaps because of this lack of player movement there was plenty of story-telling in the lobbies. No doubt one of the best was a story about Rube Waddell. It was said that one day Rube was visiting his home and a team of bloomer girls came to town. A makeshift squad was assembled to play the girls, with Waddell on the mound. It was supposed that the future Hall of Famer would toss the ball to the girls nice and easy, but instead he fired it in "as he might if opposed to Mathewson." It was feared that if he hit one of the young ladies she would be killed, so the girls took to the bench and refused to proceed with the game. After some discussion Rube went to first base and the game continued.[16]

National League Meeting

The National League held its winter meeting at the Victoria Hotel in New York December 12–14. What was billed to be a "featureless, routine" meeting proved, however, to be very interesting.[17]

The usual preliminaries took place with the awarding of the 1905 pennant to the New York Giants and the approval of the accounts of league President Harry Pulliam. The books showed that the 1905 season had produced the largest receipts in the history of the league, bringing the NL out of debt and giving it its largest cash reserve since the league was reduced to eight clubs in 1899.[18]

The next order of business was the announcement by James A. Hart that he had sold the Chicago Cubs to Charles W. Murphy. The NL magnates thought so much of Hart that he was elected an honorary member of the organization for life.[19]

The owners amended the league constitution to add one position to the league's board of directors. In the coming season it would have representatives from Boston, Pittsburgh, Brooklyn, Philadelphia, and Chicago. Various committees were set up, and sentiment prevailed to continue the 154-game schedule. The Spalding ball was approved as the official ball of the NL for the next six years.[20]

To tighten player discipline, the league strengthened a previous resolution that any player removed from a game by the umpire would be fined $10, and if the offense resulted in a suspension by the league president, the player would owe an additional $10 for each day of the suspension, and would be ineligible to play until the fine was paid. Moreover, the president was given the right to make the fine more than $10 if he deemed the offense severe enough.[21]

The major news was the battle for the re-election of Harry Pulliam as president, treasurer, and secretary of the National League. It had been anticipated that there would be no opposition to his re-election, but on the day before the meeting began, New York Giants owner John T. Brush produced a new candidate for the presidency: John Montgomery Ward, the former player and labor leader who was now a successful lawyer in New York.[22] Garry Herrmann of Cincinnati also announced his opposition to Pulliam. Brush and Herrmann asserted that Pulliam had made too many mistakes and lacked the "depth and breadth necessary" for the position. The bone of contention was Pulliam's handling of a row between New York manager John McGraw and Pittsburgh owner Barney Dreyfuss during the season. Pulliam fined and suspended McGraw, who took his case to court and had the suspension lifted. Pulliam then lifted the fines of all NL players.[23] It was thought Dreyfuss would join Brush and Herrmann, as would the owners in Boston and Brooklyn. The Philadelphia and Chicago owners were not expected to make much of a fight for Pulliam. Arthur Soden of Boston went so far as to tell Tim Murnane of the *Boston Globe* that he felt sure Ward would be the next president of the NL.[24] However, there was doubt that Ward would give up his lucrative law practice, even for a salary of $10,000.[25] More to the point, AL President Johnson said he would not sit with Ward on the National Commission. Johnson was quoted as saying he had no use for Ward and did not trust him after the lawyer had argued against the White Sox in a reserve clause case involving George Davis a few years earlier.[26]

William Shettsline, president of the Philadelphia Phillies, and Frederick Knowles of the Giants were lobbied to seek the job, but took no interest. It was believed that if Shettsline accepted the nomination, Boston and either St. Louis or Brooklyn would have voted for him, and thus Herrmann and Brush would have at least five votes (no doubt Philadelphia would go with Shettsline), enough to end Pulliam's presidency. But Shettsline declined the nomination, making Pulliam a little more secure. Even Ban Johnson voiced his support for the NL president. Herrmann said he would not support Ward, and Hart was urged to put his name in the hat. Hart refused, and the anti-Pulliam faction had no alternative candidate.[27]

The next day James Potter, a stockholder in the Phillies and former president of the club, came to New York from Philadelphia to lead the fight for Pulliam. That day new Chicago Cubs owner Murphy let it be known he was in favor of Pulliam, and Dreyfuss said he would not permit his personal feelings to interfere with his conviction that the best interests of the NL required Pulliam to remain as its head. Soden of Boston soon planted himself in the Pulliam camp, saying he could see no reason for change, as the NL was doing so well. Brooklyn's Charlie Ebbets also placed himself in the Pulliam camp.[28]

It soon became apparent that the anti-Pulliam faction would not get enough votes for even a tie. However, this did not stop Brush. After Pulliam was nominated for the president's position (by none other than Dreyfuss) and this was seconded, Brush nominated Hart. This was not seconded. Hart then protested against his nomination, assuring everyone he would under no circumstances run against his friend and protégé Pulliam. Still, Brush would not withdraw the nomination and the election was held. Pulliam received six votes. Hart got the votes of New York and Cincinnati. Hart was "thoroughly displeased" with votes being cast for him. To appease him, the league passed a resolution stating that even though there had been "a complimentary vote" for him, he was in no respect a candidate for the office.[29]

While the NL was meeting, the minor leagues (National Association of Professional Base Ball Leagues) met at the Fifth Avenue Hotel in New York.[30] The issue that concerned the minor leagues (and the majors as well) was the draft rules, which the American League magnates had authorized Ban Johnson to discuss with the minor leagues. The minors proposed that the majors be allowed to draft no more than one player from a Class-A club at $1,500, with full payment at the time of draft (instead of the current two-payment system). Draft prices would be $750 for Class B, $500 for Class C, and $300 for Class D, with no player limits in these classifications. In addition, no player could be sold within a 10-day period prior to the draft. The proposal was accepted by National Commission members Johnson and Herrmann, except for the price for a Class-A player; they cut it to $1,000.[31] This was accepted by all parties in January, and made part of the National Agreement.[32]

Personnel Movement

Although not a player movement, there was news on the managerial front. The Cincinnati Reds signed Ned Hanlon as their manager. Hanlon had been managing in Brooklyn for the previous seven seasons (he won back-to-back National League titles in 1899 and 1900), but Ebbets was reluctant to sign him for 1906. The Reds offered Hanlon $8,000, and Brooklyn would only go as high as $6,000. One condition Hanlon made to sign with Cincinnati was that ex-manager Joe Kelley would be retained as player-captain at his old salary.[33] Ebbets then signed Patsy Donovan to skipper his team, as well as to play the outfield.[34] The St. Louis Cardinals were also looking for a manager, but failed to sign one at the meeting.[35]

A number of multi-player deals involving bigger-name players were transacted at the meeting. Pittsburgh sent third baseman Dave Brain, second sacker Del Howard, and right-handed pitcher Vive Lindaman (who had won 24 games with Jersey City in 1905) to the Boston Beaneaters for future Hall of Fame pitcher Vic Willis; the righty immediately became the ace of the Pirates' staff. Boston also traded catcher Pat Moran to Chicago for right-handed pitcher Francis "Big Jeff" Pfeffer and catcher Jack O'Neill. Donovan had only been on the job for Ebbets for a matter of hours when he traded outfielder Jimmy Sheckard to the Chicago Cubs for right-handed pitcher Herbert

"Buttons" Briggs, third baseman James "Doc" Carey, outfielders Jack McCarthy and Bill Maloney, and cash.36

NOTES

1. *Sporting Life*, November 25, 1905: 8, December 2, 1905: 2, 3, 5; *Boston Globe*, November 21, 23, 1905; *Chicago Tribune*, November 22, 1905; *New York Times*, November 23, 1905; *Washington Post*, November 23, 1905.
2. *Sporting Life*, December 2, 1905: 5.
3. *Boston Globe*, November 23, 1905; *Sporting Life*, December 2, 1905: 5.
4. *Sporting Life*, December 9, 1905: 9.
5. *Sporting Life*, December 9, 1905: 5, 8.
6. *Sporting Life*, December 2, 1905: 5, 8; *Chicago Tribune*, November 22, 1905.
7. *Chicago Tribune*, November 22, 1905.
8. *Boston Globe*, November 23, 1905; *Sporting Life*, December 2, 1905: 5, 8.
9. *Sporting Life*, December 9, 1905: 7.
10. *New York Times*, November 23, 1905; *Sporting Life*, December 2, 1905: 2, 3, 5.
11. *New York Times*, November 24, 1905; *Chicago Tribune*, November 24, 1905; *Sporting Life*, December 2, 1905: 5, 9, 10.
12. *Boston Globe*, November 23, 1905; *Chicago Tribune*, November 24, 1905; *Sporting Life*, December 2, 1905: 5.
13. *New York Times*, November 24, 1905; *Sporting Life*, December 2, 1905: 2, and December 9, 1905: 5.
14. *Chicago Tribune*, November 24, 1905; *The Sporting News*, December 23, 1905: 1.
15. *The Sporting News*, December 9, 1905: 5, 9; *Chicago Tribune*, November 24, 1905. Kitson was swapped just a couple of weeks later to the Washington Senators for right-hander John "Happy" Townsend, who was then flipped to Cleveland for yet one more righty, Francis "Red" Donahue.
16. *Sporting Life*, December 9, 1905: 9.
17. *Sporting Life*, December 9, 1905: 3, and December 23, 1905: 4.
18. *Sporting Life*, December 23, 1905: 4.
19. *Chicago Tribune*, December 13, 1905; *Washington Post*, December 13, 1905; *Sporting Life*, December 23, 1905: 4.
20. *Sporting Life*, December 23, 1905: 3, 4.
21. *Sporting Life*, December 23, 1905: 4.
22. *Boston Globe*, December 12, 1905.
23. *New York Times*, December 13, 1905; Frederick G. Lieb, *The Pittsburgh Pirates* (New York: G.P. Putnam's Sons, 1948), 115-119; *Sporting Life*, December 23, 1905: 6.
24. *Boston Globe*, January 12, 1905; *The Sporting News*, December 23, 1905: 1; *Sporting Life*, December 23, 1905: 4.
25. *New York Times*, December 13, 1905.
26. *Sporting Life*, December 23, 1905: 6; SABR BioProject article on George Davis by Nicole DiCicco.
27. *The Sporting News*, December 23, 1905: 1; *Sporting Life*, December 23, 1905: 4, 7.
28. *Chicago Tribune*, December 13, 1905; *Washington Post*, December 13, 1905; *Sporting Life*, December 23, 1905: 4; *The Sporting News*, December 23, 1905: 1.
29. *Sporting Life*, December 23, 1905: 4.
30. *New York Times*, December 13, 1905.
31. *Sporting Life*, December 23, 2905: 4, 5.
32. *Sporting Life*, February 10, 1906: 8.
33. *Sporting Life*, December 23, 1905: 4.
34. *Sporting Life*, December 23, 1905: 4; *The Sporting News*, December 23, 1905: 1.
35. *Sporting Life*, December, 23, 1905: 4.
36. *Sporting Life*, December 23, 1905: 4.

— 1906 —
GRADUAL DÉTENTE, GROWING PAINS

By Christopher Matthews

Introduction and Context

BY THE TIME THE NATIONAL AND American Leagues had held their winter meetings in New York and Chicago, respectively, the internecine trade war that had transpired between the two had been over for three years. Though formal conflict between the two leagues had been extinguished, rivalries between the individual team magnates still remained. In the more established National League, one of these conflicts broke out over the presidency of the league. Harry Pulliam had been president of the National League since the National and American Leagues had called a truce, and full major-league status was granted to the latter, in 1903.[1] The truce led to more economic stability for both leagues by limiting the competition for fans and players. With the passage of more than a century, reliable information about team finances at that time is now hard to verify, but at the 1906 meetings Pulliam claimed that the previous season had been the most financially successful ever for the league.[2] Team owners were no doubt happy with such fiscal stability, and the relative health of each franchise led to many owners having little reason to part with their best players. Conditions were therefore right for many unsuccessful cash bids to be made for star players.

Though the truce had stabilized baseball's finances, the young major leagues still had to suffer through many more growing pains. Resentment remained between owners of the two leagues, especially between owners located in the same city, and those National League owners whose players had been poached from them by their upstart counterparts. These conflicts manifested themselves most saliently at the 1906 meetings through disagreements over scheduling. In the years after the two leagues joined forces, they would continue to compete over Sunday and holiday dates in cities with more than one team, as well as doubleheader dates, the start and end of seasons, and the number of games that should be played.[3] The number of games to be held in the regular season and postseason was an annual disagreement between the two leagues, with many owners from the American League wanting to shorten the regular season from 154 games and add games to the World Series. National League owners, on balance, wished to pack as many games into the schedule as possible, with some wanting to add games to both the regular season and the World Series.[4]

Conflict wasn't limited to owners in opposite leagues. Intraleague scuffles were commonplace, and they often sprang from league presidents' attempts to reinforce the authority of umpires and promote proper conduct of team personnel through fines and other measures. Public and often vulgar denunciations of umpire decisions were much more common, and both Pulliam in the National League and Ban Johnson, president of the American League, fought this behavior. John T. Brush, owner of the New York Giants, campaigned vigorously in 1906 and beyond to oust Pulliam from his presidency because of a fine and suspension Pulliam had levied on Brush's manager, John McGraw.[5] In addition, a temporary reconciliation between Johnson and White Sox owner Charles Comiskey received a great deal of attention in the newspapers during the 1906 winter meetings.[6] The genesis of this particular quarrel (the two had a chronically rocky relationship, spanning many years) was Johnson's fining one of Comiskey's players for using foul language.[7]

Player Movement

In advance of the winter meetings, the newspapers buzzed with excitement over what promised to be eventful sessions, with many players changing hands. In fact, few players were traded, but it wasn't for lack of effort on the part of owners trying to improve their teams. Healthy finances meant owners had cash to throw around, and several large offers were indeed made.

The top two National League teams, the Chicago Cubs and New York Giants, were illustrative of this dynamic, as they began a bidding war for two of the Brooklyn Dodgers' best players. Chicago's 1906 squad won 116 games, but owner Charles Murphy wasn't content with such a historically good squad. He offered $10,000 in cash and three players — pitcher Ed Reulbach, utilityman Solly Hofman, and outfielder Jimmy Slagle — for Brooklyn's star outfielder Harry Lumley, who had led the league in slugging average in 1906. The New York Giants countered with an offer of $25,000 for Lumley and Brooklyn's other star, first baseman Tim Jordan, who had led the league with 12 home runs.[8] Many other rumors filled newspaper columns in the days leading up to the meetings, but nearly all of them amounted to nothing. Explaining the lack of movement in the American League specifically, Johnson said, "Any one of the eight clubs would be willing to unbelt from $25,000 to $30,000 in a minute at this meeting to strengthen its team, but a bank roll cuts small figure in the talk of trades and only playing material of experience or excellent promise has any temptation for the men who control the clubs."[9] Such a dynamic could surely be attributed to the National League as well.

The one major move that did take place went through due to unusual circumstances. Infielder Ed "Batty" Abbaticchio was traded by the Boston Beaneaters to the Pittsburgh Pirates for outfielder Ginger Beaumont, pitcher (and occasional outfielder) Patsy Flaherty, and infielder Claude Ritchey. Abbaticchio was under Boston control in 1906, but had not played because he was living in Pittsburgh and tending to a hotel. The Pirates, naturally, were the only team Abbaticchio was willing to play for, so the Boston club wisely worked out a deal that netted it something for a player who was no longer willing to don its uniform.[10]

Business and Politics

Perhaps the most conspicuous difference between the two leagues was in the strength of their presidents. The American League was Johnson's creation and many American League owners came to own their teams through his machinations. In the National League, however, the presidency was far weaker, and the owners kept its power in check by, at least initially, granting Pulliam one-year terms.[11] Even so, Pulliam managed his post assertively and made honest efforts to control what was known as "rowdyism," or coarse language and behavior, from players and managers toward each other and the umpires.

As he had the previous year, Pulliam faced significant opposition during the 1906 meetings from John T. Brush and August "Garry" Herrmann, owners of the New York and Cincinnati teams, respectively. The conflict between Brush and Pulliam began in 1905 when Pulliam fined and suspended Giants manager John McGraw for publicly accusing Pittsburgh Pirates owner Barney Dreyfuss of bribing umpires. Brush tried but failed to get his fellow owners to replace Pulliam with John Montgomery Ward, a former player and player rights activist now a lawyer. When that move failed, Brush put up James A. Hart, the former owner of the Chicago Cubs. Pulliam was re-elected. Brush and Herrmann campaigned vigorously against Pulliam during the 1906 winter meetings. The final vote however, was 6 to 1 in favor of Pulliam, with Herrmann abstaining and Brush the only nay vote.[12] Before the votes were cast, Brush sought to nominate A.H. Soden, the Boston owner, who was in the process of selling the club, to be president. Soden, however, wouldn't accept the nomination and the coup was a failure.[13]

Besides political and personnel considerations, the winter meetings were the forum where rule changes were debated and implemented. These campaigns often amount to little, and in 1906 no rule changes were actually voted in. The two main changes that were debated were placing numbers on uniforms (at the NL meeting) and the elimination of the foul-strike rule (in the AL meeting). The owner of the Cubs, Charles Murphy, proposed that numbers be placed on the sleeves or backs of the players' uniforms with corresponding numbers on the scorecards, so that fans could better identify the players.[14] Movements to number the players date back to at least the 1890s, but this practical idea didn't become official until the American League adopted it in 1931.[15]

The movement to abolish the foul-strike rule[16] was indicative of the dearth of offense in the first decade of the 20th century. The 1906 Chicago Cubs, with their lusty .763 winning percentage, had no player with a slugging percentage higher than .430. The 1906 Chicago White Sox, American League and World Series champions, were known as the Hitless Wonders for their success in spite of their offensive futility.[17]

The foul-strike rule had only been adopted in 1901, so removing it was not such a radical option for boosting the chances of beleaguered offenses as it would seem today. Its repeal, however, was voted down in 1906,[18] and the problem of defensive dominance was ameliorated four years later with the introduction of a new, livelier baseball.

Conclusion

The 1906 winter meetings were a snapshot of the gradual détente between the two leagues, and the financial success it brought to team owners. The truce, along with the reserve clause, reinstated control of players by the owners, which allowed salary costs to be controlled once again. Lingering animosity between owners led to minor conflicts, but overall the owners knew they stood to gain more by working together than through unbridled competition.

This collective spirit showed itself in the gradual strengthening of the governing bodies of the individual leagues and the major leagues as a whole. The American League was created with a strong executive already in place, but the National League had to ease itself into such a state of affairs. Owners didn't like to see their players and managers fined, as the case of John T. Brush illustrates. Most owners, however, understood that the game benefited when law and order was imposed by strong league presidents. A modern baseball fan is used to seeing ownership generally speak with a unified voice, through the commissioner's office, and with the 1906 meetings one can see this management philosophy in its embryonic stages.

NOTES

1. Harold Seymour and Dorothy Z. Seymour, *Baseball: The Golden Age*, Vol. 2 (New York: Oxford Paperbacks) (Kindle Locations 141-142). Kindle Edition.
2. "Candidates for Pulliam's Place," *Hartford Courant*, December 12, 1906: 9.
3. Seymour and Seymour, Kindle Location 209.
4. "Food for the 'Fans' is Being Prepared," *New York Times*, December 9, 1906: SN15;

"No Baseball Trouble Over Presidency," *New York Times*, December 11, 1906: 7.
5. Seymour and Seymour, Kindle Location 383.
6. *Boston Globe*, December 14, 1906; *Chicago Tribune*, December 16, 1906.
7. Seymour and Seymour, Kindle Location 344.
8. "Bank Roll Battle On in Baseball" *Chicago Tribune* December 9, 1906: A1.
9. "Magnates Here to Meet" *Chicago Tribune*; December 12, 1906: 12.
10. "Votes Pulliam Full Approval" *Chicago Tribune*, December 12, 1906: 12.
11. Seymour and Seymour, Kindle Locations 363, 364. 209.
12. "Pulliam is Reelected," *Boston Globe*, December 13, 1906: 9.
13. Ibid.
14. "Votes Pulliam Full Approval."
15. Seymour and Seymour, Kindle Location 852.
16. Before adoption of the foul-strike rule (by the NL in 1901, the AL in 1903), foul balls did not count as strikes.
17. Seymour and Seymour, Kindle Location 1839.
18. "Pulliam is Reelected."

— 1907 —
THE NEW COOPERATION— "THE MANIFEST DESIRE TO ELEVATE THE GAME"

By Bill Nowlin

THE MAJOR-LEAGUE PORTION OF the 1907 winter meetings were held by both leagues on the same days, Tuesday through Thursday, December 10-12. It was the second year they'd met simultaneously. The National League met in New York City at the Waldorf Astoria while the American League met in Chicago.

New York was the home of both sets of minor-league meetings, which were held in different New York hotels. The National Association of Professional Baseball Leagues held its sixth annual meeting, assembling at the Fifth Avenue Hotel, also on a Tuesday through Thursday schedule, October 29-November 1. The Eastern League held its meeting on Monday, October 28, at the Victoria Hotel, beginning at noon. There was some thought that the American Association might break away from the National Association.

In general, though, baseball had continued since 1905 to enjoy a period of prosperity.

For the second year in a row, the Chicago Cubs had won the NL pennant, this time facing the Detroit Tigers in the World Series. The Tigers had won the franchise's first flag. After being beaten by their South Side counterparts in Chicago during the 1906 World Series, the Cubs grabbed their first world championship, sweeping the Tigers in four games. The two teams would repeat, with nearly identical results, in 1908, providing back-to-back World Series wins for the Cubs. That was only the fifth World Series played, and the Cubs were the first team to have won two.

Under Hughie Jennings, Detroit had climbed from sixth place to first in the AL, beating out Connie Mack's Philadelphia Athletics by a game and a half. The 1908 race would prove even closer, the Tigers finishing by just a half-game ahead of Cleveland and a game and a half ahead of the White Sox.

A number of other postseason series were also played, for instance the seven games played in Boston's City Series between the city's NL and AL ballclubs. There were some 40 interleague contests in all with the National League winning 22 games to the AL's 18. It was the first year in which the senior circuit teams had beaten their junior rivals.

As had the Eastern League, the National Board met the day before the minor-league meetings, also on October 28, and elected California League President Cal Ewing to take the place on the board of Eugene Bert, who had resigned. Agreement was quickly reached on a point designed to prevent ballclubs from releasing players merely to avoid the draft; it was determined that any player released in the last 30 days of the season would instead become a free agent and could sign with any club except the one that had released him. There was discussion of the abuse of "over-drafting," with some clubs claiming too many players and stockpiling them.

In another preliminary, Pat Powers was unanimously re-elected as head of the Eastern League. Powers was also the head of the National Association.

Tim Murnane wrote in the *Boston Globe* that the American Association would arrive "with a large chip on its shoulder." It wanted to place a team in Chicago since both Milwaukee and St. Paul "have turned out to be weak sisters."[1] The placing of a third team in

Chicago would not be welcomed by either of the major leagues. The American Association thought about refusing to attend and just going its own way, but elected at the last minute to send President Joseph D. O'Brien.

Every club was present for the Eastern League meeting, which was harmonious, with "no disputes of any consequence," and the meeting was concluded rather quickly.[2]

For the National Association meeting, over 80 delegates represented 23 leagues on the Association's roster, comprising 195 clubs.[3] The other seven leagues were represented by proxy; in all, 244 clubs were represented. It was the largest turnout of any meeting to date and on two days the room was too small to accommodate everyone, delegates as well as magnates, managers, and ballplayers. There was some talk abroad regarding a possible third major league, but most of the serious discussion related to defending the integrity of the minor leagues vis-à-vis the existing majors. Even then, the meetings were workmanlike with the minors "practically a unit on every proposition."[4]

It was agreed that no player could play in an Eastern League game unless under regular contract to one of the teams in the league; though this might seem logical enough, a number of younger players had been farmed to one or another Eastern League club by NL and AL clubs, particularly after the minor-league seasons had ended. The *New York Times* said the practice had "become very prevalent during the last two years."[5] The agreement also proscribed players from traveling to the West Coast to play in the longer California League season.[6]

There was one controversial plan advanced by the Eastern League: to ask the National Commission to bestow Double-A status (AA) on the Eastern League, ranking it above the Class A distinction enjoyed by the American Association. The matter was never introduced, though *Sporting Life* suggested that "had they done so they might have secured important concessions, as the storm of the previous day had subsided, and there was manifest a disposition to placate them with a view to harmonizing the discordant elements in the Association."[7] A committee was appointed to study the matter, basically a sop. A Class AA was created in 1911.

When the National Association meeting began, the first day was mostly routine. The Eastern League and American Association met by themselves later in the day to talk about their own issues and planned to meet separately again on the second day. AA President O'Brien said that the talk about them seceding was just talk and there was nothing to it. NL President Harry Pulliam spoke by invitation to those assembled and announced his own opposition to unrestricted farming. He also told delegates that NL players were banned from playing for the outlaw California League and subject to a $100 fine.

The National Board was given the authority to punish anyone for assault on an umpire. An attempt that would have reinstated some 22 players who had been banned for jumping to the Tristate League was beaten back.

On the second day, Wednesday, President O'Brien did introduce a resolution that four leagues would be reduced from Class A to Class B and that there would be a restructuring of the national board of arbitration, but virtually no one saw any benefit in the restructuring and it was argued that the Western League was a charter member of the association and could not be demoted, and it was pointed out that one of the conditions of the Pacific Coast League joining the National Association was the promise that it would never be lower than Class A. The vote was 20 to 3 to table the motion. The New York League joined the Eastern League and the American Association in the minority.

Most delegates left for home on the 31st. A six-hour session on the final day, November 1, was largely been devoted to hearing protests and appeals. One such resulted in placing A.J. Laws on the permanent ineligible list. Laws was the former president of the Western Pennsylvania League who had "organized a club at Butler, Pa., and offered a diamond ring to the young woman who sold the most season tickets and that the ring was never presented."[8]

All in all, relatively few changes were legislated, simply because there was a sense that 1907 had been a successful season.

1907 Winter Meetings — the Major-League Portion

The two leagues met separately but simultaneously in December, the American League wrapping up its work in two days while the National League meetings extended to four days. The most notable feature of both was the internal harmony, as well as the fraternal peace between the two leagues.

Indeed, each league president sent the other a telegram wishing his counterpart well. Ban Johnson congratulated Harry Pulliam on the Cubs winning the World Series and Pulliam replied with thanks, concluding, "Long life to the American League and its president." Anything along those lines would have been unimaginable just a few years earlier.

Matters that might have divided the two leagues, such as scheduling and rules, were referred to those respective joint committees, which would meet in February. The NL would no longer arbitrarily declare the start to its league schedule, as it had done prior to the 1903 season. Pulliam wired Johnson just before the meetings began that the NL would appoint men to a schedule committee and work things out in concert with the AL. It was, wrote the *Boston Globe*, a "minor discrepancy" and with Pulliam's undertaking "the last difference between the American league and the National league has been wiped out."[9]

The AL met at the Auditorium Annex in Chicago, a hotel complex built in 1893 and in the early 21st century known as the Congress Plaza Hotel. The meeting began at 3 P.M. on December 11 and ended on the 12th. The NL met at the Waldorf Astoria in New York City from the afternoon of December 10 into the 13th, the final day added on when things ran a bit longer than anticipated.

There were some rumors before the gatherings hinting at possible discord. One was that Charles Comiskey would attempt to unseat Johnson. There was always bound to be some friction over one matter or another, particularly in the AL, which had only seven years under its belt. But no fractious issues materialized in either league. Prosperity seemed to have bred satisfaction.

A few issues came up that one league or the other favored, but after peace had been declared and a joint rules committee had been created, no change could be made unilaterally.

It had taken a full two hours to read the minutes from the previous meeting and then there followed reports from the various league officers. Pulliam's report to the NL magnates recommended that no liquids in bottles be sold in ballparks and that no intoxicants be sold in grandstands. He also came out against "artificial doubleheaders"—ones declared by a club looking for advantage of one sort or another—and that league procedures be implemented for the rescheduling of postponed games, rather than having them be left to the home club to decide. He wanted there to be no more seven-inning games as the second games of doubleheaders. The *New York Times* dubbed it a "stand against bargain baseball."[10] He suggested that a ballclub not be permitted to recall a player once he had been placed on waivers. Lastly, he said that dressing rooms in four of the parks were substandard and should be upgraded.

It was not as though there was unanimity of opinion within each league. John T. Brush of the Giants, for instance, cast a lone vote against Pulliam's re-election as president, voting instead for Frank DeHass Robison. In the AL, Johnson's term ran to 1910, so he was not up for re-election. In appointing members to the rules committee, the AL substituted Comiskey for Thomas C. Noyes of Washington, and the league also asked Boston's John I. Taylor to stay on the board of directors for one more year rather than rotate off as planned in favor of Washington. Both could be seen as rebukes to Washington, but none of this seemed to engender any ill will on the part of the Washington club.[11]

Before the two concurrent meetings had begun, both leagues had agreed to discuss the possibility of lengthening the World Series to a "best-of-nine" competition, as had been the case in 1903 but not since. The National League was in favor and initially it seemed the AL was, too.

That was the only matter which went to a vote at the AL meeting on December 11; the vote was 7 to 1 in favor. All other matters were resolved unanimously. The White Sox cast the vote in opposition, the vote cast by the team secretary in Comiskey's absence. The following day, Comiskey was asked to explain why he had wanted to oppose the motion and he said it was because the AL races were much more competitive than the NL races (this had been the case for four years running) and that consequently the pennant-winning teams in the AL were more exhausted at the end of a 154-game season. Should they agree to revert to a 140-game schedule, he would withdraw his opposition. His argument was persuasive and the 7-to-1 vote in favor of a "best-of-nine" series was rescinded on December 12; a unanimous vote to retain the best-of-seven system, was substituted.[12]

There was a discussion after Boston Doves president George Dovey suggested the limiting of rosters to 18 players, but no resolution occurred.

At prior meetings, when the leagues referred matters to the joint rules committee, they had typically done so with instructions. This year, neither league issued any "hard and fast instructions to either of its joint committees."[13]

Pulliam had proposed that there be no pitcher's mound at all, that the pitcher's slab be on the same level as the playing field so the pitcher was not pitching downhill, giving him an advantage. There was even a suggestion by Max Fleischmann of the Cincinnati Reds that the number of balls required for a base on balls be reduced from four to three, to help with offense.

Fleischmann suggested that a batter who advanced a baserunner by means of a fly ball be credited with a sacrifice hit. And he suggested some changes in when umpires were allowed to call "time." These proposals were discussed but no actions were taken.[14]

The American League suggested that pitchers not be permitted to take a new baseball and rub it on the grass and dirt to make it less slick and shiny—it was called "ball-soiling" and reportedly burned up a great deal of time.

The language adopted by the AL on postponed games read: "All postponed games of the first series shall be played on the first or succeeding days of the second series; all postponed games of the second and third series shall be played on the next day or succeeding day of the same series."[15]

Considerable time was spent discussing the relationship between the majors and minors, and player movement back and forth — for instance, would a major-league player sent back to the minors be permitted to keep his big-league salary? There was also discussion about "covering up" players and farming. The AL adopted a rule that "restricts the practice of acquiring a player by refusing waiver on him and then immediately turning him over to a club outside the league."[16] A new system was put in place to regularize waiver rules; it seemed the sort of thing that a new league would need to address in its early years.

Although there was said to be a larger than usual number of players and minor-league men present at the two meetings, relatively few trades were consummated. At midnight on the eve of the NL meeting, Dovey had signed Joe Kelley to a deal to manage in Boston. The Tigers purchased catcher Ira Thomas from the New York Highlanders, and handed Hughie Jennings a new two-year deal as manager. The White Sox purchased John Anderson from Washington. Boston brought Fred Tenney to the NL meetings, seemingly to help market him. On the final day, December 13, Tenney, Al Bridwell, and Tom Needham were traded to the New York Giants for Frank Bowerman, George Browne, Bill Dahlen, Cecil Ferguson, and Dan McGann.

All in all, the fact that business was good no doubt contributed to the pacific nature of the two sessions and the relations between the leagues. Francis C. Richter wrote in *Sporting Life* of the AL meeting that there "was not the slightest approach to friction."[17] Feeling was so good that Detroit declined to collect a $300 fine that had been levied on Cleveland during the season for delaying a game.

All in all, *Sporting Life* editorialized, the two meetings reflected a "New Era" characterized by "amicable spirit, "mutual toleration," and, perhaps above all else, "the manifest desire to elevate the game."[18]

NOTES

1. *Boston Globe*, October 29, 1907: 5.
2. *New York Times*, October 29, 1907: 9.
3. *Hartford Courant*, October 29, 1907: 14. The *Courant* had said 30 leagues would be represented but only 23 were.
4. *Boston Globe*, November 1, 1907: 4. The *Washington Post* wrote that President Powers had heard rumors about a third league but that "the national officers had no intimation of such a plan, and he did not believe there was anything in it." See *Washington Post*, October 30, 1907: 8.
5. *New York Times*, October 29, 1907: 9.
6. *The Sporting News*, October 31, 1907: 1.
7. *Sporting Life*, November 9, 1907: 6.
8. *Chicago Tribune*, November 2, 1907: 10.
9. *Boston Globe*, December 11, 1907: 4.
10. *New York Times*, December 8, 1907: S3.
11. *Washington Post*, December 13, 1907: 8.
12. The best summary of the discussion is in the December 15, 1907 *Chicago Tribune*.
13. *Chicago Tribune*, December 15, 1907: C1.
14. *Hartford Courant*, December 12, 1907: 12.
15. *Sporting Life*, December 21, 1907: 5.
16. Ibid.
17. Ibid.
18. Ibid.

— 1908 —
MAJOR ISSUES IN THE MINORS, BRIBERY CHARGES AND WORLD SERIES TICKET SCANDAL

By Dennis Pajot

Introduction

After what some call the greatest baseball season of all time, the winter meetings of 1908 produced much thunder, especially on the minor-league level, that had implications for the majors. Two minor leagues looking to be ranked almost on the level of the major leagues dominated the minor-league proceedings. Two major issues during the 1908 season and World Series—both involving the National League—were the major focus of much of the problems at the big-league meetings. However, much of what was started at these meetings was not finished—some never really concluded—until months after the meetings ended. Only minor changes in draft procedures and game rules were passed by the major-league magnates.

Minor League and First National Commission Meetings

The National Association of Professional Baseball Leagues held its eighth annual meeting in Chicago on November 10 to 12, 1908. The meeting was held at the same time and in the same city as baseball's National Commission meeting. The chairman of the National Commission, Garry Herrmann, could not attend the meeting, so his secretary and the two major league presidents (the NL's Harry Pulliam and the AL's Ban Johnson) conducted the National Commission meeting.[1] In regard to major-league activities, the Commission ruled on a player playing in a minor league under an assumed name, (the club fined and the player declared ineligible to organized baseball). They also approved the design of World Series emblems in the future.

The Commission took up the mishandling of the tickets by the Chicago Cubs in the 1908 World Series, but made no decision. All the Commission would say at this time was that there was no merit in charges of deliberate graft, or that Cub officials were in collusion with ticket speculators. However, the club was "reprimanded for the crude and unbusiness-like manner in which the tickets were handled, causing annoyance and disappointment to many supporters of the Cubs."[2] However, the Commission made no formal report on the matter. The ticket scandal would be handled later.[3] (See below) A large number of minor-league cases were heard by the Commission, including player salary grievances, decisions on ineligible players, some league circuit changes, and player appeals. But soon all attention shifted to the minor-league meeting at the Chicago Auditorium Annex.[4]

The NAPBL meeting started in routine fashion, taking up the case of some Minneapolis and Milwaukee players (among others) who played in some barnstorming games against the outlaw Logan Squares of Chicago. The players were suspended and would be reinstated after payment of light fines.[5] There was discussion on raising the minimum admission price in the higher-level minor leagues to 50 cents. The *Milwaukee Journal* was concise in its thoughts on this: "That might be all right in the eastern cities but not in Milwaukee."[6] This idea did not get off the ground.

After hearing arguments regarding the contested ownership of the Hot Springs club, a plea to have the player draft price raised from $200 to $300, plus a request for the shortening of the drafting period to help the Class-C and D leagues (known as the "Microbes"), the minor-league delegates retired for the day.[7]

The meeting then became something of a sensation in the press.

First, a little background: the NAPBL had been formed in November 1901 as a way of ruling the various minor leagues and protecting each other, both from the warring major leagues and from themselves. One year later the recently-formed American Association, having been an "outlaw" league during the 1902 season, joined the National Association. The minors, having waived rights to representation on the National Commission, were under the rule of major-league baseball, without any say in the process.[8] The minor leagues were placed in various classifications according to the aggregate population (from the latest U.S. census) of cities forming the league, from Class A (1,000,000 total population and over) to Class B (400,000 to 1,000,000), Class C (200,000 to 400,000), and Class D (under 200,000).[9] Originally the American Association, Eastern League, and Western League were classified as Class-A leagues. The Western had been given special Class-A status, as its population was below the classification, as a condition of ending the baseball war with the American Association.[10] The Pacific Coast League was admitted to organized baseball as a Class-A league in 1904, even though its population was below the Class-A limit. The status was given under special circumstances to end another baseball war on the West Coast.[11] At the 1905 winter meetings the Southern League was elevated to Class-A status. This was done primarily as a reward to Southern League president William Kavanaugh for his part in defeating a scheme to reclassify the bigger minor leagues and raise draft prices. Thus three of the five Class-A leagues had populations under the constitutional limit.[12] These reclassifications, and an enlargement of the National Association's board from five to seven members, gave the smaller minor leagues the upper hand over the larger-populated Eastern League and American Association in the National Association.[13]

In 1907 the American Association was demanding that the Western, Pacific Coast, and Southern Leagues either be dropped to Class-B leagues, or the American Association and Eastern Leagues be given a new AA status. This demand went nowhere and now, in November 1908, the American Association was changing its tactics. League President Joseph O'Brien said his owners no longer wanted Class-AA status, as that required a change in the National Agreement, which no doubt would fail again. He stated if the NAPBL would enforce its constitution there would be no need for a new status for the American Association and Eastern League, and therefore no need to change anything in the National Agreement.[14] O'Brien presented a resolution that the Southern and Western Leagues be demoted to Class-B status, and the Board of Arbitration be reduced from seven to five members, three of those members coming from Class-A leagues. The Eastern League supported this demand, while the Pacific Coast League told the National Association members it would not join in on this request. After much debate the measure was voted down in the constitutional committee by a vote of 3 to 2. O'Brien insisted the resolution be placed before the entire delegation for a vote. After debate on the main floor, the resolution was defeated by a vote of 17 to 4, with the Missouri-Illinois League and the Pacific Coast League joining in with the American Association and Eastern League.[15]

O'Brien next asked permission for the American Association and Eastern League to withdraw from the NAPBL so they could form a working agreement directly with the major leagues. The two leagues wished to have contracts and reserves honored by the other minor leagues. Of course, this was a bombshell and caused much debate. The two requesting leagues claimed their intention was to withdraw temporarily to seek advice from the National Commission, while the other delegates saw it as the two leagues seeking permanent withdrawal from the NAPBL. This request was put to a vote, resulting in a 19 to 2 defeat. The delegates of the American Association and Eastern League left the meeting room, refusing to work on an appointment of a committee to lay the matter before the National Commission; a committee was then appointed in their absence.[16] This entire situation placed Pat Powers in an uncomfortable situation, as he was both president of the Eastern League and head of the National Association of Professional Base Ball Leagues. He stepped down as head of the minors and D. M. Shively of the Western Association took over the convention.[17]

O'Brien tried to play down any talk of revolution by saying: "We have done nothing more serious than to withdraw from the meeting. We have not withdrawn from organized baseball nor have we severed our connection with the national association by our action. We have not become 'outlaws'."[18]

The minor leagues did conduct two further pieces of important business at the meeting. The lower minors gained a victory when it was decided that players who had been drafted would be returned to the same league they had been drafted from when the drafting team cut the player. It was also voted to increase the number of cities in the Western League from six to eight by adding clubs in Wichita and Topeka.[19]

Meanwhile, the National Commission members discussed the impasse and announced it had decided the NAPBL was clearly within its rights and the Commission would not receive any delegates from the Eastern League or American Association, as they had no legal standing. Section 4, Article VI, of the National Agreement clearly stated "The National Association shall have the classification of its leagues and the adoption of a salary limit for clubs according to classification." However, in an effort to settle the matter, it was decided that National Commission chairman Herrmann be asked to come to Chicago so the Commission could deliberate as a whole. Herrmann, however, was immobilized due to a sprained ankle, so the American Association and Eastern League delegates announced they would hold a full meeting of their two leagues in Buffalo on November 18 to map out any future plans and then make a statement to the public. The Commission, by and large, was trying to stay out of the matter, but did make clear it was going to stop this type of last-minute sensationalism by adopting a new rule that, in the future, all proposed amendments to the National Association constitution must be sent to the secretary 60 days in advance of the annual meeting.[20]

Eastern League president Pat Powers explained in a circular letter sent to the owners of the Eastern League that what the American Association and Eastern League wanted was representation on the National Commission. This would enable the leagues to push through new draft rules. The two leagues wanted the privilege to draft one man from the clubs of the other three Class-A leagues and two from the Class-B clubs at the same time as the major leagues were drafting, and at the same price. These players would then be allowed to remain with the club during the season in which they were purchased. The American Association and Eastern League also wanted the right to draft territory from the lesser minor leagues for a fixed compensation. In addition they wished to prevent the majors from drafting players below Class-B leagues.[21]

The Sporting News acknowledged the two "bolting" leagues had some legitimate grievances, but thought the thread of secession was stultifying. The editor did not believe the two minors were economically prepared for a baseball war, not even for a single season. And the final statement of the editorial was perhaps a warning from the two major leagues: "The National and American Leagues will not admit a representative of the National Association to the Commission, nor will the majors make any other concession to the minor leagues, as a body, or to its members as individual organizations. Under no circumstances will protection be extended to a league or association of leagues that is not a party to the National Agreement, a major league or a league in the fold of the National Association. And as a corollary, the American Association and Eastern League must continue in the National Association to enjoy the benefits of organized base ball."[22]

Of course, rumors of a new baseball war were all around. It was asserted the Eastern League planned to withdraw from Montreal and place a club in New York, with the specific location said to be in the Bronx. It also was hinted that the Toronto club might be moved to Detroit. The American Association reportedly was expected to invade St. Louis and Pittsburgh, as well as Chicago, abandoning St. Paul and Minneapolis, though where the third franchise would be taken from was undecided, at least in the minds of the rumor spreaders. Charles Havenor, president of the Milwaukee Brewers, was in the meantime denying the American Association was planning on putting a franchise in any American or National League cities.[23]

Representatives of the Eastern League and American Association did meet in Buffalo on November 18. A committee was formed, with O'Brien as chairman. No information was released at this time, but it was believed the leagues were still pressing the points in the Powers' letter. It was decided the leagues' requests would be put in writing and given to the National Commission at its next meeting on December 7. The two minor leagues were scheduled to meet again on December 6.[24]

Second National Commission Meeting

At the December 7 meeting, after taking up some minor issues of player salaries and draft disputes, the Commission took up the minor-league "bolter" issue.[25]

The Eastern League and American Association had met on December 6 at the Victoria Hotel in New York City. They drew up the complaints that they would put before the National Commission, but gave out no details. The lawyer representing the group, Henry Killilea of Milwaukee, stated the two leagues only wanted to be classed higher than the other minor leagues and be allowed to manage their own internal affairs. He thought these two leagues were important enough to be given these considerations. To make his point Killilea said the American Association and Eastern League represented a population of 5,000,000 people, more than twice as many as were represented by all the other minor leagues put together. In addition to that, the attendance at games in the two leagues was twice as much as in all the other minor leagues combined. He said the two big minors were not looking for a baseball war, but he did hint at that possibility.[26]

The major leagues were certainly not shaking in their boots. National League president Pulliam told reporters before the meetings: "We are prepared for anything that comes along. Of course, the game of freeze out would be very unwelcome. 'War is sure hell' for the man who has to pay the piper. But organized baseball is better able to stand the strain than are the minors, and if it comes to a showdown we will all be doing business after 'outlawry' is suppressed."[27]

The American Association/Eastern League petition was presented to the National Commission in Pulliam's office in the St. James Building on December 8, with the "loyal" minor leagues also present.[28] Henry Killilea masterfully presented the concerns of the "bolting" leagues to the Commission. His petition asked for the following: 1) to conduct their affairs as a separate organization under organized baseball; 2) that the American Association and Eastern League be permitted to draft players from all other leagues except the American League and National League, provided only one player could be drafted from Class-A minor-league clubs; 3) that draft and purchase rules be amended so that players drafted by the major leagues from Class-B, C, or D leagues and later not kept, be offered to the American Association or Eastern League before being returned to their original club; 4) that major-league player reserve rosters be capped at 25, and at 20 after May 15; 5) that the American Association and Eastern League be permitted to draft players from other minor leagues for a period of 15 days after the majors had drafted, and the draft price be $750 for Class-A league players, $500 for Class B, $300 for Class C, and $200 for Class D; 6) the major-league draft period for players from the American Association/Eastern League be from September 15 to October 1; 7) that the American Association and Eastern League be permitted to draft territory from other minor leagues; and 8) that no individual player could be sold more than once under an optional agreement.[29]

One of the points in Killilea's argument for the American Association and Eastern League to obtain a higher status was his belief that the NAPBL legally expired on September 6, 1906. His argument was based on the fact that the NAPBL was created on September

6, 1901 for a period of five years. A resolution was later passed verbally to extend this period to September 6, 1911, but Killilea argued the added five years was not legally binding and that the NAPBL was simply a voluntary organization from which any member could withdraw without violating any contract. He went one step further, saying that with the contract between the parties to the National Agreement thus ended, the major leagues had any legal "as well as moral right" to change the conditions of the National Agreement and accept the "bolters" as partners. This argument would take away the National Commission's reasoning for staying out of the minor-league issue.[30]

Michael Sexton, a board member of the NAPBL, said Killilea's statement was not correct. He looked at the minutes of the inaugural meeting of the National Association and found there was nothing in them relative to the length of the life of the NAPBL. He found in subsequent minutes that the 10-year agreement had been adopted by a unanimous vote and was binding upon all organizations that were members at that time, "and upon all associations, leagues and clubs hereafter becoming parties to this National Agreement."[31]

The National Commission asked for more time to look at the petition, as it was different than had been anticipated. It was decided the National Commission would report on the issues at its annual meeting in Cincinnati on January 4.[32] This delay did not sit well with the American Association/Eastern League combine, who were now reported to be in a state of mind to withdraw from organized baseball. However, Milwaukeeans Killilea and Charles Havenor calmed the group down, saying the National Commission did not even have to take the matter up and the delay put the NAPBL on the defensive. In a face-saving move Killilea, O'Brien, and Powers were granted an audience before both the National and American Leagues to present their case and ask for future negotiations. The "bolters" were granted permission to attend the January meeting "in an advisory capacity."[33]

Many American Association owners thought the two big minor leagues had secured a victory. Havenor told the *Milwaukee Sentinel* the demands of the American Association/Eastern League were perfectly just, and he was certain they would all be granted by the major leagues in January.[34] But Havenor was not listening to what American League president and Commission member Johnson was saying: "I have great respect for Mr. Killilea, but he was not furnished with the facts and it was only too plain that there was no real grievance named by the Milwaukee man."[35]

National League Winter Meeting

The National League held its annual winter meeting at the Waldorf-Astoria in New York on December 8, 9, and 10. The New York Giants did not send a delegate at the meeting, until forced to attend on the final day. League president Pulliam acted as chairman for all the sessions. The meetings consisted of the usual activities, including the awarding of the league championship to the Chicago Cubs, the president's report on the season just past, Pulliam's re-election to the post, the election of a Board of Directors and the forming of committees. All clubs agreed to take "extra precautions" in enforcing the league's law against gambling on their grounds. A number of other items were discussed, but held over for a later meeting. One item of sentimental importance was the decision to make up any deficit in the fund to erect a monument to the late Henry Chadwick, and to make an annual appropriation for its care.[36]

Regarding player matters, the National League voted to reduce the time limit for the return of a player on waivers during the season from 10 days to 5 days. The "Microbes" request to increase the draft prices for players was approved and recommended to the National Commission for incorporation into the National Agreement. The delegates also adopted the National Agreement amendment to limit the major-league drafting period from September 1 to September 15, a cut back from October 1. The NL also heard the requests of the American Association and Eastern League, presented by attorney Killilea, and told the minor leagues they would have the National League's sympathy in its struggles.[37]

At the same time of the baseball meetings President-elect William Howard Taft was in town, and Pulliam had the opportunity to meet him at the

> ## BRUSH REMAINED STEAMED OVER THE "MERKLE GAME" DECISION
>
> In October, New York Mayor McClellan wrote to John Brush congratulating the team on a great season. Brush expressed gratitude, but acknowledged his ire over the ultimate ruling.
>
> "Mr. Mayor—I am in receipt of your congratulatory letter of the 9th instant, in which you compliment Manager McGraw and the players of the New York National League Baseball Club for their efforts to bring the highest base ball honors for 1908 to this city. It is gratifying to both managers and players to receive from you such expressions of appreciation and regard, and to know that while some things may be taken from this city, that in equity belongs to it, such encomiums as you bestow are beyond the reach of those who were called upon to sit in judgment and interpret base ball law."
>
> Manager McGraw, the players, Mr. Knowles and myself are grateful to you, as representing the city of New York, and to you personally for your kind expressions and good wishes for the future.
>
> "Brush Thanks the Mayor," *New York Times*, October 13, 1908: 16.

Hotel Astor. The President-elect told the National League president: "Glad to meet you, Mr. Pulliam. We are going to be rival Presidents, but I hope we shall always get along pleasantly." Pulliam responded by saying he would not try to appoint the Ambassador to England, provided Mr. Taft would agree not to rob him of any of his umpires.[38]

The third day of the meeting produced a first in major-league history. The National League received a visit from an American League delegation, a request that had been made by AL president Johnson, for an exchange of courtesies. The remarks made were the expected ones with hopes of future harmony. According to *Sporting Life* "the last germ of ill-will between rival majors was wiped out."[39]

After this show of harmony and unity it appeared the National League executives could adjourn with a calm, ho-hum meeting under their belts. But Pulliam sprang a sensational charge—being "like the bursting of an anarchistic bomb in a family of royalty"— that an attempt had been made to bribe umpires James Johnstone and Bill Klem in the extra game between the New York Giants and Chicago Cubs played on October 8—the game ordered to play off the tie game of September 23 (which had featured the famous Merkle play at second base). The umpires had filed formal charges, including the name of the person who initiated the bribe and the names of the persons he claimed to represent. This sensation necessitated an extra, unscheduled, day for discussion, the issuance of a formal statement, and the appearance of New York owner Brush, who had not been present at the earlier sessions, claiming illness—although some thought it was to show his disgust of the throwing out of the "Merkle game."[40] The National League statement—signed by all eight club officials—gave an outline of the attempted bribery, then continued:

"We are of the opinion that a most thorough and searching investigation of this matter be made in order to maintain the high standard and honesty of the game throughout the entire country, and if possible, to punish all persons connected with this disreputable proceeding.

"To make such an investigation as the undersigned desire, we deem it unwise to give any names of persons claimed to have been connected with this matter, as we have grave doubts as to the truths of certain statements alleged by the person who approached one of the umpires; and it is for that reason, as well as having in mind the proper punishment of all guilty parties, that all names be withheld for the present.

"We desire, however, to state that none of the persons whose names are withheld at this time is in any way connected with organized base ball."

The statement further went on to commend Klem and Johnstone for refusing to become parties to the bribe and reporting it to the league.[41]

It was the opinion of some in the press that the two umpires had been approached by a gambler representing a syndicate that wanted to wage a large sum on the game. The gambler wanted Klem and Johnstone to "see" that the Giants won the game. It was stated the umpires were offered $10,000 if the Giants won. The only identification at this time was that the man who approached the umpires was "a prominent businessman of New York, who also represented many other big men of that city."[42]

A committee was formed, consisting of John T. Brush (chairman), Charles Ebbets, Garry Herrmann, and Pulliam to investigate the matter.[43] Some have found it odd that Brush was the chairman, since his club was involved in the scandal. However, Philadelphia newsman Horace Fogel thought it not only appropriate, but a good move, writing: "If his club is involved, it was a good stroke of policy to put him at the head of this committee, so that the evidence can be adduced in his presence and he can not afterwards charge unfairness, trumped-up charges, etc. and rush into court for an injunction or any redress."[44] The matter would take months to settle. (See below).

American League Winter Meeting

The American League held its meeting at the Hotel Wolcott in New York on December 9 and 10. All the clubs were represented, with AL president Ban Johnson chairing. This meeting was unassuming. A Board of Directors was named and committees formed. The Detroit Tigers were awarded the 1908 league championship. As the National League did, the Americans decided to recommend to the National Commission the request for a higher draft price of the Class-C and D leagues for incorporation into the National Agreement. The AL also voted for the National Agreement amendment to limit the major-league drafting period from September 1 to September 15, thus making this time frame baseball law.[45] J. M. Cummings, of Baltimore thought this of little practical benefit to the minor leagues, as most of the majors had determined who they would draft days, if not weeks, before the draft period started.[46] The American League also heard the American Association/Eastern League grievances and assured Killilea of the major league's "sincere desire to aid those leading minor leagues to a better condition with a view to conserving the peace and prosperity of all connected with the National game."[47]

A number of new rules and practices were passed by American League delegates. Among the more important that there would be 40 minutes before each game for practice, the first 30 minutes for the visitors, then 10 minutes for the home team. The rule was put into place to prevent the indiscriminate throwing and batting of balls in the park. An important, and lasting, rule change prevented a runner from advancing more than two bases when a thrown ball went into the stands. Prior to this the runner was allowed to continue to run until he scored. The American League also decided no passes to games were to be issued to members of the visiting team, as this practice was being abused. A new rule was put into effect regarding something modern fans take for granted—all clubs were ordered to maintain a large bulletin board giving the batting order accurately and indicating all changes as they were made.[48]

After business was finished Johnson suggested his league delegates and those of the National League meet. The NL men accepted and the meeting mentioned above took place. The American League meeting adjourned shortly after 2:00 p.m. on December 10.[49]

Player and Manager Transactions

As at most winter meetings, trades and signing of players were done with more frequency than at other times of the year. Perhaps the major occurrence at the 1908 National League meeting in this regard was the signing by the Cincinnati Reds of Clark Griffith as the team's manager. It was reported Griffith's salary was to be $7,000, with a privilege of renewal. This signing set in motion a three-club deal. The Reds traded catcher George Schlei to the St. Louis Cardinals for left-handed pitcher Ed Karger and right-handed pitcher Art Fromme. Schlei and outfielder John "Red" Murray and righty Arthur "Bugs" Raymond were then traded by the Cardinals to the New York Giants for catcher Roger Bresnahan. The future Hall of Famer would be the St. Louis player/manager.[50]

Another managerial maneuver involved another future Hall of Famer. It was reported during the National League meeting that veteran catcher Frank Bowerman would be elevated to the Boston Braves' manager's job, succeeding Joe Kelley. Kelley, who was present at the meeting, had one year remaining on his two-year contract and threatened legal troubles to Braves owner George Dovey. Pulliam mediated an arrangement for Toronto of the Eastern League to take Kelley's contract and manage in that Canadian city. As the Future Hall of Famer's contract called for an amount over the Eastern League salary limit, the Braves would pay the excess.[51]

The major trade in the American League was that of catcher Lou Criger from the Boston club to the St. Louis Browns for catcher Ed "Tubby" Spencer and $5,000.[52]

Conclusion of Matters Taken Up at Winter Meetings

World Series Ticket Scandal

Later in December of 1908, the National Commission gave its ruling on the Chicago World Series ticket scandal. In summary the Commission found that the Cub management had told the public tickets would be on sale at Spalding's store on Friday morning, October 9. Tickets for all four scheduled home games—the first in Chicago to be on Sunday, October 11—had to be purchased in one block. The public assembled at Spalding's only to be told later in the afternoon that the tickets would not be available until the next morning at the box office of the ball park. However, while the public was in line at Spalding's the club was selling tickets at its own office to bands of "scalpers." These tickets were then sold to the public at exorbitant prices. When the public did assemble at the ball park on Saturday morning, they were told only those who had arranged for reserved seats would be accommodated. While this was happening the club was still selling tickets at its office to scalpers. The public was never notified of the sale of tickets at the club's office, and no other tickets except those purchased by scalper's could have been out in the public. The Chicago club officials admitted 630 tickets were sold to one person at their office.[53]

The National Commission found "the Chicago Club is deserving of the severest criticism and censure for the manner in which they handled the sale of tickets during the last world's series, and that they must be held responsible for the great annoyance they caused many patrons of the game in Chicago." As there was no direct charge, or proof offered, that anyone employed by the Cubs was in collusion with the scalpers, it was requested that Cubs president Charles Murphy—whom the Commission acknowledged was not in Chicago on the days this took place—look into how these tickets were secured by these persons. The commission called for clubs to make an effort to have local authorities in their city pass proper laws and ordinances to prevent the scalping of tickets. The Commission "was strongly of the opinion" that hereafter all World Series ticket sales be handled by the Commission to prevent future similar occurrences.[54]

Murphy made a short statement after the Commission reported its findings, saying that the Commission's statement there were no ticket sales at the park was incorrect. He said the sale of tickets began at the park offices at 1:00 p.m. and continued until the line of buyers had melted away. Murphy said that the tickets were not on sale at Spalding's at the advertised time due to a delay in the preparation of the tickets, which had not been delivered in time to the printer. He took the "mea culpa," saying: "My own illness was doubtless responsible for much of the trouble and confusion."[55]

Chicago sportswriter William A. Phelon wrote of the National Commission's investigation and ruling that…: "everybody is laughing raucously." He went on to say that the "Commission's report soaked nobody and everybody, satisfied no one, and left things just where they began. The report did not do justice either way. If the employees of the club were really guilty of any scalping, they escape exposure, punishment and condemnation; if they were innocent, they are not given any vindication, and are left with a cloud hanging over them…(t)he fans, who loudly insisted that somebody must be shown up as either guilty or innocent, get nothing—they are not shown wherein the ticket-men did wrong, nor are they shown where the unlucky officials were in the right."[56]

Attempted Bribe of Umpires

The inquiry of the attempted bribery of umpires Klem and Johnstone took longer. In late January, Joe Vila, the New York correspondent to *The Sporting News*, was urging the committee of Brush, Pulliam, Ebbets, and Herrmann to issue a statement on what evidence it had gathered.[57] A month later H. G. Merrill from Wilkes-Barre made the same plea.[58] The matter was finally turned over to the National Commission who ruled on the matter on April 19, 1909. In its official statement the Commission ruled that "after a full and thorough investigation of all of the matters that have been presented" the statements of the umpires were true and the two were "deserving of the highest commendation" in spurning the bribe attempt and reporting it to the National League. The Commission declined to give out the name of the person who offered the bribe, but took this action: 'In this matter the Commission would not hesitate a moment to instigate a most rigid prosecution against the offender if they had the power to do so, and the corroborative testimony to sustain the charges as made by the umpires. We feel, however, that in the absence of this, the party charged with this offense by the umpires should not go unpunished, and for that reason we will furnish to every major league club owner the name of the person who attempted this offense, with instructions to such club owners to bar him from their respective grounds for all time to come."[59] The *Chicago Tribune* soon gave the name of the man as Joseph Creamer, the Giants' team physician, and stated the money offered was first $2,500 and later raised to $3,000.[60]

Decision of Status of Minor-League "Bolters"

On January 4, 1909, the National Commission met in Cincinnati. After the usual player reinstatement issues, the members took up the American Association/Eastern League issue. Owners and representatives from the NAPBL and the "bolters" were in attendance, both giving their side again.[61] According to the *Milwaukee Journal*: "The session waxed warm at times and there was more than one exchange of hot words."[62]

After the first day adjournment, attorney Killilea and NAPBL secretary John Farrell met in an attempt to reach some type of compromise to present to their respective parties. The compromise they ironed out provided for a separate classification of the American Association, Eastern League, and Pacific Coast League, plus additional drafting privileges of players and territory for these three leagues. Another point would be that the three big minor leagues could have control of their own affairs, except where a lower class player was involved and subject to appeal to the National Commission. This compromise solution did not address the matter of the "bolters" withdrawal from the NAPBL and separate admission to the National Agreement. It was felt this was a matter for the National Commission to decide.[63]

On the second day this compromise proposal was presented to all members of both sides. With some tweaking, all issues were adjusted to everyone's satisfaction in the NAPBL, except for the American Association and Eastern League leaving the National Association. Members of the American Association and Eastern League had some issues with the compromise.

John Farrell then submitted to the National Commission what the minor leagues were willing to concede to the three big minors: 1) The Eastern League and American Association would have the privilege of settling their own internal disputes; 2) Disputes involving the "bolters" and other National Association clubs would be passed on to the NAPBL board; 3) All leagues would have the right to draft territory from leagues next lowest in classification at the same time and in the same manner that players were drafted. Prices would be set for the territory in each class; 4) The big minors could draft from Classes B, C, and D only at $100 less than that paid by the major league. This drafting would take place in the 15 days immediately following the draft period of the majors; 5) There would be no objection to the secondary draft—meaning a player not kept by the majors must be offered to a minor league of a higher class than the player was originally drafted from, starting with Class AA and working down; and 6) The Eastern League, American Association, and Pacific Coast League would be designated as Class AA, without any further privileges.

The "bolters" were willing to accept most of the conditions. However, the limitation on drafting territory only from the classification immediately below their class was of little use to either the American Association or Eastern League. This would limit them to only claiming a city from the Southern or Western League—something not useful to either big minor. The "bolters" also demanded the right to draft players from the Southern and Western Leagues. Of course, the American Association/Eastern League combine was still insisting upon its primary goal—the privilege of withdrawing from the National Association in order to become a separate party to the National Agreement.

The National Commission chairman, Herrmann, stated the commission thought the territorial drafting complaint of the American Association and Eastern League was well founded, but under no circumstances would the National Commission agree to the "bolters" demand for recognition as a separate party to the National Agreement, even if the minor-league association would agree to this demand. Herrmann, "in courteous terms," advised the two leagues to accept the compromise offered by the NAPBL.[64]

After the day's adjournment the Eastern League and American Association committee met to discuss the situation. There was much sentiment in favor of withdrawal from the NAPBL, an action that would mean outlawry and war. Henry Killilea pleaded with the excited delegates to rethink this position. Cooler heads prevailed and after some time the delegates decided to accept the NABL proposal, with the exception of the territorial draft clause and the additional right to draft players from the Southern and Western Leagues. In regard to the territorial rights a compromise was decided in which it was "understood" the price for rights to a city would be $5,000 for a Class-A city, $4,000 for a Class-B city, $3,000 and $2,000 respectively for Class-C and D territories.[65]

The loyal minors accepted these proposals, with some modifications—most notably that Class-AA leagues could draft one man from each Class-A club, only in cases where the major leagues had not previously selected a man. The National Commission took over the territorial issue and decided any league had the right to draft territory from any contiguous class upon certain terms. These terms were to include a set price for the territory in each class, three months' notice of intention and three more for consummation, notice to the National Board for the reasons for drafting territory, and additional money to be determined for the value of the franchise, plant and team.[66]

With the matters in this satisfactory state, the National Commission adjourned and delegates from the minor leagues made arrangements to go home. The American Association and Eastern League held a joint business meeting to make some adjustments in regard to the new conditions. AA president Joseph O'Brien resigned his seat on the NAPBL board, and Patrick Powers formally resigned his office as president of the NAPBL (Michael Sexton was soon elected to the post).[67]

Upon returning to Milwaukee, O'Brien told reporters: "We got all we wanted, and both the Eastern League and the Association should flourish under the new conditions. Our request to be allowed to act as a third part to the agreement with representation on the National Commission was not allowed, but that was only a minor detail to the other conditions. Great credit is due to Mr. Killilea for the part he played in securing the concessions."[68]

The winner in this agreement, without really entering the battle, was the Pacific Coast League. They were granted the privilege of gaining the new higher classification because of the promise made to it when it entered organized baseball that it would never be asked to accept a classification more than one step below the major leagues. Pacific Coast League president Cal Ewing said he would not be doing his duty to his league unless he took everything that was handed him.[69]

In March 1909 the revised National Agreement was published, incorporating the concessions granted the Eastern League, American Association, and Pacific Coast League, with the exception of the territorial draft, which had not yet been approved by the big leagues and minor leagues.[70]

Then on May 4 all these bitterly fought gains evaporated when the National Commission abrogated the entire new National Agreement, and announced all baseball rules and regulations would go back to what they had been before the concessions were made to the big minors. The National Commission said the revised Agreement had been sent to the American Association and Eastern League to be ratified and approved, but neither had done so. Thus "no league or club operating under organized base ball will be required to pay attention to any of the new features embodied in the revised Agreement." Garry Herrmann said there was no ulterior motive in all this, only that they two leagues never replied and the National Commission was forced to do something to avoid confusion throughout the baseball world.[71] It was reported the American Association and Eastern League refused to ratify the new agreement because the major league magnates would not put a definite price on the territorial rights of any league. The National Commission told the American Association/Eastern League combine to sign the agreement and an amount would be inserted later. At the earlier meeting it was "understood" what the territorial prices would be, but wording of new National Agreement stated a league "may draft a city from a league of lower classification upon terms and conditions to be proscribed by the National Commission within 30 days from the signing." In other words, the price of a territory would not be known until after the purchase.[72] As J. M. Cummings wrote in *The Sporting News*: "A child knows that there are no 'understandings' in law. Black and white goes and only that."[73] As the new AA classification gave the Big Three little or no additional power, they decided to ignore the agreement and continue under the old one.[74]

Thus the big three minors lost their AA classification. Southern League president William Kavanaugh had no objection to the National Commission abrogating the revised National Agreement, but did object to the wording of the announcement. In his opinion the new Agreement became binding when the National Association of Professional Base Ball Leagues ratified it, and the ratification and approval of the American Association and Eastern League was not necessary.[75]

With this news there were the usual rumors of a baseball war, especially the renewed story of the American Association planning an invasion of Chicago. It was thought the American Association was more eager to go to war than the Eastern League, as the Eastern had no interest in placing a team in any of the major league cities in the east.[76] O'Brien pretty much put the entire matter behind him when he said: "We are too busy catering to the base ball public. This is no time to meddle with the politics of the game."[77] Havenor was quoted as saying "I guess that we are about as well off this way as we would have been the other, if not better".[78]

The American Association and Eastern League would have to wait until the 1912 season to obtain Class-AA status.

NOTES

1 *Sporting Life*, November 21, 1908: 1.
2 *Sporting Life*, November 21, 1908: 7.
3 *Sporting Life*, November 21, 1908: 1, and November 28, 1908: 6, 7.
4 *Sporting Life*, November 21, 1908: 6.
5 *The Sporting News*, November 12, 1908: 1.
6 *Milwaukee Journal*, November 9 and 11, 1908.
7 *Chicago Tribune*, November 11, 1908:61; *Washington Post*, November 11, 1908:8; *Milwaukee Journal*, November 11, 1908.
8 *Sporting Life*, November 21, 1908: 1.
9 *The Sporting News*, November 19, 1908: 4; *Sporting Life*, November 21, 1908: 1.
10 *Sporting Life* November 21, 1908: 6.
11 *Milwaukee Sentinel*, November 10, 1908; *Hartford Courant* November 10, 1908; *Sporting Life*, November 21, 1908: 6.
12 *Milwaukee Sentinel*, November 10, 1908.
13 *Sporting Life*, November 21, 1908: 2.
14 *Milwaukee Sentinel*, November 10, 1908.

15 *Sporting Life*, November 21, 1908: 6; *The Sporting News*, November 12, 1908: 1.

16 *Sporting Life*, November 21, 1908: 7.

17 *Milwaukee Sentinel*, November 12, 1908.

18 *Hartford Courant*, November 12, 1908.

19 *Hartford Courant*, November 12, 1908; *Sporting Life* November 21, 1908: 2; *Milwaukee Journal*, November 14, 1908.

20 *The Sporting News*, November 19, 1908: 4; *Sporting Life*, November 21, 1908: 6, 7.

21 *Sporting Life*, November 21, 1908: 7; *Milwaukee Journal*, November 19, 1908.

22 *The Sporting News*, November 19, 1908: 4.

23 *Milwaukee Sentinel*, November 14, 1908; *Milwaukee Journal*, November 13, 1908; *The Sporting News*, November 19, 1908: 3.

24 *Sporting Life*, November 28, 1908: 6.

25 *The Sporting News*, December 10, 1908: 5.

26 *Sporting Life*, December 1, 1908; *Washington Post*, December 7, 1908: 4.

27 *Milwaukee Journal*, December 7, 1908.

28 *Milwaukee Journal*, December 8, 1908; *The Sporting News*, December 10, 1908: 1, December 17, 1908: 2.

29 *Sporting Life*, December 19, 1908: 1; *The Sporting News*, December 10, 1908: 1.

30 *Sporting Life*, December 26, 1908: 6.

31 *Sporting Life*, January 2, 1909: 10; *The Sporting News*, December 24, 1908: 4.

32 *Sporting Life*, December 19, 1908: 1, 2.

33 *Sporting Life*, December 19, 1908: 2; *Milwaukee Sentinel*, December 11, 1908.

34 *Milwaukee Sentinel*, December 13, 1908.

35 *Boston Globe*, December 13, 1908.

36 *Sporting Life*, December 19, 1908: 4; *Milwaukee Sentinel*, December 10, 1908.

37 *Sporting Life*, December 19, 1908: 4; *Milwaukee Sentinel*, December 9, 1908.

38 *Sporting Life*, December 19, 1908: 5.

39 *Sporting Life*, December 19, 1908: 4.

40 *Boston Globe*, December 9, 1908; *Sporting Life*, December 19, 1908: 4; *Milwaukee Sentinel*, December 12, 1908; *The Sporting News*, December 17, 1908: 1.

41 *Sporting Life*, December 19, 1908: 4.

42 *Sporting Life*, December 19, 1908: 4.

43 *Sporting Life*, December 19, 1908: 4.

44 *The Sporting News*, December 17, 1908: 5.

45 *Sporting Life*, December 26, 1908: 2.

46 *The Sporting News*, February 17, 1908: 2.

47 *Sporting Life*, December 19, 1908: 4.

48 *Sporting Life*, December 19, 1908:4; *Milwaukee Sentinel*, December 11, 1908.

49 *Sporting Life*, December 19, 1908: 4.

50 *Sporting Life*, December 19, 1908: 5.

51 *Sporting Life*, December 19, 1908: 5.

52 *Sporting Life*, December 19, 1908: 5.

53 *Sporting Life*, December 26, 1908: 1; *The Sporting News*, December 24, 1908: 2.

54 *Sporting Life*, December 26, 1908: 1, 2; *The Sporting News*, December 24, 1908: 2.

55 *Sporting Life*, December 26, 1908: 2.

56 *Sporting Life*, January 2, 1909: 5.

57 *The Sporting News*, January 28, 1909: 1.

58 *The Sporting News*, February 18, 1909.

59 *Sporting Life*, April 24, 1909: 7.

60 *The Sporting News*, April 29, 1909: 2. The entire matter is too lengthy and falls out of the compass of this article, but is interesting. The best reading on the details and possible full involvement in the matter can be found in David W. Anderson, *More than Merkle, A History of the Best and Most Baseball Season in Human History* (Lincoln: University of Nebraska Press, 1999), 210-222; and Cait Murphy, *Crazy '08, How a Cast of Cranks, Rogues, Boneheads, and Magnates Created the Greatest Year in Baseball History*, (New York: HarperCollins, 2007), 261-263, 284-286.

61 *Sporting Life*, January 16, 1909: 1.

62 *Milwaukee Journal*, January 5, 1909.

63 *Sporting Life*, January 16, 1909: 1.

64 *Sporting Life*, January 16, 1909: 2.

65 *Sporting Life*, January 16, 1909: 2; *The Sporting News*, May 20, 1909: 4.

66 *Sporting Life*, January 16, 1909: 2; *The Sporting News*, January 14, 1909: 4.

67 *Sporting Life*, January 16, 1909: 2.

68 *Milwaukee Journal*, January 7, 1909.

69 *Sporting Life*, January 16, 1909: 2.

70 *Sporting Life*, April 3, 1909: 10.

71 *Sporting Life*, May 15, 1909: 1.

72 *The Sporting News*, May 13, 1909: 2, 6; June 2, 1909: 2.

73 *The Sporting News*, June 2, 1909: 2.

74 *Sporting Life*, May 15, 1909: 1.

75 *The Sporting News*, May 13, 1909: 4; *Sporting Life*, May 15, 1909: 1.

76 *The Sporting News*, May 13, 1909: 4; *Sporting Life*, June 5, 1909: 16.

77 *Sporting Life*, May 15, 1909: 2.

78 *Milwaukee Journal*, May 5, 1909.

— 1909 —
IF IT TAKES ALL WINTER

By Marshall Adesman

MOVING INTO 1909, CHANGE WAS in the wind. All ballparks had been, up to that point, made of wood, but Pittsburgh's Forbes Field, Philadelphia's Shibe Park, and St. Louis' rebuilt Sportsman's Park opened that year as baseball's first steel-and-concrete facilities.[1] More umpires were hired so that the majority of big-league games would now feature two arbiters, the better for keeping the peace as well as making it more likely that the correct call would be made.[2] And the Reds experimented with night games, allowing a semipro team to use lights to play a game in its park after dark.[3]

But the 1909 season will always be remembered by one shattering event.

Harry Pulliam was a Kentucky native with an eclectic background. He was a law school graduate who chose to write for a newspaper in Louisville rather than practice law, and he also served for a time in the Kentucky Assembly.[4] Somewhere along the way he made the acquaintance of Barney Dreyfuss and joined his organization, first as secretary of the Louisville Colonels (then in the National League), and later as president of the team, which moved to Pittsburgh and became the Pirates. Pulliam has been described as an idealist, a dreamer, a lover of solitude and nature.[5] He was known to be sensitive and a gentleman in a sport where being rough and tough was a hallmark.

Pulliam's health suffered in February of 1909, and he decided to take a leave of absence. Pulliam was back at his desk by late June of 1909, but he "lacked his usual effervescence."[6] One month later he left the office early, saying he wasn't feeling well, went back to his apartment, and put a bullet in his head. He was just 40 years old, and baseball canceled all games on August 2 as a tribute to him.[7] They also made Heydler—who filled in during Pulliam's leave of absence—the interim president, and scheduled a new election for the winter meetings.

The Calm Before the Storm

The minor leagues were relatively unaffected by these events, and proceeded with their Winter Meetings, which began on November 8 in Memphis, Tennessee, the first time that the NAPBL had held their annual convention in the South.[8] Of the 37 leagues that made up the organization, 19 were present.[9]

Business was brisk in Memphis from the very first day. Mike Sexton, the minor leagues' president, appointed a committee to revise their bylaws. John Farrell, secretary of the organization, gave a report that included a lot of numbers: there were now 257 member cities; the American League had drafted 86 players in

---

PULLIAM'S ILLNESS

Reportedly, no note was found in Harry Pulliam's room where he shot himself, and he had been in good spirits since his return to work.

Friends of Pulliam indicated that his suicide was an emotional reaction to the moment, and consisted of no planning.

However, friends also noted that Pulliam was vulnerable to severe attacks of melancholia, and his attendants had been fearful he would make an attempt on his life.

"Pulliam Shoots Self," *Washington Post*, July 29, 1909: 1.

"Harry Pulliam Shoots Self," *Chicago Daily Tribune*, July 29, 1909: 1.

1909, 9 more than the National League; 484 players had been suspended and another 11 declared ineligible, while 161 men were reinstated. And the owners of the Wichita team in the (Class-A) Western League won a judgment in a case involving a pitcher named Hunt, who had been purchased by the Boston Doves (the name used for a time by the National League club as a paean to owner Dovey).[10]

The next day the executives got down to serious business, foremost of which was admitting the California State League into the NAPBL. This league had been considered an "outlaw," operating outside the purview of Organized Baseball; today we would simply call it an independent. The agreement that brought them into the fold allowed each team in the league to keep all of their players, even those who had violated their previous reserve clause contracts. Most players were bound to play in the league for two seasons, but a few of them were tied to the newly-assigned Class-D association for four full years. Fresno, Oakland, Sacramento, San Francisco, and Stockton were admitted as member cities, and one other town (which would prove to be San Jose) would be named later.[11]

The Class-B Northwestern League was also heard from on this day. Officially they argued that, because of their unique Pacific Northwest location, they ought to lose only one player to each Class-A league and no more than two to the major leagues, but in reality they were angling to be "re-zoned" as an A league, which at the time was the highest level in the minors. Their request was referred to committee and — no doubt to their regret — they never did get to advance.[12]

Drafting of players was a topic at a great many conventions during the early part of the twentieth century, and the 1909 meetings were no exception. The President of the Class-B Central League, Dr. Frank Carson, stumped to have major-league teams pay the same price for any players they drafted, regardless of classification. At the time a player from a higher level cost more, but Dr. Carson argued that if a Class-C athlete, for instance, was considered to be draft-worthy by a big-league general manager, then that elevated his status and the price ought to go up accordingly. This idea was also referred to committee;[13] it is unlikely that the majors ultimately looked very favorably upon this suggestion. Meanwhile, the Class-C and D leagues petitioned the minors to allow them to keep drafted players until their seasons had concluded, as opposed to the rule in effect at the time, which required those players to be delivered on August 23. This also went to committee, as did Dr. Carson's idea that if a player had not returned his signed contract by a to-be-determined period of time, he would incur a fine.[14] Dr. Carson was also involved in one more piece of business, which had to do with possible re-districting. The Presidents of the Central, Ohio-Pennsylvania (Class C), Ohio State, and Pennsylvania-West Virginia Leagues (the latter two were in Class D) were to get together to see if, perhaps, there were too many teams in too close proximity to one another.[15] Those discussions would bring about the demise of the Pennsylvania-West Virginia, the move of Mansfield from the Ohio State to the Ohio-Pennsylvania, and the addition of three new towns into the Ohio State.

Day Two ended with a birth and a re-birth. The Virginia Valley League was admitted to the Class-D ranks, with teams in Charleston, Huntington, and Parkersburg, West Virginia, plus Ashland, Kentucky.[16] An interesting side note about this league was that the 1910 pennant was won by the Huntington club, managed by Cy Young, who was still able to find the time to get into 21 games, and throw 163 innings, for Cleveland.

Despite a rumor to the contrary prior to the start of this gathering in Memphis, Mike Sexton was re-elected as president of the NAPBL. It was a position he held for the next 24 years.[17]

The final day saw a flurry of activity. The minors leagues in effect renewed themselves as an organization for another 10 years, and they passed a rule requiring players to formally be under contract before they could play in a game; while this may seem obvious to us today, at that time different leagues had different rules that basically gave ballclubs the ability to "test-drive" players for a week or two.[18] In another contractual matter, it was decided that any player who broke the signed agreement with his team would be suspended for five years.[19]

Several more new leagues sprang into existence. Based in Santa Ana, the uniquely-named Southern California Trolley League became part of the NAPBL's Class-D level, but despite fielding two teams in Los Angeles and four others nearby, they only wound up playing a handful of games before disbanding.[20] The Southwest Texas League was also admitted as a D-level loop, and they lasted for two full seasons.[21] Other attempts, however, never fulfilled their promise. Despite receiving NAPBL approval that included applications from six towns, an Iowa league did not get off the ground, and the same fate met would-be entrepreneurs in both Pennsylvania and Mississippi.[22]

Charles Murphy, owner of the Chicago Cubs, came to Memphis to arrange for spring training for his team, and he announced that they, along with Cleveland, would spend most of their time working the kinks out in New Orleans before barnstorming their way north.[23] And the final order of business was choosing a site for the minor leagues' 1910 Winter Meetings, and the lucky winner proved to be Chicago, which out-polled Louisville.[24]

There Are Battle Lines Being Drawn

As was the custom of the day, both major leagues met separately, with the National League convening in New York on December 14 and the American League gathering at the Hotel Wolcott, also in New York, the next day. With no major issues on the docket, Ban Johnson's group expected to take care of all its business in a single day.[25]

The Senior Circuit, however, could not make that statement. Since Pulliam's suicide, a triumvirate of NL owners had banded together to try and make sure the "right man" would be selected as the new president. What parameters were being considered? Just one — according to the *New York Times*, all this trio wanted was a leader who did not back his umpires, as Pulliam had done and as Heydler had done in his short time in office. Ebbets of the Dodgers, Brush of the Giants, and the Cubs' Murphy wanted someone "they can influence on this umpire question as in the old days...when it was possible for certain umpires to be barred from working in some baseball parks by the President of the League at the request of managers."[26] Curiously, the person they had chosen to carry their flag was someone who had been a thorn in the side of ownership just 20 years before — John Montgomery Ward. The former infielder and pitcher had helped to organize perhaps the first union in professional sports, the Brotherhood of Professional Baseball Players, and also the Players League, which had been formed as a challenge to the National League and its salary cap.[27] The league, however, only lasted for one season (1890), and after his retirement Ward became a practicing attorney who at times represented players in their lawsuits against baseball.[28] Despite this track record, however, Messrs Ebbets, Brush, and Murphy apparently felt he would be a malleable leader.

Barney Dreyfuss of the Pirates and Herrmann of the Reds were the primary owners stumping for Heydler's election, with Herrmann by far the most outspoken. Arriving in New York several days ahead of the Winter Meetings, he said that Heydler's consistent backing of his umpires had given the public great faith in his administration and had therefore lifted baseball to "a high standard."[29] He thought that the objections raised against Heydler were "silly," and went on to say that "it looks...as if some of the managers wanted to go on the diamond and umpire their own games... (e)ven then some of them would not be satisfied."[30]

Dovey and Stanley Robison, owner of the St. Louis Cardinals, aligned themselves with Dreyfuss and Herrmann, which meant that Heydler needed just one more vote to be elected, and that vote resided in Philadelphia. Which is exactly what Murphy wanted.

Even to this day no one can be quite sure if, and why, the Cubs' owner hated Heydler. When asked point-blank why he was opposed to retaining the league president, Murphy "rose to heights of indignation...and said that it was none of the public's business."[31] This was a typical statement by the often blunt and obstinate Murphy, whose teams were perhaps the best in the history of the franchise but whose actions, machinations and words earned him numerous enemies throughout the game and made him (along with John McGraw), "the most hated man in baseball."[32] He was, however, also very well

THE POTENTIAL ISSUE OF "SYNDICATE BALL"

Throughout the National League presidency controversy, hints of hurt feelings over syndicate ball—in this case, potential set alliances of clubs at the expense of other clubs—emerged on several occasions. Below are a few examples.

> "Mr. Murphy has nothing to do with my affairs. I will vote for whom I think has the business interests of the National League at heard."
> M. Stanley Robison

> "I do not believe that Mr. Murphy is trying to syndicate baseball, nor that he has any interest in the Philadelphia club, which recently changed ownership. I know absolutely that there is no truth that he tried to purchase the Boston club."
> John Dovey

> "As for syndicate baseball, I have always been opposed to it, and I don't propose to stand for it now. The Philadelphia club will be managed as a purely business proposition and in an honest effort to give Philadelphia a winning ball team."
> Horace Fogel

"Baseball War Clouds Parting," *Boston Daily Globe*, November 30, 1909: 4.

connected. He had begun his professional career as a sportswriter for the *Cincinnati Enquirer*, which was owned by Charles Taft, the older half-brother of William Howard Taft, the future 27th President of the United States and 10th Chief Justice of the U.S. Supreme Court.[33] Murphy and Taft struck up a lifelong friendship, which led to his becoming sports editor of the newspaper, which led to a rapport with New York Giants owner Brush and his eventual purchase of the Cubs in 1905, made possible by a $100,000 loan from Taft.[34] And when the Phillies franchise became available, Murphy and Taft made sure that it was bought by a group headed by another former sportswriter, Horace Fogel.[35]

A Pennsylvania native, Fogel worked for newspapers in Baltimore and Philadelphia, as well as *Sporting Life*, a weekly publication that was a competitor to *The Sporting News* for more than 30 years. Fogel also briefly managed two major-league teams, including the New York Giants, but his career mark of 38-72 attests to his skill on the bench. He was not much of an evaluator of talent, either, as he auditioned 21-year-old Christy Mathewson at both first base and the outfield.[36] After Fogel's dismissal, Mathewson went back to the mound for good.

Back in the newspaper business, Fogel was described as "a loudmouth front-runner with little-to-no credibility…and (who) often feuded with players in print,"[37] yet somehow he was able to come up with the $500,000 necessary to purchase a major-league ballclub. Despite repeated denials, speculation quickly focused on Murphy and Taft being the true source of the money,[38] and their reasoning became apparent when Fogel aligned himself with the anti-Heydler, pro-Ward faction, which deadlocked the vote.

Despite the fact that this matter had nothing whatsoever to do with his teams, American League president Johnson decided to throw gasoline on the already-smoldering fire. He told reporters that he and all eight AL owners were firmly opposed to Ward, citing the 1903 case involving infielder George Davis, who had jumped from the Giants to the White Sox when the fledgling AL was offering lucrative contracts to NL players. Davis went to court, where his legal counsel was none other than Ward.[39] Even though the American League won the case and Davis wound up concluding his career in Chicago, Johnson had not forgotten the incident and was obviously holding a grudge. He told reporters that he could not work with Ward, that the "good will between the leagues would be a thing of the past…," and it could foment a new internal baseball war.[40] Charles Comiskey, owner of the White Sox (and Johnson's hunting buddy) and Charles Somers of Cleveland both agreed with their leader, with Comiskey stating flatly, "I am absolutely for war. I can't see how we can avoid it...I think a little war now and then helps the game..."[41]

This, then, was the backdrop as the National League owners arrived at New York's famous Waldorf-Astoria Hotel. There was, of course, other business on the docket. The Boston Doves, for instance, signed a new manager by pirating Fred Lake away from the crosstown Red Sox,[42] while another manager chose to stay put: in spite of rumors that he would retire, Fred Clarke signed a multi-year contract to remain at the helm of the Pirates, for a salary reported to be $15,000 per year.[43] Another personnel matter to be disposed of involved pitcher Bill Torrey, who was being claimed by both the Giants and Reds, as well as the Springfield club of the (Class B) Three-I League and an outfit named the Logan Squares of Chicago.[44]

There were issues on the agenda that would be debated by both major leagues, headlined by the possibility of lengthening the schedule to 168 games. The Cubs' Murphy brazenly predicted that both leagues would adopt the longer season, which would open around mid-April and end in mid-October and still leave enough time for the World Series.[45] Yet Pittsburgh's Dreyfuss objected, saying he had no interest in playing 168 games and would, in fact, favor a reduction in the number of contests.[46]

There was also much talk about banning both the spiked shoe and the spitball. A representative from the Class B Three-I League was scheduled to demonstrate a new device that was said to be blunt and would therefore not cut another player, yet was strong enough to dig into the dirt.[47] But Grillo of the *Washington Post* correctly predicted "it is not at all likely that any change will be made in the rules...(i)t is generally admitted that to do away with the spike will...make the game slower...accidents resulting from the wearing of spikes are really very few...players are spiked simply because they are clumsy."[48] Meanwhile, the spitball was also causing a great deal of discussion. In a poll of more than two dozen sportswriters, nearly 60 percent favored abolishing the pitch, while the rest were evenly divided between those who wanted to keep it and those who really had no strong opinion either way.[49] A year earlier Pulliam had advocated against the pitch, and now Frank Chance, the Cubs' player-manager, came to New York to try and have it banned.[50] It would, however, be another decade before the spitter was declared illegal.

The owners also were casting at least furtive glances towards Wilkes-Barre, Pennsylvania. The Barons, a (Class-B) New York State League team, had purchased a pitcher, Joseph Pelequin, from the Allentown team,[51] paying $300 in cash along with a $200 promissory note. When Allentown did not receive the balance, they went to court, and Wilkes-Barre filed a most unusual defense, saying that "the sale of a baseball player is (in) direct violation of the Thirteenth Amendment to the Federal Constitution," thus not making them liable for the remaining $200.[52] The Thirteenth Amendment famously prohibits slavery, so the Barons were, in effect, telling the court that they shouldn't have to fulfill their financial obligation because they were engaging in an unconstitutional practice. In an editorial, the *Washington Post* prophesized that "professional players may one day learn definitely what their rights are under the thirteenth amendment."[53] That day, however, would not come for more than six decades.

The Phillies seemed to be everywhere. In addition to all the speculation as to whose money was behind Fogel, another matter occupied the owners in the early phase of the meetings. The Philadelphians had been in New York on October 4 for a doubleheader and, after dropping the opener, a brouhaha occurred in the nightcap. With the score tied at one in the fourth inning, right-hander Lew Moren complained when one of his pitches was called a ball. The argument grew heated and Moren was tossed out of the game, along with his catcher, Red Dooin, and second baseman Otto Knabe. The two position players, however, refused to leave the playing field, which resulted in the game being forfeited to the Giants.[54] Not content with the sweep, the Polo Grounders asked the league to extract $1,000 from the Phils, no doubt to make up for lost revenue, since the game was not official at the point of forfeiture. The league took the matter under advisement, but did rule that the three players would be ineligible to play in 1910 unless they paid the fines that had been levied upon them.[55] Since all were Phillie regulars in 1910, it is fair to assume the league received their money. Dooin, in fact, became the player-manager after Fogel fired Billy Murray, who actively lobbied for his job in New York by brandishing his contract, which still had two years to run. Despite a winning record and published sympathy from the *New York Times* and the *Los Angeles Times*[56], Murray was not retained and never managed in any league again.

Meanwhile, Just A Couple Of Blocks Away...

The eyes of baseball may have been on the National League and their contentious presidential election, but the American League also had a meeting of their own, which commenced a day after the senior circuit's festivities began. And while they were anticipating a concise, one-day affair, they were going to have to deal with an important issue during their time at the Hotel Wolcott.

The basic business was relatively easy. A committee consisting of President Johnson and two league owners—Frank Navin of Detroit and T.C. Noyes of Washington—was charged with drawing up a new agreement to perpetuate the league and to revise their constitution.[57] A team's active roster was set at 25 players from May 1 through August 20, and 35 players from August 20 until the following May 1.[58] And though more noise was made about a 168-game schedule, the AL voted to continue playing 154 games.[59]

Johnson also placed his pet peeve—barnstorming—on the docket. A common practice of the time, it consisted of players getting together and playing exhibition games in small towns all around the country once the World Series had concluded. The reason for doing this was simply to earn extra money, since salaries were very low in those pre-union days. Owners hated barnstorming because it just increased the chances for injuries, but rather than pay their players enough money to keep them at home, they sought to end the practice via the rulebook, and Johnson was happy to carry the ball, proposing that players be under contract to their teams for a full 12 months, which would obligate them to receive permission to barnstorm, an OK they were not likely to receive because, as Johnson said, "it cheapens our game."[60]

Nothing, however, can be more damaging to the sport than an accusation of cheating. The New York club, then known as the Highlanders, had been a mediocre squad in 1909, finishing fifth with their 74-77 record, 23 ½ games behind Detroit. But they had a terrific September, posting a championship-caliber record of 20-11. Was it simply a salary drive? Not according to Joe Cantillon and Hughie Jennings, managers of the Senators and Tigers, respectively. Cantillon believed that the New Yorkers were involved in a "wigwag scheme"—stealing signs from opposing catchers—and was happy to say so publicly.[61] Future Hall of Famer Jennings decided to investigate when his team went east in late September, and he sent a couple of people to check out all the nooks and crannies of their upper Manhattan ballpark. One of those "detectives" was trainer Harry Tuthill, and he noticed that "the crossbar in the 'H' of a Young's Hats sign in center field was changing colors."[62] A closer look produced the reason: a man, outfitted with a pair of binoculars, was sitting up there and, using a lever and a mirror, was letting New York batters know if the next pitch would be a fastball or not.[63]

Highlander manager George Stallings and Johnson had been enemies for almost a decade, and now it appeared as if the AL prexy could drop the hammer on his foe. Instead, when the season ended, it was Cantillon who lost his job. Now, in truth, that was primarily on merit: the Senators had a record of 158-297 in Cantillon's three seasons, including a 110-loss campaign in 1909. But the official reason given for his dismissal was disloyalty to the (Washington) organization, a charge which upset him enough that he demanded complete vindication or else he would go to court.[64]

Unlike the civil war taking place over at the Waldorf, however, Johnson was able to contain this potential stink. Unwilling to butt heads against two of his stronger franchises (New York and Detroit), Stallings and the Highlanders were allowed to skate,[65] and Cantillon received his complete exoneration.⁶⁶ A former minor-league infielder and major-league umpire, Cantillon remained in baseball as a minor-league owner and manager, though he never did return to the big leagues.

One thing these meetings lacked was player movement. Only two deals of any note were made, both by New York. The Highlanders acquired journeyman catcher Lou Criger from the St. Louis Browns in exchange for outfielder Ray Demmitt and right-hander Joe Lake, who was the only one from this trio to have any semblance of success in 1910, winning 11 games with a 2.20 ERA, though he did also lose 17 times. The New Yorkers also sold infielder and former manager Norman "Kid" Elberfeld to Washington for $5,000.⁶⁷ This was rumored to be the precursor to a much larger deal, one in which 22-year-old right-hander Walter Johnson—a 25-game loser in 1909 despite a 2.22 ERA—plus catcher Charles "Gabby" Street, would move to the Big Apple.⁶⁸ Nothing came of it, however, and Johnson would turn around and win 25 in 1910, the first of 10 straight 20-game seasons for the Big Train.

However, as always, there were some good rumors going around. One of them had outfielder George Stone, the 1906 American League batting champion, plus an unnamed Browns teammate, heading to the White Sox for right-hander Frank Smith, a 25-game winner in 1909.⁶⁹ Another had infielder/outfielder Freddy Parent moving from the White Sox to Cleveland in exchange for infielder George Stovall;⁷⁰ both proved to be unfounded. There were, however, a few deals made with minor league clubs, with perhaps the most notable being Pittsburgh's acquisition of first baseman Jack Flynn from St. Paul of the (Class-A) American Association.⁷¹ Flynn would take over for Bill Abstein, who was waived to the St. Louis Browns and who was out of the majors by 1911.

Minor League Interlude

The minors made a bit of news while these major-league meetings were being held. Henry Berry, president of the Los Angeles Angels of the Pacific Coast League, was hoping to force the resignation of Danny Long as league secretary. Berry was upset with the shoddy way in which the PCL's final statistics were distributed to newspapers in league cities, as well as with the league utilizing the field manager of the San Francisco Seals in an administrative capacity, and was hoping to push Long out the door, but he was not successful at this time.⁷² Also in the PCL, former major-league infielder Harry Wolverton was hired to manage the Oakland Oaks.⁷³ This would be the first of eight seasons in which Wolverton would lead clubs out on the west coast, though he would have less success when he went east in 1912, losing 100 games as the skipper of the Highlanders. A couple of other minor league clubs brought in new field leaders. Ed Ashenbach, who had managed Altoona in the Tri-State League, was tapped to take over Syracuse in the New York State League, while another Tri-State man, George Heckert, simply moved from Harrisburg to Trenton.⁷⁴ Meanwhile, back in the New York State, Scranton owner E.J. Coleman reportedly offered his managerial job to three people—Sam Strang, Monte Cross, and Hugh Hearne, with former big-league shortstop Cross accepting the position.⁷⁵ And there was talk that the American Association would be bringing back Joseph O'Brien as its president after a one-year hiatus, but that proved to be nothing more than talk.⁷⁶

The Ghost Of Merkle

Dennis Pajot has already thoroughly described the charge that the two umpires who worked the October 8, 1908 "playoff" game (the Merkle follow-up), had both been offered a bribe. (See the chapter on the 1908 Winter Meetings.) The matter threatened to explode again at the 1909 meetings. While the public had been told about the bribe attempt, the official conclusions were kept secret until the spring of 1909, when Harvey Woodruff of the *Chicago Tribune* broke the story.⁷⁷ But unlike today, when a cable media volcano would have erupted, the matter just withered and died. And Dr. Creamer, after threatening to sue everyone for defamation of character, quietly accepted his banishment and retreated from the spotlight and returned to his medical practice.⁷⁸ But then Ban Johnson told reporters that he had "considerable new evidence" in the case, information that included different names and proved that Dr. Creamer was "merely a scapegoat for others."[79] And then...nothing more was ever said!

So was there really new evidence and, if so, what was it? Assuming Johnson, arguably the most powerful man in the game at the time, really knew the truth, why would he issue a teaser like that and then stay quiet? Was he, perhaps, using his knowledge to try and influence the National League's choice of a new president, as intimated in a *Chicago Tribune* article?[80] We shall never know.

And Now For The Main Event

As if he were firmly perched in the eye of a hurricane, Heydler began the second day of his league's meetings with a "State of the League" report. He told the assembled executives that attendance and gate receipts had virtually doubled since the war with the American League had been settled back in 1903, and the league was debt-free for the first time in the 20th century.[81] Heydler did make it a point to mention that six games had been protested in 1909, which he felt were six too many, and he urged team owners to forgo this practice and support the decisions made by the umpires.[82]

The moguls took care of one piece of old business. A proposal had been made to put up a monument to their fallen leader, Pulliam, but it turned out that one had already been erected on the family plot in Louisville, so instead it was decided to pay Mr. Pulliam's sister "a sum of money" as well as money which may have been equal to a portion of his $5,000 salary.[83]

But the main event was the election of a president. Heydler told reporters that he was in the fight to stay, but that he thought too much importance was being given to the matter. "If I am not elected," he said, "I shall continue to exist, and probably will be much happier...."[84]

In a move which caught everyone by surprise, Heydler's name was not formally put forward in nomination. After some five hours of discussion and debate behind closed doors, National League owners finally decided to call for a vote. Ward was nominated, as expected, and then Cincinnati's Herrmann told his colleagues that he had been "authorized to withdraw the name of. Heydler if it was presented in nomination."[85] At this point Stanley Robison of the Cardinals nominated Robert Brown, a Louisville newspaperman and friend of Herrmann's who was, no doubt, serving as a "stalking horse" for Heydler.[86] No matter, the vote ended up in a tie, with Brooklyn, Chicago, New York, and Philadelphia supporting Ward, while Boston, Cincinnati, Pittsburgh, and St. Louis were lined up for Brown/Heydler. Two more ballots did not change anyone's minds, and with that the moguls adjourned for the day.[87]

Immediately there was speculation that a compromise candidate would have to be found, and one did not need the deductive skills of Sherlock Holmes to know who was hoping to be tapped. The name of Edward "Ned" Hanlon, who had managed pennant winners in both Baltimore and Brooklyn in the previous decade, was being tossed about freely, and Adrian "Cap" Anson, one of the game's early stars and the first man in history to collect 3,000 hits, had deliberately made the trip into New York so he would be available to take the position should it be offered. Meanwhile, O'Brien, the one-time American Association president who was seeking the office again, may have also dropped hints that he could be persuaded to lead the NL before stating publicly that his only interest was in the minor-league job.[88]

Johnson's supposed "new evidence" in the 1908 umpire bribery case was not the only attempt at exercising political pressure. A story began making the rounds that two of the four clubs supporting Brown or Heydler, the Pirates and Reds, were ready to bolt over to the American League if Ward became the new National League president. Attributed to an "unnamed friend" of Reds owner Herrmann, it stated that the AL would operate for one year as a 10-team circuit and then "Detroit and some other city (would be) handed over to the American association."[89] More ridiculousness came from Brush of the Giants, who told his fellow owners that since New York and Chicago were the "biggest money-making clubs in the circuit" and they wanted Ward as their leader, then "their demands should be granted."⁹⁰ All this hogwash emanating from the Waldorf-Astoria, as well as the entire tenor of the proceedings, caused the New York *Times* to, first, tacitly come out in support of Heydler—"...whose administration of the office seems to be satisfactory to every one except Murphy, Brush, and Ebbets..."—and then lambast that trio by stating that their "objections to Mr. Heydler have caused the baseball world to sneer at their absurdity."⁹¹ And the *Times* reminded readers that the owners had been in a similar spot in 1902, when Nicholas Young, the NL President since 1885, was challenged by Albert Spalding. Each candidate received support from four teams, with the deadlock eventually being broken by the selection of a compromise candidate, who turned out to be none other than Pulliam.⁹²

With the stalemate continuing, Johnson once again inserted himself into the proceedings. He sent a telegram to his friend Herrmann, informing the National League owners that their American League counterparts had concluded their business and departed from New York, which "should indicate forcibly to you...that we do not wish to influence...to the slightest degree your organization in the election of an officer."⁹³ Johnson's words shocked the assemblage and were seen as a retreat from his previous position, in which he said he would never be able to co-exist with Ward. It strengthened the resolve of the Ward faction, with Brush indicating he could wait it out all winter, if it came to that.⁹⁴

And what if it did, what would happen then? Three possible scenarios emerged:
- Heydler would remain in office indefinitely until a successor could be named;
- A "regency" would be named, a commission made up of three owners;
- One owner would be named to the post, probably on an interim basis.

The first option was not seen as likely because it was assumed, probably correctly, that this would simply strengthen Heydler's position and his ultimate hold on the presidency. The other two were not probable because, according to Ebbets, owners' responsibilities with their own teams precluded anyone finding the time to devote themselves to league-wide duties.⁹⁵

So now the back-room machinations began in earnest. Brush was given the opportunity to name a compromise candidate, but he fatefully declined because he still held out hope for a Ward victory.⁹⁶ He countered with a unique, though convoluted idea: each side would select an attorney and then those two would name a third, presumably neutral, lawyer. The 1903 George Davis case (described earlier) would then be brought out of mothballs and re-examined by this new three-man panel. Why? As explained by the *Washington Post*: "...if these lawyers decided that Ward, as attorney for Davis, had acted illegally or unprofessionally, Ward would agree to withdraw as a candidate, but if the lawyers decided in Ward's favor Herrmann and his friends would have to vote for his election."⁹⁷

This strange brew apparently was discussed but then, mercifully, rejected. The Ward faction then may have turned to an old-fashioned remedy, bribery. Rumors were rampant that both the Giants' Brush and the Cubs' Murphy had approached Stanley Robison of the Cardinals and assured him that he "can obtain sufficient players to make an almost pennant winning club..." if he came over to the Ward side.⁹⁸ (It should be noted that the Cards had not had a winning season since 1901.)

> **FOGEL DENIES ILL-WILL AGAINST HEYDLER**
>
> "... I suppose I may be held responsible for preventing the election of John Heydler to the presidency of the National League. I certainly voted against him and thus caused the deadlock which resulted in his defeat. But in all this I had no personal feeling against Mr. Heydler, none whatever. I consider him a fine man and able one, and well-fitted for the big office he came so near securing."
>
> "The Man Who is Trying to Wreck Baseball," *Baseball Magazine*, June 1913, XI (2), 21-32.

Perhaps these intrigues got to be too much for the other owners, because Herrmann met privately with Robert Hedges, the owner of the St. Louis Browns. One of the premier baseball reporters of the era, Sanborn, realized that Hedges was the only AL owner still hanging around and concluded that he had not remained in New York "to do some…early Christmas shopping…but for the purpose of being consulted as to the acceptability to the American League of numerous compromise candidates for the National League presidency."[99] And shortly thereafter, a subcommittee of Herrmann, Murphy, and William Locke, an official with the Pirates who was "trusted implicitly by members of both factions,"[100] was put together; while their mission was not made public, it was widely presumed that they were charged with identifying compromise candidates.

The next day the impasse came to an end with the selection of Thomas Lynch as the new National League president. A minor- and major-league umpire, primarily in the 1880s, Lynch had built up a reputation for honesty and integrity before going home to New Britain, Connecticut to manage a theater, disenchanted by the treatment he had received from those in uniform and the lack of support he had received from those in business suits.[101] Brush put his name forward and, because of his reputation and availability, he proved to be acceptable to all parties. Lynch insisted that Heydler return to his old position as secretary-treasurer and the owners agreed, electing him to a three-year term-[102]which, according to Sanborn, was a clear victory for Dreyfuss and Herrmann and "a practical vindication of Heydler" because it kept "the details of handling the National League's affairs in the hands of John Heydler."[103]

There was no doubt, however, that the whole matter left a bad taste in the mouths of many, and their feelings were summed up by. Grillo. In what we would now call an op-ed piece, written just prior to Lynch's election, Grillo said the game was in "deplorable condition," which he blamed on the owners, "men who… have enjoyed too much prosperity and are determined to tear down what it has taken years to build up."[104] Presaging sentiments that continue to be expressed more than a century later, he decried the lack of "true sportsmen" among the moguls, calling them "a mercenary lot whose interest ceases with the box office…"[105] But there was no shortage of other materialistic types seeking membership into this exclusive club. An anonymous executive thought that a third major league was likely to be formed within two or three years, because the "immense profits… have opened…eyes, and…they are now casting about for a favorable opportunity…"[106] While there would be at least three attempts over the years to form a third major league, none of them would prove to be successful; however, those "favorable opportunities" did translate into expansion, with the first growth spurt taking place after the 1960 season. For half a century, major-league baseball was played by the same 16 franchises, housed in the same 11 cities, but today the big-league landscape has practically been doubled, with 30 teams located in all regions of the country.

Tying Up Loose Ends

With the league's leadership question now settled, the final bits of business could be dealt with speedily. With the exception of the Boston Doves, all spring training sites were finalized. Arkansas proved to be the most popular state, with the Pirates and Reds opting to join the Red Sox in Hot Springs, while the Cardinals chose to be in Little Rock. Three teams went to Texas—Marlin Springs would host the Giants, San Antonio got the Tigers while Houston welcomed the Browns. The Cubs and Indians chose New Orleans, while the Yankees (Athens) and the A's (Atlanta) both planned to camp out in Georgia. The Dodgers selected Columbia, South Carolina while the Phillies went to Southern Pines, North Carolina, and the Senators chose to be relatively close to home with their Norfolk, Virginia locale. The White Sox were the most daring, splitting their squad between Los Angeles and San Francisco.[107]

The NL adopted a roster rule similar to that of their Junior Circuit counterparts. Just like the American League, they set the active roster at 25 players, but their dates were May 10 through August 10, unlike the AL's May 1 through August 20. The waiver rule was also changed back to its former wording, so that if a player were to be claimed on waivers, his team could withdraw him and not send him to the claiming club.[108]

And with that, the very eventful 1909 Winter Meetings came to a close.

Summary

The contentious battle for the National League presidency was easily the highlight of the Winter Meetings of 1909, with both intransigent sides standing firm for their candidates until it became apparent that neither could win and a compromise would have to be effected. While Lynch was elected to the office, the battle in reality demonstrated the power and influence of American League President Johnson, whose outspoken opposition to Ward's candidacy helped to keep the former infielder/pitcher out of power. It also showed the esteem in which Heydler was held in most circles. While he did not remain in the President's chair, he was given a three-year contract to return to his former position as secretary-treasurer, which today we might call the Chief Operating Officer. And nine years later he did, in fact, become the NL's chief executive, a position he would hold for 16 years.

The 1909 meetings also gave glimpses into the future. Interest in the profitability of franchises forecast baseball's eventual expansion. There was a challenge to the reserve clause, there was a look at the possibility of night games and, perhaps most importantly, the influence and pervasiveness of betting was glossed over, further empowering the gamblers. Over the next decade their shadow would loom larger over the game until the scandal of the 1919 World Series exploded, causing public outrage, threatening the very fabric of the National Pastime, and finally forcing baseball's leadership to change their structure in order to confront the problem head-on.

SOURCES

In addition to the sources cited in the notes, the author also consulted:

"Baseball Meetings Here This Week," *New York Times*, December 11, 1909: S1.

"Baseball Warclouds Vanish," *Chicago Daily Tribune*, December 19, 1909: C1.

"Big Series in Doubt," *Washington Post*, December 21, 1909: 8.

"Elect Tom Lynch," *Washington Post*, December 19, 1909: S1.

"Fogel on the Grill," *Washington Post*, December 12, 1909: S1.

"Full Salary for President Lynch," *New York Times*, December 20, 1909: 10.

"John Heydler is Dubious," *Chicago Daily Tribune*, December 12, 1909: C1.

Lowry, Philip J. *Green Cathedrals: The Ultimate Celebration of Major League and Negro League Ballparks* (New York, NY: Walker Publishing Company, 2006).

Murnane, T.H. "Ward? Heydler? Base Ball Fight Area Spreading," *Boston Globe*, December 13, 1909: 5.

Simpkins, Terry, "Kid Elberfeld," SABR Baseball Biography Project, http://sabr.org/bioproj/person/f51f274d, undated, accessed March 31, 2014.

"Still Opposed to Ward," *New York Times*, December 13, 1909: 7.

Stout, Glenn. *Yankees Century, 100 Years of New York Yankees Baseball* (Boston: Houghton Mifflin Company, 2002).

Thorn, John; Pete Palmer; Michael Gershman; and David Pietrusza, editors. *Total Baseball: The Official Encyclopedia of Major League Baseball, Fifth Edition* (New York: Viking Penguin, 1997).

"Ward Cannot Be President," *Los Angeles Times*, December 12, 1909: 16.

NOTES

1. Gary Gillette and Eric Enders with Stuart Shea and Matthew Silverman, *Big League Ballparks: The Complete Illustrated History* (New York: Metro Books, 2009), 38.
2. Ibid., xxv.
3. Ibid., xxiii and 155.
4. Bill Lamberty, "Harry Pulliam," SABR Baseball Biography Project, (http://sabr.org/bioproj/person/6e05b19c), undated, accessed January 28, 2014.
5. Ibid.
6. Ibid.
7. Ibid.
8. "Baseball Men to Meet," *New York Times*, November 7, 1909: S-2.
9. "Minors to Admit 'Outlaws'," *Chicago Tribune*, November 10, 1909: 12.
10. "Boom in the Minors," *Washington Post*, November 10, 1909: 8.
11. "Sexton is Reelected," *Washington Post*, November 11, 1909: 8.
12. Ibid.
13. Ibid.
14. Ibid.
15. Ibid.

16 By opening day, two other franchises would be added—one in Montgomery, West Virginia, and one that split its home games between Gallipolis, Ohio and Point Pleasant, West Virginia. http://en.wikipedia.org/wiki/Virginia_Valley_League, accessed March 17, 2014.

17 http://www.baseball-reference.com/bullpen/Michael_Sexton

18 "National Agreement: Extended by Baseball Clubs Until 1921," *Hartford Courant*, November 12, 1909: 14.

19 Ibid.

20 "Minor Magnates Plan for Future," *Chicago Tribune*, November 12, 1909: 14; *The Encyclopedia of Minor League Baseball*, 2nd edition. W. Lloyd Johnson and Miles Wolff, editors. (Durham, North Carolina: Baseball America, Inc.), 1997.

21 "New Life for Ball Leaders," *Los Angeles Times*, November 12, 1909: 16.

22 "Minor Magnates Plan for Future," *Chicago Tribune*, November 12, 1909: 14; "Baseball Men Adjourn," *New York Times*, November 12, 1909: 16; "Minors Renew Pact," *Washington Post*, November 12, 1909: 8.

23 "Minors Renew Pact," *Washington Post*, November 12, 1909: 8.

24 Ibid.

25 "Baseball Magnates Ready to Tackle Big Problems," *Chicago Tribune*, December 13, 1909: 14.

26 "Baseball Magnates Coming to New York," *New York Times*, December 9, 1909: 12.

27 Jessica Tully, "Meet John Montgomery Ward, Penn State's Only Baseball Hall of Fame Player," Onward State, http://onwardstate.com/2014/01/21/meet-john-montgomery-ward-penn-states-only-baseball-hall-of-famer, undated, accessed March 21, 2014.

28 Ibid.

29 "Herrmann is Here to Elect Heydler," *New York Times*, December 10, 1909: 12.

30 Ibid.

31 "C.W. Murphy's Plans for Baseball Meet," *New York Times*, December 11, 1909: 9.

32 Lenny Jacobsen, "Charles Murphy," SABR Baseball Biography Project, http://sabr.org/bioproj/person/e707728f, undated, accessed March 22, 2014.

33 Ibid. The Taft family, by the way, has been one of this country's most prominent political families for many years and have included Senators, Congressmen, governors and cabinet officers.

34 Ibid.

35 "Philadelphia Club Changes Ownership," *New York Times*, November 27, 1909.

36 Michael Lalli, "Horace Fogel: The Strangest Owner in Phillies History," Philly Sports History, phillysportshistory.com/2011/07/06/horace-fogel-the strangest-owner in-phillies-history, undated, accessed January 27, 2014.

37 Ibid.

38 I. E. Sanborn, "Baseball Fireworks at New York," *Chicago Daily Tribune*, December 14, 1909: 14.

39 "Ban B. Johnson Booms Heydler," *Hartford Courant*, December 14, 1909: 14.

40 "Back Ban Johnson," *Washington Post*, December 12, 1909: S1.

41 T. H. Murnane, "Eager for War," *Boston Globe*, December 16, 1909: 4.

42 "Lake to Lead Doves," *Washington Post*, December 10, 1909: 8.

43 I. E. Sanborn, "Baseball Fireworks at New York," *Chicago Tribune*, December 14, 1909: 14.

44 "Baseball Rumors in Air at Waldorf," *New York Times*, December 14, 1909: 9. The Logan Squares are an interesting little part of baseball's early history. They were founded by a man named Jimmy Callahan, who was both a pitcher (99 career wins) and infielder (901 career hits) for the Cubs and White Sox, but who retired after the 1905 season to form his own semipro team in Chicago. He purchased and renovated an old ballpark in the Logan Square neighborhood and made money playing a slate of games, including victorious October exhibitions against his former major league employers. Callahan had no compunction about signing professional players who had been suspended or were, for whatever reason, currently not in uniform, which spurred the majors to adopt a rule in 1908 that prohibited players from appearing in any games in which anyone—players, managers or even owners—had previously been declared ineligible. And then in 1909 Callahan got involved in that four-way dispute over Bill Torrey, which saw the National Commission (a three-man panel made up of the two league presidents and Cincinnati's Herrmann) rule in favor of the Reds.

45 "C.W. Murphy's Plans for Baseball Meet," *New York Times*, December 11, 1909: 9.

46 "Dreyfuss Believes Heydler Will Win," *New York Times*, December 13, 1909: 7.

47 I. E. Sanborn, "Baseball Fireworks at New York," *Chicago Tribune*, December 14, 1909: 14.

48 J. Ed. Grillo., "Men in Control of Baseball are Injuring the Sport," *Washington Post*, December 19, 1909: S1.

49 Anderson, 123-125.

50 Anderson, 125.

51 There is no listing for an Allentown team in *The Encyclopedia of Minor League Baseball*, so it is likely that it was either a semipro or independent ballclub.

52 "Baseball is Slavery," *Washington Post*, December 19, 1909: S1.

53 "Baseball and Slavery," *Washington Post*, December 21, 1909: 6.

54 1909 Philadelphia Phillies Season, http://melaman2.com/phillies/1909/1909-september.html, accessed March 29, 2014.

55. I. E. Sanborn, "Magnates Postpone Election for Banquet," *Chicago Tribune*, December 16, 1909: 16.

56. "Baseball Men Adjourn," *New York Times*, November 12, 1909, p. 16; "Ball Magnates Still Talking," *Los Angeles Times*, December 15, 1909: 16.

57. T. H. Murnane, "Eager for War," *Boston Globe*, December 16, 1909: 4.

58. "American League For 154-Game Season," *New York Times*, December 16, 1909: 10. This contrasts with the present day, when rosters are set at 25 on Opening Day and remain at that level until September 1, when they can then be expanded to 40.

59. R. W. Lardner, "Johnson Courts War With Rivals," *Chicago Tribune*, December 12, 1909: C1; "American League For 154-Game Season," *New York Times*, December 16, 1909: 10. Except for the World War I season of 1918, the 154-game schedule would remain in effect until the AL expanded by two clubs, and eight games, for the 1961 season; the NL followed suit in 1962.

60. Lardner, "Johnson Courts War With Rivals."

61. Mike Lynch, "The Great Wigwag Scheme of 1909," http://www.thenationalpastimemuseum.com/article/great-wigwag-scheme-1909, accessed March 3, 2014.

62. Ibid.

63. Ibid.

64. J. Ed. Grillo, "Many Important Matters Up To Baseball Magnates," *Washington Post*, December 12, 1909: S1; J. Ed. Grillo, "Heydler is Doomed," *Washington Post*, December 14, 1909: 8.

65. In an official statement, "the New York club is free from all complicity in such a tipping affair..."; Lynch, op. cit.

66. An official league resolution expressed "confidence in the loyalty to the American League of Joe Cantillon during the time he acted as manager of the Washington Baseball Club, and expresses to him its best wishes for his future prosperity."; "American League For 154-Game Season," *New York Times*, December 16, 1909: 10.

67. "Ball Magnates Still Talking," *Los Angeles Times*, December 15, 1909: 16.

68. "American League For 154-Game Season," *New York Times*, December 16, 1909: 10.

69. "Baseball Notes From Big League Meetings," *Washington Post*, December 15, 1909: 8.

70. I. E. Sanborn, "Magnates Postpone Election for Banquet," *Chicago Tribune*, December 16, 1909: 16.

71. "Banner Year for Baseball in 1909," *New York Times*, December 16, 1909: 10.

72. He would, however, succeed a year later, when the league elected a new president. "Ball Magnates Still Talking," *Los Angeles Times*, December 15, 1909: 16; personal e-mail from Dick Beverage, April 9, 2014.

73. "Baseball Notes From Big League Meetings," *Washington Post*, December 15, 1909: 8.

74. I. E. Sanborn, "Magnates Postpone Election for Banquet," *Chicago Tribune*, December 16, 1909: 16.

75. "Magnates Deadlock," *Washington Post*, December 17, 1909: 8.

76. "O'Brien's Chances Improve," *Chicago Tribune*, December 19, 1909: C2.

77. Charles C. Alexander, *John McGraw* (New York: Viking Press, 1988), 140.

78. David W. Anderson, David W. *More Than Merkle: A History of the Best and Most Exciting Baseball Season in Human History*, 217.

79. "Back Ban Johnson," *Washington Post*, December 12, 1909: S1.

80. "Baseball Magnates Ready to Tackle Big Problems," *Chicago Tribune*, December 13, 1909: 14.

81. "Banner Year for Baseball in 1909," *New York Times*, December 16, 1909: 10.

82. Ibid.

83. Ibid.

84. I. E. Sanborn, "Magnates Postpone Election for Banquet," *Chicago Tribune*, December 16, 1909: 16.

85. "Heydler Drops Out of Baseball Fight," *New York Times*, December 17, 1909: 13.

86. I. E. Sanborn, "National League Magnates in Deadlock Over Election of President," *Chicago Tribune*, December 17, 1909: 17.

87. "Heydler Drops Out of Baseball Fight," *New York Times*, December 17, 1909: 13.

88. I. E. Sanborn, "National League Magnates in Deadlock Over Election of President," *Chicago Tribune*, December 17, 1909: 17; "Ball Magnates Still Talking," *Los Angeles Times*, December 15, 1909: 16; "Baseball Rumors Fly Thick and Fast," *New York Times*, December 15, 1909: 12. Ironically, O'Brien wound up being passed over by both the National League and the American Association.

89. "Baseball Magnates Ready to Tackle Big Problems," *Chicago Tribune*, December 13, 1909: 14.

90. "Magnates Deadlock," *Washington Post*, December 17, 1909: 8.

91. "Baseball Rumors Fly Thick and Fast," *New York Times*, December 15, 1909: 12.

92. Ibid.

93. "Baseball Deadlock Remains Unbroken," *New York Times*, December 18, 1909: 11.

94. I. E. Sanborn, "Deadlock Balloting in National League Ends Ward's Chance of Victory," *Chicago Tribune*, December 18, 1909: 10.

95. Ibid.

96. Ibid.

97 "Deadlock is Still On," *Washington Post*, December 18, 1909: 8.

98 "Big Leaguers' Horns Locked," *Los Angeles Times*, December 18, 1909: 17.

99 I. E. Sanborn, I.E., "Deadlock Balloting in National League Ends Ward's Chance of Victory," *Chicago Tribune*, December 18, 1909: 10.

100 Ibid.

101 I. E. Sanborn, "National League Elects T.J. Lynch," *Chicago Tribune*, December 19, 1909: C1.

102 Jon Daly, "Tom Lynch," SABR Baseball Biography Project (http://sabr.org/bioproj/person/c633b89f), undated, accessed January 27, 2014. Heydler remained the league's secretary-treasurer until 1918, when he was, finally, elected the National League's president, a position he would hold until 1934. Among his accomplishments, he hired the Elias brothers to keep official statistics, he pushed for the selection of Judge Landis to serve as Commissioner, he helped to establish the Hall of Fame, and in 1929 he suggested something akin to the modern designated hitter. Amazingly, he has never been enshrined in Cooperstown. (Biography of John Arnold Heydler, http://en.wikipedia.org/wiki/John_Heydler, accessed February 27, 2014.)

103 I. E. Sanborn, "National League Elects T.J. Lynch," *Chicago Tribune*, December 19, 1909: C1.

104 J. Ed. Grillo, "Men in Control of Baseball are Injuring the Sport," *Washington Post*, December 19, 1909: S1.

105 Ibid.

106 "O'Brien's Chances Improve," *Chicago Tribune*, December 19, 1909: C2.

107 "Heydler Drops Out of Baseball Fight," *New York Times*, December 17, 1909: 13.

108 "Rumors of War are Silenced," *Los Angeles Times*, December 19, 1909: 17.

— 1910 —
HO-HUM AFFAIRS

By Dennis Pajot

Introduction

IT WAS DECIDED BOTH MAJOR LEAGUES would hold their annual winter meetings in New York City in December 1910. Although it would not be a joint meeting, this would be of great convenience to the writers and help centralize interest in the meetings.[1]

The National Association of Professional Baseball Leagues (the minor leagues) had met in Chicago on November 15, 16, and 17. After the election of officers, some constitutional amendments were adopted. These included increasing the size of the National Association's board to eight members, clarifying how money would be seized by the secretary in case of defaulting clubs and leagues, allowing contract jumpers to be reinstated "under certain conditions," and moving up the date to secure protection from the National Association, from October 15 to September 1.[2] The minors then got to the meat of their business.

By its constitution, the association was forced to reclassify some of its leagues because of constitutional requirements setting minimum population figures for league classifications; the 1910 federal census thus dictated these changes. In addition, the American Association and Eastern League were asking for the establishment of a new, higher AA standing. (At the time, Class A was the highest classification in the minor leagues.) Other leagues, however, especially the Class-A Western League, were opposed. The Western League cited the 10-year agreement, signed before the 1903 season, that it could not be demoted from the highest minor-league status, a quid pro quo for the Western's agreeing to give up the Kansas City and Milwaukee territories to the American Association. The Three-I (Indiana-Illinois-Iowa) League was also protesting its demotion. The most recent census had put the league population about 25,000 shy of the 400,000 required to maintain its Class-B status, but league officials contended that when the five-mile radius of each club was included, the population would exceed the minimum. In the end the American Association and Eastern League decided not to push for an "AA" level, and the National Association decided not to demote any of its leagues. It was felt that any demotions would be harmful to fan interest and, of course, would also mean less money received for a drafted player. Later, at the major-league winter meetings, the non-demotions were approved.[3]

The Business Side

The National League meeting began on December 13 at the Hotel Breslin. The opening day was occupied with a few minor player issues, the approval of the treasurer's accounts, the reading of the minutes from the previous year's meeting, and the formal awarding of the championship to the Chicago Cubs. On the humanitarian side, the league voted to continue monthly sums to Mrs. Johnson, the sister of the late National League President Harry Pulliam, who had committed suicide in July 1909.[4]

The second day's meeting took up various loose ends and reports, including such items as the league using 484 dozen baseballs during the 1910 season, before the league proceeded to election of a president. There had been talk of unseating Pulliam's elected successor, Thomas J. Lynch, with the names of John Montgomery Ward and James A Hart being tossed around. In the end, Lynch was unanimously re-elected to a one-year term. John A. Heydler, in the middle of his three-year term, remained as secretary-treasurer.[5]

BASEBALL'S BUSINESS: THE WINTER MEETINGS

The third day, December 15, started with the discussion of the umpires' work on the diamond. In what might seem like the age-old joke of umpires being blind, the league decided that when the arbiters were appointed for the next season, each would have to visit an oculist and have his eyes examined. Among the other minor business conducted this day was the offer from a Detroit automobile company to give a car to each league's batting champion. Remembering the controversy over the conclusion of the Cobb-Lajoie batting race in the fall, with a Chalmers automobile as the prize, the owners placed the offer on file, where it stayed. A self-printing ticket machine was exhibited at the meeting at the insistence of the Giants' John T. Brush. It seemed to interest his fellow owners.[6]

For various reasons, the 1911 playing schedule was discussed on different days. On day two a resolution directing the league president to work on the schedule was voted down, and President Lynch then formed a scheduling committee consisting of himself, John Heydler, and Pittsburgh owner Barney Dreyfuss. Surprisingly, after having served on this committee for more than a quarter of a century, Brooklyn's Charles Ebbets was dropped, despite the wide belief that he was highly qualified for this type of work. Some felt his being dropped "was the result of personal spleen,"[7] but Ebbets did not seem put out by being relieved of the hard work necessary for this thankless job.[8] At that day's meeting the owners also directed Lynch to confer with the American League about reducing conflicting Sunday dates in the Western cities. On the final day of the meetings the length and dates of the 1911 schedule were discussed at length. Garry Herrmann, the Cincinnati magnate, put forth a 112-game season plan, with postseason interleague play, but his scheme was not taken seriously. Some owners had favored a 168-game schedule, but the 154-game season was kept, with the playing days scheduled from April 12 to "on or about" October 12, which was Columbus Day. Though not yet an official national holiday, it was observed in every state in which there was a National League team, and it was important to owners like Ebbets, who said this had been a profitable day for his club the previous season. As the National League season was three days longer than that of the American League, a suspension of the rule requiring all teams in the league to approve any transferring of games was put in place. This allowed a team with possibilities of winning the championship to pull back late-season games with the consent of the opponent. It was enacted to ward off any delay of the World Series.[9]

Of the few constitutional amendments passed at the meeting, perhaps the most important was the abolition of the fund to which each club gave 5 percent of its base gate receipts to pay for league expenses. On a percentage basis, clubs with larger attendance were forced to pay more. It was decided that the expenses would now be defrayed by equal assessments upon each club annually. Another amendment attempted to stop the practice of a team refusing to waive a player and then turning that player back to the original team. Should this be tried, the team involved would be fined $250.[10]

The major order of business for the league was the sale of a 95 percent interest in the Boston Doves to a Boston syndicate for $100,000. The deal would have been finished before the meetings, but the incumbent owner, John P. Harris, stayed at the helm to vote for Lynch in the potentially tight election for the NL presidency. The four new principal owners were William Hepburn Russell, a New York lawyer and city official; brothers George A. and Lewis C. Page, publishers; and Frederic J. Murphy, an insurance executive. Russell was elected president of the club,[11] and beginning the next season the team would be called the Rustlers.[12] A few days after the meetings ended, John Harris purchased a block of stock in the Pittsburgh franchise and became a member of the Pirates board of directors.[13]

The American League began its meeting on December 14 at the Hotel Wolcott. The opening activities consisted of the reading of the minutes, the treasurer's report, election of a new board of directors and the formal awarding of the 1910 pennant to the Athletics. After little discussion, the league adopted a 154-game schedule, beginning on April 12 and running through October 8; President Ban Johnson promised to work out the specifics of the schedule at a later date.[14]

The league also dealt with the transfer of controlling interest in a club, a matter that was taken up the second day. Colonel Robert Lee Hedges wanted to sell his 65 percent interest in the St. Louis Browns to a local syndicate made up primarily of E. Manning Hodgman of St. Louis, Mark and Nathaniel Ewing, Louis M. Hall, and Edward Prendergast. It was reported that the Ewing brothers, owners of a stock brokerage firm worth $4 million, would pay Hedges $535,000 for the franchise and the ballpark. Even though the Browns were not successful on the field it was reported the club consistently earned a net profit averaging $30,000 a year.[15]

There was speculation that Hedges was being forced out of the AL because of differences with Chicago owner Charles Comiskey. It was reported that Hedges wanted to hire Fielder Jones as manager and give him part-ownership of the club. Comiskey refused to waive his rights to Jones, who had been refusing to play for the White Sox for the last two years because the salary offered by Comiskey was too low. Jones and Hedges both denied this. Another reason given why the American League wanted Hedges out was the poor showing of the Browns in recent years, but Ban Johnson denied this. Hedges said he wanted some local men to take over the "disorganized" Browns, as he did not feel he was able to undertake the hard task of improving the team.[16] Yet another opinion was offered by Hedges' personal counsel, who said the Browns were sold because of the owner's health issues. "Mr. Hedges' health has been impaired by worry and hard work, since the close of last season, and his friends and his wife finally prevailed upon him to sell the club, and accordingly the deal with the Hodgman syndicate was closed," the lawyer said.[17] The new owners would assume all liabilities of the club, including the salary of Jack O'Connor, the deposed manager of the 1910 Browns.[18]

The local St. Louis syndicate was not the American League's first choice for new ownership. Reports had been published that Washington Nationals manager Jimmy McAleer had been urged to form a group to purchase the Browns from Hedges. McAleer said he was interested until he learned the asking price, and "decided that I would perhaps tie myself up for life, and that I might be better off without such a tremendous burden."[19]

A committee composed of Ban Johnson, Comiskey, and Frank Farrell (New York Highlanders) was assigned to visit St. Louis and report back on the financial status of the new syndicate. This the trio did the following week, and reported favorably upon the new owners.[20]

But the deal hit snags almost immediately. The new syndicate made its first payment of $30,000 on January 10, but did not make the second payment, due later in January. It was reported that there was internal squabbling, and that it was proving more difficult than expected to raise the money. The date to pay for the franchise in full was extended to February 10. As it appeared the deal would fall through, Colonel Hedges' health "rapidly recovered, and he [said] he never felt better in his life, and eager to get to work and resurrect the lowly Browns from the graveyard brigade."[21] Hedges was re-elected president of the Browns, and named Rhoderick "Bobby" Wallace to manage the team in 1911. On February 19 Hedges announced the deal had fallen through and he remained the head of the Browns.[22]

Although not affiliated with the major leagues in any way, the Base Ball Writers' Association of America held its second annual meeting in the Hotel Breslin on December 14, with members present from 11 major-league cities. Joseph S. Jackson of the *Washington Post* was re-elected president, Jack Ryder of the *Cincinnati Enquirer* was elected vice president, and William G. Weart of the *Philadelphia Evening Telegraph* won election as secretary and treasurer, at a salary of $100 a year. About the only noteworthy event of this meeting was that the local representatives in each city were given the responsibility to make sure that no outsiders were admitted to the press boxes.[23]

Player Movement at Meetings

Few trades were made at the league meetings. Bill Dahlen of the Brooklyn Superbas said, "I didn't hear a lot of people hankering to make base ball trades. Guess there were two or three of them who would not have objected to a trade of some kind, but they held their goods too high."[24] Comiskey said, "Every time a manager came to me and talks trade, the first thing he does is to say he is willing to take Walsh off my hands. That stops the negotiations before they have reached even the infancy stage."[25]

In the only trade involving major-league players on both sides, the St. Louis Browns sent Art Griggs to Cleveland in exchange for catcher Nig Clarke. Griggs, a valuable utilityman, had hit only .236 in 1910, but played both outfield and infield for the Browns. The left-handed-hitting Jay Justin Clarke had hit .155 in 21 games with the Naps in 1910.[26]

A number of deals involving minor-league teams were completed. The St. Louis Cardinals, for instance, sold right-handed pitcher Frank Corridon to Buffalo of the Eastern League. The 30-year-old veteran had won only six of his 20 decisions with the Cardinals in 1910. The Cardinals also sent left-hander Johnny Lush (14-13 in 1910) and right-hander Lester Backman (6-7), plus catcher Ed Phelps (.263 in 93 games in 1910), to Toronto of the Eastern League.[27]

Willie Keeler was sold by the New York Giants, who had signed the veteran in May, to the Toronto Maple Leafs. It was the end of the line for the future Hall of Famer, who played just 39 games for the Leafs before calling it a career.[28] Yet another veteran player to go to Toronto was third baseman Bill Bradley, sold by Cleveland. The 32-year-old's leg had been bothering him for the past few seasons and in fact he would never play another major-league game. Pittsburgh asked waivers on first baseman Jack Flynn in order to sell him to Kansas City of the American Association, which then attempted to deal Flynn to Washington of the American League. However, the Cubs claimed Flynn, and the Pirates withdrew the waiver. Flynn wound up playing part of the 1911 season in Pittsburgh but also spent time in St. Paul and Kansas City before the Senators finally picked him up in the Rule 5 draft of 1911.[29]

As in all winter meetings there were plenty of rumors relating to potential trades. One report had the Chicago Cubs sending three right-handed pitchers, Harry McIntire (13-9 in 1910), Ed Reulbach (12-8), and Lew Richie (11-4), to Cincinnati for right-hander George McQuillan, whom the Reds had recently acquired from the Phillies after he had posted a 9-6 mark in Philadelphia. Cubs owner Charles Murphy was said to be willing to add veteran lefty Jack Pfiester to the deal if Clark Griffith would throw in third baseman Eddie Grant, also acquired in the trade that had brought McQuillan to the Reds, but the deal did not materialize.[30]

Summary

The 1910 winter meetings produced very little in the way of player movement, but the sale of two clubs (even though one fell through) led to a great deal of interest in the meetings. New Boston owner William Hepburn Russell died on November 21, 1911, and thus was not able to see his team, by then known as the Braves, win the World Series in 1914. The meetings did, however, plant the seeds for the creation of new, higher classifications in the minor leagues.

SOURCES

In addition to the sources included in the notes, the author read many additional articles in the publications listed, as well as coverage in the *Milwaukee Journal* and Harold Kaese's book *The Boston Braves* (New York: Putman, 1948).

NOTES

1 *Sporting Life*, December 3, 1901: 1.
2 *Sporting Life*, November 26, 1910: 6; *The Sporting News*, November 24, 1910: 1; *Milwaukee Sentinel*, November 17, 1910.
3 *Sporting Life*, November 26, 1910: 6; December 24, 1910: 9; *The Sporting News*, November 24, 1910: 1; *Milwaukee Sentinel*, November 17, 1910.
4 *Sporting Life*, December 24, 1910: 10.
5 *Sporting Life*, December 3, 1910: 1; December 24, 1910: 10.
6 *Sporting Life*, December 24, 1910: 10.
7 Ibid.
8 *Sporting Life, December 24, 1910: 6*.
9 *Sporting Life*, December 3, 1910: 1; December 24, 1910: 4; *The Sporting News*, December 21, 1910: 5.
10 *Sporting Life*, December 24, 1910: 10.
11 *Sporting Life*, December 24, 1910: 1, 2.
12 *Sporting Life*, January 7, 1911: 5.

13 *Sporting Life*, January 7, 1911: 11.
14 *Sporting Life*, December 24, 1910: 11.
15 *Sporting Life*, December 24, 1910: 1, 11; *Milwaukee Sentinel*, December 16, 1910.
16 *Sporting Life*, December 24, 1910: 11,
17 *Sporting Life*, December 24, 1910: 1.
18 Ibid.
19 *Sporting Life*, December 24, 1910: 11.
20 *Sporting Life*, December 24, 1910: 11; February 25, 1911: 1.
21 *Sporting Life*, January 21, 1911: 1.
22 *Sporting Life*, January 21, 1911: 1; February 25, 1911: 1, 2.
23 *Sporting Life*, December 24, 1910: 11.
24 *Sporting Life*, December 24, 1910: 6.
25 *Sporting Life*, December 24, 1910: 12.
26 Ibid.
27 *Sporting Life*, December 24, 1910: 7.
28 Ibid.
29 *Milwaukee Journal*, December 15, 1910; *Sporting Life*, December 24, 1910: 3.
30 *Milwaukee Sentinel*, December 14, 1910

— 1911 —
SCANDAL? WHAT SCANDAL?

by R.J. Lesch

THE 1911 WINTER MEETINGS PLAYED out in the press as well as in the meeting rooms.

Two days before the start of the 1911 World Series, which matched the New York Giants against the Philadelphia Athletics, the newspapers in both cities noticed that large blocks of World Series tickets had fallen into the hands of known ticket speculators, even before the games were reported as sold out. None of the fans denied seats at the biggest games of the year, or forced to pay inflated prices for them, could have been angrier than AL President Ban Johnson. He vowed that after the World Series was over, the National Commission would investigate the handling of ticket sales, particularly in New York.

The ticket scandal, of course, wasn't on the table at the National Association gathering in San Antonio November 13-18. Representatives of the 47 member leagues, encompassing 332 cities and towns across the United States and Canada,[1] were more concerned about proposals to revise the 10-year-old National Agreement and suggestions for curbing gambling on baseball. Well, that and enjoying the entertainments provided by the Texas League and the businesses of San Antonio. Nearly 1,000 delegates to the convention enjoyed a military parade at nearby Fort Sam Houston, a sumptuous banquet, and an East-West All-Star Game for charity featuring such players as Jim O'Rourke, Dick "Dad" Phelan, Jack Holland, Harry Wolverton, Wallace "Happy" Hogan, and Roger Bresnahan.[2] Brooklyn owner Charles Ebbets started the game as the umpire, but after he had Billy Clymer, the East's second baseman, put out of the game, he played second base himself. The East was ahead, 6-2, when the game was called on account of darkness in the top of the sixth inning.[3]

Revisions to the National Agreement focused on a proposal by three of the five Class-A leagues to create a separate classification, Class AA. The Eastern League, American Association, and Pacific Coast League had grown to the point where for a while it seemed they would be able to challenge the National and American for major-league status. As measured by the census, the three leagues had teams in 17 of the 30 largest cities in the United States, as well as the two largest Canadian cities, and had been rumbling for some time about following the precedent set by the AL in 1901, going their own way as independent major leagues. Barring that, the three leagues wanted, at least, to keep the majors from taking their star players without fair compensation.

Charles Murphy of the Chicago Cubs, however, felt that the majors were the aggrieved parties, pointing to the lack of salary limits in the minor leagues. "Players come to the big leagues from the minors and grossly misrepresent the salaries that they have been paid," said Murphy, "and as the minor leagues seem to consider information about players sacred, we are held up times without number. There is only one way to overcome this evil, and that is for the leagues to play on the square."[4] For their part, the minor leagues wanted to be able to restore the minor-league salary of ballplayers sent back to them after major-league trials. Wilbur P. Allen, president of the Texas League, proposed that a central board fix a salary limit for each league in a certain classification, and set the penalties for violations of such limits. The magnates contended that the very existence of some leagues depended upon the adoption of such a rule. Most of the November 16 business session was devoted to "the salary limit problem," which was referred to a committee.

League officials and magnates proposed other ways to keep their hard-earned nickels from falling into the pockets of greedy ballplayers. Ebbets suggested that league presidents and club owners be bonded to ensure observance of salary limits. Michael Sexton, president of the National Association, suggested discontinuing or regulating payments of railroad fares and expenses of players and their families reporting in the spring or returning home after the season. The convention voted to include language in player contracts prohibiting ballplayers from using the uniform of any club without the club's consent, and "at the expiration of each season he shall turn in his uniform before he receives his final pay,"[5] presumably to curb barnstorming.

Meanwhile, the two smaller Class-A circuits, the Western League and Southern Association, mustered enough votes to block the proposed AA classification, mindful that the arrangement would put them into a subservient position. Some skillful parliamentary maneuvering postponed the vote on November 17, and it seems some all-hours negotiation peeled away most of the anti-AA votes. The next morning, only three leagues (the Western, Three-I, and MINK) voted against the proposal. The vote made the San Antonio gathering "one of the most important meetings ever held," wrote the *Chicago Tribune*, apparently in all seriousness.[6]

As for gambling, much was said, but little was done. The leagues felt that they could act on open gambling in their ballparks or by their employees, but that it would take federal or state legislative action to curb the activities of pool sellers, lotteries, and other methods of gambling on baseball. The members adopted resolutions calling for federal prohibition of these devices, as well as betting via mail or wire, and left it at that.

The World Series ticket scandal would return to center stage during the major-league meetings in New York, December 10-14. Ever since the World Series, Johnson had traded "courteous and sharp" open letters with Giants owner John T. Brush on the topic.[7] Johnson, in an October 30 *Tribune* article, insisted he would start an investigation into the matter provided the other two National Commission members, Chairman August Herrmann and NL President Thomas Lynch, would consent. Johnson claimed to have "strong evidence" that an employee of the Giants had turned over 8,000 or 9,000 tickets to brokers, who sold them at inflated prices. "I was firmly led to believe," wrote Johnson, "that the leading ticket brokers of New York were abundantly provided with tickets, and in consecutive sectional numbers. It seemed to me that this condition could not have happened unless there was collusion between someone in your office and the scalpers."[8]

Brush, in his letter, said that Johnson could proceed with his investigation at any time, with the New York club's full cooperation. Johnson replied, curiously, that Brush himself should take up the investigation, not the National Commission. Brush responded, "You have information which I do not possess, which gives you an advantage in developing the facts," and noted the absurdity of asking the New York club to investigate its own conduct.[9] In the end the National Commission put up $1,500 to collect information on the matter, and expected Johnson to present his evidence at the New York meeting in December.

The controversy simmered in the weeks prior to the league meetings. *The Sporting News* correspondent from Brooklyn, Thomas S. Rice, defended the Giants, asserting that the Athletics had also let World Series tickets slip into the hands of speculators. Rice blamed "cheap, grafting, short-sighted politicians" in both cities, who blackmailed both clubs by threatening to make life difficult for the ballclubs—by building roads through the ballpark properties, for example—unless gratified. "Precisely the same conditions which existed in New York existed in Philadelphia, and for precisely the same reason. It is known of all men and an investigation could accomplish nothing except to create bitter feelings and keep alive a controversy that should be allowed to fade away."[10]

Washington sportswriter Joe S. Jackson agreed that the affair would go nowhere, and wrote that Johnson was raising the scandal for less than high-minded purposes. "It is expected that President Johnson, who is forcing an inquiry, will get through a report that will make the Giants office force look bad, but that will pin nobody down."[11] If so, and if the Yankees fielded a stronger team in 1912, this might draw disaffected New York fans to the AL club, achieving one of Johnson's long-term goals.

The main editorial in the December 21 issue of *The Sporting News* acknowledged the point "that the New York Club, as is every other public enterprise, is at the mercy of these vampires." The editorial opined, however, that Brush should have gone public about the problem, especially since Brush, after a quarter-century in the game, and clearly in failing health, is retiring. "Could he have better marked that retirement than by going before the public and exposing some of the evils that he has had to contend against, with his valedictory a plea that the honest public rise up and for the good of the great national game, rescue it from the slimy clutches of Tammany graft?"[12] Easy to say, of course, when you publish your paper a thousand miles from Tammany Hall.

Everyone had ideas, in the meantime, for dealing with ticket scalping. Calls were made for the National Commission to take charge of the sale and distribution of World Series tickets, and for state and local ordinances to prohibit ticket scalping. More extreme proposals aimed to extend the World Series to as many as 15 games, to dilute the value of one game's tickets, or, conversely, to scrap the World Series entirely.

At its November 12 meeting in Chicago, however, far from scrapping the fall classic, the National Commission set the start date for the 1912 World Series as October 7. The two major leagues were expected to end their seasons before that date. This ended a two-year senior circuit experiment with Columbus Day doubleheaders, a pet project of Ebbets, which had failed dismally. Herrmann had been willing to go along, but when the Reds' share of their 1911 Columbus Day revenues came to $68, he withheld his support, and Ebbets decided to let it drop.

Nobody expected any other controversies. The major leagues were expected to add their huzzahs to the Class-AA recommendation proposed by the National Association. The National League was expected to re-elect President Lynch, whose two-year tenure had been rocky but respectable. Murphy wanted a committee of umpires and writers to review the baseball rules, standardize the inconsistent, and weed out the archaic. The agendas held a few other routine matters, but by and large, people agreed with the *Boston Globe*'s Tim Murnane:

The National Commission had its troubles for several years, but finally got into a position where it could handle the disturbing element, so that now, while there is not absolute harmony, the men with large sums of money invested have come to realize that success lies only in cooperation.

With a cemented front the major leagues have now become absolute masters of the situation, and with loyal support, through the National agreement, of the 50 minor leagues, professional baseball today has become the strongest combination ever devised by man.[13]

The only serious spectator sport left was the ticket scandal, and by the time August Herrmann arrived at the Waldorf-Astoria on December 8, many doubted whether the investigation would bear any fruit, with Herrmann himself one of the doubters. "I have received a long communication from John T. Brush," Herrmann told the *Washington Post*, "and his report certainly clears the New York club of suspicion. To date I have received no evidence damaging to the Giants or Giant officials. Whether or not the sales were regularly conducted I am not in a position to state. But so far we have no absolute proof to the contrary. The commission has detectives employed in the investigation. Additional reports are expected before Mr. Johnson arrives on Monday morning."[14]

The Giants' team secretary, William H. Gray, had resigned, though he had not been formally implicated in the ticket scandal. "We haven't sent for him yet," said Herrmann, "and probably will not require his presence. Mr. Brush has exonerated him."[15] Gray's replacement was Joseph D. O'Brien, the respected former American Association president, who would represent the Giants at the league meetings, along with team treasurer John Whalen. Brush, as was his custom, was convalescing in San Antonio for the winter.

When Johnson did arrive, a day later than planned, the remaining enthusiasm for the investigation fizzled.

He was said to have news of two ticket brokers who received large blocks of seats, as well as evidence of the sale of blocks of seats to speculators before the public sale opened.[16] What evidence he had is not clearly known, but Herrmann and Lynch were even less convinced than they had been before. Neither thought the evidence would stand up in court, if it came to that, and little was disclosed to the public about what was alleged.

Most of the rest of the league meetings was given over to routine business and "an unusual number of trades and deals," as *The Sporting News* noted.[17] None of the deals involved star players, but Herrmann ended several days of suspense among the writers by unveiling his new manager—Hank O'Day. The umpire and former pitcher got the Reds off to a fast start in 1912, but finished in fourth place with a 75-78 record. O'Day returned to umpiring in 1913.

The National League did indeed re-elect Lynch to another one-year term. When reporters asked whether he would want a 10-year term such as the American League had given Johnson, Lynch told them he would decline such a deal. Murphy had tempered his resistance to Lynch, though he suggested that maybe the NL should simply elect Johnson as its president instead. Since Johnson controlled the league anyway, Murphy barbed, perhaps Johnson ought to be paid for the service.[18]

The National League also approved the sale of the Boston club to a syndicate led by John M. Ward and James E. Gaffney, pending the settlement of the estate of the recently deceased owner, William H. Russell, and agreed to most of the suggestions from the National Association's San Antonio meeting, including setting new salary limits and draft prices for all minor leagues.

The Eastern League re-elected its president, Ed Barrow, as well, and also voted to extend his term from one year to five. More momentous, as had long been anticipated, the owners voted to call themselves the International League, the name used to this day.[19]

Both major leagues authorized their presidents to deal with the Class-AA proposal, and the National Commission subsequently adopted the measure at its January meeting.

While the American League completed its business "in record time," to no one's surprise, the junior circuit was clearly miffed by attacks in the New York press on the conduct of the Philadelphia ticket sales, and surprised everyone by passing this resolution:

> Resolved, that the American League will continue to exercise its privileges and observe its obligations under the National Agreement, but will decline to have further official intercourse with the National League, except so far as may be requisite for the safeguarding of its territorial and player rights.
>
> Be it further resolved, that the American League will not be represented in another series for the championship of the world or in any other interleague event unless accorded sole charge of the sales of tickets to games played on its own grounds, under an arrangement, and with the understanding that it shall not assume responsibility for the conduct of the business department of games at the park of the other contesting club.[20]

The National League held a closed-door session to discuss the American League's apparent breakup letter, then voted to table it. Ebbets wanted to send a sternly worded reply, but for once, cooler heads prevailed in the NL. A diplomatic Lynch merely told reporters afterward, "We could not make out what it meant."[21]

In the end, Johnson signed off on National Commission Decision Number 839, dated January 6, 1912. Its conclusion was that while speculators in both New York and Philadelphia had acquired large numbers of World Series tickets and sold them at exorbitant prices, "there has nothing whatever been developed, even by intimation, that would in any way implicate any of them [the ballclubs] as having been in collusion with the ticket speculators. On the contrary, it has been shown that every reasonable precaution was taken by both clubs to protect the public. Therefore, the club owners and the regular officials of each club are completely exonerated."[22] The decision went on to acknowledge that one or more club employees might have colluded with scalpers, "although such a condition was almost impossible in Philadelphia when the manner of the distribution of the tickets in that city is taken into account." However, the National Commission decided it could not hold the clubs responsible for those actions without definite proof.

The decision also hinted at the possibility of the commission's taking over World Series ticket sales, but stopped short of taking that step. As with the gambling issue, the commission called for state and local ordinances to prohibit ticket scalping, pointing to a Pittsburgh ordinance as a model.

On that uncomfortable perch, the matter rested.

NOTES

1. *Chicago Tribune*, November 16, 1911: 6.
2. *Los Angeles Times*, November 17, 1911: III4.
3. *Chicago Tribune*, November 19, 1911: C3.
4. *Boston Globe*, November 17, 1911: 6.
5. *New York Times*, November 18, 1911: 14.
6. *Chicago Tribune*, November 19, 1911: C3.
7. *Chicago Tribune*, November 4, 1911: 12.
8. Ibid.
9. Ibid.
10. *The Sporting News*, November 9, 1911: 3.
11. *Washington Post*, December 3, 1911: S1.
12. *The Sporting News*, December 21, 1911: 3.
13. *Boston Globe*, November 12, 1911: 32.
14. *Washington Post*, December 10, 1911: S1.
15. Ibid.
16. *New York Times*, December 10, 1911: part 5, 5-7.
17. *The Sporting News*, December 21, 1911: 3.
18. Ibid.
19. *The Sporting News*, December 14, 1911: 1.
20. *The Sporting News*, December 21, 1911: 3.
21. Ibid.
22. *Decisions of the National Commission*, No. 839. "In re Investigation of Ticket Sale During World's Series," January 6, 1912, 3-8.

— 1912 —
DISCUSSING INTERLEAGUE PLAY AND THE SLOW PACE OF THE GAME

By Andy Bokser

AMONG THE ANTICIPATED BUSINESS of the National and American Leagues at their postseason winter meetings in 1912 were trades, policy discussions, appointments to league posts and boards of directors. The National League convened on Tuesday, December 11, at the Waldorf-Astoria in New York City, and the American League meeting on the next day at the Congress Hotel in Chicago.

Earlier, from November 12 to 15, the National Association of Professional Baseball Leagues (the minor leagues) met in Milwaukee. It was reported at the meeting that the National Association controlled about 6,500 players with a combined annual salary of over $3 million (maybe enough to pay a single back-end-of-the-rotation pitcher on a current major-league contender). The National Association estimated team travel and hotel expenses as close to a million dollars, and umpire costs of about $200,000. With attendance revenues reported at $6 million, it appeared that there were ample profits for at least some of the minor-league owners.[1]

Nevertheless, it was clear that those profits did not satisfy all of the minor-league owners. Some urged the National Association to adopt a sliding-scale salary cap (the scale depending on the league's classification). Some members of the Double-A International League and American Association expressed opposition to the plan since such a restriction could "impair the quality of baseball."[2] After much negotiating, the leagues agreed that monthly player payroll limits would be put in place. For example, the total players' payroll of Class-A teams were to be limited to $3,600 per month, and Class-B teams to $2,500.[3] The ceiling excluded managers' salaries.[4] While the leagues debated how the limits should be enforced (e.g., via audit or affidavit), the consensus was that the owners would be placed on their honor.[5]

At the National League meeting, Secretary John Heydler presented a new pitching statistic, earned-run average, to evaluate pitchers' 1912 seasons. He announced that Jeff Tesreau had allowed 1.96 earned runs per nine innings. His teammate Christy Mathewson was second with an earned-run average of 2.12.[6] The American League did not adopt earned-run average as an official statistic until 1913, when Walter Johnson won the crown with a microscopic 1.14 ERA.[7]

The senior circuit re-elected Thomas J. Lynch as president of the league, and elected Heydler (who later served as National League president from 1918-1934) for a three-year term as secretary and treasurer.[8] Heydler was awarded a salary increase.[9]

The National League awarded a pennant for good behavior to the Philadelphia team, whose players went through the season of 1912 with no suspensions and only one fine. The one transgressor on the Phillies was pitcher Ad Brennan, who had been thrown out of a game for "soiling a new ball."[10]

The NL reported that its eight teams used 12,060 baseballs during the 1912 season. The average of 1,500 per team was attributed in part to the fact that many fans were not returning foul balls hit into the crowd. (By contrast, Major League Baseball public-relations manager Jeff Heckleman reported in June 2010 that the 30 major-league teams used about 900,000 baseballs for the season, although only 200,000 of them were used during games.[11]) The 1912 National League schedule included 88 postponements, 119 doubleheaders, and 78 unplayed games. Six protests were lodged during the season. The one upheld was made by the Cubs against the Pirates.

The National League addressed a vexing situation. Umpire Charles "Cy" Rigler was being paid $2,200 by the Philadelphia Phillies for his role in having the team sign a pitcher, Eppa Rixey. The league concluded that an umpire officiating in a game involving a team that he was being paid by or was having a financial dispute with would be "against the best interest of the game." As a consequence, the league ruled that umpires could no longer act as scouts.[12] (Considering that Rixey was voted into the Hall of Fame by the Veterans Committee in 1963, perhaps Rigler would have had a more lucrative career as a talent scout than an umpire. However, Rigler did not have to beat the bushes to find Rixey. He was on the baseball staff at the University of Virginia, where he saw Rixey pitch as a student pursuing a degree in chemistry.[3]

Among the baseball elite appearing at the meetings in New York were Christy Mathewson, John Montgomery Ward, George Stallings, Charles Ebbets Jr., Fred Clark, and Joe Tinker.[14] (Stallings, the new manager of the Boston Braves, Toronto of the International League to obtain pitcher Dick Rudolph.[15])

As with many meetings and conventions, not all of the issues before the National League were resolved. For example, the magnates postponed a decision on whether the NL champion New York Giants should share 25 percent of their World Series earnings with the other seven teams in the league.

A matter that received much attention before, during, and after the winter meetings concerned Roger Bresnahan,[16] who had signed to manage the St. Louis Cardinals for five years starting in 1912 at $10,000 per year plus 10 percent of the team's profits.[17] After the 1912 team finished in sixth place, going 63-90, the Cardinals fired the future Hall of Famer. He maintained that he was entitled to be paid for the balance of his contract plus his share of any profits.

Lawyers for Bresnahan and the Cardinals sought to select arbitrators to resolve the situation. It was also reported that Cincinnati Reds president Gary

> ## HELENE BRITTON, ST. LOUIS OWNER, REPORTEDLY SENDS RELEASE LETTER TO ROGER BRESNAHAN
>
> [Excerpt]
> "I have decided to make a change in managers and will not need your services any longer. I feel that you have not tried hard during the past year. The club has not made nearly as much money as it did in 1911. You do not seem to take much interest in the club."
>
> "Roger Didn't Try Hard," *New York Times*, November 26, 1912: 13.

Herrmann and Barney Dreyfuss of the Pirates were bidding for Bresnahan's services.[18] With the matter still unresolved, Bresnahan brought his grievance to the NL meeting. He was being offered to several teams including Pittsburgh, Cincinnati, and Chicago.[19] The matter remained unresolved at the meetings, but the National League eventually declared him a free agent and he signed with the Chicago Cubs, getting a $25,000 signing bonus. He also settled a lawsuit against the Cardinals for $20,000.[20]

Another topic that garnered attention at the winter meetings was the future of the Giants. John T. Brush, the club's combative owner, had recently died while on a train traveling to the West Coast on November 25, 1912. It was reported that he was suffered from locomotor ataxia and other maladies, knew he was very ill and prior to his death appointed his daughter's husband as vice president of the club.[21] In his will he named his son-in-law Harry N. Hempstead and N. Ashley Lloyd, a minority partner in the team, the executors, giving them authority to vote his stock and, if they chose, to sell the team. There was no sale of the team during the meetings.[22]

T.H. Murnane, a former major-league player and now the baseball editor of the *Boston Globe*, wrote that winter meetings were becoming "little more than getting together for a good time." He wrote that he had attended at least 26 winter meetings that he found more fascinating than the 1912 NL session. He said the National Commission handled most of the business, which left the other baseball officials to do little more than to meet for the social gathering.[23]

In the eyes of another sportswriter, the American League meetings were hardly less dull. Henry P. Edwards of *The Sporting News* opined that the junior circuit meeting could have been mailed in and "not overtaxed the postman at that."[24]

Among the more recognizable names at the AL meetings were Charles Comiskey of the White Sox, Frank Navin of the Detroit Tigers, Charles W. Somers of the Cleveland Indians, and Connie Mack of the Philadelphia Athletics. Somers was re-elected vice president of the league and the presidents of the Chicago, New York, Cleveland, and Boston clubs were appointed to the league board of directors. The league executives also agreed to hold a preseason meeting in New York in February 1913.[25] One of the noteworthy deals involved a National League stalwart, Frank Chance. The New York Highlanders/Yankees hired Chance as their manager. League President Ban Johnson was all in favor. The American League was hoping to capitalize on the Cubs' rivalry with the Giants to spur fans' interest in the Yankees. Chance's efforts were in vain; the Yankees finished in seventh place in 1913 with a record of 57-94. Chance did not last the 1914 season with the Yankees, resigning with three weeks to go.[26]

It was announced that the Yankees' home games would be played at the Giants' Polo Grounds in 1913. The league said the arrangement would last for one year, and the Yankees would then have "a plant of their own." [27] As it turned out, the Yankees were Giants tenants until 1923, when Yankee Stadium was opened.

In other AL matters, Ban Johnson was asked his opinion of an idea floated by Gary Herrmann of having a 64-game interleague series. Johnson said there was no chance of Herrmann's "scheme" being adopted in 1913, and his interviewer inferred that the AL president did not want to see the plan ever implemented. The American League issued an order directing the owners and managers to work together to shorten the length of the games. The clubs bemoaned the fact that the average time of the games was close to two hours and that some low-scoring games even lasted longer than two hours. Reasons included time spent changing sides between innings, players getting back to position after foul balls were hit, the time needed to switch position players or pitchers, and catchers taking too long putting their equipment on.

In addition, the American League, acting at least partly in response to the "base ball writers," deliberated to continue the contract giving Western Union the exclusive right to install wires in league ballparks. Western Union sent a representative to the meeting to try to prevent termination of the agreement, but the league gave Johnson the authority to cancel the agreement unless a "satisfactory agreement" was reached.[28]

A minor transaction completed at the meeting was the Yankees' agreement to allowing Branch Rickey to become the St. Louis Browns' team secretary. Rickey had been on the Yankees' ineligible list for several years because of his refusal to report to the team. If this deal was not made, would the course of baseball have changed?[29]

While the 1912 winter meetings may not have satisfied the cravings of writers Murnane and Edwards for interesting developments, significant issues were indeed addressed, including the implementation of a popular statistical tool (earned-run average), the trials and tribulations of Chance and Bresnahan, discussions of how baseball games were too long, and the launching of Branch Rickey's career as one of baseball's 20th-century pioneers.

NOTES

1 "Minor League Moguls Meet," *The Sporting News*, November 7, 1912; *Washington Post* November 12, 1912.

2 "National Association of Minor Leagues Likely to Adopt Limit," *New York Times*, November 13, 1912: 13.

3 "Fixing Salaries Tedious Task," *The Sporting News*, November 21, 1912. The Class-B Northwestern League teams were allowed an extra $1,000 per month over other Class-B teams due in part to the limited population of the league's cities.

4 "Minor Leagues Are Still in Session, Salary Limit Fixed," *Christian Science Monitor*, November 14, 1912.

5. Harry Neily, "Minors Make Some Progress Toward Regulation of Salary Abuses," *The Sporting News*, November 21, 1912.
6. "Tesreau's Pitching Record," *New York Times*, December 9, 1912.
7. *The Sporting News Complete Baseball Record Book*, 2001, 154.
8. "Lynch Re-Elected by National League," *Hartford Courant*, December 11, 1912: 16.
9. "Matters of Moment in National League," *The Sporting News*, December 19, 1912.
10. "National League Re-Elects Lynch," *New York Times*, December 11, 1912.
11. Matt Ehalt, "Once a Treasured Commodity of Teams, Baseballs Become an Everyday Giveaway for Fans at Ballparks," *New York Daily News*, June 15, 2010.
12. "National League Re-Elects Lynch," *New York Times*, December 11, 1912.
13. "Eppa Rixey," in *The National Baseball Hall of Fame Almanac*, 2014.
14. W.J.M., "Arbitrate Is Plan," *The Sporting News*, December 12, 1912.
15. T.H. Murnane, "Stallings Releases Houser," *Boston Globe*, December 11, 1912. Rudolph went 26-10 for the 1914 "Miracle Braves" and won two games in the Braves' sweep of Philadelphia in the World Series.
16. "'Rajah' Ends Peace Parley," *Chicago Tribune*, December 14, 1912.
17. Joan M. Thomas, SABR BioProject, sabr.org/bioproj/person90202b76.
18. T.H. Murnane, *Boston Globe*, December 11, 2012.
19. *Los Angeles Times*, December 8, 1912: V119.
20. Joan M. Thomas.
21. "Brush Dead," *The Sporting News*, November 28, 1912.
22. "Giants Are Left in Trust," *The Sporting News*, December 12, 1912.
23. T.H. Murhane, "Tim Notes Changes—League Meetings Do Not Have Business as of Old," *The Sporting News*, December 19, 1912.
24. Henry P. Edwards, *The Sporting News*, December 19, 1912.
25. *Christian Science Monitor*, December 12, 1912: 3.
26. Peter M. Gordon, "Roger Peckinpaugh," SABR BioProject, sabr.org/bioproj/person/829dbefb.
27. I.E. Sanborn, "Magnates Loosen on Chance Deal," *Chicago Tribune*, December 13, 1912.
28. "Good of Game Keynote of American League's Meeting," *The Sporting News*, December 19, 1912.
29. Ibid.

— 1913 —
PREPARING FOR THE FIGHTS AHEAD

By Travis Stern

Introduction

THE OFFSEASON AFTER THE 1913 championship season was one of turmoil. It saw the players taking formal steps to improve their working conditions, the ouster of a league president, and the opening salvos of a new war with an "outlaw" major league.

American League

Because of the impending world tour, set to depart on November 19, and the resulting absence of magnates Charles A. Comiskey of Chicago and James McAleer of Boston, the American League meeting was held slightly earlier in the month than in previous years.[1] The league's Board of Directors meeting was originally scheduled for Wednesday, November 6, in the Congress Hotel in Chicago, but was moved to the next morning, before Thursday's larger general meeting, because some of the owners were slow in arriving.[2] The board—consisting of Cleveland's Charles W. Somers, New York's Frank Farrell, Boston's McAleer, and Chicago's Comiskey—officially wrapped up the season by formally awarding the pennant to the Philadelphia Athletics and allocating $100 for the purchase of a championship pennant.[3] Before adjourning, the board heard and accepted the president-treasurer's report showing the most profitable season on record for the 13-year-old league. In the 1913 season, the American League exceeded the previous year's attendance by "a third of a million paid admissions," according to *The Sporting News*, which argued that the numbers were reliable due to the way the clubs were required to pay into the league treasury. The league was a half a million ahead of the previous year's attendance until numbers fell away during the season's final month.

Still, every city except Boston showed an increase in attendance from the year before. Cleveland led the league in attendance, while Washington beat out the pennant-winning Athletics as the biggest road draw by a wide margin.[4]

The general meeting itself was brief; it reportedly took only 2½ hours.[5] The four members of the Board of Directors—from Cleveland, New York, Boston, and Chicago—were replaced by the presidents of the league's other four teams, and Somers was unanimously re-elected vice president.[6] Somers and Philadelphia's Connie Mack were selected by Johnson to sit alongside him on a Rules Committee set to meet with its National League counterparts to clarify and unify how some of the game's rules should be interpreted. The league also decided to suggest to the National League a shortening of the season so it would run from April 14 through October 7. AL President Ban Johnson announced that he and Barney Dreyfuss, president of the National League's Pittsburgh club and the NL's chief schedule-maker, had agreed on the opening date but that the closing date was still unsettled. Johnson suggested that starting the season later by four days would not jeopardize the October 8 beginning of the World Series.[7] (The scheduling meeting between the leagues was held in February, and the proposed date change was approved.)

In a significant action, the AL magnates voted unanimously against altering the nature of the World Series. August "Garry" Herrmann, president of Cincinnati's National League club and the president of the National Commission, had proposed shortening the season to 126 games and then having all 16 teams play in a round-robin tournament to decide the champion. Another plan that had been floated was to replace the World Series entirely with a best-of-nine series between two all-league teams of 20 players apiece, selected by a committee of baseball writers.[8] While not in favor of the Herrmann plan, Ban Johnson believed the postseason could stand some tweaking. Johnson noted the lack of monetary incentive for players to try to win as many games as they could and finish as high as possible in the standings once their team had been eliminated from winning the pennant. But Johnson did not favor a drastic reduction of games during the season.[9] He reportedly would consider extending the World Series to a best of nine, but only if admission prices were reduced.[10] (Later, Johnson denied he had ever favored a change.[11])

The demands of the Players' Fraternity for improved working conditions were discussed only informally since the league had yet to receive the particulars from the group. Relying on information sent to each club owner by the National Commission, the league asked that its discussion be referred to strictly as "informal" because no representative of the players was present. Even if the American League magnates had decided upon an official response, the Players' Fraternity's request had to first be submitted to the National Commission for consideration and subsequent recommendation to the leagues.[12]

The players' list of demands, printed in the *Sporting Life* issue of November 15, had 17 requests accompanied by Players' Fraternity president David L. Fultz's explanation for each item. Among them were requests that every club provide each player with two complete uniforms exclusive of shoes. This had become standard for all teams except for those in the National League, which required a payment of $30 for the two uniforms. Besides the economic hardship suffered by players transferred between clubs during a year, Fultz recounted tales of players receiving second-hand uniforms after paying for new ones or having to borrow from other players before going on the field of play because they had not received a uniform at all.

In the name of player safety, the Fraternity requested the universal adoption of a blank wall in center field aligned with the pitching rubber and home plate and painted dark green, to serve as a background and help prevent serious injuries to batters. The players also requested that teams pay players' traveling expenses to spring training, so long as it did not exceed the expense from the team's home city to the spring site. Fultz argued that the players did not draw a salary for the six-week exhibition season and that at the very least, the teams could afford to pay these expenses.

The players wanted notification of fines or suspension to be in writing, hoping this would keep clubs from levying punishments out of spite or for otherwise unspecified reasons. Several of the other demands followed this impulse toward maintaining a written record, with requests that players receive a written copy of their contracts and that all written agreements be binding on both club and player. When a player was transferred, the Fraternity demanded, he should get written notice indicating the teams that had a claim on him as well as the nature of the claim. The Fraternity wanted the terms of a player's pre-transfer contract to be kept in his new contract.[13]

While most of the requests were deemed acceptable by the American League and several had already been put into effect, the owners expressed serious objection to the request that players be notified in writing when waivers were asked on them. Many times waivers were asked on a player not with the intention of dealing him, but rather to gauge other clubs' interest and to open negotiations for a trade. There had been a few breaches in this secrecy during the past year, and it was speculated that far from opening up the process, the league might seek to add a stiff penalty for disclosing waiver requests.[14]

The brief meeting did not see any trades occur, and several in attendance said player trades were never a topic of conversation during or after the gathering.[15] *The Sporting News* reported only two American League managers visible in the hotel lobby, Cleveland's Joe Birmingham and St. Louis's Branch Rickey, and neither entered while the executive session was in progress. Birmingham denied a rumor that he might trade an outfielder to the Chicago Cubs, and speculated that he might play first base in the coming season. (He did not.) National League managers Joe Tinker of Cincinnati and Miller Huggins of St. Louis were also present.[16]

National Association of Professional Base Ball Leagues

The National Association of Professional Base Ball Leagues met November 11 through 13 at the Virginia Hotel in Columbus, Ohio. Twenty-four of the 43 member leagues had representatives present at the initial roll call, with several more league presidents arriving later, held up by inclement weather halting departures from Cleveland. National Association President Mike H. Sexton opened the meeting and made way for remarks from Ohio Governor (and future Democratic presidential nominee) James Cox, Columbus Mayor G.J. Karb, and Governor Ben Hooper of Tennessee, who made an appeal for the next year's meeting to be held in Nashville. To conclude the first day's gathering, Secretary John H. Farrell presented the annual report, noting 302 member teams from the United States and Canada. During the year 88 players had been drafted into the major leagues from the minors—the National League took 45 and the American League 43— and more than 8,500 player contracts were received and processed.[17] Farrell, as chairman of the National Board of Arbitration, opened the hearings in 167 appeals to the board, which required daily morning and nighttime sessions to complete. Among the 24 claims left unsettled was an application for membership by the Cuban League. The reluctance to accept the league into the organization was attributed to the use of "colored players on teams."[18]

The second day began with the appointment of committees. Besides panels on auditing, resolutions, amending the constitution, and one for drafting a resolution to honor the late Philadelphia Phillies president William H. Locke, a committee was set up to report on the feasibility of a uniform contract for all leagues in the National Association. The idea was controversial, and it was agreed that such a uniform contract would be impracticable. The primary objection was the inclusion of 10 days' notice of release, which was opposed by the B, C, and D leagues over the cost of having to pay a player for 10 days without being able to use him.[19] The delegates voted to let all leagues adopt their own form of contract; a change in Class-AA contracts was allowed to make them more in line with major-league contracts. The International League would use a three- or five-day release notice rather than 10 days, and the lower leagues planned to keep their current practices.

A committee to discuss the requests of the Players' Fraternity was planned but never appointed. The National Board was told to be ready to meet with the National Commission and the Fraternity.

On the third day the delegates considered revisions to the constitution. Among the issues clarified were allowing Class-AA clubs to draft only one player off a Class-A club; requiring that agreements on a player's sale be filed with the secretary's office within 10 days; and voiding the sale of an injured player to another team unless the purchasing club was notified of the injury first. The farming of players was forbidden. Several delegates protested against major-league clubs claiming a large number of players and then canceling the draft, and the major leagues pledged to cease the practice.[20] Omaha rather than Nashville was chosen as the site of the 1914 meeting, due in part to the Tennessee governor's promise to a temperance organization that his state would be dry in the next year.[21] The final act of the meeting was a vote requiring Secretary Farrell to take the entire month of December as vacation because of the work he had accomplished throughout the year.

Two of the Class-AA leagues—the International League and the American Association—discussed adopting a postseason interleague tournament similar to Herrmann's proposal for a major-league round-robin. After discussion at each league's meetings and an address to the International League by American Association President T.M. Chivington, it was determined that such a series would not be feasible. Despite initial widespread support, it was feared that the amount of time several teams would have to be away from their home ballparks left open an advantage that could be exploited by potential Federal League teams. The International League demanded that

American Association teams travel east and play them before returning west, while the American Association favored a coin toss to determine the arrangement. International League President Edward Barrow noted that the stakes of such a tournament would be relatively low since the winner would still have to play the Pacific Coast League pennant winner to determine a true Class-AA champion.[22]

At the banquet on Wednesday evening, National Commission Chairman Garry Herrmann's speech provided the first formal public remarks on both the leadership of the Players' Fraternity and the ever-encroaching Federal League. Herrmann began by noting Organized Baseball's successes under the purview of the National Commission for 11 years: better behavior by fans and players; better facilities; higher player salaries for the more than 8,000 players employed each season on average; and the elimination of much litigation. Proclaiming, "We are proud of our national game—base ball," Herrmann lamented that a proposed congressional inquiry into baseball did not come to pass in the last year, and said it would have been invited, rather than feared, because the game had nothing to conceal. He said the formation of the Players' Fraternity would "contribute materially to the betterment of baseball," and said the National Commission would be happy to formally discuss player complaints, as well as any suggestions the club owners might have.

However, the commission insisted on discussions only with players rather than nonplayers—specifically the Fraternity's president, David Fultz. Herrmann detailed the National Commission's objection to Fultz: He had been critical of its actions in a monthly newspaper piece he was writing without—according to Herrmann—having full knowledge of al the facts and any evidence of the work the commission was doing. Herrmann was also critical of two recent articles in New York newspapers predicting that certain clauses in the National Agreement would not be allowed.[23] (Fultz acknowledged that players he called "black sheep" members of the Fraternity had been in contact with the National Commission.)

ANOTHER GALLAGHER RESOLUTION

With Congress interested in the dissolution of trusts, Representative Thomas Gallagher of Illinois submitted a resolution on April 22, 1913, as he also had done in 1912.

[Excerpt]

"Whereas the most audacious and autocratic trust in the country is the one which presumes the control of baseball; its officials announcing daily through the press of the country the dictates of a governing commission: how competition is stifled: how territory and games are apportioned: how the prices are fixed which millions must pay to witness the sport: how men are enslaved and forced to accept salaries and terms or forever be barred from playing, and other acts incident to trafficking in a national pastime for pecuniary gain."

Banned from baseball, scorned former owner Horace Fogel seemingly sought revenge on those who had wronged him.

Fogel sent a letter to Gallagher offering to "lay the foundation for the investigation and to subpoena witnesses necessary to easily make out a clear case to turn over to the department of justice for immediate action to bust up this arrogant baseball trust."

United States Congress. Bills and Debates in Congress Relating to Trusts: 1902-1913. Government Printing Office. 1914. p3181.

"Baseball in House," *Washington Post*, April 23, 1913: 1.

Most damning for club owners, Herrmann said, was Fultz's request for a pledge by players to strike at a moment's notice. Since no grievances, complaints, or demands had been filed with the Commission, there was no cause for a strike, Herrmann said. There would be no objection to having Fultz present when issues were discussed, provided that a committee of players was also present. Herrmann concluded his remarks on the Players' Fraternity by recognizing three categories of players — those still developing, those in the prime of their careers, and those in the waning stages — and asserted that legislation benefiting one of these groups at the expense of the others would be damaging to the game itself.

Herrmann indicated he didn't think the new Federal League, operating outside the bounds of the National Agreement, would be a threat to the established leagues, and he welcomed the existence of the potential new league because baseball should not be confined to those in "organized ball." He promised no interference with their operations unless they violated contractual obligations or vested rights. Asserting that players of all kinds should be free to make their own choices, Herrmann and the Commission promised to ensure that all legal provisions would be enforced, especially once a contract had been signed. He asserted that players and owners who did not respect those obligations would have no place in Organized Baseball "either now or in the future." Herrmann also addressed the reserve clause, stating that the previous "inequitable arrangement" had been changed for the better now that players were being compensated for signing a contract that contained the clause.[24]

National League

The story that dominated the National League's offseason was the process of replacing Thomas J. Lynch as league president. Ever since assuming the post in 1910, Lynch, a former NL umpire, had endured persistent opposition from some of the owners. The search for Lynch's successor was focused at first on Robert P. Brown, a newspaperman from Louisville, who was favored by Cincinnati's Garry Herrmann, Pittsburgh's Barney Dreyfuss, and Brooklyn's Charles Ebbets. Needing five votes to make the change, the trio might have been able to persuade St. Louis president Schuyler Britton to vote for Brown but no one else, which would mean another year of unease with Lynch remaining in charge. The newly elected president of the Philadelphia club, William F. Baker, declared that he would support Lynch unless a better man could be secured.[25] The "better man" Baker had in mind was the governor of Pennsylvania, John K. Tener, a former major-league pitcher. Baker had intended to gather sufficient support to offer the position on their first meeting, but a leak occurred, possibly by Cincinnati's Herrmann in an effort to derail the plan altogether. Tener was still open to the possibility, however, and though he refrained from public comment before the vote, the move was widely lauded as a positive one for the National League. Seeing defeat, the other faction withdrew their support for Brown, and Tener was unanimously elected on the National League's first day of meetings, December 9 at the Waldorf-Astoria in New York City.[26]

Before the election took place, however, President Lynch submitted the President's Report, detailing the league's statistics from 1913. There had been 76 postponed games, 73 doubleheaders, 15 ties, 12 games that were never played, and five that were protested with four of those disallowed and the remaining one withdrawn. The league used 13,728 baseballs during the year. Lynch noted a general decline in "rowdyism" on the field despite two notable confrontations between players and managers. In a final bit of defiance, Lynch wished the league and its new president success and stated to the room before leaving, "I hope you will inject some of that dignity expected of him into yourselves, and be a help instead of a hindrance." He then left the room and delivered a printed copy of his final remarks for proper quotation to the Base Ball Writers Association, meeting in session in another part of the hotel. Taken aback, the National League magnates then tabled a proposal that had been brought forth to give Lynch a gold watch as a token of gratitude.[27] Later, Lynch denied a report that he would head the Federal League, stating unequivocally, "I am a National Leaguer."[28] Rumors that he might be retained as head of the umpires in the National League did not come to pass, however, and Lynch retired from baseball altogether.

On the second day, Tener was officially installed as the National League's eighth president for a four-year term at a yearly salary for $25,000, though day-to-day management would be handled by Secretary John A.

Heydler until Tener's governorship ended in January 1915. During Tener's brief acceptance remarks, he fondly recalled playing for Cap Anson's Chicago teams. It was then decided that the National League attendees would go en masse to Anson's nearby theatrical performance that night as a show of support. In the afternoon the group considered the demands of the Players' Fraternity. They decided to leave the case with the new president while refusing to publicly divulge any decisions that had been reached. Tener, who once had been secretary of John Montgomery Ward's Brotherhood of Professional Players, would consult with the National Commission's Herrmann and Johnson at their next meeting.

The final day of the meeting was largely devoted to work, though the owners were visited by Morgan G. Bulkeley, the first president of the league, who spoke briefly of his reminiscences and the progress that had been made since he served in 1876. Of note was the presence of Helene Hathaway Robison Britton, the female owner of the St. Louis club, which Bulkeley admitted was an "innovation, but a very good one."[29] Among the business conducted was approval by the league for the National Commission to release $36,000 to be divided equally among the league's eight clubs. The money was 25 percent of the New York Giants' receipts from the 1912 World Series. The club objected to a recently established league rule that required such distribution of receipts among league members. A New York judge upheld the rule, but the Giants refused to concede the matter of $20,000 being held back from the 1913 World Series, so action on that was tabled until a later date.

The attendees discussed at length a proposal previously offered by Brooklyn's Charles Ebbets to create a new draft system for all major-league clubs based on the reverse order of each league's final standings, while allotting all even picks to one league and all odd to the other. While the plan garnered wide appeal, it was decided to postpone an official decision until the American League could similarly deliberate. The final bits of business disposed of before adjourning to President Tener's end-of-meeting dinner included granting the Brooklyn club the lone exception to a constitutional prohibition against two teams occupying the same city, and forbidding a player, manager, or owner of a rival club to discuss player transfers or sales without knowledge and consent of that player's owner and club representatives.[30]

By the official end of the meetings, no significant player deals had occurred. A day after adjournment, however, St. Louis traded first baseman Ed Konetchy to Pittsburgh, along with third baseman Mike Mowery and right-handed pitcher Bob Harmon, for first baseman Jack "Dots" Miller, infielders Art Butler and Al "Cozy" Dolan, outfielder J.O. "Chief" Wilson, and left-handed pitcher Hank Robinson. Konetchy had long been dissatisfied with consistently poor finishes in St. Louis and pushed for a trade to New York. Rumors had the Giants' Fred Merkle, Fred Snodgrass, and Buck Herzog being exchanged for the first baseman and outfielder Lee Magee, but Herzog was adamant against playing for a club that far west with a threat to go "outlaw" if dealt.[31] While Konetchy apparently entertained a three-year, $10,000-a-year contract to manage a St. Louis Federal League team, he eventually committed to his new Pittsburgh club.

The most notable player movement in both name and result after the meetings was that of Joe Tinker from Cincinnati to Brooklyn. After much speculation and rumor, the Cincinnati shortstop and manager was sold to Brooklyn for $25,000 with the promise that Cincinnati would pay him $10,000 as an enticement to get him to accept the transfer. Tinker, however, wanted to return to Chicago and used the resulting salary dispute to jump to the Chicago Federal League club as player-manager on December 27, 1913, for a salary of $36,000 spread out over three years.[32] He was the first major player acquired by the fledgling league, and it forced both of the established major leagues to reconsider their previous position of dismissing the new organization.

Spring Meetings

It was in the wake of several large Federal League splashes that the National and American Leagues met in the middle of February 1914 to finalize their schedules. The National League met at the Waldorf-

Astoria in New York for three days beginning on Tuesday, February 10, while the American League gathered at the Biltmore in New York for one day, Wednesday February 11. Both leagues ratified their schedules, which had them open on April 14 and close on October 7 per the American League's original suggestion.[33]

Behind the perennially strong leadership of President Ban Johnson, the American League owners refused to appoint a "war committee" as the National League had done to fight the Federal League, choosing instead to put Johnson in charge of all matters. Johnson then deferred to the National Commission (of which he was a member) to serve as a de-facto war committee.[34] The National League had appointed President Tener, Cincinnati's Herrmann, and Boston's John C. Toole on the first day of its meeting. Since the American League had declined to follow suit, on the second day the NL rescinded its original vote and similarly chose to place its trust in the National Commission, allowing the two established leagues to stand shoulder-to-shoulder in any dispute with the Federal League.

President Tener and the rest of the league were then able to turn their attention to the issue between Chicago president Charles Murphy and his deposed manager, Johnny Evers. Tener ruled that Murphy must pay Evers the $40,000 called for by his contract as player and manager. Murphy argued that a letter from Evers in which he requested more money or might not ever play ball again constituted his resignation. Murphy admitted, however, that he had failed to give Evers the 10 days' notice required by all contracts signed in the National League under the National Agreement.[35] Within the month Murphy, who had few friends among National League magnates, was forced out of the club's ownership as Charles Taft purchased his stock for $500,000.[36]

TAFTS AND MURPHY

Annie Taft—wife of Charles Taft and sister-in-law to President William Howard Taft—owned the Philadelphia National league grounds, and eventually co-owned the Chicago National League grounds on the west side.

Charles Murphy was the personal representative of the Tafts when they purchased the Philadelphia grounds in 1909.

The ongoing close relationship between Murphy and the Tafts sometimes brought into question who was really running the Cubs. In November, 1914 - after Murphy was removed from baseball - he issued a written statement that Charles Weeghman never had an option on the Cubs.

Weeghman replied, "I simply desire to request that Mr. Murphy ask Mr. Taft whether or not I had an option, and I'm willing to stand by what Mr. Taft has to say. I do not care to answer Mr. Murphy's statement further because he is a neighbor of mine and I have a fine bulldog at home which I prize very highly, and I'm afraid Mr. Murphy might poison my dog."

"Taft to Keep Cubs; Bresnahan Will be Manager," *Chicago Daily Tribune*, November 19, 1914: 9.

NOTES

1. "The American League Holds an Uneventful Meeting in Chicago," *Sporting Life*, November 15, 1913: 10; "Americans Fancy Tener in National," *The Sporting News*, November 13, 1913: 1.
2. "American League Will Ignore Fraternity," *Hartford Courant*, November 6, 1913: 18.
3. "The American League Holds."
4. "American Leaguers to Hear Story of Success," *The Sporting News*, November 6, 1913: 1.
5. "Americans Fancy Tener."
6. "American League Meets in Chicago," *New York Times*, November 7, 1913: 10.
7. Ibid.; "The American League Holds."
8. "A Series Plan," *Washington Post*, December 7, 1913: S3.
9. "Johnson's Amendments," *Sporting Life*, November 8, 1913: 7.
10. "American Leaguers to Hear."
11. "American League Will."
12. "The American League Holds."
13. Ibid.

14 "American Leaguers to Hear."

15 "Americans Fancy Tener."

16 "Americans Sit on Herrmann's Idea," *The Sporting News*, November 13, 1913: 5; "American League Meets."

17 "National Association Starts Its Twelfth Annual Meeting at Columbus, O.," *Sporting Life*, November 15, 1913: 6.

18 "Minor Leaguers Hand a Rebuff to the Commission," *The Sporting News*, November 20, 1913: 5.

19 "National Association: The Twelfth Annual Meeting at Columbus, Ohio, the Most Successful in a Decade," *Sporting Life*, November 22, 1913: 5; "Seeking Uniform Baseball Contract," *Hartford Courant*, November 13, 1913: 19.

20 "Seeking Uniform."

21 "National Association Starts Its Twelfth."

22 "Late News Items," *The Sporting News*, December 11, 1913: 1; "International Passes Up Interleague Series With AA," *The Sporting News*, December 18, 1913: 3.

23 These clauses asked for (3) transferral of a contract subject to all terms of the original contract, (5) written notification of an unconditional release or request of waivers on a player, (10) free agency if not tendered a contract after the 45-day probationary period, and (13) inability of clubs to withdraw a request for waivers on a player once asked.

24 "The Powers' Policy!" *Sporting Life*, November 22, 1913: 1, 18.

25 "Phillies Again to Be King Makers in Their League," *The Sporting News*, November 13, 1913: 1.

26 "The National League Holds a Most Successful Spring Meeting," *Sporting Life*, December 20, 1913: 6.

27 Ibid.

28 "National League Meeting[:] John K. Tener Elected President for Four Years," *Sporting Life*, December 13, 1913: 2; "The National League Holds."

29 "The National League Holds": 7.

30 "The National League Holds": 6-8.

31 "Gives Feds Chance to Sling the Ink," *The Sporting News*, November 6, 1913: 1; "Discussion of Demands," *Los Angeles Times*, December 11, 1913: III4.

32 Daniel R. Levitt, *The Battle That Forged Modern Baseball: The Federal League Challenge and Its Legacy*. (Blue Ridge Summit, Pennsylvania: Ivan R. Dee, 2012); ProQuest ebrary. Web. June 17, 2015, 3-10.

33 "National League Schedule," *Sporting Life*, February 14, 1914: 6; "American League Schedule," *Sporting Life*, February 14, 1914: 7.

34 "The American League Holds One of Its Usual Quiet Meetings," *Sporting Life*, February 21, 1914: 11.

35 "The National League Comes Into Line With Defensive Policy," *Sporting Life*, February 21, 1914: 10.

36 Lenny Jacobsen, "Charles Murphy," The Baseball Biography Project, sabr.org/bioproj/person/e707728f, accessed July 31, 2015.

1914
WARS AT HOME AND ABROAD

By Travis Stern

Introduction

IN THE MONTHS FOLLOWING THE FIRST year of play in the Federal League, the two established major leagues showed different approaches to this new rival. While a desire for peace persisted throughout the winter months, it was tempered by fervent desires for one entity to be a clear loser in any compromise. Though the Federal League held its own meeting at the Biltmore Hotel in New York City on October 23 and 24, little more was accomplished than just setting the stage for the rest of the offseason.

American League

The annual meeting of the American League was originally scheduled for the middle of December, but league President Ban Johnson alerted club owners that the gathering would be moved up a month in order to discuss "business of great importance."[1] In moving the meeting to just before the annual meeting of the minor leagues, the speculation was that Johnson wanted to decide on a plan of action before departing for Omaha. It was under these circumstances that representatives from each American League club met at the Congress Hotel in Chicago on November 5 and 6.

The absence of New York Yankees president Frank Farrell for both the directors' meeting in the morning and the closed executive session in the afternoon further fueled speculation that the sale of that franchise was imminent. Rumors that Farrell was being ousted from the league had been flying for weeks. One of the most interesting was that the new owners would be Jim Gaffney and George Stallings, president and manager, respectively, of the past year's World Series champion Boston National League club. Gaffney, a native and loyal New Yorker, was said to crave a bigger stage, but it also appeared that no formal overtures for the New York franchise were actually made.[2] The most persistent rumor was that the franchise would be sold to brothers Robert and George Ward as part of an agreement to secure peace with the Federal League. The Wards owned the Federal League club in Brooklyn (the Tip-Tops) and were the financial buoys that helped keep the league afloat. While it was acknowledged even among Federal League detractors that the Wards would be a welcome addition to Organized Baseball, they seemed to be steadfast in their allegiance to the Federal League. Under one rumored plan the Wards would purchase the Yankees if it would not interfere with their Federal League franchise and if they could secure the lease on the Polo Grounds to move their Brooklyn team there. Negotiations seem not to have gone very far, if in fact they ever occurred.[3] Upon arriving at the hotel Thursday afternoon as the meeting was breaking up, Farrell emphatically denied that his New York club was available for purchase at all.[4]

The session Farrell missed was largely devoted to discussing the Feds. Despite all the talk about bringing the Wards into the fold, no group in Organized Baseball was more ardent in its opposition to the presence of another major-league than the one that had fought that fight on the opposite side more than a decade earlier. After talking to Ban Johnson, Chicago White Sox president Charles Comiskey, and Boston Red Sox president Joseph Lannin, Chicago writer George S. Robbins believed any semblance of peace could come only if the American League magnates softened their tough position toward the Feds.[5] The prevailing opinion was that the upstarts had already done all the damage they could possibly do, and that the American League would make no concessions to them. Johnson stated frankly that "the Federal League should be a dead issue."[6] Should the Federal League magnates have their clubs absorbed into the established minor leagues or buy National League clubs, Johnson allowed, there would be no strong objection on the part of the AL.[7] The official position that emerged from the Thursday afternoon meeting was a unanimous agreement that "there is no room for a third league."[8]

The morning session, at the league directors' meeting, saw business handled in the quick and efficient manner typical of American League meetings. President Johnson's report was received, and for the fourth time in five years the league pennant was formally awarded to the Philadelphia Athletics. While nothing was officially noted regarding the reports that Washington manager Clark Griffith had pointed out Philadelphia's weaknesses to Boston before their World Series sweep, Connie Mack did accept apologies from another of the league's managers.[9] In violation of the league's policy of secrecy about players on waivers, Detroit manager Hugh Jennings had divulged that Philadelphia was removing veteran pitchers Eddie Plank, Jack Coombs, and Chief Bender from its roster. Though left with very little leverage in seeking any potential return for the players, Mack refused to make a formal complaint, having already accepted a personal apology from Jennings. Mack acknowledged that some changes were in store for his club, and it was reported that both third baseman Frank "Home Run" Baker and second baseman Eddie Collins were being made available.[10]

On the second day, Cleveland president Charles Somers was re-elected to a one-year term as league vice president and, in a move that seemed to assert his place in the league, Frank Farrell was elected to the board of directors along with Somers, Comiskey, and Lannin. The owners passed a resolution to erect a monument at the grave of umpire Jack Sheridan. Finding that the games played in the past year took much longer than was deemed necessary, a directive was issued to players, managers, and umpires to increase their pace. Unable to act without the National League's joint approval, the attendees favored a reduction of rosters from 25 players to 20, and they advocated lowering ticket prices to the World Series so that they exceeded the regular-season price by only a small margin.[11] While some discussion included extending the number of games as well, writer William Weart argued that neither proposed solution would fix the issue. Fans had shown themselves willing to pay up to $5 for a ticket, he wrote. The fans' primary concern, according to Weart, was how to get the ticket.[12]

On the evening of the second day, with all business concluded or tabled until the spring meeting and awaiting National League consideration, the group attended the annual banquet, held at the Chicago Automobile Club and hosted by Charles Comiskey.[13] In an effort to ensure that some of the players on league payrolls could be successfully distributed among the minor leagues without being picked off by the Federals, Johnson and Comiskey led a contingent of American League personnel attending the minor-league gathering the next month in Omaha.

National Association of Professional Base Ball Leagues

The 1914 season had not been financially successful for much of Organized Baseball, and the minor leagues were particularly challenged. At the 14th annual meeting of the National Association of Professional Base Ball Leagues in Omaha's Rome Hotel on November 10, 11, and 12, the positives were highlighted and reasons for the negatives were discussed. National Association Secretary John H. Farrell reported that even with all the difficulties, 39 of the 42 member leagues starting the year saw their seasons through to the finish, close to the best mark in the organization's history.[14] Similarly, the convention was very well attended, with more than 200 registered from all over North America. There were eventually 27 leagues represented in person and several others by proxy.[15] The high number of attendees was somewhat of a surprise, given the economic hardships of the past year and Omaha's distance from major population centers.[16] Farrell's report said the year might not have been as dire as many had feared, with 8,403 player contracts received and promulgated, and 43 players drafted into the major leagues (28 by the National League, 15 by the American League), which paid a total of $56,500 for them.[17] Though both figures were down from previous years, the decline was slight.

Most magnates cited the general depression resulting from the wars in Europe and Mexico as the primary cause for their sorrows, while admitting to some reckless maneuvers by a few individual magnates.[18] President Al Tearney of the Three-I League was vocal in his attribution of his league's losses to the existence of the Federals, but Western League President Norris O'Neill felt differently. While acknowledging that some of his league's clubs had lost players to the Feds, he believed any argument that an outlaw league in a different part of the country would hurt his league's attendance was a ridiculous proposition. *The Sporting News* noted a variety of reasons other than the Feds why Tearney's league suffered a disappointing year, including the closing of the coal mines in one league town and a prominent financial backer withdrawing in another.[19]

The Federal League hoped to poach a few leagues away from the National Association and Organized Baseball and persuade them to affiliate with the Feds instead, or, failing that, to use the depressed conditions throughout the minors to compel those owners to force the two major leagues to seek peace on favorable terms.[20] The Feds were confident that several teams would jump from Organized Baseball to join them if the money was right.[21] They already had an agreement of sorts with the Class-C Colonial League to develop talent. The six-team league was a member of the National Association and still operated under its terms and conditions. Run by President A.J. Winn, it had an unusual operating structure: The league president effectively owned all of the property of the league. He signed all the players, collected all the money, and paid all the bills, with the general acknowledgment that the primary financial backing came from the Wards of the Federal League. For the 1914 season, it was reported that the league lost $21,000. Still President Winn planned to ask for Class-B status for the coming season under the threat that it would formally abandon Organized Baseball if the request was not granted.[22]

In view of the Federal League's posturing, the first order of business for the convention was a vote on adopting President Mike Sexton's resolution affirming loyalty to Organized Baseball, and it was passed unanimously by the 26 represented leagues. A Pacific Coast League representative spoke briefly to dispel newspaper reports that his league had been negotiating with the Feds. To stress the importance of Sexton's resolution, it was reported that for the first time, a verification of credentials was required for all voters.[23] Though the symbolism of such a resolution was important as the first and only significant act by the whole body on the first day, it did not mean there wasn't dissension in the ranks. Don E. Brees, president of the Wichita club in the Class-A Western League, announced his resignation immediately upon returning from the meeting. He was a vocal advocate for the minors using their power to demand immediate peace and was upset when it was decided that they would only endorse any action the major leagues took.[24]

The serious business continued the next day as the chairman of the National Commission, August "Garry" Herrmann, spoke of the need for immediate and drastic action in light of the previous year's financial difficulties. In the name of economy and elimination of extravagance, Herrmann advocated for a salary limit for each league that was in line with the gate receipts of the smallest club in each league, rather than the largest. As a result, the Committee on Constitutional Revision recommended a reduction of the player salary limit by 20 percent, with specific amounts detailed for each class. The Class-A limit of $3,200 a month for the Southern League and $2,800 for the Western League was accepted without protest. The Class-B limit of $2,000 was also accepted but with some reluctance by the Texas League and the New York State League. President William Davidson of the Texas League argued against the $500 reduction but was placated by the intimation that his league could receive a special dispensation if it demonstrated the ability to pay the higher salaries. The Double-A leagues, in direct competition with the Federal League clubs, protested the announced $5,000 cap as it made the leagues' salary arrangement public knowledge. They were given special leave to set their limit privately, and the club owners pledged themselves to economy. The most spirited discussions came from the C and D leagues, with the Central League leading the fight, and after two days of arguments they were allowed to keep their current limits. The revision committee also recommended a reduction in the roster limits in each classification, and this proved not to be particularly objectionable to those in attendance.[25]

A good portion of the meeting dealt with territorial concerns, with the most notable and bitterest battle being between the Class-D Central Association and the Class-B Three-I League for the rights to Rock Island, Illinois. While nearby Iowa cities Moline and Davenport had Three-I clubs, Rock Island wanted the Central Association's Ottumwa franchise. As a special compliment to National Association President Sexton and his hometown, Rock Island requested bending the rule forbidding a club to operate within five miles of another without consent. Though the convention was agreeable to complimenting the Association's president, it was reluctant to set a precedent that could extend the Western League's desire to put a club in Kansas City, Kansas, across the river from the American Association's Kansas City, Missouri, franchise, which was already competing with a Federal League club in the same city. As a concession, Three-I President Tearney, who had already announced the relocation of the Springfield, Illinois, franchise to Rock Island so that it couldn't be deemed unoccupied territory, allowed that if Rock Island would not support a Three-I team, he would concede the territory to the Central Association. Many believed a contentious year was in store as members of the Rock Island delegation immediately began plans for a boycott.[26]

Al Tearney had an active and vocal presence at the meeting. In addition to a failed proposal to hold all future National Association meetings in Chicago, he proposed to reorganize the National Board of Arbitration by reducing the number of members from 10 and making it a permanent sitting with one member from each of the five classes. Though Tearney agreed to table the proposal and resubmit it next year after being told the present board couldn't be removed legally with a year left on its contract, some changes were made.[27] The National Board, which was led by Secretary John H. Farrell and served as the Supreme Court of baseball, regularly undertook a tremendous amount of work during the week of the convention and drew no salary for its service. Meeting for many long sessions each day, the board faced 250 cases at the 1914 meeting alone, which kept them working beyond the conclusion of the convention by at least one day. The congestion of cases was due in part to procrastination on the part of the claimants, as most were filed in the last month before the meeting though many of them could have been filed and adjudicated well before then.[28] In an effort to reduce the workload, it was proposed that all claims within a league must first be presented to the league president for decision. In these cases, the board would be used just for appeals and interleague disputes. Near the end of the convention, the board was granted absolute power to act for the whole of the National Association in any settlement made with the Federal League, and it was given a full endorsement and expression of confidence from the convention. Upon completion of his duties, Secretary Farrell was once again given a mandatory 30-day vacation.[29]

Among the many cases heard by the National Board was an unusual petition by the Class-D Western Canada League. While both the Federal League and Organized Baseball continued to cloak themselves in the rhetoric of war, actual fighting had begun in Europe into which Canada, part of the British Empire, had been thrust in August. Unsure of the duration of the war, the Western Canada League believed it would have to suspend operations for the 1915 season. The league requested the ability to loan its players to clubs in other leagues but retain their rights upon resumption of operations. Details such as which club would receive the profit if a loaned player was drafted into a higher league had to be settled, but a general uncertainty remained. Charley Stis, the manager of the Regina team, attended the conference actively seeking both placements for his players if the league chose to suspend and players to help his club if the season continued as planned. He was offered the Cedar Rapids manager position in the Central Association but was embarrassed to be unable to make a decision to accept until the league finalized its decision.[30] On December 17, five weeks after the meeting, the league suspended operations, with four of the six clubs voting in favor and two, Stis' Regina club and Saskatoon, wanting to play.[31] The league would lie dormant until the 1919 season, when it returned as a Class-C league for one year and then two seasons at Class B before ceasing operations.[32]

National League

The National League met for three days, starting Tuesday, December 8, at the Waldorf-Astoria in New York. As in years past, the board of directors gathered immediately beforehand to conduct year-end business, including officially awarding the league pennant to the World Series champion Boston Braves. Once the general meeting commenced, the league considered the reduction of the player limit for each team that the American League had proposed earlier in the offseason.[33] Waiting to make a final decision until after the National League could consider it, the American League had proposed lowering the limit of players per club from 25 to 20. Writer Joe Vila wrote that if both leagues agreed to a reduction, a large number of players would be released or sent to the minors, thereby strengthening other leagues.[34] The National League decided on a 21-player cap but made a concession to the New York club's objections. From September 1 through May 1, teams were allowed to carry 35 players, but the limit would be 21 from May to September—the majority of the playing season. It was reported that several teams rarely carried more than 21 due to their finances, and setting the limit at 21 would lessen the more prosperous clubs' advantage. New York, for instance, had about 50 players under contract at the time with 16 on multiyear deals. The limit would not include managers, coaches, or other uniformed personnel.[35]

To further aid the financially struggling clubs, it was decided that no team could begin spring training or journey to the South before March 1. A ban on series held before the season between major-league teams in the same city was recommended for presentation to the American League as a way to redirect focus onto Opening Day. The league also sought to curtail unsanctioned barnstorming tours in the offseason that were not conducted by the league owners themselves, like one that had recently been undertaken by Frank Bancroft. Before the first day ended, the league accepted the request of Tommy Rice of the Base Ball Writers Association of America to have the umpire present the press box with the correct batting order for each team before the game, and the league voted to allow a representative from the National Association onto the Joint Playing Rules committee.[36]

Among the most persistent elements of the many proposed peace plans between the major leagues and the Federal League was the sale of the Chicago Cubs to Charles Weeghman, the owner of the Chicago Federal League team. The National League had ousted former Chicago owner Charles Murphy from its ranks during the previous offseason, and the current team president, Charles Thomas, was removed from the league's board of directors on the first day of the current meetings. Garry Herrmann had been in conversations with Weeghman for several months, but only, he stressed, on his own and not in any official capacity for the National Commission or the National League.[37] Negotiations between Weeghman and Charles Taft, who had purchased control of the franchise from Murphy, broke off when Taft held as a condition of the sale that the club could not be moved from West Side Park. Aware that Charles Comiskey's American League team dominated the South Side of the city, Weeghman had planned to move the Cubs to his Federal League team's ballpark at Clark and Addison on the city's North Side.[38] Herrmann brought the gathering up to date on his endeavors, reiterating once again that no overtures for peace had been made by Organized Baseball. The specifics of his negotiations with Weeghman, however, were not disclosed.[39]

So much of the second day was spent on debating the waiver rules that planned discussions about the World Series had to be moved to the next day. The issue brought forth by Julius Fleischmann of the Cincinnati Reds was the practice of placing a player on waivers and then pulling him back once it was ascertained what clubs might benefit from his services. He argued that this was bad for baseball, as it prevented weaker teams from getting better and allowed the best players to play, which became more imperative under the new player limit. New York's John Toole proposed to prevent waivers from being withdrawn once asked. The discussion continued into the third day with the weaker clubs advocating for its adoption and Toole's own New York club arguing that the rule would prevent clubs from sufficiently developing players, as asking waivers would be equivalent to a release to some other club. Final decision was deferred until the February meeting so that the two leagues could reach a joint decision. Also on that final day, the league declined to take any action on altering the World Series from its current best-of-seven format.[40]

Throughout the week the National Commission had also met several times to confer on a variety of issues. Despite reports that it had enacted the ban on intercity, preseason series that the National League had advocated, Commission Chairman Herrmann said no such prohibition was adopted and that he personally held no objection to such series. While they spent much of their time dealing with an adjustment to the International League's configuration, the hope was that a uniform policy decision would be made on contract jumpers and violators of the reserve clause who now wished to rejoin Organized Baseball. If such a policy was determined, it was not publicly disclosed during the week.[41] The issue had been reignited in light of Rube Marquard's re-signing with the Giants for two years in July. In the offseason, after seeking and being denied a $1,500 advance on his 1915 salary, Marquard told Brooklyn Federal League club owner Robert B. Ward he was free to sign and was willing to sign an affidavit to affirm that he had obtained his legal freedom from New York. Ward thereupon signed the left-hander to a two-year, $10,000 contract and gave him his desired $1,500 in cash. Immediately Marquard was denounced as a contract jumper, as the New York club produced the contract, signed on July 27, that secured him for 1915 and 1916 at $3,000 a year, plus an option for 1917. Both Ward and Giants president Harry Hempstead threatened legal action, but ultimately Marquard continued to pitch in the National League in 1915.[42]

Though the National League had no significant player movement or ownership changes during its meeting, the American League made news in both areas that would have great importance in future years. Rumors had persisted since the end of the season that Philadelphia would release second baseman Eddie Collins, the reigning MVP, so he become manager of the Yankees. Instead, Collins was sole to the White Sox. Philadelphia received $50,000 for Collins, while the player himself got a new five-year contract valued at around $12,000 per year.[43] The subsequent 12 years that Collins spent in Chicago proved to be quite eventful.

The other significant move was the sale of the Yankees franchise. The American League had strenuously asserted during its meeting the previous month that the club would not be sold to the Wards of the Federal League as part of any peace agreement, and that owner Frank Farrell would remain in control. Keeping true to half of that assertion, the league announced that negotiations were expected to be completed soon on a sale to a group led by Jacob Ruppert Jr., whose wealth had come from real estate and breweries. The final hurdle—a $100,000 difference between Farrell and partner William Devery's $500,000 asking price and Ruppert's $400,000 cap—was expected to be cleared in short order. Ruppert had big plans for his new purchase and unsuccessfully attempted to induce Connie Mack to take over management of the club. It was announced that the team would continue playing at the Polo Grounds in 1915 and possibly 1916, but that Ruppert's group would build a new ballpark on a plot of land he owned on Lenox Avenue between 136th and 138th Streets.[44] These plans were never realized and the club continued its tenure at the Polo Grounds until Yankee Stadium opened in 1923.

Spring Meetings

Wrapping up and finalizing their schedules, the NL and AL met within a week of each other in New York City in February 1915. The American League's meeting on February 4 was held at the Hotel Belmont and was finished in less than four hours. The meeting featured the official admission of Colonel Jacob Ruppert and Tillinghast "Cap" Huston as new representatives of the Yankees, with Ruppert also succeeding Frank Farrell on the league's Board of Directors. After setting the season's opening and closing dates at April 14 and October 7, the league turned to other matters. At the behest of its managers, the league rescinded the player limit it had placed on clubs in November, with teams allowed to continue carrying 25 players from May 15 through August 15, and 35 players during the offseason, instead of the proposed cap of 20. Unlike the National League, the American League owners decided not to place any restrictions on when their spring-training period should begin. In addition to granting two season passes to any American League ballpark for each of the league's players, the group declared war on the "emery ball" pitch used by Boston and New York in the previous season. Umpires were instructed to be vigilant right from the outset and crack down on the first rule-breaker who used a piece of emery paper to scuff a new ball, so an example could be set by punishing the violator with a suspension and hefty fine.[45]

The National League gathered, once again at the Waldorf-Astoria, on February 9 and 10. Despite the belief that it might follow the AL in rescinding the new player limit, the NL decided to maintain the 21-player roster for the 1915 season. The league established that player-managers would count against the limit, so the bench manager would be unable to insert himself in any game during the season without forfeiting the right to carry one of the players on his roster. The penalty for violating the rule was steep—forfeiture of the game. Concerns were expressed that by carrying four more players per team, the American League might have a competitive advantage throughout the season. The NL also declined to alter the March 1 start date for spring preseason activities. Wrapping up the unfinished business from December, it passed the prohibition on withdrawing waivers on players once asked or claimed, 6-2, with only the New York Giants and Pittsburgh objecting. Managers were no longer permitted to ask for waivers on or claim a player under the new rule, with only club presidents allowed to make those transactions.

Of special historical note was the presence of St. Louis Cardinals owner Helene Hathaway Britton. Not only was she the first woman to own a major-league franchise, but she addressed the delegates during the debate on the waiver question, thus becoming the first woman to do so in the game's history.[46] Prior to this time, she attended numerous meetings, but had only listened.

NOTES

1. "The League to Meet in Chicago November 6," *Sporting Life*, November 7, 1914: 9; "American Will Have Something to Say," *The Sporting News*, November 5, 1914: 6

2. "Tim Murnane Hears Little of Federals in Windy City," *The Sporting News*, November 12, 1914: 1.

3. "No Peace Note in Federal Meeting," *The Sporting News*, October 29, 1914: 2; "NY Scribes Fail to Oust Farrell," *The Sporting News*, November 12, 1914: 1.

4. "The League to Meet."

5. "Robbins Fails to Find Peace Dove," *The Sporting News*, October 29, 1914: 1.

6. "Prospects of Early Peace Fade as Issues are Joined," *The Sporting News*, November 19, 1914: 1.

7. Ibid.; "AL Meet Shows Johnson's Position," *The Sporting News*, November 12, 1914: 1.

8. "Details of the Annual Meeting in Chicago," *Sporting Life*, November 14, 1914: 9.

9. Ibid.

10. Ibid.; "American Magnates Attend Strictly to Own Business," *The Sporting News*, November 12, 1914: 3

11. "Details of the Annual': "American Magnates."

12. "Wards Finding It Hard to Break In," *The Sporting News*, November 19, 1914: 1.

13. "Details of the Annual"; "AL Meet Shows."

14. "Tim Murnane Hears."

15. "Over 200 Register on Omaha Convention Roll," *The Sporting News*, November 19, 1914: 2.

16 "Fourteenth Annual Meeting Held at Omaha," *Sporting Life*, November 21, 1914: 14-15.

17 "Minors at Omaha Spurn Idea of Peace," *The Sporting News*, November 12, 1914: 1; "Minor Leagues are Lined Up," *Sporting Life*, November 14, 1914: 1; "Thirteenth Annual Report of Secretary Farrell," *Sporting Life*, November 14, 1914: 14.

18 "Minors at Omaha."

19 "The Feds and the Minors," *The Sporting News*, October 29, 1914: 4; "No Apologies for This," *The Sporting News*, October 29, 1914: 4.

20 "There Can Be No Peace," *The Sporting News*, October 29, 914: 4.

21 "No Peace Note."

22 "Boston Feels its Dignity Lowered," *The Sporting News*, October 29, 1914: 2.

23 "Fourteenth Annual Meeting"; "Omaha Convention Leaves No Doubt as to Where It Stands," *The Sporting News*, November 19, 1914: 2-3.

24 "Herrmann Finds Peace Hope Fading," *The Sporting News*, November 19, 1914: 1.

25 "Omaha Convention"; "Fourteenth Annual Meeting."

26 "Omaha Convention"; "Fourteenth Annual Meeting"; "Three-I Leaguers Worked Fast to Fortify Their Claim to Rock Island," *The Sporting News*, November 19, 1914: 2.

27 "Omaha Convention."

28 Ibid.; "Congestion of Claims Awaiting Decision Not Fault of the National Board but of Litigants," *The Sporting News*, November 19, 1914: 3.

29 "Omaha Convention."

30 "Congestion of Claims"; "A Dearth of Deals," *The Sporting News*, November 19, 1914: 3; "Western Canada League," *Sporting Life*, November 21, 1914: 15; "Western Canada League," *Sporting Life*, November 28, 1914: 20; "Western Canada League," *Sporting Life*, December 5, 1914: 18; "Minor—and Major—Bits Picked Up in the Lobbies," *The Sporting News*, November 19, 1914: 2.

31 "Western Canada League," *Sporting Life*, December 26, 1914: 18; "Moguls Warlike as They Gather," *The Sporting News* December 10, 1914: 1.

32 Western Canada League (D) Encyclopedia and History, Baseball-Reference.com baseball-reference.com/minors/league.cgi?code=WCAN&class=D), accessed August 14, 2015.

33 "National Leaguers in Annual Meeting Take Radical Action for Retrenchment," *The Sporting News*, December 17, 1914: 3; "Fortieth Annual Meeting of the Senior League," *Sporting Life*, December 19, 1914: 2.

34 "NY Scribes Fail." Vila argued that at least 100 players would be affected; however, five players eliminated from each of the 16 teams would be 80 players. Regardless, the result would be a 20 to 25 percent reduction in player jobs in the major leagues.

35 "National Leaguers"; "Fortieth Annual Meeting."

36 Ibid.

37 "Prospects of Early Peace."

38 "No Peace Note."

39 "Fortieth Annual Meeting.".

40 "National Leaguers"; "Fortieth Annual Meeting."

41 "American League to Fore with Two Big News Stories," *The Sporting News*, December 17, 1914: 3.

42 "Rube Marquard's Stunt Gets Him in Bad with All Hands," *The Sporting News*, December 10, 1914: 1.

43 "American League to Fore"; "Eddie Collins Sold to Chicago White Sox," *Sporting Life*, December 12, 1914: 1.

44 "American League to Fore"; "A Great Base Ball Park for Farrell's Club," *Sporting Life*, December 19, 1914: 5.

45 "The Schedule Meeting of the Junior Major League," *Sporting Life*, February 13, 1915: 4.

46 "The Spring Meeting of the Senior Major League," *Sporting Life*, February 20, 1915: 2.

— 1915 —
PEACE TIME FOR THE NATIONAL PASTIME

By Rich Bogovich

THE 1915 SEASON HAD BEEN A TOUGH one for Organized Baseball, and murky moods were probably spread widely across the sport as the annual meetings approached in November and December. As noted in a *Sporting Life* preview of the four-day meeting of the National Association of Professional Baseball Leagues (NAPBL), membership had plunged from 47 minor leagues a year earlier to 22.[1] Meanwhile, the National and American Leagues played the entire season under the dark cloud of the antitrust suit that had been filed in January.[2] There was talk that the majors were pursuing a settlement with the rival Federal League, including at a meeting in Cincinnati in early November, but *The Sporting News* threw a wet blanket on that, telling its nationwide readership all it needed to know in the headline of its November 11 edition—"Little Likely to Come Out of All This Talk of Peace."

Nevertheless, interest in the NAPBL gathering in San Francisco should have been heightened because Federal League franchises had provided stiff competition in four top minor-league cities. The International League had continued to lock horns with the Federal League in Buffalo but had moved out of Baltimore before Opening Day and out of Newark by midseason, while the American Association battled a Federal League team in Kansas City throughout 1915. Another reason for interest in the meeting from November 9 through 12 was highlighted in *Sporting Life*: Rebels were going to try supplanting NABPL leaders at some point during the four days. Conversely, the leadership was considering a plan to expand the duties of the NAPBL secretary by tacking on those of the president; Michael Sexton, a former head of the Three-I League and the Western League, had become the second president in 1909 but had already announced his disinterest in running for re-election. Among the few bright spots forecast was the attendance "by representatives of the Carranza government, looking for a franchise for a base ball league in Northern Mexico next year, under the auspices of Organized Ball."[3]

One important firsthand account of the goings-on was decidedly unkind. "The National Association convention of 1915 will go down in the records as that which compelled the delegates to travel farthest, at which the sessions were prolonged over more days, and at which less of real moment was accomplished than at any previous meeting of the minor leagues," wrote Al C. Joy, sports editor of the *San Francisco Examiner*.[4] Still, the two weeklies devoted a full page each to the NAPBL proceedings, despite their being closed to the general public for the first time in their 15 years. Reports indicated that business would be expedited, if the public was kept away.[5]

The only prominent attendee from the major leagues was president Charles Ebbets of Brooklyn's NL team, though scouts from other teams were noticed. On the first day, Sexton was one of several dignitaries who offered opening or welcoming remarks. "For several years I have been convinced that it would take a catastrophe such as we have suffered to bring the owners to their senses and make them realize that they have thrown their money away," he said. "Not alone in salary limits, but in other expense accounts, such as cutting down of spring training, can we reduce."[6] Contrary to the wishes he expressed before the event,

Sexton was re-elected president on the final day (and remained in the post through 1931).

The NABPL made at least tentative decisions on some important topics, including adjustments to salary regulations, restrictions on drafting players from lower leagues, and punishments for playing with an ineligible or disqualified player, but neither weekly found those developments worthy of much ink. However, *The Sporting News* did offer commentary and analysis on a few fronts. For one, it reported that due to the ample use of proxies, too few club owners and managers were actually in attendance to pull off many player deals. The most significant exception was the sale of four Milwaukee players to Oakland. The paper explained the absence of the delegation from the Mexican government as a misunderstanding of an effort by John J. McCloskey, who was attempting (without success) to revive the Rio Grande Association, which had folded in July during its inaugural season, and he wanted territorial rights in northern Mexico for additional teams. The owners and managers present apparently didn't sugar-coat the sorry state of the minor leagues, but they avoided blaming or giving credit to the Federal League, whose triumphs in Baltimore and Newark seem to have been ignored in favor of the minor-league representatives from Kansas City and Buffalo bragging about having dealt major blows to the Federal League franchises in their two cities.[7]

The National and American League meetings were more than a month away, but the Federal League meeting happened to overlap with the start of the NAPBL's conference. The Federal League magnates met in Indianapolis on November 9, amid speculation that upon adjournment the leaders would hasten to a resort in French Lick, 100 miles to the south, for more discussions with their major-league rivals.

Given the competitive circumstances, it should have come as no surprise that after receiving reports from the eight clubs during its internal session, the Federal League issued a statement declaring that "after consideration of all the facts, we were well rewarded for our operations in 1915."[8] The leadership did not avoid public comment on the situations in Kansas City and Buffalo. The *Indianapolis Star* printed details provided by the league:

> The franchises of Kansas City and Buffalo were forfeited for certain defaults upon their respective parts. The Kansas City franchise will be transferred to New York city and the team will be strengthened to the extent of making it a representative New York club, which will surely merit the support of New York fans. It is believed that the Buffalo situation later

WHERE'S BARNEY?

Separating fact from strategic positioning during the war between the Federal League and the majors could, at times, prove difficult.

According to Barney Dreyfuss, French Lick was a coincidence.

"What I desired was rest and a little recreation on the golf links. On learning that the Federals intended on visiting French Lick, I naturally changed plans because there would be little rest among a crowd of baseball men, and besides, my presence there would have caused all sorts of yarns to be sent out to the effect that I was on hand by appointment. I have no appointment to meet any baseball people at present, and was unaware that Col. Ruppert was at the resort until tonight. He goes to French Lick about four times a year, however, so there could be no surprise in his presence there."

Barney Dreyfuss

Ruppert reportedly was part of the entourage that met and discussed peace with a band of Federal League owners during the World Series. Dreyfuss was dispatched, in December, from the National League meetings to discuss Federal League peace plans with American League.

"Dreyfuss Purposely Avoids Fed Magnates," *Evening Star* (Washington D.C.), November 11, 1915: 19.

will be properly taken care of by the citizens of that community.

> The grounds on Manhattan Island have been obtained, plans have been drawn for the stand to seat 55,000 people and we will be ready for operation in New York city at the beginning of the season of 1916.[9]

But was the talk about New York mostly posturing, pointed squarely at the other two major leagues? *Star* sports editor Ralston Goss suggested as much, when his account began, "With an olive branch in one hand and a hand grenade in the other, Federal League magnates who met here yesterday moved down to French Lick Springs last night, there to continue the peace negotiations begun in Philadelphia early in October and renewed in Cincinnati last week." Goss also quoted from a "private conversation" with an unnamed Federal League magnate "who has been foremost in the peace negotiations," who said, "There are so many angles in a deal of the magnitude we are undertaking, though, that one can not say what will come of the negotiations. I think both sides are actuated by a sincere motive to get together and that the experience we have gained since the peace negotiations of a year ago has taught us that it would be folly to continue the war if it is possible to obtain peace with honor."[10]

Alas, as the *New York Times* reported, the only owner from the two established major leagues to meet with Federal League potentates in French Lick was Jacob Ruppert, the relatively new owner of the Yankees. Given the Federal League's new announcement about New York, that may have had more significance than the *Times* perceived. In any case, there was also apparently speculation that Barney Dreyfuss of the Pirates was at the resort, but the Federal League representatives didn't report seeing him.[11]

The most significant developments relating to the peace negotiations during the remainder of November centered on the Federal League's scheme for New York. The front page of *The Sporting News* on November 25 reported on those plans for Manhattan in three separate articles. In the second column was a short article saying that Federal League officials had just spent time on the island but they wouldn't reveal anything about the site of the new ballpark. Meanwhile, the entire fourth column was devoted to word that an unnamed Boston millionaire would be the new club's key funder. The topic was also covered in the first column in an article primarily about the American League. In the paper's first article a week later, Joe Vila, sports editor of *The Sun* in New York, suggested that the Federal League effort was stalling. Regardless, in the weekly's first article of its December 9 edition, it provided AL President Ban Johnson with a forum to comment at length about the situation:

> If the National League takes any action in regard to the Feds that is up to them. We won't attempt to dictate to the National League. The American League stands where it always has stood on the Federal League question. We consider them a failure. They batted into baseball as a business venture and they have discovered they made a big mistake. They are ready to quit, so why should we bother about them. The Feds have defeated themselves and are responsible for their own mistakes.
>
> So far as putting a team in New York is concerned, that is one monumental bluff. They simply want to scare somebody to get out as cheaply as possible and save something from this wreck. Prospects for a successful season in the American League next season are bright so why should we bother about the Federal League?[12]

And with that setting the tone, the AL's magnates headed to Chicago for their annual meeting on Wednesday, December 15. The NL had convened the day before but finished one day after the AL. Chicago's unusual ad-free daily tabloid, *The Day Book*, didn't exactly roll out the red carpet for the American League dignitaries on that day when it opined:

> Maybe peace is in sight. Maybe it isn't. It is something that gets no red-faced cheers from us and really makes little difference to the great fan family. Reorganization may bring better baseball, but in the past with two leagues

the magnates never showed any especial consideration for the public which makes baseball possible. Their very indifference gave the Feds their opening.[13]

Despite this attitude, in that edition the paper wrote at length about the peace talks. In the midst of the NL's internal sessions in New York, Federal League leaders were dialoguing with their counterparts there.

James Crusinberry of the *Chicago Tribune* reported about the dominance of the Federal League negotiations in discussions among early arrivals for the AL meeting. That didn't keep owners or managers of at least four of the clubs from also talking about trades. In particular, he recorded one conversation initiated by Robert Hedges, owner of the St. Louis Browns, with Chicago White Sox skipper Pants Rowland:

> Once Hedges bumped into Manager Rowland of the Sox and asked the following question:
>
> "Can you fix up a deal so that the Browns can get Schalk, Scott, and Fournier?"
>
> "Perhaps I can," answered Rowland. "If you can give us Pratt, Sisler, Koob, Shotton, and Austin."
>
> "Don't you want me to throw in the north end of my grand stand?" concluded Hedges as he walked away.[14]

Hedges had expressed interest in three stars of the White Sox, including a future Hall of Famer in catcher Ray Schalk. Rowland had countered by naming three starting position players for the Browns, and wasn't too greedy in adding pitcher Ernie Koob, St. Louis's fifth starter. Rowland most astutely included so-so rookie George Sisler, another future Hall of Famer.

Hedges may not have been making a serious inquiry, but according to Jack Fournier's SABR biography online, Browns manager Branch Rickey wanted the White Sox first baseman, though he wouldn't reveal to reporters whom he dangled in exchange. Washington manager Clark Griffith, meanwhile, offered first baseman Chick Gandil for Fournier.[15] Fournier ended up staying put.

In hindsight, the most interesting trade talk was probably that stemming from Chicago's strong interest in filling a glaring void at third base. As historians Mark Armour and Daniel Levitt noted, the White Sox were so desperate in 1915 "that Rowland played outfielder Braggo Roth at third for thirty-five games. Roth's fielding percentage of .837 is the lowest since 1910 for anyone who played in at least thirty games. Roth made an error on nearly one of every six chances." The White Sox pursued Yankee third baseman Fritz Maisel, coming off a .281 average in his second full season, but he ended up hitting .215 over the remainder of his major-league career. To acquire Maisel, Chicago had reportedly considered trading none other than Shoeless Joe Jackson.[16] When the dust settled, however, the only steal from White Sox magnates was the new motor car parked outside the Congress Hotel by Louis Comiskey, son of the team's owner.[17]

The American League did conduct some actual business during its meeting. For example, Charles Somers of Cleveland was re-elected the league's vice president, presumably as a vote of confidence that he would remain head of his team despite financial difficulties.[18] This optimism was misplaced, because in early 1916 Somers' creditors forced him to sell the franchise to James Dunn.

The day after the meeting, Crusinberry of the *Tribune* described several additional votes. The moguls approved resolutions barring players from writing for newspapers or magazines (even nominally) and from barnstorming after the regular season. They also voted in support of keeping the World Series a best-of-seven format, contrary to the nine-game proposal from some NL owners.

However, Crusinberry called it "the most exciting and most mysterious meeting the American league has had since the war days of fifteen years ago" because of scuttlebutt that an agreement with the Federal League was suddenly mere days away. "The invasion of the dove of peace rather killed the talk of everything else, even including the proposed trades," he wrote.[19]

Sporting Life dutifully reported on the National League's internal decision-making from Tuesday through Thursday, including a rule interpretation declaring that a player's bat would be considered part of him until a ball in play is fielded. Most everything else was dismissed by reporter Francis Richter as minor, with the real news emanating from fruitful negotiations on Friday and Saturday with the Federal League and the American League.[20]

The outcome and aftermath of those intense discussions have been well documented.[21] By the middle of the following week, three days before Christmas, a full agreement was wrapped up in a bow for baseball fans. The Federal League would disband, which it did for all intents and purposes by February 7. In a nutshell, NL and AL owners bought out the owners of the Federal League franchises in Pittsburgh, Brooklyn, Newark, and Buffalo.[22] More significantly, the owners of the Federal League teams in Chicago and St. Louis, Charles Weeghman and Phil Ball, were permitted to purchase the Cubs and Browns, respectively. For 1916 the Cubs began playing in Weeghman's ballpark, known widely today as Wrigley Field. There was no remnant of a Kansas City ownership to compensate, so that left the Baltimore franchise as the lone holdout. The Terrapins ownership rejected any deal, and their antitrust lawsuit (specifically naming the NL), which went up to the US Supreme Court, wasn't resolved until 1922.

The Cubs had numerous Chicago Whales on their roster in 1916, and the Browns likewise played many former St. Louis Terriers. The agreement had reinstated all players who had been blacklisted by Organized Baseball, and men from the other six Federal League teams became available to the highest bidder among the AL and NL teams. Only the Cardinals, White Sox, Red Sox, and Athletics avoided signing former Federals for 1916. As the main headline of *The Sporting News* had declared on December 30, 1915, the "Way Is Clearing for Baseball to Enjoy Its Greatest Boom."[23]

NOTES

1. R.S. Ranson, "National Association Meeting," *Sporting Life*, November 13, 1915: 16. This article and one a week later referred to the National Association of Professional Baseball Leagues as the "National Association of Minor Leagues."

2. This was the noted *Federal Base Ball Club of Baltimore, Inc. v. National League of Professional Base Ball Clubs et al.*, 259 US 200), which was ultimately decided in 1922.

3. Ranson.

4. Al C. Joy, "Minor Magnates Go Far to Transact a Small Amount of Business," *The Sporting News*, November 18, 1915: 2.

5. "Annual Meeting of the National Association," *Sporting Life*, November 20, 1915: 10.

6. Ibid.

7. "Pickups from the Meeting of the Minor Magnates," *The Sporting News*, November 18, 1915: 2.

8. E.W. Cochrane, "The Federal League Prepares for the Future," *Sporting Life*, November 20, 1915: 12.

9. Ralston Goss, "Federals Threaten Invasion," *Indianapolis Star*, November 10, 1915: 10.

10. Ibid.

11. "Federal Leaguers' Futile Meeting," *New York Times*, November 11, 1915: 11.

12. George S. Robbins, "American Hews Strictly to Its Own Line of Conduct," *The Sporting News*, December 9, 1915: 1.

13. "Baseball—Sports of All Kinds—Boxing," *The Day Book* (Chicago), December 15, 1915: 9.

14. James Crusinberry, "A.L. Magnates Arrive Today to Talk Peace," *Chicago Tribune*, December 15, 1915: 15.

15. Nelson "Chip" Greene, "Jack Fournier," sabr.org/bioproj/person/81af331c.

16. Mark L. Armour and Daniel R. Levitt, *Paths to Glory: How Great Baseball Teams Got That Way* (Washington, D.C.: Potomac Books, 2011), 62.

17. "Commylou Loses Car! No Peace for Him," *Chicago Tribune*, December 16, 1915: 16.

18. "The American League's Annual Meeting," *Sporting Life*, December 25, 1915: 7. The situation in Cleveland was discussed in the first column and in the article's second column as well.

19. James Crusinberry, "Cubs to Weeghman by Terms of Baseball Peace," *Chicago Tribune*, December 16, 1915: 16.

20. Francis C. Richter, "National League's Eventful Meet," *Sporting Life*, December 25, 1915: 5.

21. See, for instance, Daniel R. Levitt, *The Battle That Forged Modern Baseball: The Federal League Challenge and Its Legacy* (Lanham, Maryland: Ivan R. Dee, 2012).

22. See, for instance, Mark S. Halfon, *Tales from the Deadball Era* (Lincoln: University of Nebraska Press, 2014), 10; Steven A. Riess, Ed., *Sports in America from Colonial Times to the Twenty-First Century* (New York: Routledge, 2015), 132.

23. "Way Is Clearing for Baseball to Enjoy Its Greatest Boom," *The Sporting News*, December 30, 1915: 1.

— 1916 —
THE MINORS AND PLAYERS ARE RESTLESS

By Rich Bogovich

MAJOR-LEAGUE ATTENDANCE surged nicely in 1916 without Federal League franchises competing with six NL and AL teams in four cities, Chicago, St. Louis, Brooklyn, and Pittsburgh. The combined attendance of 6.5 million—up from 4.8 million in 1915—was only returning to 1911 levels, but major-league magnates had to be relieved that the recovery occurred promptly. Though the Cardinals' attendance slipped slightly, the other five major-league teams in Federal League cities—the Cubs, White Sox, Browns, Robins (Dodgers), and Pirates—saw their combined attendance increase by about 775,000, or close to half of the total increase in major-league baseball. In addition, the two teams bought by Federal League owners, the Cubs and Browns, saw their attendance more than double. Nevertheless, there were several significant controversies and threats looming over Organized Baseball as the leagues' annual meetings drew near in November and December.

New Orleans hosted the annual conclave of the National Association of Professional Baseball Leagues (NAPBL) for 1916, from November 14 through 16. The *Boston Globe* had the benefit of a preview provided by its own Tim Murnane, who doubled as the NAPBL's vice president, elected a year earlier by virtue of his league leadership in the Northeast. Murnane began by focusing on a big negative. He noted that in 1914 the major leagues had paid $300,000 into the minor-league treasury for purchasing and drafting its players. Complications caused by the Federal League's existence apparently prevented any such deposit in 1915, but during the fall of 1916 the payment was less than $100,000, due to the many signings of former Federal Leaguers in the AL and NL, in place of minor leaguers, to round out rosters.

Murnane highlighted a second potential agenda item that involved the two major leagues: making a minor-league representative a fourth member of the National Commission, the body that had governed baseball since 1902. There was also talk of a fifth member who would represent the players. The National Commission had always consisted of the AL and NL presidents plus a member on whom they mutually agreed. From the onset, that third member was Cincinnati Reds president August "Garry" Herrmann. American League President Ban Johnson, however, was reportedly finding it difficult to work with National League President John Tener, who was finishing his third year in that position. The elimination of the Federal League must not have changed the relationship between the AL and NL at its core, as Murnane declared, "No matter how pleasant everything may look on the surface, the fact is that the magnates of the two major leagues look on each other with suspicion." Murnane also commented that in recent years the NL, AL, and NAPBL had "worked together in the most friendly manner."[1] The implication was that, assuming no desire by the NL to replace Tener on the commission, adding a minor-league representative may have been the most promising cure. It wasn't until he wrote a shorter preview two days later that Murnane brought up an aspect of the NAPBL discussions likely to be of greater interest to fans, under the headline, "Many Trades Are Expected," but he didn't elaborate in the article.[2]

NAPBL President Michael Sexton circulated a letter shortly before the meeting that was reminiscent of his call for frugality during his opening remarks a year earlier. As it turned out, a family illness kept him back home, so Murnane served as chairman. That afforded him the opportunity to refer to himself in the third person in his account of the first day. At the time of the NAPBL meeting a year earlier, its membership consisted of 22 leagues, and it had grown to 26 by the time of the gathering in New Orleans. However, a few had experienced or were continuing to cope with complications, most notably the Canadian League. Its teams didn't play at all during 1916 due to Canada's participation in the Great War across Europe. In fact, the league would never resume play.

Murnane also framed some labor intrigue scheduled for the next day, in the form of a presentation by major leaguer-turned-attorney Dave Fultz, leader of the four-year-old Fraternity of Baseball Players. "It is well known that all the minor league players have signed an agreement to withhold their signatures from new contracts until after March 1 or until notified by Fultz that all is well," Murnane wrote. "The minor league magnates will not worry very much if they are forced by the players to close their ball parks until Memorial Day. It would cost the leagues nearly $20,000 each season to meet the demands of Mr. Fultz, who has asked the convention to make it a law requiring the clubs to pay for the transportation of players to and from home."[3]

Fultz did prove to be the big story of the second day, and as a result the specter of a strike surfaced. The NAPBL's leaders voted unanimously to table indefinitely each of four demands presented by Fultz, essentially rejecting them. Those demands were to prohibit certain contractual clauses that allowed teams to stop paying injured players, to permit unconditionally released players to sign immediately with other clubs, to provide players with travel money to attend spring-training camps, and to revise procedures of the minor leagues' National Board when it heard claims filed by players. NAPBL Secretary John Farrell, its only paid employee, asserted that the first demand had been met three years earlier but argued against the other three demands.[4]

Decisions on the NAPBL's third and final day included submitting a request to the two major leagues to form a second National Commission that would include minor-league representation and act only on appealed rulings of the minor leagues' National Board. As formulated, the new panel would have two minor-league and two major-league slots, plus a member selected by the other four. According to Murnane, "many baseball men" favored offering that fifth seat to federal Judge Kenesaw Mountain Landis of Chicago, who in 1914 had been assigned to preside over the Federal League's injunction suit against the NL and AL. An internal decision made was to a repeal the year-old regulation under which the NAPBL set player and salary limits for all of the minor leagues. As a result, each league would again set its own limits.[5]

The NAPBL apparently didn't take seriously a major proposal floating around Organized Baseball at the time: to form a new American Association as a third major league. At a minimum, the plan was endorsed by AL President Johnson. The idea was to combine Milwaukee, Indianapolis, Toledo, and Louisville of the existing American Association with Baltimore, Buffalo, Newark, and Toronto of the International League. One vision for a reformed International League had existing franchises in Providence, Rochester, and Montreal joined by Syracuse, Albany, Utica, and Binghamton, with Jersey City possibly supplanting Richmond. IL President Ed Barrow rejected the concept upon his return from New Orleans, though it had been discussed.[6]

On November 23, about a week after the NAPBL's labor decisions, Dave Fultz responded publicly:

> The National Association simply must grant these requests; that is all there is to it. We have pledges from virtually all our players not to sign contracts unless they get word from officers of the Fraternity.
>
> I am more sure than ever that we have the majority of the players behind us on this issue. Since the minor leagues conference ignored our requests in New Orleans, I have received

letters from dozens of players asking that we "sit tight."[7]

That, in turn, provoked a prompt warning from none other than NL President Tener:

> Should the major league players declare a sympathetic strike because of the refusal of the National Association to grant certain requests of the Baseball Players Fraternity it will be a strike not against the National Commission but against the very game of baseball itself.
>
> I cannot conceive that young men like our players can talk of attempting to tie up their business over such a trivial matter as is involved in the dispute between the Players Fraternity and the minor leagues. A strike of this kind would simply mean that big league players would have to bear the entire brunt of it. The Class AA and A minor leagues could easily pick up 16 men for their teams, while the big leagues were idle.
>
> Everything that has been accomplished for the benefit and advancement of the player has come through the national commission. Mr. Fultz says the commission has always been fair and just. I will go farther than that and say that in disputes between the players and club owners the commission always has leaned toward the player.[8]

Fultz, on behalf of a Fraternity membership reported at 1,215, publicly rebutted Tener about two weeks later and took issue with a particular adjective that the NL leader used:

> These minor league matters are not trivial and are of as much importance to major league players as they are to the men in the minors. There are about 5,000 minor league players and only 360 major leaguers. And sooner or later every one of those 360 men will drift back to the minors or retire from the game. That is why the failure of the National Association to recognize the Fraternity's just requests involves the major league player as well as the minor league player and why he is willing to go to any length to support the minors. Furthermore, of what use would the Fraternity be if its members failed to band together in such times as these?"[9]

Meanwhile, on November 24 it was announced that a special meeting of the National Commission was called for December 1 in Chicago, on changes to the form of players' contracts. Tener's fellow members both had public comments to offer. "There will be no renewal of high salaried 'war' contracts," Ban Johnson said a few days before the meeting, alluding to the inflation caused by competition with the Federal League.[10] That position couldn't have come as much of a surprise to observers of the game.

After the meeting, Garry Herrmann's public comments mentioned Fultz at least three times. "The new contract, adopted today, means that a player, if injured, will be paid in full and the contract cannot, under any circumstances, be terminated until it expires. The clause is the most beneficial that could possibly be arranged for the player, and I am sure it will more than satisfy the contentions of the Players' Fraternity," Herrmann concluded.[11]

On November 23 *The Sporting News* had printed a long editorial about these labor issues that was critical of Fultz, but in other commentaries, both before and after the November 23 piece, the paper instead blasted the NAPBL on the governance issues it was pushing. In the first, the weekly predicted doom for any continued effort to add a minor-league representative and a players' counterpart to the National Commission: "Quick to denounce Dave Fultz and his Fraternity for manufacturing 'grievances,' the minors themselves with an inconsistency that is amazing to those who have followed baseball administration closely, conjure up 'grievances' of their own against the majors and the Commission that are as baseless as anything Fultz ever imagined in his most radical nightmare." In the other editorial minor-league magnates were scolded for not stomaching the National Commission's ability to set aside rulings of the minors' National Board.[12]

It may be that these stances influenced subsequent coverage, and made at least some sportswriters view the NAPBL's positions as a bigger deal. An extreme example came out of the New York bureau of the *Los Angeles Times* on December 11, the day of the International League's annual meeting in New York: "Organized baseball peace is once more seriously threatened," the dispatch said. "The minor leagues are ready to secede and rid themselves of the yoke of the national commission."[13]

Thus, there was plenty for National League magnates to discuss at New York's Waldorf Hotel from December 12 through 14, and for AL leaders in Chicago on the latter date. On the NL's first day, President Tener made his annual report, in which he endorsed Herrmann's idea of diverting some of the World Series money currently allocated to the pennant winners' players to all of the other players in the two leagues. Secretary John Heydler's report followed, and it included the calculation that 14,744 baseballs were used during the season, an increase of 1,526 over the previous year.[14] After these talks the league took some action regarding roster limits, abolishing the "disability list" and increasing by one, from 21 to 22, the number of players that a team could carry from May 15 to August 31. The Cubs and Giants were the lone votes in favor of increasing rosters to 25 during that span.[15]

The magnates then heard three representatives of the NAPBL press their case for a new counterpart to the National Commission. The trio consisted of Murnane, Pacific Coast League Vice President J. Cal Ewing, and Eastern League President Dan O'Neil. Afterward, the presidents of the three Double-A leagues — Edward Barrow of the International League, Thomas Hickey of the American Association, and Allen Baum of the PCL — requested that drafting players from their leagues be eliminated. The NL leaders decided to wait two days before taking any action on these matters.

On the second day the NL leaders discussed and debated but did little deciding. Pittsburgh's Barney Dreyfuss was largely successful in fending off attempts by the Giants to allow exceptions to the 22-player limit, though the issue was ultimately referred to the Committee on Constitution. Similarly, though a suggestion by Phillies' president William Baker to prohibit trades after August 1 was popular, the alternative date of August 15 advocated by Brooklyn's Charles Ebbets caused the matter to be sent to the same committee. It was expected to make recommendations in time for another league meeting in February.

Two hours on the third day were spent discussing possible rule changes. Boston Braves president Percy Haughton advocated changes that would increase scoring, including awarding a walk after three pitched balls and banning the spitball. Various suggestions were referred to the Joint Rules Committee. The magnates referred the two requests from the minor leagues to the National Commission, though according to *Sporting Life*, the NL delegates announced their endorsement of a new counterpart to that board.[16] The National Commission was also asked to address a concern about the contractual framework it had developed on December 1. Someone noticed that it contained a clause that allowed a player to appeal his salary directly to the commission, which owners argued would place far too much authority in the commission's hands.

The NL added a fourth day of discussions, and an early controversy was Dreyfuss' unsuccessful attempt to push Herrmann off the National Commission in favor of someone unconnected to Organized Baseball. The league later sent to the National Commission a new scheme for drafting minor leaguers. The major change supported was to give the earliest picks to the poorer performing clubs rather than those at the top of the two leagues' standings.

Only one significant deal was made between teams during the NL's conclave, but it was an unusual one. In an effort to replace Joe Tinker as manager, the Cubs traded outfielder Joe Kelly plus cash to the Boston Braves for coach Fred Mitchell, who became Chicago's new skipper.

In the meantime, the American League was able to confine its meeting to December 14. One new policy approved applied to World Series games played in AL parks. The price of tickets could only be doubled, meaning that bleacher seats would cost no more than 50 cents. An exception allowed for a $5 tax on box seats.

Like the NL, the AL's leaders permitted two groups of minor-league representatives to speak about the same requests. The club owners empowered Ban Johnson to decide the matters, presumably through the National Commission. "President Johnson, however, did not give the minor league applicants any positive answers," according to the *Sporting News* account. "Rather he questioned them, debated with them and gave them pointers on his own ideas of the needs of baseball as a whole—then sent them on their way pondering and with ideas on new propositions expected to develop later."[17] Other than approving the contractual framework submitted with minor modifications, no other major decisions were made during the AL's day.

Those looking for decisive action on the more important lingering issues had to wait until the National Commission met in New York on February 15, 1917. The commission did make some adjustments to how players would be drafted from the minors, but they didn't grant the bigger wishes of the three Double-A presidents. The commission also rejected the creation of a counterpart for handling appeals of decisions by the minor leagues' National Board, though it did decide it would involve the National Board's secretary and the minor leagues' president when such cases were brought before it. "This really therefore makes a board of five and gives the minor leagues representation on the Commission in all cases affecting them," concluded *Sporting Life*. Alas, Tim Murnane was no longer around to comment. He had died of a sudden heart attack eight days earlier, at the age of 64.

The other major decision made on that mid-February day was a clear statement on labor matters. About a month earlier, Dave Fultz had emerged from a Fraternity meeting in Chicago to announce a potential strike on February 20. He called it off just before the National Commission meeting, but the trio still adopted this resolution: "Resolved by the National Commission that the action of the National and American Leagues, in severing relations with the Players' Fraternity and abrogating the agreement entered into with said Fraternity, under date of January 6, 1914, be and same is hereby ratified and approved, with the understanding that the status of all interests in Organized Base Ball, club owners, and players alike, is the same as it was before the agreement hereinbefore referred to was entered into, having in mind the preamble of the National Agreement adopted in 1903, under which the game has advanced to the position of the national institution to which we point with pride today."[18] As a result, the Fraternity gradually disintegrated, and there wouldn't be a new surge of unionism among baseball players for about five years.

NOTES

1 T.H. Murnane, "Minor Leagues Meet Next Week," *Boston Globe*, November 12, 1916: 57.

2 T.H. Murnane, "Many Trades Are Expected," *Boston Globe*, November 14, 1916: 6.

3 T.H. Murnane, "Minors Balk on $20,000 Outlay," *Boston Globe*, November 15, 1916: 9.

4 "Minor Leaguers Table Demands of Fraternity," *Los Angeles Times*, November 16, 1916: III1.

5 T.H. Murnane, "Minors Want New National Commission," *Boston Globe*, November 17, 1916: 6.

6 "Barrow Against Third League," *Christian Science Monitor*, November 21, 1916: 10. Directly above that article was one in which Johnson endorsed the scheme. The concept was detailed in the first story of *The Sporting News* on November 16. Subsequently, Columbus was named in place of Milwaukee in order to form a more compact circuit, according to "Third Major League Is Still Probability," *Washington Post*, December 8, 1916: 8.

7 "Players to Refuse to Sign Contracts," *Hartford Courant*, November 24, 1916: 17.

8 "Statement Is Given by Tener on Strike Talk," *Christian Science Monitor*, November 25, 1916: 18.

9 "Fultz Calls Strike One of Principle," *Hartford Courant*, December 6, 1916: 17.

10 "To Cut Players' Salaries," *New York Times*, November 29, 1916: 8.

11 "Concession to Ball Players," *Boston Globe*, December 3, 1916: 17.

12 "Minors' Plan Will Fail" and "Saved From Own Folly," *The Sporting News*, November 23, 1916: 4.

13 "Minor League Magnates to Start Revolution," *Los Angeles Times*, December 12, 1916: III1.

14 "The Meeting of the National League," *Sporting Life*, December 23, 1916: 4.

15 "Player Limit Only Increased by One," *New York Times*, December 13, 1916: 12.

16 "Concession to Ball Players."

VOLUME 1 - 1901-1957

17 "American League Declares for Reducing Baseball Cost," *The Sporting News*, December 21, 1916: 3.

18 "Important Action by the National Commission," *Sporting Life*, February 24, 1917: 2.

— 1917 —
WAR? WHAT WAR?

By Paul Hensler

Introduction and Context

NOW FULLY INVESTED IN THE GREAT War taking place in Europe, the United States was burdened by a shift in its political and economic conditions that demanded a sharp focus on a mobilization of the nation's armed forces. On the home front, Americans were implored to sacrifice for the good of the war effort, and the national pastime was absorbing some of the impact of those perilous times. Even with the demise of the Federal League, attendance was down in both the National and American Leagues, and with no end to the war in sight, more men joined the military, either voluntarily or through conscription, thus siphoning an increasing number of players from the rosters of major- and minor-league teams.

Baseball entered the late autumn of 1917 cloaked in a pall of uncertainty. One month after the Chicago White Sox' six-game victory over the New York Giants in the World Series, Brooklyn Dodgers owner Charles Ebbets tried to counter fears over a possible suspension of the 1918 campaign by claiming, "The public will require recreation during the continuance of the war."[1] Ebbets intended those recreational endeavors to include baseball, even at the cost of a proposed schedule reduction to 140 games and the addition of a federally mandated 10 percent tax on tickets that would likely discourage more people from attending games.

As autumn wore on, several leagues met in various locations to chart a course intended to provide the game with guidance for the coming season.

The Business Side

Among the first issues to be addressed was the sorry state of the minor leagues. Convening in Louisville, Kentucky, the National Association of Professional Baseball Leagues sought to form a new league in an effort to coalesce several of its member franchises into a new Union League.

Great interest was shown by the major-league clubs in the proposed new association, because without a stable minor-league base from which to draw new major-league talent, "disruption ... and disintegration of the minors would mean too much to the big league club owners."[2] This concern over the viability of baseball's lower ranks was rooted in the fact that only 11 of 22 minor leagues completed their 1917 schedules, and trepidation over a collapse of the system underpinning "the foundation of the American and National [L]eagues" was not just idle fear-mongering.[3] Creation of a new league by redistricting those still in existence was thought to be a rational way to address the impending crisis. But the proposal was fiercely opposed by most franchise owners – those in Louisville, Indianapolis, and Toledo among the most vocal – and on November 14 the National Association voted resoundingly against such a plan.[4]

The backdrop of the war remained increasingly ominous, and on December 11, officials of the National League and the minor leagues met in New York to consider their options for 1918. The good news was that baseball would resume in the spring, but front offices were faced with the stark realization that "the game cannot go along rousing its usual interest with public attention centered on how things are going among the thousands of American soldiers in Europe."[5] The possibility of a reduced schedule grew more likely as interstate transportation logistics were expected to emphasize military-oriented objectives rather than civilian needs. This meant that railroads, which provided the majority of such transit services, "will be compelled to move more troops and supplies than they did this year, [and] conditions may be such as to interfere with the quick jumps of the baseball clubs [from city to city]."[6] The NL magnates agreed to confer with American League owners later that week to discuss the best strategy for the coming season, although this issue was controversial in its own right. August "Garry" Herrmann, the chairman of the National Commission, had already scheduled a joint meeting of the two major leagues in Chicago without the official consent of the National League clubs, and many of those team officials questioned the wisdom of rushing into a session with the AL before all of the National League's affairs could be given necessary attention during the session in New York.

Senior circuit representatives also tended to other baseball-related business by re-electing John Tener as league president, reappointing J.H. Heydler league secretary for another four-year stint, and officially awarding the 1917 pennant to the New York Giants. In a move designed to share "part of the world's series receipts" among more teams, the National League approved splitting the fall classic's gate with all clubs except the one finishing the season in last place.[7] The league declared that during the 1918 campaign one day's gate receipts at every ballpark would be donated to Clark Griffith's Ball and Bat Fund, a charitable venture that supplied baseball equipment to American troops at home and abroad. And in a matter of internal jurisprudence, the league's constitution was amended to preclude the appeal of large fines levied against players or managers for "scandalous conduct on or off the field."[8] The measure was implemented as a corrective for a case during the 1917 season in which Giants manager John McGraw appealed the $500 fine and 16-day suspension he drew for his role in a brawl with umpire Bill Byron.[9]

With the plenary session of the National and American Leagues just ahead, a meeting of International League owners in New York let it be known that they did not want to set policy for 1918 in too hasty a fashion, and for good reason. With the new season still months away, there was angst among "the more conservative owners and officers," who feared that improved conditions in the war might obviate some contingencies baseball may have committed to, among them a shorter schedule or rosters trimmed to 18 players.[10] The IL meeting was also punctuated by the decision of league President Edward Barrow to step down in February 1918. Barrow tendered his resignation in response to the slashing of his salary by the team owners from $7,500 to $2,500.

Meanwhile, officials of the American League, meeting in Chicago at the same time as their National League counterparts in New York, expressed a desire to keep their squads staffed with 25 players. One of the most vocal owners, Colonel Jacob Ruppert of the Yankees, curiously opined that teams needed a full complement of players, citing a "[necessity] to carry undeveloped minor leaguers [who are] scared to death, and it requires time for [them] to wear off [their] stage fright" after being called up to the big-league club.[11] The league also endorsed continuation of spring training in its accustomed format with no accommodations like travel or schedule alterations to be made for wartime conditions.

The convention of AL owners on December 12 re-elected Charles Comiskey vice president and presented him with the 1917 league pennant. The junior circuit's board of directors was installed, its new members being team presidents Phil Ball (St. Louis Browns), Frank Navin (Detroit), Benjamin Minor (Washington), and Ben Shibe (Philadelphia Athletics). Discussion of a possible split of World Series ticket receipts among the top four American League teams yielded no agreement, as most clubs voiced the opinion that only the league champion was entitled to the proceeds. And in a show of sympathy for the passing of a local baseball scribe, the owners sanctioned an exhibition contest between the two Philadelphia teams with all funds raised to be given to the widow of William G. Weart, baseball writer for the *Philadelphia Telegraph*.

With league-specific matters put to rest for the time being, executives of the National and American Leagues convened December 14 at the Congress Hotel in Chicago, "the first joint session held in years," said the *Chicago Tribune*.[12]

Noting the rivalry very much present between the two circuits as well as the National League's perceived superiority over the American, the *Tribune* told its readers that the junior circuit owners hesitated to take action to alter the length of the 1918 season or its starting date. "On important issues of the day the American Leaguers begged to be excused until they had had an opportunity to talk these over with the Nationals," but in terms of realistic expectations for dealing with the current dilemma, "[t]he real purpose of the joint meeting is to form some sort of working agreement between the two major leagues so that baseball can be carried on next season regardless of war conditions."[13]

The power of ownership – as vested in the reserve clause – was manifest in the intention of teams to trim their payrolls as a way to cut costs. "There is going to be some wonderful salary dipping in the next few months," the *Tribune* reported, "and naturally some stories following of players refusing to sign because of mistreatment."[14] Ban Johnson, president of the American League, further proposed the inclusion of a "war clause" in players' contracts that would not only "absolve [club owners] from all salary obligations in the event a player enlisted or is drafted" but also deem players returning from military service "still bound to the club with which he last signed."[15] Debate over another kind of expense that could not be reduced was also on the agenda. Payments were owed to a pair of ownerships of the defunct Federal League, $50,000 to the old Pittsburgh group and $60,000 to the former Brooklyn franchise. As a means of settling controversies that erupted during the brief tenure of the Federal League, both the NL and AL were expected to endorse the remittances.

When the joint session was finally held, on December 14, the team owners collectively expressed little regard for any war considerations previously discussed. Finding "no cause for alarm about baseball at present ... [t]hey agreed that if the war forces them to retrench it will be time enough to adopt a war policy when they actually face conditions."[16] The only concession to the war effort was to delay the opening of the 1918 season by one week, and the campaign itself was to consist of the full 154-game schedule, although the American League unsuccessfully lobbied for a 140-game slate. This stunning display of myopia came at a time when the need to call men to the colors was reaching a most critical point. As the historian David Kennedy noted in his detailed study of the period, "Men's willingness to come forward, so tensely relied upon in the spring of 1917, was less certain than ever [by the autumn of that year]."[17] It is incredulous that club owners who, like the rest of the American populace at large, were exposed to the dunning of organizations such as the Committee on Public Information for the purchase of war bonds – to say nothing of the incessant orations of Four-Minute Men drumming up all manner of support for the war effort – could believe that baseball on any level would be able to continue normal operations. In an era during which "100% Americanism" and "slacker raids" also painted the landscape of the United States, the moguls of the national pastime were deluding themselves if they thought that baseball would function as idyllically as it did in peacetime.[18]

Also meeting in Chicago and acquiescing to contemporaneous war demands, American Association club owners adopted a 1918 schedule beginning in May and reduced from the standard 154 contests to 140. They further sanctioned the use of two umpires per game rather than one and unanimously voted to outlaw "the spitball, 'shine' ball, 'emery' ball, and all other similar deliveries."[19]

But as printed in its December 20 edition to recap the joint AL-NL session, *The Sporting News* reported, "[T]he two majors, called together to decide on a general war policy, made no departures from previous regulations whatever, so far as was disclosed to the public."[20] Forced by the government to impose an admissions tax on tickets, the owners conceded that such a surcharge would be implemented, but this was the only indication of a straying from baseball's steady course. *The Sporting News* suggested that the "bold front" shown the public by the owners was a testament to the grandeur of the game as "an institution not even the greatest of wars can do damage to."[21]

Optimism as exuded by the owners, in the hope of playing a pat hand while the rest of the country made increasing sacrifices, eventually darkened. The reality of the conflict in Europe in 1918 would cause baseball to close down its regular season in early September and play the World Series well ahead of schedule.

Personnel Dealings

Accounts in the press in late 1917 reported the traditional offseason swapping and purchasing of players, although included in this reportage was the disclaimer that in some cases such transactions could be voided or restructured if a player was drafted into the armed forces. Nonetheless, *Baseball Magazine* reported, "Despite the worrisome uncertainty of the war – the lik[e]lihood that many of the men who might be traded would be carried off for martial service – more deals were made than were ever recorded during a similar period."[22]

The deal garnering the most attention was the trade on December 11 of catcher William Killefer and star hurler Grover Cleveland Alexander from the Philadelphia Phillies to the Chicago Cubs for right-handed pitcher Mike Prendergast, catcher William "Pickles" Dillhoefer, and a substantial cash payment, variously reported as between $55,000 and $80,000."[23] Cubs owner Charles Weeghman looked to retool his lineup by purchasing some new players and was prepared to spend lavishly; he was rumored to have $250,000 available to do so. By adding the right-handed Alexander, one of the best pitchers of the day, to his staff, Weeghman evinced his willingness to open his coffers.

Joining the spree was Boston Red Sox owner Harry Frazee, who had unsuccessfully pursued several players on the Philadelphia Athletics roster for most of 1917. Finally, on December 14, he consummated a trade with A's owner Connie Mack that delivered to Boston a trio of "great stars who did so much for the Mackmen in the days that used to be": catcher Wally Schang, outfielder Amos Strunk, and right-hander Bullet Joe Bush.[24] In return, Boston parted with southpaw Vean Gregg, catcher Chet Thomas, and outfielder Manny Kopp, plus $60,000. The Cleveland Indians had hoped to acquire Bush, but owner Jim Dunn lost out in his bid. As the joint meetings came to a close, the St. Louis Browns sent outfielder Burt Shotton and shortstop Doc Lavan to the Washington Senators for right-hander Melvin "Bert" Gallia and $15,000.

As trading continued past the end of 1917 and into the new year, the Cubs remained active as they swapped outfielders with the Phillies on December 29, Fred "Cy" Williams heading east and George "Dode" Paskert moving west. One week later, Chicago sent second baseman Larry Doyle, catcher Dutch Wilson, and $15,000 of Weeghman's funds to Boston for Braves southpaw George "Lefty" Tyler.

During the course of January 1918, four other deals were also finalized. Having expressed his desire to leave the Giants, infielder Buck Herzog anticipated a trade during the meetings, but it was not until January 8 that he was sent to the Boston Braves for the just-acquired Doyle and right-hander Jesse Barnes. The next day, the Brooklyn Dodgers traded second baseman George Cutshaw and outfielder Casey Stengel to Pittsburgh for shortstop Chuck Ward and a pair of right-handers, young Burleigh Grimes and two-time 21-game winner Al Mamaux. On January 10, first baseman Stuffy McInnis became yet another former Athletic when Connie Mack dealt him to the Red Sox for three players to be selected at Mack's option.[25] Lastly, the Yankees traded what *Baseball Magazine* termed "most of their ball club" to the Browns for second baseman Del Pratt and future Hall of Fame left-hander Eddie Plank, in addition to $15,000.[26] The Yankees surrendered catcher Les Nunamaker, right-hander Urban Shocker and southpaw Nick Cullop, as well as two infielders, Fritz Maisel and Joe Gedeon.

Observing that the early December trades boded well for the sport, *The Sporting News* opined stoically, "The big deals put through will revive interest in the national game and cause the public to realize that the magnates are of the [mindset] that war is not going to put an end to the National pastime."[27]

Summary

Much bravado was exuded by major-league baseball after the 1917 season in the hope that the Great War

– now devolved into a stalemate – could somehow be brought to a conclusion. Bold headlines proclaimed baseball's disregard for "wartime retrenchment" and the importuning of "war economists" while team owners plunged ahead making "big player deals [that] indicate confidence in the future."[28] Had a settlement been reached to end the conflict, baseball doubtless would have fared well.

However, as the loss of players to the war effort continued, leagues on the major- and minor-league levels were to find that coping with the reality of the times was eventually going to harm the game. Attempts at a "business as usual" approach would prove to be an exercise in poor judgment by those who ran major-league baseball, and the winter of 1917-1918 became a lost opportunity for the national pastime to gird itself for the hard times yet ahead.

SOURCES

In addition to the sources cited in the Notes, the author also consulted:

Gillette, Gary, and Pete Palmer, eds. *The ESPN Baseball Encyclopedia*, Fourth Edition. (New York: Sterling Publishing Company, 2007).

The Baseball Encyclopedia, Ninth Edition (New York: Macmillan Publishing Company, 1993).

NOTES

1. Thomas Rice, "Ebbets Outlines His Views as to Future of Baseball," *The Sporting News*, November 8, 1917: 7.
2. J.V. Fitzgerald, "Baseball's Fate During War May Hang on Meeting," *Washington Post*, November 12, 1917: 8.
3. Ibid.
4. "Chiefs Meet to Make New Baseball Map," *Los Angeles Times*, November 13, 1917: III-1; "Minor Leagues Against Change," *Christian Science Monitor*, November 15, 1917: 12.
5. "Club Owners Face Serious Problems," *New York Times*, December 9, 1917: 33.
6. Ibid.
7. "National Has Plan to Pass Series Coin Out Among 7 Clubs," *Chicago Tribune*, December 13, 1917: 21.
8. "National League Will Meet American: Johnson's Circuit Awaits Coming: Barrow Will Resign," *Hartford Courant*, December 13, 1917: 14.
9. See also Wm. A. Phelon, "Stirring Times in Baseball History," *Baseball Magazine*, Volume 19, Issue 4: 427-428.
10. "International Owners Gather," *Christian Science Monitor*, December 10, 1917: 16.
11. "American Opposes Cutting Program," *Boston Globe*, December 13, 1917: 9. Unreported were Ruppert's thoughts on any stage fright (or shellshock) experienced by troops on the Western Front. Notables who favored roster cuts were Branch Rickey, Barney Dreyfuss, and Charles Ebbets.
12. James Crusinberry, "Major Owners Gather Today to Prune Cost," *Chicago Daily Tribune*, December 14, 1917: 15.
13. Ibid.
14. Ibid.
15. "American League Makes No Changes," *New York Times*, December 14, 1917: 10.
16. "Major Leagues to Start a Week Later," *Boston Daily Globe*, December 15, 1917: 5.
17. David M. Kennedy, *Over Here: The First World War and American Society* (New York: Oxford University Press, 2004), 167.
18. Indeed, as Kennedy makes clear in his study of the United States during the Great War, "The quickening pace of the draft calls in the summer of 1918 and the extended registration in September revealed the growing desperateness of the military's manpower needs." *Over Here*, 167. Other measures that year would be attempted by the owners to excuse players from wartime service, including having their players sign affidavits requesting that their draft boards grant them deferred classification. See also copy of affidavit, Papers of August Herrmann, 1887-1938, BAMSS12, National Baseball Hall of Fame Library, National Baseball Hall of Fame, Cooperstown, New York, Box 113, Folder 4.
19. "Short Season, Late Start in Association," *The Sporting News*, December 20, 1917: 1. An experiment in which a single umpire was employed during games proved to be a failed "economizing."
20. "Majors' Joint Conference Turns Down War Economists," *The Sporting News*, December 20, 1917: 3.
21. "Concerning the Joint Conference," *The Sporting News*, December 20, 1917: 4.
22. Wm. A. Phelon, "Sensational Baseball Trades," *Baseball Magazine*, 1918, Volume 20, Issue 2: 399.
23. The *Chicago Tribune* claimed a payment of $80,000, but later figures, among them those in the Macmillan *Baseball Encyclopedia*, put the amount at $55,000.
24. Edward F. Martin, "Three Big Stars Sold to Red Sox," *Boston Globe*, December 15, 1917: 1. A sidebar to this article noted that the sale of the three Athletics was another in a series of deals in which Connie Mack sold off 17 players over the prior three years for a total of about $175,000.
25. Phelon, "Sensational Baseball Trades," 400. Phelon, more than implying that playing in Philadelphia for Mack had become less than desirable, snidely remarked, "Members of the Sox are trembling in their shoes fearing that Connie's hawk-like eye may light upon them. They have cause." Those ultimately chosen

were third baseman Larry Gardner, outfielder Tillie Walker, and backstop Hick Cady.

26 Ibid. Citing health issues, Plank had actually announced his retirement in August, shortly after losing a 1-0 classic to Walter Johnson, and he kept his word, never reporting to the Yankees. Jan Finkel, "Eddie Plank," SABR Baseball Biography Project, sabr.org/bioproj/person/339eaa5c.

27 "Cleveland Also to Pull Off Big Deal," *The Sporting News*, December 20, 1917: 3.

28 Quoted from various articles, *The Sporting News*, December 20, 1917: 3.

— 1918 —
BASEBALL RETURNS FROM THE GREAT WAR

By Jacob Pomrenke

ON NOVEMBER 11, 1918, MINOR-league owners from 40 teams, representing seven leagues, were preparing for a somber discussion about whether baseball would even be played in the 1919 season[1] when word came down that the World War had ended.

The "war to end all wars" had caused an existential crisis throughout the baseball world. The US government's "work or fight" order had forced every minor league and both major leagues to end their 1918 seasons earlier than usual. The World Series between the Boston Red Sox and Chicago Cubs wrapped up just after Labor Day and all draft-eligible ballplayers were forced to choose between joining the military or taking a job in a war-essential industry.[2] With the war now over, no one was quite sure what Organized Baseball would look like when play resumed … if play resumed.

"Not one minor league, just at this time, is certain of opening next season," Southern Association President R.H. Baugh said at the start of the 17th annual winter meetings in Peoria, Illinois, on November 12. "The prevailing opinion is to wait and see if conditions by next spring will adjust themselves to warrant baseball."[3]

Meanwhile, in Chicago, White Sox owner Charles Comiskey spent Armistice Day celebrating the end of the war. "I never was happier in my life than this morning when I knew peace was assured. The good news came sooner than expected," he said.[4]

Peace in baseball, however, was far from certain. Faced with severe financial difficulties after the premature end to the 1918 season, some minor-league owners were ready to declare war on the major leagues.[5] At issue was the majors' practice of acquiring players via the Rule 5 draft, and optional agreements that allowed major-league teams to sell players to minor-league teams with the right to repurchase the player at a later date.[6] Most minor-league owners depended on the sale of their players in order to turn a profit. Major-league teams benefited greatly from these arrangements and used them to keep costs down in developing prospects.

As historian Cliff Blau has written, "[T]he truce between the majors and minors was always an uneasy one."[7] In 1918 the gloves came off as minor-league owners adopted a stern resolution at the winter meetings protesting the Rule 5 draft. American Association President Thomas J. Hickey demanded that the minor leagues withdraw from the National Agreement, in place since 1903, if the majors did not agree to abolish the draft.[8] "It is the minor leagues that develop these stars and the smaller leagues should reap the financial reward," said A.R. Tearney, president of the Three-I League.[9]

Ban Johnson had other ideas. The American League founder and de-facto head of the National Commission, baseball's governing body, dismissed the minors' call for war and blamed their troubles on an old foe—the Federal League. The Federal League's attempt to become a third major league in 1914-15 had forced AL and NL teams to raise salaries across the board and cut into the money available for player sales. Johnson claimed that before the Federal League's formation, major-league teams had paid an average of $250,000 per year to the minors for new talent, a revenue stream that had yet to be restored by 1918.[10]

In his paternalistic way, Johnson tried to reassure minor-league owners that the majors had their best interests in mind. He intended to meet with Garry Herrmann, chairman of the National Commission, baseball's governing body, and work out a plan to keep the minor leagues afloat. "The National Association … for years has been incapable of managing its own affairs," Johnson said. "We are planning to give the minor leagues a sane, just, and forceful government in place of their own weak organization, which has proved so inefficient in the past."[11]

As these shots were being fired in the press, the major-league owners had their own differences to work out. No one except Ban Johnson was satisfied with the three-man National Commission, a chair that had been missing a leg since August, when National League President John Tener resigned after a dispute between the Philadelphia A's and Boston Braves over the rights to pitcher Scott Perry turned ugly.[12] It was one of many National Commission rulings that seemed to go the American League's way, with the dictatorial Johnson pulling the strings behind the scenes. But some AL owners weren't happy with Johnson, either. Just after the Perry decision, three owners—Comiskey, Boston's Harry Frazee, and Washington's Clark Griffith—publicly called out their president for his "bungling" of baseball's response to the War Department's "work or fight" order.[13]

Frazee, who was the first AL owner not hand-picked by Johnson[14] and believed (not without merit) that the league president was trying to run him out of baseball, made the first dramatic play to turn the tables on Johnson. Shortly after the minor-league meetings ended in November, Frazee and outgoing New York Giants owner Harry Hempstead approached former President William Howard Taft about becoming the "supreme head of baseball," which would abolish the National Commission entirely.[15] The idea of a one-man commission had been tossed around for several years as both leagues grew frustrated with the ineffective National Commission, but America's entrance into World War I in the spring of 1917 put a damper on any talk of radical realignment of baseball's power structure. Now that the war was over, the idea regained steam.

Taft was a popular choice to become baseball's commissioner. He had made a lasting contribution to the game's history in 1910, when he became the first sitting president to throw out the "first pitch" on Opening Day in Washington, D.C. His younger brother, Charles P. Taft, had been a one-time owner of the Philadelphia Phillies and briefly the Chicago Cubs. After the news broke that Taft had been approached, five NL owners quickly expressed some level of support for the idea, as did acting NL President John Heydler, who had taken over John Tener's duties and was elected to fill the permanent position in December.

Unfortunately for Frazee and Hempstead, they did not have the authority to extend a job offer to Taft or anyone else. Philadelphia Phillies owner William Baker expressed dismay that Frazee and Hempstead had approached Taft without consulting the other executives. Frazee, he said, "was acting on his own initiative … [and] was not empowered to speak for the American League."[16] For his part, Taft, a keen legal mind who would later serve as chief justice of the US Supreme Court, was only interested in a job in baseball that required him to settle contract disputes between the leagues[17] — not the all-powerful authority figure that the commissioner would become under Kenesaw Mountain Landis. He turned down the job on the last day of November. The National Commission would last another two years before dissolving in the wake of the Black Sox Scandal.

As Taft was still contemplating the offer, a furious Ban Johnson lashed out at Frazee and Hempstead for overstepping their authority. "There are no two individuals in baseball who know less about the national agreement and the rules governing baseball," Johnson snapped. "These parvenu owners have no idea of the conditions existing in baseball [when the National Commission was formed]. Their perspective in baseball is bounded by the walls of their own parks."[18] Johnson would outlast both of his adversaries: Hempstead's tenure in baseball was over before Opening Day as he sold his share of the Giants to Charles H. Stoneham in January 1919, while Johnson and Frazee continued to butt heads until financial woes forced the latter to sell the Red Sox in 1923.

In December the focus began shifting to the coming season. Ban Johnson received an encouraging letter from the War Department, which gave the green light for baseball to "resume the usual regular schedule" in 1919.[19] So the games could be played … but who would play them? In the confusion surrounding the work-or-fight order, some major- and minor-league owners — assuming the season was about to end and their revenue streams were about to dry up — had released their players before the end of their contracts in order to save money. Some players contacted the National Commission to see if they were now free agents, a fleeting challenge to the hated reserve clause that bound them to their teams in perpetuity. But the commission issued a statement that all teams would retain rights to their former players, quickly nipping that threat in the bud.[20]

Another point of contention involved the dozens of major leaguers who had quit their teams in midseason to take a war-essential job instead of joining the military — which usually took the form of playing baseball for a company team in an industry or shipyard league. Shoeless Joe Jackson of the White Sox was the most notable player to join the "paint and putty" circuit, and his team's owner, Charles Comiskey, was among the most vocal about wanting to ban these "unpatriotic" players from returning to the majors.[21] He even went so far as to support a resolution at the American League's annual meeting in December to blacklist them. But the man who had built the 1917 World Series champions did not get much support and soon relaxed his stance at the urging of his new manager, Kid Gleason. Jackson, Lefty Williams, and the other shipyard players were all in uniform on Opening Day.

At the AL meeting in Chicago, the cautious league owners decided to adopt a 140-game schedule and set a roster limit of 21 players instead of the usual 25, keeping expenses down just in case fans chose not to return to the ballparks after the war.[22] The National League followed suit at its own meeting in New York. In another attempt to cut costs, NL owners in January approved an $11,000-per-month player salary cap, which worked out to a team payroll of less than $58,000, according to baseball historian Bob Hoie.[23] But the AL teams refused to go along with the idea and the plan was mostly ignored by the time the season began. Still, all salaries under a shortened 140-game schedule were lower since most players got paid only while they were playing.

Because of the uncertainty around baseball, there were few major deals at any of the league meetings during the winter of 1918-19. The New York Yankees bolstered their rotation by acquiring veteran pitchers Dutch Leonard and Ernie Shore from the Boston Red Sox, and signing right-hander Pete Schneider from the Cincinnati Reds, but none proved to have a lasting impact with the team. Later, a three-way deal was completed by the Tigers, Red Sox, and Senators involving, most notably, infielder Ossie Vitt and catcher Eddie Ainsmith. But the most significant (and surprising) move at the winter meetings was the Phillies' release of their manager, Pat Moran, who had led Philadelphia to its first pennant in 1915. The Cincinnati Reds promptly signed him to replace Christy Mathewson, who was still overseas on military duty. The hiring paid immediate dividends, as Moran — dubbed the "Miracle Man" by Reds fans — led Cincinnati to its first pennant and a World Series championship in 1919.

As the new year rolled around, the big issues on the table were still the future of the National Commission and the overall relationship between the major leagues and minors. A special joint meeting between the American and National Leagues was called for January 16, 1919, at the Hotel Biltmore in New York. After former President Taft's rejection of the tentative "offer" to be baseball's commissioner, no other candidates had been introduced. Each league agreed to form a committee to study the issue and recommend potential candidates for the job. The NL appointed William Veeck of the Chicago Cubs and William Baker of the Philadelphia Phillies, while the AL selected Jacob Ruppert of the Yankees and Frank Navin of the Detroit Tigers. In the meantime, the National Commission would continue overseeing the game with Cincinnati Reds president Garry Herrmann as chairman, the same position he had held since 1903.[24]

The shots fired by the minor leagues back in November finally landed in January. At a stormy meeting in New York, the precarious National Agreement that had held the majors and minors together for nearly two decades was torn apart. "They wished for independence," Ban Johnson said, "and now they have it."[25] Under the tentative arrangement, the Rule 5 draft was abolished, as were all existing optional agreements between major- and minor-league teams. The only way in which major-league clubs could acquire players from the minors was by directly purchasing their contracts.[26] In announcing the new pact, Herrmann said, "When (the minor-league executives) stated that they would be the happiest men in the world if they were permitted to go their own way … we thought best to permit them to do as they desired."[27]

In spite of their bluster at the time, the decision proved to be a colossal blunder for major-league owners. The minors quickly moved to restrict access to their players and, unencumbered by the $2,500 draft fee that previously had been the ceiling, held out for higher and higher prices when the majors came calling for fresh talent. By 1921 the American and National Leagues would be ready to call a truce. "These prices now are so exorbitant and so ridiculous that it would wreck the treasury of any major-league club in baseball if it attempted to recruit an entire team from the minors," syndicated columnist Frank Menke wrote that year.[28] A new agreement was signed that reinstated the minor-league draft and resumed the steady flow of players up the ladder of professional baseball. By then, the National Commission was gone and Kenesaw Mountain Landis had been officially hired as baseball's supreme authority. The old judge held jurisdiction over all of the major and minor leagues for nearly a quarter-century.

There was one final order of business during the joint major-league meetings in New York that offseason: The National Commission began to prepare a new system to distribute World Series gate receipts to the players of the competing clubs. The 1918 World Series had been disrupted by a threatened player strike before Game Five, when the Red Sox and Cubs players refused to take the field after learning that the rules had been changed governing how much money they were to make for participating—a decision that cut their individual World Series bonuses by more than 70 percent.[29] The standoff ended after a few hours, but it put a scare into baseball officials and it did not escape notice of the Cubs' crosstown rivals, the Chicago White Sox, who won the American League pennant the following season … and decided to take matters into their own hands when it came time to get paid for the 1919 World Series.

NOTES

1. *Christian Science Monitor*, November 12, 1918.
2. *Chicago Tribune*, May 24, 1918.
3. *Chicago Tribune*, November 13, 1918.
4. *Chicago Tribune*, November 12, 1918.
5. *Hartford Courant*, November 15, 1918.
6. Cliff Blau, "League Operating Rules." Accessed online at cliffblau.ucoz.com/rules.htm on February 16, 2016.
7. Cliff Blau, "The Major League Draft." Accessed online at cliffblau.ucoz.com/ml_draft.htm on February 16, 2016.
8. *New York Times*, November 15, 1918.
9. *Hartford Courant*, November 15, 1918.
10. *Chicago Tribune*, November 16, 1918.
11. *New York Times*, November 16, 1918.
12. Daniel Ginsburg, "John Tener," SABR Biography Project. Accessed online at sabr.org/bioproj/person/c90d4ea9 on September 10, 2015.
13. *Chicago Tribune*, August 4, 1918; *New York Times*, August 7, 1918. Johnson had at first urged AL ballplayers to claim exemption from military service, while the NL took "just the opposite position." Later in the summer, Johnson made several announcements proclaiming that baseball would shut down "immediately," only to backtrack after club owners persuaded him that they could at least continue the season through Labor Day.
14. Daniel R. Levitt, Mark L. Armour, and Matthew Levitt, "History Versus Harry Frazee: Re-revising the Story," *Baseball Research Journal*, Vol. 37 (Cleveland: Society for American Baseball Research, 2008), 28.
15. *Boston Globe*, November 24, 1918.
16. *Chicago Tribune*, November 25, 1918.
17. *New York Times*, November 25, 1918, and December 1, 1918.
18. *Chicago Tribune*, November 30, 1918.
19. *New York Times*, December 5, 1918.
20. *Washington Post*, January 7, 1919.
21. Jim Leeke, "The Delaware River Shipbuilding League, 1918," *The National Pastime: From Swampoodle to South Philly* (Phoenix, Arizona: Society for American Baseball Research, 2013).

22 *New York Times*, December 13, 1918. The AL meeting began on December 12.

23 Bob Hoie, "1919 Baseball Salaries and the Mythically Underpaid Chicago White Sox." *Base Ball: A Journal of the Early Game* (Jefferson, North Carolina: McFarland & Co., Spring 2012).

24 *1919 Spalding Guide*, Internet Archive, available online at archive.org/details/spaldingsbasebal07chic.

25 *The Sporting News*, January 23, 1919.

26 *1919 Spalding Guide*.

27 *Atlanta Constitution*, January 17, 1919.

28 Frank Menke, "Effort to 'Knife' Johnson by Major Clubs Gives Minors Chance to Use Deadly Weapon," King Features Syndicate, as printed in *San Antonio Evening News*, December 16, 1921.

29 A player's share for the victorious Red Sox in the 1916 World Series had been $3,910. In 1918, because of the new system enacted by the National Commission, each Red Sox player received a bonus of just over $1,100. For further reading, see Doug Pappas' article "The World Championship That Almost Wasn't," accessed online at roadsidephotos.sabr.org/baseball/bb98-7.htm.

— 1919 —
THE END OF THE DEADBALL ERA

By Jacob Pomrenke

AS BASEBALL'S POWERS-THAT-BE prepared for the 1920 season, the national pastime was in complete turmoil behind the scenes. The American League was in the midst of a civil war over a series of controversial decisions made by its founder and president, Ban Johnson. There were steady rumors that the recent World Series between the Chicago White Sox and Cincinnati Reds had been fixed by gamblers. And there was still no working agreement between the major leagues and minor leagues, the latter having opted for financial and structural independence after the unprofitable World War I years. But the most significant story of that offseason was the sale of a talented, headstrong star from the Boston Red Sox to the New York Yankees.

By the time all the dust finally settled, baseball's governing body, the National Commission, had been dissolved and federal judge Kenesaw Mountain Landis ruled as the game's supreme authority. Eight White Sox players were banned for life in the 1919 World Series scandal, giving the game its biggest black eye. And as baseball took steps to move out of the Deadball Era, Babe Ruth became the sport's home-run king and its first transcendent superstar, establishing a dynasty in New York that would last for the rest of the 20th century.

But it was a different Red Sox player sold to the Yankees who became the center of attention during the 1919-20 offseason. Pitcher Carl Mays, not Ruth, was the catalyst for the American League's internal feud that threatened to blow up baseball's power structure and end the profitable era of peace between the two major leagues that had been in place for nearly two decades.

Since joining the Red Sox in late 1914, Mays had helped the team win three World Series and was the ace of Boston's pitching staff. However, his abrasive personality and reputation for headhunting had made him "perhaps the most disliked player of his era," according to SABR biographer Allan Wood.[1] By 1919, with the Red Sox heading for a sixth-place finish, he was frustrated and wanted out. In mid-July, Mays walked off the mound in the second inning of a game at Chicago's Comiskey Park and abruptly left the team, vowing never to pitch for the Red Sox again. "I do not care where I go," he said.[2] Red Sox owner Harry Frazee, a theater mogul who paid more attention to Broadway than to his baseball team, announced that he would seek a trade for Mays, and the other AL clubs virtually lined up to acquire the submarine-style pitcher who was in the prime of his career. On July 30 Mays was sent to the Yankees for two players and $40,000 in cash.

AL President Ban Johnson, fearful that other players might emulate Mays by refusing to play and demanding a trade—which would nullify the powerful reserve clause that bound players to their teams—responded by suspending the pitcher indefinitely. The Yankees were furious that Johnson had intervened in a deal that had already been struck between the two clubs. Following the lead of Philadelphia A's manager Connie Mack in a disputed case involving pitcher Scott Perry in 1918, the Yankees turned to the court system for justice.[3] A New York judge ruled that Johnson had overstepped his authority and issued a temporary injunction, allowing Mays to suit up for the Yankees. He made his debut in pinstripes on August 7 and posted a superb 1.65 ERA in 13 appearances, helping New York to finish in third place with an 80-59 record, a half-game ahead of the Detroit Tigers.

BASEBALL'S BUSINESS: THE WINTER MEETINGS

Some rival teams, especially those operated by supporters of Ban Johnson, weren't too happy about Mays defying the league's disciplinary action. Tigers owner Frank Navin protested that the Yankees had illegally used a pitcher under suspension and shouldn't be allowed to accept their third-place share of the World Series gate receipts. (Whether that money should fall to the fourth-place Tigers, Navin didn't say.) The three-man National Commission, which included Johnson, NL President John Heydler, and Cincinnati Reds owner Garry Herrmann, agreed to withhold the Yankees' share until the Mays case was settled.[4] This controversial decision set in motion a series of events that turned the American League's winter meetings into "open warfare" between the five owners who backed their league president and the "insurrectionists"—Boston's Harry Frazee, New York's Jacob Ruppert, and Chicago's Charles Comiskey—who were fed up with Johnson and ready to oust him.[5]

In 1919 those three owners also comprised a majority of the AL's Board of Directors, which also included Cleveland Indians owner James Dunn and Ban Johnson, serving as chair. After Johnson announced the decision to withhold the Yankees' World Series money, the directors passed a resolution, by a 3-to-2 majority with Dunn and Johnson opposed, ordering the National Commission to pay the New York owners what they were owed. The commission, led by Johnson, refused to obey the nonbinding order.

The AL directors also set the league's annual meeting for December 10 at the Biltmore Hotel in New York. A defiant Johnson replied that the annual meeting would be held in Chicago as it always had been, snapping that the renegade owners "do not possess the moral or physical courage to sit in session with the other five honest club owners of the league."[6]

In the meantime, Yankees owner Ruppert went back to court, securing an injunction from New York Supreme Court Judge Joseph Newberger that prevented the American League from holding its official meeting in Chicago … and another injunction that forbade Johnson to use league funds to fight the first order. Comiskey, who had once been Johnson's closest friend and business partner before the two had turned against each other, began taking shots at his rival in the press. "Mr. Johnson is endangering not only the value of our [teams], but the integrity of baseball," the White Sox owner said. "We therefore intend to do everything possible to rid Organized Baseball of the impediment which we believe is now attached to it."[7]

Comiskey was a key part of the triumvirate seeking to remove Johnson from power, but he was preoccupied with more serious troubles that offseason. Early on during the 1919 World Series, he had learned that eight of his White Sox players were conspiring with gamblers to throw games to the Cincinnati Reds.[8] After the Reds' surprising victory in eight games,[9] Comiskey hired a detective agency to investigate the players involved and quietly track down as much information as possible.[10] He didn't intend to reveal that information because he knew that if the fix became public knowledge, it would destroy his championship team. Ban Johnson was also aware of the fix but, although he had fought for years against the scourge of gambling and game-fixing in baseball, he didn't want to see the national pastime sink to the seedy level of boxing or horse racing in the eyes of the public. However, as World Series rumors continued to flourish during the 1920 season, Johnson saw an opportunity to get back at Comiskey, ruining his old friend's ballclub and reputation. Johnson helped lead an effort to empanel a grand jury in Chicago to investigate the World Series fix. Later, after the Black Sox players were indicted, Johnson used American League funds to aid the prosecution before their criminal trial in Chicago. Comiskey would never forgive him.

With the league's top leaders at one another's throats, Tigers owner Frank Navin tried to play peacemaker and withdrew his protest against the Yankees in early December 1919. "I have no ax to grind and I would like to see the property rights of the club owners protected," he said.[11] His efforts resulted in two signs of progress: The Yankees dropped their injunction requests, and the other AL owners agreed to travel to New York to meet as a group. But the night before the full league was set to hold its winter meeting, Comiskey learned of Johnson's plan to vote the "insurrectionists" off the Board of Directors and install new officers from among the "loyal five."[12]

The meeting that took place, according to historians Harold and Dorothy Seymour, was "the most torrid session the American League has held in the nineteen years of its existence. ... [There] probably has never been a baseball conclave in which there was such a violent display of bitterness."[13] In the end, Johnson accomplished his goal of voting Ruppert, Comiskey, and Frazee off the board. They, along with James Dunn, were replaced by Navin, Phil Ball (St. Louis Browns), Ben Shibe (Philadelphia A's), and Ben Minor (Washington Senators). The new board could be trusted to abide by Johnson's wishes.[14]

But Johnson's victory was short-lived, because Ruppert and Yankees co-owner Tillinghast L'Hommedieu Huston took the fight right back to the legal system, where the New Yorkers had enjoyed a certain kind of home-field advantage so far. The pair filed a $50,000 lawsuit in February 1920 against Johnson, alleging that he had tried to drive them out of baseball by conspiring with the New York Giants to kick the Yankees out of the Polo Grounds, the home ballpark that both teams shared.[15] Ruppert and Huston also questioned the legitimacy of Johnson's employment as league president[16] and tried to get him to turn over the league's books. The lawsuit went nowhere, but the new season was soon to begin and all league business had long since ground to a halt.

Navin once again stepped in to preserve any semblance of peace, and the American League scheduled another meeting for February 10 in Chicago.[17] The second meeting was just as ugly as the first. Phil Ball of the Browns and Ruppert at one point "seemed to be all set for a passage at fisticuffs [until] cooler heads prevailed."[18] But this time the "insurrectionists" got their way. After three "grueling" sessions that didn't end until the early morning hours, an agreement was reached in which Carl Mays was allowed to remain with the Yankees, who also were awarded their third-place share from the World Series pool. More importantly, Ban Johnson's power to issue suspensions and fines was effectively—and permanently—neutered. A board of review comprising Ruppert and Clark Griffith of the Washington Senators, was established, with broad powers over league business that turned Johnson into more of a figurehead as president than the czar he had been for the last 20 years.[19]

A day later, at a joint meeting of both major leagues, the owners formally accepted the resignation of Cincinnati Reds owner Garry Herrmann as chairman of the National Commission. Herrmann had played a key role in establishing peace between the American and National Leagues back in 1903, but his presence on the commission had been largely ceremonial over the years, as the other owners grumbled that he always seemed to lean in the same direction as Johnson when it came time to vote. Baseball's power structure was falling apart.

The Carl Mays controversy, along with other disputed cases involving pitchers Scott Perry and Jack Quinn, had seriously eroded the owners' support for the National Commission. The idea of a neutral, independent commission, or maybe even a single commissioner, to oversee Organized Baseball had been proposed earlier, most notably by Albert Lasker, an advertising executive and part-owner of the Chicago Cubs. In the fall of 1918, Red Sox owner Harry Frazee and Giants owner Harry Hempstead had approached former President William Howard Taft about the possibility of serving as baseball's sole commissioner, but the well-respected Taft wasn't interested. It would take another year, and the exposure of the Black Sox Scandal, before the Lasker Plan gained enough traction to succeed.

In addition to the aforementioned disputes, the commission's power had also been weakened by the withdrawal of the minor leagues from the National Agreement in early 1919. America's involvement in World War I had cut into the minors' profits and forced many teams and leagues to fold. The minors also felt that they were not being sufficiently compensated when big-league clubs took their best players in the Rule 5 draft. Desperate to hold onto their stars, minor-league owners opted in January 1919 to pull out of the National Agreement, which had been in place since 1903.

But with global peace at hand and baseball soaring in popularity, it turned out to be only a one-year hiatus. The minor leagues at their winter meeting on November 13-15 in Springfield, Massachusetts, voted to renew their working arrangement with the major leagues.[20] *Reach Guide* editor Francis C. Richter wrote approvingly, "The foolish notion, long entertained by both parties to the National Agreement, that each can get along without the other, has at last been dispelled. … Each is absolutely necessary to the other — the major leagues to the minor for the revenue, and the minors to the majors for the development of players."[21] The partnership between the majors and minors has been in place ever since.

In contrast to the out-of-control American League, the National League's annual meeting on December 9 at the Waldorf Astoria in New York was its most peaceful in years. The main order of business was restoring the 154-game schedule that had been cut to 140 games in 1919 because owners were fearful that fans might not return to ballparks after the end of the war. They were cured of that notion after several teams enjoyed record attendance; more than 6.5 million fans attended games in 1919, twice as many as in 1918. The 1920 season, the first in the so-called Live Ball Era characterized by high-powered offensive production, would turn out to be even more profitable.

Because of all the turmoil, relatively few player transactions were conducted at these winter meetings, but one of the most significant transactions in baseball history took place as soon as the calendar rolled over to 1920. On January 5 Red Sox owner Harry Frazee announced the sale of his biggest star, Babe Ruth, to the Yankees. In return, the financially distressed theater mogul received $100,000 for the 25-year-old Bambino, plus a $300,000 loan from Yankees co-owner Jacob Ruppert.[22] At the time, it was the highest purchase price for any player in baseball history. Although Ruth had been a pitching ace with the Red Sox for most of his career, he had moved to the outfield full-time in 1919 and set a single-season major-league record with 29 home runs. With the Yankees, he would go on to even greater heights, leading them to seven pennants and four World Series championships.

Ruth's transfer to the Yankees forever changed the balance of power in the American League. The Red Sox had won three of the previous five World Series (in 1915, '16, and '18), but they wouldn't win another one for the rest of the 20th century. The Yankees, meanwhile, continued to purchase talent from the cash-strapped Frazee. In addition to Ruth and Carl Mays, New York acquired such stars as Waite Hoyt, Wally Schang, Everett Scott, Bullet Joe Bush, Sam Jones, Joe Dugan, George Pipgras, and Herb Pennock from the Red Sox during Frazee's ownership.[23] These players formed the nucleus of the Yankees' three consecutive pennant winners (1921-23) and helped establish the Murderers' Row dynasty that dominated the AL for years.

In the seven-player deal that brought them shortstop Scott and right-handed pitchers Bush and Jones, the Yankees sent back to Boston right-hander Jack Quinn, one of the last legal spitball pitchers in the major leagues. In February 1920 the Joint Rules Committee made an important and far-reaching decision to help improve offense and bring more fans to the ballpark. Legislation was enacted to ban all "freak" pitches — including the spitball, the shine ball, the emery ball, and all other doctored pitches — which had helped many pitchers enjoy great success during the Deadball Era of 1901 to 1919.[24] The Joint Rules Committee ordered pitchers to stop throwing the spitball after the 1920 season, but eventually 17 pitchers (including future Hall of Famers Stan Coveleski, Urban "Red" Faber, and Burleigh Grimes) were given a lifetime exemption from the ban as long as they were still active in the major leagues.

Hall of Fame pitcher Walter Johnson, who did not throw the spitter, appreciated the reasoning behind the ban: "There is no getting away from the fact that the baseball public likes to see the ball walloped hard. The home runs are meat for the fans. Babe Ruth draws more people than a great pitcher does."[25]

The rule change had an immediate effect. Scoring increased from 3.9 runs per game in 1919 to 4.4 in 1920 and 4.9 in 1921, while attendance soared as well. In 1920 the Yankees became the first team to draw more than 1 million fans at home. Ruth was a national sensation, walloping 54 home runs to shatter his own record of one year earlier. (He broke his own mark again in 1921, hitting 59 homers.) Even the Black Sox Scandal could not cast a dark enough shadow to ruin the game's new prosperity. Babe Ruth is sometimes credited with "saving" baseball in the wake of the 1919 World Series fix, but the sport's popularity was already on an upward swing both before and after the scandal became widely exposed.

Meanwhile, the future of the National Commission would not be decided in the offseason of 1919-20. Garry Herrmann's resignation in February and the owners' subsequent inability to decide on a new chairman left the game without competent leadership when the Black Sox fixers Eddie Cicotte, Shoeless Joe Jackson, and Lefty Williams testified to their involvement before a Chicago grand jury in the fall of 1920. It was at that point that the baseball owners finally sprang into action and hired federal judge Kenesaw Mountain Landis to serve as the game's first commissioner. Landis would serve in that role for 24 years, guiding the sport through its darkest hour and into the modern era.

NOTES

1. Allan Wood, "Carl Mays," SABR BioProject. sabr.org/bioproj/person/99ca7c89.
2. Ibid.
3. Harold and Dorothy Seymour, *Baseball: The Golden Age* (New York: Oxford University Press, 1971), 264-66.
4. *The Reach Official American League Base Ball Guide for 1920* (Philadelphia: A.J. Reach Co., 1920). Accessed online at Smithsonian Libraries, library.si.edu/digital-library/book/reachofficialame1920phil.
5. *Washington Post*, November 20, 1919; *Chicago Tribune*, November 22, 1919.
6. *Chicago Tribune*, November 22, 1919.
7. *Washington Post*, November 22, 1919.
8. There is conflicting evidence on what Comiskey knew about the World Series fix and exactly when he first knew it, with Comiskey writing in a 1929 letter that he was aware at least by the end of Game One. Reporter Hugh Fullerton wrote in a 1935 memoir that he confronted Comiskey *before* Game One that the fix was in and Comiskey replied that he already knew about it. In any event, it was a loosely kept secret throughout baseball, with many people apparently knowledgeable about the fix. See Gene Carney, *Burying the Black Sox: How Baseball's Cover-Up of the 1919 World Series Fix Almost Succeeded* (Washington, D.C.: Potomac Books, 2006), 40-53.
9. The baseball owners had voted in 1919 to lengthen the World Series to a best-of-nine affair in hopes of boosting attendance. The experiment was dropped after three years and the Series returned to best-of-seven in 1922.
10. Gene Carney, "Comiskey's Detectives," *Baseball Research Journal*, Volume 38, Issue 2 (Cleveland: Society for American Baseball Research, Fall 2009).
11. Seymour, 269.
12. Ibid.
13. Ibid.
14. *Chicago Tribune*, December 11, 1919.
15. Since 1912, the Yankees had been tenants at the Giants-owned Polo Grounds, an uneasy agreement that ended when the AL team built its own stadium on the other side of the Harlem River in 1923.
16. At a preliminary hearing, arguments centered on Ban Johnson's claim that he had signed a 20-year contract to serve as AL president back in 1910. But he could not seem to produce any proof of such a deal. The Yankees also questioned Johnson's longstanding financial stake in the Cleveland Indians.
17. Seymour, 271.
18. Ibid.
19. Ibid.
20. *Hartford Courant*, November 16, 1919.
21. *1920 Reach Guide*.
22. Daniel R. Levitt, Mark L. Armour, and Matthew Levitt, "History Versus Harry Frazee: Re-revising the Story." *Baseball Research Journal*, Volume 37 (Cleveland: Society for American Baseball Research, 2008).
23. Ibid. In addition to the players involved — plus Hall of Fame executive Ed Barrow, who is credited with the idea for moving Ruth to the outfield when he managed the Red Sox; Barrow joined the Yankees front office in 1920 — the Yankees also paid the Red Sox close to $500,000 in cash during this period as part of the deals.
24. Steve Steinberg, "The Spitball and the End of the Deadball Era," *The National Pastime*, Number 23 (Cleveland: Society for American Baseball Research, 2003).
25. *New York Evening Telegram*, August 22, 1920.

— 1920 —
THE YEAR THAT ROCKED BASEBALL AND CHANGED IT FOREVER

By Marshall Adesman

BASEBALL FANS LOVE NUMBERS — 755, 511, 2,632, for instance, or .300 batting averages, winning 20 games, stealing 100 bases, hitting 100 mph on the radar gun — all are part of the lore of the game. Sometimes those numbers include specific years, generally the year we started watching or the year our favorite team won the World Series; Red Sox fans, no doubt, have a special place in their hearts for 2004.

Not too many of us were around for the year 1920, but all fans, even the most casual, ought to be aware of what transpired then, because the events of 1920, tinged with drama and suspense, reshaped the game so much that its influence is still being felt.

The story of the Winter Meetings of 1920, then, must be told in the context of the entire year (which also includes a bit of the tail-end of 1919), as if it were a piece of theater.

Act One — The Background

Back in the first two decades of the 20th century, baseball really was the national pastime. Fans (also known as "cranks" or "bugs") just loved their baseball and loved betting on the action, which made the game very attractive to the gambling subculture. Wagers could be placed anywhere — in homes, in shops, and even in the grandstands and bleachers. Betting on baseball was pervasive, an ever-present sideshow that was ignored by the three-man governing body, the National Commission.

But disputes over players began to chip away at this structural foundation. While still in high school, George Sisler signed a contract with his hometown Akron club of the Class-C Ohio-Pennsylvania League that was quickly declared invalid.[1] Despite this ruling, Akron peddled his rights to Columbus of the American Association, which later made a profit by selling the contract to the Pittsburgh Pirates.[2] All this time Sisler was playing for the University of Michigan and coach Branch Rickey. The National Commission ruled that Pittsburgh's claim would be "dormant" until Sisler graduated from Michigan, but the matter heated up again during his junior year and the commission ultimately granted his request for free agency, with his promise that he give the Pirates first crack at his services.[3] By this time Branch Rickey had become manager and vice president of the St. Louis Browns, and he signed his former student-athlete in 1915. Pittsburgh owner Barney Dreyfuss appealed to the National Commission but was rebuffed and, from that point on, dedicated himself to ousting Cincinnati Reds owner Garry Herrmann, chairman of the National Commission, from baseball's ruling body.[4]

Act Two — The Fallout

The 1920 season was in its final days and the White Sox were involved in one of the tightest pennant races in years, a three-way affair that also included the Cleveland Indians and New York Yankees. Despite that, Comiskey suspended seven of the eight indicted players. (First baseman Chick Gandil had retired after the 1919 World Series.) Without two starting infielders (Swede Risberg and Buck Weaver), two starting outfielders (Joe Jackson and Happy Felsch), and their two best starters (Eddie Cicotte and Lefty Williams), the depleted White Sox lost two of their final three games and finished two games behind

Cleveland, which went on to defeat Brooklyn in the World Series.

Repercussions were being felt off the field as well. National League President John Heydler criticized the National Commission (of which he was a member), calling it ineffective and saying that it was now time for baseball's government to assume a new format.[5] A change had been put forth even before the scandal broke, suggested by Albert Lasker, a Chicago advertising executive and Cubs stockholder. Lasker's thought was that a three-man panel of complete outsiders ought to be placed in charge of the game, men who had absolutely no financial interest in any of the 16 clubs. The names of a host of prominent citizens were bandied about as potential chairmen, including former President William Howard Taft, Generals John Pershing and Leonard Wood, Senator Hiram Johnson of California, former Treasury Secretary William McAdoo, and Judges Charles McDonald and Kenesaw Mountain Landis.[6] The Lasker Plan, as it became known, was ignored when first proposed but now, as new revelations were made public almost daily, it was revived and rapidly moved forward, spearheaded by the three American League "Insurrectos" and actively supported by the owners of three National League clubs (the Pirates, Giants, and Cubs). On October 1, a letter went out to all major- and minor-league owners, urging their support of the Lasker Plan; by October 7, the NL formally endorsed it and called for an October 18 meeting with the AL to discuss a complete reorganization of baseball.[7] Ban Johnson and the "Loyal Five" (Cleveland, Detroit, Philadelphia, St. Louis, and Washington) ignored this meeting, but the 11 clubs in attendance renounced the existing National Agreement; endorsed the creation of a new, three-man commission headed by a chairman; set up a six-man committee to search for the best three people to sit on this commission; and issued an ultimatum to Johnson and his group—join them in the new baseball order or this "Allied Eleven" (sometimes referred to as the "Big Eleven") would find a 12th franchise and form a new major league; this new franchise would most likely come from one of their towns and thus offer direct competition, which would essentially mean a baseball civil war.[8]

After the indictments were returned on October 22, Johnson rejected the proposal, pointing out that it did not include the minor leagues at all. He countered with a new idea: a nine-man committee (three each from the AL, the NL, and the minors) that would be charged with creating a new governmental structure for baseball.[9]

On November 8 all 16 major-league franchises met at the Congress Hotel in Chicago, with the "Allied Eleven" conferring in one room while the "Loyal Five" met in another. Washington owner Clark Griffith was chosen to be the messenger, shuttling between meeting rooms (New York's Jacob Ruppert joined him), as each side tried to sway the other before a self-imposed 4:00 P.M. deadline. When no progress was made, the larger group adopted the Lasker Plan and selected Judge Landis as commissioner. The Yankees, White Sox, and Red Sox resigned from the American League, the National League dissolved itself and a new 11-team NL was created, with a 12th franchise to be placed in whichever "Loyal Five" city defected; if all stayed the course, an expansion team would be awarded to either Cleveland or Detroit.[10]

And it was at this point that the National Association of Professional Baseball Leagues—better known as the minor leagues—held its annual Winter Meetings.

Act Three — Meetings, Meetings, and More Meetings

Scene One: The Minors

The minors had no desire to get in the middle of this powderkeg. In fact, the previous two seasons had been played without a hitch even though the Major-Minor League Agreement had actually been abrogated before the start of play in 1919; the minors had objected to the terms of the major-league draft and, unable to come to some sort of accord, the two sides had simply agreed to operate independently.[11] While overall sentiment favored maintaining neutrality, the minors did want to be part of any strong effort to rid the game of crooks and gamblers.[12] But there were those in the majors who wanted the minors to get involved, so when they gathered in Kansas City at the Hotel Muehlebach on November 9, they were greeted by requests from both factions to address the delegates. Ban Johnson got to bat first, and asked the minors to remain neutral. "(Y)ou should pursue a central course, showing no favor or partiality to either side," he said.[13] However, in his first-ever appearance before a minor-league convention,[14] he also sought to subtly influence their thinking by offering the carrot of power. "I think you should have equal representation on the national board and that you should have equal power with the American and National Leagues."[15] He also brought forth his idea of reorganizing the game from within and asked the minors to set up their three-man committee.

The next day Detroit owner Frank Navin and Cincinnati's Garry Herrmann were on hand to address the owners, but they had not gotten very far when they were handed a note—all owners had agreed to meet in Chicago the very next day, without attorneys or league presidents.[16] Something was a-stirring.

Free to deal with their own matters, the minors proceeded, first by re-electing Michael Sexton of Rock Island, Illinois, as president of the NAPBL and then, for the first time, adding a salary of $5,000 per year to the position so he would devote himself to the job full-time. John Farrell, who had been secretary-treasurer since the organization was founded in 1901, was re-elected to the post and given a raise to $7,500. It was decided that the money would come from a new "tax," a 2 percent appropriation of the purchase price of all players sold.[17]

They then named a six-man committee to help develop a plan for baseball's reorganization. Sexton was chosen to head this body, along with Thomas Hickey, president of the American Association (Class AA); John Martin, president of the Southern Association (A); George Maines, president of the Michigan-Ontario League (B); W.H. Walsh, president of the South Atlantic League (C); and Walter Morris, president of the West Texas League (D). They agreed to meet with their major-league colleagues, but only after the latter had put its house in order.[18]

They unanimously adopted a resolution urging every state legislature to adopt a bill that would punish those found guilty of bribing or attempting to bribe a player, manager, or umpire. Written along the lines of a bill drafted by Judge John Crooker, owner of the Houston team in the Texas League and set to be proposed in that state's legislature, the resolution called for a sentence of two to five years in prison, along with the punishment of any owners or other officials who were found to have been connected with the fixing of ballgames.[19]

So much was happening, so many changes were being suggested for the National Agreement. In response, Sexton was authorized to appoint a committee to prepare a new draft for either the next scheduled meeting (February 1921) or the next winter meeting. He placed himself on it and also named Farrell, Dave Fultz, president of the International League (Class AA); William Bradley, president of the Virginia League (Class B); and Bob Brown, owner of Vancouver in the Class-B Pacific Coast International League.[20] The International League, however, opted for a different voice.

Dave Fultz was a former college and professional athlete who became a lawyer and, in 1912, organized a players union, the Fraternity of Baseball Players. He was elected president of the International League in 1919 but, by the following year, had antagonized a great many people—especially major-league owners—by his opposition to reinstating the minor-league player draft, and to the selection of a single commissioner.

Fultz was simply representing his constituents. The Double-A leagues (the highest level of the minors at the time) were not particularly interested in falling under the rule of a single high commissioner or in having the draft restored, at least not without a better system of compensation, which they defined as either better prices for their players or the power to hold onto those players for a longer period of time.

The majors disagreed and took it out on Fultz. His leadership and iconoclastic views earned him a pink slip as IL owners, "influenced" by their major-league brethren, booted him out and installed John Toole, a major-league attorney.[21]

Contract-jumping, also a major problem at that time, received considerable attention. A rule had previously been adopted that banned jumpers for "a number of years," but clubs were actually getting around it by saying that particular players hadn't really jumped but "had taken vacations." In an effort to tighten up the rule, and its enforcement, it was decided that Secretary Farrell would be allowed to use his judgment as to whether players had been "mistakenly" declared ineligible. For his part, Farrell "gave his word that he'd see to it contract jumpers got what was coming to them."[22]

Some general administrative matters were settled. The Texas League was elevated from Class B to Class A, and a territorial dispute between the Western Association and Southwestern League was settled. Dan O'Neill, president of the Eastern League, spoke passionately about how major-league teams had been playing Sunday exhibitions within 10 miles of EL territories. American League teams had ceased this practice after he had spoken with Ban Johnson, but the NL had not yet responded, so the minors extended their existing five-mile rule to 10. They also raised salary limits by 50 percent, and ruled that Class-C teams would now have to pay Class-D teams $500 for a drafted player, up from $350.[23]

As always, individual leagues, teams, and owners were very active, none more so than Ernest Landgraf. The owner of the Syracuse team spent a great deal of time talking to groups from Harrisburg, Pennsylvania; Newark, New Jersey; and Montreal, all of whom wanted to purchase his franchise.[24] Montreal also expressed interested in the Akron club.[25] In the end, Landgraf held onto his club in 1920, waiting a couple of years until the St. Louis Cardinals owner, Sam Breadon, made him an offer he couldn't refuse. Meanwhile, Akron moved to Newark, and Montreal would have to wait until 1928 to ascend to the International League.

George Stallings, who gained lasting fame as the manager of the "miracle" Boston Braves of 1914, purchased the Rochester club and brought in old colleague Walter Hapgood, who resigned as business manager of the Braves for a similar position in Rochester. Stallings followed the lead of Connie Mack by installing himself as manager, which put an end to the rumors that Buck Herzog would get the job. Herzog was one of the players implicated in the alleged fix of the August 31 Cubs-Phillies game, though he was never indicted or brought to trial.[26]

Out west, the Pacific Coast League was embroiled in its own gambling scandal. While defending their 1919 championship, the Vernon Tigers, owned by Hollywood film comedian Roscoe "Fatty" Arbuckle, found themselves accused of bribing players to throw games. League President William McCarthy acted quickly, throwing Tiger first baseman Babe Borton and several other players out of the league, and turning evidence over to a Los Angeles County grand jury, which issued (lesser) criminal conspiracy indictments against the players for their alleged acts.[27] Borton then charged that the 1919 pennant had also been bought.[28] A legal technicality cleared all the players in court, but Borton, along with Salt Lake outfielders Harl Maggart and 1919 batting champ Bill Rumler, plus pitchers Tom Seaton (Portland) and Casey Smith (San Francisco), were expelled for life.[29]

The Los Angeles club found itself in a rather unusual pickle. It was informed by the city that street work would be going through part of its ballpark, so it needed to take bids from house movers to shift the grandstands east, after which it would have to rebuild the playing field. Ownership was not only concerned about the expense, but also how it could affect the series of spring-training games already scheduled with the Cubs, where any delay in getting the new site ready on time could put those games in jeopardy, a lethal double-whammy on Los Angeles's bottom line.[30]

Another West Coast association, the Class-B Pacific Coast International League, looked as though it could be in some trouble when Bob Brown, owner of the Vancouver franchise, seemed ready to move his team up to the PCL.[31] Those dire predictions came true when the Pacific Coast International ceased to exist after the 1921 season.

In response to the pervasive gambling problem in baseball, the Class-B Texas League decided to hire a new "sheriff"—it asked J. Doak Roberts to take over as league president. Roberts had been active in reviving the loop in 1902, had owned teams in Corsicana and Houston, and had even been president in the early years of the 20th century. Now he was asked to clean up the gambling mess, and he began by getting a list of gamblers and gaming resorts in each league city, then informed all players that anyone caught associating with any of the people or locales listed would be thrown out of the league. In fact, just the mere suspicion of crookedness would bring about swift action from this tough lawman.[32]

There have always been people who felt that putting money into a minor-league club was a good investment. Former Texas League player John Fagan "Barney" Burch, backed by a wealthy uncle, spent $70,000 and purchased the Omaha club of the Class-A Western League (which included a 10-year lease on the ballpark and a list of reserved players) from William "Pa" Rourke, who had been with the team as a player, manager, and owner for more than 20 years.[33] But the New Haven club in the Class-A Eastern League received more for less when it announced that Walter Johnson, the longtime ace right-hander of the Washington Senators, had agreed to purchase $5,000 worth of stock. At the age of 33 and coming off the worst season of his career, the Big Train was obviously thinking about his future, but was careful to point out that he "will not take an active part" in the team's affairs.[34]

J. Walter Morris was re-elected president of the Class-D West Texas League, and announced that it would add two new franchises,[35] a proclamation that proved to be premature. Meanwhile, a group of Kentucky businessmen formed a new association which they called the Old Kentucky League, to be helmed by Dr. Frank Bassett, former president of the Kitty League. Despite announcing four firm franchises and interest from three other states, this league never did get off the ground.[36]

Clarence "Pants" Rowland, who had won a World Series as manager of the White Sox in 1917, was hired as skipper of Columbus in the American Association. Another former major leaguer, just-retired Giant second baseman Larry Doyle, moved into the Toronto dugout, while a second International League club

RESOLUTION FROM NOVEMBER 12, 1920

Introduced by Garry Herrmann; seconded by Jim Dunn; unanimously adopted.

"Resolved, That the meeting endorse the principles of ethical control of baseball proposed in the plan submitted to all professional league clubs by four major league club owners in October last, and instruct the Drafting Committee that the spirit contained therein be embodied in the new national agreement. That the unreviewable control of all ethical matters be invested in the Chairman of the Control Board."

"Baseball Factions Sign Peace Treaty," *Des Moines Register*, November 13, 1920: 12.

changed skippers as the Reading Aces handed the reins to Dick Hoblitzel.[37] Meanwhile, Joe Tinker, the former Chicago Cubs shortstop and future Hall of Famer, sold his share of the Columbus club in the American Association to Thomas Wilson, making the Chicago businessman the team's majority owner.[38] Tinker moved to Orlando, where he spent the rest of his life, even playing shortstop there for two games at age 40, in 1921.

And finally, it was decided to hold the 1921 meetings in Buffalo, New York.[39]

As previously noted, these meetings began with Ban Johnson urging the minors to remain neutral in the majors' civil war, but the NAPBL apparently was able to gauge which way the wind was blowing, so a delegation from their National Board (including Sexton, Farrell, and several league presidents) then journeyed to Chicago, where they met with Judge Landis to inform him in person that he would be acceptable as chair of "a new major-minor Commission should one be areed to," though it was also made clear that they planned to keep their National Board intact to settle minor-league matters.[40]

Scene Two: Armistice

On the morning of November 12, the "Allied Eleven" met in Chicago at the Congress Hotel office of Alfred Austrian, Charles Comiskey's personal attorney and a significant behind-the-scenes player in this entire drama. Among those present was Albert Lasker, who had been scheduled to accompany President-elect Warren G. Harding on a trip to Panama, but was advised—by Harding!—to attend the baseball meeting instead because it was more important.[41] They were joined at noon by the "Loyal Five," and after three hours they emerged with an agreement that changed baseball forever and remains essentially in effect after more than nine decades.[42]

Federal Judge Kenesaw Mountain Landis was unanimously selected to be baseball's first commissioner. Lasker's proposal for two associate commissioners was dropped in favor of a single czar, though the two league presidents remained in place. All league matters would be taken up at joint meetings, where decisions would be made by a vote of the teams. It was hoped that the minor leagues would agree to endorse this compromise, which would then allow them to appoint a "special pleader" who would, when the need arose, appear before the commissioner.[43]

Landis desired the job, but also wanted to remain on the federal bench, where he was sure "I am doing important work in the community and the nation."[44] When one of the owners suggested that the commissioner's duties should not take up much time, he readily accepted the seven-year contract.[45] He also immediately set the tone for his office, stating, "We have got to have a higher standard of integrity and honesty in baseball than in any other walk of life—and we are going to have it. ... From now on ... (business) will be conducted in exactly the same manner as my court ...: no favors will be granted to magnates or players."[46]

There was still one more skirmish to be fought—a new National Agreement had to be hammered out. The minors had already named their six-man committee, and they would be joined by a like number of major-league moguls at a meeting set for early December.[47]

Scene Three: New World Order

Ban Johnson's influence on the game was now waning. He had strongly favored Judge Charles McDonald, a personal friend, for the commissioner's job, and now he tried to weaken the power of the new office when the 12-man committee got together in New York's Hotel Commodore to draw up the new National Agreement. The draft by the committee gave Landis the power to investigate anything that he "suspected to be detrimental to the best interests of ... baseball," and then unilaterally take action based on his findings.[48] Johnson suggested that the new commissioner should be allowed only to recommend action, an idea that infuriated Landis, who said he would not take the job if his hands were tied in any way. The owners were so desperate to recover from the Black Sox mess and its fallout that they gave the judge the powers he wanted.[49] After wordsmithing by Landis and a trio of attorneys (one of whom was John Toole, who just two days later obtained his earlier-noted post as head of the National Association of Professional Baseball Clubs), a new National Agreement was announced on Sunday, December 12. In addition to sweeping powers for the commissioner, it also created an Advisory Council made up of the commissioner and the two league presidents; created the post of secretary-treasurer; and declared that, once ratified by the major leagues, it would be the law of the baseball land for the next 25 years.[50] There was some objection from the minor leagues: George Maines, president of the Class-B Michigan-Ontario League, thought that the minors were losing their powers of self-determination,[51] while others remained fearful of a restored draft. The majority of minor leaguers, though, were expecting the draft to be resumed and hoped the fee structure would be brought more in line with the cost of doing business in the postwar economy.[52] The agreement would have to be ratified by the two major leagues and would be taken up at their coming Winter Meetings. The minors would not be discussing the matter until January 10, at which time they could accept or reject it, with a formal announcement of their decision to be made at a scheduled joint major-minor meeting on January 12.[53] The major leagues, for their part, seemed not to care that the minors were given no administrative voice or even what the minors decided; they were now satisfied with this New World Order they had created, and at long last could gather for their annual conventions.

Act Four — Talkin' Baseball

It had been a long and exhausting 14 months, since the World Series of 1919 set off this incredible chain of events, and no doubt everyone — executives, players, writers, fans — were worn out and eager to just talk about the game between the lines without also including legal proceedings or civil wars or new alliances or anything else. This may explain why lots of rumors were swirling as the National League met first, at the Waldorf Astoria in New York City, on December 14. The hometown Giants were in need of a second baseman after the retirement of Larry Doyle, and supposedly were casting their eyes on either Boston's Rabbit Maranville or St. Louis's temperamental Rogers Hornsby, who had just won the first of his six consecutive batting championships (among seven overall). The Pirates, without a pennant since 1909, felt they had a good chance if they could plug their hole at shortstop and were also looking at Maranville, as well as the Phillies' Art Fletcher.[54] The Pirates would eventually win the Maranville sweepstakes, sending three players (including future Hall of Fame manager Billy Southworth) plus money to Boston for Maranville in a deal completed about a month after the meetings ended.

George Grant, the owner of the Boston Braves, let it be known that he would be willing to sell his team if he could get his price. (It took a bit of time but Grant finally made the deal in 1922.) Meanwhile, Grant promoted 33-year-old Edwin Riley from club secretary to business manager.[55]

Fact became rumor, or something, in the Phillies' dugout. The popular Gavvy Cravath had spent nine of his 11 major-league seasons in a Phillies uniform, including the 1919 and 1920 seasons when he was the player-manager. But owner William Baker fired Cravath after the team finished last in 1920 and then stated that Mike Kelley, who had just won the American Association pennant with the St. Paul Saints, would assume the reins in Philadelphia. Well, maybe they hadn't ironed out all the details when Baker made his announcement. Or maybe Kelley agreed and then, like college basketball coach Bobby Cremins so many years later, changed his mind within a few hours. In any event, Kelley remained in St. Paul and Baker had to find a new field leader, who turned out to be former pitcher Wild Bill Donovan, who had managed the Yankees a few years earlier. Donovan would fare no better than Cravath and, in fact, was let go in midseason and would never manage again. Cravath played for Salt Lake City in the Pacific Coast League in 1921 and he too never managed another club.[56]

There were two rumors, affecting both leagues, that foreshadowed the baseball world of the future. There were eight teams in each major league, and everyone played 22 games against every other team in its league, for a total of 154. But an idea was being floated to change that, to bump that up to 24 games against each league-mate, for a 168-game schedule. That would never materialize, but expansion in 1961 (AL) and 1962 (NL) would create a 162-game season, the first change in the number of games since World War I caused the playing year to be shortened in 1918 and 1919. At the same time, there was also a rumor that the owners were considering ending the season on August 15 and then shifting to interleague play.[57] After being bantered about numerous times over the years, interleague play eventually became a reality in 1997.

So were the National League meetings all sound and fury? No, there was some activity, though not nearly as entertaining as the rumors that preceded it. As expected, the owners signed off on the new National Agreement. The league president, John Heydler, was given a long-term extension and a substantial raise; with just one year left on his contract, an additional three years were inserted, taking him through 1924, and his salary was reportedly raised by 50 percent to $15,000.[58]

There was continued discussion about the spitball and whether or not it ought to be abolished. There was a strong feeling that outlawing it altogether would be unfair to those pitchers who used it as their primary weapon, so it was decided to refer the matter to the new Advisory Council with the recommendation that only current practitioners be allowed to continue using the pitch.[59]

Charles Ebbets of the Dodgers, William Baker of the Phillies, Garry Herrmann of the Reds, and Sam Breadon of the Cardinals were elected as the league's new Board of Directors, and Dreyfuss was appointed to draft the 1921 schedule (154 games, it should be noted).[60] They proposed that the season begin on April 13, with a six-week spring-training period beginning on March 2.[61]

As for player transactions, there were only a tiny handful, two of which featured pitcher Rube Marquard. The big lefty, a future Hall of Famer, had gotten into some trouble at the World Series when it was discovered he was scalping tickets that had been given to him. The league announced that Marquard "had been sufficiently punished" and no further action would be taken against him,[62] though it didn't really say if his punishment was anything more than embarrassment. With his status now cleared up, the Dodgers then peddled Marquard to the Cincinnati Reds for another left-hander, Walter "Dutch" Reuther.[63] Marquard wound up having a good year in Cincinnati and was then traded to the Braves, while Reuther was a .500 pitcher in Brooklyn before having more success in the American League.

One deal was left over from the "late unpleasantness." Right-hander Claude Hendrix, three times a 20-game winner, and infielder Buck Herzog were both released by the Cubs. They had been implicated in the fixing of that August 31 game, and though no formal charges were ever brought against them, they never played major-league ball again.

So now it was on to the American League. After an "off day" (for the writers) on Thursday, the AL held its meetings on Friday, December 17, at the Hotel Belmont in New York City. Just as with the senior circuit, rumors abounded, many of which centered on the Boston Red Sox. After winning their fourth World Series of the decade in 1918, the Red Sox had followed up with two sub-.500 seasons, making them ripe for the rumor-mongers. The most extreme had owner Harry Frazee selling the team to a Boston-based group headed by businessman James Conway and also featuring former manager Bill Carrigan, who would return to the dugout as part of the deal. The sale price was supposed to be "up to" $1 million, though Frazee had stated publicly that he would not sell for less than $1.2 million.[64] Another bit of scuttlebutt had star outfielder Harry Hooper being traded to the Yankees, while shortstop Everett Scott and first baseman Stuffy McInnis were being eyed by the White Sox.[65] In addition to Hooper, the Yankees were also supposedly interested in infielder Jumping Joe Dugan of the Philadelphia Athletics as part of an overall effort to improve their team speed.[66]

Some of these rumors came true, just not right away. Frazee did sell the Red Sox but not until 1923, when he did indeed get his price. Bill Carrigan did return to Fenway, but not until 1927, and then turned in three straight last-place finishes. Harry Hooper did get traded, but not to New York and not during the Winter Meetings—in the very first week of spring training, he was shipped to the White Sox for outfielder-first baseman John "Shano" Collins and outfielder Harry "Nemo" Leibold.[67] Connie Mack said he had no intention of sending Dugan to the Yankees and did, in fact, keep him in Philly for the 1921 season, but eventually Dugan found his way to the Bronx and became a key member of three World Series champions. He was joined by Scott, who would play in 1,307 consecutive games, a record that was later eclipsed, first by Lou Gehrig and then by Cal Ripken Jr.

Easily the most embarrassing rumor came from the pen of *Detroit News* sports editor H.G. Salsinger. One of the great writers of the early 20th century, Salsinger had a career that spanned half a century, covering baseball, football and two Olympics; he would posthumously receive the J.G. Taylor Spink Award, which essentially put him into the baseball Hall of Fame, and he was also inducted into the Michigan Media Hall of Fame.[68] But two weeks before the American League convened its meetings, Salsinger all but guaranteed that Clarence "Pants" Rowland would become the new manager in Detroit[69] and, as we have seen, Rowland signed with the American Association team in Columbus, Ohio, while Ty Cobb was named player-manager of the Tigers at the insistence of owner Frank Navin.[70]

In the end, there were only two deals of note. In one, the White Sox purchased the contract of Earl Sheely from Salt Lake City in the Pacific Coast League.[71] Sheely had been playing in Utah for five seasons and had batted over .300 every year. He would prove to be a solid first baseman for the White Sox through 1926, batting over .300 four times and just missing on two other occasions.

The other deal was much larger and would have a far greater impact. The Red Sox shipped right-hander Waite Hoyt, southpaw Harry Harper, catcher Wally Schang, and infielder Mike McNally to the Yankees for infielder Del Pratt, catcher Muddy Ruel, left-hander Hank Thormahlen, and outfielder Sammy Vick. In his *Boston Globe* column, writer James O'Leary stated, "It looks as if the Boston people got a little the better of the deal," basing it on the promise of the 24-year-old Thormahlen and the excellent track record of Pratt, while calling the 21-year-old Hoyt "a speculation."[72] Well, Pratt held up his part of the deal, batting .300 for the final four years of his career, though only two were played at Fenway. Thormahlen proved to be a giant bust, winning just one more game in the majors. Meanwhile, Brooklyn-born Hoyt, who had a mere 10-12 record in his two Boston seasons, would shine with the Yankees, winning 157 times over the next decade on his way to six pennants, three World Series, and the Hall of Fame. Wally Schang would also prove to be a valuable addition to the New York roster, receiving a significant number of MVP votes in both 1922 and 1924.

While Branch Rickey is recognized as the "father" of the farm system, another St. Louis executive, Bob Quinn, was also putting this concept into practice. Continuing a system he had actually instituted when he ran the Columbus club, the Browns' general manager "put over a couple of treaties of alliances with minor-league clubs," agreeing to supply the players and managers.[73] Not surprisingly, Columbus was one of those teams, as were Mobile, Terre Haute, Joplin, and Flint. The Browns also released Joe Gedeon despite his having been their regular second baseman for three years. Why? He admitted to the grand jury that he had been told (probably by his friend, Swede Risberg) about the fixing of the 1919 World Series and had consequently made several hundred dollars with this inside information. After the Browns released Gedeon, no other team would touch him, and eventually he was barred for life by Commissioner Landis.[74]

A tiny note, easy to pass over, proved to have a major impact on baseball for years. Buried in a larger *New York Times* story was the information that Yankees general manager Ed Barrow had signed minor-league coach and former catcher Paul Krichell to be a scout for the New Yorkers. Krichell's "special mission" was to "comb rough diamonds from the college pools and the semipro hay mows."[75] One could say that Krichell fulfilled his task—over the next 37 years, he would discover such talent as Phil Rizzuto, Tony Lazzeri, Johnny Murphy, Charlie "King Kong" Keller, Whitey Ford, and a big Columbia University first baseman named Lou Gehrig.

Having essentially lost the struggle for power, Ban Johnson really wanted to win one fight, no matter how minor, to prove he still had some leverage in the game, and he chose the Board of Directors election as his battleground. Traditionally, owners would serve on the board on a rotating basis, and for 1921 the owners of the Yankees, White Sox, and Red Sox (plus Detroit) were scheduled to be installed. You may recall that these were the three "Insurrectos" who had been battling with Johnson and had even briefly announced their secession from the American League and subsequent hookup with the National League. Johnson exacted his revenge by denying them their seats, making sure, instead, that the board was made up of the owners from Cleveland, St. Louis, Philadelphia, and Washington.[76] As you might imagine, this slight did not go over well with the rebels, even after Johnson compromised just a bit by offering Colonel Ruppert his seat on the board, a suggestion that was summarily refused. Ruppert's business partner, Colonel Tillinghast l'Hommedieu Huston, publicly attacked Johnson and the "Loyal Five" for breaking with baseball tradition in selecting the new Board of Directors.[77] Naturally Johnson responded in print, calling Huston "undesirable" and remarking, "It was the sentiment of the majority of the club owners that two members of our league should not be elected ... as they had attempted to wreck the American league."[78] At least the league was able to agree on ratifying the new National Agreement, and the delegates also determined that they would like to make New York City the site of their meetings every year. They also endorsed April 13 as Opening Day, and approved the prohibition of the spitball once all current practitioners had retired.[79]

And with that the guns were silenced.

Summary

The Winter Meetings of 1920, which actually took place on three stages, completely wheeled around the activities of the previous year, which began with the World Series of 1919 and were kicked into high gear with the allegation that the Cubs-Phillies game of August 31 had been fixed. In order to maintain the trust of the fans and their status as America's national pastime — to say nothing of trying to salvage their primary sources of income — baseball's owners completely restructured their government by creating the office of commissioner, hiring Judge Landis, and giving him a blank check to rid the game of gambling and, essentially, run it as he saw fit. Landis readily embraced these nearly dictatorial powers for almost a quarter of a century, and the owners, by and large, meekly followed along. Given the advantage of time we can see that Landis fulfilled his original mandate. No team ever again threatened to secede, and future challenges, such as those from the Mexican League and the Continental League, were turned aside. Landis's iron rulings set the precedent for dealing with the issue of gambling, which remains in effect today.

Another long-range result of the 1920 Winter Meetings was the ascendance of the New York Yankees. The acquisition of pitcher Waite Hoyt and catcher Wally Schang from Boston solidified their team and began a dynasty that would last into the 1960s. The Red Sox, on the other hand, would not contend for a pennant until 1938, and would not go to another World Series until 1946.

SOURCES

In addition to the sources cited in the Notes, the author also consulted:

Carney, Gene. *Burying the Black Sox* (Washington, D.C.: Potomac Books, Inc., 2006).

"Free Draft Novel Idea of M'Credie," *The Sporting News*, December 16, 1920.

"Have Quinn at Sea on a Training Camp," *The Sporting News*, December 16, 1920.

Johnson, W. Lloyd, and Miles Wolff, eds. *The Encyclopedia of Minor League Baseball*, second edition (Durham, North Carolina: Baseball America Inc., 1997).

Kirby, James. "The Year They Fixed the World Series," *ABA Journal*, Vol. 74, February 1, 1988: 65.

Miner (no first name given). "Hamilton Adds Good Ones to Joplin Roster," *The Sporting News*, December 16, 1920.

"Offers For Sisler? Yes, Two of Them," *The Sporting News*, December 2, 1920.

"Ty Cobb Signs Up to Manage Tigers," *Boston Globe*, December 19, 1920.

Vila, Joe. "Landis Given All Powers Asked For to Keep Baseball Clean," *The Sporting News*, December 16, 1920.

Wood, Wilbur. "Here's Lead to New Scandal Gotham Scribes Can Follow," *The Sporting News*, December 16, 1920.

NOTES

1. Michael T. Lynch Jr., *Harry Frazee, Ban Johnson and the Feud That Nearly Destroyed the American League* (Jefferson, North Carolina: McFarland and Company, Inc., 2008), 85.
2. Lynch, 95.
3. Lynch, 97.
4. Lynch, 98.
5. Lynch, 137.
6. Lynch, 138.
7. Lynch, 139.
8. David Pietrusza, *Judge and Jury: The Life and Times of Judge Kenesaw Mountain Landis* (South Bend, Indiana: Diamond Communications, Inc., 1998), 164-165.
9. Lynch, 141.
10. Pietrusza, 166-167.
11. Robert L. Finch, L.H. Addington, and Ben H. Morgan, eds., *The Story of Minor League Baseball* (Columbus, Ohio: The Stoneman Press, 1952), 21 and 22.
12. I.E. Sanborn, "Minor Leagues to Stay Neutral in Baseball War," *Chicago Tribune*, November 10, 1920.

13 "Ban Addresses Minors," *Los Angeles Times*, November 10, 1920.

14 "Baseball Conflict Shifts to Minors," *New York Times*, November 10, 1920.

15 "Ban Addresses Minors."

16 David Pietrusza, "'The Czar is Dead—Long Live the Czar!': How Kansas City Played a Role in Creating the Commissioner's Office," *Road Trips* (Cleveland: Society for American Baseball Research, 2004) ,15.

17 "Minors Conclude Session," *New York Times*, November 12, 1920.

18 "Minors Ask for an Equal Voice," *Christian Science Monitor*, November 12, 1920.

19 Earl Obenshain, "Minors Prove Intent to Be Masters of Own Destiny," *The Sporting News*, November 18, 1920: 3 and 5; "Minor Leaguers Ask Laws in Every State on Baseball Gaming," *Chicago Tribune*, November 11, 1920.

20 Obenshain, 5.

21 Brian McKenna, "Dave Fultz," SABR Baseball Biography Project (http://sabr.org/bioproj/person/1857946b), undated, accessed May 24, 2013; Joe Vila, "Late News Item: Fultz Is Retired To Meet Major Wishes," *The Sporting News*, December 16, 1920; "Toole Takes A Chance On The International," *The Sporting News*, December 23, 1920. By the way, it is interesting to note that, more than 40 years later, the major leagues would do something similar, ousting their Commissioner, General William Eckert, and replacing him with their attorney, Bowie Kuhn.

22 Obenshain, 5.

23 Ibid.

24 "Late News Items: Knights of Columbus Will Lead In Fight," *The Sporting News*, December 2, 1920; "Toole Takes a Chance on the International," *The Sporting News*, December 23, 1920.

25 "Baseball Program for December," *The Sporting News*, December 9, 1920.

26 "Late News Items: Strongest Decision Yet Given Baseball," *The Sporting News*, December 9, 1920.

27 Matt Gallagher, "Vernon, as a Team, Gets a Clean Bill," *The Sporting News*, December 16, 1920.

28 "Roscoe 'Fatty' Arbuckle's Vernon Tigers," sportshollywood.com/vernontigers.html, accessed March 2 and May 24, 2013.

29 Ibid. Rumler was eventually reinstated by baseball, though not until 1928.

30 Matt Gallagher, "Coasters Impatient at Grand Jury's Delay," *The Sporting News*, December 9, 1920.

31 "Toole Takes a Chance on the International."

32 "Texas Has a Cleanup Man," *The Sporting News*, December 16, 1920.

33 "Rourke Sells Omaha Club," *The Sporting News*, December 9, 1920.

34 Paul W. Eaton, "Small Chance That Feds Will Fight On," *The Sporting News*, December 16, 1920. Johnson, by the way, pitched for another seven seasons.

35 Joe Vila, "Late News Item: Fultz Is Retired to Meet Major Wishes," *The Sporting News*, December 16, 1920.

36 "Old Kentucky Is Organized," *The Sporting News*, December 16, 1920.

37 Bruce Dudley, "Class AA Leaguers Merely Onlookers," *The Sporting News*, December 16, 1920; "Toole Takes a Chance on the International."

38 "Minors Urge Legislation Against Baseball Gambling," *Washington Post*, November 11, 1920.

39 "Minors Conclude Session," *New York Times*, November 12, 1920.

40 Obenshain, 5.

41 Pietrusza, *Judge and Jury*, 169

42 "Landis Takes Baseball Job; Peace Declared," *Hartford Courant*, November 13, 1920.

43 Ibid.

44 Pietrusza, *Judge and Jury*, 170.

45 Ibid. Landis did find, however, that he could not handle both jobs concurrently and stepped down from the federal bench on March 1, 1922.

46 "Landis Confers With Herrmann," *Boston Globe*, November 21, 1920.

47 I.E. Sanborn, "Major Operation on B.B. Fabric to Restore Game," *Chicago Tribune*, December 8, 1920. The major-league owners committee included Garry Herrmann of Cincinnati, Charles Ebbets of Brooklyn, Barney Dreyfuss of Pittsburgh, Tom Shibe of Philadelphia, Frank Navin of Detroit, and James Dunn of Cleveland.

48 Pietrusza, *Judge and Jury*, 173-174.

49 Pietrusza, *Judge and Jury*, 174.

50 "Agree on Terms of Baseball Pact," *New York Times*, December 10, 1920.

51 "Minors Slighted, Says M-O Leader," *Washington Post*, December 14, 1920.

52 "Agree on Terms Of Baseball Pact."

53 Ibid.

54 James C. Isaminger, "Baker Sure Before Announcing Again," *The Sporting News*, December 2, 1920; Ralph S. Davis, "Pittsburg Fancies Its Turn Has Come," *The Sporting News*, December 16, 1920.

55 James O'Leary, "Red Sox Select Hot Springs for Camp," *The Sporting News*, November 25, 1920; Melville E. Webb Jr., "Boston Boy Chosen Braves' New Business Manager," *Boston Daily Globe*, December 19, 1920.

56 James C. Isaminger, "Quaker City Fans Puzzled at Mix Between Baker and Kelley," *The Sporting News*, November 25, 1920; "Baker Sure Before Announcing Again," *The Sporting News*, December 2, 1920; "Mack Sits Pretty While Others Fret," *The Sporting News*, December 9, 1920.

57 "Longer Schedule May Be Adopted," *New York Times*, November 18, 1920.

58 James O'Leary, "New Baseball Plan Adopted," *Boston Globe*, December 16, 1920.

59 Ibid.

60 Ibid.

61 Frank Smith, "National Moves to Start Major Season April 13," *Chicago Tribune*, December 16, 1920.

62 "National League Completes Meeting," *Washington Post*, December 16, 1920.

63 "Reuther Goes to Brooklyn," *Christian Science Monitor*, December 16, 1920.

64 "Baseball Program for December," *The Sporting News*, December 9, 1920.

65 Joe Vila, "John M'Graw Talks About Next Season," *The Sporting News*, November 25, 1920.

66 Joe Vila, "Giants Falling Back on Maranville Now," *The Sporting News*, December 9, 1920.

67 http://www.baseball-reference.com/players/h/hoopeha01.shtml, accessed May 29, 2013.

68 http://www.detroitnews.com/article/20080208/SPORTS07/10620001069 H.G. Salsinger, "Here's Tipping Off the Hand of Navin," *The Sporting News*, December 2, 1920.

70 The Georgia Peach, still going strong at age 34, played for eight more seasons and batted over .300 every year, including a .401 mark in 1922.

71 Oscar Reichow, "Chicago Magnates Give Fans a Brand of Dope They Like," *The Sporting News*, December 9, 1920.

72 James O'Leary, "Big Trade Gives Red Sox a Shade," *Boston Globe*, December 15, 1920.

73 "Quinn Pretty Busy in His Idle Moments," *The Sporting News*, November 25, 1920; "Spring Atmosphere Where Rickey Sits," *The Sporting News*, December 9, 1920.

74 Rick Swaine, "Joe Gedeon," SABR Baseball Biography Project (sabr.org/bioproj/person/eded419b), undated, accessed March 2 and May 31, 2013.

75 "American League Meets Here Today," *New York Times*, December 17, 1920.

76 "Johnson's Forces Rule A.L. Session," *New York Times*, December 18, 1920.

77 "Huston Launches Attack on Johnson," *New York Times*, December 21, 1920.

78 "Johnson Defends League's Action in Electing Directors," *Chicago Tribune*, December 22, 1920.

79 "Johnson's Forces Rule A.L. Session."

1921
FIRST WITH LANDIS

By Joe Marren

Introduction and context

IT IS A TALE OF PRECEDENT SET AND precedent broken. While the combined majors and minors confab would one day be called the winter meetings, minor-league meetings were first actually held in October, so Buffalo was among the first Northeastern cities to host the meetings in December (December 5, to be precise), which is definitely winter in Buffalo. Also, Judge Kenesaw Mountain Landis, chosen the sport's first commissioner on November 12, 1920 (although he didn't formally take charge until January 12, 1921), attended his first set of winter meetings in Buffalo in 1921. An interesting sidelight is that the first winter meetings without him also occurred in Buffalo; they began on December 6, 1944, less than two weeks after Landis died on November 25, 1944, in Chicago.

When representatives from 21 of the 26 minor leagues formally opened the business meeting in Buffalo's Lafayette Hotel on Monday, December 5, the economy of the leagues and the teams was at the very top of the agenda. (Not in town were representatives from the Western Canada, Florida, West Texas, Cotton States, and Alabama-Tennessee leagues.) Another main point to be deliberated was a new plan to reinstate a player draft from the minors to the majors. But all that business took a back seat to the news that the new commissioner had fined and suspended New York Yankees slugger Babe Ruth and two teammates, outfielder Bob Meusel and pitcher William Piercy, for defying an order that prohibited barnstorming by players from World Series squads (the New York Giants had defeated the Yankees, five games to three, in the 1921 fall classic). Piercy was part of a six-player swap with the Boston Red Sox just two weeks later.[1]

So it was finances and personalities that dominated the 1921 winter meetings. Michael Sexton, president of the National Association of Professional Baseball Leagues, said near the start of the meetings that economy would be at the top of the agenda since operating expenses had increased 200 percent since 1914 and, therefore, reductions were needed to save the "little fellows."[2] In short, Sexton said, executives at the meetings were going to have to figure out a way for baseball to curb expenses. He thought the best way to do so would be to cut salaries and player expenses for travel and meals, as well as to cut the number of players allowed on rosters. He also said he wanted to use just one umpire per game.

What was also on the minds of the major-league moguls was a way to get the minor leagues to agree to a draft. News reports said that while minor-league owners and managers opposed a new big-league draft, players in the American Association, the Pacific Coast League, and the International League favored it because it could help their careers.

The Draft

The majors and minors had reached agreement on a seven-year player-movement plan at the 1920 winter meetings, and voted to approve the arrangement on January 12, 1921. But there were grumblings about the accord almost as soon as the ink was dry. In fact, the International League voted not to submit to the draft and waived its rights to draft from lower classified leagues. As *The Sporting News* noted, there were hints that the issue would come up at the winter meetings. Therefore, the paper editorialized, it would be best if all minor- and major-league executives and owners would meet together in one hotel in one city and talk until there was an agreement: "…but the majors and minors have yet to advance to the stage where they can bunch their meetings in one confab."[3]

Perhaps one of the reasons why people weren't meeting at the same place and at the same time was the differences over what was formally known as the Minor-Major Agreement, or more popularly known as the selective clause or draft. President Ban Johnson of the American League announced that he would fight to restore the old draft plan at the meetings in Buffalo. Even though the players supported a draft, the minor-league club bosses would fight against one, according to *The Sporting News*. Part of the issue came down to money: The minors wanted $7,000 for each player drafted by a big-league team, but the majors said that was too much for an untested player and thought $5,000 per player was more reasonable.

Landis also favored a new draft plan (there had been a draft until 1918), but said that the price for a player was not the issue. Rather, hindering a player from moving up the ladder and furthering his career was akin to placing "a stone wall" in front of a player, and Landis was hoping to break down that wall.[4]

No formal action was taken at the close of the meetings in Buffalo. But reading between the lines, it can be seen that the minor leagues were uneasy about what they termed "raids" by their major-league brethren. The minor-league personnel selected to attend the meeting hosted by the majors later that December in New York City[5] were all against a draft: American Association President T.J. Hickey, International League President John Conway Toole, and Pacific Coast League President William H. McCarthy. Indeed, at its December 12 meeting in the Hotel Commodore in New York City, the International League voted 6 to 2 to support the current seven-year agreement with the majors rather than negotiate a new plan that would include a draft.

The American League's response was tepid. Owners voted to ask for a meeting of baseball's Advisory Council to seek a way to revise the agreement signed in January. The National League's response was at first more boisterous. Brooklyn owner Charles Ebbets wanted the league to boycott the signing of any player from any minor league not in favor of a new draft plan (which were the three AA leagues plus the Three-I [Class B] and the Western [Class A]). But in the end the National League also voted to go to the Advisory Council to ask for an amendment to the Minor-Major Agreement to re-establish a draft.[6]

What the Advisory Council came up with was a two-step proposal that Commissioner Landis announced on December 17:

1. One player from each AA or A club would be eligible for the draft after the close of his minor-league season. The major-league club that picked him would pay an AA team $5,000 and an A team $4,000. If the player was released within one year after being drafted, then the AA or A team that he played for had the right of first refusal on re-signing him and would have to pay the major-league club half of the draft price.[7]

Predictably, the minor-league bosses did not like the plan and Pacific Coast League owners went so far as to threaten to form a rival major circuit on the Coast. To avoid being labeled an outlaw league, Dr. Charles Strub, president of the San Francisco team, said, the league would first apply for big-league status with the Advisory Council and, if denied, would then sever relations with Organized Baseball.

The Babe

Even though he had only been baseball commissioner for about a year, Landis faced down Babe Ruth after the slugger's record-setting 59-homer season of 1921. Before coming to Buffalo for the winter meetings, Landis had announced he was suspending and fining Ruth, Meusel, and Piercy for their direct violation of a 1911 rule that banned barnstorming by players who had played in the World Series.

Shortly after Game Eight of the Series on October 13, a 1-0 Giants win that clinched the Series, Ruth and the others embarked on the tour.[8] Ruth had told the new commissioner that he would violate the seldom-enforced rule about barnstorming "and I don't care what you do about it."[9] Eventually, however, Ruth abandoned the tour and slightly less than two months later Landis handed down the verdict. Each player was fined a percentage of his World Series check (in Ruth's case, $3,362) and suspended until May 20, 1922. They were being punished not just for violating the rule, but also for "a mutinous defiance, intended by the players to present the question: Which is bigger — baseball or any individual in baseball?"[10]

Ruth's reaction was to refuse comment except to say, "There's one thing, I'm not worrying, and it won't spoil my vaudeville act."[11] Landis also refused comment when he got to the meetings in Buffalo. (Meusel, though, said Landis could "go jump in the lake.")[12] Baseball writers supported the commissioner's action and quoted baseball executives as saying that what Landis did was right for the game.[13]

There was speculation that the rule would be repealed at the winter meetings, but it wasn't formally discussed. In June of 1922, the National League owners upheld the rule while the American League clubs rewrote it to say that no barnstorming could go on past October 31.

Player Deals

The winter meetings were traditionally known for the back-and-forth dealings between clubs, and 1921 was no exception, though some of the deals reported in the press were more speculative than real.

John McGraw of the Giants started things off by sending veterans George Burns, a 32-year-old outfielder who had played 149 games that season with a .299 batting average and a league-leading 80 walks, backup catcher Mike Gonzalez, and cash to the Cincinnati Reds for third baseman Heinie Groh, who had batted .331 in 97 games. This deal wasn't exactly a surprise since Groh had said during the 1921 season that he wanted to play in New York and had been suspended for part of the season because he refused to play any longer for Cincinnati, where he had manned the hot corner since 1913.

But McGraw wasn't done after the Groh deal. He also purchased the contract of left-handed outfielder Jimmy O'Connell, 19, from the San Francisco Seals of the Pacific Coast League for $75,000. The papers called O'Connell the "Babe Ruth of the Pacific Coast," and reported that he was also coveted by the Yankees and Chicago Cubs.[14] But the press also said the price was exorbitant since at the time it was the highest amount ever paid for a minor leaguer.[15] In fact, at the time of the transaction only the deals for Babe Ruth and Heinie Groh had been in the $75,000-to-$100,000 range. Terms of the contract allowed O'Connell, from the University of Santa Clara, to play with San Francisco through the 1922 season. Some writers thought that the short right-field stands at the Polo Grounds (just 258 feet away from home plate) were made to order for O'Connell. In the event, he played only two seasons in the big leagues, both for the Giants (87 games in 1923 and 52 games in '24) and had just eight career home runs. He was accused of being part of an attempt to fix games late in the 1924 season and was banned from the game for life.

In other player deals:

The Reds bought the contract of third baseman Babe Pinelli from Oakland of the Pacific Coast League for $10,000. Pinelli, 26, had played part of the 1918 season with the Chicago White Sox and part of the 1920 campaign with the Detroit Tigers. He stayed with the Reds through 1927 and eventually returned to the big leagues as an umpire, serving for 22 years. (He was behind the plate for Don Larsen's perfect game in the 1956 World Series.)

The Detroit Tigers bought the contracts of Syl Johnson and Herman Pillette, two minor-league pitchers from Portland, for $40,000 and several players to be named after spring training. The St. Louis Browns picked up journeyman outfielder Chick Shorten, 29, from the waiver wire for $2,500. Shorten's major-league career began with the Red Sox in 1915, and he was traded to the Tigers in 1919. He would last only a year with the Browns before finishing his career with the Reds in 1924. The Browns also acquired left-handed pitcher Dave Danforth, 31, from Columbus of the American Association. Danforth broke in with the Philadelphia Athletics in 1911 and pitched for them and the Baltimore Orioles of the International

League in 1912. After more time in Baltimore, and also in Louisville, he resurfaced in the majors with the Chicago White Sox in 1916, becoming an early relief specialist for four years before spending two seasons in Columbus. He finished his major-league career with the Browns, pitching in St. Louis from 1922 to 1925. The Browns sent to Columbus right-handed pitcher Bill Burwell (8-8 in two seasons), left-handed pitcher Lou Lowdermilk (who had last pitched in the majors in 1912), lefty pitcher Emilio Palmero (who would finish his five-year career with a 6-15 record with four teams), second baseman Bill Gleason (who played 40 games over three seasons), and seven players to be named later.

The Economy of Baseball

All the dealing for players and high prices paid for rookies and minor leaguers might indicate that baseball was playing in ballparks located on Easy Street. But minor-league executives saw serious financial troubles and, in spite of the prices paid for players at the winter meetings, league officials said frugality would have to be the watchword of the future.

John H. Farrell, secretary-treasurer of the National Association of Professional Baseball Leagues, said that the 28 leagues represented 191 cities and towns in the United States and Canada. Those teams had 5,401 players under contract and paid an average $700,000 per month in salaries.[16] It cost about $101,000 annually to run a Class-A club over a six-month season; between $34,000 and $53,000 a year for a Class-B club in a 4½-month season; and between $22,000 and $39,000 a year in a four-month Class-D season. Class-C clubs did not make an annual expense report, Farrell said. About one-third of the costs involved salaries, another third was paid out in taxes and to visiting teams, and the final third went to cover remaining expenses. NAPBL President Sexton said that expenses could easily be reduced, especially since there were predictions that there would be 35 leagues below the major-league level in 1922, by watching travel expenses and reorganizing spring training.

Sexton's other proposed austerity measures included shedding unprofitable teams, like the International League's Jersey City Skeeters, and finding a way of capping sums paid for minor leaguers. It was even briefly thought that the Syracuse team of the International League would be able to get a better lease on a stadium by moving to Montreal, but Syracuse owner Ernest C. Landgraf announced in Buffalo that his club had signed a new lease with the stadium owners, who would be picking up the tab for refurbishing the park. Despite their free-spending ways in Buffalo, the majors also had an idea to save money. Predictably, National League President John A. Heydler called upon the minor-league club owners to accept more "reasonable prices" for players or, he warned, the majors would find different and cheaper ways of developing talent.[17] Yet Heydler's pronouncement was a bit bizarre, considering the deals made in Buffalo. The *New York Times* weighed in on the matter by noting that the money the Giants spent on acquiring their new players "caused many baseball men to shake their heads. Time may justify such expenditures, but at this stage it is difficult to figure along lines of baseball value."[18]

Heydler even went so far as to propose that the major leagues should develop a school for players to help save on the costs of dealing with minor-league owners. At the start of the New York City meetings, he had said that there should be a cap in place when the contracts of minor leaguers were bought—"putting on a roof instead of allowing the limit to be the sky."[19] And then in Buffalo he said: "A training school under the management of several former big league stars could do wonders with a class of bright, ambitious candidates who were eager to play on the big circuits. The various clubs could select their nominees, place them in such a camp for six or eight months of intensive training under the proper instructors, and at the close of the course players would be available who, in most cases, would be as far advanced in the science of professional baseball as the average minor leaguer under the old drafting system."[20]

World Series

In the early years, the National and American Leagues could be counted on to oppose each other on almost every issue. The 1921 World Series, both on and off the field, had been the latest example. Since the entire series was played in the Polo Grounds between two New York teams, the Yankees and the Giants, it was thought that something should be done to enliven things for other fans. One fix would be to shorten the Series, which was then a best-of-nine affair. (The Series had been a best-of-nine for the first one, in 1903, and then again from 1919-21. All other series were best-of-seven.)

When the winter meetings shifted from Buffalo to New York City, the American League voted in favor of a seven-game series; predictably, the National League voted in its separate meeting to keep it as a best-of-nine.

Yet when the two leagues met together in Manhattan's Hotel Commodore on December 15, the owners informally voted 9 to 7 to switch to a shorter series, with the Chicago Cubs siding with the American League. But since each league formally voted as a single unit, the result was a tie, so Judge Landis cast the deciding vote in favor of a shorter series.

Baseball on Trial

Landis became commissioner after gamblers had fixed the 1919 series, when Cincinnati beat heavily favored Chicago, so baseball was keenly aware of its public image and looked for all opportunities to show it was clean. Such an opportunity came in Buffalo when Sexton told reporters that public confidence had returned "with the election of Judge Landis as baseball commissioner and the penalty he inflicted upon the three American League players [barnstormers Ruth, Meusel, and Piercy] for disobedience of the rules."[21]

Landis told the conferees in Buffalo that baseball was still being judged by the public and that it was up to the leaders of the sport to lead by example. "Baseball has got to be better in its morals than any other business," he said, "and it is up to the majors and minors alike to keep that thought constantly in mind."[22]

To get to that Edenic place that Landis envisioned, the National League decided to crack down on concessionaires and make them more accountable. In other words, it passed the buck to vendors to make sure that fans didn't throw soda-pop bottles onto the playing field or, as a report in the *New York Times* put it, "make such persons at least imitate human beings."[23]

Wrapping Up and Looking Ahead

Buffalo, which was the 11th largest city in the country in 1920, wanted to shine in its time on the baseball stage. The mayor came out to meet the magnates, arrangements were made for day trips to nearby Niagara Falls, programs in the shape of a catcher's mitt offered complimentary tickets to theaters, and other sundry items were given to each attendee. Sexton said it was the best winter meeting he had ever attended, and newspaper reports said it was the busiest with constant meetings.

Perhaps the praise was hyperbole, but there was one problem: Who would foot all the bills? The Buffalo Bisons of the International League wound up picking up much of the tab, but Buffalo newspaper reports complained that the American Association would often chip in for part of the cost when one of its cities hosted a winter meeting. The reports also said that the National Association would consider paying a larger share in the future.[24]

And finally, although Hamilton, Ontario, lobbied to get the 1922 winter meetings, Louisville of the American Association was awarded the prize. Manager Joe McCarthy of Buffalo had skippered Louisville to the 1921 interleague title. Delegates said that Louisville had a richer baseball history, and that Hamilton was just a little too close to Buffalo. Although Hamilton is, indeed, about 70 miles from Buffalo, the roads in winter in 1922 would not have ensured it was just an hour or so drive down the highway.

SOURCES

In addition to the sources cited in the Notes, the author also consulted these sources:

"American League Evasive On Draft," *New York Times*, December 15, 1921.

"Ball Men At Smoker Meet New Mayor," *Buffalo Express*, December 7, 1921.

"Baseball Clans Gather," *New York Times*, December 5, 1921.

"Baseball Vanguard Here For Meetings," *New York Times*, December 12, 1921.

"Coasters Will Ask Rating as Major," *The Sporting News*, December 22, 1921.

"Coast Ball League Is Ready to Fight," *New York Times*, December 25, 1921.

"Col. Ruppert Admits Judge Is a Talker," *Buffalo Express*, December 8, 1921.

"Comment on Current Events in Sports," *New York Times*, December 12, 1921.

"Consider Revised Figures on Draft," *New York Times*, December 17, 1921.

"Draft Question Still Unsettled by Magnates," *Buffalo Express*, December 17, 1921.

"Extent of Penalty Is Surprise Here," *New York Times*, December 6, 1921.

"Failed in Action on Barnstorming and Player Draft," *Buffalo Express*, December 17, 1921.

"Fight Talk Grows as Ints. Close Meeting," *Buffalo Express*, December 14, 1921.

"Have Decided to Remain In Ints' Circuit," *Buffalo Express*, December 13, 1921.

"International Will Not Permit Draft," *The Sporting News*, December 15, 1921.

"Johnson Will Fight for Old Draft Plan," *The Sporting News*, December 1, 1921.

"Judge Landis Is Out Strong for the Draft," *Buffalo Express*, December 16, 1921.

"League Votes Not to Abandon Stand," *New York Times*, December 13, 1921.

"Magnates Here for Baseball's 1921 Sessions," *Buffalo Express*, December 5, 1921.

"Major League Scouts Hover on Sidelines," *Buffalo Express*, December 7, 1921.

"Minors Frown on Draft Plan," *Boston Globe*, December 9, 1921.

"Minors Not Keen to Restore Draft," *New York Times*, December 9, 1921.

"Minors Still Protected From Draft," *Buffalo Express*, December 9, 1921.

"M'Graw Discusses Groh's Acquisition," *New York Times*, December 9, 1921.

"M'Graw Gets Groh in Deal With Reds," *New York Times*, December 7, 1921.

"Nation's Leaders of Baseball on Hand," *Buffalo Express*, December 6, 1921.

"Possible Break in Ints' League for 1922 Season," *Buffalo Express*, December 7, 1921.

"Proposals For That Revision of Draft Rule," *Buffalo Express*, December 18, 1921.

"Providence With Montreal After Int. Franchises," *Buffalo Express*, December 12, 1921.

"Rumors, facts Hold the Baseball Stage," *Buffalo Express*, December 15, 1921.

"Seek Removal of Stone Wall Minors Built," *Buffalo Express*, December 15, 1921.

"Shortened World Series Decided On," *New York Times*, December 16, 1921.

"Shows Progress of Our Baseball in Two Decades," *Buffalo Express*, December 9, 1921.

"Syracuse to Remain," *New York Times*, December 9, 1921.

"Talk Trades as Magnates Meet," *Boston Globe*, December 12, 1921.

"Trip to Falls Ends Meeting for Magnates," *Buffalo Express*, December 9, 1921.

"Will Refuse to Buy Players at Any Old Price," *Buffalo Express*, December 14, 1921.

"World Series Is Cut Down to 7 Games," *Buffalo Express*, December 16, 1921.

NOTES

1. Piercy, pitchers Rip Collins and Jack Quinn, and shortstop Roger Peckinpaugh were sent to the Red Sox for shortstop Everett Scott and pitcher "Sad" Sam Jones.

2. "Majors Want Minors Under Draft Again," *Washington Post*, December 2, 1921.

3. "Get 'Em All Together," *The Sporting News*, December 1, 1921.

4. "Draft Situation Scored by Landis," *New York Times*, December 8, 1921.

5. The International League was set to meet December 12 in the Hotel Commodore in New York City; the National League on December 13 in the Waldorf-Astoria; the American League on December 14 in the Hotel Commodore; with the joint meeting December 15 in the Hotel Commodore.

6. The Advisory Council was made up of Commissioner Landis, American League President Ban Johnson, National League President John Heydler, National Association of Professional Baseball Leagues President Michael Sexton, and Association Secretary-Treasurer John Farrell.

7. "Draft Terms Named by Major Leagues," *New York Times*, December 18, 1921.

8. The tour opened in Buffalo on October 16, three days after the World Series ended. It also stopped in Elmira, New York, and Jamestown, New York, before Ruth ended it in Scranton, Pennsylvania, on October 21. He expected to make $25,000 on the tour, but ended it early when urged to do so by Yankees

part-owner Colonel T.L. Huston, who convinced Ruth the tour would be a financial bust based on poor receipts.

9 Thomas Barthel, *Baseball Barnstorming and Exhibition Games, 1901–1962* (Jefferson, North Carolina: McFarland & Company, Inc., 2007), 95.

10 "Ruth Is Suspended; Fined Series Money," *New York Times*, December 6, 1921.

11 Ibid.

12 Barthel, 102.

13 "Numerous Disputes by Minor Leaguers," *New York Times*, December 6, 1921; "Ruth Eligible for Exhibition Games," *New York Times*, December 7, 1921; "Giants Pay $75,000 for Young Player," *New York Times*, December 8, 1921; "Landis and M'Graw Combine to put Yankees in Background," *The Sporting News*, December 15, 1921; "Draft Terms Named by Major Leaguers," *New York Times*, December 18, 1921; and "Landis Ruling for Babe Ruth Was Big Topic," *Buffalo Morning Express*, December 6, 1921.

14 "Giants Pay $75,000 for Young Player," *New York Times*, December 8, 1921.

15 "Comment on Current Events in Sports," *New York Times*, December 12, 1921; "Landis and M'Graw to Put Yankees in Background," *The Sporting News*, December 15, 1921.

16 "Sexton Points Way to Strict Economy," *New York Times*, December 7, 1921.

17 "Baseball Moguls Face a Busy Week," *New York Times*, December 11, 1921.

18 "Comment On Current Events in Sports," *New York Times*, December 12, 1921.

19 "National Leaguers to Convene Today," *New York Times*, December 13, 1921.

20 "Training for Sand Lot Stars May Come Soon," *Buffalo Express*, December 11, 1921.

21 "Just Warming Up for a Very Busy Season," *Buffalo Express*, December 7, 1921.

22 "Judge Landis Met Magnates at Banquet," *Buffalo Express*, December 8, 1921.

23 "Would Amend Rules And Restore Draft," *New York Times*, December 15, 1921.

24 "Baseball Goes on to New York for One Week," *Buffalo Morning Express*, December 10, 1921.

— 1922 —
TO MEET OR NOT TO MEET

By Chris Jones

WITH AN ATTACK ON A FUTURE Hall of Famer's batting average, a lifetime ban handed down to a minor-league executive, and a power struggle between the American League president and the commissioner, the 1922 baseball winter meetings did not lack for story lines.

Controversy abounded even before the meetings started, as there was serious concern that a joint meeting between the National and American leagues would not happen at all. Commissioner Kenesaw Mountain Landis had planned for a joint meeting in New York on December 14, 1922.[1] This plan was put into jeopardy when American League President Ban Johnson scheduled the American League's annual meeting for Chicago on the 13th, preventing American League representatives from getting to New York in time for a joint meeting the following day.[2] In making this decision, Johnson voiced displeasure with the way the National League had handled several matters involving players who violated minor-league rules, and said he saw no need for the joint meeting.[3]

Johnson's decision sparked immediate controversy, with the New York Times reporting that "most of the observers were agreed that this is only another step in Johnson's campaign against Commissioner Landis."[4] National League President John A. Heydler accused Johnson of going back on his word because Heydler, Landis, and Johnson had met during the World Series and "tacitly agreed that the two major league meetings would be held in New York on December 12 and 13, with a joint meeting to follow on the next day."[5] That contradicted a statement, attributed to President Johnson's secretary, that Johnson had no knowledge that the other baseball leaders wanted the meetings to be held in New York.[6]

Judge Landis confirmed the prior agreement, stating that "President Johnson of the American League, in the presence of several club owners of both leagues, said that the annual meeting of his organization would be held in New York."[7] Landis refused to alter his plans for a December 14 meeting, which he said would take place with or without the American League participating.[8]

The New York Yankees' co-owner, Colonel Tillinghast Huston, called the dispute "childish in the extreme," according to the New York Times.[9] Noting that Johnson's and Landis's offices were only a few blocks apart, Huston wondered, "Why doesn't one walk around the corner, call on the other and get these things settled?"[10] Huston said he would not attend the American League meeting in Chicago because personal matters would have him in New York, but scoffed at any notion that he should attend Landis's joint meeting as the lone American League representative: "Not on your life. ... What would I do there alone against eight National Leaguers? I don't want to be a hopeless minority all by myself."[11] As it turned out, Huston would have other reasons to not attend any meeting involving major-league owners.

The storm clouds began to lift when a report surfaced that Johnson had agreed to move the American League meeting in Chicago to December 12, giving the owners time to travel to New York for the December 14 joint meeting.[12] While this seemed to be Johnson's final concession, he surprisingly later reversed course again by rescinding his call for a meeting in Chicago, and instead ordered a meeting in New York ahead of Judge Landis's joint meeting.[13] Johnson may have been pressured by his American League constituents, some of whom were said to not want to meet in Chicago for business reasons, including transactions pending

— 147 —

with National League clubs.[14] Somewhat strangely, these same owners were also reported to "not see much necessity for a meeting jointly with the present league, however."[15]

MINOR LEAGUE MEETING NOTES

The Southern Association actually opened the winter meetings, on December 3. A hot discussion topic was an increase in the waiver price of $400, with most owners said to favor it.[16]

John H. Farrell, the secretary-treasurer of the National Association of Professional Baseball Leagues, presented a proposal from the major leagues to increase the player limit from 40 to 50, although the proposal was expected to be opposed.[17] Indeed it was; the National Association adopted resolutions condemning such an arrangement, which would allow each major-league club to have 25 players in the minors under option.[18] The proposal was reportedly unpalatable to the minor-league clubs because they did "not intend to consent to a condition that would practically give the majors control of the player market," according to the *Chicago Tribune*.[19]

Western League President Al Tearney informed his club owners that he was tired of their bickering and threatened to resign. After lengthy discussions, Tearney was re-elected by the owners to a new five-year term that bound the club owners to follow his decrees. In other words, said the *Chicago Tribune*, "Tearney is free to conduct the league affairs as he sees fit."[20]

Tearney, who was also president of the Three-I League, wasn't finished. He accused Commissioner Landis of discriminating against two of his clubs in favor of the White Sox.[21] Landis offered little in the way of a response, reportedly stating only that he "had no desire to enter into a controversy with Tearney."[22]

The International League adopted a 168-game schedule, with an opening date of April 18 and a closing on September 23.[23] The International League also declared the draft a "dead issue" as far as it was concerned.[24]

Klepper Barred for Life

The minor-league convention also had its share of fireworks. Three days before the meeting, it had been announced that William H. Klepper, president of the Portland club of the Pacific Coast League, was permanently banned from participating in any affairs of the National Association.[25] Klepper was accused of making false statements about the capital stock of the Tacoma club that he had organized.[26]

Klepper had reportedly purchased 51 percent of the stock in the club with Tacoma residents subscribing the balance.[27] Klepper filed a statement with National Association Secretary Farrell saying that all of the money had been paid.[28] This was false, although Klepper claimed that he "could not possibly have hoped to benefit by this shortage … and I do not know why I have been held accountable."[29] He blamed Pacific Coast League President William H. McCarthy for the actions taken against him.

This was not the first time, however, that Klepper had found himself in trouble with the governing bodies of baseball. The year before, Commissioner Landis had suspended him until 1925 for allegedly attempting to "steal" Seattle's manager. In what appeared to be one of his final acts as president of Seattle, Klepper declared manager William Kenworthy a free agent. Klepper then left Seattle to become president of the Tacoma club, and hired Kenworthy as his manager.

In the end, Landis issued a statement that the Board of Arbitration "had no jurisdiction over the Portland corporation except so far as it is connected with baseball activities."[30] Klepper was permitted to remain the president of the corporate entity, but was prohibited from signing contracts or other documents involving the business of the club or "personally tak(ing) part in baseball matters."[31]

Major-League Meetings

After all that sound and fury, the National and American Leagues did meet separately on December 13, 1922, and the controversial joint meeting was held, as scheduled, the next day.[32] Among the items on the agenda were possibly returning to a best-of-nine World Series, and limiting late-season player transactions.[33]

These and other matters were discussed at the separate meetings, but the issues were largely put off until the joint meeting and, according to one report, the leagues "did nothing save to add to the sum total of bunk they have been dishing out for years."[34]

In the National League meeting, at the Waldorf-Astoria, club owners discussed changing the barnstorming rule; permitting the commissioner and the home club to decide when playing conditions were suitable during the World Series instead of leaving the decision to umpires; and providing fixed payments for umpires officiating the World Series instead of a percentage of the gate receipts.[35] No action was taken on any of the proposals.[36] The National League did fix June 25 as the deadline after which no trades above the waiver price would be permitted.[37]

The American League gathering, at the Hotel Belmont, reportedly discussed "important matters as keeping the players' uniforms clean and restricting the sale of soft drinks."[38] The league mandated that each club provide two home uniforms to each player and extra stockings and caps when on the road.[39] The soft-drink discussion resulted in a proposal to adopt measures intended to prevent pop bottles from being used as weapons against players.[40]

The American League voted to have a committee decide the minimum distance home runs must travel.[41] Most of the owners reportedly agreed that "heavy slugging hurts the popularity of baseball," and that 300 feet should be the minimum distance for a home run.[42] Such an action would have made "two-base zones" in the bleachers necessary at the Polo Grounds and Yankee Stadium, turning some "homers" into doubles.[43] The owners left the final decision to the Rules Committee.[44] Finally, Ban Johnson's annual report attacked the National League, reportedly claiming that "the older circuit was in some measure responsible for corruption among players."[45] April 18 was fixed as Opening Day for the 1923 season.[46]

At the joint meeting, Johnson continued to make his voice heard, launching an attack on gambling in major-league parks.[47] He cited Boston's Braves Field as the site of more open gambling than any other, and requested that Landis and the National League cooperate with the American League's campaign to rid the game of the practice.[48]

The joint session did result in some progress:

A rule was passed preventing the transfer of players from one club to another after June 15 except through the waiver process.

- The leagues decided that the major-league draft would begin on the first day of the World Series, in the city where the first World Series game was held.
- Waiver rules were amended to provide that a club asking for and then withdrawing a waiver request on a player must do so within 48 hours or forfeit their rights to the player.
- The barnstorming rule, which had resulted in the suspension of Babe Ruth at the beginning of the season, was amended to prohibit players from participating in exhibition games after October 31.
- During World Series games, Commissioner Landis and the president or another official of the home team were given the authority to determine when ground conditions were suitable for play, although once a game began, the decision on whether to suspend or postpone games would rest with the umpires.
- Clubs would be permitted to carry 40 players on their roster until June 15, instead of the prior May 15 deadline.
- There was, however, no discussion of the proposed return to a best-of-nine World Series.[49]

Cobb's .400 Average in Dispute

One of the more hotly contested issues during the meetings stemmed from an innocuous groundball hit by Detroit player-manager Ty Cobb on May 15, 1922. Cobb and the Tigers were battling through the rain against the Yankees at the Polo Grounds. While it rained, the official scorer was among those seeking shelter beneath the stands.[50] Cobb hit a groundball to Yankees shortstop Everett Scott, who, the *New York Times* reported, "fumbled and kicked the ball into centre field so far that (Lu) Blue was able to score from second base."[51] While the official scorer "immediately called the play an error," an unofficial score "sent out by a reporter sitting in the press box and not in touch with the official scorer, credited Cobb with a hit."[52]

While one hit over the course of a major-league season may seem trivial, in this instance it was the difference between Cobb's hitting over .400 for a third time or not.[53] So it was news when on December 4, when the American League revealed its official batting statistics, it was learned that Ban Johnson had "(overridden) the decision of the scorer in New York on one play and changed an official error into an official hit," raising Cobb's average from .398 to .401.[54] The New York Chapter of the Baseball Writers' Association of America protested the ruling, declaring that the change was made "without proper investigation" and that "neither the official scorer nor any of the writers who saw the game were questioned by league authorities."[55]

Johnson defended the ruling, claiming that the official score of the game was "not authenticated."[56] He outlined the procedure employed by the American League in compiling official statistics:

> "Last Spring an agreement was entered into with The Associated Press that its representative should cooperate with the official scorers in all cities, in order that its service might have the official stamp. … The provision was carried out in the game in question and Cobb was credited with a hit. If change was made it was without notice to The Associated Press. The American League official statistician sensibly adopted The Associated Press account.[57]

The Associated Press scorer who had credited Cobb with the hit was Frederick G. Lieb, a sportswriter who was the incumbent president of the Baseball Writers' Association. Lieb criticized the decision to accept his "unofficial" scoring of the play.[58] Lieb stated that "the American League had no authority to accept the unofficial score of the Detroit-Yankee game … in preference to the official score" and explained why his scoring of the play differed from the official scorer:

> My failure to agree with the official scorer in the disputed play was due to the fact that it was a rainy afternoon and Mr. [John F.] Kieran, the official scorer, left the press stand for the covered section of the grandstand. Had Mr. Kieran been in the press stand The Associated Press score compiled by me would have agreed with the official score. Obviously when there was a difference of opinion between the two scores, the official and not the unofficial score would have been accepted.[59]

Cobb, for his part, suggested that while the writers were in an investigating mood, they should also look into awarding him additional hits from the 1921 season that he said were taken from him because of a scoring discrepancy: "Let them tell me and the public why it was three safe hits were taken from me during that series and two times at bat added," Cobb said.[60] The Georgia Peach added that "of course, the public understands that I had nothing to do with President Johnson awarding me the hit in question … but since the aforementioned baseball writers are reported to have threatened to protest this action, I would like the scoring in that last series at New York in 1921 to be cleared up."[61]

The New York Chapter of the Baseball Writers Association of America followed through on its threat and resolved not to recognize the average of .401.[62] The topic was on the agenda at the baseball writers' annual meeting on December 14.[63] Ban Johnson was invited to attend, but reportedly "first pleaded that he was busy, promised to communicate later, and after two hours sent word that he would communicate with President Lieb later."[64] The writers subsequently voted to support the New York Chapter's decision and "adopted a resolution refusing to accept the American League statistics as official."[65] The group ordered its members "to refuse to act as official scorers unless assured that their scores will be accepted as final."[66] In reply, Johnson said that "Cobb's average stands at .401, and will not be changed."[67] That is precisely what happened.

Yankees Sold

The chief topic of the joint meeting of the major-league clubs was said to be Tillinghast Huston's sale of his half-interest in the New York Yankees to his partner, Jacob Ruppert.[68] The parties declined to disclose the amount of money involved, but it was expected that Huston would receive between $1,250,000 and $1,500,000, a considerable return on the $250,000 his half-share had cost him.[69]

Also reportedly heading to Ruppert as a part of the transaction was Huston's "omen of good luck," that being a "faded derby hat" referred to as the "iron boiler" that Huston had worn throughout two summers (1921 and 1922) in which the Yankees won the pennant.[70] Ruppert was supremely confident in the Yankees' continued success under his sole control: "With Babe Ruth out there, and the iron boiler on my head, we can't lose."[71]

Toronto Red Sox?

Boston Red Sox owner Harry H. Frazee emphatically denied a report printed in a Toronto newspaper that a Toronto syndicate had obtained an option to purchase the team.[72] Frazee also denied that former Cubs manager Frank Chance and former automobile racing star Barney Oldfield were negotiating to purchase the team. Ban Johnson characterized the Toronto report as "pure bunk."[73] International League President John Conway Toole said he considered the report "unworthy of comment," then commented, stating that there was "absolutely no possibility of Red Sox moving to Toronto or of even considering such a proposition."[74]

MISCELLANEOUS NOTES

Third baseman George "Buck" Weaver, previously banned for life as one of the Black Sox, was denied his appeal for reinstatement by Commissioner Landis.[75] Landis defended his decision by pointing to the fact that indictments were issued against the players, including Weaver, and that Weaver had failed at trial to deny under oath the testimony of a prosecution witness that Weaver had been present at a meeting that arranged for the throwing of the World Series.[76] Landis dismissed the importance of the not-guilty verdict against Weaver, noting that "the same jury returned the same verdict in favor of Cicotte, Claude Williams, and Joe Jackson."[77]

The Giants and White Sox arranged for a 21-game spring tour, starting in San Antonio, Texas, and finishing in New York prior to the season opener.[78]

Arrangements were announced for the Red Sox to play an exhibition game in Louisville to open the team's new ballpark on April 5, 1923.[79]

Player Transactions

While no blockbuster deals were consummated at the meetings, there were a number of player transactions involving both major- and minor-league clubs:

- Veteran Cleveland right-hander James Bagby, who won 31 games in 1920, was sold to the Pittsburgh Pirates. The purchase price was not announced.[80]
- Manager-owner Connie Mack of the Philadelphia Athletics acquired third baseman Sammy Hale from the Portland (Pacific Coast League), at a cost of $75,000.[81]
- Former Cleveland first baseman Doc Johnston announced that he had purchased his release from the Philadelphia Athletics for $5,000 in order to become the manager of a Pacific Coast League team.[82] (He would play for Seattle in 1923, but was not the manager.)
- The Pittsburgh Pirates acquired right-handed pitcher George Boehler of the Western League's Tulsa Oilers for $30,000. Boehler was coming off of a 1922 season in which he compiled a 38-13 record and struck out 333 batters in 441 innings. Boehler had had brief stints with Detroit and St. Louis, but would win only one game in Pittsburgh and only six in his major-league career.[83]
- A three-team trade was reportedly discussed: "The big deal between New York, Washington and the Chicago White Sox still hung fire, although the general belief was that Chicago would get (Roger) Peckinpaugh and Waite Hoyt in a triangular trade, which would give Eddie Collins to the Yankees and perhaps send an outfielder to the Yankees.[84] The trade did not materialize.
- Pittsburgh acquired right-handed pitcher Earl D. Kunz from the Sacramento Pacific Coast League club for $7,500 and four players: right-handed pitchers Moses Yellow Horse and William

Hughes, outfielder Harry Brown, and infielder Claude Rohwer.[85] Sacramento had originally held Kunz at a value of $35,000, but relented to the trade with the inclusion of the four players.[86]
- Frank Chance agreed to a one-year contract to manage the Boston Red Sox.[87]
- Veteran infielder Donie Bush was named manager of the Washington Senators, succeeding Clyde Milan.[88]

Looking Ahead

Minor-league owners sought to help facilitate a joint meeting of all major- and minor-league teams in 1923 by resolving to hold their meetings in Chicago, provided that Commissioner Landis would call a joint session at the same time.[89] Landis had suggested such an action by expressing his desire to have all baseball leaders in the same city to meet at the same time.[90] Nashville was selected as an alternate candidate, besting West Baden, Indiana.[91]

Landis and the major leagues did their part, resolving to hold the 1923 meetings in Chicago during the second week of December.[92] In order to avoid a repeat of clubs or leagues threatening to skip the meetings, it was agreed that when a joint meeting is called, any clubs responding should constitute a quorum (although absent clubs could be represented by proxy).[93]

NOTES

1 "Plans for Meeting Upset by Johnson," *Boston Globe*, December 3, 1922.
2 "Ban Johnson Drops Wrench in Landis Plans; Names Chicago as Baseball Meeting Place," *New York Times*, December 3, 1922.
3 "Plans for Meeting."
4 "Ban Johnson Drops Wrench in Landis Plans."
5 "Plan for Meeting Known to Johnson," *New York Times*, December 5, 1922.
6 Ibid.
7 "Landis is Firm on Meeting Date," *New York Times*, December 6, 1922.
8 Ibid.
9 "Col. Huston Thinks Fight Is Childish," *New York Times*, December 6, 1922.
10 Ibid.
11 Ibid.
12 "Johnson Yields in Landis Fight," *New York Times*, December 9, 1922.
13 "Ban Shifts A.L. Meet to N.Y. and War Clouds Lift," *Chicago Tribune*, December 9, 1922.
14 Ibid.
15 Ibid.
16 "Minor Magnates Ready for Meeting," *Washington Post*, December 3, 1922.
17 "Landis Is Firm on Meeting Date," *New York Times*, December 6, 1922.
18 "Majors, Minors May Meet Here Next Year," *Chicago Tribune*, December 8, 1922.
19 Ibid.
20 Ibid.
21 "Landis Mum on Charges Hurled by Tearney," *Chicago Tribune*, November 30, 1922.
22 Ibid.
23 "Huston Wants to Sell His Interest," *Christian Science Monitor*, December 12, 1922.
24 Ibid.
25 "Minor Body Puts Ban of Klepper," *Washington Post*, December 7, 1922.
26 Ibid.
27 "Klepper Is Ruled Out of Baseball," *New York Times*, December 7, 1922.
28 Ibid.
29 Ibid.
30 Ibid.
31 Ibid.
32 "Baseball Moguls Only Palaver: Leagues Give Out Old Bunk," *Los Angeles Times*, December 14, 1922.
33 "Killefer, Veeck in New York to Start Trading," *Chicago Tribune*, December 11, 1922.
34 "Baseball Moguls Only Palaver."
35 "National Names June 25 Closing Date for Trades," *Washington Post*, December 14, 1922.
36 Ibid.
37 Ibid.
38 "American Would Limit Home Runs," *New York Times*, December 14, 1922.
39 Ibid.

40 "Aim at Reduction of Home Run Swats," *Boston Globe*, December 14, 1922.

41 Ibid.

42 Ibid.

43 "American Would Limit Home Runs."

44 Ibid.

45 Ibid.

46 Ibid.

47 "Major League Trades Fail as Big Meet Ends," *Chicago Tribune*, December 15, 1922.

48 Ibid.

49 "Major Leagues Pass Rule Curbing Late Seasons Sales and Deals After June 15," *Hartford Courant*, December 15, 1922.

50 "American League Batting Title is Won by Sisler; Cobb Second," *New York Times*, October 24, 1922; sabr.org/research/three-or-was-it-two-400-hitters-1922#footnoteref7_nxj567u.

51 Ibid.

52 Ibid.

53 "Rules for Ty Cobb on Disputed Hit," *New York Times*, December 8, 1922.

54 *New York Times*, December 4, 1922; sabr.org/research/three-or-was-it-two-400-hitters-1922#footnoteref7_nxj567u.

55 "Protest Hit Giving Cobb .401 Average," *Boston Globe*, December 7, 1922.

56 "Rules for Cobb on Ty Cobb on Disputed Hit," *New York Times*, December 8, 1922.

57 Ibid.

58 "Ty Cobb Calls for Scoring Clean-Up," *New York Times*, December 9, 1922.

59 Ibid.

60 "Cobb Seeks Investigation of Missing Hits of 1921," *Washington Post*, December 9, 1922.

61 Ibid.

62 "Writers Going After That Average of Cobb's," *Boston Globe*, December 14, 1922.

63 "Ben Fails to Appear," *Chicago Tribune*, December 15, 1922.

64 Ibid.

65 Ibid.

66 Ibid.

67 Ibid.

68 "Huston Wants to Sell His Interest," *Christian Science Monitor*, December 12, 1922.

69 "Ruppert to Be Sole Owner of Yankees," *New York Times*, December 13, 1922.

70 Huston Wants to Sell His Interest."

71 Ibid.

72 "Frazee Flatly Denies Transfer of Red Sox," *New York Times*, December 7, 1922.

73 Ibid.

74 Ibid.

75 "Weaver's Appeal Denied by Landis," *New York Times*, December 12, 1922.

76 Ibid.

77 Ibid.

78 "Klepper Is Ruled Out of Baseball," *New York Times*, December 7, 1922,

79 "Minors May Meet With Big Leagues," *New York Times*, December 8, 1922.

80 "Cleveland Sells Bagby," *New York Times*, December 6, 1922.

81 Ibid.

82 "Baseball Clubs to Fight Pools," *Christian Science Monitor*, December 7, 1922.

83 "Boehler Brings $30, 000," *Chicago Tribune*, December 9, 1922.

84 "Majors Get Late Start," *Los Angeles Times*, December 13, 1922

85 "Pirates Give Four to One," *Boston Globe*, December 14, 1922.

86 "Club Owners in Joint Session," *Christian Science Monitor*, December 14, 1922.

87 "Chance to Manage Red Sox in 1923," *New York Times*, December 12, 1922.

88 "Donnie Bush Is Appointed Manager of the Senators," *New York Times*, December 13, 1922.

89 "Majors, Minors May Meet Here Next Year," *Chicago Tribune*, December 8, 1922.

90 "Minors May Meet With Big Leagues," *New York Times*, December 8, 1922.

91 "Majors, Minors May Meet Here Next Year," *Chicago Tribune*, December 8, 1922.

92 "Major Leagues Pass Rule Curbing Late Season Sales and Deals After June 15," *Hartford Courant*, December 15, 1922.

93 Ibid.

— 1923 —
THE BATTLE OF AVALON

By Mike Lynch

AS NOVEMBER ROLLED INTO December 1923, Organized Baseball found itself with much on its plate, including a National League owner who had been indicted for perjury by a federal grand jury in the E.M. Fuller & Company bankruptcy case,[1] and a Pacific Coast League president who had been ousted by a controversial majority vote but refused to go down without a fight.

Judge Kenesaw Mountain Landis, commissioner of baseball, checked into New York's Commodore Hotel on December 1, although his reason for being there was left to conjecture, including that of one reporter who admitted "the purpose of the Judge's errand was something of a mystery."[2] Speculation was that Landis was to meet with NL President John Heydler to discuss the possible retirement of New York Giants owner Charles Stoneham, whose indictment had embarrassed baseball.[3] (Stoneham was accused of giving false testimony to investigators of Fuller's collapse.)

Landis was also believed to be interested in the sale of the International League's Newark Bears, owned by William Ashton of Baltimore, who allegedly bought the team with money he received from Baltimore Orioles owner Jack Dunn. Ashton was alleged to be acting as a figurehead for Dunn, who was eventually accused of "syndicate baseball," a practice of holding stock in multiple teams that clearly represented a conflict of interest and a competitive advantage.[4] A group of Montclair, New Jersey, men, led by Mayor Howard F. McConnell, made a failed attempt to purchase the club in late November and Landis was said to be keeping an eye on the situation.[5]

Another arrival was William H. McCarthy, who had served as president of the Pacific Coast League from 1920 until November 11, 1923, when he was overthrown and replaced by longtime *Los Angeles Times* sportswriter Harry A. Williams.[6] McCarthy had accused William Wrigley, owner of the Chicago Cubs and the Los Angeles Angels of the Pacific Coast League, of supplying the money used to purchase the PCL's Seattle club, and was thereby also guilty of syndicate baseball.[7] Wrigley was part of an anti-McCarthy faction within the league that had spent months working on a plan to replace him, and they sprang their surprise on McCarthy during the league's annual meeting in California.

In what would become known as "The Battle of Avalon," named for the Catalina Island city in which the coup took place, Williams was elected president of the PCL by a 5-3 vote, receiving support from the Salt Lake City, Los Angeles, Oakland, Portland, and Seattle clubs.[8] McCarthy refused to acknowledge Seattle's right to vote and called for a second ballot since the five votes needed for election hadn't been attained. Salt Lake's Bill Lane, who was on the verge of becoming co-vice president of the circuit, ignored McCarthy and announced that Williams was the new president of the Pacific Coast League, much to the chagrin of the Sacramento, San Francisco, and Vernon magnates who supported McCarthy.[9]

Despite his insistence that his detractors failed to garner the required votes to unseat him, McCarthy had little hope of being reinstated as head of the PCL by Commissioner Landis, but hoped that an investigation into the purchase of the Seattle club would uncover evidence that Wrigley was behind it.[10]

At the big-league level, American League President Ban Johnson moved the date of the AL meeting so as not to collide with the major-league meeting taking place in Chicago on December 10.[11] Still, some speculated that Johnson and Landis, combatants in a power struggle that had begun even before the latter became baseball's first commissioner, would "indulge in a test of strength."[12]

Among the issues that needed to be addressed at the major-league meetings were Landis's power to hear appeals in claims and salary disputes involving major-league umpires and a proposal to exclude coaches from the 25-man roster limit in force between June 15 and August 31.[13] There were also a few superstars who were rumored to be on the trading block, most notably St. Louis Cardinals four-time batting champ Rogers Hornsby, who was coveted by the Chicago Cubs; Eddie Collins, the AL's premier second baseman and, to that point, a .331 career hitter, who was expected to go to the Washington Senators as player-manager; and St. Louis Browns ace right-hander Urban Shocker, who had been suspended toward the end of the 1923 season and wanted Landis to declare him a free agent.

Besides the verification of Williams as PCL president, the minors were mostly concerned with the draft and modifying a system that their three largest circuits—the American Association, International League, and Pacific Coast League—had abandoned in 1919 when they refused to observe rules established under the National Agreement. The three were said to be open to "some sort of agreement sufficiently satisfying to the big fellows to induce them to re-establish buying and selling operations."[14]

Before any business was conducted, however, the baseball convention was stunned by the news that popular pitcher and manager Wild Bill Donovan had been killed when the train he was riding on, the Twentieth Century Limited, smashed into an abandoned car in Forsythe, New York. The train had three sections, each powered by its own locomotive. Donovan was in the second section and had survived the initial crash, but died instantly when the third section barreled into the second in an attempt to catch up after having fallen behind.[15]

The 47-year-old Donovan had spent 18 years in the majors, winning 185 games as a pitcher and 245 as a manager, and was attempting a comeback. He had spent the 1923 campaign with the New Haven Profs of the Class-A Eastern League, where he went 1-0 with a 2.65 ERA in five games while serving as the team's skipper. Speculation was that if Clark Griffith couldn't pry Eddie Collins from the White Sox, he was going to name Donovan his manager.[16]

The meetings got under way on December 10 at the Congress Hotel in Chicago. The National League spent the day discussing issues such as the use of rosin and other foreign substances on the ball, the frequency with which new balls would be introduced into games, contract bonuses, and eliminating the rule that credited a batter with a home run on a hit that bounced into the stands.[17]

The American League's board of directors voted to continue aiding former catcher Lou Criger in his recuperation from tuberculosis by paying for a trip to Arizona, and named George Sisler and Babe Ruth the most valuable players of the junior circuit for their work in 1922 and 1923, respectively.[18]

Minor-league business included a board of arbitration that listened to each side in the dispute over the PCL presidency, considering a player-draft plan that would benefit all sides, and electing John D. Martin president, secretary, and treasurer of the Southern Association.[19]

Despite all the fanfare surrounding Hornsby, Collins, and Shocker, only two deals between teams were struck on the first day of the convention. The Philadelphia Athletics purchased second baseman Max Bishop from Baltimore of the International League, and the Buffalo Bisons of the IL purchased catcher Dewey Hill from the Toronto Maple Leafs. Bishop went on to star for Connie Mack for 10 years, drawing 1,046 walks in 1,181 games with Philadelphia, which earned him the nickname "Camera Eye." Hill, on the other hand, spent all 12 of his professional seasons in the minors.[20]

Day Two of the meetings featured a "big political move," a definitely preemptive strike by the commissioner as NL owners "passed a resolution of support of Judge Landis and officially commended the commissioner for his work for the good of the National game."[21] Landis knew that an endorsement from the senior circuit—though unnecessary, according to

Mel Webb of the *Boston Globe*—would significantly weaken the attack rumored to be coming from the AL, and he was right.

League directors were elected—Frank Navin of Detroit was named vice president of the American League and placed on the board of directors with Bob Quinn of Boston, Jacob Ruppert of New York, and Phil Ball of St. Louis. The NL elected to its board of directors Christy Mathewson of Boston, Barney Dreyfuss of Pittsburgh, Bill Veeck of Chicago, and Charles Stoneham of New York, which seemed to indicate that he had no intention of retiring in the wake of his indictment.[22] (Stoneham was convicted on the perjury indictment in 1925 and was assessed a stiff fine, but given no prison time.)

The National Board of Arbitration finally settled the question about the presidency of the Pacific Coast League by backing Williams and stripping McCarthy of any rights he once had. Otherwise, no other news made much of a splash, with the possible exception of Yankees hurler Carl Mays being sold to the Cincinnati Reds and Brooklyn's Charles Ebbets offering the Cardinals $275,000 for Hornsby, which Webb reported as "the one big laugh of a dull day."[23]

The third day of the meetings, December 12, had Landis addressing both major leagues, and he started off with a bang. Whatever war Johnson and the American League magnates planned on waging against Landis was quickly quashed when the commissioner quickly took the offensive and stated loudly and in no uncertain terms that he was baseball's sole governor.[24] "Those standing sentinel without," reported the *Los Angeles Times*, "heard harsh words and strong language" that included an accusation that his opposition was "acting like a lot of swine."[25]

The *New York Times* reported that Landis had heard rumors that Johnson and the AL owners were going to take the fight to him, although not everyone was on board.[26] Yankees owner Ruppert made an impassioned speech in Landis's favor that brought applause from his fellow magnates and "did much to bring the meeting back to solid earth again."[27]

Still, Landis offered to walk away from his position without compensation for the remainder of his contract if the owners weren't satisfied with how he was running their business. He received unanimous praise from all 16 clubs, however, and the matter was put to rest.

"So the great war ended," wrote N.W. Baxter of the *Washington Post*. "The present czar not only retains his autocratic powers but had them extended in several particulars, while Ban Johnson, who enjoyed czaring [*sic*] himself, will have to be content with what little practice he can get as president of the junior circuit."[28]

The rest of the day was particularly productive as 16 of 17 rule amendments were voted on, with 14 passing, although only two were deemed "important."[29] Despite Johnson's objections, Landis was given "appellate powers in determining a dispute over a contract or right to services" by an umpire, and it was decided that coaches shouldn't count toward the player limit.

As the meetings progressed the likelihood of Eddie Collins going to the Senators in a deal with the White Sox became "as wet as the weather," according to Clark Griffith, who refused to part with second baseman Bucky Harris.[30]

On December 13 the majors and minors agreed to draft rules. As explained by Irving Vaughan in the *Chicago Tribune*:

> All players now going to the big leagues will be subject to draft, providing they are not recalled under options. Any big league club can put in a bid for a player who comes under this classification, but where two or more seek the same man he will go to the major team lowest in the percentage column. For every player drafted $5,000 will be paid but only one man can be taken from each club. Players not originally obtained from the majors are not subject to the annual "grab."[31]

Though no major transactions took place, the Chicago Cubs made some deals that included a handful of pitchers. Percy Jones, who won 16 games for Los Angeles of the PCL in 1923, and George Stueland, who went 9-6 in 45 appearances with the Cubs from 1921-1923, went to the PCL's Seattle Indians for 24-game winner Elmer Jacobs and 13-game winner Sheriff Blake. According to reports there were other unknown players involved and an undisclosed "hatfull" of cash that exchanged hands.³² The Cubs also sold third baseman John Kelleher to the Boston Braves.

December 14 marked the final day of the meetings and it was fairly uneventful. Both leagues agreed to start the 1924 season on April 15; the White Sox released four players to the minors — catcher Roy Graham, first baseman Bud Clancy, 18-year-old infielder Jess Cortazzo, and pitcher Paul Castner; and with that all the participants departed Chicago, including Clark Griffith, who was still without a manager and claimed he might pilot the Senators himself.³³

Alas, no major trades were made. "The few real stars of the game who were slated for trades remain just where they were before the confab started," wrote Irving Vaughan. "Rogers Hornsby is still with the Cards, Urban Shocker is still a Brownie and will not be sold, and Eddie Collins is second baseman of the White Sox."³⁴

NOTES

1. *Hartford Courant*, September 3, 1923.
2. *New York Times*, December 2, 1923.
3. Ibid.
4. *Boston Globe*, February 9, 1927.
5. *New York Times*, December 2, 1923.
6. *Los Angeles Times*, November 13, 1923.
7. *New York Times*, December 2, 1923.
8. *Los Angeles Times*, December 7, 1931.
9. *New York Times*, November 13, 1923.
10. *New York Times*, December 2, 1923.
11. *New York Times*, December 6, 1923.
12. *Los Angeles Times*, December 10, 1923.
13. *New York Times*, December 10, 1923.
14. *Los Angeles Times*, December 10, 1923.
15. *New York Times*, December 10, 1923; sabr.org/bioproj/person/55c38ae8.
16. sabr.org/bioproj/person/55c38ae8.
17. *Los Angeles Times*, December 11, 1923.
18. Ibid.
19. Ibid.
20. Ibid. The *Times* reported that Bishop's purchase price was $15,000, but it has been listed as $20,000 elsewhere.
21. *Boston Globe*, December 11, 1923.
22. Ibid.
23. Ibid.
24. *Washington Post*, December 13, 1923.
25. *Los Angeles Times*, December 13, 1923.
26. *New York Times*, December 13, 1923.
27. *New York Times*, December 14, 1923.
28. *Washington Post*, December 13, 1923.
29. *New York Times*, December 13, 1923.
30. Ibid.
31. *Chicago Tribune*, December 14, 1923.
32. Ibid.
33. Griffith's decision to hold on to Bucky Harris proved to be a good one. As player-manager, Harris led the Senators to back-to-back pennants in 1924 and 1925, and won a World Series title in '24.
34. *Chicago Tribune*, December 15, 1923.

THE NEGRO LEAGUES COME EAST: THE EASTERN COLORED LEAGUE AND THE AMERICAN NEGRO LEAGUE

By Jim Overmyer

1923 Eastern Colored League

AFTER THE INITIAL SUCCESS IN THE Midwest of the Negro National League, which was launched in 1920, there began a drumbeat on the East Coast for a black league there. There were enough good teams to support one, and as early as the spring of 1922 rumors of an organization were afoot among teams in the East.[1]

These Eastern teams had proved to be financially attractive opponents for the NNL squads, which would take time out from their league schedule to make Eastern swings. Andrew "Rube" Foster, the powerful president of the Midwestern loop, had taken steps to bring the Easterners partially within his league's control, hoping he could prevent the formation of a competing league. He offered the Eastern clubs, along with some from the Midwest, "associate memberships," which guaranteed those teams potentially lucrative home-and-home series with the NNL while at the same time protecting them from having their players signed by clubs in his league (and, not insignificantly, protecting NNL teams from losing players to the associates).[2] Until the NNL's founding, the top black teams were independents, bound by no firm rules preventing clubs from "raiding" rosters by offering better salaries to players on other teams. Old habits, particularly one as successful as this one, die hard, and the owner of a Negro team always had to keep an eye out for poaching by his colleagues.

When the East organized, it did so through the leadership of its most prominent black owner, Edward Bolden, who had the Hilldale team of Philadelphia. Initially cool to Foster's offer of an associate membership, Bolden had enlisted Hilldale in the NNL's anteroom in 1921, but soon became disenchanted with his decision. As he pointed out, train fares to the Midwestern cities were costly, and "we have received more money for a twilight engagement in Philadelphia, where the players could walk to the park, than a Sunday game in the West, with over a thousand miles of railroad fare to cover."[3] He also felt restrained by his inability as an associate to sign NNL players who wanted to come East, where salaries were sometimes higher.[4] The sports pages of the black papers in the East were also agitating for a league. The *New York Age*, for example, said that "the fans want to see these teams mix it, so they can tell 'who's who'" in the East."[5]

So it was that on Saturday, December 16, 1922, the owners of six top East Coast teams met at the Philadelphia YMCA (the segregated one for blacks) to found the Mutual Association of Eastern Colored Baseball Clubs. The black sporting press, ever mindful of names that could fit into snappy headlines, called it the Eastern Colored League. The teams were spread along a corridor of about 200 miles that ran roughly north and south between New York City and Baltimore. New York provided three of the six teams: the Lincoln Giants, Brooklyn Royal Giants, and Cuban Stars. The others were Bolden's Hilldale club, the Bacharach Giants of Atlantic City, and the Baltimore Black Sox. Rather than seek out a president or commissioner who had no vested interest in one of the teams, the founding owners made themselves a board of commissioners, with Bolden the chairman.

Although the ECL was a Negro League, and all the players were African-Americans or black Latinos, three of the six owners (Nat Strong of the Royal Giants, James Keenan of the Lincolns, and George Rossiter of the Black Sox) were white men. This immediately became an issue used by Foster to attack his new competition. His leading objection was the presence of the white owners, particularly Strong, a booking agent (or game arranger). Nat Strong's tight grip on non-major-league ballparks in the New York City area was resented by black team operators, who had to pay him a slice of gate receipts to get a place to play. Bolden responded in print, pointing out, among other things, that Foster himself charged booking fees to his NNL teams.[6]

The ECL continued its preseason organization and announced its 1923 schedule and team rosters in mid-April. Among the players, undoubtedly to Rube Foster's chagrin, were some NNL starters from the previous season, including catcher-infielder Biz Mackey and second baseman Frank Warfield (both on Bolden's team) and left-handed pitcher Dave Brown of the Lincoln Giants.

1924 Eastern Colored League

The Eastern Colored League's six commissioners (the individual team owners) were of the opinion that the loop's first season had been a success. At least, a December 7, 1923, article in the *Baltimore Afro-American*, containing pronounced press-release-type qualities, proclaimed that the first East Coast black major league "has been warmly received by an appreciative public and a marked degree of contentment is evidenced among the players."[7] The winter meeting the next day in Philadelphia followed this copacetic theme. Hilldale owner Edward Bolden, who had as much as anyone been responsible for the league's birth, was re-elected league chairman, while James Keenan, owner of the Lincoln Giants, was re-elected secretary-treasurer.

But more importantly, the commissioners sorted through several applications from teams seeking to join their league. They chose two to bring the ECL to eight teams, a number that not incidentally equaled the size of the white American and National Leagues, to say nothing of the rival Negro National League. C.W. Strothers, a black businessman called "Colonel" by one and all in Harrisburg, Pennsylvania, had founded the Giants of that city as an amateur sandlot team in 1908 and had made them into a well-regarded independent club. The Washington Potomacs had existed for only a year as an independent team, but their principals were owner George W. Robinson, whose Roadside Hotel in Philadelphia was a popular stopping place for black travelers, and playing manager Ben Taylor, a future Baseball Hall of Famer already becoming a black baseball legend. Before the season began Harrisburg, too, would have a famous manager—Strothers enticed future Hall of Famer Oscar Charleston to leave the Negro National League.

Charleston was the best of a number of players to forsake their NNL teams and migrate east, validating the predictions of NNL President Rube Foster that higher salary offers from the ECL would lead to defections from his organization. One of Charleston's motives for coming to Harrisburg was a chance to manage. Outfielder Pete Hill left the NNL's Milwaukee team to manage and play part-time for Baltimore. According to the *New York Age*, Keenan of the Lincoln Giants had strengthened his team by acquiring players "from other sections."[8] One of those sections was the NNL, the source of shortstop Gerald Williams and center fielder Harry Kenyon.

A subsequent meeting of the ECL's scheduling committee in April produced a balanced slate of games, in which every team played its opponent 10 times. This was true on paper, but, as was always the case with the Negro leagues, completion of the schedule didn't come to pass. Without access to the sort of capital borrowing from white-owned financial institutions that was needed to build their own ballparks, many black teams rented dates in existing minor and semipro ballparks, and could not always easily reschedule games lost to rainouts or transportation snafus. In addition, two of the ECL's original teams, the Brooklyn Royal Giants and Cuban Stars, both based in New York City, did not have any home fields (although Nat Strong, the Royals owner, had booking control over dozens of venues in and around the city). This caused those two teams, in particular, to chronically fall short of completing their schedules.

The compact geographical size of the league, and the concentration of its decision-making powers among the owners, meant that many crucial decisions were made either through the modification of decisions made at the winter meetings or by dealing "on the fly" with issues that came up during the spring and summer. One of these was the making of a measure of peace between the ECL and NNL at a six-hour joint meeting on September 8, 1924, in New York City that produced the first Negro World Series that October. For the NNL, a combination of financial problems resulted in the folding of one club and the shifting of others among cities. This, along with continued criticism of Foster's heavy-handed administration of the league and the continued leaking of players to the ECL, encouraged Foster to give in to demands of sportswriters and fans and agree to an interleague series.[9] The settlement came with a nonraiding agreement and promises to have the two leagues work better together in the future.[10] In the Negro World Series, the Kansas City Monarchs defeated Bolden's Hilldale team, five games to four, as the Negro leagues took another step toward respectability in the eyes of black writers and fans by more closely resembling the success of the white majors.

1925 Eastern Colored League

The agreement to continue cooperation between the two Negro major leagues, which made that first World Series possible, resulted in a joint meeting of the Eastern Colored League and Negro National League in Chicago on December 4-6, 1924. All eight ECL club owners, who also constituted the league commissioners, traveled west to attend. Rube Foster was unanimously elected chair of the joint meeting, and ECL Chairman Edward Bolden presented a draft of an agreement that would substantially ease tensions between the rival leagues. The result was adoption of a pact that covered territorial rights, the honoring of player contracts, and other improvements that offered protection to the teams of both leagues. "Indications are that organized baseball will have a peaceful future," is how the *New York Age* summed it up.[11]

The most important facet of the agreement was the prevention of "roster raiding," the signing of players under contract to a team in one league by a team in the other loop. There had been a steady migration of NNL players to the ECL in the first two seasons of the Eastern League's existence, which was the cause of most of the bad blood. Now, each team submitted a list of 1924 players who were considered to be its property for the coming season, which made them off-limits to teams in the other league (and in the same league, for that matter) without a written release from the original club. Waivers were also required for movement of a player between teams in the same league.[12]

Regarding territory, the leagues agreed that the ECL could locate teams only east of a line running north and south along the Pennsylvania-Ohio border, and that the territory to the west belonged to the NNL. This conformed with the existing distribution of the Negro-league teams, and while it was unlikely that the leagues had any intention of placing regular teams so far from their geographic bases (primarily for the purpose of travel expenses), the dividing line presumably also prevented a league from offering associate memberships in its rival's territory, as the NNL had done on the East Coast prior to the Eastern League's formation.

A three-member arbitration committee, with each league selecting one member and a third agreed upon by the two loops, was set up to police the agreement. And the World Series between the two pennant winners was authorized again. The agreement explicitly entitled second- and third-place teams, in addition to the pennant winners actually playing in the Series, a share of gate receipts. It set up a four-member commission, which could not include a representative of a pennant-winning team, to run the Series.[13]

The maximum size of a team roster was set at 20 players. Although the subject of an across-the-board reduction in player salaries (something that might appeal to an owner now that he was no longer locked into a bidding war) was brought up, nothing definite was decided.[14]

After this ground-breaking agreement, the representatives of the separate leagues had their own initial organizational meetings, which resulted in Bolden's being elected for a third term as ECL chairman.

Then, as arranged in advance, the ECL commissioners adjourned until January 24, 1925, when they met again in Philadelphia to take care of their league's affairs. An important matter was approval of the transfer of the Washington Potomacs to Wilmington, Delaware, after a financially disappointing season in the national capital.[15]

Another 70-game schedule was agreed upon, and promises were made to try to make sure all games were played, which would avoid the criticism leveled by fans and sportswriters in 1924 when some teams did not come close to playing their full schedules. But Philadelphia sportswriter Lloyd Thompson cut to the real cause of uncompleted schedules. Owners needed to supplement team income, which was limited by the fact that the Negro leagues' market was big-city blacks, a minority of the population with generally lower per-capita incomes. Thompson candidly observed that "although the public has a perfect right to be exacting, they must also take into consideration the fact that with the clubs paying top salaries to players and with practically only one day per week at the respective cities being a paying proposition, the owners can ill afford to pass up lucrative bookings with independent clubs in their vicinity."[16]

At a further preseason meeting on March 25 to approve the schedule, William Dallas, a white sportswriter for the *Philadelphia Evening Ledger*, was named umpire supervisor as the ECL attempted to improve the quality of its officiating. In its first two seasons, umpires were hired by the home club for each league game, and the quality of their work was uneven.

1926 Eastern Colored League

The preliminaries for the 1926 Eastern Colored League season began, as had been the case the year before, with a joint meeting with the Negro National League. This time the representatives met in Philadelphia on January 6–8, with Edward Bolden, the ECL chairman, leading the meeting. The interleague peace that had enveloped the 1925 season continued; as one reporter characterized matters, "tranquility reigned supreme."[17] There were important issues to take up, though. Although some teams did well financially, the overall economics of Negro League ball were always tenuous. An apparent general anxiety about profits led to a decision to cut costs in what for the owners was the surest way—a player salary cap of $3,000 per month per team was instituted. Although the leagues decided to admit no associate member teams, it was made clear that playing nonleague games against independent black teams was welcome, so long as the team in question did not have on its roster any players claimed by a league club. Both of these measures seemed aimed at the most powerful independent team, the Homestead Grays of Pittsburgh. Grays owner Cumberland Posey was an aggressive businessman who had no qualms about luring players away from league teams, and who had a good-enough team to offer a well-attended (and thus lucrative) game to league outfits passing through Pittsburgh. As an indication of the relative ineffectiveness of Negro League rules on player contracts, the Grays continued to poach league players in 1926, and yet still wound up with games against Negro League teams.

Although all the teams from both leagues were at this winter meeting, only one player transaction was reported, the sale of right-handed pitcher Rube Currie to Foster's Chicago American Giants from Bolden's Hilldale team.

The two leagues then proceeded to hold their separate winter meetings. The ECL elected Bolden as chairman for the fourth straight year. James Keenan of the Lincoln Giants was again elected secretary, although the treasurer post that he also held was split off and handed to Charles Spedden of the Baltimore Black Sox.

George W. Robinson's Potomacs, who had started as an ECL team in Washington in 1924 and had moved to Wilmington to start 1925, had gone out of business partway through the previous season. A new team, the Newark Stars, owned by Wilbur C. Crelin, a white regional baseball promoter, was admitted to fill the vacancy. But the team won only one league game, drew poorly, and failed to survive the first half of the season.

Newark actually began its losing streak at a subsequent ECL preseason scheduling meeting, held on February 20, when both Crelin and Cuban Stars owner Alejandro Pompez claimed the rights to right-handed pitcher Pedro San, a Dominican Republic native seeking to break into United States baseball. San had explained the confusion in a letter to the league, but it was in Spanish and the only person in the room who could read it was the bilingual Pompez. No action was taken because "apparently, the Commissioners were unwilling to accept Mr. Pompez' interpretation of the letter," although San eventually wound up with the Cuban Stars.[18]

1927 Eastern Colored League

The foundation of the league was threatened after the 1926 season when Lincoln Giants owner James Keenan, unhappy with his perceived bad treatment by the league's scheduling committee, announced he was pulling his team, a charter member, out of the league. ECL Chairman Edward Bolden was given credit for smoothing things over and keeping the Lincolns in the league, but it would be one of the last acts Bolden would perform as the ECL's head.

Bolden, who had done more than anyone to found the league and had been the only chairman it had known, had nevertheless come under increasing criticism for his inability to enforce on-field discipline—players frequently contested umpires' decisions, often arguing with them at length, which of course held up games, and sometimes even struck them.[19] Bolden, who believed that successful black baseball could come about only through cooperation with the whites in majority control of the sport, was also felt by some owners to be too accommodating to the white booking agent Nat Strong of New York, who also owned the Brooklyn Royal Giants of the ECL.

While Bolden continued to sit as a league commissioner via his control of the Hilldale team of Philadelphia, he stepped down from the chairmanship at the winter meeting on January 11, 1927. He and the other league commissioners (the club owners) handed the job to Isaac H. Nutter of Atlantic City, a leading African-American lawyer and political figure there. Nutter, while a fan of the local Bacharach Giants ECL team, had no financial stake in the team and thus was the league's first independent president. Keenan, having withdrawn his and the Lincoln Giants' resignations, was re-elected secretary, and also given back the treasurer position he had held in the past.

For the third straight year the initial league off-season meeting was held in conjunction with that of the Negro National League, this time in Detroit, an NNL city. The National League was going through a leadership change of its own, much more of a crisis than that in the ECL. Founding president and organizing stalwart Rube Foster had suffered a mental breakdown, and would never run a league meeting, nor his Chicago American Giants team, again. Foster died in an Illinois state mental institution in 1930. The team continued on under a series of owners until the declining years of the Negro leagues, going out of business in 1950.

These leadership shifts were taking place against an ominous background for Negro League baseball. The manufacturing slowdown that preceded what is recognized as the full-fledged beginning of the Great Depression had begun to noticeably impact urban black workers, who tended to hold the jobs most at risk in an economic downturn. "Last to be hired, first fired."

The fan base for black baseball was experiencing widespread unemployment. Consequently, both leagues voted to lower the $3,000 monthly team salary cap to $2,700, and to reduce the size of rosters to 14 for the ECL and 16 for the NNL.[20]

The commissioners reiterated their ban on playing any independent team that had signed away ECL players, and imposed a five-year ban on any player who jumped a league team for an independent. This was, as usual, aimed at Cumberland Posey's Homestead Grays, who specifically had signed right-handed pitcher George Britt away from the Baltimore Black Sox. As usual, these resolutions were honored as much in the breach as in the enforcement. The Grays played some games against league teams as the 1927 got further away in time from the league meeting when the bans were imposed. Britt remained with the Grays for the five-year period, but since Homestead as a team was doing better financially than Negro league ball in general, it's doubtful he wanted to return to Baltimore anyway.

The ECL announced an ambitious split-season schedule of 120 games per team, which was a fantastical notion, given the vagaries of weather, travel problems, and the lure of good gate receipts from nonleague games with white or black independent teams. The Bacharach Giants, who won both ends of the split season, were among the games-played leaders with 88. No team was admitted to the league to replace the collapsed Newark Stars of 1926, and the ECL began play with seven teams. But in June, Keenan reversed his January reversal of the Lincoln Giants' resignation, and the team became independent. The issue that led to the departure was a dispute over his signing of outfielder Alonzo Montalvo, upon whom an NNL club had a claim that was upheld by both leagues. But Keenan, who had a home field in the Bronx, had long resented a schedule that deprived him of lucrative Sunday home dates there, and may have decided that "the league will need the Lincoln Giants more than the Lincolns will need the league."[21]

1928 Eastern Colored League

The Eastern Colored League owners re-elected Isaac Nutter as league president when they convened their preseason meeting on February 11, 1928, in Philadelphia. Edward Bolden, the league's first leader before turning over the top spot to Nutter in 1927, was re-elected secretary-treasurer, a post he had taken over in the middle of the previous season. Bolden's right to not only hold a league office but to represent the Hilldale team he had founded, was challenged, however, by other Hilldale officials, who had earlier deposed him as team president. Bolden successfully maintained that despite no longer being club president, he owned a majority stock position, and the rest of the owners recognized him as Hilldale's representative.[22]

The owners made a few other decisions, such as deciding on a rotating crew of league-controlled umpires and requiring a $500 "good faith" deposit from each team to swell the league treasury. But the contretemps over Bolden's eligibility was an omen for the ECL's short and rocky future. The six teams that had finished the 1927 season had already shrunk to five with the withdrawal of the Harrisburg Giants and Brooklyn Royal Giants, partly offset by the return to the fold of the Lincoln Giants, who had left the league during the previous year. But Bolden himself made a move in March that nearly sank the league before any games were played. He took the keystone Hilldale franchise out of the league, committing it to playing more profitable independent ball. He blamed a lack of cooperation by self-interested owners and the absence of reliable home parks for all teams for "tearing the vitals from the Eastern League." It was clear that, in the beginnings of a national economic downturn, most if not all Negro League teams were losing money, but Bolden's accounting was specific—Hilldale had lost $21,000 since the beginning of 1927, a significant sum in the black baseball world of the late 1920s.[23]

The remaining owners decided on April 19 that it was useless for the ECL to go on, but reversed their position before the month was out when a potential new team, the Philadelphia Tigers, found a home park and was admitted. The ECL's resurrection surprised many who had believed it dead. A *Baltimore Afro-American* headline on April 28 captured their surprise: "Is Eastern League Dead or Fooling? Body, Last Week Reported Dead, Now Said to Be Alive and Kicking."

But two months later, also sensing that more profitable bookings could be had outside of a league schedule, Alejandro Pompez and James Keenan took their Cuban Stars and Lincoln Giants, respectively, out of the league, and all the teams turned to independent ball. Although he was writing about the initial decision to suspend play (the one that had been reversed), *Afro-American* writer Bill Gibson succinctly summed up the league's six-year history: "A child of Edward Bolden, Hilldale pilot, and spasmodically fed by the owners of seven clubs, the Eastern League always remained rather a puny thing, never developing the robustness and virility of its relative, the National League. The league led a sort of see-saw existence, assuming an ascendancy or soaring to minor heights on the wind of certain powers behind the throne who dictated to large measure the policies of its administration."[24]

1929 American Negro League

The Eastern Colored League had barely ceased operating when in August of 1928 the African-American sportswriters who had covered it began to make the case that an organized league, rather than independent baseball, was what black baseball in the East needed. "The public will never again patronize 'independent' baseball as it did in the days before it knew the association brand of the game.... The game and the men interested in it and the men who make their living by it need a strong, well-balanced circuit which will protect all of those involved," Romeo Dougherty of the *New York Amsterdam News* wrote. He added that the sportswriters also wanted Edward Bolden, owner of the Hilldale team of the Philadelphia area and founder of the first Eastern league, to lead this movement, "because Ed Bolden means more to baseball than baseball can ever mean to Ed Bolden.[25]

So the American Negro League was formed at a meeting on January 15, 1929, in Philadelphia, and Bolden was elected president. James Keenan, owner of the Lincoln Giants of New York City, was voted vice president and George Rossiter, owner of the Baltimore Black Sox, was treasurer. The league secretary position was given to W. Rollo Wilson, sports columnist for the *Pittsburgh Courier*, in an innovative move that brought a representative of the black East Coast sports journalists, who had been ever more critical of the malfunctioning ECL, into the inner circle.[26]

The new league was composed of five charter members of the old ECL: Hilldale, the Baltimore Black Sox, the Atlantic City Bacharach Giants, and the Cuban Stars and Lincoln Giants of New York City. The identity of the sixth team, like Wilson's election as league secretary, was also ground-breaking—the Homestead Grays of Pittsburgh. An aggressively run franchise located halfway between the territories of the Eastern and Midwestern black leagues, it was on the one hand a lucrative barnstorming stop, but on the other a constant threat to lure star players "jumping" their league contracts.

The ANL had rules that made it a model for Negro league ball up to that point in time. Bolden was given broader powers than either he or predecessor President Isaac Nutter had possessed in the old ECL, particularly in policing on-field attacks on umpires or other players. To keep a lid on salaries, rosters were limited to 14 players at the beginning of the season, with expansion to 16 per team by July.[27] The league also addressed the chronic early-season absences of players who had joined international barnstorming trips to the Far East and Hawaii, from which they often returned after the beginning of the Negro leagues season. This time, suspensions of one day for each late day in reporting were ordered, and made to stick.[28]

The ANL lived up to many of its goals. It had increased the number of African-Americans on its umpiring staff, enforced compliance with the official schedule, and fostered cooperation among the owners. But attendance was still down, finances were still a serious problem around the league as the Depression deepened, and 1929 would prove to be the ANL's only season.

NOTES

1. "Name This City for New League," *Atlantic City Daily Press*, April 28, 1922.
2. Michael Lomax, *Black Baseball Entrepreneurs, 1902-1931* (Syracuse, New York: Syracuse University Press, 2014), 251.
3. Neil Lanctot, *Fair Dealing and Clean Playing: The Hilldale Club and the Development of Black Professional Baseball, 1910-1932* (Jefferson, North Carolina: McFarland & Co., 1994), 93.
4. Ibid.
5. "Will Eastern Baseball Men Consolidate Their Interests?" *New York Age*, December 2, 1922.
6. "Colored Baseball Men in Sensational War of Words," *New York Amsterdam News*, January 17, 1923; "Chairman of Eastern Club Answers Charges of Foster," *Pittsburgh Courier*, January 20, 1923.
7. "Washington and Harrisburg May Join the Eastern League," Baltimore *Afro-American*, December 7, 1923.
8. "Many Changes Among Managers of Teams in Eastern League," *New York Age*, February 23, 1924.
9. Lomax, *Black Baseball Entrepreneurs*, 308.
10. "World Series October 3," *Chicago Defender*, September 13, 1924.
11. "Colored Baseball Magnates Sign National Agreement at Chicago," *New York Age*, December 13, 1924.
12. Ibid.
13. "Big Leagues Hold Annual Baseball Meeting," *Pittsburgh Courier*, December 13, 1924.

14. Ibid.
15. "Eastern League in First Meeting for Winter at Phila," *New York Age*, January 31, 1925.
16. Ibid.
17. "Baseball Magnates in Harmonious Meeting," *New York Amsterdam News*, January 20, 1926.
18. "Eastern League Defers Action on 1926 Schedule Until March 12," *New York Age*, February 27, 1926.
19. Lanctot, *Fair Dealing and Clean Playing*, 107-8.
20. "Eastern League Elects Nutter Pres. to Succeed Bolden," *Pittsburgh Courier*, January 22, 1927.
21. "Keenan at the Bat," *New York Amsterdam News*, June 29, 1927.
22. "Isaac Nutter Reelected President of Eastern Baseball League at Annual Meeting in Philadelphia," *New York Age*, February 18, 1928.
23. "Ed Bolden Explains Hilldale's Position," *Pittsburgh Courier*, March 31, 1928.
24. "Eastern League Collapse Far-Reaching in Its Effects," Baltimore *Afro-American*, April 28, 1928.
25. "Need of Baseball League in the East Apparent to Lovers of the National Game," *New York Amsterdam News*, August 15, 1928.
26. "Eastern League Formed; Grays Join," *Pittsburgh Courier*, January 19, 1929.
27. Lanctot, *Fair Dealing and Clean Playing*, 192-3.
28. "The Passing Review," Baltimore *Afro-American*, May 4, 1929.

— 1924 —
BIG DRAMA IN THE BIG APPLE

By Aimee Gonzalez

Introduction and Context

AS THE AMERICAN AND NATIONAL Leagues prepared for the 1924 winter meetings in New York City, drama laced the usual business agenda of trades, rulings, and discussion of regulations. The NL had faced trouble internally since the end of September, when its president, John Heydler, disclosed, first to Commissioner Kenesaw Mountain Landis and then to the NL club owners, that outfielder-first baseman Jimmy O'Connell of the New York Giants had attempted to bribe infielder Heinie Sand of the Philadelphia Phillies to throw games in the Phillies' last series of the season, against Brooklyn. This became known as the O'Connell-Dolan scandal (Albert "Cozy" Dolan was a Giants coach who was accused of urging O'Connell to offer the bribe[1]), partly for what purportedly happened and partly because some NL club owners wanted to keep it quiet.

The way this problem was handled caused rifts in the league and hindered business as usual. American League President Ban Johnson had accused the Pacific Coast League of having a gambling problem, and threatened to bring evidence to the AL board of directors. That alone antagonized William Wrigley Jr., the chewing-gum magnate and owner of the Los Angeles team in the PCL (as well as the Chicago Cubs), who dominated PCL policy-making. When Johnson also decided to publicize his hostile attitude about the National League and his feelings about how Commissioner Landis was handling the O'Connell-Dolan scandal, Wrigley was ready to declare war. Although Johnson's American League was going strong and had earned points with the public for its commitment to clean baseball, by the time the winter meetings began, quiet rumors had emerged that Johnson's dismissal was imminent.[2] Although this turned out not to be the case, it was a miracle that any business was accomplished at all, with attention focused largely on the issue of Commissioner Landis's judgment and authority pitted against Ban Johnson's assertions. Although there was extensive discussion of trades, "it seems that most of the owners and managers [were] willing to swap [only] provided the Statue of Liberty and Woolworth building [were] thrown in."[3] Against this backdrop, the NL convened on December 9 and the AL the following day. The leagues met for a joint session on Thursday the 11th at Commissioner Landis's instruction. Landis himself ultimately was unable to attend the New York meeting, and so the session adjourned with few conclusions reached until the following week in Chicago, at the Congress Hotel, when the commissioner would be able to participate.[4]

The week before the major league meetings, the National Association of Professional Baseball Leagues (the official name of the minor leagues) had a much smoother and more productive meeting, in Hartford, Connecticut. The Bond Hotel hosted a robust crowd from December 2 to 4, with strong representation from every minor-league club, as well as the major-league clubs. Headlining attendees included Bucky Harris, player-manager of the World Series champion Washington Senators, and George Sisler the St. Louis Browns' player-manager.[5]

Player Movement

National Association

Much of the commotion surrounding the National Association's meeting in Hartford had to do with business items; making deals proved to be much more challenging, although many did come to pass. The Boston Braves went into the meeting looking to acquire outfielder Ty Tyson of the Louisville Colonels, but could not make it happen. The Colonels' owner, William Knebelkamp, for his part was on record as frustrated at the way trading in general turned out, declaring that "we have had several deals on the fire, but everything has fallen through."[6]

Toledo Mud Hens president Joe O'Brien and manager Jimmy Burke also could not close any deals. Jack Dunn, manager of the Baltimore Orioles, finally had to record a no-sale on shortstop Joe Boley; after several seasons he still had no bids from the major-league clubs, which should have indicated that his price continued to be too high. There was considerable demand for first baseman Lu Blue from Ty Cobb's Detroit Tigers, but Cobb quickly clarified that Blue was not on the market. The meeting's course of events then consisted primarily of efforts to persuade Cobb to simply consider talking about a swap. Even Nashville Volunteers manager Jimmy Hamilton, widely known for his ability to close a deal, struck just one in 1924, purchasing pitcher Larry Bennett, who had been with Bridgeport.[7]

Some teams had better luck, however, including Jersey City. Manager Patsy Donovan signed free-agent right-hander Johnny Tillman before the Norfolk Tars had a chance to make him a better offer. The Boston Red Sox obtained Joseph Earl Lucey from Jersey City, intending to put him on the mound. Previously he had played both shortstop and in the outfield for the New York Yankees after college, then went down to the minor leagues and developed his pitching skills with Jersey City. Walter Mails, a left-handed pitcher for the Oakland Oaks, went to the St. Louis Cardinals, while the Indianapolis Indians acquired outfielder Sumpter Clarke and third baseman Elmer Yoter from the Cleveland Indians.[8] Cleveland sent infielder Frank Ellerbe to the Kansas City Blues. First baseman and outfielder Elmer Bowman went to the Birmingham Barons from the Seattle Indians, and Minneapolis Millers pitcher Eric Erickson went to the Toronto Maple Leafs. For all the difficulty in closing some of the desired traditional trade deals in Hartford, 1924 did see the first airplane-for-player deal, struck between Omaha Buffaloes president Barney Burch and St. Joseph (Missouri) Saints president Edward Tracey. Burch sent pitcher Roy Luebbe and catcher Fred Wilder to Tracey in exchange for the airplane; this was deemed to be legal.[9]

American and National Leagues

One deal had been agreed upon going into the meetings, between the Chicago Cubs and the Pittsburgh Pirates, which drew attention because it was a three-for-three player trade with no money involved. The Cubs obtained middle infielder Walter "Rabbit" Maranville, first baseman Charley Grimm, and pitcher Wilbur "Lefty" Cooper in exchange for second baseman George Grantham, right-handed pitcher Vic Aldridge, and rookie first baseman Albert Niehaus.[10] Grimm would eventually become manager of the Cubs and take them to the World Series three times.

The headline prospective trade was Washington's bid for star right-hander Urban Shocker of the St. Louis Browns, which became public in early November.[11] Clark Griffith, the Nationals' owner, was anticipating the departure of his longtime franchise player, pitcher Walter Johnson, as the latter had expressed an interest in buying into a minor-league team as manager-pitcher, and Griffith hoped to plug Shocker into Johnson's rotation spot. Connie Mack, the Philadelphia Athletics manager, had already struck a significant deal with the Pacific Coast League's Portland Beavers in November; he sent pitchers Dennis Burns and Bob Hasty, infielder Harry Riconda, outfielder Ed Sherling, and minor-league catcher Chuck Rowland, plus a cash consideration, to the City of Roses, all for just one man—catcher Mickey Cochrane, and it was expected that this would be finalized during the winter meeting.[12] It was also public knowledge that the Detroit Tigers were on the hunt for a new second baseman.

As it turned out, trading was tough in the major leagues as well—at the adjournment of the New York part of the winter meetings Detroit had not found anyone who met the specifications they wanted, and Washington did not get Urban Shocker. By the time the winter meetings finally concluded a week later in Chicago, Shocker was once again a Yankee—the Browns traded him for pitchers Joe Bush, Milt Gaston, and rookie left-hander Joe Giard, whom the Yankees had acquired from Toledo of the American Association.[13] In the meantime, Clark Griffith moved to protect his team from Walter Johnson's potential departure, stipulating that Johnson must acquire a significant interest in a Pacific Coast League club and present the contract to him for examination. Only if Griffith found the contract acceptable would Johnson be allowed to leave. (Johnson had engaged in talks with St. Paul, but let it go in favor of pursuing Oakland.) If no deal could be struck, Johnson would have to return to the nation's capital. *The Sporting News* called Griffith "the only club owner … who has ever consented to let a real star go while he was still useful without receiving a large equivalent for his services."[14] At the same time, as Johnson's search continued to run into dead ends, Griffith offered him two contract choices—one for a single season and one for two– both of which Johnson rejected. The Nationals went ahead and acquired right-handed pitcher Stanley Coveleski (a future Hall of Famer, just like Johnson) from the Cleveland Indians, in exchange for righty Byron Speece and rookie outfielder E. Carr Smith.[15] Although Griffith was willing to take a risk, ultimately Johnson did not buy into a club and stayed in Washington, where he enjoyed his final 20-win season in 1925 and led the team back to the World Series.

The Business Side

For both the minor and major leagues, 1924 was a busy year. Although the minors and majors met separately, on different dates and in different cities, much of their business agenda items overlapped.

National Association

The largest theme in the business discussions at the meeting in Hartford revolved around scaling back operations—capping salaries and reducing bonuses, and amending rules regarding the number of optioned players on a team roster.[16] Optioned players are those who can be moved freely between the major-league team and the minor leagues. The other key topic was the minor leagues' relationship with the major leagues, which included a serious reflection on how the minor-league system was structured and whether this structure continued to make sense. Then as now, the minor leagues functioned as a gateway to the majors. Unlike now, there was concern at the time that there were not enough aspiring ballplayers to fill the minor-league rosters. Although this was largely a matter of survival for the minor leagues, the major leagues clearly had a stake in the issue as well. The minor leagues realized that baseball was up against heavy competition for public interest—golf, and tennis, boxing, and college football were the sports of the day; Little League was a fledgling notion and would not gather the strength it needed to become organized for more than a decade. In order to engage those who did play the sport, and cultivate those who expressed an interest, the National Association's president, Mike Sexton, proposed a new level for amateurs, particularly those who were not yet eligible for the minor or major leagues. Dubbed Class E, this level would allow promising players in lower or community leagues to begin training with professional baseball staff and get a sense of what a career in baseball could be like. Having the National Association offer this class option would also allow these lower leagues to unload some of their financial responsibilities and thus reduce the risk of folding.[17] Pursuant to this discussion was how the minor-league rosters would be filled—specifically, the minor leagues felt that it should be their task to scout the "sandlots and colleges and [work with] undeveloped athletes" and that the major leagues should stay out of it entirely.[18]

In addition to its own business items, the National Association certainly could not ignore the storm brewing between the National and American Leagues, especially the comments from AL President Ban Johnson, whose allegations of gambling concerned the Pacific Coast League, one of the Association's own. After its meetings ended, the Association went public with a denunciation of Johnson, and took the extra step of reaffirming its confidence in Commissioner Landis's ability to head Organized Baseball.[19]

American and National Leagues

The business side of the major-league meetings opened with the establishment of sides—the NL's first order was to pledge unconditional support for Landis while condemning Ban Johnson's criticisms of him. However, the camps were not evenly divided—the AL also adopted a resolution supporting Landis and criticizing their president's public actions.[20] NL President John Heydler was unanimously re-elected, contrary to circulating reports that he was to be replaced.

Pitcher Walter Johnson received the AL Most Valuable Player award. The NL MVP award went to pitcher Dazzy Vance; having been decided prior to the meeting, this had only to be authorized. This award prompted outcry from the St. Louis chapter of the Baseball Writers Association of America, who believed that their second baseman, Rogers Hornsby, was the rightful recipient of the honor. The winners were decided by a committee consisting of baseball writers from each major-league city, and the St. Louis chapter asked that the two major leagues publicize the balloting process so that the writers could discern who had failed to include Hornsby on his list of winners.

When the New York portion of the meetings adjourned, the troubling, unresolved question was whether the two major leagues would be able to repair their relationship and move on. Efforts had begun, and before the Chicago half of the meeting it was reported that Ban Johnson had "shown a disposition to 'go along' with the magnates … but it remains for the commissioner and his cohorts to make this end possible."[21] However, until the eve of the Chicago meeting, there was speculation that if Landis and Johnson could not solve their difficulties, one of them would quit by the end of the day.[22] As it turned out, the AL backed its condemnation of its leader in New York with new action in Chicago, choosing to remove Johnson from the Advisory Council with a warning, in order to ensure peace between the commissioner and the AL. This effectively stripped Johnson of all power except that of fulfilling the immediate duties of his position. Detroit Tigers president Frank J. Navin replaced him on the Advisory Council.[23] Johnson did not resign, and neither he nor Landis spoke publicly of their conflict after the meeting adjourned.

This did not mean that others refrained from speaking publicly, and soon the owners who had voted to remove Johnson from the Advisory Council began to worry that he might change his mind and resign after all. Remorse set in—after all, Ban Johnson was the man who had led the effort to clean up baseball, turning it into a classy and respectable sport, worth watching as well as playing. He always had his eye on the big picture. In the words of one imaginative reporter, he "cleared the jungle, surmounted the fever-stricken and crocodile-infested swamps and carried a new, healthy legion safely to the promised land of success. He [had] been accused of being dictatorial … but when he pounded his fist [it was] for the American League."[24]

WHAT DOES "MOST VALUABLE" MEAN?

Rogers Hornsby won his fifth batting title in a row in 1924, a year that also happened to be the first year of the new National League award for the most valuable player.* (The American League started its incarnation of the award in 1922.)

When Dazzy Vance was chosen as the National League MVP in 1924, Branch Rickey expressed befuddlement.

"I can't understand on what basis the committee worked out its decision," Rickey said. "It was my understanding that the award was to have been given to the most valuable player in the league. The committee must have had a different understanding."**

Rogers Hornsby won the batting championship again in 1925, and this time won the award.

* "National League to Reward Stars," *New York Times*, February 13, 1924: 23.
** "Rickey Is Disappointed," *New York Times*, December 3, 1924: 17.

In Summary: Looking to the Future

The 1924 winter meetings proved to be anything but business as usual. Overshadowing much of the proceedings was the drama that unfolded between Commissioner Kenesaw Landis and AL President Ban Johnson. They butted heads over how the NL bribery scandal during that year's World Series was handled, and Johnson further exacerbated the baseball community when he decided to go after the Pacific Coast League for an alleged gambling problem.

Although he ended up being severely curtailed, Johnson did achieve his perpetual goal of sustained adherence to honest, clean baseball. Since the proportions to which the conflict grew made it unavoidably public, baseball was forced to start holding itself more accountable to its audience. Transparency facilitates fans' ability to relate to the sport, which in turn facilitates growth. Although the leagues' relationships may have continued to be tense going into 1925, their common goal of creating a sport on par with those that had already gained a strong foothold in American culture was much more likely to be reached after that tumultuous winter.

NOTES

1. O'Connell and Dolan were suspended for life by Commissioner Landis. Lowell Blaisdell, "Mystery and Tragedy: The O'Connell-Dolan Scandal," *The Baseball Research Journal* (SABR Baseball Research Journal Archive: 1982). research.sabr.org/journals/oconnell-dolan-scandal, accessed February 4, 2012.

2. The December 11, 1924, edition of *The Sporting News* discussed the continuation of the O'Connell-Dolan case and narrated the issues stemming from Ban Johnson's antagonizing public statements. It provided an illustration of the numerous relationships involved that caused these incidents to gather force.

3. "Big Leagues Hold Annual Meetings," *The Sporting News*, December 11, 1924.

4. "Landis Established as Czar of Baseball—Joint Meeting Adjourns to Next Wednesday in Chicago," *Boston Globe*, December 12, 1924. Commissioner Landis's wife had been admitted to the Mayo Clinic and her sister had died the week before the meetings.

5. Because of his sister-in-law's death, Landis did not attend the National Association meetings, but there was appreciation that he had intended to be there. Paul Rickart, "Looking 'Em Over at the Bond Hotel," *The Sporting News*, December 11, 1924: 3. Landis had failed to appear at all at the National Association meetings the year before, held in his home base of Chicago. His change of heart held promise.

6. Rickart.

7. Ibid.

8. Rickart: 8.

9. "Omaha Club Trades a Battery to St. Joseph for an Airplane," *New York Times*, December 3, 1924: 17.

10. Irving Vaughan, "Grimm, Cooper, and Maranville Traded to Cubs," *Chicago Tribune*, October 28, 1924.

11. Frank H. Young, "Nats to Make Bid for Urban Shocker, Vet Brown Hurler," *Washington Post*, November 11, 1924: S1.

12. "Mack Pays $50,000 for Coast Catcher," *New York Times*, November 18, 1924: 29.

13. The resulting lineup after this trade and commentary on the matter was treated in "It Could Be Worse, Sighs Connie Mack," *The Sporting News*, November 27, 1924: 1. "Shocker a Yankee; Traded for Bush," *New York Times*, December 18, 1924, also provides a summary of negotiations, an editorial on the Yankees having fared better in the deal, and a short history of Urban Shocker's previous stint with the Yankees.

14. "Griff Draws Line on Walt's Going," *The Sporting News*, December 4, 1924.

15. "Stan Coveleksie (sic) and Mike M'Nally Obtained by Nats," *Washington Post*, December 12, 1924: S1; "Sox Get Prothro in Trade for McNally: Coveleskie [sic] of Indians Goes to Senators for Speece and Outfield Rookie," *Boston Globe*, December 12, 1924.

16. "Minor Leaguers Meet Tomorrow," *New York Times*, December 1, 1924.

17. "Mike Sexton Expresses Need for Circuits of Class E Rating," *The Sporting News*, December 11 1924.

18. "Plenty of Action Expected at Minor League Conference," *The Sporting News*, November 27, 1924.

19. "Comment on Current Events in Sports," *New York Times*, December 8, 1924.

20. "Storm Session Looms When Baseball Moguls Gather for Annual Meeting," *Los Angeles Times*, December 9, 1924.

21. "Peace Seems to Rest in Hands of Landis," *The Sporting News*, December 18, 1924.

22. "Everybody Mum on Eve of Big Baseball Meet," *Chicago Tribune*, December 17, 1924.

23. "American League Owners Join National in Endorsing Landis," *The Sporting News*, December 25, 1924.

24. "Owners Now Seeing Error of Their Way," *The Sporting News*, December 25, 1924.

— 1925 —
DIFFERENT SCRIPT, SAME CAST

By Aimee Gonzalez

Introduction and Context

ONCE AGAIN THE AMERICAN AND National Leagues met in New York City, December 7 to 9, 1925. The stormy drama that engulfed the winter meeting proceedings in 1924 gave way to clear skies this winter, and it was expected to be business as usual based on last year's understood agreements. Hence the NL was taken completely by surprise when the same people from last year's AL emerged from their session at the Belmont Hotel on December 8 and announced that President Ban Johnson's contract had been thrown out and a new one drawn up that extended his term by five years, to 1935, with a $10,000 pay increase. AL magnates demonstrated regret after their 1924 decision to remove Johnson from the Advisory Board, which had effectively rendered him powerless in any matter not directly related to his role as president, and now made up for it with these actions.

Besides this seeming snub to the National League, the American League also drafted a change to the regular-season schedule that would have it end a week earlier in September than it had. The NL had also drafted a changed schedule and presented it for discussion at their session at the Waldorf Hotel on December 7, but it had games scheduled through the first week of October instead. This became another point of contention that caused Commissioner Kenesaw Mountain Landis to intervene at the joint session on the last of the three scheduled days of meetings, December 9.

Members of the National Association of Professional Baseball Leagues were busy in anticipation of their meeting at the St. Catherine hotel on Catalina Island, off the coast of California January 12 to 14, 1926 this was a far cry from the Hartford, Connecticut, scene of the prior year's meetings. In preparation for Cataline, the Pacific Coast League made extensive preparations so that the trek for the rest of the member leagues would be worthwhile. The PCL appropriated $3,500 for meeting expenses and it got cooperation from various chambers of commerce. Boating trips, golf, and souvenirs were planned to top off the lavish affair.[1] As a final touch, William Wrigley Jr., owner of the island as well as the PCL's Los Angeles Angels and the Chicago Cubs, staged the first-ever radio broadcast of baseball meetings.[2] The turnout was excellent and included Commissioner Landis, who made his first trip to California for this session.

Player Movement

National Association

Although there were a few trades between minor- and major-league teams, the majority of deals were among the minor leagues themselves, with at least 100 players changing places. The San Antonio Bears of the Texas League were the busiest, purchasing third baseman Tibbie Serre and outfielder George Bliss from Syracuse, pitcher William Ward from Fort Smith, pitcher Leon Drake from Hartford, pitcher Guilford Paulson from the St. Louis Cardinals, and second baseman John Henzes from Bridgeport. San Antonio sold outfielder Leslie Meyers to New Orleans and pitcher Earl Collard to Evansville. The Nashville Volunteers were also active, obtaining pitcher Charley Brown from Salisbury for pitcher Cliff Ross. Nashville also purchased second baseman Carrol Butler from Topeka and first baseman Otto Pahlmann from Danville. Nashville sold outfielder Yank Davis to Beaumont and infielder Frank Parkinson to Shreveport. A fan of the limelight, Houston's manager Joe Mathes began talking trades on the train out to Los Angeles. By the time he arrived he had managed to obtain pitchers Claude Davenport and Harold Haid from St. Joseph (Missouri) of the Western League for pitcher Lefty Schwartz, a player to be named later, and cash. Manager Mathes continued dealing on the island, acquiring pitcher Ken Penner from Wichita for outfielder Pete Compton, an optional release of pitcher John Berly, and a cash consideration.[3]

American and National Leagues

Money talks, and everyone was listening to what Chicago Cubs owner William Wrigley Jr.'s one million dollars might have to say when he sent President William Veeck Sr. to New York with a blank check and — as a result of having publicly declared his intention to spend[4] — Cubs fans' hopes in his suitcase. Unfortunately if a player is not for sale he cannot be bought, so Veeck did not walk away with the pitchers the Cubs needed. He did not leave completely empty-handed, though, re-signing infielder Clark Pittenger and closing deals for outfielder Joe Kelly, second baseman Clyde Beck and infielder Maurice "Red" Shannon from the minors. He also traded right-handed pitcher Vic Keen for Cardinals shortstop Jimmy Cooney. Although the value of these acquisitions did not come near the $1 million available to spend, the Cubs accomplished more than other teams. The Cardinals fared well, obtaining Keen, whom manager Rogers Hornsby had recommended strongly to club president Sam Breadon.

The Detroit Tigers also had a busy time of it with the minors, as they needed to square away an obligation to the Fort Worth Panthers, who had supplied Detroit with third baseman Billy Mullen. Owner Frank Navin, in response to Fort Worth's adamant request for an infielder and outfielder, first swapped third baseman Fred Haney to the Boston Red Sox for outfielder Ernie Vache and third baseman Homer Ezzell, and then sent the two to the Panthers. The Philadelphia Athletics transferred third baseman Francis Sigafoos and first baseman Jim Keesey to the International League Reading Keystones, while the Cincinnati Reds sold right-handed pitcher Neal Brady to another International League team, the Buffalo Bisons. Cincinnati manager Jack Hendricks made it known that he wanted to do what he could to help out Bill Clymer, his former sidekick on the Reds coaching staff, who was now the manager in Buffalo.

Pittsburgh, on the other end of the spectrum, acquired no new players through either trade or deal with other major-league clubs. Given their prevailing status as World Series champions, owner Barney Dreyfuss was not surprised — the common sentiment was that no one wanted to trade with the champions, fearing the prices would be too high and/or that the Pirates would not want to move anyone. They did, however, sell second baseman Lafayette Thomas to Buffalo. The Washington Senators also anticipated shedding a player — shortstop Everett Scott, who left baseball to pursue the bowling and billiards business in Indiana. Scott came back to baseball in 1926, spending time with the White Sox and the Cincinnati Reds before leaving the majors again, this time permanently.[5]

The Business Side

National Association

Some individual league meetings yielded decisions that would resonate with the Association as a whole when it assembled in California. The International League re-elected president John Conway Toole with a bit of drama, as Sam Robertson of Buffalo, the lone dissident, tried unsuccessfully to overturn the decision. The Eastern League decided to continue with a 154-game schedule and to restore the player limit to 16 after trying out a 15-player limit for the 1925 season.

Once all of the member leagues convened on Catalina Island, everything ran smoothly. Commissioner Landis gave a short speech on the way the baseball meetings used to be run, noting the improved relationship between himself and the Association, and between the member leagues themselves. And despite the long trip for some attendees, the eeting was one of the best-attended sessions ever.[6]

Although fanfare took center stage, a few key business items were addressed. President Michael Sexton was unanimously re-elected for a five-year term but discussion stopped there; no pay raise was discussed. The Association rejected the major leagues' proposal to extend the period during which a player could be optioned from two to three years. The Association maintained that two years was sufficient, and furthermore viewed an extension as an infringement on their ability to develop and sell their own players—in other words, it was another move by the majors to extend control, which the minors would not tolerate. The Association had also blocked a proposal the previous year that would have raised from 8 to 15 the number of 15 players a major-league team could send out on option. The delegates grappled with other matters of major-league/minor-league relations. Major-league clubs' selections were capped at 40 unless written notice was given of intention to release or reassign players (meaning that the limit stayed at 40). Payment to major-league clubs for players optioned to Class AA or A was to be maintained at $300, with a minimum of $100 for all other classifications. The meetings concluded with the dedication of the new tower at Los Angeles' Wrigley Field in memory of those who killed in the Great War.

American and National Leagues

After the previous year, the individual and joint sessions of the major leagues were fairly quiet, aside from the buzz of the multiple trades and sales going on between the majors and minors. The two big issues facing the major leagues were the calendar changes and the fallout from the contract extension and raise for Ban Johnson. This meant that Landis's term would be up for renewal before Johnson's, giving the latter a bit of a power edge. The uncertainty of what he might do with that leverage worried the commissioner. The AL also wanted to end the regular season a week earlier, thereby starting the World Series earlier. Bad weather was their primary consideration. The NL also proposed a change in the schedule, but wanted the season to end a week later, in the beginning of October, due to the laws against Sunday baseball prevalent at the time, as well as the weather in league cities. Although football had expanded beyond college campuses and walked into the baseball diamond—teams like the Cubs and the Giants were lending their space and some financial assets to the nascent gridiron teams, the Bears and (Football) Giants, respectively—the pro football season and potential conflicts with the baseball season were not a consideration. The major-league magnates had no reason (yet) to believe that football was a threat to baseball despite speculation from some sportswriters that fans' attention would be stolen in the offseason by this newly emerging version of the college pastime.

Another big agenda item, which was ultimately sent to the Joint Rules Committee for resolution, was the use of rosin in pitching. The National League proposed that this be permitted again, and the American League flatly opposed it.[7] The NL believed that it would improve the game and reduce the number of balls used. In conjunction with this conversation was discussion of the new baseball structure. The primary manufacturer for the major leagues had changed the composition of the ball's core, which was supposed to reduce home runs. (It did not.) It was made clear that this was done without league approval.

Another issue that ended up going to the Joint Rules Committee was a proposal from Pittsburgh Pirates owner Barney Dreyfuss that games halted by rain before the fifth inning be replayed from the point of interruption, rather than resumed.

Commissioner Landis had recently barred players from playing in offseason games after October 31. Intended largely for Single-A and Double-A player, a number of them would be prevented a number of them from playing in a Miami Winter League. (Player-managers such as George Sisler, Bucky Harris, and Frankie Frisch could get around the ban by only carrying out managerial duties for their Miami teams.)

The other extra-curricular venture that ballplayers were into at the time—guest writing for the press—was less of a problem for Landis, but did trouble the sportswriters, who felt it was an infringement on their role.

In Summary/Looking to the Future

The skies cleared for the 1925 winter gatherings. While the AL and NL returned to New York with no battle cries to be heard, the National Association went west to Catalina Island and William Wrigley's lavish hospitality. It was astounding, for the NL especially, to be in the same city exactly one year later with the

AL owners, who, now regretting how they had treated Ban Johnson, changed their tune entirely. Choosing to recall last year's sequence of events to defuse the showdown between Landis and Johnson as a force of hand by the NL (and conveniently downplaying their role), the AL now pushed back by rejecting the proposals for both the season calendar changes and pitching rules that the NL had put forth. It had to have stung, to say the least, when Landis ultimately sided with the AL on the calendar face-off after the NL had provided him with unwavering support the previous year in his battle against Johnson. The pitching issue was sent to the Joint Rules Committee for further debate; eventually it passed with a majority vote, and rosin bags started appearing in 1926.

Other than that, it was business as usual, with the minors especially experiencing a high volume of trade and dealing, and the majors spawning a high volume of gossip about what William Wrigley Jr.'s $1 million could buy.

Although the heart and soul of the winter meetings is the business among baseball clubs, this was the first year that football appeared on the scene, emerging as a professional market and gaining more media and fan attention going into 1926. The Chicago Cubs and New York Giants had embraced football in 1925, even making money from it, and if more clubs were not paying attention then, they would be soon enough.

SOURCES

In addition to the sources cited in the Notes, the author also consulted:

Addington, L.H. "Minor Meeting Runs Smoothly; Sexton Unanimously Re-Elected," *The Sporting News*, January 21, 1926.

Bray, E.D. "Speaking of Ill Luck, Prize Goes to Augusta," *The Sporting News*, December 17, 1925.

Chester, Carl W. "Bill Clymer Already at Work on His Bisons," *The Sporting News*, December 3, 1925.

Coates, Les. "Bill Lane Puts It Up to Yankee Officials," *The Sporting News*, December 10, 1925.

Davis, Ralph S. "Clarke Not Likely to Desert Pirates," *The Sporting News*, November 12, 1925.

—. "Clarke to Return as M'Kechnie's Aid," *The Sporting News*, December 17, 1925.

—. "Dreyfuss Leaves Door Trifle Ajar," *The Sporting News*, December 3, 1925.

—. "Pittsburg Cheers Our All-Star Team," *The Sporting News*, November 26, 1925.

Eaton, Paul W. "Clark Griffith Has Best Foot in Front," *The Sporting News*, January 14, 1926.

Gallagher, Matt. "Big Turn-Over Begun on Los Angeles Team," *The Sporting News*, December 24, 1925.

— "Los Angeles Dealing in Futures With Cubs," *The Sporting News*, November 12, 1925.

Greene, Sam. "One Thousand Stolen Bases? It Isn't Likely, Even For Cobb," *The Sporting News*, November 12, 1925.

—. "Tigers Make Deal But Get Nothing," *The Sporting News*, December 17, 1925.

Hale, C.E. "Providence Shift Completed," *The Sporting News*, November 26, 1925.

Harrison, James B. "Baseball Leagues Convene This Week," *New York Times*, December 6, 1925.

Isaminger, James C. "Philadelphia Fans Proud of Two A's," *The Sporting News*, November 26, 1925.

Jowers, Francis J. "All Not So Selfish in Game After All," *The Sporting News*, December 10, 1925.

Kennedy, Lou M. "Ernie Johnson Slated to Manage Portland," *The Sporting News*, December 3, 1925.

Loose, S.R. "Tulsa Oilers Will Give Backyard Another Try," *The Sporting News*, January 14, 1926.

M.A.C. "Virginia May Go Back to East Club Circuit," *The Sporting News*, December 10, 1925.

McBride, C.E. "Toole's Retention Victory For Dunn," *The Sporting News*, December 17, 1925.

O'Phelan, J.E. "Association Sent 22 Players to Big League Clubs in 1925," *The Sporting News*, November 26, 1925.

Pollan, H.L. "Breadon and Rickey In Control at Houston," *The Sporting News*, December 17, 1925.

— "Gainer Steers Clear of Managerial Cares," *The Sporting News*, November 12, 1925.

Powers, Francis J. "Fewster's Going Has Tragic Touch," *The Sporting News*, December 17, 1925.

R.I.L. "They're Getting Ready to Export Beaumont," *The Sporting News*, December 24, 1925.

Reichow, Oscar O. "If You Fail, Try, Try Again!" *The Sporting News*, December 17, 1925.

Rice, Thomas S. "'Resin Ball' Brings Friction in Majors," *The Sporting News*, December 24, 1925.

Riley, Don. "Jack Dunn Sells One, Asks Waivers on Four," *The Sporting News*, November 26, 1925.

Stoecker, Herbert J. "Eastern to Continue on 154-Game Program," *The Sporting News*, December 17, 1925.

Vaughan, Irving. "Be Gorra! Th' Cubs Are Changing Fast," *The Sporting News*, December 24, 1925.

—. "Cubs Give Up Hope in Hollocher Case," *The Sporting News*, December 10, 1925.

—. "Landis, In Effect, Approves 'Ghosting,'" *The Sporting News*, November 26, 1925.

—. "Veeck Tries to Keep His Word With Fans," *The Sporting News*, December 17, 1925.

Vila, Joe. "Huggins Is Wearing His Spurs Although It's Only December," *The Sporting News*, December 10, 1925.

—. "If There's Any Boiling to Be Done, Yankee Heads Will Do It," *The Sporting News*, December 24, 1925.

—. "Some Optics Smarting From Smoke of Big Ban's Victory," *The Sporting News*, December 17, 1925.

—. "When Baseball Men Were Bold and Heavier of Fist Often Told," *The Sporting News*, December 3, 1925.

Whitman, Burt. "Bob Quinn Answers Critics of Lee Fohl," *The Sporting News*, December 10, 1925.

—. "Braves Drop One Via Waiver Route," *The Sporting News*, November 12, 1925.

"Southern Club Owners Amend Player Limit," *The Sporting News*, December 17, 1925.

"Browns Purchase Fielding Sensation," *The Sporting News*, November 12, 1925.

"Caught in the Trade Winds Off Catalina," *The Sporting News*, January 21, 1926.

"Dove of Peace to Flutter Back as Baseball Moguls Gather," *Chicago Tribune*, December 6, 1925.

"Echoes from the Lobbies," *The Sporting News*, December 17, 1925.

"'Johnson Program' Is Carried Out at Joint Meeting of Major Owners," *The Sporting News*, December 17, 1925.

"Landis Puts Lid on Majors in Florida," *The Sporting News*, November 12, 1925.

"Major League Folks Gathering in New York for Seven Days of Anticipated Serenity," *Hartford Courant*, December 7, 1925.

"Minors Are Urged to Encourage Kids," *The Sporting News*, January 14, 1926.

"N.L. Wants Resin, But Not at Cost of Peace," *The Sporting News*, December 24, 1925.

"Otto Williams Joins Cardinals as Coach," *The Sporting News*, December 17, 1925.

"Phil Ball Weighs Top With Bottom," *The Sporting News*, December 24, 1925.

"Re-Election of Toole Opens 'Meeting Week,'" *The Sporting News*, December 10, 1925.

"Robertson Says Toole Was Not Voted Raise," *The Sporting News*, December 17, 1925.

"Sam Breadon Tells It to Rog With 'K's,'" *The Sporting News*, December 17, 1925.

"Sisler To Manage Winter Loop Team," *The Sporting News*, December 3, 1925.

NOTES

1. Matt Gallagher, "Royal Entertainment for Minor Delegates," *The Sporting News*, November 26, 1925.

2. Oscar C. Reichow, "Minors' Meet to be Broadcast," *The Sporting News*, December 17, 1925.

3. "Caught in the Trade Winds Off Catalina," *The Sporting News*, January 21, 1926.

4. Irving Vaughan, "Cub Fans Anxious Over That Million," *The Sporting News*, December 3, 1925.

5. Scott was only able to go to White Sox because he was able to secure his unconditional release from Washington. Washington couldn't send him to the minors because he was a 10-year tenured player. So, effectively, Scott forced their hand. Scott played more than 100 games in the minors in 1927 and 1928.

6. "Minor Meeting Runs Smoothly; Sexton Unanimously Re-elected," *The Sporting News*, January 21, 1926.

7. Rosin had been banned as part of the foreign-substance rule passed in 1920. The argument to allow rosin again focused on the idea that it made it easier for a pitcher to grip the curveball, avoiding slippage from sweat. Rosin received approval in January 1926, though the two leagues continued to disagree over usage through the 1926 season. See, for, example, "Big Leagues Will Permit Use of Resin," *Atlanta Constitution*, January 30, 1926.

— 1926 —
CHANGING OF THE GUARD

By Abigail Miskowiec

National Association of Professional Baseball Leagues

THE CITIZENS OF ASHEVILLE, NORTH Carolina, rolled out the red carpet for the minor-league meetings in 1926. The 25th annual meeting of the National Association was held December 7 to 9, with a record number of executives from both the big leagues and the NAPBL descending upon the Southern city in the Blue Ridge Mountains. With several committees formed by Asheville locals, visiting delegates were offered tours of the Biltmore mansion, a trip to Chimney Rock mountain, and a day on the golf links, among other recreations.

But a dark cloud hung over the meetings: NAPBL President Mike Sexton's son, Leo J. Sexton, had died just a few days before the assembly.

Rule Changes and Reelections

For years, the NAPBL had been looking to shut down winter baseball. The owners wanted players to rest during the offseason rather than risk injury in the winter leagues. In order to combat the issue, the NAPBL considered signing players to year-round contracts, but in the end, executives simply banned the practice outright. The ruling ended winter baseball in the Pacific Coast League and by several Eastern League clubs.

The next order of business was the re-election of several executives. Thomas J. Hickey was re-elected president of the American Association and given a pay raise of $2,000 annually for the life of his three-year contract. Association Secretary J.H. Farrell also reaped the benefits of the record-breaking year, earning a $5,000 raise. Herman J. Weisman replaced interim President D.J. Haylon as the head of the Eastern League.

Both major- and minor-league scouts attempted to organize during the NABPL meetings. They went so far as to nominate a president, longtime scout Eddie Herr, who declined the position by saying he was "too dumb."[1]

The Chicago Cubs used the meetings as an opportunity to announce major organizational changes. John Seys was promoted from secretary to vice president and, most notably, the name of Cubs Park was changed to Wrigley Field, in honor of owner William Wrigley Jr.

Major Moves Spurred by Aging Players

Several big-league managers attended the minor-league meetings in hopes of picking up the next star. Brooklyn Robins manager Wilbert Robinson made the trip to Asheville, as did Cubs manager Joe McCarthy. Robinson was rumored to be interested in infielder Billy Rhiel of Greenville (South Atlantic League), but no deals were made.

The St. Louis Browns raised doubts as to the future of star George Sisler by acquiring first baseman Guy Sturdy from the Tulsa Oilers. Sturdy would replace the future Hall of Famer in the final five games of 1927, ending Sisler's 12-year career with the Browns. The Philadelphia Athletics signed Dud Branom, the first baseman of the Kansas City Blues. However, Branom floundered in his one season with the A's before being sent back to the minors.

National League

Little was accomplished when the National League executives met at the Hotel Astor in New York. The bigwigs convened on December 14-15. The NL executives voted to re-elect Kenesaw Mountain Landis as the commissioner, setting up a battle between Landis and American League founder and President Ban Johnson when the two leagues met in Chicago. The senior circuit also tried to set a $20,000 limit on the amount that major-league teams had to pay for minor-league players, but this proposal was shot down in the joint meetings.

Rogers Hornsby Causes Trouble for World Champs

St. Louis Cardinals player-manager Rogers Hornsby and team president Sam Breadon were locked in a bitter feud during the 1926 NL meetings. Hornsby, who had just led the Cardinals to their first World Series championship, demanded a pay raise, despite collapsing statistically and physically down the stretch. He claimed he had received $33,000 on his player contract and no extra money as manager. Breadon refused Hornsby the three-year, $45,000-$50,000 contract he wanted. The bad blood between the two was so great that league President John Heydler threatened to get involved. Breadon found a cheaper deal when he hired catcher Bob O'Farrell as player-manager for $20,000.

A few days after the NL meetings wrapped up, Breadon traded Hornsby to the New York Giants for infielder Frankie Frisch and pitcher Jimmy Ring. Hornsby got his pay raise, and the Giants got a star to compete with the Babe. Unfortunately, the Cardinals weren't clear of Hornsby yet. The Rajah owned 12.5 percent of the franchise, having been a part of the group that purchased the club in 1925, and this posed a conflict of interest now that he was a Giant. Commissioner Landis stepped in and worked out a deal that saw Hornsby relinquish his stake in the team in return for a hefty sum.[2] Hornsby had the last laugh, too, when he finished 1927 as the league leader in runs and came in third in the MVP voting.

Managerial Changes for Pennsylvania Clubs

The Pittsburgh Pirates, one year removed from a World Series title, fired manager Bill McKechnie. In August 1926, Pirates players had attempted to oust vice president and assistant manager Fred Clarke. The coup resulted in team captain Max Carey being traded to Brooklyn. Veterans Babe Adams and Carson Bigbee were unconditionally released. The team's mid-season collapse and further internal strife seemed to be the cause of McKechnie's firing. President Barney Dreyfuss signed Donie Bush, a veteran manager and player, to one-year contract to helm the team. Fred Clarke announced his resignation from the team the same week.

In Philadelphia, Stuffy McInnis signed on as manager of the flailing Phillies, replacing Art Fletcher. The two-year contract marked a homecoming of sorts for McInnis, who first rose to stardom as a member of the Athletics' "$100,000 infield."

American League

A potential baseball war was looming over Chicago when the AL met on December 14-15, on the same days the National League magnates were meeting in New York. Landis's contract would end after the 1927 season, and Ban Johnson was angling for one last shot at power. However, the junior circuit followed the NL's lead and nominated Landis for another term. Johnson was thrown a bone and granted a position on the advisory board.

Original AL Stars Fade

Four future Hall of Famers from the early days of the American League found themselves in new positions heading into the winter meetings. After the 1926 season, the Chicago White Sox released 39-year-old player-manager Eddie Collins after a sharp decline in his speed on the basepaths. Collins had piloted the club for three seasons and was one of the few White Sox players to come out of the Black Sox scandal clean. On Christmas Eve Collins elected to return to where he had started his career and signed with the Philadelphia A's. Catcher Ray Schalk replaced Collins as player-manager.

On November 9 Ty Cobb resigned after six years as player-manager of the Detroit Tigers. Rumors that team president Frank Navin planned to fire Cobb prompted the retirement.[3] Cobb didn't stay retired for long. In February 1927 the 40-year-old signed a one-year, $60,000 contract, the largest in baseball history at the time, to join Collins on the Athletics.[4] The Tigers hired George Moriarty, an umpire and former player, to run the team.

BASEBALL'S BUSINESS: THE WINTER MEETINGS

The St. Louis Browns felt that their player-manager, George Sisler, was showing signs of decline. In 1926, at the age of 43, he batted under .300 for the first time since his rookie season. The Browns finished the season with a 62-92 record and fired Sisler as manager, although he was kept on as the starting first baseman. Dan Howley became the new manager.

Despite finishing second in the AL behind the New York Yankees, the Cleveland Indians released player-manager Tris Speaker. The former MVP, who had led the Tribe to the World Series title in 1920, signed as a free agent with the Washington Senators before the 1927 season and then joined Cobb and Collins on the A's in 1928 for what would be his final season as an active player. The Indians replaced Speaker with veteran scout and coach Jack McCallister. A once-promising prospect, McCallister started scouting for Cleveland after splitting his kneecap sliding into home in a benefit game. McCallister managed the Indians for one season (66-87) before Roger Peckinpaugh, the 1925 American League MVP and future general manager, stepped in.

The Boston Red Sox, mired in the worst decade in their history, accepted manager Lee Fohl's resignation at the close of the 1926 season. In his two years as manager, the Red Sox lost more than 200 games. Fohl cited rumors of changes in management as his reasons for leaving. Fohl's assistant manager, Lefty Leifield, also jumped ship, joining Moriarty in Detroit. Fohl replaced Dan Howley (the new manager of the Browns), as skipper of the defending International League champion Toronto Maple Leafs. The Red Sox summoned legendary manager Bill Carrigan out of retirement to pilot the 1927 club.

More Scandal Rocks Baseball

The national pastime is no stranger to controversy; the Black Sox Scandal is still remembered nearly a century later. Other transgressions have not achieved that level of fame. In December 1926 pitcher Dutch Leonard, whom the Detroit Tigers had released before the 1926 season, declared that he and Indians outfielder Smoky Joe Wood had conspired to fix a late-season game in 1919. Leonard bet $600 on the match while Wood bet $250, Leonard said.[5]

Leonard handed correspondence with Wood and Ty Cobb over to AL President Ban Johnson, who passed it up the chain to Commissioner Landis. Leonard said that Wood, Cobb, and Tris Speaker colluded to fix the results of the game so that Detroit would clinch third place in the pennant race (first and second being locked up by Chicago and Cleveland). According to Wood's letter, though Cobb had knowledge of the fix, he refused to put down money on the game. Cobb's letter denied all knowledge and involvement. Gossip tied the recent departures of Cobb and Speaker from their managing jobs to the allegations. Landis cleared both Cobb and Speaker of the charges.

As the investigation wrapped up, a new accusation roped Eddie Collins into the mix of the accused. Swede Risberg, one of the Black Sox, alleged that the White Sox paid $1,100 to members of the Detroit Tigers to throw a four-game series in 1917. Collins survived the Black Sox Scandal in 1919, but Risberg accused him of funding this fix.

Eventually, Landis exonerated all players and managers, but in the light of the rampant accusations, he suggested new rules to curb fixing of games.[6] He proposed a statute of limitations in line with federal and state laws to prevent decades-old accusations from surfacing. Landis also suggested one-year bans for players and managers found to have fixed games or to have bet on games in which the player or manager was not directly involved. Finally, Landis proposed a lifetime ban for anyone who bet on a game in which he was directly involved.[7] All of these proposals were adopted and they still exist.

Joint Meeting of AL and NL

The two major leagues met at the Congress Hotel in Chicago to settle the matter of the commissioner's tenure. Although both sides had earlier agreed to support Landis, the official announcement was reserved until the joint meeting. Landis's contract was renewed for a seven-year term, and he earned a raise to $65,000 per year.

The only other buzz from the meeting came when former Red Sox manager Bill Carrigan returned to the team after 10 years. Carrigan, Babe Ruth's first major-league skipper, had managed Boston's World Series winners in 1915 and 1916.

Conclusion

Despite rumors of tension between Kenesaw Landis and Ban Johnson, the 1926 winter meetings enjoyed a pleasant, peaceful atmosphere. The eight managerial changes set a record but caused few issues within clubs. The passing of the torch from the first American League stars to the next generation worried some, who thought the league would be overshadowed by the NL. However, the 1927 Yankees Murderers' Row lineup, and Connie Mack's great Philadelphia team from 1928 through 1933, would buoy the AL for years to come.

SOURCES

In addition to the sources cited in the Notes, the author also consulted:

"Charges Cobb-Speaker Bet on a 'Fixed' Game," *Boston Globe*, December 22, 1926: 1.

"McCallister Chosen to Pilot Indians," *Boston Globe*, December 12, 1926: B24.

"Fohl Resigns as Manager of Red Sox," *Boston Globe*, October 24, 1924: B23.

"Cobb Quits Tigers, Moriarity Manager," *Boston Globe*, November 4, 1926: 1.

"M'Kechnie Let Out as Pirate Manager," *New York Times*, October 19, 1926: 32.

"Dreyfuss Signs Donie Bush to Succeed McKechnie as Pirate Manager," *New York Times*, October 26, 1926: 32.

"Clarke Severs All Ties With Pirates," *Boston Globe*, October 29, 1926: 31.

"O'Farrell Agrees to Manage Cards," *New York Times*, December 28, 1926: 14.

"Deposing of 8 Major League Managers This Year Sets New Record in Baseball," *New York Times*, December 26, 1926: S4.

"Winter Baseball Banned By Minors," *New York Times*, December 10, 1926: 32.

"Minor Leagues Act to Curb Draft Law," *New York Times*, December 9, 1926: 35.

"Baseball Scandal Told in Nutshell," *Leatherneck*, February 1927: 47.

"M'Innis is Named Manager of Phils," *New York Times*, October 22, 1926: 25.

"White Sox Bought Four Detroit Games in 1917, New Charge," *New York Times*, January 2, 1927: 1.

NOTES

1 "Just Notes," *The Sporting News*, December 16, 1926: 3.

2 "Rogers Hornsby-Management Problems." sports.jrank.org/pages/2134/Hornsby-Rogers-Management-Problems.html.

3 "I owe a great debt to Cobb, but I am not willing to pay it by keeping Detroit in the baseball ruck." *New York Times*, October 25, 1926: 25.

4 The 1927 A's team would also feature Jimmie Foxx, Mickey Cochrane, and Lefty Grove, who helped lead the next generation of American League stars.

5 "Baseball Scandal Up Again, With Cobb and Speaker Named," *New York Times*, December 22, 1926: 1.

6 There is a lot more information available regarding the alleged bribe incidents, but they go beyond the scope of the winter meetings.

7 "Landis Exonerates Accused Players," *New York Times*, January 13, 1927: 30.

— 1927 —
A LITTLE ON THE DRAFTY SIDE

By Marshall Adesman

Introduction

DEEP IN THE HEART OF TEXAS, THE National Association of Professional Baseball Leagues (better known as the minor leagues) huffed and puffed at their major-league brethren and tried to … well … not blow the house down but remodel it into something they could live with more comfortably. But from New York, the majors basically told them the house was fine the way it was and if they didn't like it, they were free to move out and find their own place. It was a dispute that could have only one ending, but it was allowed to percolate for more than a year before becoming a major issue at the 1928 conventions.

The Eyes of Baseball Are Upon You

The minor leagues kicked off the annual series of winter baseball meetings when they gathered at the Baker Hotel in Dallas, Texas, on December 6. Not quite three years old, the hotel was looking for a position of prominence in a city experiencing a population explosion,[1] and was happy to play host to delegates from two dozen leagues, spread out from coast to coast.

The meetings began with a bang. Mike Sexton, president of the NAPBL, gave his annual State of the Minors address and went right after what he termed the big-league teams' indiscriminate signing of young players. This may sound strange to many twenty-first-century readers, but at that time players were generally signed by minor-league clubs, which would eventually sell them to teams in higher classifications, including the major leagues; this money often proved to be the difference between a profitable minor-league season and the need to find funds to make it through the winter. But big-league owners were beginning to think about cutting out the middleman — namely the minors — and Sexton decried the "mad scramble" for talent that made it "almost impossible for minors to recruit talent."[2] Sexton went on to say that the majors signed the bulk of these players at "inflated" salaries, more for trading purposes than for replacing aging stars, even though the young athletes were under the "gross misconception that professional baseball is the easy money route to prosperity."[3] He noted that these players were rarely placed on a major-league club's reserve list. Rather than call for an outright ban on the signing of young talent by the majors, Sexton proposed a rule that required an athlete to play at least one year with a minor-league team; in other words, he would be signed off the sandlots or the college campuses and first play in the minors before his contract could be purchased by any team in a higher classification.[4] It was, simply, a call to make a rule out of what had been heretofore the standard procedure.

But that wasn't the only thing Sexton had on his mind, or that was of concern to at least some of his constituents. More and more major-league or high-level minor-league teams were buying up control of lower NAPBL clubs, which was causing some rumblings of discontent from among the brethren. Sexton suggested that before it "leads to an open rupture,"[5] the majors and minors work out an arrangement to eliminate "some objectionable features,"[6] which he did not specify.

And this led directly to another point. The Major-Minor Agreement between the American, National, and minor leagues, which remains to this day as the governing contract that delineates exactly what is expected of all parties (now known as the Basic

Agreement), was originally drawn up and signed in 1920. But how long was it supposed to last? One part of the document mentioned seven years, another 25 years, and still another seemed to indicate that it was to be law throughout the life of the commissioner, Judge Kenesaw Landis.[7] Having reached the seven-year benchmark, many minor-league clubs were hoping, for one reason or another, that a new agreement could be legally negotiated, and thus formally charged their Committee on Constitutional Changes to draw up a recommendation that would then be carried to the majors.[8]

Sexton also proposed setting new population limits for minor leagues, to go into effect prior to the 1930 US census. His thought was that operation costs could be held down if the aggregate population requirements for all classifications (that is, adding together the number of people in each Double-A city, in each A-ball city, etc.) were raised, and those populations "confined to the corporate limits of (each) city, as determined by the Federal census."[9] His suggested numbers were 80,000-199,999 for Class D, 200,000-399,999 for Class C, 400,000-999,999 for Class B, one million to two million for Class A, and over two million for Class AA. He also recommended the establishment of a new Class E, which would total less than 80,000 and which, if adopted, might see the inclusion of some cities currently listed as Class D.[10] It is worth noting that a Class E never became a reality (except for the Twin Ports League, a four-team league in the Duluth, Minnesota-Superior, Wisconsin, area that began in 1943 and folded after six weeks).

John Farrell was officially the secretary-treasurer of the NAPBL (nowadays we would classify him as the chief operating officer), and every year he gave a report to the assembled executives on the season that had just ended. For 1927, Secretary Farrell announced that the minors began the year with 24 leagues and closed with the same 24, representing 174 cities. A total of 410 disputed cases were formally adjudicated by his office. Farrell also stated that in November he had journeyed to Washington to argue before the US House Ways and Means Committee against keeping the war tax on admissions, which had been in effect for a decade already, even though the fighting in Europe had ended nine years ago;[11] it must be noted that Congress officially ended this tax a few months later, in June of 1928.

An annual topic of concern was the drafting of players, and the Dallas meetings were no exception. Minor-league executives were basically opposed to any sort of draft, desiring, as mentioned, to sign their own talent and then freely sell them in an open market for the best possible price. Judge Landis and major-league moguls, however, favored an unlimited selection of players.[12] This dispute was not new and had, in fact, caused a rupture back in 1918,[13] but in 1925 a compromise was worked out that allowed players on the rosters of lower-level teams to be drafted by clubs in higher classifications. There was — of course! — an exception: the three Double-A organizations (the highest classification at this time), in addition to the Class-A Western League and the Class-B Three-I League, had raised enough of a fuss that they were allowed to operate under a "modified draft" system, in which players could be drafted only if they had already been sent down by a major-league team.[14] And now these five "renegade" loops hoped the other leagues would push the Committee on Constitutional Changes to recommend the modified system to the majors.

But the majority of NAPBL executives knew how the powerful and autocratic Judge Landis felt about this matter and were wary about antagonizing him; he already believed that some Double-A teams were using the draft to implement their own version of a farm system, which he vigorously and vociferously opposed.[15] They therefore voted to recommend to the majors a "standard" draft system, and furthermore ordered the five renegade leagues to fall into line,[16] which led to bitterness and the possibility of "war within the ranks of the National Association."[17]

Bitter feelings were also present on at least one other front. Two teams in the Class A Western League, Tulsa and Oklahoma City, were seeking to move into the Class A Texas League, a change prompted by geography and, no doubt, economics. In a classic "who said what?" the two clubs claimed that league officials had told them earlier in the year that they could depart as long as they found two other franchises ready to take their places, and St. Joseph, Missouri, and Pueblo, Colorado, were being offered as possibilities.[18] But now the Western League decided it would rather keep the two Oklahoma cities, which prompted outrage and a formal petition before the minor leagues' Board of Arbitration. Set up in 1902, this body primarily ruled on disputes between players and owners and had the power to hand out suspensions. Every year it seemed to have one major case thrown in its lap, and in 1927 it was this Western League conflict. The board's decision was that territorial rights were "one of the pillar principles of Organized Baseball," and thus Tulsa and Oklahoma City did not have the right to move into another league just because they wanted to do so.[19]

With all these internal battles being fought, it was still necessary to take care of the normal business of baseball. Fresh from its victory in the boardroom, the Western League looked toward the diamond and announced it would play a 168-game split-season schedule, beginning on April 12 and ending on September 23, followed by a best-of-five postseason featuring the champions of each half.[20] The Western was not the only league to opt for a split season, as the Pacific Coast (Class AA) and Southern Association and Texas League (both Class A) also went that route. In 1927, 10 of the 24 leagues had used that format, but in 1928 more than half chose to break up their seasons—16 leagues out of 29.[21]

The Central League had a legacy in the Midwest that stretched back to 1903, but it had been dormant for the previous five years, except for a few weeks in 1926.[22] But the announcement was made that it would be back in 1928 as a Class-B loop, featuring four Ohio cities—Akron, Canton, Dayton, and Springfield—plus Erie, Pennsylvania, and Fort Wayne, Indiana. The president of the (Class B) Three-I League, L.J. Wylie, would also helm the Central.[23]

There was speculation that the (Class B) Virginia League might go out of business, but that proved to be erroneous. While they did lose two North Carolina clubs—Kinston moved to the (Class D) Eastern Carolina League and Wilson dropped out of baseball—the four teams based in Virginia decided to operate as a compact, four-team league.[24] Meanwhile, the proposed Bright Belt League became the aforementioned (and more appropriately named) Eastern Carolina League, and featured the North Carolina towns of Fayetteville, Goldsboro, Greenville, Rocky Mount, and Wilmington, in addition to Kinston. William Bramham, already the president of the South Atlantic Association and the Virginia League in Class B and the Piedmont League in Class C, added the Eastern Carolina to his Durham-based portfolio[25] and, as we shall see, was about to begin exercising his growing influence.

Taking a page from Mike Sexton's address that opened the convention, the Louisville club of the American Association introduced a resolution that would prohibit any team in the Double-A loop from being owned by a major-league club. (The Cincinnati Reds' recent purchase of the Columbus franchise was specifically grandfathered in.) The motion was defeated, but a milder resolution was approved, which required a team to notify the league president 20 days in advance if a sale was pending. It was felt this would be enough time for the league to investigate the purchaser and, if deemed undesirable, to find a new buyer for the franchise.[26] In this way, the American Association felt it could keep itself free from big-league domination.

While the convention buzzed with activity, the city of Charleston, South Carolina, was simply trying to get its foot in the door. Representatives were quite visible in Dallas, telling everyone about the new 10,000-seat ballpark just built in the hopes the city could either become a major-league spring-training site or join the NAPBL. Despite being "hungry for baseball" with "interest now at a peak,"[27] the city, out of Organized Baseball since 1923, would not get back in until 1940.

Perhaps overwhelmed by the contentiousness of the Western League case, the Board of Arbitration decided to formally petition Secretary Farrell to move its annual assemblage to September, rather than during the Winter Meetings. They felt they had too much to do and too many cases to decide, and this may have subconsciously affected some decisions while also preventing the board members from missing some of the other business, as well as much of the fun, of the convention.[28]

Some player personnel moves did take place in Dallas, with perhaps the most prominent name being Francis "Lefty" O'Doul. A star pitcher in the minors, he injured his arm in a throwing contest held during his first spring training (1919) with the Yankees, which ultimately altered the course of his career. Always a good hitter, he took his chronically sore arm back to the Pacific Coast League after he was found wanting as a pitcher by both the Yankees and Red Sox and remade himself as a mediocre (at best) outfielder but one of the best hitters of his generation. He batted .375 for Salt Lake City in 1925, .338 for Hollywood in 1926, and .378 for San Francisco in 1927, with 33 home runs and 278 hits in 196 games,[29] winning the first Most Valuable Player Award ever given in the PCL.[30] Those gaudy numbers led to his being acquired by the New York Giants where, it was predicted, "he will become the ace pinch-hitter" if he did not become an outfield regular.[31] O'Doul went on to win two National League batting titles and fashion a career mark of .349, and in 1929 he collected 254 hits, still the single-season record in the senior circuit.

Another player with an interesting backstory was Harry "Socks" Seibold, a diminutive right-handed pitcher. First appearing in the majors with the Philadelphia Athletics, Seibold won just seven games over parts of three seasons and was eventually farmed out. Over the next few years he played in the minors (Pacific Coast League and Western League, to name just two), but he also played independent and semipro ball because, in his own words, "I made more money ... and I enjoyed it, too."[32] He may also have battled arm problems as well as authority as he bounced from coast to coast. Formally suspended by Organized Baseball for refusing to be sent to Nashville in 1924, Seibold continued to play independently until he was reinstated in the winter of 1927 and signed at these Dallas meetings by Reading of the (Class AA) International League.[33] He would have a tremendous season in 1928, going 22-8 before being one of five players sent by the Chicago Cubs to the Boston Braves for Rogers Hornsby. Pitching for the Braves in 1929 meant Seibold was making his first major-league appearance in a decade.

Determined to improve on their fourth-place finish, the Cubs had already picked up slugging outfielder Hazen "Kiki" Cuyler from Pittsburgh. They now struck a deal with Minneapolis for the American Association's strikeout leader, right-hander Pat Malone, a deal that included southpaw Jim Brillheart.[34] Malone immediately became the ace of the Cubs staff, winning 18 games in his rookie year, followed by back-to-back 20-win campaigns.

Several teams also hired new managers. Ray Kennedy, who had been the skipper at Charlotte of the (Class B) South Atlantic Association for the previous four years, went up the road to the league's Asheville team, and to replace him the Hornets brought in Heinie Groh.[35] The former New York Giants infielder, however, did not last the season in Asheville. Howard Gregory was another manager who moved to a different team in the same league, going from Wichita to Oklahoma City in the Western League.[36] William "Wild Bill" Rodgers moved up a level, leaving Peoria in the Three-I League for Little Rock of the Southern Association.[37] Like Groh, however, Rodgers would be fired before the 1928 season concluded.

For 16 years Frank Snyder was a major-league catcher, splitting his time almost evenly between the Cardinals and Giants; he was, in fact, the regular backstop when New York won back-to-back World Series in 1921 and 1922. But for each of the past two seasons he had collected fewer than 200 at-bats, so when the Cardinals, for whom he played in 1927, asked him if he wanted to pilot the Houston team in the Texas League, he jumped at the chance.[38] This proved to be a good move, as the Buffaloes won both the regular-season title and the postseason playoff. Snyder replaced Joe Mathes, who seems to have been fired by St. Louis but who landed on his feet by becoming the skipper of the Chattanooga Lookouts of the Southern Association.[39]

Like his Cardinals teammate Frank Snyder, outfielder Billy Southworth saw his playing time diminished in 1927, and at the age of 34 (a year older than Snyder), must have also begun thinking about life beyond his playing days, so he accepted the post of player-manager for Syracuse of the International League. Then a game of musical chairs began, with the Rochester franchise relocating to Montreal, which then enabled St. Louis to move its Syracuse farm team to Rochester.[40] Southworth simply went about his business and led the Red Wings to the pennant as a rookie skipper. It may have been his first taste of success but not his last, as he fashioned a long career that included four National League pennants, two World Series triumphs, and posthumous induction into the Baseball Hall of Fame.

Not all older players were able to land on their feet like Snyder and Southworth, and it was for them that the Association of Professional Ball Players of America was founded in 1924. Designed to help former players (both major and minor leaguers), umpires, coaches, scouts, even clubhouse men, who had fallen on hard times, the organization sought formal recognition from the NAPBL at the Dallas meetings. And the minors responded with a pledge of $5,000, made up of $750 from each Double-A league, $400 from the Class-A leagues and $300 from every Class-B league.[41] Written into the agreement was a clause stating that if the organization ever had $50,000 in the bank, the minor leagues would be relieved of their annual pledges unless it once again became necessary. The money would be controlled by Judge Landis, but Mike Sexton was appointed to serve as the minor leagues' official representative.[42]

In another example of thinking outside the box, the Shreveport team of the Texas League announced it was setting up a "clearing house" and selling subscriptions. Its purpose was to keep tabs on players who were released, and try to match up an athlete looking for work with a team that needed someone at his position. Shreveport was able to say it had already signed up 25 clubs, and hoped that more would join its fledgling effort.[43]

After all this activity, only one bit of business remained: the selection of a site for the 1928 meeting. By a vote of 13 to 10, Toronto defeated Chattanooga, effectively closing the minor-league portion of the 1927 Winter Meetings.[44]

A City That Doesn't Sleep

Far less emotional than the Dallas gathering, the major-league meetings took place in New York City December 13-15. The National League went first, holding its meeting at the Hotel Waldorf, followed the next day by the American League at the Belmont Hotel, and finally wrapping up with a joint session at the Roosevelt Hotel on the 15th.[45] John Drebinger, a *New York Times* baseball beat writer, did not expect anything "startling" to develop, and for the most part he proved to be correct.[46]

The Steering Committee of the two leagues met, for instance, and made no formal announcement, just one example of how quiet things were on the administrative front.[47] National League President John Heydler told his owners that a record number of baseballs were used in 1927, almost 52,000, and 86 games were postponed during the year, an all-time high for losing or rescheduling contests because of weather. Along those lines, he suggested that, in the interests of completing the entire 154-game schedule, late-season makeup games be permitted in two-team cities (New York, Chicago, St. Louis, Boston, and Philadelphia) even if the team(s) in the other league happened to be at home at the time.[48] Other stop-the-presses moments included the NL decision to continue using three umpires in every game, and the announcement of the dedication of the Mathewson Gateway, a 36-foot-tall structure at the Bucknell University athletic field.[49] Paid for in part by donations from major-league baseball, the NAPBL and even the Baseball Writers Association of America and named in honor of the school's most famous athletic alumnus, New York Giants great Christy Mathewson, the gate would be formally dedicated in June.[50] But the National League gathering was a veritable Mardi Gras when compared to the American League, whose lone bit of news was that it was the first Winter Meeting not dominated by the presence of Ban Johnson. The league's founder, once the most powerful executive in the game, had seen his standing and influence decline throughout the decade, and had resigned on October 17. Ernest Bernard, president of the Cleveland Indians, was chosen two weeks later to succeed Johnson and was now presiding over his first formal league-wide gathering.[51]

Things did pick up, however, when it came to player transactions, and then again when the two loops got together on the final day. First, a look at the deals.

The 1927 St. Louis Browns had finished with a 59-94 mark, which placed them seventh in the eight-team American League, 50½ games behind the "Murderer's Row" New York Yankees. Owner Phil Ball, no doubt embarrassed and frustrated and locked in a struggle with the crosstown Cardinals (World Series winners in 1926) for the region's entertainment dollar, authorized a series of moves to try to improve the team. Before the Winter Meetings, the Browns sent their best pitcher, Milt Gaston, plus fellow right-hander Sam Jones, to the Washington Senators for righty Dick Coffman and outfielder-first baseman Earl McNeely.[52] Upon arriving in New York, however, the Browns became Ground Zero for trade rumors, and foremost among them was the thought that they might deal their star player, George Sisler.

Sisler, of course, was one of the best players in the game, had batted .400 twice in his career and had set the major-league record (since broken) by collecting 257 hits in a season (1920). But he had been forced to miss the entire 1923 campaign with a severe sinus infection that impaired an optic nerve, which left him with chronic headaches and double vision.[53] Though he did return in 1924, he was never quite as dominant again and, despite his having batted .327 in 1927 with 201 hits and a league-leading 27 stolen bases, the Browns were aware that he would be 35 years old by Opening Day, and let it be known that he was available for the right price, news that dominated the baseball gossip. Nationally syndicated columnist Westbrook Pegler, covering the convention for the *Chicago Tribune*, hinted that Sisler had been the cause of discontent in the Browns' clubhouse.[54] The Senators and A's were rumored to have the edge over the Indians, Red Sox, and White Sox in the Sisler sweepstakes,[55] and ultimately that proved to be correct as he went to Washington. The price, however, surprised all—a straight cash deal for $25,000, with no players coming to St. Louis for a man who eventually entered the Hall of Fame with a .340 lifetime batting average.[56]

To replace Sisler, the Browns engineered a deal with Detroit, swapping outfielder Harry Rice, right-hander Elam Vangilder, and infielder Chick Galloway (who was joining his fourth team in less than a month!) to the Tigers in exchange for their first baseman, Lu Blue, and hard-hitting outfielder Henry "Heinie" Manush, the 1926 American League batting champion and a future Hall of Famer.[57] Then, to complete their makeover, the Browns sold aging slugger Ken Williams to the Red Sox for $10,000, and traded another outfielder, Edmund "Bing" Miller, to the A's for right-handed pitcher Sam Gray.[58] This meant that manager Dan Howley's starting 1927 outfield of Rice, Miller, and Williams would all be elsewhere in 1928, to be replaced by Manush, McNeely, and young Fred Schulte. It would also help catapult the Browns into third place with an 82-72 mark. Gray would win 20 games, a career best, and Blue and Manush would lead the offensive charge, especially the latter, who topped the AL with 241 hits and finished just two points behind Mickey Cochrane in the MVP balloting.

With Sisler headed for Washington, speculation began as to the fate of Joe Judge, who had been manning first base for the Senators since 1916. A year younger than Sisler, Judge wound up meeting the challenge—he batted .306 with 93 RBIs and finished right behind Manush in the final MVP tally. Well, what did that mean for Sisler? He played just 20 games in a Washington uniform before he was sold (for just $7,500) to the Boston Braves, where he turned in three good seasons before retiring.[59]

A couple of other future Hall of Famers were packing their bags. Though center fielder Tris Speaker had batted .327 for Washington, Senators owner Clark Griffith said he would be happy to release Speaker to any club that wanted his services.[60] While age may have been a factor—Speaker would be 40 by Opening Day—the fact that the penurious Griffith didn't try to at least make a sale is rather curious. Connie Mack signed Speaker and the Grey Eagle served as a backup outfielder for the A's before announcing his retirement. Meanwhile, young Red Sox right-hander Charley

"Red" Ruffing was being pursued by the Yankees. Boston president Bob Quinn said he was willing to listen to offers but was not interested in making a deal "for a lot of bench-warmers that aren't any use to the Yankees."[61] He wanted at least one regular from New York, which probably shied away from paying too steep a price for a hurler with a career record of 20-46. After another 50 losses, the Red Sox finally swapped the enigmatic righty to the Yankees early in 1930 for cash and utility player Cedric Durst, and Ruffing blossomed in New York, being a member of six World Series champions and winning 231 games over the next 15 seasons on his way to Cooperstown.[62]

In the National League, the Cardinals must have felt they needed to make a little noise to counteract all the Browns' activity. Right-hander Jimmy Ring and catcher John Schulte went to the Phillies for infielder Jimmy Cooney, outfielder Johnny Mokan, and catcher Clarence "Bubber" Jonnard.[63] They also bought catcher Frank Gibson from the Braves, but interestingly, none of these men saw any playing time in St. Louis in 1928. Having finished just two games behind Pittsburgh in 1927, the Cards already had one of the best teams in the league, and they would ride their great pitching staff to a second pennant in three years. Meanwhile, the Phillies—losers of 103 games in 1927—caused a bit of a ripple when owner Will Baker supposedly gave his new manager, Burt Shotton, $500 and told him to see what he could get in the open market.[64] Pegler reported that this "aroused an outcry ... that Mr. Baker was trying to buy a pennant ... contrary to the true competitive spirit of the great national game."[65] Pegler was no doubt writing tongue-in-cheek, because even in this pre-free-agency era, $500 would not buy very much, and the Phillies truly did get what they paid for as their 1928 loss total soared to 109.

There was one significant managerial change. After seven-plus years at Cleveland's helm and a World Series triumph in 1920, Tris Speaker was forced to resign under a cloud of suspicion after the 1926 season.[66] He was replaced by Jack McCallister, who had been what we would today term the team's bench coach throughout Speaker's reign, but the Indians finished a disappointing sixth with a 66-87 record, and McCallister was dismissed. There was a recurring rumor that Yankees coach Art Fletcher was the Indians' top choice, with one report stating that the Yankees simply needed to release Fletcher from his contract for this to become a fact.[67] But Cleveland general manager Billy Evans, a former major-league umpire, denied this report and Fletcher himself supposedly hinted to friends that he was not really interested in the position.[68] Evans ultimately went local and hired Roger Peckinpaugh, the veteran shortstop who had been the American League's MVP in 1925. Having made a name for himself as a youth on the Cleveland sandlots, Peckinpaugh became the regular shortstop in the Bronx at age 22, served briefly as Yankees manager late in the 1923 season, and helped the Washington Senators to back-to-back American League pennants and their only World Series triumph in 1924.[69]

The business of baseball was taken care of when the two leagues got together at the Roosevelt Hotel, with the draft dispute with the minors taking center stage. Knowing they had the upper hand, the majors told the NAPBL that they had no problem allowing the Major-Minor Agreement to expire as of January 14, 1928, which would mean both organizations would operate independently of one another and be in direct competition for talent. If that came to fruition, the majors would undoubtedly then set up their own minor-league network, making it completely unnecessary for them to buy players from NAPBL clubs. Answering the question as to the length of the agreement, the majors bluntly told the minors that the Major-Minor Agreement was in effect for "as long as Mr. Landis is Commissioner."[70]

While no one really expected this possible rupture to become a fact, the minors quickly responded. A three-man committee, consisting of NAPBL Secretary John Farrell, multi-league president William Bramham and (Class A) Eastern League President Herman Weisman, was quickly able to meet with major-league leaders and a small extension, to February 1, was agreed upon.[71] It was also decided that the two organizations would meet in early February to discuss the draft and the signing of new talent,[72] and it was later learned by Jack Ryder of the *Cincinnati Enquirer* that

Judge Bramham was the primary voice of reason and the person most directly responsible for "smoothing matters over."[73]

Two of the more prominent major-league managers took opposite views on the flap with the minor leagues. John McGraw of the New York Giants supported the majors' hard-line approach, feeling that the minors had it pretty good and "haven't got a kick coming." But Yankees skipper Miller Huggins countered that he thought relations between the two entities needed to be reorganized, and that major-league ownership of minor-league franchises was "inevitable."[74] Huggins compared baseball to the automobile industry, pointing out that Henry Ford produced cars cheaply because he owned the raw materials, and that baseball ought to follow that example and own the players and the minor-league teams for which they played. The influential voice of *The Sporting News* disagreed, however, saying such a plan would be "disastrous" and "would sound the death-knell for many minor leagues."[75] With the hindsight of almost nine decades, we can see that both sides were right—the NAPBL did shrink in size and has been totally dependent on the majors for more than half a century. On the other hand, the farm system has proved to be an excellent way to steadily and systematically develop talent.

At the 1926 Winter Meetings, the Cardinals had traded Rogers Hornsby to the Giants for Frankie Frisch (and the aforementioned Jimmy Ring), which opened up an unusual can of worms. It turned out that Hornsby also had a financial stake in the Cardinals, which meant that his loyalties could be divided when New York was playing St. Louis. The owners sought to remedy that by passing a rule expressly prohibiting any player from having a monetary interest in a club if he was not playing for that club. It also prohibited any nonuniformed baseball employee from having any financial involvement whatsoever in any major-league team, and prohibited any club or member of that club (player or nonplayer) from lending money or underwriting a loan to an umpire or any player on another team.[76] It was also resolved that if any player attempted to bribe another to "bear down" against a third team, he was to be suspended for three years, and the same would hold true for the man accepting such a bribe. A related resolution was passed that still reverberates today: If a player was caught betting on a game in which he and his team were not involved, he would be suspended for one year; if it concerned a game in which he and/or his team was playing, he would be banned for life.[77]

Several teams announced their spring-training sites for 1928: The White Sox, for instance, chose Shreveport, Louisiana, while the Indians opted to go a little farther south, to New Orleans.[78] After four years in Sarasota, Florida, the Giants decided to move their headquarters to Augusta, Georgia, because manager John McGraw was of the opinion that Florida was just too darned hot in March, and the change from those temperatures to the much cooler spring air found in New York could be the cause for many early-season injuries.[79] *The Sporting News* tended to agree, suggesting that even Georgia would be too warm and advocating that teams train in climates more akin to "that they would have to face in the first month or so of the regular season."[80] (One wonders what they would make of the modern Grapefruit and Cactus Leagues.) One person who would not be terribly concerned about spring-training sites was Hank O'Day. Having been a player, manager, and umpire for more than 40 years (including the previous three decades as one of the game's premier arbiters), O'Day retired but was hired for a newly created position in which he would scour the country in search of new umpiring talent.[81] The regular-season schedule was also made public, with Opening Day set for April 11 and the final game listed for September 30. This was the first time baseball released its playing dates before the new calendar year had actually begun.[82] The Senators, meanwhile, stated their intention to invite President Calvin Coolidge to throw out the first ball.[83]

Two small items are worthy of mention. When the major leagues met in joint session at the Roosevelt Hotel on December 15, one resolution they failed to pass was a recommendation from their Advisory Council for the establishment of a disabled list.[84] While modern fans take the lists, of various lengths, for granted, the disabled list would not be established until 1941.[85]

And while we have seen that John McGraw's feelings about Florida training sites have not been shared by succeeding generations of baseball people, he did hit the nail on the head when it came to getting clubs from city to city. At these 1927 meetings, he predicted that before too long, all major-league teams would do all of their traveling by air, saying "(i)t is the safest method of travel there is. … I shall be perfectly willing to transport my team by airplane as soon as they perfect ships with four or more motors."[86]

Summary

The minor leagues attempted to flex their muscles when it came to the Major-Minor Agreement in general and the draft in particular, but ultimately they lost out as the majors showed who was the dominant partner in this relationship. Longtime stars like George Sisler and Tris Speaker were coming to the end of the line, while new stars like Red Ruffing and Lefty O'Doul were ascending. And no one could predict that, in just two years, the Roaring Twenties would come crashing down, altering the minor-league landscape and, despite Judge Landis's strong objections, making the farm system a fiscal necessity.

SOURCES

In addition to the sources cited in the notes, the author also consulted:

Surdam, David G. *Wins, Losses, and Empty Seats: How Baseball Outlasted the Great Depression* (Lincoln: University of Nebraska Press, 2011).

apbpa.org/.

"League Scouts Under Fire at Baseball Meet," *St. Petersburg Times*, December 8, 1927.

Obenshain, Earl. "Majors Spend Vast Sum for Minor Talent," *The Sporting News*, December 15, 1927: 5.

O'Phelan, J.E. "New St. Paul Pilot? You Never Can Tell," *The Sporting News*, December 8, 1927: 1.

"Peck Emerges From Cover," *The Sporting News*, December 15, 1927: 1.

"Scribbled By Scribes," *The Sporting News*, December 22, 1927: 4.

NOTES

1 According to the 1920 US Census, there were, officially, 158,976 people in Dallas; by 1930, that figure would shoot up to 260,475, an increase of 64.4 percent. Jackie McElhaney and Michael V. Hazel, "DALLAS, TX," *Handbook of Texas Online* (tshaonline.org/handbook/online/articles/hdd01), published by the Texas State Historical Association, accessed January 10, 2015.

2 "Sexton Tells of Rookie Signing," *Boston Globe*, December 7, 1927: 26; "Minors Urge Curb on Scouting Evil," *New York Times*, December 7, 1927: 35.

3 "Minors Seek to Curb Scouts," *Washington Post*, December 7, 1927: 15.

4 Ibid.

5 "Minors Urge Curb on Scouting Evil," *New York Times*, December 7, 1927: 35.

6 Ibid.

7 "Minors in Doubt on Baseball Pact," *New York Times*, December 8, 1927: 37.

8 Ibid.

9 "Minors Seek to Curb Scouts."

10 Ibid.

11 "Secretary Farrell Reports to Minors," *The Sporting News*, December 8, 1927: 1.

12 Jerold J. Duquette, *Regulating the National Pastime: Baseball and Antitrust* (Westport, Connecticut: Praeger Publishers, 1999), 32.

13 Thomas A. Pendleton, "The 1919 Orioles," *The National Pastime: A Review of Baseball History* 21 (2001), 83-84.

14 Robert L. Finch, L.H. Addington, and Ben H. Morgan, eds., *The Story of Minor League Baseball* (Columbus, Ohio: The Stoneman Press, 1952), 27. The Double-A leagues were the American Association, the International League, and the Pacific Coast League.

15 Ibid.

16 "Five Circuits to Discontinue Draft System," *St. Petersburg Times*, December 9, 1927.

17 "National Association Nullifies Modified Draft System," *The Sporting News*, December 15, 1927: 3. It should be noted that it was not until 1931 that the minor leagues finally capitulated to Landis and the major leaguers (Duquette, 33).

18 Fred Turbyville, "Tulsa-Oklahoma City Must Remain in Western League," *The Sporting News*, December 8, 1927: 1.

19 "'Headliners' of Dallas Meeting," *The Sporting News*, December 15, 1927: 3. The Western League did bring Pueblo into the fold for the 1928 season, replacing the franchise in Lincoln, Nebraska, which dropped down to the Class-D Nebraska State League. And by 1933 both Tulsa and Oklahoma City were finally able to migrate to the Texas League.

20 "Minors Urge Curb on Scouting Evil."

21 "Casual Comment by the Observer," *The Sporting News*, December 15, 1927: 4.

22 An attempt was made to revive it in 1926, but by mid-June its four teams were absorbed by the (Class B) Michigan State League. W. Lloyd Johnson and Miles Wolff, eds., *The Encyclopedia of Minor League Baseball, 2nd edition* (Durham, North Carolina: Baseball America, Inc., 1997), 244.

23 "Minors in Doubt on Baseball Pact."; "Central League Comes Back," *The Sporting News*, December 15, 1927: 4.

24 Turbyville; *The Encyclopedia of Minor League Baseball, 2nd edition*.

25 "Piedmont Meeting This Week," *The Sporting News*, December 15, 1927: 5.

26 "Scribbled By Scribes," *The Sporting News*, December 15, 1927: 4; "Minor League Split on Ownership Rule," *New York Times*, December 5, 1927: 31; Turbyville.

27 "Charleston Runs a Temperature," *The Sporting News*, December 15, 1927: 5.

28 "Board Seeks Early Date," *The Sporting News*, December 15, 1927: 5.

29 Due to the good California weather, the PCL played extended schedules in those years.

30 Brian McKenna, "Lefty O'Doul," sabr.org/bioproj/person/b820a06c, undated, accessed February 13, 2015.

31 "Turns Around—Comes Back," *The Sporting News*, December 8, 1927: 1.

32 Terry Bohn, "Socks Seibold," SABR Baseball Biography Project sabr.org/bioproj/person/0dae01bf, undated, accessed December 1, 2014, and February 13, 2015.

33 "War Cloud Looms Up As Big Leagues Meet," *The Sporting News*, December 15, 1927: 1.

34 "Minor Leagues Fight Present Draft System," *St. Petersburg Times*, December 8, 1927.

35 Ibid.

36 "Secretary Farrell Reports to Minors," *The Sporting News*, December 8, 1927: 1.

37 Ibid.

38 "Managers For Two Card Sub-Stations," *The Sporting News*, December 15, 1927: 1.

39 H.L. Pollan, "Houston Is Surprised, But Well Pleased With New Deal," *The Sporting News*, December 15, 1927: 5.

40 "Managers For Two Card Sub-Stations."

41 "Minor Leaguers Behind Plan to Aid Sick-Aged," *The Sporting News*, December 15, 1927: 3.

42 Ibid.

43 Ibid.

44 "Rebounds From the Baker Lobby," *The Sporting News*, December 15, 1927: 3.

45 John Drebinger, "Major Leaguers Meet This Week," *New York Times*, December 11, 1927: S1-2.

46 Ibid.

47 James R. Harrison, "Trade Winds Blow as Magnates Meet," *New York Times*, December 13, 1927: 35.

48 James R. Harrison, "Manush and Blue Sent To Browns," *New York Times*, December 14, 1927: 36.

49 Ibid.

50 Ibid.

51 John Drebinger, "Major Leaguers Meet This Week"; Mark Armour, "Will Harridge," SABR Baseball Biography Project sabr.org/bioproj/person/111c653a, undated, accessed November 29, 2014, and February 15, 2015.

52 "Genuine Bravery, Believe It or Not," *The Sporting News*, December 22, 1927: 4.

53 Bill Lamberty, "George Sisler," SABR Baseball Biography Project sabr.org/bioproj/person/f67a9d5c, undated, accessed February 17, 2015.

54 Westbrook Pegler, "Cards and Phils, Browns And Tigers Trade 10 Men" *Chicago Tribune*, December 14, 1927: 25.

55 James R. Harrison, "Manush and Blue Sent to Browns," *New York Times*, December 14, 1927: 36.

56 "Genuine Bravery, Believe It Or Not."

57 Ibid. Galloway had spent his entire major-league career with the Philadelphia A's until the beginning of December, when he was traded to Milwaukee of the American Association. Three weeks later the Double-A team sent him to St. Louis, where the Browns then used him to land Blue and Manush.

58 Ibid.

59 baseball-reference.com.

60 Frank H. Young, "Player Market at New York Is Closed," *Washington Post*, December 16, 1927: 17.

61 James R. Harrison, "Trade Winds Blow as Magnates Meet."

62 baseball-reference.com.

63 "Majors Agree With Minors That New Deal Is Fair Enough," *The Sporting News*, December 22, 1927: 3.

64 Westbrook Pegler, "Cards and Phils, Browns And Tigers Trade 10 Men."

65 Ibid.

66 Speaker and Ty Cobb were accused of conspiring to fix a game back in 1919. While officially exonerated, both men were "persuaded" by Ban Johnson to give up their player-manager posts. Don Jensen, "Tris Speaker," SABR Baseball Biography Project sabr.org/bioproj/person/6d9f34bd, undated, accessed February 17, 2015. Also see Gerald C. Wood, *Smoky Joe Wood: The Biography of a Baseball Legend* (Lincoln: University of Nebraska Press, 2014), 249-254, and 288-291.

67 "Minor Leagues Fight Present Draft System."

68 "Fletcher Not Tribe Manager," *St. Petersburg Times*, December 9, 1927.

69 As of 2016 Peckinpaugh was still the youngest manager in major-league history, having compiled a 10-10 mark at age 23. "Roger Peckinpaugh, American League's Veteran Shortstop, Indian Manager," *Hartford Courant*, December 11, 1927: C-1; Peter M. Gordon, "Roger Peckinpaugh, SABR Baseball Biography Project sabr.org/bioproj/person/829dbefb, undated, accessed February 17, 2015.

70 James R. Harrison, "Majors Would End Pact With Minors," *New York Times*, December 16, 1927: 10.

71 Ibid.

72 "Majors Agree With Minors That New Deal Is Fair Enough."

73 "Tactful Bramham Stilled the Storm," *The Sporting News*, December 22, 1927: 1.

74 John Drebinger, "Major Leaguers Meet This Week."

75 "Scribbled By Scribes."

76 "Majors Agree With Minors That New Deal Is Fair Enough"; Westbrook Pegler, "Magnates Close Confab In Blaze of Resolutions" *Chicago Tribune*, December 16, 1927: 27.

77 James R. Harrison, "Majors Would End Pact With Minors."

78 Irving Vaughan, "Only One Nick Put in Commy's Wallet," *The Sporting News*, December 15, 1927: 1; "Secretary Farrell Reports to Minors," *The Sporting News*, December 8, 1927: 1.

79 "Casual Comment by the Observer."

80 Ibid.

81 Westbrook Pegler, "Cards and Phils, Browns And Tigers Trade 10 Men."

82 "Major League Schedule Out," *Los Angeles Times*, December 2, 1927: B-1.

83 "Majors Agree With Minors That New Deal Is Fair Enough."

84 John Drebinger, "Major Leaguers Meet This Week."

85 Corey Dawkins and Rebecca Glass, "Collateral Damage—The Disabled List: A History," Baseball Prospectus, baseballprospectus.com/article.php?articleid=15967, February 3, 2012, accessed February 18, 2015.

86 "McGraw Predicts Travel by Plane," *St. Petersburg Times*, December 9, 1927.

— 1928 —
THE DRAFT MESS AND GLIMPSES INTO THE FUTURE

By Silvio Sansano and Marshall Adesman

Introduction

THE ANNUAL BASEBALL WINTER meetings of 1928 took place in three cities. The National Association of Professional Baseball Leagues (the minors) went north for its 27th annual convention, filling the King Edward Hotel in Toronto from December 5 to 7. The chief topic of conversation was a continuation of 1927's primary sticking point, the drafting of players by teams in higher classifications, including the major leagues. The National League met on December 10 and 11 at the Waldorf Astoria Hotel in New York, and American League moguls were in Chicago's Congress Hotel on December 11 and 12. Just for good measure, all major-league owners got together at the Congress Hotel on December 13, with Commissioner Kenesaw Mountain Landis presiding. At that session a surprise topic was a radical idea unexpectedly proposed by John Heydler, president of the National League.

Northern Exposure

The minor-league gathering in Toronto was described as "the biggest meeting the minor leagues ever held."[1] There were, in fact, some 500 delegates to this convention, including a large contingent of major-league "observers,"[2] who were there for two reasons: to make trades or at least begin talking about deals that might be completed the next week when the big leaguers met in New York and Chicago; and to see what sort of draft recommendations the NAPBL would put forth.

As usual the first order of business was the annual report by Secretary-Treasurer John Farrell, in which he announced that 208 teams in 30 leagues had qualified for membership in 1928; three leagues folded during the course of the season while one failed to start altogether.[3] President Mike Sexton, in his annual address, deplored the fact that some smaller leagues could not afford to journey to the convention and suggested that future gatherings be held in central locations, like West Baden, Indiana.[4] This recommendation was eventually rejected by the membership when they selected Chattanooga, Tennessee, as the site for their 1929 meeting.[5]

As you might expect when so many people are gathered in the same place, a great deal of activity took place on several fronts, including rumors that proved to be unfounded. There were reports, for instance, that Harry Williams, president of the Pacific Coast League (Class AA), was investigating the possibility of putting together a new league that would feature cities in Washington state and western Canada and would serve, in effect, as a farm for his PCL. On the other side of the country, John Toole, president of the Class AA International League, said that George Stallings, the manager of the 1914 Miracle Braves of Boston, would return to the helm of the Montreal Royals. Stallings had been forced by health concerns to step down during the 1928 season. As it turned out, the PCL rumor was untrue, and Stallings died just five months after the meetings.[6]

By and large the Toronto meetings proved to be a lively affair, with several former major leaguers signing to manage in the minors, including former New York Giants teammates Jack Bentley and Heinie Groh, who took over York (Class-B New York-Pennsylvania) and

Hartford (Class-A Eastern), respectively.[7] George Burns, who had played in the Polo Grounds before Bentley and Groh, agreed to manage Springfield in the Eastern League, while Eugene "Bubbles" Hargrave, the first catcher to win a major-league batting championship (he hit .353 with Cincinnati in 1926), was sent to St. Paul of the Class-AA American Association as manager, with right-hander Paul Zahniser going to Cincinnati in return.[8] Former White Sox skipper Clarence "Pants" Rowland took charge of the Nashville Volunteers of the Class-A Southern Association; former Yankees infielder Fritz Maisel moved into the Class-AA Baltimore Orioles' (International League) dugout; and Steve O'Neill also went to the IL as the leader of the Toronto Maple Leafs. This proved to be the first of numerous managerial assignments for the former catcher, highlighted by a World Series triumph with Detroit in 1945.[9]

There were some interesting twists to a handful of managerial assignments. Former major-league righty Allan Sothoron became a first-time skipper, with Louisville of the Class-AA American Association. This took place, however, after Bert Niehoff had already been told the job was his! Nowadays one would expect a noisy lawsuit, but the former Atlanta Crackers leader landed on his feet by joining the New York Giants as a coach.[10] Future Hall of Famer Tris Speaker hung up his spikes to manage Newark in the Class-AA International League. Speaker having been Cleveland's player-manager for eight years (and winning the 1920 World Series), it was natural to assume, as Francis Powers did in *The Sporting News*, that "(it) will only be a matter of time until Spoke is recalled to the majors as a manager."[11] It never happened, however, and after the 1933 season Speaker was only occasionally involved with baseball.

Other managerial moves found Wilbur Good agreeing to lead Atlanta in the Class-A Southern Association, Frank "Pop" Kitchens taking the reins in Tampa (Class-B Southeastern League), and Lester "Pat" Patterson going to Dubuque of the Class-D Mississippi Valley League.[12]

There were also some small player transactions generated in Toronto that involved men whose names have pretty much passed into history. For example, a couple of Pacific Coast League teams made moves: The Los Angeles Angels sold the rights to second baseman Gale Staley to Portland for cash, and the neighboring Hollywood Stars purchased outfielder Joe Bonowitz and infielder Hod Kibbie.[13] A couple of trades involved players who would make more of a mark in succeeding years. The Red Sox shipped infielder Billy Rogell and right-hander William "Slim" Harriss to St. Paul of the (Class-AA) American Association in exchange for catcher Alex Gaston and outfielder Russ Scarritt.[14] While Scarritt had a couple of good seasons in Boston before washing out, Rogell would resurface in Detroit in 1930 and became the starting shortstop for the Tigers' back-to-back American League champions of 1934 and 1935. The Tigers sent three players to Toronto of the International League in exchange for first baseman Dale Alexander and righty John Prudhomme, plus cash.[15] Prudhomme won exactly one game for Detroit but Alexander was a solid hitter, compiling a lifetime batting average of .331. He led the AL with 215 hits in 1929 and won the batting title in 1932 with a .367 mark. (He started the season with the Tigers and was traded to Boston in June.)

In other action, the Class-C Piedmont League allowed its teams to carry as many as four rookies on their 14-man rosters, up from two in 1928. It set its season to end on the Saturday after Labor Day, after which the top two teams would play a best-of-seven series to determine the league champion.[16] Former major-league executive Joe Cantillon became the American Association's umpire-in-chief, while Dale Gear was re-elected president of the Class-A Western League.[17] International League President John Toole was also re-elected, but his powers were cut. A move to oust Toole was thwarted by a compromise in which a three-man executive committee was appointed to take over most presidential duties, making Toole little more than a figurehead.[18]

Several teams announced spring-training sites. Rochester of the International League moved from Monroe, Louisiana, to Plant City, Florida, while Buffalo announced it would be in Palmetto, Florida. The Dallas Stars of the Texas League, having given the White Sox permission to train in their park, said they would work out the kinks in Corsicana, Texas.[19]

The Washington Senators announced that they would train in Tampa, Florida, but the Southeastern League, of which Tampa was a member, told Washington owner Clark Griffith that it would either like a share of the Sunday gate receipts, or be allowed to play a couple of Sunday exhibition games. Griffith was not interested in turning over any money, and reminded the mayor of Tampa that he had a lease on the playing field and, what's more, had paid off the team's debts in 1927 in exchange for his current spring-training arrangement. The Old Fox got his way—money always speaks loudly—but he did not forget. After training in Tampa in 1929, the Senators moved their spring base to Biloxi, Mississippi, in 1930 and then to Orlando in 1936, where they stayed for many years, except for the travel-restricted World War II seasons of 1943-1945.[20]

An entire league got stonewalled. A proposed revival of the Michigan-Ontario League was put off when NAPBL Secretary John Farrell informed organizers that there were financial claims still outstanding against one or two of the proposed franchises.[21] An Ontario League came into being in 1930 (does this mean that the cities at fault were in Michigan?), but it folded after just one season. And a team tried to stonewall its association, as the Piedmont League had to hold up many of its operations –especially creating its schedule—while waiting for the Greensboro Patriots to try to come up with $3,500 to guarantee that it would be able to operate in 1929.[22]

Several franchises were openly for sale. The Baltimore Orioles, a training ground for so many great players over the years, including Babe Ruth and Lefty Grove, went on the market after owner Jack Dunn died in an accident just weeks before the Toronto meetings.[23] Akron of the Class-B Central League was also available, as was Columbus (Georgia) of the Southeastern League, which announced it was taking sealed bids.[24] In Nashville, owner Rogers Caldwell was buying out his partners so he could become the sole owner of the Southern Association's Volunteers. Since he was a close business associate of the Yankees' principal owner, Jacob Ruppert, this led to speculation that he would sell all or part of the club to the reigning World Series champions, or at least sign on as one of their affiliates.[25] The Yankees, meanwhile, bought control of the Syracuse team in the Class-B New York-Pennsylvania League, and were poised to take charge of the Chambersburg club of the Class-D Blue Ridge League, while across the Harlem River, the Giants purchased "a controlling interest" in Bridgeport of the Eastern League.[26]

All of this, however, took a back seat to two important pieces of business. One was the rule that allowed a franchise to control the territory for 10 miles around it (from home plate, to be specific). This was brought up because there was talk of placing teams in Kansas City (Kansas) and Windsor, Ontario. The 10-mile rule was invoked by Kansas City (Missouri) of the American Association and the Detroit Tigers in the American League, blocking any new club.[27] Dale Gear, president of the Western League, fearing the rule would be successfully challenged in court, suggested that an exception be permitted when a state line was crossed. This would have allowed the Western League to move to Kansas City, Kansas. His idea was voted down.[28]

While the 10-mile regulation was important and had long-lasting ramifications, it was the draft rule that was the talk of Toronto. Adopted seven years earlier in order to help guide relations between teams in the majors and minors, it was now proving to be a bone of contention within the NAPBL itself. Most minor-league teams were in favor of unlimited selection of players, allowing a team from a higher classification to claim the contracts of players from teams in lower classifications. At that time the modern farm system was not only just in its infancy, but was openly discouraged by Commissioner Landis. Selecting players from a lower classification was an established method for bringing fresh talent to the higher-level club and for providing the lower-level team with much-needed cash. But the three Double-A leagues, plus the Western League (Class A) and Three-I League (Class B), preferred a different approach, lobbying for a system in which players could be drafted only if they had already been sent down by a major-league team.[29] This greatly favored the top classifications, making it less than popular with the majority of the NAPBL rank-and-file.

Judge William Bramham, who was the head of three minor leagues and would later become president of the NAPBL,[30] brought a compromise to Toronto. Bramham suggested that if a player had originally been signed into a league in which the draft was in effect, he would always be subject to the draft, no matter where he had played in any given year.[31] In this way, all leagues would be treated equally when it came to drafting players.

Baseball's five-man Advisory Council also weighed in with a proposal. This committee was made up of Landis, John Heydler and Ernest Barnard, presidents of the National and American Leagues, respectively, and Mike Sexton and John Farrell of the NAPBL. Under their proposal, a major-league team could option up to 12 players to the minors (up from the 1928 limit of eight); it could sign no more than four players without any minor-league experience in 1929, three in 1930 and then just two thereafter; no Double-A player could be drafted by a major-league team if he had not been in Organized Baseball for at least four years; and higher draft prices, originally proposed in 1926, would be adopted.[32]

Neither of the compromises could muster enough support. In fact, despite the fact that a majority of teams and leagues favored unlimited selection, the power wielded by the three Double-A leagues and their two lower-level cohorts prevented the NAPBL from making a firm decision in Toronto. It was decided that the matter would be dealt with at a separate conference dedicated solely to resolving the issue. Mike Sexton's favorite gathering spot, West Baden, Indiana, was chosen as the site for a January 10 meeting that would feature three representatives from Class AA, one from each Class A league, and five other men to speak for all the other classifications. The major leagues would also be asked to send people to West Baden so that their interests could be heard.[33]

Before leaving Canada, the delegates were treated to a speech by Commissioner Landis, who paid tribute to Toronto, acknowledging the importance of its recreational and sporting development, and thanked all Canadians for their efforts during the Great War.[3434] And with that, having deferred the important draft issue for another month and having already chosen Chattanooga to be the site for the 1929 confab, the lively NAPBL meetings came to a close.

New York State of Mind

The National League set up shop at New York's swank Waldorf-Astoria Hotel on December 10 for two days of meetings preparing for the 1929 season. Early speculation on personnel changes centered on the local teams. Having finished just two games behind the Cardinals in the 1928 pennant race, Giants manager John McGraw decided he needed a little more pitching and set his sights on one of two right-handers deemed expendable by the Cincinnati Reds, Dolph Luque and Peter Donohue. The *New York Times's* John Drebinger, one of the leading sportswriters of his day, stated explicitly that the Giants had "virtually ... closed a deal with ... the Reds" that would bring either or both of these veterans to the Polo Grounds,[35] no deal came to pass. Meanwhile, in Brooklyn, there were rumors that Wilbert Robinson, who had been managing the Robins since 1914 (and had been team president since 1925), might lose both of those posts. Since they won the pennant in 1920, the Robins had finished in the first division only once, and the frequent odd occurrences that took place during their games had made them better known as the Daffiness Boys than for being serious pennant contenders.[36] Two of Robinson's veteran players, outfielder Max Carey and shortstop Dave Bancroft (both future Hall of Famers) were rumored to be interested in taking over the team's managerial duties if Uncle Robbie got the sack.[37]

None of that scuttlebutt proved to have any substance. Brooklyn did make news, though, by completing a major trade, sending southpaw Jess Petty and infielder Harry Riconda to the Pittsburgh Pirates for shortstop Glenn Wright.[38] This immediately brought up the question of Bancroft's future in Brooklyn, but Robinson said he planned to keep him because "he is too good a man to let go."[39] Robinson kept his word on Bancroft but would lose the presidency a year later, and was fired as manager after the 1931 season, and replaced by Max Carey.

There was one other deal involving a notable name. After an eight-year absence, Boston brought shortstop Rabbit Maranville back to his original club, purchasing his contract (and that of outfielder George Harper) from the Cardinals.[40] Despite having just turned 37 years old, Maranville would be the Braves' everyday shortstop for the next three years before moving over to second base for his final two seasons as a regular, on his way to a 1954 Hall of Fame induction.

A few other people made some news during these NL meetings. One of the league's most distinguished umpires, Bill Klem, resigned.[41] While no official reason was given, two stories circulated. One was that he was upset over not having been asked to officiate at either of the past two World Series; the other said his continuing problems with the Giants, which included serious threats to his safety, prevented him from continuing in the post he had held since 1905.[42] Writing in *The Sporting News*, Joe Vila commented that the future Hall of Famer was "a capable, fearless and honest official," and that league President Heydler "will persuade him to change his mind, for his permanent retirement would be a detriment to the National Game." And in fact Heydler did prove to be successful in keeping Klem around, with the Old Arbitrator staying on until 1941, when he became the National League's umpire-in-chief until his death in 1951.[43]

While Klem was, temporarily at least, eager to give up the life of an umpire, another person eagerly embraced it; The Pacific Coast League sold the contract of arbiter George Magerkurth to the National League. A former professional boxer, he would become known over the next 19 years for being cantankerous and pugnacious, and was indirectly responsible for the addition of a screen attached to the inside of the foul poles.[44] At the time of his move to the NL, the *Christian Science Monitor* rather amusingly wrote that Magerkurth "has been an efficient umpire on the coast. His name, however, is too long. ... (W)hen he comes to the majors he will be known as 'Mager.'"[45] He actually was called "Mage" throughout his career.

Judge Emil Fuchs had been part of a small group, fronted by Christy Mathewson, that had purchased the Boston Braves in 1922. Mathewson was scheduled to be the team president but when his tuberculosis made that impossible, Fuchs assumed the role. In 1928 the Braves lost 103 games under two managers, and when dire financial straits forced Fuchs to sell off his star player-manager Rogers Hornsby, Fuchs announced that he would manage the club in 1929. Modern-day commissioners might have stepped in and told him no (Bowie Kuhn did just that with Ted Turner), but Landis didn't say a word and Fuchs would lead the Braves to a 56-98 record in 1929, good for dead last in the National League. In 1930 Bill McKechnie was the manager; Fuchs sold the team in 1935.[46]

A couple of old catchers found major-league employment. Hank Gowdy, whose .545 batting average and five extra-base hits had led the Miracle Braves to a World Series triumph in 1914, returned to the team as a coach.[47] And Gabby Street, whose chief claim to fame as a player had been catching a baseball dropped from the Washington Monument in 1908, was signed to be a manager in the Cardinals' farm system.[48] He had been leading minor-league teams since 1920 and had spent the previous three years in the Class-B South Atlantic League. The new connection benefited Street. McKechnie's Cardinals had won the pennant in 1928, but were swept by the Yankees in the World Series. St. Louis fired him and hired Billy Southworth to be their skipper; Southworth added Street as one of his coaches. Things did not go well for the defending champs (who finished fourth), with Southworth being booted after just 88 games in favor of McKechnie. Deacon Bill, however, bolted for Boston at the end of the season, at which time Street was handed the reins and won back-to-back National League pennants in 1930 and '31, topped by a World Series triumph in the latter year.

In administrative matters, Heydler reported that NL attendance for 1928 had fallen below 5 million, a decrease of 400,000 from 1927. To no one's surprise, he was re-elected as league president.[49] In a very forward-thinking action that still resonates today, National League owners decided that all of their fields needed to have telephone hookups between the dugouts and the press boxes.[50] Two pieces of business were deferred until a meeting to be held in New York in February. Boston residents had just voted, by better than three to one, to allow Sunday baseball. The City Council was required by law to wait at least 30 days before they could act, but they were expected to ratify the voters' overwhelming decision, which would, naturally, affect the 1929 schedule.[51] Also placed on the agenda for February was the rule about interference and blocking a runner, especially at home plate, which was based on a Cubs-Giants game played at the Polo Grounds in late September.[52]

The Cubs sent several players down to the minors. One eventually resurfaced and etched his name into the record books. Earl Webb was a left-handed-hitting outfielder who had been a part-time player for the Cubs when they sent him to their Los Angeles farm team.[53] After a big year on the Coast, Webb found his way to the Red Sox, and in 1931 he cracked out 67 doubles, as of 2015 still the major-league single-season record. It would not be the last time that a player thrived, even for a short time, after leaving Wrigley Field.

Other items needed to be dealt with, but since they would affect both leagues, they were held for the joint session scheduled for later in the week. So the NL owners found their way to Chicago while their American League counterparts prepared for their own meeting.

Let's Make a Deal

The final day of the National League meeting, December 11, was the first day for the AL conclave, held at the Congress Hotel in Chicago. Perhaps because of the league's competitive imbalance—the Yankees had won 101 games in 1928 and the A's had won 98, but only one other club (the Browns) had finished above .500—there were few trades of note in addition to the Dale Alexander deal, which had already been completed at the minor-league convention.

The player who generated the most interest was Red Sox third baseman Buddy Myer, who was being eyed by several clubs. Myer had originally come up with Washington, but was traded to Boston early in the 1927 season and proceeded to become one of the top infielders in the game, batting .313 and stealing a league-leading 30 bases. The last-place Red Sox were in the midst of rebuilding and were willing to part with Myer, though according to Washington owner Clark Griffith, Boston wanted "a whole flock of players for him."[54] With several suitors, it was no wonder that Red Sox president Bob Quinn could place a high price on Myer, and the much-anticipated deal was completed on December 15 (shortly after the meetings concluded), with the winner being the Senators (or Nationals; both names were used by sportswriters of the era). Five players were sent to the Red Sox for Myer: right-handed pitchers Hod Lisenbee and Milt Gaston, infielders Bob Reeves and Grant Gillis, and outfielder Elliot Bigelow.[55] Despite the odds, Washington came out way ahead in this deal. The two pitchers both had losing records in Boston, with Gaston losing 20 games in 1930 and leading the league in wild pitches twice. Reeves was handed the third-base job and batted just .248 in 1929 before becoming a part-time player, while Gillis and Bigelow made marginal contributions before heading back to the minors. For Washington, however, the addition of Myer solved long-term infield problems. Third baseman Ossie Bluege was moved to shortstop, but when he was injured, young Joe Cronin entered the lineup and began his Hall of Fame career. In 1930, Bluege went back to third base and Myer moved to second, where he would become one of the top players of the 1930s, helping the Senators reach the World Series in 1933 and winning the 1935 American League batting title with a .349 average.

Washington also traded Bucky Harris, who had not only played second base for the Senators since 1920 but had also been their manager since 1924, to Detroit for infielder Jack Warner, who wound up never playing an inning in the nation's capital but instead split the 1929 season between Toledo and Brooklyn. Harris's playing career was at its tag end, but he would manage in the majors almost continually until 1956. The Senators also announced that Walter Johnson would not pitch in 1929. The Big Train had been hired two months earlier as the team's new manager (replacing Harris), and had not been an active player for more than a year. Johnson, who had managed Newark of the International League in 1928, would in fact never throw another competitive pitch again.

The Cleveland Indians were also active in Chicago. First general manager Billy Evans sent $50,000 to the San Francisco Seals of the Pacific Coast League for hard-hitting outfielder Earl Averill.[56] Averill injected instant offense into the Indians lineup, batting .332 with 18 home runs (including one in his first major league at-bat) and 96 RBIs in his rookie season, and he went on to be a six-time All-Star and a 1975 Hall of Fame inductee. The Indians sent money and a couple of players to Kansas City (American Association) for 34-year-old left-hander Jim Zinn, who hadn't pitched in the big leagues since 1922.[57] That deal didn't pan out, as Zinn went 4-6 with an ERA of 5.04, and spent 10 more years in the minor leagues. Finally, Evans pulled the trigger on the second big trade of the AL meetings when he sent 29-year-old right-hander George Uhle to Detroit for shortstop Jackie Tavener and pitcher Ken Holloway. Uhle had been a mainstay in Cleveland, winning 20 or more games three times, including two years when he led the league in victories. But he had been under .500 for two straight seasons and, in spite of also being a good hitter (a .286 average with 17 RBIs in 1928, and a .289 lifetime average), he was thought to be a poor influence on a couple of players, which paved the way for the trade.[58] The deal worked out a little better for the Tigers than for the Indians. Holloway won just seven games in a Cleveland uniform, Tavener batted just .212, and both were back in the minors by 1931. Uhle had a good year in 1929 but was mediocre after that. One of the long-term outcomes of this trade, however, was that Uhle was credited with the invention of the slider. Pitching batting practice against teammate Harry Heilman one day, Uhle experimented with a new pitch, releasing the baseball off his middle finger. Heilman had never seen that pitch before and thought it was a new curveball, but Uhle said, "Hey, that's not a curve. That ball was sliding."[59]

At least three clubs were thinking spring: The Giants declared they would train in San Antonio, while the Tigers said they would be in Phoenix. The Red Sox announced that they would head back to Bradenton, Florida, for the second straight spring, and they were also debating the merits of offering a contract to a college outfielder named Ken Strong. Strong was the Bo Jackson of his era, a multidimensional football star at New York University who excelled as a running back, placekicker, punter, and passer, and was expected to join the NFL after graduation. Like Jackson (and John Elway and numerous others), Strong wound up playing both sports, and was elected to both the college and professional football Halls of Fame. He played three years of minor-league baseball — probably to help supplement his income — while starring in the NFL.[60]

Under the category of "sound and fury," Yankees manager Miller Huggins let it be known that he was willing to "dismantle" his club if he could complete certain trades.[61] Over the years many teams have been torn apart, but rarely after winning a World Series (the 1997 Florida Marlins immediately come to mind), but Huggins, for whatever reason, was threatening to do just that. It did not happen; the Yankees, in fact, made no significant changes heading into 1929 and won a very respectable 88 games, good enough for second place. Huggins died suddenly just before the season ended.

The Future Is Just Around the Corner

On December 13 the two leagues met together under the overall auspices of Commissioner Landis, in the same Chicago hotel, the Congress, that had just played host to the AL moguls. Landis was unequivocally opposed to the minor leagues serving as a farm system for the majors, believing that this system, dubbed "chain-store baseball," restricted player movement. So when it came to his attention that several teams already owned or controlled minor-league clubs and several more were thinking of following suit, he asked for all owners to give him an accounting of their current or potential holdings.[62] It was unclear what the commissioner planned to do with this information; indeed, if he was working behind the scenes to maintain the independence of the minor leagues, he failed completely. The one matter that had been the chief issue in Toronto was quickly shot down—both major leagues agreed that they would not attend the draft conference the minors had scheduled for January which, according to *The Sporting News*, "was equivalent to telling the minors to get busy and straighten out the troublesome question among themselves."[63] (The minors quickly canceled their West Baden meeting and issued a statement that the draft rules would remain the same for the immediate future, which did not thrill the Double-A leagues, who hinted at a possible secession from the NAPBL.[64] Cooler heads eventually prevailed.)

With one other exception, the one-day joint session took up administrative matters of interest to both leagues. Having suffered through a series of springtime postponements and subsequent doubleheaders later in the season because of inclement weather, the leagues decided that the 1929 season would begin and end a week later, running from April 16 until October 6. It was recognized that this would bring baseball into conflict with football, but that was felt to be a necessary evil.[65] *The Sporting News* applauded this move, saying there would be plenty of room for the complete schedule to be played without doubleheaders being crammed into September,[66] and added this interesting comment: "*If there is a World Series* (italics added) it will be an easier matter to arrange it in October. ..."[67]

A rule change ended the practice of minor-league teams selling a star prospect to a friendly major-league club for a high price, having the player returned at a later date and then, when it put him back on the open market, forcing another big-league club to pay the already established price. In addition, the leagues banned the signing of any player under the age of 17, and set a pricetag of $7,500 on any first-year player.[68]

The magnates agreed to donate $50,000 to the American Legion to help finance a tournament of junior ballplayers.[69] It was also agreed that the major leagues and minor leagues would each donate $5,000 a year for the next five years to the Association of Professional Ball Players, an organization that had been formed to help out former players who were struggling financially.[70]

And beyond the discussion of the schedule and playing into the football season, there were other glimpses into a future era. The Baseball Writers Association of America appointed a committee to speak with the American and National League presidents to discuss ways to improve the scoring system. The BBWAA was hoping to get the leagues to hire independent and impartial people to serve as official scorers at all games so that its members would not feel beholden to any major-league club.[71] It would take more than 50 years to effect this change.

Then there was the suggestion made by National League President John Heydler. Never previously mistaken for a radical or Bolshevik, at the joint meeting Heydler surprisingly asked the assembled owners to consider an idea that would, quite simply, revolutionize the game. Saying only that he wanted to "give club owners ... something to think over ... at a future meeting," Heydler suggested turning the traditional starting nine into a 10-man team with the addition of a permanent pinch-hitter for the pitcher, i.e., a designated hitter.[72]

It is impossible to determine, all these years later, what made Heydler think of this, but it certainly had the capability of changing the game in a variety of ways. Managers would have to rethink the batting order from top to bottom, while pitchers would need to focus only on pitching. It was thought that some outfielders might protest against this idea, since for many years the outfield had been the last haven for an aging slugger. On the other hand, good-hitting pitchers (like George Uhle) might also object, since they enjoyed swinging the bat. Most pitchers, however, took little batting practice, so they were not very well prepared when they stepped into the batter's box. They also wasted a lot of energy running the bases, thus possibly hurting their effectiveness when they got back on the mound. Heydler asserted that quite frequently a pitcher was replaced by a pinch-hitter not because he was tiring, but because it was simply his turn to bat, and his idea would allow managers to keep an effective pitcher in the game.[73] Heydler also believed that hurlers would be able to improve their pitching skills if they did not have to worry about hitting, and he also thought his idea could help speed up the game.[74]

Heydler also speculated that minor-league clubs could possibly benefit from the new rule change. The majors were often reluctant to spend upward of $50,000 for a great hitter who was not nearly as good in the field. With this designated-hitter rule, a player's defensive shortcomings would be a secondary concern, making it possible for minor-league teams to ask for, and receive, top dollar for top batting prospects.[75]

Heydler's revolutionary proposal, however, fell flat at the joint meetings. No one from the American League expressed any interest, with new Tigers manager Bucky Harris saying it would ruin baseball and Indians skipper Roger Peckinpaugh adding that a "manager would not have a chance to do any masterminding."[76] The National League supported their leader, and the *Washington Post* found that the idea had its supporters and detractors among fans interviewed at random.[77] But it had its impact: In an editorial, *The Sporting News* wrote that "there may come a time when such a departure (from tradition) is welcomed without anybody shrinking with fear. ..."[78] And that time would come more than 40 years later, on April 6, 1973, when Ron Blomberg of the New York Yankees faced Luis Tiant of the Boston Red Sox as the game's first designated hitter.[79] The DH is now used in virtually every league and conference, from kids games to the major leagues; ironically, it is not in effect in the National League, despite having first been proposed in 1928 by its president, John Heydler.

Summary

In contrast with many previous gatherings, the 1928 Winter Meetings were filled with hot topics and a couple of major transactions, plus numerous managerial hirings on the minor-league level. The battle over the draft, the possible introduction of Sunday baseball in Boston, the increasing development of the farm system, and the overlapping schedule with football were all matters that would evolve as the years went on, but chief among them was John Heydler's shocking idea to institute a designated hitter. Though it took more than four decades for this proposal to become a reality, Heydler proved to be a baseball visionary, and his initiative has left a lasting legacy on all levels of the game.

SOURCES

In addition to the sources cited in the Notes, the author also consulted:

Anderson, David. "Bill Klem," SABR Baseball Biography Project, sabr.org/bioproj/person/31461b94, undated, accessed August 16, 2014.

Baseball Library 2006. "Charlton's Baseball Chronology—1928." baseballlibrary.com/chronology/byyear.php?year=1928#November (accessed May 29, 2011).

Cooper, George S. "Middle Atlantic Makeup Stands," *The Sporting News*, December 6, 1928: 2.

Davis, Ralph. "Garden Directors Approve Sharkey-Stribling Go; Klem to Remain," *Pittsburgh Press*, January 15, 1929: 35.

Drebinger, John. "Baseball Sessions Carded This Week," *New York Times*, December 9, 1928: S-2.

Drebinger, John. "Detroit Gets Dale Alexander and Prudhomme from Toronto in $100,000 Deal," *New York Times*, December 6, 1928: 42.

Dunkley, Charles W. "Heydler's Idea Unsound, Is Decision," *Washington Post*, December 13, 1928: 15.

Greene, Sam. "Detroit Jumps Into Big Money to Beat Off Rival Major Bidding," *The Sporting News*, December 13, 1928: 1.

Pegler, Westbrook. "Ghost Hitters for Pitchers is New Plan for Old Idea," *Washington Post*, December 23, 1928: 15.

Semchuck, Alex. "Wilbert Robinson," SABR Baseball Biography Project sabr.org/bioproj/person/5536caf5, undated, accessed August 18, 2014.

Thorn, John, Pete Palmer, Michael Gershman and David Pietrusza, eds. *Total Baseball: The Official Encyclopedia of Major League Baseball, Fifth Edition* (New York: Viking Penguin, 1997).

Young, Frank H. "Griffith Plays Waiting Game as Buddy Myer deal nears," *Washington Post*, December 12, 1928: 17.

——— "Nats Angle for Hunnefield In Triple Exchange if Deal for Myer Proves Failure," *Washington Post*, December 13, 1928: 15.

——— "Red Sox Asked to Hold Open Offer," *Washington Post*, December 14, 1928: 15.

——— "Nats Obtain Myer, Trading 5 Players," *Washington Post*, December 16, 1928: 1, 21.

——— "Red Sox Rate 3rd Baseman Highly," *Washington Post*, December 8, 1928: 13.

"Draft Meet Spurned by Heydler," *Washington Post*, December 11, 1928: 14.

sportsencyclopedia.com/al/wasdc/nats.html

"Indians Trade Uhle for 2 Detroit Men," *New York Times*, December 12, 1928: 44.

"Minor League Men Gather at Toronto: International and American Association Meetings Today," *New York Times*, December 3, 2011: 33.

"Minor Leagues May Talk Draft at Session Today," *Washington Post*, December 6, 1928: 18.

"Myer Decision by Griffith Due Today," *Washington Post*, December 15, 1928: 15.

NOTES

1. "Yankees Seek Buddy Myer or Bluege," *Washington Post*, December 5, 1928:15.

2. "Major Leaguers Arrive at Minors' Convention" *Hartford Courant*, December 5, 1928: 19.

3. "Report of Secretary Opens Minor Session," *The Sporting News*, December 6, 1928: 1.

4. Brian Bell, "Baseball Heads to Talk Over Draft Today," *Los Angeles Times*, December 6, 1928: B-1.

5. "Convention of Owners Shelves Baseball Draft," *Hartford Courant*, December 7, 1928: 22.

6. "Trading Rapid on First Day," *Christian Science Monitor*, December 6, 1928: 8; Joe Vila, "National League to Lose Klem, Who Is Peeved, New York Hears," *The Sporting News*, December 6, 1928: 1; baseball-reference.com.

7. "Trading Rapid on First Day," *Christian Science Monitor*, December 6, 1928: 8.

8. "Baseball Trade Winds Blow Gale at Toronto Meet," *Chicago Daily Tribune*, December 6, 1928: 25; Charles Dunkley, "10-Man Team Proposal is Tabled," *Washington Post*, December 14, 1928: 15.

9. John Drebinger, "M'Graw Is on Trail of Luque-Donohue," *New York Times*, December 7, 1928: 35; "Report of Secretary Opens Minor Session," *The Sporting News*, December 6, 1928: 1; L.H. Addington, "Shopping and Swapping With the Minor Leaguers," *The Sporting News*, December 13, 1928: 3, 7.

10. "Trading Rapid on First Day," *Christian Science Monitor*, December 6, 1928: 8; L.H. Addington, "Shopping and Swapping."

11. Francis J. Powers, "Evans Thumbs Over His Trading Stock," *The Sporting News*, December 6, 1928: 2.

12. "Shopping and Swapping."; "Caught on the Fly," *The Sporting News*, December 13, 1928: 7.

13. "Angels Sell Staley to Ducks, Stars Buy Pair," *Los Angeles Times*, December 9, 1928: A-1.

14. "Trading Rapid on First Day."

15. Ibid.

16. "Piedmont Magnates Broaden Rookie Rule," *The Sporting News*, December 6, 1928: 2.

17. L.H. Addington, "Modified Draft Loops Allied Against Any Change in Policy," *The Sporting News*, December 6, 1928: 1.

18. Ibid.

19. "Trading Rapid on First Day"; "East Carolina Loop Stands," *The Sporting News*, December 6, 1928: 2; "Shopping and Swapping"; "Caught on the Fly"; Paul Moore, "Dallas to Train in Corsicana," *The Sporting News*, December 6, 1928: 2.

20. Paul W. Eaton, "Tampa Smokes Up One on Senators," *The Sporting News*, December 6, 1928: 2.

21. "Shopping and Swapping."

22. They obviously found the money—the Patriots won the 1929 Piedmont League title. J. Chris Holaday, *Professional Baseball in North Carolina* (Jefferson, North Carolina: McFarland & Company, 1998), 75; "Piedmont Magnates Broaden Rookie Rule"; George Netherwood, "Outlook Bright for Patriots," *Greensboro Daily News*, December 4, 1928: 13; George Netherwood, "Extension Granted the Patriots," *Greensboro Daily News*, December 16, 1928: 4, 1.

23. "Shopping and Swapping."; W. Lloyd Johnson and Miles Wolff, eds., *The Encyclopedia of Minor League Baseball*, 2nd edition (Durham, North Carolina: Baseball America Inc., 1997), 256.

24. "Shopping and Swapping."; "Southeastern Club on Block," *The Sporting News*, December 13, 1928: 1.

25. Joe Hatcher, "Rowland Comes Back in Managerial Field," *The Sporting News*, December 13, 1928: 1.

26. Joe Vila, "Retirement Plans Confirmed By Klem," *The Sporting News*, December 13, 1928: 1; John Drebinger, "Giants Adopt the Chain-Store Idea By Purchasing Bridgeport Club," *New York Times*, December 18, 1928: 44.

27. Brian Bell, "Draft Matter Given Go-Bye," *Los Angeles Times*, December 7, 1928: B-1. A territorial rule is still in effect today although, due to better roads and modes of transportation, a minor-league club nowadays controls a diameter of 35 miles.

28. "Shopping and Swapping."; "Minor League Territorial Question Brings Warm Debate," *The Sporting News*, December 13, 1928: 3.

29. "Trading Rapid on First Day"; Robert L. Finch, L.H. Addington, and Ben H. Morgan, eds., *The Story of Minor League Baseball* (Columbus, Ohio: The Stoneman Press, 1952), 26-27. Double-A was the highest level of the minors at that time and would be until 1946. That level included the American Association, the International League and the Pacific Coast League.

30. He led the Class-B South Atlantic Association, Class-C Piedmont League, and Class-D Eastern Carolina League; he became head of the NAPBL at the end of 1931. *The Encyclopedia of Minor League Baseball*, 2nd edition, and *The Story of Minor League Baseball*.

31. "Trading Rapid on First Day."

32. John Drebinger, "Important Trade by Yankees Looms," *New York Times*, December 5, 1928: 37.

33 "Minors Disband; Leave Draft as Muddled as Ever," *Chicago Tribune*, December 8, 1928: 30; "M'Graw Is On Trail Of Luque-Donohue"; "Convention of Owners Shelves Baseball Draft," *Hartford Courant*, December 7, 1928: 22.

34 "M'Graw Is on Trail of Luque-Donohue."

35 Ibid.

36 Peter Golenbock, *Bums* (New York: Pocket Books, 1984), 5.

37 John Drebinger, "Baseball Owners Leave for Chicago," *New York Times*, December 13, 1928: 37; "N.L. Washes Its Hands of Minor Draft Fight," *The Sporting News*, December 13, 1928: 1.

38 "Baseball Owners Leave for Chicago."

39 Ibid. It was a good thing for the Robins that they didn't move Bancroft. Wright was hurt early on and made only 30 plate appearances for the year, so Bancroft wound up reclaiming his shortstop post and batted .277. Overall, the trade proved to be fairly inconsequential for both clubs. Wright did come back in 1930 with a good season, but that was the last one of his career. Petty won 11 games for Pittsburgh in 1929 but then only two more in the majors, while Riconda wound up playing in just nine more major-league games.

40 James C. O'Leary, "Braves Get Harper, Maranville, Gowdy," *Boston Globe*, December 9, 1928: A-32.

41 "National League to Lose Klem, Who Is Peeved, New York Hears."

42 Ibid.

43 "Klem to Remain," *Pittsburgh Press*, January 15, 1929: 36.

44 In 1939 during a dispute over whether a ball was a home run or foul ball, Magerkurth and Billy Jurges spit at each other. Both were fined and suspended, but more importantly, National League President Ford Frick ordered that a two-foot-wide wire screen be installed inside the foul poles to help the umpires determine whether a ball was fair or foul. *Evening News of Sault Sainte Marie*, July 19, 1939: 10; *Kingston* (New York) *Daily Freeman*, July 19, 1939: 1; *Rhinelander* (Wisconsin) *Daily News*, July 24, 1939: 5; Paul Geisler Jr., "Billy Jurges," SABR Baseball Biography Project, sabr.org/bioproj/person/aada6293#sdendnote14sym, undated, accessed July 7, 2016.

45 "Committees to Discuss Draft," *Christian Science Monitor*, December 8, 1928: 7.

46 Burt Whitman, "Hub Marking Time on Council Action," *The Sporting News*, December 6, 1928: 1; en.wikipedia.org/wiki/Emil_Fuchs_(baseball), accessed August 30, 2014.

47 baseball-almanac.com/treasure/autont2002b.shtml, accessed August 31, 2014; "Minors Disband; Leave Draft as Muddled as Ever," *Chicago Tribune*, December 8, 1928: 30.

48 "M'Graw Is on Trail of Luque-Donohue."

49 "Landis Polls Major Owners on Farms, But No Action Is Taken," *The Sporting News*, December 20, 1928: 3.

50 Ibid.

51 "Hub Marking Time on Council Action"; "N.L. Washes Its Hands of Minor Draft Fight," *The Sporting News*, December 13, 1928: 1.

52 "N.L. Washes Its Hands of Minor Draft Fight"; In the Cubs-Giants game, as a Giants runner attempted to score, the Cubs' Gabby Hartnett hit him with his shoulder and knocked him down, even though the catcher did not have the ball. Hartnett then held the runner down until his third baseman came down the line and applied the tag. The umpire ruled that there was no interference and the runner was out. The umpire was Bill Klem, and this may have been the reason for the threats made against him. Dom Forker, Wayne Stewart, and Michael Pellowski, *Baffling Baseball Trivia* (New York: Sterling Publishing Company, 2004), 220-221.

53 Irving Vaughn, "Cub Ranks Shrink at Minor Session," *The Sporting News*, December 13, 1928: 1.

54 Frank H. Young, "Red Sox Rate 3rd Baseman Highly," *Washington Post*, December 8, 1928: 13.

55 Burt Whitman, "Bob Quinn's One-For-Five Deal Should Help Boston Red Sox," *The Sporting News*, December 20, 1928: 3.

56 "Evans Thumbs Over His Trading Stock"; baseball-reference.com/bullpen/Earl_Averill_(averiea01), accessed September 1, 2014.

57 Francis J. Powers, "Billy Evans Adds as He Subtracts," *The Sporting News*, December 13, 1928: 1.

58 Joseph Wancho, "George Uhle," SABR Baseball Biography Project (sabr.org/bioproj/person/1d015def), undated, accessed September 11, 2011.

59 Ibid.

60 "Business Lags, But Baseballers Chin and Chin," *Chicago Tribune*, December 5, 1928: 29; "Caught on the Fly"; profootball-hof.com/hof/member.aspx?PLAYER_ID=206.

61 "Important Trade by Yankees Looms."

62 "Landis Polls Major Owners on Farms, but No Action Is Taken"; John Drebinger, "Giants Adopt the Chain-Store Idea By Purchasing Bridgeport Club," *New York Times*, December 18, 1928: 44.

63 "West Baden Conference Off; Present Draft Pact to Stand," *The Sporting News*, December 20, 1928: 3.

64 Ibid.

65 Charles Dunkley, "10-Man Team Proposal Is Tabled," *Washington Post*, December 14, 1928: 15. One has to wonder what those 1920s owners would think of the twenty-first-century baseball and football schedules.

66 "Landis Polls Major Owners on Farms, But No Action Is Taken."

67 Ibid.

68 Ibid.

69 "10-Man Team Proposal Is Tabled."

70 "Pickups and Rebounds From the Major League Meetings," *The Sporting News*, December 20, 1928: 3.

71 Ibid.

72 "10-Man Team Proposal Is Tabled."

73 "Heydler's Plan Receives Favor," *Christian Science Monitor*, December 12, 1928: 10.

74 Brian Bell, "Many Hurlers Star at Bat, Others Hard to Convince, Los Angeles Times-Washington Post News Service archive, December 13, 1928: 15-16.

75 Ibid.

76 Charles Dunkley, "American League Managers Condemn Heydler Proposal for Batless Pitchers," *Hartford Courant*, December 13, 1928: 20.

77 "National Firm in Radical Proposal," *Washington Post*, December 13, 1928: 15.

78 "The Ten-Man Team," *The Sporting News*, December 20, 1928: 4.

79 Marty Noble, "First DH Blomberg thankful for his place in history," m.mlb.com/news/article/36452472/, accessed August 22 and September 2, 2014.

— 1929 —
LET'S ALL PLAY BY THE SAME RULES

By Frederick C. Bush

Introduction

THE NATIONAL ASSOCIATION OF Professional Baseball Leagues (minor leagues) and the National and American Leagues held their annual winter meetings one week apart in December 1929. Though there were different points of contention for both the minors and majors, some issues were relevant to all the organizations and leagues. The draft, the signing of college players, and major-league clubs' ownership of minor-league franchises — called "common ownership" but derisively referred to as "chain store"[1] baseball by Commissioner Kenesaw Mountain Landis — were all discussed, though few important agreements were reached.

There was abundant trade activity among the NAPBL clubs during the December 4-6 meetings in Chattanooga, Tennessee, but little else of note was accomplished. The most compelling event of the meetings was the dual hearings of the cases of Rochester Red Wings second baseman George "Specs" Toporcer and manager Billy Southworth, with the fiasco surrounding their situation leading Branch Rickey to plead on behalf of Toporcer.

The National and American League meetings were held in New York City on December 10-12 and also lacked major developments, with only one noteworthy trade taking place and few policy changes, so that they were best summarized as "three loquacious but unfruitful days."[2] Attendance at major-league games in 1929 had been outstanding for most clubs, especially in the National League, which had attendance figures that were second only to 1927, so there was little desire for any drastic changes. Thus, as was the situation at the NAPBL meetings, one of the more noteworthy items involved a debacle, in this case the war between the two ownership factions of the National League's Brooklyn Robins that would determine the fate of Wilbert Robinson as the club's president and manager.

NAPBL Meeting

Nearly 1,000 baseball personnel, including the presidents of 21 minor leagues, convened in Chattanooga, Tennessee, on December 4 for the NAPBL's annual meeting with the dual goals of making trades to improve their clubs and addressing issues vital to the leagues in order to reverse the trend of increasingly lower attendance.

The draft was expected to be foremost on the owners' minds since it had been discussed at length at the previous year's meetings without any resolution, but the NAPBL did not give serious consideration to this issue in 1929 because, perhaps, as one reporter observed, "A curious feature of the draft question is that scarcely anyone understands it."[3] The lone effort concerning the draft was a proposal by William Bramham, the president of the South Atlantic Association as well as the Piedmont and Eastern Carolina Leagues, "that a player shall not be subject to draft until he has been credited with participation in 200 games, for all players except pitchers."[4] The proposal failed; it won the support of two-thirds of the NAPBL's membership but needed a three-fourths majority.

The delegates did approve a new rule dealing with the scouts who evaluated talent, whether for the draft or other means by which players were obtained. It stated that the NAPBL "would not recognize a claim presented by any person acting as a scout for a member club of the National Association, unless a written contract between the club and scout should be filed with the secretary of the association."[5]

Scouts often signed college players. Byrd Douglas, Princeton University's baseball coach, asked the convention to declare the practice unethical. In response, the NAPBL adopted a 'hands-off' policy toward college athletes, agreeing that clubs should wait until the players had completed their studies before signing them to professional contracts. It declared that it was "the sense of this association that any attempt on the part of organized baseball to induce directly or indirectly any college or schoolboy athlete to sign a contract or give an option on his services for pay while he is still enrolled or in the process of his education at any institution should be deprecated."[6]

The NAPBL did nothing to improve the fortunes of the minor leagues. Ideas that might have extended the reach of the minors or improved attendance were usually presented in vain.

Havana, Cuba, had applied for a franchise in the Southeastern League, which could have expanded the market for that league. Air travel was still in its nascent stages, though, and some players were afraid to fly. The NAPBL's Board of Arbitration declared that it would not sanction the suspension of players who refused to travel by airplane, saying it regarded airplane travel as safe but considered the question "a matter for individuals to pass upon. It would not countenance a blanket rule requiring the players to fly."[7] Thus, the potentially lucrative Cuban market remained out of reach.

Rather than making a foray into a new market, E.L. Keyser, the president of the Western League's team in Des Moines, believed that his club could succeed in a new time slot and intended to try nighttime baseball. He cited the success colleges had experienced with night football, asserting that "schools that used to be poor now have money" and saying he believed it would "offset the use of the auto and give the working man a chance to attend."[8]

Beyond Keyser's plan, no one else seemed to have any money-making ideas. Outdoor advertising was discussed; however, the norm at these meetings prevailed and nothing was decided. One money-saving idea, proposed by the American Association's Louisville club, that the price to option a player be reduced from $100 to $1, was rejected.

While ideas were being rejected and trades were being made, high drama was taking place at a joint hearing for player George "Specs" Toporcer and manager Billy Southworth of the International League's Rochester Red Wings in their appeal against penalties arising from their actions in the ninth and final game of the Little World Series between Rochester and the Kansas City Blues of the American Association. At an earlier hearing in Chicago, Toporcer had been fined $200 and suspended for one season, while Southworth had been fined $500. They complained that they had not received notice to appear at the Chicago hearing, and a second hearing had been granted by NAPBL President M.H. Sexton.

The fines and suspension stemmed from an incident in the game of October 13, 1929, won by Kansas City. Toporcer objected too vigorously to a called third strike by home-plate umpire Larry Goetz and was ejected from the game. As Sexton described the events in his official decision, Toporcer's actions "consisted in a vehement protest, some profanity and gesticulations of a character which led to commotion and an outbreak by the spectators, which verged very closely upon a riot and mob scene."[9] Manager Southworth was fined for further inflaming the situation.

Since Rochester was the St. Louis Cardinals' International League affiliate, Branch Rickey, the Cardinals' general manager, came to Chattanooga and — "inundating the National Board with his eloquence"[10] — testified on Toporcer's behalf. Rickey portrayed Goetz as being hot-headed himself, asserted that Toporcer's punishment did not fit the crime, and said it was unfair to make Toporcer sit out an entire season. Weighing Rickey's arguments along with the fact that Toporcer "was not guilty of any physical attack upon the umpire" and had heretofore maintained "a clean and honorable record." Sexton rescinded the suspension but increased Toporcer's fine from $200 to $500.[11] Sexton made it clear that Toporcer had to pay the fine himself by March 1, 1930; it could not be paid by the Rochester club.

Commenting that Southworth "was remiss in his effort to quell the disturbance, but I do not find that he incited the crowd,"[12] Sexton reduced the manager's fine to $200.

The only other controversy at the meetings was stirred up by Commissioner Landis, the principal speaker at the NAPBL's banquet on December 5, who gave his opinion about the rise of "common ownership"—the farm system—in which major-league clubs purchased minor-league franchises to develop their players. Landis said all baseball clubs should be individual interests rather than what he termed "chain store" baseball operations. He asserted, "We must solve the problem of the little fellows," and predicted the complete demise of minor-league baseball unless "a remedy can be found to restore baseball to its former high favor."[13] Landis derided the farm system as a bane to the minors, and said he believed it was "a contributing factor to the despondency in which the game rests in many sections of the country today."[14] The following week's major-league meetings, however, indicated that Landis had no intention of trying to end common ownership. In fact, the "do-nothing" approach of the NAPBL's convention would infect both the National and American League meetings as well.

Major-League Meetings

Landis fired an opening salvo against common ownership on December 10, the opening day of the major-league meetings, with a proposal that both major- and minor-league clubs be required "to file official notification with baseball authorities upon acquiring control of a smaller baseball property."[15] He reasoned that since clubs were required to provide notification when they purchased a player, they should have to do the same when they purchased a franchise.

American League President E.S. Barnard believed that the farm system "was not a success and was on its way to dying a natural death,"[16] and that it was not a matter for concern. Thus, while the National League supported Landis's measure, the American League favored restoration of the universal draft instead; the fact that Landis would cast the deciding vote in the event of a tie guaranteed that the commissioner would prevail.

Landis's primary objection to farm teams appeared to be his belief "that fans in minor league towns resented alien ownership,"[17] which was why he thought the farm system had contributed to declining attendance in the minors. St. Louis Cardinals president Sam Breadon, whose team owned nine minor-league clubs at the time, read telegrams from the presidents of minor-league teams throughout the country that indicated they endorsed major-league ownership of minor-league franchises.

Contrary to Landis's objections, Breadon's evidence showed that the benefits of farm systems were becoming clear to an increasing number of owners. Minor-league cities saw better players when they had a major-league club developing its top prospects on their squads; this was more likely to raise attendance rather than lower it. Also, many minor-league franchises had folded for lack of financial support, a situation that could be avoided if the club were owned by a major-league team. It was evident "that practically the only clubs hurt by 'chain store' ownership are those in major leagues which can't afford to go into the business on a big scale."[18]

In the end, Landis's proposal was a mere potshot, rather than a barrage that ended the practice of common ownership, and no more was said or done about the matter at these meetings.

Jacob Ruppert, president of the New York Yankees, had a more substantial plan that would affect both the major and minor leagues. He proposed two changes to the option system: Teams should be allowed to have 15 players on option to the minors, rather than the current eight; and they should be allowed to option out a player for three years rather than two. Both leagues agreed to the idea, but they would have to obtain the consent of the minor leagues before the plan could be implemented. They were prepared to make concessions in order to gain the necessary support, including the possibility of an agreement not to sign college players.

One additional policy that affected the transfer of players was the edict that players whose contracts were transferred from one club to another now had to report to their new team within 72 hours; exceptions would be made only for players who had to travel from one coast to another.

In addition to player movement, attention was also given to the rules of the game, which were not standard for both leagues. Accordingly, the Baseball Writers Association of America agreed to prepare instructions for official scorers so that the rules would be "codified, unified, and clarified."[19]

The leagues accepted a BBWAA proposal that their presidents appoint the official scorers for each team based on the recommendations of the club presidents and local BBWAA chapters. Official scorers would be appointed to one-year terms and could be dismissed immediately if they failed "to measure up to the exacting standards of efficient scoring."[20] Two alternates would be appointed to serve in the absence (or dismissal) of a scorer.

The standardization of both rules and scoring was one of only two agreements of any true significance reached at the meetings. The other was the shortening of the season from 176 to 170 playing days for the 154-game schedule, with a mid-April start and a September 28 finish. All other issues either turned out to be minor or failed to gain consensus for any plan of action.

The topic of radio broadcasts of major-league games had seemed important when St. Louis Browns president Phil Ball announced at the beginning of December that he would address the issue at the winter meetings. Ball believed that broadcasts of Browns games had cut into the team's attendance in 1929, and he wanted the American League to prohibit the broadcasting of ballgames.

Ball appeared to have an ally in American League President E.S. Barnard, whose primary objection to radio broadcasts was that "broadcasters are reaping a golden harvest from the major-league clubs without any financial return to the clubs which provide the entertainment."[21] He wanted to charge each radio station $50,000 to broadcast games, with $25,000 going to the club and $25,000 to the league, reiterating, "There is no reason why baseball should not share in the profits of a venture that it makes possible."[22]

The *Chicago Tribune* asserted that some owners were opposed to radio broadcasts "because of the traditional suspicion with which some of the magnates view anything which smacks of progress,"[23] but profits were clearly the heart of the matter. In the end, the owners were unable to come to any agreement and decided to leave the issue of broadcasts to the clubs.

Whatever losses Ball thought his Browns had incurred from radio broadcasts would be offset by the new lease the St. Louis Cardinals signed to remain in Sportsman's Park, owned by Ball's Dodier Realty Company, for another 10 years. The new lease called for the Cardinals to pay $35,000 per year, a $5,000 increase over their previous rent. The Cardinals had announced the deal at the beginning of December to quell rumors that the team might leave St. Louis.

While a Cardinals move had been mere conjecture, the Brooklyn Robins were engaged in a legitimate controversy. Wilbert Robinson, the president and manager of the Robins, was in a power struggle over his future role with the team once his contract expired on January 1, 1930. Robinson had the continued support of Joseph Guilleaudeau, who represented the half of the franchise owned by the Ebbets estate, but he was vehemently opposed by Steve McKeever, who owned the other half of the club, and McKeever's director, Frank York. If the deadlock over the contract continued, he would automatically remain president of the club as stipulated in its constitution, but there remained the question of who would be the manager.

National League President John Heydler conceived a plan to settle the controversy and summoned the Robins' four leaders to meet with him and Commissioner Landis on the second day of the league meetings. None of the participants would say what was discussed during the meeting, but the *New York Times* wrote, "(I)t can be reported with authority that Mr. Heydler's well-laid plans were handsomely torn into shreds."[24] Landis admitted that he had never seen anything like the Robins' front-office squabble and, as was the norm throughout these winter meetings, nothing was resolved.

Discussion of the increase in home runs in 1929 was another case of much ado about nothing. The 1,349 home runs hit that season were cited as the major factor in 55,980 baseballs (4,665 dozen) having been used during the season, 387 dozen over 1928.[25] AL President Barnard was cold to the idea that the ball "might be wound a bit more loosely or deadened in any way" and exclaimed, "I think that beyond question the present type is the best baseball we have had in the history of the game."[26] Not everyone agreed with Barnard's assessment, but the only change the owners decided upon was to request that baseball manufacturers remove the gloss from the balls before they delivered them to the leagues. The rationale for their request was that home runs had decreased after umpires had begun to remove the gloss from the balls in the latter half of the 1929 season.

While trades had hit a record number during the minor-league meetings, the major-league meetings saw a dearth of deals and wound down with only one player of note being traded. The St. Louis Cardinals traded the venerable pitcher Grover Cleveland Alexander and catcher Harry McCurdy to the Philadelphia Phillies for outfielder Homer Peel and right-handed pitcher Robert McGraw. Exactly 12 years previously the Phillies had traded him to the Chicago Cubs. He entered the 1930 season with 373 victories but would pitch in only nine games for the Phillies in 1930, posting a 0-3 record with a 9.14 ERA before his career was over.

As the meetings wound down, the owners agreed to make donations including $50,000 to support the American Legion Junior Baseball program, which had just completed its second season. According to a report delivered at the meetings, more than 300,000 youths participated in the program in the summer of 1929, with Illinois leading all states by fielding 1,468 registered teams.[27]

They gave $10,000 to the National Amateur Athletic Federation with part of the sum earmarked for "providing expert instruction to coaches of sandlot and school teams throughout the country."[28]

A donation of $5,000 was given to the Association of Professional Baseball Players of America, an organization that helped former major- and minor-league players who were now invalids, indigent, or both.

To pay the $65,000 total in donations, Commissioner Landis would deduct 15 percent of the gross receipts of the 1930 World Series, an increase of 5 percent over recent years. Taking care to donate funds to these three organizations was perhaps the most prescient move of the 1929 winter meetings, as each group contributed to the well-being of baseball in its own way, thus nurturing the growth of the sport and ensuring also that there would be annual winter meetings into the future.

NOTES

1 Frank H. Young, "Czar Is Silent on Evils of System," *Washington Post*, December 14, 1929.

2 Brian Bell, "Robins Send Ballou to Minors," *Washington Post*, December 14, 1929.

3 John Drebinger, "Baseball Owners Set for Meetings," *New York Times*, December 1, 1929.

4 "Minor Leagues Pick Montreal," *Christian Science Monitor*, December 6, 1929.

5 "Minor League Clubs Gather," *Christian Science Monitor*, December 3, 1929.

6 "Minor Leagues End Convention," *Christian Science Monitor*, December 7, 1929.

7 "Year's Suspension of Toporcer Lifted," *New York Times*, December 5, 1929.

8 "E.L. Keyser Urges Baseball at Night," *Christian Science Monitor*, December 5, 1929.

9 "Branch Rickey's Eloquent Plea Lifts Toporcer Suspension; Player Fined $500 and Manager Southworth Must Pay $200," *The Sporting News*, December 12, 1929: 3.

10 Ibid.

11 Ibid.

12 Ibid.

13 "Minor Leagues Pick Montreal."

14 Ibid.

15 "Shorter Season Gains Favor at Winter Meeting," *Chicago Tribune*, December 11, 1929.

16 Roscoe McGowen, "American League Re-Elects Navin," *New York Times*, December 11, 1929.

17 "Czar Is Silent on Evils of System."

18 Ibid.

19 "Two Major Leagues Combine in Joint Baseball Meeting," *Christian Science Monitor*, December 13, 1929.

20 Ibid.

21 "American League to Weigh Radiocasts," *Christian Science Monitor*, December 6, 1929.

22 "Barnard Favors $50,000 Broadcasting Charge," *The Sporting News*, December 5, 1929: 1.

23 "Major Leagues Ponder Closing Season Earlier," *Chicago Tribune*, December 9, 1929.

24 John Drebinger, "Landis Peace Plea to Robins Fails," *New York Times*, December 12, 1929.

25 John Drebinger, "4,925,713 at Games in National League," *New York Times*, December 11, 1929.

26 "American League Re-Elects Navin."

27 "4,925,713 at Games in National League."

28 "Two Major Leagues Combine in Joint Baseball Meeting."

— 1930 —
THE JUDGE AND THE MAHATMA DEBATE THE CHAIN STORE SYSTEM

By Gary Levy

Prologue

THE AMERICAN NATIONAL LEAGUES each held individual annual meetings on December 9, 1930, in New York City. Although the National League was bound by its constitution to meet in New York City, its American League counterpart had originally planned to meet in Chicago. However, league President E.S. Barnard later changed this arrangement so the AL's annual meeting would be in New York City on the same date as the NL meetings. The two leagues' annual joint winter meetings took place later in the week, on December 10-12, also in Gotham.

National Association of Professional Baseball Leagues Convention

The annual convention of the National Association of Professional Baseball Leagues (NAPBL) was held in the frosty hinterlands of Montreal over December 2-5, 1930. Although the long trek to Canada might have been viewed as peculiar, the fact that the United States was in a state of Prohibition (which would be repealed in 1933) but its neighbors to the north were not may help to explain it. "Montreal is a long rumble from St. Louis (where *The Sporting News* was headquartered) … and cold …14 under 0… but numerous antifreeze stations are convenient."[1]

The National Association comprised 21 minor leagues, representing "nearly every club in the minor leagues which is embraced by Organized Baseball."[2] National Association Secretary J.H. Farrell reported at the opening event of the convention that 8,937 players had been employed in minor-league baseball the summer before, and that during the 1930 season the association had encompassed 23 leagues involving 165 cities and towns across North America, although two of the leagues had since disbanded. Farrell reported total income of almost $2.9 million, with most revenues coming from contract assignments: from minors to majors ($1,377,250), from minors to minors ($768,758), and from majors to minors ($460,901).[3] Since player transactions accounted for more than 80 percent of the revenue for minor-league teams and the National Association, this would foretell later issues involving the major leagues' great desire to ensure a "universal draft" of players from the minor leagues.

The Pacific Coast League (Class AA) was deadlocked on the election of a league president: Incumbent President Harry Williams and J. Cal Ewing of the Oakland club each had four votes. International League (AA) met and discussed the coming 1931 season. Charles Knapp of Baltimore was re-elected president, Lawrence Solman of Toronto, vice president, and William T. Manley of New York, secretary-treasurer. Tom Hickey was reappointed president of the Class-AA American Association, and later had his pocket picked of $180, but before the meetings concluded he purchased a "stylish new derby" nonetheless.[4]

As in the recent past, the annual convention of the National Association revolved greatly around the need to renew the agreement between the minors and majors, most specifically the so-called "universal draft." Major-league owners wanted this draft because it allowed them to obtain players from any minor-league team (or from high schools or colleges, for that

WILLIAM BAKER AT THE WINTER MEETINGS

When Philadelphia Phillies owner William Baker arrived in reported good health – despite a heart ailment over the last few months – at the Mount Royal Hotel in Montreal for the minor-league meetings, he greeted friends in the lobby.* Baker suffered a slight attack on the evening of December 3, but quickly recovered. He proceeded to have dinner with his wife, Phillies business manager Gerald P. Nugent, and their wives. By 10 P.M., Baker felt ill enough that a doctor was summoned to his Ritz-Carlton suite. By 5:30 the following morning, Baker had died.**

The minor-league convention met at 11 A.M., and adjourned until 1 P.M. out of respect for Baker.***

National League President John Heydler commented, "I was deeply shocked and grieved to learn of the sudden death of Mr. Baker. He was second in length of service among the club presidents, having been at the head of our Philadelphia club for more than 17 years. Mr. Baker was a man of fine principles, impartial in action, and with a courage to stand up to his convictions."****

---

* "Baseball Man Dies Suddenly," *Ottawa Journal*, December 4, 1930: 1.
** "W.F. Baker Dies Suddenly; Cobb May Become Owner of Philadelphia Nationals," *Cincinnati Enquirer*, December 5, 1930: 3.
*** "Delegates Decree Baseball Players Must Stay Out of Ring," *Ottawa Journal*, December 5, 1930: 27.
**** "W.F. Baker Dead; Head of Phillies," *New York Times*, December 5, 1930: 25.

---

matter) for as little as possible and at a set amount. This last point was important—owners had no love for bidding wars, where small-market teams could be outspent by teams in larger markets. Another concern from major-league owners was that if they could not draft talent cheaply, they would have to hold onto higher-paid veteran players longer, at a cost to their bottom line.[5] Minor-league teams argued that they developed player talent and so should benefit financially when their player was drafted by a major-league team.[6] If minor-league teams were exempt from the universal draft, they would be able to charge more for drafting their players. These pressures, brewing since the late nineteenth century, led some clubs to begin to build their own farm systems to avoid draft expenses. Commissioner Kenesaw Mountain Landis greatly disliked what he termed this "chain-store" model of ownership.[7]

Rumors had been circulating that the major and minor leagues had settled questions regarding the draft prior to the December meetings, but accounts seemed to indicate that neither NL President John Heydler nor AL President E.S. Barnard had agreed to such a settlement.[8] The overwhelming sentiment of the meetings was that there would be a minimal number of transfers—maybe even none at all!—between minor- and major-league teams until a new agreement regarding the player draft was established.[9]

Making matters worse, there existed substantial confusion and controversy as to whether the player draft and related issues of player option and control practices would remain in effect, or whether it was time for renewal of the current agreement as long as Commissioner Landis held office. If the current understanding regarding the player draft continued, then the majors planned to move forward with their mutual understanding with minor-league teams that allowed them to sign college players. If, however, any minor-league teams decided to disregard the current selection rules, major-league teams declared they could sign any free agents, "be they college players, semi-professional players or Independent players."[10]

Perhaps because of the draft issue being primary on owners' minds, fewer high-profile trades were made during the meetings. Although many trades and sales of players were apparently begun during the National Association meetings, most went unfinished by the time the meetings ended on December 5. "While the business of tossing about the draft ultimatum progressed in the convention chambers, the majority of magnates stood around hotel lobbies with their hands clutched around bank rolls, and with check books and fountain pens securely fixed in their pockets," *The Sporting News* wrote. "Fewer player transactions were competed than at any National Association meeting in many years."[11] The paper also reported, "There was not a trade of any importance between a major and minor club. That never happened before. There have been some big deals made now and then at the meetings of the minors … this year not one."[12]

Shortly after the close of convention business, NL and AL Presidents Heydler and Barnard announced that the major leagues rejected the minor leagues' request to revise the draft "provided that the majors would first withdraw their ultimatum in reference to not transacting any business with non-draft leagues."[13] They asserted that major-league baseball teams would not engage in player transactions with non-draft teams after December 1.

Nonetheless, there was some modest player movement activity as Wichita outfielder Woody Jensen, batting champion of the Western League, and a teammate, catcher Jack Mealey, were purchased by the Pittsburgh Pirates, along with infielders Howard Groskloss and Pep Young, and right-handed pitchers J. Bernard Walter and Clay Mahaffey, who were all considered "recruits" and would be going to Wichita. Big Boy Walsh, the son of famed former White Sox pitcher Ed Walsh, was set to break camp with the New York Yankees after spending the summer with Hazleton in the New York-Penn League.[14] The Cleveland Indians picked up two right-handed pitchers, Oral Hildebrand from Indianapolis of the American Association and Howard Craghead from Oakland in the Pacific Coast League. The Detroit Tigers acquired catcher John Grabowski from St. Paul of the American Association. The Baltimore Orioles traded right-handed pitcher Jim Weaver and catcher Tom Padden to the Yankees for right-handed pitchers John Hopkins and Kenneth Holloway and cash. Cincinnati added lefty first baseman Mickey Heath from Hollywood of the Pacific Coast League for cash and two players to be named later (outfielder Marty Callaghan and infielder Pat Crawford).

The National Association changed six rules in Montreal. Five changes affected players, and the sixth allowed the group to meet in any city, not just ones that had clubs in the Association itself. (Whereupon West Baden, Indiana, was selected for the 1931 convention.)

The five new rules involving players forbade them to compete in professional boxing or wrestling; prohibited the offering of a contract to a player under 18; attempted to curb fighting by authorizing "in case of a physical attack on an umpire by a player or a player by an umpire," suspensions of between 90 days and one year"[15]; lowered from 80 days to 15 days, the required notice of a proposed amendment change regarding league rules; and raised the roster limit in Class-C leagues from 14 players to 15 players.

Likely in anticipation of the stance by the major-league presidents, the National Association selected a nine-man committee (three from each Double-A league) and sent them to the National and American League meetings in New York City to seek agreement between the minors and majors on the player-draft issue. The committee was granted complete authority to act on behalf of the National Association. John McGraw and William L. Veeck, both of the NL, agreed to meet with the committee.[16]

The National Association delegates were shaken by the death of William Frazer Baker, owner of the Philadelphia Phillies, of a heart attack in Montreal at the age of 64. Baker was recalled by some as a miserly owner who had sold Grover Cleveland Alexander to the Chicago Cubs in 1917 rather than give him a pay raise. Over the three-year period 1915-1917, Alexander had compiled a won-lost record of 94-35. After Baker's death Branch Rickey and Ty Cobb were quickly mentioned as candidates for purchasing the Phillies, but Baker's will left control of the club with his widow and the wife of the club's business manager, Gerald P. Nugent, who became the team's acting president.[17]

Joint Major League Meetings

The 1930 meetings of the American and National leagues in New York City December 10-12 were characterized as "the winter of the big wind," since the owners were apparently "too busy rushing from one meeting to another and squabbling with the minor league committee on the draft even to get together on the matter of ivory exchanges."[18]

It was not the case that the teams didn't want to make trades. Players often mentioned as available included star (but pricey) third baseman Willie Kamm of the White Sox (the A's, Red Sox Indians, and Yankees were interested), veteran first baseman Lew Fonseca of the Indians (the White Sox were listening), right-handed pitchers Ed Morris of Cleveland and Danny MacFayden of the Red Sox (sought by the Yankees), colorful right-handed pitcher Flint Rhem of St. Louis (Brooklyn was interested), first baseman Jim Bottomley of the Cardinals (the Cubs were interested), and catcher Muddy Ruel of the Senators (sought by Cleveland). In addition, Braves lefty Ed Brandt was being dangled as bait for hitters, most notably utility player Harvey Hendrick of Brooklyn. Teams including the Yankees, the Giants, the Indians (needing a catcher), the Boston Braves (needing hitters), the Brooklyn Robins (in the market for pitching), the Phillies, and the Washington Senators were most vocal in their desire to swap players.[19] But it was all for naught as the most significant deals completed at the meetings were Detroit signing catcher Wally Schang (who had been released by the Athletics) and infielder Joe Dugan (released by the Braves), and the Yankees acquiring catcher Cy Perkins (released by the Athletics).[20]

The 1930 meetings were remembered more for what did not get accomplished than for what did. Some minor issues were discussed and decided upon, such as an American League proposal to reduce the number of home runs being hit by adding 40-foot screening to the top of fences that were less than 300 feet from home plate; a 30-foot-high fence on outfield walls less than 325 feet from home plate; and a 20-foot fence on walls less than 350 feet from home plate. Not surprisingly, Yankees owner Jacob Ruppert, whose ballpark had well-known short porches, did not support the screen notion. National League President Heydler also stated his opposition. Another look at why the ball was so lively was proposed. The Giants' McGraw acknowledged that the current ball was livelier than it once was and more than it should be.[21] Reports surfaced that the 1931 baseball would have a thicker cover and looser sewing and would be less lively.[22]

The sacrifice fly rule was scrutinized by the Joint Rules Committee. This body included three National League members (Heydler, the Cardinals' Sam Breadon, and the Cubs' William L. Veeck); three American League members (Barnard, the Senators' Clark Griffith, and Philadelphia player-coach Eddie Collins); National Association President William Bramham; major-league umpires Tom Connolly and Bob Emslie; and John B. Foster, a noted baseball authority and the editor of the 1931 *Spalding Official Baseball Guide*. The discussion centered on getting rid of the 1926 rule under which a batter was not charged with an at-bat if his fly ball advanced any runner. National Leaguers suggested simply amending the rule so that a batter could be credited with a sacrifice fly only if a runner scored on his fly ball. The committee decided to abolish the sacrifice fly altogether, allowing a batter to be charged with an at-bat even if a run scored.[23] (The modified sacrifice fly rule suggested by the NL was enacted after the 1953 season.)

Other rules changes: Any ball hit in fair territory and bounding into the grandstand would be a double in both leagues. (The AL had adopted this rule the previous year.) The National League rule basing whether a ball is fair or foul on where it left the playing field rather than where the umpire last saw it, became a standard major-league rule.[24] AL President Barnard pressed managers to shorten game times, "as many big-scoring, heavy slugging" games were taking too long, in his opinion.[25] The National League softened its rules regarding barnstorming teams, which thus allowed a squad of major leaguers to go to Japan. The NL also approved a rule that only people in uniform be allowed on the playing field after ballpark gates were opened, and the NL Board of Directors upheld President Heydler's decision to deny the Reds' claim of $4,000 against the Cubs, plus the waiver price, for first baseman George Kelly. Much to the delight of the press, the American League agreed that all players would henceforth wear numbers on their uniforms.[26] Cleveland, New York, and Washington had begun wearing numbers the previous season. The NL took no action on this matter.

Two major issues loomed large as the two leagues met during what was a very cold and unpleasant December in New York City—the continued and growing anxiety about the financial (and general) health of major-league baseball as the nation entered the second year of the Great Depression; and the need for the major and minor leagues to come to an agreement regarding the player draft. Inherent in the latter matter were unresolved and increasingly unpleasant battles between the majors and minors over the ownership and drafting of players, the specifics of when a player's options have been used up, and the ownership of minor-league clubs by major-league teams. Consternation over these issues was far from new, and had, in fact, been percolating for several years.

Concern over baseball's financial situation was tempered by NL President Heydler's report that 1930 had been the best year ever for the league despite the depression. Attendance was up 500,000 from 1929's total of about 5,000,000, led by the Cubs with 1,463,624. Even Brooklyn surpassed a million in attendance. The New York Giants were the best road draw, and the Boston Braves, with a gate figure just shy of 465,000, had their best year ever despite a sixth-place finish. However, "high salaries and soaring operating expenses" were said to prevent some clubs from making any significant profits in this record-setting attendance year.

There had also been much gossip but little action about attempting to get Commissioner Landis to change his views about major-league team owners also owning minor-league teams. Landis was vociferous in his disdain of the practice, and again tales flew that the owners might try to induce him to mellow his stance on what was termed the "chain-store" model of ownership. Sitting on the other side of the issue was Branch Rickey, vice president of the Cardinals and regarded as "King of the Chain Store System,"[27] who had loudly and frequently voiced his opposition to Landis's claims.[28]

Word was that major-league team owners might attempt to override Landis's ruling that owners register with the major-league office whenever they purchased a minor-league team. Meanwhile Cubs owner William L. Veeck indicated that his organization planned to sell its Reading franchise as soon as possible. "We do not want any minor-league teams on our shoulders and we want to be free to purchase or trade for any players who we believe will aid the Cubs," Veeck said.[29] Similarly, Indians GM Billy Evans also announced that Cleveland would "abandon the chain-store program" and sell its interests in minor-league teams.[30]

Making matters worse was the fact that Branch Rickey, at the opening of the National Association convention in Montreal earlier in the week, had demanded that the minor leagues to seek resolution of the rules regarding ownership of minor-league teams by major-league clubs. Criticizing Landis's position, Rickey maintained that the "chain-store" model was essential to minor-league baseball, and that it (and not night baseball) was the main reason small teams were able to remain in business. His remarks were viewed by some as "a slap to the face of the National Board of Arbitration and at the commissioner."[31] Rickey expressed hope that someday there would be rules in place that would give "clubs in minor leagues ... owned by major-league interests the same rights in dealing with players as independently owned clubs," and he pleaded with attendees to make a clear and definitive decision as to whether they wanted minor-league teams to be owned by major-league organizations.[32]

Rickey contended that major-league owners sought guarantees that minor leaguers on teams owned by major-league clubs would be treated identically to players on independently owned minor-league clubs. He maintained that this arrangement would allow the moving of a minor leaguer on a major-league-owned club to another club owned by the major-league organization without the move being considered an option for a period of no more than two years. Delegates at the meeting viewed this as an effort by the major leagues to be allowed to move players among their teams indefinitely, until a player's skills and value had diminished. Not surprisingly, Rickey's comments received only a lukewarm reception.

Rickey was clearly speaking about Landis's ruling that George Toporcer of the Cardinals' Rochester team must either be sold to a minor-league team not owned by the Cardinals or put on the Cardinals' major-league roster. Toporcer had played for the better part of eight years with the Cardinals' major-league club. However, in 1928 St. Louis sent him to Rochester, where he spent the next several years, winning the International League MVP award in 1929 and 1930, and was player-manager from 1932 to 1934.

Apparently Leslie O'Connor, secretary to Commissioner Landis, had revealed during the major leagues' joint meeting that St. Louis had asked Landis to "interpret the rules of the major-league agreement without discrimination against clubs which happened to have minor-league holdings."[33] The request was taken to be a shot at the commissioner, and was withdrawn before being put to a vote.

The National Association committee of nine (with three members from each of the three Class-AA leagues) attended the meetings, and were initially scheduled to meet with delegates from the AL and NL on the first day of the gathering. The American League representatives failed to appear, so the meeting was rescheduled for the next day. When the joint meeting did convene, the outcome proved to be very disappointing for the minors — the committee from the major leagues simply refused to consider any deal regarding the drafting of players from minor-league teams. The minor leagues wanted a $10,000 draft price; the majors offered $7,500. The minor leagues wanted a ban on drafting players with less than four years' experience; the majors countered with three years.[34]

Given the impasse, minor-league committee members suggested that these questions be submitted to Landis, but the major-league group objected, and members of both committees ended up feeling rebuffed and angry. The minor-league members left the meeting with a sense of being coerced and disrespected, and conversations began among several Double-A owners about creating their own organization, which could possibly lead to the creation of a third major league. The major-league members would not disclose the reason for their objection, and were adamant in their stance. Major-league teams were left to wonder where they could put players who did not make the major-league roster after the season began; minor-league teams wondered how and where they would be able to lure talent without the interchange with the major-league clubs. Pessimism pervaded the rank-and-file of Organized Baseball.

After the meetings, major-league owners sent to every member of the National Association a "definite statement of the proposition made to them in the last conference on the draft that was held in New York." NL President Heydler went so far as to make certain that the letter and proposal would be published in *The Sporting News*, noting that "there is nothing to conceal. On the contrary we would like to have the public and all of the minor organizations know exactly where the major leagues stand."[35] AL President Barnard asserted that he believed the entire disagreement would be cleared up in short time, and certainly before exhibition games were to begin in the spring.

In their proposal the majors offered a new price scale: $7,000 for players drafted from Double-A $6,000 for players drafted from A leagues, $5,000 for players drafted from B leagues, $2,500 for players drafted from C leagues, and $2,000 for players drafted from D leagues. They offered these concessions — a minor-league club that loses a player to the majors is not subject to a further selection by Double-A teams; a player whose contract has never been assigned to a minor-league club by a major-league team shall not be subject to selection by Double-A teams until he has the same three-year service time that would make him eligible to be selected by a major-league team. Several other points of lesser importance were also included in the proposal.[36]

Later in the month the stalemate was broken when the American Association and Western League reluctantly accepted the proposal. The Pacific Coast League was also believed to be in favor of the universal draft language, although it had prospered financially from the previous arrangement. Nonetheless, there was no official announcement of acceptance from any minor-league clubs. The hope was that Santa might provide a special gift as the holiday season approached.[37]

NOTES

1. Gene Kessler, "So They Say," *The Sporting News*, December 11, 1930: 3.
2. "National Association Reserve Bulletin Lists Personnel of 142 Clubs," *The Sporting News*, December 4, 1930: 6.
3. "Farrell Makes 1930 Report at Montreal." *The Sporting News*, December 4, 1930: 1.
4. "So They Say."
5. Robert F. Burk, *Much More Than a Game: Players, Owners, and American Baseball Since 1921* (Chapel Hill: University of North Carolina Press: 2001), 34.
6. Neil J. Sullivan, *The Dodgers Move West* (New York: Oxford University Press, 1989), 92.
7. "Minors Prepare at Montreal to Submit Majors Peace Pact," *The Sporting News*, December 11, 1930: 5.
8. "Majors' 1931 Plans Ignore Draft Issue," *The Sporting News*, November 27, 1930: 5.
9. "Coast League Deadlock on President Unbroken," *The Sporting News*, December 4, 1930: 2.
10. Gene Kessler, "Picked Up in Corridors of Mount Royal Hotel during Pow-Wow at Montreal," *The Sporting News*, December 11, 1930: 3.
11. "Minors Prepare at Montreal to Submit Majors Peace Pact."
12. "Scribbled by Scribes," *The Sporting News*, December 4, 1930: 4
13. "Picked Up in Corridors of Mount Royal Hotel during Pow-Wow at Montreal."
14. "N.Y. Clubs Pry Into Trade Mart While Acting as Hosts to Majors," *The Sporting News*, December 11, 1930: 1.
15. "Minors Adopt Six Rule Amendments," *The Sporting News*, December 11, 1930: 5.
16. "Majors Agree to Hear Terms of Minors' Offer," *The Sporting News*, December 11, 1930: 1.
17. "Many Ready to Bid for Baker Holdings," *The Sporting News*, December 11, 1930: 1; "Ruch, Baker's Heirs Will Retain Phillies," *The Sporting News*, December 18, 1930: 1; "Two Women Share Baker's Club Stock," *The Sporting News*, December 18, 1930: 2.
18. "Frank York, Seeking Pitchers, Gets Case of 'Convention Feet,'" *The Sporting News*, December 11, 1930: 1.
19. "N.Y. Clubs Pry Into Trade Mart While Acting as Hosts to Majors."
20. "Caught in the Draft of Corridors at Majors' Conclave," *The Sporting News*, December 18, 1930: 6.
21. "Listening In at Majors' Gabfest," "Summary of Major Leagues' Decisions."
22. "New York Sessions Fail to Bring End to Draft Dispute," *The Sporting News*, December 18, 1930: 2.
23. "Summary of Major Leagues' Decisions"; "The Major League Meetings," *The Sporting News*, December 18, 1930: 1.
24. "Summary of Major Leagues' Decisions."
25. "Listening In at Majors' Gabfest." "Summary of Major Leagues' Decisions."
26. "Rickey Demands Equal Rights for 'Farms,'" *The Sporting News*, December 11, 1930: 7.
27. "Majors Agree to Hear Terms of Minors' Offer," *The Sporting News*, December 11, 1930: 1.
28. "Picked Up in Corridors of Mount Royal Hotel during Pow-Wow at Montreal."
29. "Indians' Heart Set on Ruel and Kamm," *The Sporting News*, December 11, 1930: 5.
30. "Rickey Demands Equal Rights for 'Farms.'"
31. "Minors Prepare at Montreal to Submit Majors Peace Pact," *The Sporting News*, December 11, 1930: 6.
32. Ibid.
33. "Browns will Start With Young Infield," *The Sporting News*, December 18, 1930: 2.
34. "Major Leagues Offer to End Strife over Draft by Agreeing to Graduate Pay Increases for Selected Players and Liberalizing of Option Provisions," *The Sporting News*, December 25, 1930: 8.
35. "Synopsis of Majors' Draft Concessions," *The Sporting News*, December 25, 1930: 1.
36. "American Association Leads Way for Universal Draft Agreement," *The Sporting News*, December 25, 1930: 1.
37. Ibid.

— 1931 —
BASEBALL GETS A TASTE OF DEPRESSION

By Ted Leavengood

AS THE MAJOR-LEAGUE OWNERSHIP gathered in Chicago, Illinois from December 8 through 10, 1931, the Great Depression was a silent partner to the discussions. Unemployment rose dramatically in 1931, topping out at 16 percent and showing no signs of relenting. Attendance dropped at almost every ballpark during the 1931 season, and overall attendance for the major leagues fell by 17 percent. In 1930 three teams — the Dodgers, Yankees, and Cubs — had all topped the one million mark in attendance, but only the Cubs exceeded that mark in 1931 and they lost almost 400,000 fans. Baseball was a powerful antidote to the bad economic news that beset the nation and the sport was still in relatively robust financial condition, but the effects of the worst fiscal downturn in American history were being felt even by the National Pastime as Americans curtailed their attendance at games, and those that could afford a trip to the ballpark had far less money to spend.

The annual gathering of baseball executives began with the meeting of the National Association of Professional Baseball Leagues, with the 16 existing minor leagues gathering at the West Baden Springs Hotel and Resort in southern Indiana from December 2 through 4. The hotel was known as the "Eighth Wonder of the World" and the resort featured a mineral spring spa similar to its European counterpart in Baden Baden, Germany. A casino, race track, and baseball field were part of the attraction, but as baseball magnates perambulated its posh hallways and meeting rooms, the hotel was actually in desperate straits and would close for good early the next year.

The setting was perfect however, given the focus of the minor-league leadership on their worsening economic conditions. The 1930 season had ended with 22 leagues but only 19 were able to open in 1931 and just 16 had completed their seasons; in addition, a number of teams had been forced to fold throughout the year. Preliminary meetings had been held to discuss the failures of teams in Toledo, Ohio and Mobile, Alabama, both of which had been relocated. Major-league officials in general attended the meetings, but Branch Rickey, who was deeply invested in the viability of the minors as a "farm" system for his Cardinals ballclub, attended these preliminary meetings. More than anyone, Rickey was a prime mover in the affairs in West Baden.

The hot topics for the meetings included reducing National Association staff and consolidating its offices to curb overhead expenses, and electing a new leader to replace Michael Sexton, who was viewed as partially responsible for the economic overreach of the organization. Sexton had become the salaried president of the association in 1920 and he had expanded its financial commitments, all of which were on the table in 1931. Secretary-Treasurer John Farrell, who had been with the association since its inception, was retained for a year.[1]

Five men jockeyed to succeed Sexton at the meetings and eventually a five-person executive committee, rather than one man, was chosen to replace Sexton. The group included Warren Giles, president of the Rochester team in the (Class-AA) International League (and future National League president), Joe Carr from the St. Paul club of the (Class-AA) American Association, Alvin Gardner, president of the (Class-A) Texas League, Ross Harriott of the Terre Haute club in the (Class-B) Three-I League, and W.G. Branham, president of the (Class-C) Piedmont League and eventual successor to Sexton, and they were charged with studying conditions and governing for one year and reporting their findings and recommendations back to the NAPBL at the 1932 Winter Meetings.[2] Branch Rickey was said to have been a major actor in the re-organization of the minor leagues and these personnel changes. He noted for the *New York Times* that the minor leagues had been reduced from 52 leagues in 1922 to the 16 operating in 1931 and he said of the new minor-league regime, "We don't expect the committee to work wonders," but he believed that progressive action was needed.[3] The word "progressive" dominated the descriptions of the meetings and what was needed to right the ship of baseball's lower levels.

In addition to the re-organization, a new collective agreement was reached in which player salaries were lowered and various unsavory practices, such as signing players under assumed names and aliases, would be abandoned, but ultimately little comment was offered on the promise made going into the meetings to ask Commissioner Landis to set aside funds to assist the minors in moving back into many of the small towns where teams had recently failed. The most common source of cash for minor-league teams—purchase of their players by major-league teams—was far less common in 1931, a sure sign that the pinch was being felt by all.[4] Rickey was less active in personnel matters affecting his own team, but did pay $12,500, one of the highest sums ever, for an outfielder, Nick Cullop, who broke the American Association home run record in 1930 would play for the Cardinals affiliate in Columbus, Ohio.

Many major-league teams sought to answer nagging roster concerns by purchasing minor-league standouts. The White Sox purchased outfielder Harold Anderson from St. Paul to add to their major-league roster, which would make a later deal with the Washington Nationals possible. Bill Veeck, Sr. of the Cubs told *The Sporting News* that he saw his team being aggressive at the meetings in pursuit of any talent to help the club

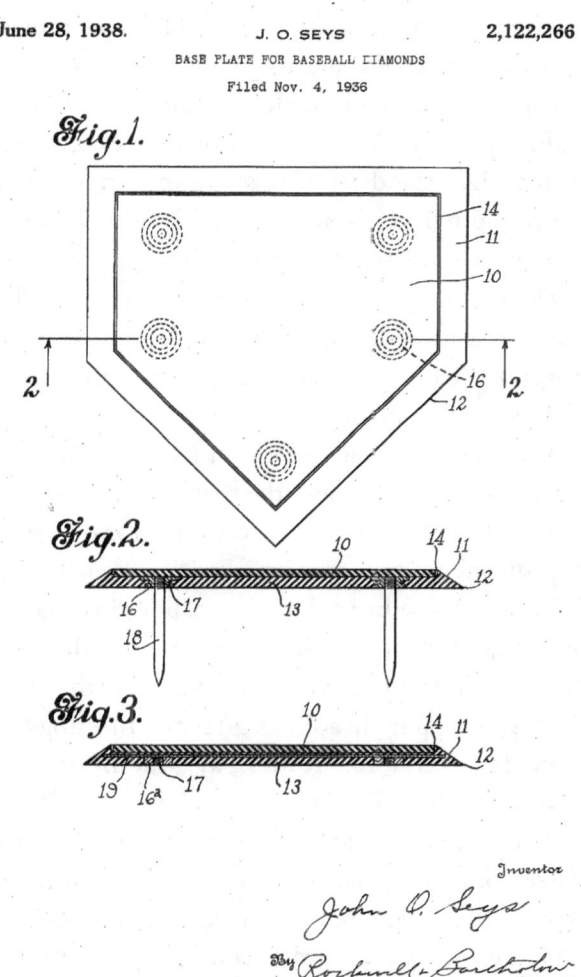

in the 1932 season.[5] There were similar comments from Connie Mack of the Athletics and Gabby Street of the Cardinals, but it was the Boston Red Sox which purchased two minor-league pitchers, John Michaels and Bob Weiland, in an attempt to add that elusive left-hander who might emerge and lead them back to prominence. The Philadelphia Athletics, coming off their third American League pennant in a row, had failed to beat the Cardinals in the World Series and Mack was looking at Cleveland shortstop Eddie Morgan as perhaps the missing piece that might give them enough to win it all in 1932.

Following the death of Charlie Comiskey on October 26, 1931 the White Sox team was taken over by his son, Louis. In his first Winter Meetings, the son hoped to establish his bona fides with an aggressive attempt to upgrade his father's team. The Sox had been mired in the lower division for the years following the Black Sox scandal of 1919. He consummated the first trade of the meetings by sending outfielder Chuck Reynolds and infielder Johnny Kerr to Clark Griffith of the Washington Nationals in exchange for a pair of right-handers: 40-year-old veteran Sam Jones and young reliever Irving "Bump" Hadley (who had fallen from grace with manager Walter Johnson), and infielder Minter Hayes. Comiskey and manager Lou Fonseca expressed repeatedly that other than young prospect Vic Fraser, every other name on the existing roster was available in trade.[6]

The 1931 major-league Winter Meetings began on a Tuesday in Chicago and the news was all about the salary cuts and the tough road to hoe for ownership in confronting the economic crisis.[7] Baseball was selling an escape from the grim realities in which far too many Americans were engulfed, but there was no escaping the overwhelming tenor of the times. *The Sporting News* headlines after the meetings had concluded said it all: "Ruth's Pay May Be Reduced to $50,000"; "Cards Not to Play Santa Claus."[8] Babe Ruth had been paid $80,000 annually each of the prior two seasons and Yankee owner Colonel Jacob Rupert reported the reduction. The Cardinals were determined not to give away the newly-acquired Hack Wilson.

The meetings produced an explicit agreement that major-league rosters were to be reduced from 25 to 23 for the 1932 season, a move that was applauded by *The Sporting News* in an under-the-masthead summary of the 1931 Winter Meetings. The reduction, which had to be achieved by June 15, also required the 40-man roster to be reduced to 38. *The Sporting News* believed that there were too many players on the major-league rosters who did not belong there, regardless of whether or not money would be saved. The two leagues differed on the number, with the American League preferring 22 and the National League 23. Commissioner Landis had settled the issue by voting for 23.[9]

Whether the roster sizes were cut for monetary or aesthetic reasons, the rationale in trimming salaries was without question a bow to the winds of economic despair that gripped the country. A formal resolution was voted to extend to all players and staff, which stated that, "by reason of prevailing conditions and the decrease in attendance at our games, it becomes necessary that the general operating expenses including salaries of ball players in both leagues, be substantially reduced."[10] *The Sporting News* opined that baseball was following the lead of the rest of American industry, but conceded that the sport could not *mandate* a reduction without giving impetus for a re-examination of the ruling that the major leagues did *not* constitute a trust in violation of American law. Almost immediately, there was a new impetus for a new players union, and it was rumored that former players such as Ty Cobb and George Sisler were being sought to lead it.

The meetings discussed a wide range of issues, including broadcasting of games on radio (a practice that had begun a decade earlier), but which also saw some clubs deriving greater income than others. These meetings continued the wariness of many toward the new technology, as ownership believed that radio broadcasts cut into home attendance without giving them adequate compensation. *The Sporting News* warned in fact that radio would be employed at the discretion of individual owners, though there was "intimation that it would be barred in all parks in 1933."[11] The sentiments of the major-league owners may have been colored by the request from the minor leagues in West Baden a week earlier to tax radio broadcasts as a means of support for the farm systems being cultivated increasingly by major-league franchises.

The meetings forbade "synthetic doubleheaders" that were not scheduled officially but agreed to by owners trying to pack greater attendance into two weekend games instead of a weekday game. Although not in a mood to structure a money-sharing arrangement with the National Association, in a show of largesse, the otherwise conservative major-league philanthropists agreed to donate $50,000 to support the American Legion tournament. And in a final matter of business, the owners responded to rumors that the ball had been too lively in 1930 and had been replaced with something less prone to leaving the park in 1931. The owners said in an official resolution that no changes to the ball were to be made for the 1932 season, calculating perhaps that keeping balls in the park meant less to be spent on horsehide.

There were few trades made during the meetings in Chicago. But the most talked about transaction occurred between two of the most notable figures of the time — Branch Rickey, who was formally named vice president of the St. Louis Cardinals at the meetings, and Bill Veeck, Sr. of the Chicago Cubs. Branch Rickey had not sought out Lewis "Hack" Wilson, but in one of the most interesting deals of the 1931 Winter Meetings he acquired the slugging outfielder, and left-handed pitcher Arthur "Bud" Teachout from the Chicago Cubs for future Hall of Fame righty Burleigh Grimes. In the preceding World Series, Grimes had won the decisive Game Seven for the Cardinals as they defeated Connie Mack's Philadelphia Athletics. Grimes had won Game Three as well and was regarded as a hero by St. Louis fans. Yet Rickey believed it was better to trade a player a year too early than a year too late and he told *The Sporting News* that he saw Wilson as an "attractive bond," one that would bring a productive yield in trade.[12]

Correspondingly, the Cubs' Veeck had promised several weeks earlier he would be active in reshaping his roster, and trading Hack Wilson for Burleigh Grimes got rid of a player on the decline, and one (accurately) rumored to be drinking far too much, for a World Series standout. Grimes had won 25 games against the Cubs over the course of his career and from the perspective of the Chicago brain trust, they could not have been happier to have him on their side for the 1932 season. Given Wilson's reputation for carousing and heavy drinking, it was difficult to believe that Rickey had not outsmarted himself, but no sooner had the trade hit the wires than Rickey was able to convince Brooklyn to invest $45,000 (and minor-league outfielder/first baseman Bob Parham) in Wilson, one of the few cash deals made prior to the 1932 season and made at a time when owners were not as awash in cash as they had once been.[13]

Branch Rickey was likely motivated by two external issues. The first was the demands of a burgeoning minor-league operation matched by none. Money to support that operation was no doubt part of Rickey's motivation in trading for Wilson. Additionally, Grimes was 38 years old and Rickey had the 22-year-old Dizzy Dean waiting in the wings. Dean had first appeared for the Cardinals in 1930 in a single game that he won impressively. But Rickey gave the outspoken Dean another year of seasoning in the minors in 1931, to which he responded by winning 26 games, throwing 304 innings and posting a 1.57 ERA. Dean was ready and he would step in for Burleigh Grimes capably from the start of the 1932 season, throwing 286 innings and winning 18 games for a team that finished sixth in the National League. The Cubs did wind up winning the pennant, but it was not the addition of Burleigh Grimes that pushed them to the top of the league. The future Hall of Famer slumped and won only six games with an ERA of 4.78. Rickey got the better end of the trade, even if the return did not manifest itself in obvious terms.

It is possible that the economic reserves of various teams served to diminish the usual trade discussions. There was considerable discussion, for instance, that the Yankees desired to trade infielder Tony Lazzeri. There were numerous capable infielders in the New York minor-league farm system, the most notable of which was Frankie Crosetti. Lazzeri would weather these trade winds, however, and teamed with Crosetti in a formidable Yankee middle infield until 1938, when the then-33-year-old Lazzeri was released and picked up by the Cubs.

The most sought-after player at the Winter Meetings was outfielder Chuck Klein of the Philadelphia Phillies. Klein had led the National League in home runs in 1929 with 43 and had followed with two more seasons at or near the top of the league in power categories. Though the Phillies had featured Lefty O'Doul with Klein in 1929, the team had managed nothing better than a fifth place finish. They had dropped to last in 1930 and, though they won 14 more games in 1931, concluded another losing season, this time in sixth place in the National League. The conventional wisdom was that they would be well-served to trade Klein for a good arm, but the meetings concluded with Klein still playing in Philadelphia.

The meetings were quiet in contrast to other years where numerous high-profile players changed teams. But the sport had deepening concerns about the economy and at these meetings made important progress in meeting the challenges that beset the country. That so many measures directly affecting players could be initiated by the owners without question or redress is unimaginable from the modern perspective, where the Major League Baseball Players Association (MLBPA) requires negotiation on issues of much less significance that minimum roster sizes or resolutions to reduce pay across the board. Unionization became a fact of life for American industry in the 1930's with the passage of the National Labor Relations Act in 1935, and would ultimately lead to the formation of the MLBPA 30 years later.

The roster size reductions at the major-league level were of far less consequence than in the minors, where whole leagues had ceased to exist due simply to economics. The draconian situation facing many players at the lower levels was detailed in a piece in *The Sporting News* two weeks after all meetings had ended. The Pacific Coast League particularly targeted veteran players, like Hugh McQuillan and Hank Severeid, whose big-league experience and name recognition had previously helped provide legitimacy to minor-league teams and sell tickets. But their salaries began to outweigh the benefits and many recognizable names were given pink slips in the weeks just before Christmas 1931.[14]

The Negro National League had met January 27 to January 29, 1931 to confront the extreme economic issues that beset all professional baseball. The league was forced to contract its size by dropping the Memphis Red Sox, Birmingham Black Barons, and Cuban Stars, and adding the Louisville White Sox and Indianapolis ABC's. The league memorialized Rube Foster on Opening Day of the 1931 season. Foster, known as the Father of Black Baseball and the principal organizer and first president of the National Negro League, died December 9, 1930. The changes adopted at the January meeting did not prevent the demise of the National Negro League that ceased to operate after the 1931 season.[15]

All of baseball was now just beginning to confront the changing economic landscape. More would come in the seasons that followed as Connie Mack and Clark Griffith would be forced to sell off their best players just to meet payroll for the coming season. The 1931 Winter Meetings were the beginning of a decade of change for major-league baseball, when the pain being felt by the country as a whole touched home for the National Pastime.

NOTES

1. Edgar G. Brands. "Minors All Set for Busy Session at West Baden Next Week," *The Sporting News*, November 26, 1931: 3; Brands. "Committee of Five Assumes Administration of National Association," *The Sporting News*, December 10, 1931: 3. Farrell ultimately remained as treasurer through 1937.

2. Edgar G. Brands. "Committee of Five Assumes Administration of National Association."

3. Associated Press, "Minor Leagues End Regime of Sexton," *New York Times*, December 4, 1931: 30.

4. "Few Deals for Cash Made in West Baden," *The Sporting News*, December 10, 1931: 5.

5. Edward Burns. "Veeck Promises Answers to Cubs Riddles in 1932 Within Few Days," *The Sporting News*, December 3, 1931: 1.

6. Edward Burns. "All of White Sox, Except Fraser, Put on Block For Sale or Barter," *The Sporting News*, December 10, 1931: 1.

7. Edgar G. Brands. "Economy Made Watchword of Majors at Annual Conference," *The Sporting News*, December 17, 1931: 3.

8. Joe Vila. "Ruth's Pay May Be Reduced to $50,000," *The Sporting News*, December 17, 1931: 1.

9. "The Cut in Players," *The Sporting News*, December 17, 1931: 4.

10. "Conforming to National Conditions," *The Sporting News*, December 4, 1931: 4.

11. Brands, "Economy Made Watchword at Majors."

12. "Cardinals Not To Play Santa Claus By Giving Wilson Away for Song," *The Sporting News*, December 17, 1931: 1.

13. Lee Lowenfish, *Branch Rickey, Baseball's Ferocious Gentleman* (Lincoln: University of Nebraska Press, 2009), 220.

14. "Coast Owners Sharpen Knives to Cut Salaries," *The Sporting News*, December 10, 1931: 7.

15. Thanks to Robert Reeder. See John B. Holway. *The Complete Book of Baseball's Negro Leagues: The Other Half of Baseball History*, 2nd edition (Winter Park, Florida: Hastings House, 2001), passim.

— 1932 —
WEALTH OF CHANGES REVITALIZES BASEBALL IN POOR TIMES

By Ely Sussman

Introduction and Context

AMERICA WAS ENGULFED IN THE Great Depression when the 1932 Winter Meetings arrived, and like everything else, its greatest pastime was affected negatively. For lack of funds, only 16 minor-league circuits completed the 1932 season, down from the 25 that did so three years prior.[1] As a result, many baseball players were forced into unemployment. It was necessary for the National Association to reorganize in accordance with the plans that had been conceived at their West Baden, Indiana, meeting in 1931. "The annual convention," reported Edgar G. Brands of *The Sporting News*, was expected to be "the most important [for the National Association] since its organization."[2]

Delegates met December 7-9 in Columbus, Ohio, at the Deshler-Wallick Hotel, at the time considered one of the most luxurious hotels in the city. With an approximate population of 290,000, Columbus was not cluttered or difficult to navigate.[3]

Meanwhile, major-league baseball was prepared to discuss everything from competitive balance to World Series shares to attendance figures to radio broadcasting rights. Though the major-league teams were in a less dire condition than their minor-league brethren, few were coming off profitable seasons and steps had to be taken to ensure that the sport could weather the economic storm. Everything took place in New York City at the Commodore Hotel in Midtown Manhattan. The American and National Leagues held separate sessions on December 13-14 and convened for a joint meeting on the 15th.

Player/Personnel Movement (National Association)

The player market was largely untouched during the Columbus meetings. The inactivity was unsurprising because movement had been minimal throughout the summer and fall, too. The majors didn't execute any deals between themselves and the minors during the three days.

However, a couple of unusual transactions were announced. Two American Association umpires (R.W. Snyder and Joe Rue) were swapped for a pair from the Pacific Coast League (Tom Dunn and Eddie McLaughlin).[4] This was simply for the convenience of the men involved, allowing them to work closer to home. Also, a manager and coach effectively swapped places. Del Baker, manager of the Beaumont Exporters, the Texas League affiliate of the Detroit Tigers, headed to the major-league club as a coach for manager Bucky Harris and Detroit coach Bob Coleman was named manager of Beaumont. Baker later managed the Tigers for several seasons, winning the AL pennant in 1940. Coleman, a veteran minor-league skipper, took the reins in Beaumont and later resurfaced in the majors at the helm of the Boston Braves (1943-1945).

Player/Personnel Movement in the Majors

Covering the Winter Meetings for *The Sporting News*, Daniel M. Daniel reported that major-league executives "certainly set a record" in making no fewer than 12 trades. "Most of them were of primary importance," he added.[5]

BASEBALL'S BUSINESS: THE WINTER MEETINGS

Brooklyn Dodgers manager Max Carey made it known that he was interested in adding pitching depth. He offered second baseman Neal Finn, third baseman Jack Warner, right-handed reliever Austin "Cy" Moore, and $15,000 to the Philadelphia Phillies for right-handed starter Ray Benge. Originally, the Phillies were unwilling to accept until Finn was included. Although not known for his hitting ability, Finn was the premier defensive player they needed to fill a gaping hole in the infield. Tragically, Finn needed midseason surgery to repair an ulcer, and he died on July 7.[6]

Outfielder and third baseman Freddie Lindstrom of the New York Giants was eager to be dealt during the meetings. Longtime manager John McGraw had retired in June, and Lindstrom didn't enjoy playing under the direction of his successor, first baseman Bill Terry. The Giants' sixth-place finish only lowered his spirits further. Three teams had to get involved, but ultimately Lindstrom became a Pittsburgh Pirate. To acquire him, the Bucs traded right-hander Glenn Spencer to the Giants and outfielder Gus Dugas and $15,000 to the Phillies. The Phillies received outfielder Chick Fullis from the Giants and sent them center fielder George "Kiddo" Davis to fill the vacancy left by Lindstrom's departure.

President Clark Griffith of the Washington Senators was concerned with bulking up his bullpen. He gladly moved Harley Boss, the first baseman for his Southern Association affiliate in Chattanooga, to the Cleveland Indians for right-handed reliever Jack Russell and minor-league first baseman Bruce Connatser. Russell rewarded his new team in 1933 with 12 wins and a 2.69 earned-run average.

Struggling left-handed pitcher Carl Fischer was dealt twice before the "wild trading orgy" was through.[7] On December 13 the St. Louis Browns swapped him for Washington righty Dick Coffman. Only hours after changing teams, Fischer was packaged with the steady right-handed reliever Firpo Marberry and sent to the Tigers for 10-year veteran Earl Whitehill. This also paid immediate dividends for the Senators, as the left-handed Whitehill logged 270 innings and won 22 games in 1933, leading them to the pennant. And St. Louis and Washington weren't through dealing with each other. The Browns gave up outfielders Goose Goslin and Fred Schulte, along with starting pitcher Lefty Stewart, and their compensation included outfielders Carl Reynolds and Sam West, southpaw Lloyd Brown and $20,000. This deal was warmly received in the nation's capital. Goslin, a future Hall of Famer, had broken into the majors with the Senators and spent parts of 10 seasons with them before his stint with the Browns. They also knew of Stewart's ability firsthand, as he had defeated the Nationals 10 times in 1931 and '32. While Goslin and Schulte played key roles in the Senators' pennant-winning campaign, St. Louis fell into the cellar the next year for the first time since 1913.

Desperate to rebound from miserable seasons, the Boston Red Sox (43-111) and Chicago White Sox (49-102) did a bit of business. Boston sent shortstop Al Rhyne and right-handed starting pitcher Eddie Durham to Chicago for outfielders Bob Fothergill and Bob Seeds, shortstop Gregory Mulleavy, and infielder Johnny Hodapp. None of these six players contributed much to their new teams, but both clubs fared far better in 1933 (the White Sox won 67 games, the Red Sox, 63).

Several teams plucked promising young players from the minor leagues. By sending shortstop Doc Marshall plus $5,000 to the Buffalo Bisons of the International League, the Giants added third baseman Blondy Ryan. The Brooklyn Dodgers obtained coveted shortstop Linus Frey of the Southern Association's Nashville Vols for right-handed pitcher Earl Mattingly and $10,000. The Boston Braves purchased infielders Dick Gyselman and Al Wright from the Mission Reds of the Pacific Coast League for $60,000, and threw in pitcher-third baseman Bucky Walters. Though the 23-year-old Walters hadn't accomplished much at this point in his career, he eventually developed into a six-time All-Star and the National League's Most Valuable Player in 1939.

All but three of the 16 major-league franchises made trades during the Winter Meetings. The exceptions were the pennant-winning Chicago Cubs (90-64) and New York Yankees (107-47), and the Philadelphia

Athletics, winners of 94 games. Yankees business manager Ed Barrow and skipper Joe McCarthy considered a couple of deals, but felt little pressure to make a move after winning close to 70 percent of their games. "I've got the best club in the world," McCarthy said, "and it hasn't started to slip yet."[8] This may have jinxed the Yankees, who would finish second in the standings in 1933. The Cubs and A's followed up their 1932 seasons by dropping into third place.

Rule Changes and Other Business (National Association)

As was necessary, the Columbus meeting of the National Association led to "revolutionary changes."[9] Contrary to what had been reported earlier in the offseason, Judge William G. Bramham was willing to run for president and he was elected unanimously. New officers were chosen to comprise the Executive Committee, which replaced the National Board of Arbitration. Warren Giles, general manager of the International League's Rochester Red Wings; J. Alvin Gardner, Texas League president; and Dale Gear, president of the Western League and the Western Association, were selected as representatives of the Class AA (Giles), Class A (Gardner), and Class B, C, and D leagues (Gear). Bramham's election filled the hole created when Michael H. Sexton, National Association president since 1909, was ousted in 1931. Sexton's tenure as president remained in 2016 the longest in the history of the minors.

From the first sessions on December 7, the Committee of Five, the executives temporarily running the Association after Sexton was ousted, urged the minor leagues to establish salary limits that would aid competitive balance while safeguarding the clubs in uncertain economic times. Most circuits obliged, but because the Class-AA leagues were unable to agree upon a satisfactory figure, each one was allowed to determine its own limit.[10]

The Association's charter was amended to reflect the expansive reorganization. It was decided that annual meetings would be moved up to the third Wednesday in November. To raise funds for the maintenance of the Association, the president was directed to keep 2 percent of the money paid to clubs whenever they reassigned players. Similarly, 3 percent of the gross gate receipts of all postseason series were to be paid to the treasury. Together with the president, the new Executive Committee was to approve league membership applications and require applicants to pay a fee for admittance.

Illness — the flu in most cases — prevented several key figures from attending. Presidents William E. Benswanger of the Pittsburgh Pirates and Bob Quinn of the Boston Red Sox, and Brooklyn's manager Max Carey were absent. Those who checked in but were physically limited included Perry B. Farrell, Thomas J. Hickey, and Clarence Howland, presidents of the New York-Penn League, American Association, and International League respectively.[11]

Galveston, Texas, was chosen to host the 1933 convention, thanks to the efforts of Ray Koehler and Billy Webb of the Galveston minor-league club. Indianapolis, Louisville, and Springfield, Massachusetts, also made bids.

Rule Changes and Other Business (Major Leagues)

Radio broadcasting was a hotly contested topic at the New York gathering. Owners William L. Veeck Sr. (Cubs), Judge Emil Fuchs (Braves), and Quinn (Red Sox) were known advocates, while some club owners, including those of all three New York clubs, were opposed. They felt broadcasts cut into ticket sales by deterring people from attending the games. The issue was put to rest at the joint meeting on December 15, when it was announced that each club could do whatever was in its best interests.[12]

A general reduction in salaries was inevitable. All umpires had to take pay cuts, and every club except the Yankees decided to drop one or more coaches to shed expenses.[13] Yankees business manager Ed Barrow, however, was no less motivated to save money. He was steadfast with the soon-to-be 38-year-old Babe Ruth and lowered his pay from $75,000 to $52,000.[14] The player limit was left at 23, but clubs were required to reach that number by May 15. The annual cutoff had previously been June 15, a date that was retained as the major-league trade deadline.

John A. Heydler, reelected president of the National League for a fifth term, said he would work for a smaller salary because of the economy. Steve McKeever (Brooklyn), Gerald Nugent (Philadelphia), Sam Breadon (St. Louis), and Sidney Weil (Cincinnati) comprised his board of directors for 1933.

Summary

"The majors are like a big building," Heydler declared in Columbus. "If the foundation lacks strength the structure is in grave danger."[15] Minor-league baseball was the "foundation" to which he was referring and after the 1932 Winter Meetings, it was far sturdier thanks to "the willingness of all, from top to bottom, to shoulder the burdens and accept the responsibilities placed upon them."[16] Now reorganized, the National Association was better prepared to endure the harsh economic times.

SOURCES

In addition to the sources cited in the Notes, the author also consulted:

Altenburg, Jess, Edgar G. Brands, and Bill Wambsganss. "Radical Changes to Be Made in Baseball Map and Regulations at Minors' Meeting at Columbus," *The Sporting News*, December 1, 1932: 6.

Lentz, Ed. *Columbus: The Story of a City* (Charleston, South Carolina: Arcadia Publishing, 2003), 116-118.

Thompson, Denman. "Griff Considering Bids for Young First Sacker," *The Sporting News*, December 8, 1932: 1.

NOTES

1. "The 3rd President," on The Official Site of Minor League Baseball, July 8, 2011. Accessed January 1, 2012: louisville.bats.milb.com/milb/history/presidents.jsp?mc=_bramham.
2. Edgar G. Brands, "Battle Lines Drawn as Minors Get Ready to Tackle Problems," *The Sporting News*, December 1, 1932: 1.
3. Irven Schelback, "Ambitious Programs Outlined for Delegates to Meeting," *The Sporting News*, December 8, 1932: 3.
4. "Class AA Ball Loops Can Set Own Pay Rolls," *San Diego Union*, December 10, 1932: 8.
5. Daniel M. Daniel, "Twelve Deals, Involving total of 42 Athletes, to Bring About Unusual Changes in Rosters," *The Sporting News*, December 22, 1932: 3.
6. "Mickey Finn Dies; Phils Infielder," *Boston Herald*, July 8, 1933: 6.
7. Tom Swope, "Cincy Fans Smiling the Sunny Jim Way," *The Sporting News*, December 22, 1932: 1.
8. Joe Vila, "'Why Should I Want to Deal?'" *The Sporting News*, December 22, 1932: 5.
9. "Revolutionary Changes Voted Into the National Agreement," *The Sporting News*, December 15, 1932: 5.
10. Edgar G. Brands, "National Association Revamped, Judge Bramham Named Head, Headquarters Moved to Durham," *The Sporting News*, December 15, 1932: 5.
11. "National Association Revamped," 5.
12. "Commissioner Will Find Farms 'Posted,'" *The Sporting News*, December 22, 1932: 3.
13. Harry Neily, "Heydler Gives Note of Cheer to Minors," *The Sporting News*, December 15, 1932: 3.
14. Daniel R. Levitt, *Ed Barrow: The Bulldog Who Built the Yankees' First Dynasty* (Lincoln: University of Nebraska Press, 2008), 285.
15. "Heydler Gives Note of Cheer to Minors."
16. "Revolutionary Changes Voted Into the National Agreement."

1933
THE SELL-OFF

By Jason C. Long

Introduction and Context

SOME OF THE BEST PLAYERS IN BASEball traded places at the 1933 winter meetings. The meetings opened amid optimism, with a feeling that baseball was recovering from the Depression and could "be expected to gain steadily" as it moved forward.[1] During 1933, all 14 minor leagues that began the season completed it; most teams did not suffer the expected losses; and a few even earned a profit. Nevertheless, at the minor-league meetings, the business focused on ousting "shoestring operators" to further ensure team and league solvency. As the action shifted to Chicago for the big leagues, big moves were rumored. Teams did in fact deal star players, including future Hall of Famers like Mickey Cochrane, Chuck Klein, and Lefty Grove. But in contrast with the optimistic atmosphere, the teams that traded away those players did so for financial reasons.

Blue Laws Lifted

Contributing to the optimism heading into the meetings was Philadelphia and Pittsburgh lifting their "Blue Laws." These laws had prohibited Sunday games. National League President John Heydler welcomed the change, saying that it "would do much to stabilize our circuit, especially in the case of the Phillies, who always have suffered under a heavy financial burden because they were unable to play their Sunday games at home."[2] The change ensured that, for the first time, all major-league clubs could play at home on Sundays.

The Minor League Meetings in Galveston

Eight days after those votes, the National Association of Professional Baseball Leagues (NAPBL) met on November 15 in Galveston, Texas, at the Buccaneer Hotel. Attendees were advised to bring their bathing suits and be ready for deep-sea fishing and a cruise on the US Coast Guard cutter *Saranac*.

The Business Side

When business began, the delegates considered proposed amendments to the National Association and Major-Minor Agreements. In general, these were minor and technical, although Commissioner Kenesaw Mountain Landis had recommended a provision to forfeit owners' rights to their teams if the teams fell into receivership. The Southern Association and American Association led the opposition to this provision; they questioned its legality and reasoned that the receiverships in place were helpful and should not be discarded. Apparently the other delegates shared this opposition, as they rejected the provision without a single vote in support.

Other business saw NAPBL President William G. Bramham assailing "shoestring" operators. He identified these as team owners who capitalize on civic pride to raise funds, then stall players and other creditors, and in some cases abscond with the funds.[3] The delegates adopted a rule to constrain these "bootleggers of franchises," as Bramham put it, by stipulating that any compensation due to a team owner or operator must first be transmitted through the NAPBL office. The NAPBL office could apply the funds to claims due, before the owner or operator could then receive the income.[4]

Bramham also spoke out against Shaughnessy playoffs, so called because Montreal Royals general manager Frank Shaughnessy devised the system for the International League. The system — familiar today — provided for the top four teams in a league to face off in postseason series, with the first- and fourth-place finishers and the second- and third-place finishers playing in the first round, followed by the winner of each series facing off for the league championship. In addition to the International League, the American Association, the Texas League, and several other leagues had adopted this system in 1933. Shaughnessy himself was "one of the busiest men at the convention," dealing not only with his club's business but also defending his playoff plan.[5] He insisted that no league that had adopted his plan would drop it for 1934. Bramham, on the other hand, said that playoffs were "not a test of real merit. It is commercializing the sport to a degree that must inevitably meet with popular disfavor."[6]

The meetings further saw Bramham warn against "chain store" operations, the beginnings of the modern minor-league system, in which teams in different leagues were owned by the same person or group, including big-league clubs. This made it easy to move players between them. Though prohibited by many leagues, it was still practiced via secret agreements and other violations that Bramham sought to punish with "severe penalties, which include free agency" for the players.[7] Indeed, heading into the meetings, the American Association resolved to prohibit any of its teams from using a player who had played for any team that had common ownership with the Association club. Otherwise, rules prohibiting chain-store systems were already in place, so the meetings offered only admonitions for teams to comply.

A few changes were aimed at play on the field as well. One that caused some discussion was the Southern Association adopting a new rule that allowed runners to advance on an intentional walk with two outs. A fan first suggested the rule, which provided that if there were two outs and the pitcher threw four consecutive balls to a batter, the batter was entitled to first base and any baserunners could advance two bases, except if runners were on second and third, in which case the runner on third would score but the runner on second would move to third. Officials of other leagues, including Frank Shaughnessy, exclaimed that the Southern Association had done "something great," but suggested that the rule should not apply if the pitcher threw a strike.[8]

Player Movement

In contrast with 1932, there was significant player movement during the minor-league meetings. Early on, the Cardinals and Phillies announced a trade of catchers, with Spud Davis heading to St. Louis in exchange for Jimmie Wilson. Both were well-regarded backstops: Davis hit .349 with nine home runs in 1933, while Wilson, noted for his defense and coming off an All-Star Game appearance (the first All-Star Game had been played during the season), hit .256. This was the second time the two catchers were dealt for each other: On May 11, 1928, they moved in opposite directions in a trade that occurred during a game. Wilson caught two innings of that game for the Phillies and was then told of the trade.[9] He went to the Cardinals' clubhouse, changed, and sat on their bench for the rest of the game. The 1933 trade also included the Cardinals acquiring infielder Ed Delker. The Phillies had acquired Delker from the Cardinals during the 1932 season, but he played poorly and was rumored to be injured. Reports were that the Phillies insisted that the Cardinals take him back for the same price that the Phillies had paid for him in 1932 as a condition of the Davis trade.[10]

Other trades saw the Browns and the White Sox swapping catchers, with St. Louis sending Mervyn Shea to Chicago for Frank Grube, and the Pirates acquiring right-handed pitcher Red Lucas and outfielder Walter Roettger from the Reds for outfielder Adam Comorosky and infielder Tony Piet. The Pirates were looking to bolster their staff, and Lucas had posted a 3.40 ERA in 219 innings in 1933. For the Reds, second baseman Piet was the prize, having hit .323 in 107 games in his third big-league season. The Reds traded infielder George Grantham to the Giants for righty Glenn Spencer, primarily a relief pitcher. The Dodgers and Cubs added to their teams as well, purchasing players from the minors during the meetings, while many minor-league players were traded or sold between minor-league clubs.

Summary

The Galveston meetings were described as the "most active player trading mart in years," which was attributed to the "the changed attitude toward the immediate future of the game—one of optimism."[11] With the location in Galveston, attendance had been expected to suffer, but registration unexpectedly reached 350 delegates. The sense of better times on the horizon led not only to the active trade market, but also to the minors increasing roster limits, player salaries, and executive salaries, while planning for several new leagues in 1934. And though all reports praised Galveston as host, the NAPBL sought a more central location for the 1934 meetings and chose Louisville, Kentucky.

The Major League Meetings in Chicago

Almost a month later the action shifted to Chicago for the major-league meetings. The big leaguers were expected to address topics including a uniform ball, radio broadcasts, the All-Star Game, and possibly extending Commissioner Landis's contract. There were also rumors of star players being moved; many expected the two Philadelphia teams to be most active at meetings anticipated to bring "the biggest turnover of talent in many years."[12]

The Chuck Klein Trade

The meetings were scheduled to begin on December 12, but the Phillies continued with their head start on trading. They followed up the Spud Davis deal by sending another key piece of their lineup, future Hall of Fame outfielder Chuck Klein, to the Cubs. The 1932 MVP and reigning National League batting champion (.368), Klein had also hit 28 home runs. Phillies president Gerald Nugent regretted that economics made Klein's trade necessary, but commented,

"… We are forced to make the trade through continued and heavy loss of money, not only last season but the season before as well.[13]

In exchange, the Phillies received first baseman Harvey Hendrick and infielder Mark Koenig from the Cubs, left-hander Ted Kleinhans from Atlanta of the Southern Association, and cash "in the neighborhood of $100,000." Nugent acknowledged that it "may appear that the Cubs are getting the better of the deal," but asked fans to "remember that the players coming [to Philadelphia] aren't our only profit from the transaction."[14]

The League Meetings

The formal meetings opened on Tuesday, December 12, with the American and National Leagues scheduled to hold their own meetings Tuesday and Wednesday, and the joint meeting set for Thursday, all at the Palmer House hotel. In the American League meeting, one of the first priorities was re-electing Will Harridge as league president, secretary, and treasurer for a five-year term. This contrasted with Harridge's previous one-year terms and was considered a tribute to his operations in trying times. On the topic of the uniform baseball, for instance, Harridge said that uniformity would both improve the game and save money:

> A uniform baseball for all organized baseball not only would improve the game but would result in the saving of vast sums of money now wasted. … For years club owners have been wasting big sums of cash on players who are permitted to compile staggering and dizzy batting averages with unusually live baseballs.[15]

Despite the American League having a livelier ball, the AL owners took no action to change their ball; they were confident that the National League would adopt their ball. Finally, the delegates at the AL meeting unanimously supported continuing the All-Star Game.

In contrast, the National League did not achieve much unanimity. Some teams opposed continuing the All-Star Game. President Heydler solicited a vote on a uniform ball, and five teams supported adopting a livelier ball like the American League's. Only

Bill Terry, manager of the World Series champion Giants, voted against it. The Giants' pitching led to their championship and they did not want a change. Neither the Phillies nor the Reds voted on the issue.

Each league voted to extend Commissioner Landis's contract for seven years and one month, so that he would remain commissioner through the end of the 1941 winter meetings. A committee consisting of Harridge, Heydler, Yankees owner Jacob Ruppert, Giants owner Charles Stoneham, Indians owner Alva Bradley, and Braves owner Emil Fuchs was authorized to present the extension to Landis as "a token of the owners esteem, gratitude," and "confidence in his administration."[16]

The Joint Session

Commissioner Landis then presided over the joint meeting, which lasted for three hours. The owners agreed to adopt a uniform ball, although they did not simply adopt the American League version, but authorized Harridge and Heydler to meet with manufacturers and settle on a ball for both leagues. Afterward, Heydler said it was "a little difficult to talk intelligently as to the exact texture, cover, and qualities of the ball," but noted that the differences in the American and National League versions were in the "stitching and thickness of the cover."[17] He acknowledged that the ball would be livelier than the version the NL had used in 1933, but was prepared for that:

> Maybe we won't have such marvelous pitching records in the National League next season, but it will be fair all around, and the good pitchers will rise above the mediocre ones as always.[18]

The big leagues also intended to persuade all minor leagues to use the same ball.

Although some National League teams opposed continuing the All-Star Game, the majority of all clubs prevailed and a 1934 game was planned for New York. There was no formal vote to continue the game permanently, but there was an understanding that the game would become an annual event and that Cleveland would host in 1935.[19]

Doubleheaders were another topic, with the leagues agreeing to prohibit "synthetic" doubleheaders on Sundays — i.e., twin bills created by postponing weekday games – until after June 15. This was a compromise between AL and NL owners, as some clubs wanted to prohibit planned twin bills. The leagues resolved that they would study the impact of the June 15 rule, and if it appeared that planned doubleheaders were unnecessary to bolster attendance, then each league would be permitted to place further restrictions on home clubs' discretion to schedule them.[20]

In other business, the leagues altered the practices governing counting players on option toward team limits and salary responsibility for optioned players, but left intact the rules governing radio broadcasts.[21] The existing rule allowed each club to decide for itself whether to broadcast its games. Only Cleveland and the two St. Louis clubs were selling broadcast rights at that time, with most of the other teams wanting no part of such an arrangement, believing that it cut into attendance. Finally, A's vice president John Shibe received permission to recruit an all-star team for a world exhibition tour after the 1934 season. His team would have to come from the American League; the NL declined to participate.

Connie Mack's Sell-off

The main attraction in Chicago did not take place in a meeting room. Instead, in the hotel's lobbies and suites, teams hammered out deals that moved some of the best players in the game. On the first day of the meetings, an "outwardly sad" Connie Mack announced that he had traded catcher Mickey Cochrane to the Tigers; left-handed pitchers Lefty Grove and Rube Walberg and second baseman Max Bishop to the Red Sox; and right-handed pitcher George Earnshaw to the White Sox.[22] These deals dismantled Mack's most recent powerhouse. Of the starting lineup that won three straight pennants from 1929 to 1931 and back-to-back World Series in 1929 and 1930, only Jimmie Foxx, the reigning AL MVP and Triple Crown winner, remained.

Though startling, the deals had been rumored for months. Since the end of the 1933 season, Tigers owner Frank Navin had been saying he would acquire Cochrane to lead the Tigers as player-manager in 1934. Before leaving Detroit for the meetings, he said he had scheduled "an appointment with Mack" and expected they would make a deal "without difficulty."[23] In turn, while the deal was still only a rumor, Cochrane reportedly told a friend that he "would be happy to manage the Tigers."[24] Mack reportedly asked the Tigers for $125,000 and catcher Ray Hayworth, but accepted catcher Johnny Pasek and $100,000. The Tigers announced immediately that Cochrane, who was at the meeting, would both manage and catch in 1934.

The deal with the Red Sox had also been churning for some time, though the principals were less explicit before Mack announced the trade. Lefty Grove had tied for the AL lead with 24 victories while sporting a 3.20 ERA (fourth in the league) in 1933. After the trade, Grove seemed pleased to be leaving the A's, saying he was "tickled to hear of it." He said he would be "glad to go" to Boston, which he admired as a baseball city, and was "sure [he would] have more enthusiasm for [his] pitching next year and the years thereafter than for some time."[25]

Max Bishop and Rube Walberg also moved from Philadelphia to Boston in the deal. Bishop hit .294 in 1933 with a stellar .446 on-base percentage. Walberg's statistics were less gaudy; he had a losing record (9-13) in 1933 and a 4.88 ERA, with the third-place Athletics. In return, the A's received shortstop Rabbit Warstler, right-hander Robert Kline, $125,000 for Grove, and $50,000 combined for Bishop and Walberg. Warstler, standing only 5-feet-7, was the quintessential all-glove, no-bat infielder, and the 6-foot-4 Kline had not achieved great success either, with a career ERA of 4.88 through 1933.

Connie Mack's third deal involved another big right-hander, the 6-foot-4 George Earnshaw. Mack traded Earnshaw and catcher John Pasek, just acquired in the Cochrane deal, to the White Sox for catcher Charlie Berry and a reported $25,000. Earnshaw had been a hero in the A's World Series wins, but fell on hard times in 1933. Mack sent Earnshaw home early in the year for being out of shape, and again during August, telling him not to return. Mack said that the A's clubhouse was "more congenial" without Earnshaw. The truth may have been that Earnshaw had a drinking problem.[26] In any event, the White Sox insisted on getting a catcher to replace Berry, so the A's sent Pasek to Chicago, too.

Other Player Movement

A day after acquiring Cochrane and Grove respectively, the Tigers and Red Sox continued to deal. The Tigers traded 27-year-old outfielder John Stone to the AL champion Senators for veteran outfielder Leon "Goose" Goslin. Stone was considered an improving hitter and excellent defender. In fact, the Senators tried to trade for him before the 1933 season. They offered outfielders Sam West and Carl Reynolds as well as left-hander Lloyd Brown to the Tigers, who declined. After the 1933 season, the Tigers discussed trading Stone to the St. Louis Browns for Reynolds, whom the Senators had sent to St. Louis, but no deal resulted. At the winter meetings, then, when Washington offered Goslin, who had a .325 career batting average, the Tigers agreed. Despite Goslin's long track record as a hitter, the Senators lauded the deal. Player-manager Joe Cronin said that the deal "materially strengthened the offense, as well as the defense. Stone's ability to drive in runs and his youth made him attractive to me."[27] Cronin and Goslin may have feuded during the 1933 season, which may have really made Goslin's departure attractive to Cronin.[28]

The Red Sox also traded for an outfielder, acquiring Carl Reynolds from the St. Louis Browns. They were looking to upgrade their outfield with Reynolds, who had hit .286 with eight home runs in his only season in St. Louis. In exchange, the Red Sox gave up Smead Jolley, an outfielder with a poor defensive reputation, in addition to right-hander Ivy Andrews and an undisclosed amount of cash.

Smead Jolley, whose unusual name was a tribute to a family friend, was not long for the Browns. St. Louis manager Rogers Hornsby immediately packaged Jolley, left-hander Wally Hebert, and shortstop Jim Levey in a deal with Hollywood of the Pacific Coast League for prize shortstop prospect Alan Strange. Strange had hit .324 with Hollywood and was considered to be excellent defensively. The Browns also purchased George Puccinelli and Ray Pepper, outfielders from the Cardinals organization, for $15,000. By heading back to the West Coast, meanwhile, Jolley was able to resume a career that made him a Pacific Coast League icon and one of the minor leagues' all-time great hitters.

Rumors

Amid the trades at the meetings, there were some rumored deals that never came to fruition. The White Sox and the Yankees discussed a deal that would have sent shortstop Luke Appling to New York. Chicago apparently sought right-handed pitcher Red Ruffing, shortstop Lyn Lary, and outfielder Sammy Byrd, but nothing came of the teams' conversations. Likewise, nothing came of a two-hour meeting between representatives of the Cubs, Braves, Pirates, and Cardinals. In that meeting the Cubs were reportedly offering right-hander Pat Malone, infielder Billy Herman, and shortstop Billy Jurges, while seeking some combination of Braves third baseman Pinky Whitney, catcher Tommy Padden and first baseman Gus Suhr of the Pirates, and first baseman Rip Collins from the Cardinals, while the Braves sought Cubs outfielder Kiki Cuyler. The Cardinals, however, were unwilling to trade any front-line players, so no deals resulted.

Summary

Most of the delegates left Chicago on Friday. *The Sporting News* called the meetings the "liveliest market the big leaguers had witnessed at their winter meetings for a long time."[29] From the close of the 1933 season through the end of the winter meetings, 45 players changed teams, with the bulk of them moving between teams in the American League.

Conclusion

The optimism that opened the 1933 meetings was justified in many respects. Instead of minor leagues folding, as they had in the past, new leagues were planned for 1934 and six new leagues actually formed for that year. Shaughnessy playoffs were partly responsible for providing the minors with a new source of revenue.[30] Big-league teams were also doing somewhat better under the changes adopted in 1932.

With this background, the 1933 meetings represented an active trade market. Much of the activity resulted from the A's—a team with significantly declining attendance—selling their star players. It was widely reported that Connie Mack was under pressure from lenders and investors, but after the meetings he suggested a slightly different reason for the sell-off: The A's could not afford the star players' salaries any longer. Mack insisted that he "was not breaking up" the A's, but instead had acquired "funds with which to rebuild. In fact," he said, the team had "already spent a considerable portion for new players."[31] Nevertheless, the A's fell from a third-place finish in 1933 to fifth place in 1934, even with Jimmie Foxx still in the fold, and would not have another winning season for many years after the sell-off.

Lefty Grove was viewed as a savior when he arrived in Boston, and he capitalized on that status. He did not train on Sundays during spring training, and was the only Red Sox player to have his own room on the road. But Grove developed a sore arm and scuffled to an 8-8 record with a 6.50 ERA in 1934 as the Red Sox finished exactly .500 at 76-76. That was still a marked improvement for what had been a losing team, but critics considered Grove a bust. Their analysis was short-sighted—from 1935 through 1939, Grove returned to form as one of the best pitchers in the game.

Mickey Cochrane fared much better with his new team. He hit .320 while catching and managing the Tigers, who also benefited from Goose Goslin's .305 batting average, 13 home runs, and 100 RBIs. Despite having only two home runs, Cochrane beat Lou Gehrig, who won the Triple Crown in 1934 with a .363 batting average and 49 home runs, for the AL MVP award. Many credited Cochrane's leadership as the Tigers broke through to the American League pennant. Cochrane could not quite get them over the hump, however, as the Tigers fell to the Cardinals in seven games in the World Series before the action shifted to New York City for the 1934 winter meetings.

NOTES

1. "Baseball Men Hail End of Sunday Ban," *New York Times*, November 9, 1933: 30 (quoting John A. Heydler, National League president).
2. Ibid.
3. "Phils Trade Davis for Wilson, Cards," *New York Times*, November 16, 1933: 34.
4. "Bramham Chosen by Minor Leagues," *New York Times*, November 17, 1933: 25.
5. "Gathered on Promenade Along Galveston Sea Wall," *The Sporting News*, November 23, 1933: 6.
6. "Phils Trade Davis for Wilson, Cards."
7. Ibid.
8. "Adopt Rule to End Intentional Pass," *New York Times*, November 18, 1933: 22.
9. Gary Livacari, "Jimmie Wilson," SABR BioProject, sabr.org/bioproj/person/e9fa0e9d#, most recently accessed December 6, 2015. Wilson thus became "the only player in major league history who was a member of two teams during one game." Ibid.
10. Dick Farrington, "Cards, Browns Keep Irons Hot to Forge Other Likely Deals," *The Sporting News*, November 23, 1933: 1.
11. "Trading of Players Heaviest for Years," *The Sporting News*, November 23, 1933: 7.
12. "Big Deals Loom in Major Leagues," *New York Times*, December 12, 1933: 32.
13. "Klein of Phillies Goes to the Cubs," *New York Times*, November 22, 1933: 25.
14. Ibid.
15. "Harridge Favors Uniform Baseball," *New York Times*, December 6, 1933: 32.
16. E.G. Brands, "Uniform Ball to Be in Use Next Season," *The Sporting News*, December 21, 1933: 5.
17. "Big Leagues Vote for Uniform Ball," *New York Times*, December 15, 1933: 31.
18. Ibid.
19. "Uniform Ball to Be in Use Next Season."
20. Ibid.
21. Ibid.
22. "Mack Sells Grove and 4 Other Stars," *New York Times*, December 13, 1933: 32.
23. Sam Greene, "Navin to Dangle $100,000 Check as Cochrane Offer at Confab," *The Sporting News*, December 7, 1933: 1.
24. C. William Duncan, "Mickey Cochrane, Always a Fighter, Should Bring Back Detroit Tigers Scrappy Ways of Ty Cobb," *The Sporting News*, December 21, 1933: 3.
25. "'Tickled,' Say Grove and Bishop on Trade; Each Calls Boston a Great Baseball City," *New York Times*, December 14, 1933: 30.
26. "Mack Says He'll Consider Bids for George Earnshaw," *Washington Post*, September 1, 1933: 17.
27. Shirley Povich, "Stone Picked to Bat Fourth for Nats," *Washington Post*, February 10, 1935: 35.
28. Shirley L. Povich, "This Morning," *Washington Post*, December 14, 1933: 18.
29. "Sales of A's Stars Feature of Trading," *The Sporting News*, December 21, 1933: 5.
30. David Pietrusza, *Judge and Jury: The Life and Times of Kenesaw Mountain Landis* (Dallas: Taylor, 2001), 352.
31. "Mack Lays Deals to Wage Demands," *New York Times*, December 19, 1933: 28.

— 1934 —
THE REDS GO UNDER THE LIGHTS WHILE THE BRAVES GO TO THE DOGS

By Bob LeMoine

THE 1934 BASEBALL WINTER MEETings could very easily have just gone to the dogs. The talk leading up to the convention was the desperate attempt of the Boston Braves owner, Judge Emil Fuchs, to pull his team out of the red by requesting that Braves Field host nightly greyhound racing. These were desperate times during the Depression, and Fuchs saw the dogs as a chance to save his Braves. The immediate response from baseball was overwhelmingly negative, as baseball's stained history with greedy bettors was recalled. As teams attempted to survive, the issues of economics versus purity of the old-fashioned game were at odds. The issue had already stirred up a commotion among the delegates, but it was soon overshadowed by another proposal that some saw as just as desperate.

The minor leagues had been playing night baseball for seven years and experiments in the venture had been attempted since 1880. Some minor-league clubs were able to survive the Depression by embracing this novelty, but major-league clubs continued to refuse to play after dark. Taking a risk, Cincinnati Reds owner Powel Crosley and GM Larry MacPhail presented the case for night games as a way to bolster slumping attendance.

These were the issues of the 1934 baseball winter meetings, which saw very few trades. In fact, the most talked-about player was a has-been, out-of-shape, injury-prone legend about to turn 40. Rarely would anyone care about the future of such a player, yet everything he did still made headlines, which made people wonder what was next for Babe Ruth?

In a sign that baseball was on the rebound, major-league attendance in 1934 had increased by 874,680, or 14 percent, over 1933 after dropping almost 40 percent from a high of 10.1 million in 1930 to 6,09 million in 1933.[1] The biggest losers were the Boston Braves (down 214,598), Chicago White Sox (down 161,230), Washington Senators (down 107,459), and Brooklyn Dodgers (down 92,627).

Of the 16 clubs, only six were able to show a profit as of September 30, 1934.[2] Economics, thus, was the foremost thought for baseball club owners who were finding themselves in desperate straits as the Depression lingered. Playing night baseball, greyhound racing, and the peddling of radio rights were three such examples of owners trying to attract a new audience, which needed a new spark to attend the old national pastime.

The Minor Leagues Convention

The 33rd annual winter meetings of the National Association of Professional Baseball Leagues (the minor leagues) were held on November 21-23 in Louisville, Kentucky. In an event described by the Associated Press as "the melting pot of the game, where magnates, players, scouts, umpires and others gather once a year to swap players and yarns, legislate a bit and partake of the usual elaborate program of entertainment that is mapped out for them,"[3] 900-plus delegates were present. Many major-league clubs had representation as well, looking for a chance to "wheel and deal." There were 19 minor leagues and 128 teams in 1934, a gain over the previous year's 14 and 95.[4] Much of the success in the minor leagues could be credited to the leadership of William Bramham, who took over as NAPBL President in 1933. With the help of his skills in promotion and organization, the minor leagues grew to 43 at the onset of World War II.[5] Of Bramham, a reporter wrote in 1934, "Baseball big wigs throughout the country have given him much of the credit for the return of the game to its old plane, following the depression."[6]

Each year since 1916 (except for 1918, during World War I), a Little World Series[7] had been held between the champions of the Double-A American Association and International League. The champions of each league had been determined by postseason playoffs involving the leagues' top teams. The American Association felt the playoffs lessened the quality of the Little World Series and in 1934 voted to scrap its playoff tournament and declare one pennant winner. The Association asked the International League to do the same, threatening to pull out of the Little World Series if the IL refused to change.[8] The International League refused to consider the proposal, pointing out that their four playoff teams gained financially from the series. The AA began negotiations with the Pacific Coast League for a similar series,[9] but that plan failed when the geographical obstacles were realized.[10] Instead, the AA planned to hold a postseason all-star game or series.[11]

Making news during the convention was Oklahoma oil baron and philanthropist Lew Wentz, who was seeking to purchase the St. Louis Cardinals. Wentz, Dick Farrington of *The Sporting News* wrote, "rolls in wealth,"[12] and was one of the richest men in the United States, paying $5 million in income tax in 1926.[13] He was impressed with the Cardinals farm system and success. "Then there is the fact that I like to go places in my airplane," Wentz said. "What would be more fun than taking a jump from St. Louis to Rochester, to Columbus or to Houston?"[14] (The latter three teams were St. Louis farm clubs.) Wentz was looking to buy out Sam Breadon's shares of the team for $1,250,000 (other reports gave the sum as between $1,000,000 and $1,250,000), or 77 percent of the club. The sale also included the Cardinals' minor-league system. Wentz's net worth was $10 million (more than $179 million in 2016).[15] Wentz felt the farm system was overvalued, and eventually backed out of the deal.[16]

On November 21 the Chicago Cubs sent $50,000 and right-handed pitchers Bud Tinning and Dick Ward to St. Louis for another righty, Tex Carleton, and later Cincinnati sent $40,000 for two Cardinals farmhands, third baseman Lew Riggs and outfielder Ival Goodman.[17] Their crosstown rivals, the St. Louis Browns, under the leadership of Rogers Hornsby, were also busy on the trade front. The Browns received $20,000, left-handed pitcher Bob Weiland and infielder Johnny Burnett from Cleveland for outfielder Bruce Campbell. Hornsby "was showered with congratulations by the other traders for that one, but the Indians seemed well pleased," wrote the Associated Press.[18]

Cleveland also sent a minor-league outfielder, left-handed pitcher Forrest Twogood, and a player to be named later to Toledo of the American Association for its manager, Steve O'Neill, a former catcher for the Indians who would now serve as pitching coach under manager Walter Johnson (and who would take over the helm of the team after Johnson resigned in early August).[19] The Chicago White Sox "also parted with a big bank roll," sending righty pitcher Phil Gallivan and infielder Billy Sullivan to Indianapolis of the American Association in exchange for outfielder Vernon Washington.[20] Twenty minutes later Indianapolis traded Sullivan to St. Paul for third baseman Otto Bluege.[21] Al Schacht was released by Washington and moved on to Boston as the Red Sox' third-base coach. This effectively broke up the vaudeville-like pregame comedy routine performed by Schacht and teammate Nick Altrock.

With Babe Ruth in a steep decline, the Yankees were in need of an outfielder. The face of the Yankees and baseball itself for 14 years since coming over from the Red Sox, Ruth had played his last game as a Yankee, although he was still on the team's roster at the time of the meetings. Ruth was gone to the Boston Braves before the 1935 season, but another Yankee legend was soon to arrive. New York sent four players to the San Francisco Seals of the Pacific Coast League for young outfielder Joe DiMaggio. Because DiMaggio had injured his knee during the 1934 season, the Yankees were hesitant about his health, so two of the players were sent on option (which meant they could be recalled), while the other two were sent outright to the Seals. But the *New York Times* said DiMaggio, the holder of a 61-game hitting streak in 1933, "was even a better prospect than Paul Waner was when he came from the Pacific Coast League to the Pirates."[22]

In other transactions on November 21, the Pittsburgh Pirates acquired right-hander Mace Brown from Kansas City of the American Association, and Ike Boone, an eight-year major leaguer, signed a two-year contract to manage Toronto in the International League.[23]

On November 22 the Chicago Cubs were active again, and were finally able to acquire the left-handed starter they had been coveting. Sending right-handed pitchers Guy Bush and Jim Weaver and outfielder Babe Herman to the Pittsburgh Pirates, the Cubs received southpaw Larry French and future Hall of Fame outfielder-third baseman Freddie Lindstrom. The deal was called the largest in the history of the minor-league convention; the player salaries totaled around $200,000.[24] In the first two days of meetings, the Cubs had acquired two new pitchers and an outfielder, as team president Philip K. Wrigley and manager Charlie Grimm were anxious to reshape the club. In October they had traded right-handed pitcher Pat Malone for catcher Jimmy O'Dea, and nine players so far had been dealt away.[25] Their efforts proved to be successful: The Cubs won the National League pennant in 1935.

"I am glad that Louisville has a chance to see me," announced St. Louis Cardinals pitching ace Dizzy Dean, making a surprise appearance at the convention. Dean, saying he was on hand to conduct business with Cardinals treasurer Bill DeWitt, happened to mention that he and his brother Paul, also a Cardinals pitcher, were prepared to hold out over the club's contract offers. Dizzy was offered $15,000 and declared that he would not take a penny more or less than $25,000. Paul Dean was offered $7,500.[26] In early December Dean threatened to quit baseball temporarily, as a movie production company had offered him $35,000 to star in a film based on his life.[27] Dizzy prevailed, signing with the Cardinals for an amount reported to be between $20,000 and $26,000.[28]

Other deals on November 22 included the Cincinnati Reds purchasing right-handed pitcher Danny MacFayden from the Yankees, the New York Giants selling righty Herman Bell to Kansas City, and the Boston Red Sox selling the contract of first baseman Ed Morgan to Rochester, the Cardinals' farm club in the International League. The Red Sox also signed a working agreement with Knoxville of the Southern Association.[29]

At the close of the minor-league convention, 105 players had been involved in deals, affecting 11 of the 16 major-league clubs and a majority of the minor-league clubs.[30] Other offseason moves followed. Chicago White Sox right-hander George Earnshaw reacted to a salary cut by threatening to retire to his insurance business.[31] He thought better of it, however, and signed a week later for a $500 bonus.[32] Mae Nugent, wife of Philadelphia Phillies president Gerald Nugent, became the team's vice president, the first female club vice president in the National League.[33] The Amateur Baseball League moved its headquarters from Springfield, Massachusetts, to Miami.[34]

Major League Meetings

The major-league meetings were held December 11-13 in New York City. For the first two days, the National League met at the Waldorf-Astoria Hotel and the American League met at the Commodore. On the final day, both leagues combined for a joint meeting at the Roosevelt Hotel, and were addressed by Commissioner Kenesaw Mountain Landis. But even the evening before the official beginning of the convention, "everyone seemed to be wrapped up entirely in arguments relating to dog racing," reported John Drebinger of the *New York Times*.[35]

Judge Fuchs, the Braves' owner, was already a major story before he arrived. "It looks as though I've already talked too much," Fuchs said upon arriving in New York. "I am not combating anybody. In Boston we have a proposition that looks very good to us and one that will in no way cast any reflections on baseball. … But I am still confident that when other owners have heard my complete story they will take another view of the situation."36

Horse-racing tracks were barred within 15 miles of the Boston city limits, but entrepreneurs were seeking out greyhound dog-racing permits. Fuchs and the Braves board of directors were among them, seeking a permit to build a track at Braves Field and hold greyhound racing at night. Fuchs received a favorable response from the Massachusetts Racing Commission but now "found himself the center of what may develop into quite a verbal tempest before it's all over."37

NL President-elect Ford C. Frick called the proposal "absolutely preposterous."38 He said, "It is entirely at variance with the principles for which baseball has battled so strenuously. … Organized Baseball has outlawed players for gambling and it is ridiculous to conceive that baseball now could permit a sport founded on gambling to move into the same premises with it."39 Reaction from Fuchs's fellow owners and Commissioner Landis was mostly negative.40 A National League rule stipulated that a club would lose its membership in the league if it allowed "open gambling or betting pools on its grounds or any of the buildings that are the property of that club."41

"I don't believe that Frick said that," Fuchs responded.42 "I am sure that the other directors will sanction every action of mine when I present them with the facts."43 Because a portable structure for dog races was impractical, Fuchs was also reported to be negotiating with the Red Sox about holding Braves home games at Fenway Park.44 Despite all the fury, the issue was never addressed.

At their separate meetings on December 11, both leagues voted to continue the All-Star Game, begun in 1933 and already called "a baseball fixture" by Edward Burns of the *Chicago Tribune*.45 Some club owners opposed the game since "the rivalry among the cities had become somewhat bitter and there were those in favor of abandoning the feature," Burns wrote. Such opposition, however, was not actually voiced at the convention. The 1935 game would be held at Municipal Stadium in Cleveland. Burns wrote that there was little substance to any of the rest of the day's convention news, wryly noting that St. Louis and Detroit were officially awarded the NL and AL pennants. "This news previously had been a substantial rumor, widely circulated around the nation," Burns quipped. "Tomorrow the sage nabobs are expected to vote and announce that St. Louis officially won the World Series. This too, was a matter that had leaked out in early October."46

The NL formally installed Frick as its president, succeeding the retiring John Heydler; Harvey Traband as secretary and treasurer; and Sam Breadon (St. Louis), Powel Crosley (Cincinnati), Gerry Nugent (Philadelphia), and Stephen McKeever (Brooklyn) as league directors. The only trade of the day was a deal of right-handers, with the New York Giants sending Jack Salveson to Pittsburgh for Leon Chagnon.47

Despite the warning of Commissioner Landis that "not in my lifetime or yours will you ever see a baseball game played at night in the majors," Cincinnati president Larry MacPhail spoke to the convention for three hours and convinced the delegates that night baseball would be good for the game.48 Cincinnati owner Powel Crosley said his club was giving serious consideration to playing seven night games during the 1935 season. Crosley said 70 percent of the Reds' total attendance in 1934 was drawn from Opening Day, Sundays, and holidays. "I feel there is something wrong with a business which finds it necessary to operate on a losing basis on all but 15 days during the season," Crosley said. One game would be played against each opponent in the league.49

"Otherwise," reported the Associated Press on the events of December 11, "the managers, filling the lobbies with cigar smoke as the magnates met in the conference rooms, talked and talked and got exactly nowhere."50 Rogers Hornsby was willing to entertain offers for anyone on the St. Louis Browns' roster, but was flustered and came up empty. He tried to lure outfielder Gerald Walker from Detroit, but Mickey Cochrane wouldn't budge. Then he desired Washington infielder Ossie Bluege, but Clark Griffith wanted nothing to do with the offer. Griffith sought Browns' right-handed pitchers Bump Hadley and

Buck Newsom, offering what Hornsby called "a sight seeing [sic] out of Washington and a basket lunch, with pickles."[51] The White Sox refused all offers for outfielder Al Simmons, and the Dodgers did the same for those inquiring about right-handed pitcher Van Lingle Mungo. Washington tried in vain to persuade the White Sox to take catcher Luke Sewell.

In other business on December 11, outgoing National League President John Heydler remained with the league in the newly created office of chairman of the board of directors, a lifetime position. Heydler wrote in his last report as president that though attendance had risen in 1934, he doubted that any club but the world champion Cardinals had turned a profit. He credited the livelier ball for a more exciting product on the field, saying, "… Our games last season were marked by more hitting and consequently more action. The number of runs scored increased by 799 in 1934; there were 665 more singles, 229 more doubles, 10 more triples and 195 more home runs. The league batting average rose from .266 to .280. "[F]ears that the livelier ball would upset our well-established team balance were, of course, proved groundless by the close race which ensued," Heydler's report said.[52]

Heydler's also warned of tax levies that "present a serious situation in these times when all leagues are pressed to maintain their existing circuits and when the break of one club may menace the welfare of all."[53] The NL also returned to a staff of 12 umpires for the 1935 season.[54]

On the topic of Babe Ruth, Yankees owner Jacob Ruppert commented, "The Babe is on our reserve list, and as such is like any other player. Anything Ruth wants to do, I will try to help him do. There have been no offers for him as a manager or a player. When the time comes for contracts to go out for 1935, I will send him one. I will dicker with him if he cares to continue to play with us, and will meet him halfway as I always have in the past." Would Ruth become the Yankees manager? That was not on the horizon. "I have no idea of releasing [Yankee manager Joe] McCarthy before his contract expires at the end of the 1935 season. I can find no fault with him. … When the time comes to pick his successor, I cannot say that Ruth would come in for any more consideration than any one of say 10 others."[55]

Reading dispatches from the convention while he was in Manila on a barnstorming tour, Ruth politely said, "Whatever baseball does to me is all right with me. The game has been good to me. I'm ready to quit if there's no place for me." Ruth also denied a rumor that he would manage the Yankees' Newark farm team, saying, "No minor-league club for me."[56] He played a round of golf, "walloping the ball long distances, but consistently slicing, much to his disgust," the Associated Press reported. "I am not worried about the future. I am having a good time," Ruth said.[57] Lefty Gomez thought of playing a round with the Babe, until he was told a cobra had been killed near the clubhouse.[58]

On December 12 the National League finally decided to allow night baseball. The minor leagues had implemented this innovation seven years before, and unauthorized attempts at temporary or permanent lighting structures at ballparks dated back to 1880. National League clubs were now allowed to schedule up to seven night games for 1935, and any club scheduling more would be fined $15,000 and have its gate receipts confiscated.[59] Though Cincinnati made the original request, the resolution allowing night ball was sponsored by the Cubs, Cardinals, and Braves in addition to the Reds. The Phillies favored the innovation but reserved the right to change their mind, while the Pirates voted no but reserved the right to change their mind if the idea worked. Both the Giants and Dodgers voted a flat no. The resolution said no club was obligated to accept an invitation to play a night game on the road, and neither did any club announce plans to install lighting. Philip K. Wrigley, the Cubs' president, stated his support for night baseball, but said there was no current plan to install lights. (Wrigley Field actually became the last ballpark to add lights, more than 50 years later).

After he announced the results of the voting on night baseball, Ford Frick was able to turn his attention to the issue of greyhound racing at ballparks, and he circulated a statement from Judge Fuchs:

"Nothing will be done by me which will embarrass baseball or the National League. Under the constitution of the National League, betting, legal or otherwise, is prohibited in its ballparks, where baseball is played. I have and always will abide by the constitution of the National League. This statement is simply a reiteration of the only statement for publication ever issued affecting this subject or authorized by me as published by the Associated Press."[60]

In response, Edward Burns of the *Chicago Tribune* wrote, "Reporters, especially those from Boston, who have been all worked over the matter, considered Fuchs' statement a gem of ambiguity and were greatly distressed when the gentleman refused to enlarge upon the typed handout."[61] Some focused on the phrase "where baseball is played," and thought Fuchs must have worked out a deal for the Braves to play home games at Fenway Park so dog-racing at Braves Field would not be a conflict. Commissioner Landis followed with a statement that "Judge Fuchs had assured him that no activities involving gambling will be conducted by the Boston National League club or on any properties under its control."[62] No further discussion was held on the issue.

Philip Wrigley announced that Wrigley Field would admit children to Cubs games at half-price. J. Louis Comiskey, owner of Wrigley's crosstown rival, said the White Sox had been charging 25 cents admission for children in the bleachers, but didn't see the need to extend this practice to the grandstand unless the league made it an official policy.

Other events of December 12 included retaining the "lively ball" used in 1934, and providing retired major-league players with at least 10 years of experience free admission to any ballpark. The NL also increased the waiver price from $4,000 to $6,000, and reduced the time limit on waivers from five days to three.[63]

At the combined session on December 13, "[S]cores of old-timers deplored the National League's decision even to take a seven-game fling at playing baseball under the big arc lights at night. We found the general opinion that this was very much a minor rather than a major league move," wrote Melville E. Webb if the *Boston Globe*.[64] The AL was against night baseball altogether, calling the NL "the burlesque circuit."[65]

In other events at the joint session, L.C. McEvoy, vice president of the St. Louis Browns, proposed that both leagues ban radio broadcasting of games. The motion failed, and teams continued to make their own choices on the issue. Sam Breadon said the sale of the Cardinals was all but over when the Wentz negotiations fell through, and added, "I look for better times in baseball, beginning with the new season." Former major-league shortstop Glenn Wright flew in from San Bernardino, California, to pitch the California town as a great place for spring training. The Pittsburgh Pirates were sold on their former shortstop's idea, and trained there in 1935.[66]

The meetings closed with two more trades by the Giants, who were involved in all three trades at the major-league meetings. They traded right-handed pitcher Joe Bowman to the Philadelphia Phillies for outfielder Kiddo Davis, and infielder Billy Myers to Cincinnati for shortstop Mark Koenig and right-handed pitcher Allyn Stout.

As the meetings concluded and the owners embarked on their plans for the 1935 season, Ruth was setting sail from Manila on a two-month trip via Java and Europe. He would arrive back in the United States in late February of 1935 and begin the last stop of his major-league career, the Boston Braves. He never would manage, and his playing career would end on June 2. Ruth never played under the lights, although Cincinnati inaugurated night baseball on May 24. In Ruth's abbreviated stay with the Braves, he sparred with Fuchs; Fuchs himself gave up control of the club on August 1; and the financially troubled team wobbled to a 38-115 record.

Even without greyhounds, the Braves still went to the dogs.

NOTES

1   Figures gathered from baseballchronology.com/Baseball/Teams/Background/Attendance/default.asp.
2   Jimmy Powers, "Here's New Twist in News: Dog Bites Baseball; Only 6 Big League Clubs Showed Profit in '34," *Washington Post*, December 11, 1934: 19.

3. "Baseball Men Plan Meeting at Louisville," *Hartford Courant*, November 15, 1934: 18.

4. "19 Minor Leagues Reserve 1,799 Players, Gain of 493 Over 1933," *The Sporting News*, November 22, 1934: 6.

5. "William Bramham," retrieved from baseball-reference.com/bullpen/William_Bramham.

6. Dix Sarfield, "Judge William Bramham, President of Minor League Baseball Clubs, Is Ranked Among Game's Big Figures," *St. Petersburg Times*, June 22, 1934.

7. The series was renamed the Junior World Series in 1932, according to baseball-reference.com (baseball-reference.com/bullpen/Junior_World_Series), but newspapers continued to call it the Little World Series.

8. "Wentz in Evidence as Minors Meet," *Boston Globe*, November 21, 1934: 20.

9. "Cardinals Reap a Rich Harvest by Player Sales," *Christian Science Monitor*, November 22, 1934: 6.

10. "Series Abandoned by Minor Leagues," *New York Times*, November 23, 1934: 24.

11. "Baseball Meetings in Louisville Are Brought to a Close," *Christian Science Monitor*, November 24, 1934: 4; While no series was held in 1935, it resumed in 1936 and continued for several years (baseball-reference.com/bullpen/Junior_World_Series).

12. Dick Farrington, "Sale Talk Reveals Cards Drew 334, 821," *The Sporting News*, November 22, 1934: 1.

13. Ibid.

14. Ibid.

15. "Cards May Be Sold; Harris Senator Pilot," *Chicago Tribune*, November 14, 1934: 21; To determine today's equivalent of Wentz's net worth, the author used the online inflation calculator dollartimes.com/inflation/inflation.php?amount=250&year=1934.

16. "Sam Breadon," in Donald Dewey and Nick Acocella, eds., *The New Biographical History of Baseball* (Chicago: Triumph Books, 2002), 39-40. Lee Lowenfish, in *Branch Rickey: Baseball's Ferocious Gentleman* (Lincoln: University of Nebraska Press, 2009), 262, pondered some interesting "what-if's" in regard to what might have happened if Lentz had bought the club. Rickey shared much in common with Lentz. Lowenfish wrote, "A similar devotee of aviation, Rickey would have loved to accompany Wentz on his journeys, for he was a man the passionate executive admired for his sincere philanthropy and staunch Republicanism. Although Wentz was not a spendthrift, the budget for farm system development and Major League salaries would have increased. … The two men remained good friends and occasional hunting buddies." When Rickey was with the Dodgers and they were up for sale 10 years later, he suggested that Wentz consider the purchase, but Wentz declined.

17. "Cardinals Reap a Rich Harvest."

18. Ibid.

19. Ibid.; Adam Ulrey, "Steve O'Neill," sabr.org/bioproj/person/ef6e78f2.

20. "Cardinals Reap a Rich Harvest."

21. "Yankees Obtain DiMaggio, Coast League Batting Star, in Player Transaction," *New York Times*, November 22, 1934: 28.

22. Ibid. The deal was completed on December 19, 1934. San Francisco received Floyd Newkirk, Jimmy Densmore, and Ted Norbert. Doc Farrell, also included in the trade, refused to report to San Francisco, so the Yankees sent $5,000 to the Seals in 1935. retrosheet.org/boxesetc/D/Pdimaj101.htm.

23. "Yankees Obtain DiMaggio."

24. "Cubs and Pirates in $200,000 Trade," *Los Angeles Times*, November 23, 1934: A11.

25. "Chicago Cubs Secure Larry French and Freddie Lindstrom From Pittsburgh," *Hartford Courant*, November 23, 1934: 17; "Cubs and Pirates in $200,000 Trade."

26. "Dizzy Dean Will Charge Champion Cardinals $25,000 for His Services in 1935," *Hartford Courant*, November 23, 1934: 20.

27. "Dean Threatens to Quit," *New York Times*, December 2, 1934: S5.

28. "Cardinals Sign Dizzy Dean; Give Him Big Raise," *Chicago Tribune*, December 6, 1934: 21.

29. "Cubs and Pirates in $200,000 Trade."

30. "105 Players Figure in Louisville Deals," *The Sporting News*, November 29, 1934: 5.

31. "George Earnshaw May Quit Baseball," *Hartford Courant*, November 23, 1934: 17.

32. "Earnshaw Will Pitch for Sox," *Washington Post*, November 29, 1934: 19.

33. "Mrs. Nugent Vice-President," *Christian Science Monitor*, December 4, 1934: 6; Philadelphia Phillies Timeline: philadelphia.phillies.mlb.com/phi/history/timeline.jsp (1930s section).

34. "Amateur Ball League Will Move Its Offices," *Washington Post*, December 5, 1934: 19.

35. John Drebinger, "Major Problems Confront Baseball Magnates at Conventions Opening Today," *New York Times*, December 11, 1934: 30.

36. John Drebinger, "Major Problems Confront Baseball Magnates."

37. Associated Press, "Braves President Plans to Conduct Dog-Racing Track," *Christian Science Monitor*, December 8, 1934: 8.

38. Victor O. Jones, "Frick Opposes Fuchs' Action. Would Bar Dog Racing in Baseball Parks," *Boston Globe*, December 8, 1934: 1.

39. "Braves President Plans to Conduct Dog-Racing Track," *Christian Science Monitor*, December 8, 1934: 8.

40. "National League Won't Allow Braves to use Park for Ball Games and Dog Racing," Associated Press, *Hartford Courant*, December 8, 1934: 13.

41. John Drebinger, "Major Problems Confront Baseball Magnates."

42 Jones, "Frick Opposes Fuchs' Action."

43 "Dog-Race License Sought by Braves," *New York Times*, December 8, 1934: 22.

44 Ibid.

45 Edward Burns, "Major Leagues Give Cleveland All-Star Game," *Chicago Tribune*, December 12, 1934: 23.

46 Ibid.

47 Ibid.

48 Peter Morris, "Night Baseball," in *Game of Inches* (Chicago: Ivan R. Dee, 2010), 379.

49 "Night Baseball May Be Launched by Cincinnati," *Chicago Tribune*, December 12, 1934: 24.

50 Associated Press, "Major League Magnates Do Plenty of Talking but Fail to Accomplish Anything," *Hartford Courant*, December 12, 1934: 15.

51 "Major League Magnates Do Plenty of Talking."

52 "Heydler Farewell a Warning on Taxes," *The Sporting News*, December 20, 1934: 3.

53 "Major League Magnates Do Plenty of Talking."

54 Ibid.

55 Ibid.

56 "Ruth Willing to Quit, He Says; Spurns Minor League Post," *Washington Post*, December 13, 1934: 19.

57 Associated Press, "Ruth Shows No Sign of Worry," *Wilkes-Barre (Pennsylvania) Record*, December 12, 1934: 29.

58 Associated Press, "Ruth Watches Developments From Manila," *Klamath News* (Klamath Falls, Oregon), December 13, 1934: 2.

59 Edward Burns, "Night Games Approved by National League," *Chicago Tribune*, December 13, 1934: 25.

60 Ibid.

61 Ibid.

62 Ibid.

63 Ibid.

64 Melville E. Webb Jr., "Cochrane, Cronin and Collins Confer," *Boston Globe*, December 14, 1934: 31.

65 Daniel M. Daniel, "Reds Likely to Be Alone in Experiment With Night Ball," *The Sporting News*, December 20, 1934: 3.

66 "Seen and Heard at the Major Meetings," *The Sporting News*, December 20, 1934: 3.

1935
INSPIRATIONAL DELEGATES CHURN CREAM INTO BUTTER

By Ely Sussman

Introduction and Context

THE NATIONAL ASSOCIATION DIDN'T just survive during the summer of 1935—it flourished. "The past season," recalled promotional department head Joe Carr, "was one of the very best that minor league baseball has experienced in years."[1] For the Association's 34th annual meeting, about 2,000 baseball people convened in Dayton, Ohio, to maintain the momentum. The city was home to the Class-C Dayton Ducks; it was the first time the Association congregated in a city without a more advanced club. Dayton had ample facilities to accommodate the delegates. The Biltmore Hotel, a luxurious building that opened in 1929, hosted the meeting, held November 20-22.

Chicago, meanwhile, had just the year before concluded its Century of Progress international exposition, a wildly popular fair that stimulated consumer spending and coincided with the city's centennial celebration. The city was bustling with excitement, which made it an ideal host for Major League Baseball's winter meetings. The American and National Leagues met separately for the first two days, December 10-11, with the Palmer House housing the AL, while the NL settled in the Congress Hotel. A joint session was held on the 12th in the Palmer House.

Player Movement (National Association Convention)

A record 135 players changed teams in deals at the National Association meeting, compared with the 80 and 105 who were moved in 1933 and 1934 respectively. The Double-A Milwaukee Brewers were relieved to unload their aging pieces, including catchers Paul Florence and Tony Rensa and outfielder Earl Webb. The St. Louis Browns traded 32-year-old right-hander Fay Thomas to the Chicago Cubs for righty Mike Meola, who had amassed 39 wins in his two summers with the Los Angeles Angels of the Pacific Coast League. This was the first transaction of the offseason to involve both American and National League teams.

Larry MacPhail of the Cincinnati Reds was particularly active. He added first baseman George McQuinn and five other players to his team on November 22, the final day of the minor-league meetings. McQuinn had been praised for his fielding while in the New York-Penn and International Leagues, and MacPhail was counting on him to take over for Jim Bottomley, whose ailing back was sapping his power—107 games played and only one home run in 1935—and threatening his career. Also that Friday, the Boston Red Sox paid $75,000 to the Hollywood Stars of the Pacific Coast League for infielders Bobby Doerr and George Myatt.

One trade constructed in Dayton featured only major-league players. Catcher Earl Grace and 6-foot-3 right-hander Claude Passeau (who had been brought up from the minors and pitched in one game at the end of the 1935 season) were swapped from the Pittsburgh Pirates to the Philadelphia Phillies for catcher Al Todd. Rumors circulated that the New York Yankees were looking to make a deal for Philadelphia Athletics third baseman Pinky Higgins. Those were flatly denied, however, by Yankees business manager Ed Barrow and, in fact, Higgins remained in Philadelphia.

Player Movement (American League and National League Meetings)

"One or two established stars will be added to the lineup," Detroit Tigers owner Walter O. Briggs said before the sessions, "if it is possible to secure them by trade or purchase."[2] Manager Mickey Cochrane came through for his boss by bagging outfielder Al Simmons. The reigning world champions were confident that the future Hall of Famer would be an upgrade in center field over their 1935 platoon of Gee Walker and Jo-Jo White. The three-time All-Star was acquired from the Chicago White Sox for the bargain price of $75,000 after totaling a career-low 79 RBIs in 1935.

A's manager Connie Mack was eager to exchange his star first baseman, Jimmie Foxx, for cash upon checking in at the Palmer House. "The game's greatest auctioneer of playing talent"[3] did so successfully on December 10 when he moved Foxx and right-handed pitcher Johnny Marcum to the Boston Red Sox. In return, Mack received $150,000, veteran right-hander Gordon Rhodes, and catcher George Savino. With that, Foxx became the last member of Philadelphia's 1929 championship team to leave the organization.

The Yankees eventually got involved at the winter meetings. They came to an all-right-handed-pitching agreement with the Cleveland Indians, sending Johnny Allen westward in exchange for Monte Pearson and Steve Sundra.

Of course, there was action at the Congress Hotel, too. J. Roy Stockton of the *St. Louis Post-Dispatch* reported that New York Giants manager Bill Terry "would like to retire to the bench" after four seasons of dual responsibility as the club's first baseman and skipper. Though Terry didn't decide on an heir during his time in Chicago, he improved an already strong roster. The Giants dealt right-handed starting pitcher Roy Parmelee, reserve infielder-outfielder Phil Weintraub, and cash to the St. Louis Cardinals for Burgess Whitehead, a defensive-minded second baseman. In 1935 Terry had given three players, Hughie Critz, Al Cuccinello, and Mark Koenig, long trials at second base, but none showed much skill with the glove. The expectation was that Cardinals general manager Branch Rickey would move several more players at the meetings. Aside from brothers Dizzy and Paul Dean, "all of the other fellows" were being discussed in trade talks.[4] In the end, though, the rest of the roster was kept intact.

Rule Changes and Other Business (National Association Convention)

At the National Association business meeting, "a sweeping change in the administrative system of the minor leagues was made without a dissenting vote."[5] Powers previously delegated to the Executive Committee were allocated to President William G. Bramham. The National Association Agreement was amended to give him the authority to check gambling and protect umpires from harassment. By unanimous vote, Bramham's annual salary was increased from $8,500 to $12,500.[6]

The A-1 league classification—a step above Class A and one below AA—was created, for which the Southern Association and Texas League both qualified.[7] All 21 leagues active during the 1935 season were expected to continue operating. Additionally, a new eight-team Class-D circuit made up of US and Canadian teams, was one of several that were in the early stages of formation.

Commissioner Kenesaw Mountain Landis, American League President William Harridge, and National League President Ford C. Frick were present in Dayton, an indication of the growing importance of the National Association in the world of professional baseball. Delegates voted to hold the 1936 meetings in Montreal; Little Rock was the only other city to gain significant support. The meetings were tentatively scheduled for November 18-20.[8]

Rule Changes and Other Business (MLB Meetings)

Cleveland Indians GM Billy Evans announced his resignation two days before the start of the National Association convention. Evans had spent the past eight years with the Indians organization after 22 seasons as an American League umpire.

In Chicago, the American League owners discussed numerous topics, but night baseball was their chief concern. They agreed to an indefinite ban, with even the installation of lights disallowed.⁹

In other news, Jacob Ruppert of the Yankees continued to ban broadcasting of his team's games, fearing that attendance would suffer if fans could simply follow the action on the radio. The Athletics, on the other hand, announced that they would allow the practice for the first time in 1936. President Harridge seemed keen on barring "butterfly nets," elongated gloves used by some AL first basemen. Such gloves, he felt, gave their wearers a significant advantage, a violation of the league's rules.¹⁰ It was decided that players could not begin barnstorming until 10 days after the close of the season.¹¹ Briggs was officially introduced as sole owner of the Tigers after his partner, Frank Navin, died on November 13.

Speaking to Reds owner Larry MacPhail after the 1934 season, Commissioner Landis had been pessimistic that the major leagues would ever play on artificially illuminated fields. "Young man," he told MacPhail, "not in my lifetime or yours will you ever see a baseball game played at night in the majors."¹² This proved to be wildly off the mark; Cincinnati hosted seven after-dark contests in 1935. Attendance at the games was encouraging and MacPhail opted to renew that schedule for the following summer. Other National League clubs were also given the freedom to arrange their own night games.¹³

The NL paid considerable attention to its umpires. A pension list was created to reward retired officials who worked at least 15 years in the league. It was decided that umpires would be required to report to spring training — at no personal expense — to officiate in exhibition games. Like the American League owners, they banned barnstorming for the first 10 days after the season. They gave Ford Frick another two-year term as president and gave Secretary Harvey Traband vice presidential responsibilities.¹⁴

At the joint session on December 12, an AL plan to reduce admission prices for children under 13 failed. The two leagues had an understanding that ticket pricing would not be changed by one without the consent of the other, and the National League opposed the plan. The 1936 All-Star Game was awarded to

SCHOOL OF INSTRUCTION

Recognizing the need to educate club officials around the business side of baseball, the National Association offered its first school of instruction at the 1935 session. Led by George Trautman, president of the Columbus Red Birds of the American Association, the session included exhibits and speakers on the topic of promotions by clubs aimed at boosting the popularity of the game in their community.*

Speakers included Trautman; Leo Miller (on giving away automobiles and also on attracting female fans); C.O. Brown (on promoting sandlot baseball); Warren Giles (on knothole gangs); Jack Corbett (on extending the radius of the community); E.G. Brands (on the importance of publicity); Frank Shaughnessy (on Mickey Cochrane's ambassadorial work to boost Detroit's attendance); and Ray Kennedy (on feature days).** Topics of the exhibits included Syracuse's new kind of netting used as a screen for the backstop; Toledo's use of matchbooks to advertise the club; Scranton's stamping advertising for that day's game on papers delivered to hotels; Palestine's use of a mock wedding with their catcher as the blushing bride; and Cincinnati's diagram of seating arrangements that gave the ticket buyer immediate knowledge of his seat location.

The school of instruction returned in 1936, when the number of exhibits increased from 35 to 52.*** The session was skipped in 1937,**** but returned in 1938.*****

---

* "'How to Sell Game' Hints Given Owners: Exhibit Showing Promotion Work and Talks Feature 'School,'" *The Sporting News*, November 28, 1935: 8.
** Ibid.
*** "School of Instruction Plays Big Role in Program of Minors," *The Sporting News*, December 10, 1936: 3.
**** "Minors' Record-Breaking Convention," *The Sporting News*, December 9, 1937: 4.
***** "Minors Move Forward," *The Sporting News*, December 15, 1938: 4.

the Boston Braves, though a specific date was not determined. Three proposals for changes in the Major-Minor Agreement were accepted: Clubs and leagues would now be subject to punishment if they did not pay official scorers; the selection period that had to elapse during reacquisition of optioned players was voided; and the Class A-1 rating was officially created.

Summary

Just by tweaking the administrative structure, delegates at the National Association convention ensured that minor-league baseball would continue to rise in prominence, as it did until the full effect of World War II was felt in 1943.

MacPhail was wise to return night baseball to Crosley Field. According to the National Baseball Hall of Fame Library, the seven night games he scheduled for the 1936 season drew 136,722 fans, an average of 19,532 that was more than four times the size of the usual daytime crowd.[15] However, his club wasn't the only one to sell more tickets in 1936; according to Baseball-Reference.com, 13 of the 16 MLB franchises had higher attendance that season despite the still-depressed economic climate.

SOURCES

In addition to the sources cited in the Notes, the author also consulted:

"1936 Major League Baseball Attendance and Miscellaneous." Baseball-Reference.com. Accessed June 23, 2012.

Bang, Ed. "Tribe Deals Remain Just So Much Talk," *The Sporting News*, November 28, 1935: 1.

Brands, Edgar G. "Many Changes in Major, Minor Official Personnel to Be Made," *The Sporting News*, November 28, 1935: 1.

Brands, Edgar G. "Inspirational Meeting at Dayton Centralizes Power in President, Cements Major League Alliance," *The Sporting News*, November 28, 1935.

Burns, Ed. "N.L. Goes Own Way on Meeting Plans," *The Sporting News*, December 5, 1935: 1.

Drebinger, John. "Acquisition of Pearson by Yanks Features Active Day at Baseball Meetings," *New York Times*, December 12, 1935: 34.

Drebinger, John. "Higgins Purchase Denied by Barrow," *New York Times*, November 23, 1935: 15.

"Giants and Cardinals in Midst of Sensational Player Trade," *The Sporting News*, November 28, 1935: 1-2.

Harwell, W.E. "Richards Fortifies Atlanta Behind Bat," *The Sporting News*, November 28, 1935: 5.

Isaminger, James C. "Foxx and Marcum Are Sold to Red Sox," *The Sporting News*, December 12, 1935: 1.

Levy, Sam. "Detroit Helps Milwaukee Brew New Team," *The Sporting News*, November 28, 1935: 1.

Moloughney, M.J. "U.S. and Canadian Cities Plan New Class D Loop," *The Sporting News*, December 12, 1935: 1.

"Night Lights Burning Low in the Majors," *The Sporting News*, December 5, 1935: 1.

Swope, Tom. "Reds Invest $25,000 in New First Sacker," *The Sporting News*, November 28, 1935: 7.

"Yawkey's Bankroll, Mack's Talent Enlivens Auctions," *Brownsville Herald*, December 11, 1935: 5.

NOTES

1. Edgar G. Brands, "48 of 90 Amendments Would Give President More Authority," *The Sporting News*, November 14, 1935: 3.
2. Charles P. Ward, "Briggs Will Follow Liberal Tiger Policy," *The Sporting News*, November 28, 1935: 5.
3. Associated Press, "Yawkey, Mack Stir Other Ball Magnates," *Reading Eagle*, December 11, 1935: 16.
4. Dick Farrington, "Rickey Lays Cards on Swapping Table," *The Sporting News*, November 28, 1935: 1.
5. Edgar G. Brands, "Minors Strengthen Organization for the Coming Years," *The Sporting News*, November 28, 1935: 3.
6. Ibid.
7. Ibid.
8. Ibid.
9. Edgar G. Brands, "American Thumbs Down on Night Games," *The Sporting News*, December 19, 1935: 3.
10. Ibid.
11. Ibid.
12. Robert B. Payne and Tom Pierett, *Let There Be Light: A History of Night Baseball 1880-2008* (Bloomington, Indiana: AuthorHouse, 2010), 2.
13. Edgar G. Brands, "National Renames Frick for Two More Years," *The Sporting News*, December 19, 1935: 3.
14. Ibid.
15. Payne and Pierett, 179.

— 1936 —
HOME PLATE AND HURLERS

By Stephen R. Keeney

THE 1936 WINTER MEETINGS WERE not the most exciting session. At the time, it seemed as though little history was made during those three days, but some of the changes made did have an important impact on the game, and some of the smaller changes are still in use. The 1936 meetings gave us innovations to the game and equipment, action on perennial issues that would change the future of the game, and, as always, player trades. The most anticipated event of the 1936 meetings was Commissioner Kenesaw M. Landis's decision on the status of Bob Feller, which threatened to create a "baseball revolution" by team owners.

Minor-League Meetings

The National Association (the minor leagues) held its sessions on December 2-4 at the Mount Royal Hotel in Montreal. The schedule included business sessions each morning and organized activities like brewery visits, hockey games, and sightseeing each afternoon. More than 600 people registered for the meetings, and about 800 attended various events.[1]

The convention highlighted the growth of the minor leagues during the year. Minor-league rosters listed 2,258 active players, despite 12 teams not submitting their rosters in time.[2] The National Association announced that all five leagues started in 1936 had survived to the end of the season, and that preliminary work was under way to start 18 more leagues.[3] Attendance and exhibits increased at the school of instruction sessions, in their second year of existence. The sessions spotlighted new ideas for marketing and promotion, including how to partner with businesses, civic groups, and other organizations. The sessions taught that winning was not, in fact, "a primary essential to a successful season."[4]

Delegates voted on 20 changes to the Association's constitution, far fewer than the previous year's 100.[5] They approved higher player limits for teams in all classifications; ending automatic ineligibility for players for failing to report 10 days after the start of the season; and rules strengthening the territorial rights of both leagues and clubs. They rejected proposals to eliminate the Association's commission on trades in which no cash changed hands, and to require players to have five years at Class-AA before they could be drafted. Probably the most important change was allowing major-league teams to recommend the signing of certain players to minor-league teams. The minors did, however, vote down a proposal that all such recommendations be sent to the commissioner's office.

Trading among clubs was heavy at the minor-league meetings. More than 100 players[6] were swapped among the minor leagues and between minor- and major-league teams. Most were players for players, rather than cash for players. One of the most noteworthy deals was the trade of outfielder Vince DiMaggio, brother of Joe DiMaggio, from the minor-league San Diego Padres to the Boston Bees of the National League; the Padres received right-handed pitcher James "Tiny" Chaplin, utilityman Rupert "Tommy" Thompson, and cash.

Major-League Meetings

The major-league meetings were held December 8-10 in New York City. On the first two days, the National League met under President Ford Frick at the Waldorf-Astoria while the American League met under President Will Harridge at the Commodore. On the final day the two leagues met together before Commissioner Kenesaw Mountain Landis at the Roosevelt.

Innovations

Some of the new ideas introduced at the meetings never had much chance of making it to the professional level. One proposal that failed was the no-pitch intentional walk. New York Yankees business manager Ed Barrow suggested that "pitchers be allowed to tell the umpire to send a man to first when an intentional pass is intended, and thus save the time lost with four bad pitches."[7] National League President Frick proposed that for part of the season all Sunday dates be doubleheaders, with teams taking Mondays off. Instead it was decided that teams by agreement could change a Sunday-Monday schedule to a Sunday doubleheader with Monday off.[8]

Cubs president P.K. Wrigley proposed that teams be allowed to sell tickets for children at the reduced price of 50 cents. That plan was left to the discretion of individual teams.[9]

The one innovation of the 1936 meetings that still exists in today's game was the addition of black beveled edges to home plate. Called "the most radical move"[10] of the second day of the National League meetings, the change was adopted by the joint session the next day. The new design was created by Cubs vice president John O. Seys. (A month before the meetings he applied for a patent for the design, which he assigned to the Seamless Rubber Company.) Home plates at the time were buried in the ground so that the top of the plate was flush with the ground. However, as the dirt was moved around, the top edges of the plate became higher than the surrounding dirt. Players sliding into home often faced injuries (and ripped pants). The new design gave home plate five spikes—one for each corner of the "home" shape—which secured it into the ground, and a beveled edge of dark rubber that eliminated the sharp edges but allowed the white of the plate to be above the dirt and visible to players and umpires.[11]

"The Hardy Perennials"

The 1936 meetings gave the club owners another chance to decide on what *New York Times* sportswriter John Drebinger dubbed "the hardy perennials"—issues for years before and after the 1936 meetings.[12] They were night baseball, radio broadcasting, and the ball itself.

Night baseball expanded from the National League to the American League at the 1936 meetings. The NL allowed teams to play up to seven night games per season at home as long as the visiting team agreed. The AL followed suit in what was thought to be a favor to the new owners of the St. Louis Browns, who were trying to increase attendance and revenue, and whose plan for a nighttime exhibition with the Cardinals had previously been denied. All American League teams except the Yankees and the Tigers agreed to at least one night game against the Browns in St. Louis. The two leagues did not come up with a rule for night baseball, but both had the same optional rules for all teams.[13]

As for broadcasting, radio broadcasts of games had been around long enough for teams to form opinions on their impact. The teams seemed to be split regionally on whether the broadcasts were good or bad for business. The Chicago, Cincinnati, and St. Louis clubs[14] all saw broadcasting as a way to drum up public interest in the game, while the New York clubs saw radio as a drain on attendance and thus on profits. Neither league reached a consensus and the clubs were allowed to decide for themselves whether to broadcast games. The American League assigned former Browns business manager L.C. McEvoy to draft contracts between AL clubs and broadcasters that would ensure "provisions for censorship and adequate compensation for the clubs."[15] The National League discussed a similar move, but instead allowed clubs to work out the details themselves.[16]

The last of the "hardy perennials" was the baseball itself. Calls to change the ball were to some degree started by St. Louis Browns manager Rogers Hornsby, echoed by baseball fans, and endorsed by the Boston Red Sox. As a result of changes to the ball over the last few years, the 1936 season had the worst ERAs and the most runs scored per game since 1895 with the exception of the 1930 season, which featured the "jack rabbit" baseball.[17] Batting averages, slugging percentages, and home runs per game were higher than they had been since the end of the jack-rabbit era. After 1930 the leagues moved to a less lively ball, only to move back to a livelier ball for the 1934 season. At the 1936 meetings it was decided to make the ball slightly "deader" once again.[18] The only team resistant to the change was the Yankees, who had led the AL in runs, home runs, RBIs, and slugging percentage in 1936. But they did not protest much after seeing the overwhelming support for a change and learning that no changes would be made until the 1938 campaign anyway.[19]

The adjustment could not be implemented immediately because almost all the balls for 1937 had already been produced. The league presidents were assigned to work with the manufacturer to design a new ball. Different variations would be tried during spring training, and the new ball would be selected. The ball, the leagues decided, would no longer be labeled with the league's name, but would be stamped "Official Major League Baseball," to allay fans' suspicions that each league had a different level of "liveliness."[20] One person disappointed with the new balls was President Franklin Delano Roosevelt, who wrote to the annual baseball writers' dinner in February that he got "the biggest kick out of the biggest score" and that his favorite games had at least 15 runs with one team winning by a single run.[21]

Trades and Transactions

Trading at the 1936 meeting was disappointing in both volume and impact. Coming on the heels of the minor-league meetings in Montreal, where 12 of the 16 major-league clubs had swapped over 100 players, everyone expected many trades to be completed in New York. Cubs owner Philip K. Wrigley said he was open to trading any player on his roster, and said the Cubs had contacted every major-league team except the Phillies about potential trades.[22]

The biggest trade bait offered up was Dizzy Dean. The Cardinals right-hander was one of the best pitchers of his era. In 1936 he led the majors in innings pitched, WHIP, and strikeout/walk ration, while finishing second in strikeouts and fifth in ERA. Cardinals owner Sam Breadon and general manager Branch Rickey, however, decided that Dean's clubhouse and media antics resulted in more damage than his talent was worth.[23] Dean and his brother and teammate Paul once trashed the Cardinals' locker room and ripped their uniforms after being fined for missing an exhibition game.[24] When reporters got into the locker room to take pictures of the scene, the brothers obliged by doing it all over again. Despite these pranks, such a valuable starter coming onto the trade market in the reserve-clause era was rare, and many teams were interested. The Cardinals expected a "stampede" of teams clamoring for Dean's services, despite the fact that in October Dean, without being asked or prompted and without having been given an offer for 1937, told reporters that whatever the Cardinals were going to offer him, he was going to reject it because he wanted more.

But neither the Cardinals nor any of their potential trade partners would make the deal at any price. The Cincinnati Reds reportedly offered $200,000 in cash plus players for Dean, but the players offered were not the right ones, according to Rickey. At various times reports came out that the star hurler had been dealt to the Reds, the Giants, the Pirates, and the Cubs, each of which involved the buyer sending $150,000 to $200,000 plus players to the Cardinals. In the end, however, no deal was completed, leaving the Cardinals with the difficult task of re-signing a player they had publicly denounced and tried to move out of town.

With the top prospect for a swap going nowhere and the Cubs' fire sale unattended, the 1936 Winter Meetings ended with nothing but disappointment in the trade department. A piece in *The Sporting News* summed up the mood of the baseball world:

> Over-cautious club owners and managers turned what was expected to be an active player mart at the major league meetings into practically a stalemate. There was plenty of talk and rumors, but when sifted down to realities, little in the way of exchange of talent was accomplished. It is possible that the groundwork was laid for future deals, but viewed in the light of actual results, there is little basis for belief that the demand for new faces on a number of teams is being met.[25]

Those words essentially held true—there was not much player movement and as a result there was almost no movement in the standings. In the National League, not only did the Giants win the pennant in both 1936 and 1937, but the top four and bottom four teams remained the same in both seasons (though in a slightly different order). In the American League, the Yankees won the pennant both seasons, going 102-51 in 1936 and 102-52 in 1937. Both seasons ended with the Yankees defeating the Giants in the World Series in six (1936) and five (1937) games.

Despite the disappointing lack of high-end, impactful trades, there was some player movement during those three days in December. The Phillies sent third baseman Lou Chiozza to the Giants for $25,000 and rookie shortstop George Scharein. The Philadelphia Athletics traded third baseman Pinky Higgins to the Red Sox for utilityman Billy Werber. A three-team trade in the American League sent left-handed pitcher Earl Whitehill from Washington to Cleveland, lefty pitcher Thornton Lee from Cleveland to the White Sox, and right-hander Jack Salveson from the White Sox to Washington.

The Bob Feller Case

By far the most anticipated story line of the meetings was the status of rookie sensation Bob Feller. Feller had made his major-league debut during the 1936 season for the Cleveland Indians at age 17. He pitched in 14 games and finished with an ERA of 3.34 and a strikeout-to-walk ratio of 1.62, which would have ranked second and fourth in the American League had he pitched enough innings to qualify.[26]

The controversy involved the way Cleveland obtained Feller's contract rights. At the time—almost three decades before the first amateur draft—the majors and minors had an agreement under which major-league clubs could acquire players only by signing college players or purchasing players' rights from minor-league clubs. All other players were labeled "sandlot" players and were off-limits to major-league teams. The Indians was not supposed to be able to sign the 17-year-old Feller directly because he was still in high school.

The case against Cleveland was brought by the Des Moines Demons of the Class-A Western League, which had tried to sign Feller. The question for Commissioner Landis was whether this was an elaborate ploy by Cleveland to avoid the rule against major-league teams signing sandlot players. Feller was from Van Meter, Iowa, about 20 miles from Des Moines. Cleveland scout Cy Slapnicka had arranged for Feller to be signed by the Fargo-Moorhead Twins of the Class-D Northern League. Fargo-Moorhead immediately assigned Feller to the Class-A1 Southern Association team in New Orleans, but Feller never reported to either team. New Orleans, which had a working agreement with Cleveland, "retired" Feller so that he could pitch in an exhibition for Cleveland against the St. Louis Cardinals. Feller performed so well that he was reinstated by New Orleans and immediately transferred to Cleveland.[27]

Leading up to the meetings, the Feller case and Landis's decision were hugely important topics that hung heavy over the game. Just before the minor-league meetings, Landis had ruled on somewhat similar cases involving two Cincinnati Reds players. Landis ruled that Cincinnati had improperly used the Toronto minor-league club to do its bidding in the signing of infielder Lee Handley and catcher John Peacock, and declared both players free agents, free to sign with any club except Cincinnati.[28] This decision invalidated a trade the Reds had made with Brooklyn that had included Handley.[29]

For the Indians, there would be no such finality before the meetings. Speculation by major-league clubs at the minor-league meetings was divided, with some expecting the Indians to retain Feller's services while others thought they would lose his rights and also face a fine. Regardless of how teams felt, Cleveland was handcuffed by Landis's delay. Even if they kept the rights to Feller, they could not negotiate any deals involving him because other teams feared such a trade would be invalidated by Landis, just like the Cincinnati-Brooklyn deal.

CREATING A NEW RADIO GIG

In 1932 Leo McEvoy went on the record stating that he saw radio broadcasting as an issue that should be regulated at the league level. "Broadcasting, player limits, admission prices and such things are problems for the leagues and if a league decided that it is wise to adopt a certain policy, the clubs will have to fall in line,"* he said. Four years later, at the winter meetings, McEvoy became the American League radio czar.**

McEvoy's 1937 job description involved drawing up the contracts under which stations could broadcast accounts of games. This included oversight of provisions for sponsorship and compensation for clubs.*** Perhaps the most difficult challenge facing McEvoy was making a convincing counterargument to the belief that the American League wished to eliminate radio broadcasts. At what was said to be the first nationwide conference of baseball announcers, McEvoy said, "Whether the broadcasting of games was thought to be beneficial or harmful to the gate, there still remains the fact that radio has suddenly jumped into a most prominent and influential position among methods of news dissemination, that radio broadcasting is here to stay and to improve."****

---

* "Extra Innings," *St. Louis Post-Dispatch*, November 22, 1932: 31.
** "Over-Caution Rules Player Mart," *The Sporting News*, December 17, 1936: 4.
*** Ibid.
**** "M'Evoy Outlines Air Policy," *The Sporting News*, April 15, 1937: 9.

Clubs and leagues began taking steps to prevent the uncertainty of Cleveland's situation from occurring in the future. In Montreal the minor leagues adopted the "Baltimore amendment," which allowed major-league clubs to "recommend" to a minor-league club that they should sign a "sandlot" player.[30] Landis tried to get the clubs to also agree to require that all such recommendations be filed with the commissioner's office, but that idea was voted down. The next week in New York, major-league clubs similarly agreed to the "recommendation" amendment, and also rejected the "Landis rider."[31]

Some wondered whether a decision against Cleveland would cost Landis his job. Some argued that by rejecting the "Landis rider," the owners were signaling their intent to Landis. But others argued that this was just the latest of several times during his now 15-year reign when many thought Landis was about to be fired. Some suggested that if Landis ruled Feller a free agent, the owners would revolt out of fear of the uncertainty of their player rights.[32] Most owners felt that Cleveland should retain Feller's rights even if they did break the rules.[33] Despite all this uproar, at least one reporter noted that

> Among the more keen and cool-headed observers, however, there is the feeling that regardless of what the commissioner's final decision is, the result will be the same as it has been ever since the post was created for Landis in 1921.
>
> There may be some undercurrent grumbling, but all eventually will express satisfaction with the verdict whether they like it or not, for always it is generally understood the commissioner holds the whip hand.[34]

So a baseball revolution was unlikely, but a decision had to be made. And Landis's ruling proved to be intriguing, inasmuch as it contradicted itself.

It was fair to assume that Landis would either rule Cleveland had violated the major-minor agreement, thus making Feller a free agent and possibly resulting in a fine for the Indians, or that Cleveland had not violated the rules and would be able to keep Feller. The result was neither. Landis ruled that Cleveland did in fact violate the agreement, but he also decided that the "recommendation" amendment, voted on just the day before, prevented him from making Feller a free agent.[35] This of course was not true—he should have applied the rules as they existed at the time of the incident.

In the end, practicality won the day. Landis worked for the owners, who thought that Feller should stay with Cleveland, and Landis thus obliged his employers. He also noted that invalidating Cleveland's claim to Feller would not really help Des Moines, because Feller would sign with a major-league club, not with Des Moines. Instead, acknowledging that Cleveland had broken the rules, Landis made the Indians pay Des Moines $7,500—the amount the Des Moines club had offered Feller for his services.[36] The ruling was also inconsistent with Landis's rulings in the Cincinnati cases just weeks before. But everything was all right because, ultimately, the decision was the one that major-league owners wanted. Or, as one writer put it, "[T]he Feller decision looks inconsistent, is frankly retroactive, but since it is satisfactory to baseball, it is accepted without further comment here."[37]

One person who lost out was Feller himself. He was happy to still be playing for Cleveland, but he was also disappointed at what could have been. Red Sox owner Tom Yawkey and Yankees owner Jacob Ruppert reportedly said that if Feller became a free agent they would be willing to offer him $100,000 to sign.[38] As it was, Feller tried to sign with Cleveland for $20,000. He ended up signing for $14,000 for the 1937 season, and did not make $20,000 until the 1939 season.

The experience of the 1936 Winter Meetings likely had a major impact on Feller. Upon his death he was hailed by some as a "union activist," and he was always a staunch advocate of player rights.[39] Feller was a big fan of barnstorming and even ran barnstorming teams as a side business.[40] He believed players in the Negro Leagues weren't getting a fair chance to show what they could do, and his barnstorming teams helped give them that chance.[41] In 1945 Feller persuaded Commissioner Happy Chandler, Landis's successor, to increase the number of barnstorming games players could appear in during the offseason.[42] In 1956 he was elected the first president of the Major League Baseball Players' Association, and was the first star player to advocate against the reserve clause. He once told Mike Wallace that the arrangement was "medieval" because "you're obligated to the ball club for the entire life of your baseball career, but the ballclub is obligated to you for 30 days."[43] While the 1936 Winter Meetings may not have been the busiest or most impactful session, they played a large role in the legend of Bob Feller.

SOURCES

In addition to the sources cited in the Notes, the author also consulted Baseball-Reference.com and the following materials:

Drebinger, John. "Indians Will Keep Rookie Mound Ace," *New York Times*, December 11, 1936.

———. "Major League Club Owners and Officers Open Winter Conclave Here Today: Verdict on Feller Due at Convention," *New York Times*, December 8, 1936.

Kieran, John. "The Great Diamond Mystery," *New York Times*, October 30, 1936.

———. "Uneasy Lies the Head," *New York Times*, December 8, 1936.

McGowen, Roscoe. "Cards Now Likely to See Dean Antics," *New York Times*, December 10, 1936.

———. "Dean's 1937 Affiliation Is Still Deep Mystery to Baseball Men," *New York Times*, December 8, 1936.

———. "Giants Get Chiozza From Phils in Deal Said to Involve Camilli," *New York Times*, December 9, 1936.

———. "Promise of Important Trades Unfulfilled as Meetings End," *New York Times*, December 11, 1936.

Rabinowitz, Amanda. "Cleveland Pitching Great Bob Feller Dies at 92," NPR.org, npr.org/2010/12/16/132101192/Pitching-Great-Bob-Feller-Dies-At-92.

Spink, J.G. Taylor. "'Three and One' Looking Them Over With J.G. Taylor Spink," *The Sporting News*, December 24, 1936: 4.

"Big Leagues Agree on Livelier Ball," *New York Times*, January 6, 1934.

"Brief Bits of Montreal Gossip," *The Sporting News*, December 10, 1936: 8.

"Diz May Be Foolin', But Cards Are Not," *The Sporting News*, November 12, 1936: 1.

"Feller, Losing $100,000 Chance, Is 'Glad'; Schoolboy Will Demand $20,000 as Salary," *New York Times*, December 11, 1936.

"Landis' Blue Pencil Trims Cincy Roster," *The Sporting News*, December 3, 1936.

"Landis' Decision on Feller Holds Revised Regulations Validated Acts of Cleveland," *The Sporting News*, December 17, 1936: 8.

"Montreal Counting on Record Meeting," *The Sporting News*, November 26, 1936.

"Players' Group Selects Feller," *New York Times*, October 2, 1956.

"Reds' Money-Talk Isn't Loud Enough," *The Sporting News*, December 10, 1936: 2.

"San Diego Welcomes Players Received for Vince DiMaggio," *The Sporting News*, December 10, 1936.

"The Biggest News at the Meeting!," Advertisement, *The Sporting News*, December 10, 1936: 2.

"Wrigley's Aces Up, But Nobody Calls," *The Sporting News*, November 12, 1936: 1.

NOTES

1. Edgar G. Brands, "Montreal Meet Caps Fine Year for Minors," *The Sporting News*, December 10, 1936: 3.
2. "Minors' Reserve List for 1937 Reflects Steady Comeback of Game," *The Sporting News*, December 3, 1936: 8.
3. Edgar G. Brands, "Montreal Meet Caps Fine Year for Minors."
4. E.G. Brands, "School of Instruction Plays Big Role in Promotion of Minors," *The Sporting News*, December 10, 1936: 3.
5. "Minors to Consider 20 Changes in Rules," *The Sporting News*, November 26, 1936: 1.
6. "Heavy Traffic Clogs Market for Players," *The Sporting News*, December 10, 1936: 1.
7. "Frick for Charting Sunday Twin Bills," *The Sporting News*, November 19, 1936: 10.
8. Ibid.
9. "Deadening of Ball Put Off Until '38," *The Sporting News*, December 17, 1936: 3.
10. John Drebinger, "Landis Will Rule on Title to Hurler," *New York Times*, December 10, 1936.
11. John O. Seys, Base Plate for Baseball Diamonds. Seamless Rubber Company, Inc., assignee. Patent US2122266. 28 June 1938. Print. Available at worldwide.espacenet.com/publicationDetails/originalDocument?CC=US&NR=2122266A&KC=A&FT=D&ND=2&date=19380628&DB=&locale=en_EP (last accessed 12/2/2015).
12. John Drebinger, "Major League Club Owners and Officers Open Winter Conclave Here Today: Verdict on Feller Due at Convention," *New York Times*, December 8, 1936.
13. John Drebinger, "Landis Will Rule on Title to Hurler," *New York Times*, December 10, 1936.
14. Both Chicago and St. Louis had two teams at the time. The sources used here do not specifically mention which team from each city agreed with the "Midwest" view on radio broadcasting, but since the sources refer to a regional rather than a league-based split, it's safe to assume the teams that supported radio were either a mix of leagues or most of the teams from these cities.
15. "Over-Caution Rules Player Mart," *The Sporting News*, December 17, 1936: 4.
16. Ibid.
17. Frederick G. Lieb, "Baseball Is Still the National Sport," *Baseball Research Journal*, 1972, available at sabr.org/research/baseball-still-national-sport.
18. The composition and design of the ball could be changed to make the ball more "lively" or more "dead." Livelier balls are generally harder, allowing for more "pop" off the bat, while deader balls are generally softer and less resilient to give the ball less pop off the bat. Consider the difference between a fully inflated or underinflated ball (soccer ball or kickball) or between a racquetball and a handball.
19. "Deadening of Ball Put Off Until '38," *The Sporting News*, December 17, 1936: 3; John Drebinger, "Magnates Reject Amendment Rider," *New York Times*, December 9, 1936.
20. J.G. Taylor Spink, "'Three and One' Looking Them Over With J.G. Taylor Spink: 'Official Major League Ball' New Idea," *The Sporting News*, December 24, 1936: 4.
21. "Roosevelt Letter Read Amid Cheers," *New York Times*, February 8, 1937.
22. "Wrigley's Aces Up, But Nobody Calls," *The Sporting News*, November 12, 1936: 1.
23. Roscoe McGowen, "Cards Now Likely to See Dean Antics," *New York Times*, December 10, 1936; Roscoe McGowen, "Dean's 1937 Affiliation Is Still Deep Mystery to Baseball Men," *New York Times*, December 8, 1936; "Diz May Be Foolin', But Cards Are Not," *The Sporting News*, November 12, 1936: 1.
24. "1934—Dizzy, Daffy, and Ducky," ThisGreatGame.com, thisgreatgame.com/1934-baseball-history.html.
25. "Over-Caution Rules Player Mart."
26. The lowest number of innings pitched by a qualifying pitcher that season was 160, and the highest number of innings pitched by a nonqualifying pitcher was 148⅓. According to Baseball-Reference.com, in order to qualify for rate-based rankings a pitcher must pitch an average equal to or greater than one inning per league game that season.
27. "A Wise Decision by Landis," *The Sporting News*, December 17, 1936: 4
28. "Landis' Blue Pencil Trims Cincy Roster," *The Sporting News*, December 3, 1936.
29. Ibid.
30. John Drebinger, "Magnates Reject Amendment Rider," *New York Times*, December 9, 1936.
31. Ibid.
32. "Deadening of Ball Put Off Until '38," *The Sporting News*, December 17, 1936: 3; John Drebinger, "Landis Will Rule on Title to Hurler," *New York Times*, December 10, 1936.
33. "Landis Will Rule."
34. Ibid.
35. "Landis' Decision on Feller Holds Revised Regulations Validated Acts of Cleveland," *The Sporting News*, December 17, 1936: 8.
36. Ibid.

37 "Deadening of Ball Put Off Until '38," *The Sporting News*, December 17, 1936: 3.

38 Ibid.

39 "RIP Bob Feller, Union Activist," TeamsterNation, teamsternation.blogspot.com/2010/12/rip-bob-feller-union-activist.html.

40 "Barnstorming Green Light for Feller," *Lewiston Daily Sun*, September 12, 1945, accessible at https://news.google.com/newspapers?id=WJogAAAAIBAJ&sjid=OmgFAAAAIBAJ&pg=3607,4894856&dq=bob+feller+barnstorming&hl=en, and Amanda Rabinowitz, "Cleveland Pitching Great Bob Feller Dies at 92," NPR.org, http://www.npr.org/2010/12/16/132101192/Pitching-Great-Bob-Feller-Dies-At-92.

41 Rabinowitz, "Cleveland Pitching Great Bob Feller Dies at 92," *supra*.

42 "Barnstorming Green Light for Feller," *Lewiston* (Maine) *Daily Sun*, September 12, 1945, accessible at news.google.com/newspapers?id=WJogAAAAIBAJ&sjid=OmgFAAAAIBAJ&pg=3607,4894856&dq=bob+feller+barnstorming&hl=en.

43 "Bob Feller: The Mike Wallace Interview," Harry Ransom Center at the University of Texas at Austin, accessible at hrc.utexas.edu/multimedia/video/2008/wallace/feller_bob_t.html (last accessed December 18, 2015).

— 1937 —
MORE BUSINESS THAN BASEBALL

By Zak Schmoll

Introduction and Context

IN 1937, BOTH THE NATIONAL AND THE American Leagues held their Winter Meetings in Chicago, while the National Association met a few days earlier in Milwaukee. Rumors aplenty swirled around these gatherings, but very few teams actually pulled the trigger and made significant deals. The deals that did take place, however (and even a few that did not), created quite a bit of debate and controversy.

From December 1-3, the National Association met in Milwaukee's Schroeder Hotel. Milwaukee had a rich baseball history and had always fielded a team somewhere in Organized Baseball. (It was one of the original eight cities in the American League when it was established in 1901.) Because of these deep roots, the city was a clear choice for the National Association meetings.

On December 6 and 7 the National and American Leagues met separately in Chicago, at the Palmer House and the Congress Hotel respectively. The leagues then came together on the 8th, when Commissioner Kenesaw Mountain Landis convened a joint session.

Player Movement

One of the biggest questions surrounding the 1937 meetings was whether right-hander Van Lingle Mungo would be traded away from the Brooklyn Dodgers and manager Burleigh Grimes.

In 1937 Mungo had missed significant time to injury. It began relatively simply with a strained side, but Grimes continued pitching Mungo throughout the season. Mungo claimed that Grimes did not give him enough time to heal, but Grimes countered by saying, "When Mungo complained of a lame arm, I used him in a few games to see whether he could pitch despite his condition. I know that I had a lame arm all one year and yet managed to win 19 games that season."[1]

The difference of opinion on Mungo's injury led to greater tension. While Mungo claimed that he wasn't given time to properly heal, he also was not attending the prescribed diathermic therapy sessions that would help him heal more effectively.[2] As a result, Grimes suspended Mungo until he got himself into shape and was ready to play.

That never happened because Mungo simply left the Dodgers and went home. This action was the final straw, and most people around baseball assumed the pitcher would be traded before spring training.

Yet despite this tension, the 26-year-old was not traded that winter, primarily because the Dodgers were looking for a king's ransom in return for their three-time All-Star. "Mel Ott of the Giants would have been acceptable," one sportswriter suggested, adding, "So would Frank Demaree of the Cubs. Or Arky Vaughan, the Pirates shortstop, who would have been converted to an outfielder had Brooklyn obtained him."[3]

This type of blockbuster offer was never forthcoming, and Mungo was never the same pitcher after that year. He pitched for parts of seven more seasons, but he never made another All-Star Team and fashioned a modest 27-32 mark over that time.

While this deal never materialized, the Detroit Tigers and manager Mickey Cochrane did make a trade that generated its fair share of bad feelings in the Motor City.

The Tigers swapped their extremely popular outfielder, Gerald "Gee" Walker, plus infielder Marvin Owen and catcher Mike Tresh to the Chicago White

Sox for right-hander Vernon Kennedy, outfielder Dixie Walker and infielder Tony Piet. In 1936 Gee Walker had hit .335 with 18 home runs, 113 RBIs, and 23 stolen bases.

Cochrane knew that this would not be a popular move, but he decided that acquiring Kennedy, a 21-game winner in 1936, to strengthen their pitching staff was worth the sacrifice of the veterans Walker and Owen, along with the relatively promising prospect Tresh. "I knew I was putting myself on the spot," said Cochrane, "but I had to do something to strengthen our pitching. ... We had to have somebody who figures to win 18 or 20 games, if we are to improve our position. In my opinion, Kennedy will give us the needed help."[4]

The reaction was moderated somewhat when Walker himself came out in support of the trade. "Don't be too harsh on Mike. He had to have a pitcher. ... I'm sure he did what he thought was best for the club."[5] Regardless, the trade was still quite unpopular in Detroit.

If the fans had their way, Mungo would have been traded and Walker would have not. However, that is not what happened in 1937, and their situations became the biggest player-movement stories of the winter.

The Business Side

The main business at the National Association meetings in Milwaukee reflected a mood of caution. In his keynote address, Association President William G. Bramham cautioned teams about taking on too much payroll. In the previous season, a record 13,500,000 people had attended National Association games. While this was obviously a cause for celebration, Bramham did not want teams to begin spending recklessly simply because they suddenly had some more money in the till.

There was also a discussion about who should be allowed to use National Association facilities, with President Bramham warning minor-league teams about allowing exhibition games to be played in their ballparks. He reasoned that barnstorming teams were potential competitors for talent and could draw players away from the organization. Because of this, he felt that it was best to simply not allow those teams access to minor-league parks. Not coincidentally, a delegation from the National Semi-Pro Baseball Congress, led by president Raymond Dumont, attended the meetings in Milwaukee to try to find minor-league support. In particular, they were offering commissionerships to minor-league owners over district and state tournaments, in exchange for allowing these sanctioned tournaments to be held in the National Association teams' home fields. Obviously, this was contrary to what was being advocated by President Bramham. The National Semi-Pro Baseball Congress survives today as the National Baseball Congress and conducts a national semipro tournament annually in Wichita, Kansas. The tournament is played in a stadium shared with the Wichita Wingnuts, an independent team not affiliated with MLB.

At the joint meeting of the major leagues, it was decided that the All-Star teams would again be returned to a fan vote. American League President Will Harridge said his clubs always wanted the All-Star Game to be open to fan participation and that it was the National League that had changed that tradition a few years earlier.[6] True or not, fans around the country now had the All-Star vote returned to them.

There was also a discussion regarding college athletes and their eligibility to play professional baseball. Major- and minor-league teams had for years been accused of stealing players away from colleges. National League President Ford Frick proposed that college players either have been awarded their degrees or receive a signed permission letter from the school's president before playing professional baseball. However, the issue was essentially tabled. Even though it would be a while before any restrictions came into play, the discussion about forbidding undergraduates from leaving during their college career was already being given serious consideration and is still being dealt with today, most recently in the 2011 Collective Bargaining Agreement between major-league owners and the Players Association.

Finally, five people were voted into the Baseball Hall of Fame: New York Giants manager John McGraw; the original National League president, Morgan Bulkeley; talented nineteenth-century shortstop George Wright; American League founder and President Ban Johnson; and Connie Mack, one of the most recognizable figures in baseball history, who was still active as owner and manager of the Philadelphia Athletics.

Summary

The 1937 Winter Meetings focused more on business discussions and there was not very much player movement. Van Lingle Mungo was almost certainly on the move, but the Brooklyn Dodgers' staggeringly high demands for him ended any possibility of a deal taking place.

The most significant trade proved to be extremely unpopular in Detroit because of the departure of Gerald Walker. Not only was he a great ballplayer for the Tigers, but he also had a very strong following among fans.

On the business side, the National Association delegates heard a message of caution despite their recent success. They were told not to sacrifice any competitive advantage they might have over barnstorming teams by sharing ballparks, and they were urged to keep their budgets in line.

They did decide to return the All-Star Game to the fans, elected five new members to the Hall of Fame, and opened the discussion on collegiate eligibility.

These meetings did not necessarily provide major changes, but there were some fascinating story lines that made for interesting Hot Stove discussions.

SOURCES

In addition to the sources indicated in the Notes, the author also consulted Baseball-Reference.com and the following sources:

"Semi-Pros at Convention," *The Sporting News*, December 2, 1937.

Associated Press. "Heavy Majority of Major League Owners Seen in Favor of Less Lively Baseball," *Hartford Courant*, December 7, 1937.

Associated Press. "Trade Talk Fills Milwaukee Hotels," *New York Times*, November 30, 1937.

Brands, Edgar. "Bramham Sounds Note of Caution in Optimistic Report," *The Sporting News*, December 2, 1937.

———. "Registration of 1,002 Set Records for Minor League Conventions," *The Sporting News*, December 9, 1937.

"History of the NBC—NBC Baseball World Series—National Baseball Congress." NBC Baseball World Series—National Baseball Congress. nbcbaseball.com/nbchistory.html (accessed January 6, 2012).

Levy, Sam. "Milwaukee, Site of Minors' Convention, Rich in Diamond History," *The Sporting News*, November 25, 1937.

NOTES

1 Tommy Holmes, "Mungo Steams Up and Boils Over on Grimes," *The Sporting News*, November 25, 1937.
2 Ibid.
3 Tommy Holmes, "Grimes Still Seeks Mauler for Mungo," *The Sporting News*, December 16, 1937.
4 Sam Greene, "Detroit Fans Deride Cochrane for Swapping Walker to Dykes," *The Sporting News*, December 9, 1937.
5 Sam Greene, "Gerry Walker Comes to Defense of Cochrane for White Sox Trade," *The Sporting News*, December 16, 1937.
6 Edgar Brands, "Major Leagues Split on Changing Ball and Increasing Player Limit," *The Sporting News*, December 16, 1937.

1938
OUT OF THE HAT

By Jason C. Long

Introduction and Context

IN 1938, THE MAJOR LEAGUES RETURNED to New York City for the winter meetings, while the minor leagues held their meetings in New Orleans for the first time since 1916. The minor leagues sought to promote uniformity, and with the nation's economy beginning to emerge from the Great Depression, several minor leagues adopted increases in salary limits. In the same vein, the major-league teams voted to increase their rosters to 25, after having trimmed to 23 during the depth of the Depression a few years earlier. The American and National Leagues also agreed on a uniform ball for 1939. Other business saw an increase in night games, rule changes, and several teams announcing radio deals. There was also important player movement, with the Cubs and Giants striking a six-player deal to exchange All-Star shortstops, the Tigers making a surprise pitching acquisition and filling their need for a third baseman, Washington trading first baseman Zeke Bonura to the Giants, and a trade between the Dodgers and Bees that apparently resulted from pulling names out of a hat.

The Minor League Meetings in New Orleans

The 37th meeting of the National Association of Professional Baseball Leagues (NAPBL) began on Wednesday, December 7, at the Roosevelt Hotel in New Orleans. Mayor Robert Maestri sent an official welcome to NAPBL President William G. Bramham stating that attendees would have "an experience of a memorable character that will last ... a lifetime."[1] Indeed, the City of New Orleans expected the meetings to provide a "great benefit" that "money could not buy" in publicity and tourism.[2]

The Dodgers' Broadcast Announcement

Baseball activity was under way in New Orleans well before the meeting's official start. Brooklyn Dodgers general manager Larry MacPhail, in New Orleans for the meetings, announced the day before they began that all Dodgers games in 1939 would be broadcast on radio. The three New York teams had agreed not to broadcast games during 1938, 1939, and 1940. In the spring of 1938, however, MacPhail had declared that he considered this agreement to be inoperative, and his announcement made clear that the Dodgers would move on from the arrangement altogether. Neither Giants owner Horace Stoneham nor National League President Ford Frick had any comment. But Yankees business manager Ed Barrow declared that MacPhail, the Yankees and Giants were "no longer bound by it and can move as they see fit."[3] Though the *New York Daily Mirror* suggested that the Dodgers had been "on the air" like "dead horses" for years, General Mills and Socony Vacuum Oil reportedly paid $77,000 for the broadcast rights for 1939 and 1940.[4]

The Cubs and Giants Strike a Six-Player Deal

The same day the Cubs and Giants made a trade in which each team sent a shortstop, catcher, and outfielder to the other. Stoneham and Giants manager Bill Terry completed the deal in New Orleans with Cubs scout Clarence "Pants" Rowland, sending shortstop Dick Bartell, outfielder Hank Lieber, and catcher Gus Mancuso, each a former All-Star, to Chicago. The Cubs sent back shortstop Billy Jurges and outfielder Frank Demaree, former All-Stars, and catcher Ken

O'Dea. Apparently the Cubs had a deal in place a year earlier to trade the same players to the Pirates, but owner P.K. Wrigley vetoed the deal. His approval this time resulted from his confidence in Gabby Hartnett, who had taken over the third-place Cubs in July and led them to the National League pennant. Hartnett, who was walking around the Roosevelt Hotel with his pockets full of cigars, had re-signed with the Cubs on December 1 for a salary of $27,500, a $5,000 raise. After the trade with the Giants, somebody in New Orleans suggested to Hartnett that Leiber might be disagreeable. Hartnett responded, "Well, so am I," and warned that anybody who would not play hard for him would not "be around very long."[5] Leiber had puzzled the Giants; after he hit .331 with 22 home runs in 1935, his performance at the plate had deteriorated. Some attributed this to Bob Feller beaning Leiber in the head during an April 1937 exhibition game that coincidentally was played in New Orleans. But Leiber's 1936 season had already showed a decline, producing only nine homers and a .279 average. In any event, Stoneham recognized that Leiber might "come back with another club and beat" the Giants, but said that the Giants had "gone the limit" and had to "give up" on him.[6]

The Official NAPBL Meetings

When the meetings officially began in the Roosevelt Hotel's Tip-Top Room at 10:00 A.M. on Wednesday, more than 1,000 delegates were on hand. Attendees included Commissioner Kenesaw Mountain Landis and representatives from each major-league club.

One focus for the delegates was the lack of uniform rules across the minor leagues on such things as determining player status, calculating batting averages, and determining league champions. Delegates approved changes in minor-league agreements to establish uniformity in scoring to mimic the major leagues, particularly in batting averages; the number of players teams could have on option; offseason roster limits; restricting Class B, C, and D-league teams to six players with more than three years' professional experience; and player classifications. President Bramham himself introduced the proposal that was adopted to remedy variations in the bases for classifying players as amateurs, rookies, or otherwise, based on their playing experience.

In addition to the proposals designed to promote uniformity across the minor leagues, several others reflected improving economic conditions. Minor-league attendance in 1938 had increased by 2 million over 1937, so player salary limits were increased in several leagues, and the roster changes needed to achieve uniformity resulted in teams carrying more players rather than fewer.

Nevertheless, a few proposals that stemmed from improving economic conditions were withdrawn. For example, the Southern Association and Texas League had proposed allowing a player (and the manager as well) to receive a portion of the purchase price when he was sold. Similarly, the Western Association and Three-I League suggested allowing leagues from Class C up to pay signing bonuses to free agents. President Bramham argued against the proposals, warning that they would lead teams back into financial problems. After a long discussion, the sponsors withdrew the proposals.

Among the proposals that the NAPBL rejected was Commissioner Landis' recommendation to rescind the "Baltimore Agreement." Adopted two years earlier in Montreal, it permitted scouts from one club to recommend that a player sign with another club. The majors began using the agreement to scout players and sign them for a minor-league club, with the intention of having them actually play for the major-league club. A notable example was Bob Feller, whom the Indians scouted and recommended to Fargo; Feller signed with Fargo, but reported directly to the Indians. Landis called this practice "authorized subterfuge" because it allowed major-league clubs to effectively sign players who had no professional experience. Otherwise, the National Agreement prohibited major-league clubs from signing amateurs except college players. When Landis and Bramham proposed altering the Baltimore Agreement to end this "subterfuge," the NAPBL delegates declined in short order. As one delegate explained, the practice would continue regardless of prohibitions, "So why not let the bars down?"[7]

Thus, instead of prohibiting major-league clubs from using the Baltimore Agreement to sign inexperienced players, the delegates resolved to permit this practice. This proposal would require approval at the major-league meetings in New York.

Clark Griffith introduced a proposal to limit each major-league team to one minor-league affiliate per classification, with no more than seven total. After the minors had taken actions favoring major-minor affiliations, Griffith's proposal arrived like a "thunderbolt" that left the meetings "speechless."[8] It was referred to the majors, with the minors planning a vote by mail after the majors considered the matter.

Other Activity at the NAPBL Meetings

The NAPBL conducted business in three sessions, with Wednesday's session beginning at 10:00 A.M. and lasting past noon. While the delegates were in session on Wednesday, the NAPBL scheduled a sightseeing tour and lunch in the French Quarter for women accompanying delegates to the meetings. The men had their turn later, with a "stag party" scheduled for Wednesday night. Thursday's session also began at 10:00 A.M., and the annual banquet took place that evening. The final session was held on Friday morning starting at 10:00 A.M.

The meetings featured the return of the "business school" for team officials. The NAPBL had offered the school at previous winter meetings, but skipped it in 1937. American Association President George Trautman presided over the school, which offered instruction for owners, business managers, and business secretaries on matters including player transfers, dealing with the press, team relations with the NAPBL, radio broadcasts, promotional activity, and accounting.

Of the 35 proposals on the agenda to alter the National Agreement, plus two introduced during the meetings, the delegates passed 28 proposals, declined four, and deferred one, while the other proposals were withdrawn. Many minor leagues held their own meetings in conjunction with the NAPBL convention, including the Middle Atlantic League, the Southern Association, the Western Association, the Texas League, and the Piedmont League, which used the gathering as an opportunity to order the Durham Bulls to stop wearing red pants

The Major League Meetings in New York

After the Friday session in New Orleans, the action shifted to New York for the major-league meetings. For the first time, the American and National Leagues held their respective meetings at the same hotel, the Waldorf Astoria. The leagues chose one hotel in response to demands from the press, which did not want to shuffle between two sites for the league meetings. Nevertheless, the big leagues' joint session would be held at the Roosevelt Hotel, a few blocks away.

The Giants Trade for Zeke Bonura

As the teams left New Orleans, one loose end was Zeke Bonura's waiver status. Bonura hit .289 with 22 home runs for Washington in 1938, having come from the White Sox after the 1937 season. But the Senators were unhappy with Bonura's fielding at first base and believed that the right-hander was a poor fit for Griffith Stadium with its deep left field. The Senators thus placed Bonura on waivers. Initially, the White Sox claimed Bonura. He had been a fan favorite in Chicago, and the White Sox did not want Washington to trade Bonura to the crosstown Cubs. Once Clark Griffith assured the White Sox that he would not do so, the White Sox passed on Bonura. The A's also expressed interest, with Connie Mack saying that Bonura would "hit a lot of home runs for us in Shibe Park," but ultimately they also waived on Bonura, with a statement that Clark Griffith "would want too much in the way of playing strength in exchange for Zeke."[9] Griffith met with the Giants' Horace Stoneham and Bill Terry at an NFL game between the NFL's Giants and Packers at the Polo Grounds on Sunday, December 11, where they finalized a deal. The Giants sent right-handed pitcher Tom Baker, infielder Jim Carlin, and a reported $25,000 to the Senators for Bonura. This led to backlash in Washington, since Baker had already flopped with the Dodgers and Cubs, and Carlin was a career minor leaguer without a position. Griffith and manager Bucky Harris were reportedly "half apologetic" in announcing the deal.[10] In New York, manager Bill Terry, a "stickler" for fielding himself, said he knew "all about" Bonura's fielding and that he was "prepared to worry along on that," but that "what counts most" was that the Giants "finally got somebody" to "give that ball plenty of riding."[11]

The Tigers Acquire Fred Hutchinson

On the eve of the official opening, Tigers manager Del Baker arrived in New York and announced "one of the biggest surprises of the major league offseason."[12] At the last minute, the Tigers outbid the Pirates and the Yankees to acquire Seattle Rainiers pitcher Fred Hutchinson. In his first minor-league season, in 1938, the 19-year-old righty threw 290 innings, posting a 2.48 ERA and a 25-7 record. As the minor-league meetings were winding down, the Pirates had Hutchinson within their grasp. Pittsburgh president Bill Benswanger was coy, responding to a rumor that the Pirates had acquired Hutchinson by saying, "I won't say that we won't buy him."[13] Yankees manager Joe McCarthy, who had also been trying to acquire Hutchinson, was more frank: "Pittsburgh beat us to him."[14] But the Tigers quietly made a deal, sending $50,000 and four players — outfielder JoJo White and infielder Tony Piet from Detroit, and first baseman George Archie and right-handed pitcher Ed Selway from the minor leagues — to Seattle. In exchange, Detroit insisted on Hutchinson pitching for the Tigers in 1939; Seattle had wanted him to pitch for the Rainiers in 1939 and join the major leagues afterward. When Baker arrived in New York on Monday night and announced that Hutchinson would be wearing a Tigers uniform in 1939, a Pittsburgh official remarked, "Guess shaking hands on a deal no longer binds a bargain in baseball, as in the old days."[15]

The Official Meetings

The major-league meetings officially opened on the morning of Tuesday, December 13, with the leagues' individual sessions scheduled for Tuesday and Wednesday at the Waldorf-Astoria and the joint session scheduled for Thursday at the Roosevelt Hotel.

One of the prime issues for both leagues was the baseball itself. Although the ball that each league had been using contained the same interior, one year earlier the National League had adopted a thicker covering and added threads to the stitching. Both moves were designed to assist pitchers, deadening the ball and providing pitchers a better grip.

The American League Meeting

In a contentious session that lasted more than seven hours, the American League addressed matters including night baseball, which ball to use, and roster size. The National League began to allow night baseball after then-Reds president Larry MacPhail lobbied for it at the 1934 winter meetings. Despite the Reds averaging 20,000 fans at their night games, the AL continued to shun night baseball. This resulted in no small part from the sentiment among AL owners like Clark Griffith, who in the early 1930s called night games "bush league stuff" and "just a step above dog racing," and Yankees president Ed Barrow, who called night baseball a "novelty" that would "never last."[16] Cleveland and Philadelphia, however, sought permission to play under the lights in 1939. Heading into the meetings, the AL was split: Boston, Detroit, New York, and Washington opposed the request, while Cleveland, Philadelphia, Chicago, and St. Louis were in favor. Connie Mack sorely wanted the financial boost that night games would provide, so he made a deal with Clark Griffith, privately telling Griffith that if the Senators would support night baseball in Philadelphia, Mack would pass on Bonura. They agreed, Mack passed on Bonura, and Griffith broke the deadlock; the league approved up to seven night games in Philadelphia and Cleveland.[17] There could be no night games on Saturday, Sunday, or holidays, and no inning could start after 11:50 P.M. These were the same limitations that the National League employed, except that the NL allowed Saturday night games.

With respect to the ball, the AL voted to retain its covering but adopt the NL's stitching. Led by former pitcher and longtime Yankees antagonist Clark Griffith, and after consulting with representatives from the National League, the AL sought a less lively ball at least in part to blunt the home-run power that had propelled the Yankees to the past three World Series championships.

Finally, the AL unanimously re-elected President Will Harridge for a 10-year term; resolved to retain the 23-man roster instead of moving back to a 25-man limit, though it did propose a two-player disabled list that would not count against the roster; declined Griffith's proposal to ban signing bonuses (which were already prohibited in the NL); decided that Connie Mack would manage the 1939 AL All-Star Team; and voted to start the 1939 season on April 17 with the Yankees traveling to Washington to take on the Senators.

The National League Meeting

The National League meetings were less contentious and not as long as the AL meeting, with the NL waiting on the AL for several issues. For example, NL President Ford Frick announced that the NL was satisfied with its ball, though it was toying with the idea of allowing a yellow covering instead of a white exterior to promote the ball's visibility. Thus, the NL delayed a final decision because it wanted to play with the same ball as the AL. Frick stated that if the NL could not reach an agreement with the junior circuit, then the NL might consider using a yellow ball. Differing with the AL, however, the NL voted 4 to 3 to return to the 25-man roster. (The Cubs abstaining but owner Wrigley advised that he would vote with the majority.) Under the NL proposal, teams would have until May 15 to comply with the 25-player limit. Before May 15, and after September 1, the NL proposed that teams could have a 40-man roster.

Otherwise, the NL was busy only with routine business. It adopted all the minor-league amendments proposed in New Orleans, deferred Clark Griffith's proposal to limit teams to one minor-league affiliate per classification, and declined the Yankees' proposal to extend the length of player contracts to cover spring training. The NL scheduled the Reds to host the Pirates at Crosley Field to open the season on April 17, 1939, with all the other teams opening the next day.

The Joint Session

Commissioner Landis presided over the joint session of the American and National Leagues on Thursday at the Roosevelt Hotel. One of the first issues that the meeting addressed was roster size. With the leagues deadlocked, it was up to Landis to cast the deciding vote. After its 4-to-3 vote, the NL agreed to make it unanimous in the joint session. Seven AL teams supported the 23-man limit, the Yankees being the only holdout. Landis sided with the majority to break the tie between the leagues, thus adopting the NL proposal for a 25-man roster between May 15 and September 1, with a 40-man roster the rest of the season.

The joint session also addressed several proposals to change the rules of play. One change that was adopted was an addition to the rule on infield flies, making it apply to certain outfield flies. The addition to the rule provided: "If before two are out, while first and second, or first, second and third are occupied, an outfielder, in the judgment of the umpire, intentionally drops a fly or line drive, the umpire shall immediately rule the ball has been caught."[18] Clark Griffith proposed another change to provide that pitchers would have to keep only one foot on the pitching rubber before throwing a pitch, rather than two. The leagues adopted the new rule, which provided:

Preliminary to pitching, the pitcher shall take his position facing the batsman with both feet squarely on the ground but his pivot foot must be on or in front in contact with the pitchers' plate, his other foot may be directly behind or in front (not on the side of) the pitchers' plate. In the act of delivering the ball to the batsman, he must keep one foot in contact with the pitchers' plate defined in Rule 9. The pitcher shall not raise either foot until in the act of delivering the ball to batsman, or in throwing to a base, nor may he make more than one step in such delivery.[19]

A committee consisting of NL President Ford Frick, AL President Will Harridge, and Henry P. Edwards, a Cleveland sportswriter and one of the BBWAA's founders, was convened to consider other amendments to the rules including whether to count a fly scoring a run as a sacrifice and whether to award an RBI to a batter hitting into a double play.

In addition to the rule change concerning the pitching rubber, Griffith submitted several other proposals in the joint session. He again proposed his rule change to limit teams to one affiliate per minor-league classification, which he had sponsored in each of the AL and NL meetings. But he withdrew it because Yankees owner Jacob Ruppert did not attend the meetings due to his failing health and the proposal was aimed primarily at the Yankees. He also proposed banning planned doubleheaders on Sundays, even though they appealed to most owners because they generally were among the best-attended games. The leagues declined and allowed teams to continue scheduling Sunday doubleheaders after the third Sunday of the season.

Other business saw the leagues agree that if a team's claim of a player on waivers would put the team over the roster limit, it must immediately notify Commissioner Landis which player it would drop to make room for the newcomer. (This would be the case even if the team later withdrew the waiver claim.) The leagues renewed their annual $20,000 appropriation to support the American Legion's baseball program and heard from Christy Walsh, director of sports for the New York World's Fair (scheduled to begin in 1939), about baseball's place at the fair. Walsh presented a letter from Jacob Ruppert, chairman of the fair's sports committee, urging that baseball should "dominate all other sports with an outstanding exhibit in the Academy of Sport."[20]

The 1939 major-league meetings were awarded to Cincinnati after the American League consented to vary from the standard rotation that would have seen Chicago serve as the host city. The move was part of the plan to celebrate the 100th anniversary of baseball, based on the story of Abner Doubleday inventing the game in 1839. The minor leagues were invited to meet in Cincinnati too, and while that required President Bramham and the NAPBL executive committee to agree, the expectation was that they would do so. This would represent one of the few instances when the minor leagues joined the majors in the same city, or in a city that did not host a minor-league team, or when the majors met in a city other than Chicago or New York.

Other Player Movement

With Fred Hutchinson and Zeke Bonura moving to new teams, player movement continued as the meetings progressed. The Tigers went into the meetings looking for a third baseman; this had been a soft spot in their lineup for some time. While Marv Owen had hit for a decent average in the mid-1930s while manning Detroit's hot corner, the Tigers shipped him to Chicago after the 1937 season seeking better alternatives. But Owen's replacements at third had hit .248 with only 3 home runs in the 1938 season. At the meetings, the Tigers reportedly talked to Clark Griffith about Senators shortstop Cecil Travis, whom the Tigers would shift to third. Griffith asked for Tigers starter Elden Auker, outfielder Roy Cullenbine, and catcher Birdie Tebbetts for Travis and catcher Rick Ferrell, but the Tigers declined. They went on to talk to the Athletics about Bill Werber and to the Browns about Harlond Clift. Ultimately, the Tigers agreed to send the right-handed Auker, left-hander Jake Wade, and reserve outfielder Chet Morgan to the Red Sox for third-baseman Pinky Higgins and southpaw reliever Archie McKain. Higgins did not have Clift's power or Werber's speed, but he had hit .300 every year but two since breaking into the majors in 1934. Likewise, the submarining Auker had been a mainstay of Detroit's rotation, winning at least 13 games in four of his six big-league seasons.

Cleveland had wanted Auker too, with manager Oscar Vitt saying that he had offered second baseman Odell Hale and righty reliever Denny Galehouse to Detroit. The Tigers reportedly were willing to deal Auker and shortstop Billy Rogell to Cleveland in exchange for Indians shortstop Lyn Lary and righty reliever Johnny Humphries or outfield Moose Solters. The Indians wanted Rogell and Auker, but were unwilling to meet the Tigers' price. Thus, the Tigers kept Rogell and sent Auker to Boston to solve their longstanding need for a third baseman.

Another third baseman was traded in a deal that arose from much more fortuitous circumstances.

As owner of the reigning National League pennant winner, Phil Wrigley gave a dinner for the owners on December 13. While stories varied, apparently Larry MacPhail took the opportunity to suggest a new tradition at the annual dinner to trade players by throwing names into a hat:

Let each club throw the name of a player into a hat ... The player has to be some bird which is on the active roster on August 15 the previous year. Then everybody digs in for a player ... In that way, we do some trading.[21]

Wrigley asked MacPhail whose name he would put in the hat; MacPhail identified right-handed pitcher Fred Frankhouse. Next, Wrigley asked Bees owner Bob Quinn who he would throw in, and he identified third baseman Joe Stripp. Wrigley then asked, "Why can't you two go ahead?"[22] Quinn and MacPhail consented, and that was the trade. MacPhail apparently planned to suggest doing this again the next year. Although Cardinals owner Sam Breadon said his team did not have a player whose name he would throw into a hat, Quinn, Wrigley, and the Pirates' Bill Benswanger seemed to want to continue MacPhail's tradition.

The Dodgers made a few conventional trades, too. Before the meetings Larry MacPhail said he was "very likely" to swing a deal involving first baseman Buddy Hassett.[23] First the Dodgers sent minor-league right-hander Lew Krausse to the Cardinals for outfielder Jimmy Outlaw. Then MacPhail fulfilled his prophecy, sending Hassett and Outlaw to the Bees for outfielder Gene Moore and righty Ira Hutchinson. The Dodgers also wanted Phillies pitcher Hugh "Losing Pitcher" Mulcahy (the right-hander had earned his nickname by losing 18 games in 1937 and 20 games in 1938), but Brooklyn offered Joe Stripp (acquired in the hat deal), infielder Woody Williams, and right-handers Bill Posedel and Johnny Gaddy. The Phillies, however, said they required some combination of first baseman Bert Haas, second baseman Pete Coscarart, and infielder Johnny Hudson in exchange. In light of that, the Dodgers' desire for Mulcahy faded and there was no deal.

The Red Sox were looking for starting pitching at the meetings, and in addition to landing Auker, they sent infielder-outfielder Ben Chapman to Cleveland for pitcher Denny Galehouse and infielder Tom Irwin. Chapman was a former All-Star who hit .340 in 1938, but the Red Sox wanted the 26-year-old Galehouse to shore up the rotation and provide pitching depth.

Other trades saw the Bees and Pirates swap catchers; Boston sent Ray Mueller to Pittsburgh for Al Todd and outfielder John Dickshot, and a trade of Sox; the Red Sox sending infielder Eric McNair to the White Sox for infielder Boze Berger. Boston had granted White Sox skipper Jimmy Dykes permission to examine McNair at McNair's Mississippi home, and when the White Sox were satisfied with his health, the deal was completed.

Trade Rumors

A few trades were rumored at the meetings but never came to fruition. The Phillies offered Hugh Mulcahy to the Cubs for second baseman Billy Herman and $25,000. Meanwhile, the Giants offered the Phillies second baseman Alex Kampouris for shortstop Del Young and outfielder Gibby Brack. Young and Kampouris were glove-first infielders, but Brack was an effective batter in limited action and Herman was a lifetime .300 hitter who was eventually elected to the Hall of Fame. The Giants also wanted Phillies righty Claude Passeau, offering a package of outfielder Jimmy Ripple, right-handed reliever Bill Lohrman, and cash. Nothing came of any of these teams' pursuits.

First base was a source of rumors for both Philadelphia teams. The Phillies sought a power-hitting first baseman. They ended up with a first baseman named Powers, purchasing minor leaguer Les Powers, who had slugged for the Giants' Jersey City affiliate. Even after this purchase, the Phillies inquired about the Cubs' young first baseman Phil Cavarretta, but no deal resulted. On the AL side, in addition to flirting with Zeke Bonura, Connie Mack reportedly wanted Rudy York from the Tigers. He was willing to offer third baseman Bill Werber, whom Mack called "one of the league's best third basemen,"[24] but the Tigers acquired Pinky Higgins and no deal for Werber transpired. The A's received an offer for their first baseman, Lou Finney, who had hit .275 with 10 home runs in 1938; the White Sox offered outfielder Rip Radcliff, but Connie Mack held onto Finney.

Finally, the Indians wanted second baseman Don Heffner from the Browns, and offered St. Louis a wide choice of players. The Browns could choose from right-handed pitchers Willis Hudlin and Bill Zuber, southpaws Earl Whitehill and Al Milnar, plus outfielders Earl Averill, Moose Solters, Bruce Campbell, or Roy Weatherly. Heffner was a light-hitting second baseman, the players the Indians offered were similarly unremarkable, and ultimately both teams stood pat.

Conclusion

Though the 1938 winter meetings saw a number of developments both on and off the field, the results ranged from ineffective to inconclusive. For example, although the night games approved in Cleveland and Philadelphia attracted larger crowds than the average day games, they did not significantly affect the teams' overall attendance. Cleveland drew more than 55,000 fans to the first night game at Municipal Stadium, on June 27, 1939. But the team's total attendance in 1939 declined by more than 88,000 fans from 1938, even though the Indians finished in third place each year with nearly identical records. At best, night baseball in Cleveland may be viewed as having simply forestalled a greater overall decline in attendance. In Philadelphia, only a few more than 15,000 attended the A's first night game at Shibe Park, though poor weather was a factor. Indeed, critics suggested that Connie Mack undermined his night games by scheduling them too early in the season, before the weather was warm enough. And the Phillies, who moved into Shibe Park during July 1938 and therefore also featured night games during the 1939 season, fared worst of all, averaging only slightly more than 14,000 fans for each of their seven night games.

In the same vein, it is not clear that the changes in the ball suppressed offense. Although American Leaguers hit 68 fewer home runs in 1939 than in 1938, slugging percentages and batting averages in 1939 remained within a few points of their 1938 totals. And changes aimed at the Yankees also failed; the Bronx Bombers led the league in slugging and homers, just as they had in 1938, as they claimed their fourth straight pennant. In the National League, slugging increased slightly in 1939 while home runs increased from 611 to 649 with the new ball.

Finally, the teams that acquired players at the winter meetings did not see great improvement in the standings. For the Giants, Billy Jurges hit .285 and was an All-Star in 1939, but Zeke Bonura did not give the ball too much "riding," hitting just 11 homers as the team fell from third place in 1938 to fifth in 1939. Likewise, the Cubs fell from pennant winners in 1938 to fourth place in 1939, even though Hank Leiber did find Wrigley Field agreeable as he bounced back with a .310 average and 24 home runs. The Tigers fell from a fourth-place finish in 1938 to fifth place in 1939. Even though Pinky Higgins was solid at third base, hitting .276 with eight homers, Fred Hutchinson posted a 5.21 ERA and claimed only three wins as the Tigers went 5-7 in his 12 starts. Elden Auker, whom the Tigers sent to the Red Sox in exchange for Higgins, also did not post a great 1939, posting a 5.36 ERA as he went just 9-10 and Boston again finished second to the Yankees, who went on to sweep the Reds in the 1939 World Series as both the majors and minors headed to Cincinnati for the 1939 winter meetings.

NOTES

1 "Welcome From New Orleans," *The Sporting News*, December 1, 1938: 4.

2 Harry Martinez, "Sports From the Crow's Nest," *New Orleans Times-Picayune*, December 4, 1938: Sec. 4, 7.

3 "Dodger Baseball to Be Broadcast," *New York Times*, December 7, 1938: 29.

4 "Scribbled by Scribes," *The Sporting News*, December 15, 1938: 4.

5 Ibid.

6 Roscoe McGowen, "Giants Get Jurges, O'Dea and Demaree in Deal With Cubs," *New York Times*, December 7, 1938: 29.

7 "Frisch, Seeking Post in Majors, Rules Out New Orleans Pilot Job," *New York Times*, December 9, 1938: 33.

8 Edgar S. Brands, "Minors Loosen Bands of Economy, Invite Majors to Do Likewise," *The Sporting News*, December 15, 1938: 7.

9 "Powers No. 1 Catch in Phil Power Hunt," *The Sporting News*, December 15, 1938: 1.

10 Denman Thompson, "Capital Can't Make Bonura Deal Add Up," *The Sporting News*, December 15, 1938: 11.

11 John Drebinger, "Senators Send Bonura, First Baseman, to Giants," *New York Times*, December 12, 1938: 24.

12 Sam Greene, "Detroit Goes High to Land Hill Prize," *The Sporting News*, December 15, 1938: 1.

13 "Sale of Coast Ace to Pirates Is Seen," *New York Times*, December 10, 1938: 22.

14 Ibid.

15 "Tigers and Red Sox Both Fill Old Voids," *The Sporting News*, December 22, 1938: 7.

16 John Helyar, *Lords of the Realm* (New York: Villard Books, 1994), 40.

17 Griffith's vote represented an about-face from his earlier statements, but his opposition to night baseball had become equivocal. While Griffith initially described night games as "bush league stuff," he later began to consider them. See David G. Surdam, *Wins, Losses, and Empty Seats: How Baseball Outlasted the Great Depression* (Lincoln: University of Nebraska Press, 2011), 233-35. And while he supported the AL banning night games for the 1938 season, by July of that year he acknowledged to American League president Will Harridge that "night baseball in Washington would pack them in." See "Night Baseball Trend Is Seen by Harridge in Major Leagues," *New York Times*, July 3, 1938.

18 E.G. Brands, "New Player Limit, Uniform Ball for Majors," *The Sporting News*, December 22, 1938: 7.

19 Ibid.

20 John Drebinger, "Major Leagues Raise Player Limit to 25; Red Sox and Tigers Complete Deal," *New York Times*, December 16, 1938: 34.

21 Dan Daniel, "Over … the Fence," *The Sporting News*, December 22, 1938: 7.

22 Ibid.

23 "Traders Turn to N.Y. Session," *Baltimore Sun*, December 10, 1938: 15.

24 "Powers No. 1 Catch in Phil Power Hunt."

— 1939 —
THE TIE GOES TO THE COMMISSIONER

By Jason C. Long

Introduction and Context

THE 1939 BASEBALL WINTER MEETings were held in Cincinnati, with the major and minor leagues meeting together for the first time since 1923. But meeting together provided little impetus for agreement. The minor leagues approved several measures to govern major-minor affiliations, but when the American and National Leagues split on whether to approve them, Commissioner Kenesaw Mountain Landis cast his tie-breaking vote against them. The meetings similarly saw no player movement that would be meaningful for the 1940 season.

The American and National Leagues had always held their meetings in New York or Chicago, but decided to meet in Cincinnati as part of the yearlong celebration of baseball's centennial. Based on the story that Abner Doubleday invented baseball in 1839, the centennial celebrations included the Hall of Fame opening in Cooperstown, New York; each major league producing a film about baseball; and more than $100,000 spent on other promotions. Cincinnati was chosen as the winter meetings' location because it was the home of the first professional baseball team, the Red Stockings; coincidentally, the present-day Reds were the reigning National League champions.

About 1,500 people attended the meetings, representing more than 40 leagues and some 300 baseball clubs. The meetings opened at the Netherland Plaza Hotel in downtown Cincinnati on December 4. The minor leagues conducted business on the 4th through the 6th, followed by the major leagues, which were scheduled to meet on the 7th and 8th and conclude with a joint session on Saturday, December 9.

On the Field

As the meetings approached, there was buzz that teams would trade star players. For example, there was wide speculation that the Boston Bees would trade Max West. At least seven teams were interested in the outfielder, who hit .285 with 19 home runs during his sophomore season in 1939. Cardinals outfielder and future Hall of Famer Joe Medwick was also rumored to be on the move, with Dodgers president Larry MacPhail stating that he would bid "as high as any club" for him.[1] Other stories had the Tigers trading Hank Greenberg, who had demanded a raise in exchange for moving from first base to left field to make room for Rudy York; the Yankees acquiring Browns All-Star first baseman George McQuinn; several clubs pining for Phillies All-Star outfielder Morrie Arnovich; and the Giants, coming off a fifth-place finish, pledging that they "must do something for 1940."[2]

One of the first moves came from the hometown Reds, who re-signed the key members of their pennant-winning pitching staff. Bucky Walters, who won 27 games and the National League MVP Award in 1939, signed a $20,000 contract for 1940. Paul Derringer, who went 25-7, signed a two-year contract for an amount close to $20,000 per year. Pitcher Johnny Vander Meer and utilityman Bill Werber also re-signed.

The Dodgers provided a highlight of the meetings' opening day when MacPhail, "holding court" in the Netherland Plaza's Presidential Suite, announced a contract extension for Leo Durocher. Durocher had led the Dodgers to a 15-game improvement in his first year as manager, so the extension was no surprise. But when MacPhail held a press conference wearing "the latest cut" in white flannel pajamas to announce that there was "never any question" about Durocher's return, it was "hilarious." Durocher got in on the act too, stating that he had agreed to "keep MacPhail for another year."[3]

In more serious business, the White Sox were offering outfielder Gerald "Gee" Walker around, seeking a catcher, but ultimately traded him to Washington for pitcher Pete Appleton and outfielder Taft Wright. The deal followed a late-night meeting that stretched into the early morning between Chicago manager Jimmy Dykes, Senators manager Bucky Harris and team president Clark Griffith. Chicago also traded outfielder Rip Radcliff to the Browns for outfielder Moose Solters and sold third baseman Marv Owen to the Red Sox.

The Cubs were also shopping for a shortstop. Dick Bartell, an All-Star with the Giants in 1937, was the Cubs shortstop in 1939. But his poor season led the Cubs to eye the Dodgers' Johnny Hudson, the Pirates' Arkie Vaughn, and the Bees' Eddie Miller as possible replacements. Nothing came of that, so the Cubs traded "worn-out shortstops" with the Tigers, exchanging Bartell for Billy Rogell.[4] Recognizing Rogell's limitations, the Cubs subsequently attempted to acquire Marty Marion, a minor-league shortstop in the Cardinals system. But the Cardinals declined, and Marion went on to become a seven-time All-Star and the 1944 National League MVP.

The Cubs were also in the market for a catcher and were rumored to be seeking Dodgers All-Star Babe Phelps. Instead, they traded catcher Gus Mancuso and minor-league pitcher Newel Kimball to the Dodgers for catcher Al Todd. The trade placed Todd on his fifth National League team and made him teammates with pitcher Dizzy Dean, with whom Todd brawled when both were in the Texas League in 1931.

The Boston Bees were another team dealing at the winter meetings. First the Bees traded Jim Turner, the "gray bearded rookie sensation of 1937," to the Reds for first baseman Les Scarsella and cash.[5] This reunited Turner with Bill McKechnie, the Reds manager who had managed Boston in 1937 when Turner won 20 games; Turner had gone just 4-11 in 1939. The Bees also traded pitcher Johnny Lanning to the Pirates for pitcher Jim Tobin and cash. In a separate deal, the Pirates sent pitcher Bill Swift and cash to the Bees for pitcher Danny McFayden. The Bees also signed reliever Dick Coffman, who was a free agent after the Giants released him, and purchased outfielder Hubert Bates from the Phillies for the waiver price.

Finally, the A's and Tigers made a last-minute deal that lasted only about a month. The A's offered outfielder Wally Moses to the Tigers, reportedly seeking Rudy York, who hit .307 with 20 home runs in 1939. But as the meetings wound down, the A's agreed to send Moses to Detroit for second baseman Benny McCoy and pitcher George Coffman. Based on the Tigers violating minor-league rules, however, in January 1940 Commissioner Landis declared McCoy and 92 other players in the Tigers system to be free agents. As a result, the trade was void; Moses and Coffman returned to the A's and Tigers, respectively, and McCoy was free to sign with any team. Quite a courtship followed for the 23-year-old, who was considered a top prospect after hitting .302 with 13 doubles and 6 triples in 227 plate appearances in 1939. McCoy signed with the A's, whose $45,000 signing bonus with a $10,000 salary for two years was the highest of 10 reported offers. This proved to be only a moderately successful investment for the A's; McCoy's best season came in 1941 when he hit .271 with eight home runs. After that, he went off to World War II and never played in the major leagues again.

The star players who had been the subject of speculation stayed with their teams. Bees manager Casey Stengel did not "expect to get anyone any good" for Max West, and he did not; potential trading partners refused the Bees' demands. Reds coach Jewel Ens quipped that Boston was asking for so many players for West that a trade would put the Bees "way over the limit." Otherwise, Boston sought star quality, not, as Stengel put it, "four or five guys named 'Joe' who couldn't play regular."[6] In fact, Stengel deadpanned that the Bees would "trade West to anybody—for Medwick."[7] As for Medwick, Dodgers president MacPhail gave up hope of trading for him, at least at the winter meetings. The lack of any major player movement was described as "a striking feature" of the winter meetings.[8]

The Business of Baseball

Whatever drama the 1939 meetings lacked in player movement, they made up in wrangling between the major and minor leagues. Heading into the meetings, the headliner was Commissioner Landis addressing the "evils of farm clubs."[9] Baseball's rules neither provided for nor prohibited affiliations between major-league and minor-league teams. But after the World Series, Landis had refused to approve any new major-minor working agreements, and there was tension over existing affiliations. Indeed, not only had Landis rebuked major-league teams for their minor-league relationships, but heading into the meetings he fined the Tigers, the Dodgers, and two minor-league teams for their handling of minor-league players. As the meetings opened, however, the news from the commissioner struck a different note. Judge William G. Bramham, president of the National Association of Professional Baseball Leagues, the minors' umbrella group, announced that Landis had instructed him to issue a bulletin approving working agreements between major- and minor-league teams.

The Minor-League Meetings

With this concession in hand, the minor leagues set about to strike the "biggest blow ever" at Landis' opposition to major-minor affiliations.[10] On December 5 the NAPBL unanimously adopted four proposed amendments to the rules governing these relationships:

- The first explicitly authorized working agreements between major- and minor-league teams. Notably, this was an amendment to the minor-league rules that did not require approval from the major leagues.
- The second amendment allowed major-league clubs to sign players and assign them to their minor-league affiliates, and later obtain the players themselves. In the past, major-league clubs could recommend players to minor-league clubs only if they wanted to later have the players on their own rosters. This too was a minor-league rule that did not require major-league approval.
- A third amendment provided that each club in an affiliated system must be considered a separate entity. Landis had interpreted the existing rules to treat all affiliated clubs as one entity, and this amendment would overrule his interpretation. This rule required major-league approval.
- The fourth amendment would preclude the commissioner from placing interpretations on any rules, requiring that each rule must be applied strictly according to its text without the commissioner's gloss. This rule also required approval from the major leagues.

These amendments were expected to "revolutionize" major-minor affiliations. Moreover, several major-league teams building large farm systems supported the amendments, suggesting that the major leagues would approve them. But when Landis, who had not even arrived at the meetings when the NAPBL adopted the amendments, was advised of them, he said, "I haven't a thing to say about it. Goodbye."[11]

The NAPBL also adopted a rule requiring a major-league team that wished to move into a Double-A league's territory to pay the league compensation to be determined by a board. Previously, the rules called for $5,000 in compensation. This proposal also required major-league approval.

The Major-League Meetings

After the minor leagues completed their business, each major league began its meeting on Thursday. In the National League, the Reds and Dodgers co-sponsored the NAPBL amendments. Addressing these amendments took up most of the day, but in the end the National League unanimously approved them. On the other hand, every American League team but the Yankees voted to reject the measures. Other American League clubs viewed loosened restrictions on farm systems as a benefit to the Yankees, whom they were trying to limit.

The National League addressed other matters beginning with Larry MacPhail's proposal to expand the postseason. In addition to the league champions meeting in the World Series, MacPhail called for a postseason series between the teams that finished second, third, and so forth. The plan was derided before the meetings, but the league surprisingly referred it to a study committee. Next, the National League adopted a rule that when a Sunday game in a city with a baseball curfew was not completed to 4½ or five innings, the game would resume later with the same score and player positioning as when the game was called. The league also increased its internal waiver price from $6,000 to $7,500, matching the American League price. Finally, the league named Boston's Bob Quinn, Chicago's Philip Wrigley, Horace Stoneham of New York, and Pittsburgh's Bill Benswanger as its new Board of Directors.

The American League likewise addressed some specific provisions, including an effort to curb the Yankees. At a league meeting over the summer, Senators owner Clark Griffith, who had long been trying to limit the Yankees, proposed a rule that would prohibit the league champion from making nonwaiver trades. Griffith was apparently motivated by the Yankees trading bench players Joe Glenn and Myril Hoag to the Browns for Oral Hildebrand, a useful pitcher, after the 1938 season. The league tabled the proposal, but Griffith continued lobbying the owners. Yankees president Ed Barrow, who had a sometimes "abrasive" personality and no longer had beloved but recently deceased Yankees owner Jacob Ruppert as his backstop, did not effectively counter Griffith's salesmanship.[12] Thus, when Griffith revived his proposal at the winter meetings the league unanimously—that is, including the Yankees' vote—adopted the rule barring the league champion from making nonwaiver trades.

The National League rejected this rule in short order, so it applied only to the American League. But it applied immediately, ending the Yankees' pursuit of the Browns' McQuinn, for whom the Yankees were rumored to have offered Babe Dahlgren, other players, and $75,000. Explaining the Yankees' vote to adopt the rule, Barrow publicly proclaimed that the rule did not matter because the Yankees relied on their farm system for talent, though Barrow privately recognized the need for trades to obtain the right mix of players. In any event, in another move aimed at the Yankees, Griffith proposed to limit major-league farm teams to one per class. When league President Will Harridge considered the proposal so drastic that it required further study, Griffith withdrew the proposal.

The non-Yankees business in the American League meeting involved the league flatly rejecting MacPhail's postseason plan and changing the means of selecting its All-Star manager. Instead of the reigning pennant winner's manager running the American League team, Red Sox manager Joe Cronin was chosen for the job. Larry MacPhail reacted with disdain:

Those American League babies figure it this way. Cronin knows he's not going to win the pennant anyway, see, so he can concentrate on preparing for the All-Star Game … They're always cutting corners, those guys.[13]

The American League also named New York's Ed Barrow, Boston's Tom Yawkey, Alva Bradley of Cleveland, and Chicago's Harry Grabiner as its new Board of Directors.

In other business, both leagues approved a rule allowing Saturday night games, lifting the previous rule limiting teams to seven night games per season. Both major leagues rejected the NAPBL's proposed rule for compensating Double-A leagues. And officials from the Yankees and Browns met with American League President Harridge in a private session to discuss means of helping the downtrodden St. Louis club, though they emerged with nothing to report.

The Hall of Fame

After the leagues' individual meetings, the Baseball Writers Association of America voted Lou Gehrig into the Hall of Fame without an election to commemorate the end of his consecutive games streak. Gehrig's 2,130-game streak ended in Detroit on May 2, 1939, when the Iron Horse benched himself and was later found to be suffering from amyotrophic lateral sclerosis, now commonly called Lou Gehrig's disease.

The AL-NL Joint Session

The American and National Leagues were scheduled to meet jointly on Saturday, December 9. But the National League met late into the night on Thursday to finish its business, allowing the joint session with Commissioner Landis to begin on Friday. Landis began the session by reading each NAPBL proposal; after each, the National League voiced its "yes" vote and the American League voiced its "no." The tie between the leagues empowered Landis to cast the tie-breaking vote. His replies to the league votes were variously described as "solemn" or "gruff," but he replied in each instance by stating, that "The Commissioner votes 'no.'"[14] National League President Ford Frick sought a poll of each league, as in the past Landis had sometimes voted with the overall majority of clubs notwithstanding the league votes. Landis refused Frick's request and went on to the next order of business. MacPhail, who drafted the amendments, stormed out of the joint session "in a rage" before 15 minutes had passed.

Although major-minor relationships were the primary order of business, they were not the only one. Landis continued casting his tie-breaking vote with the American League to approve a rule requiring unanimous approval for a major-league team to move into a location where a team from the other major league already played. Previously, such a move required only approval from a majority of teams. The American League adopted this rule with an apparent concern that the Cardinals were considering a move to Detroit. The National League had rejected the rule, empowering Landis to break the tie in favor of the requirement.

The leagues also addressed a few rules of play on the field. In an effort to boost flagging batting averages, the leagues reinstated the sacrifice fly rule, which did not charge a batter with an at-bat if he hit a run-scoring fly ball. That rule had been adopted in 1926 but eliminated after the 1930 season. In a move less favorable to batters, the leagues decided that a batter would not get a run batted in when a run scored as a result of the batter hitting into a double play. Yankees president Barrow proposed a rule to allow a pitcher to notify the umpire that he wanted to intentionally walk a batter and eliminate the formality of throwing four wide pitches. Barrow's proposal was tabled.

In any event, with Landis proceeding in a "staccato" fashion, the entire session was complete in less than 40 minutes. Afterward, farm system supporters were outspoken. MacPhail expressed exasperation with Landis' stance:

> What is the use? . . . Here we have gone to all the trouble of clarifying rules governing farming systems. But the commissioner's mind is made up. He has always been dead set against chain-store baseball, and a group of American Leaguers, determined to tear down the Yankees, are using this as a means toward gaining their end.[15]

A National League team official who did not want to be identified predicted that Landis' votes would damage the minor leagues:

> Chain-store baseball . . . has been the lifeblood of minor-league baseball for the past eight or nine years. Back in 1931 there were only about ten or eleven minor leagues. Today we have forty-one . . . I predict that today's failure to pass these amendments will see more than twenty of these minor leagues fold up . . .[16]

Officials from the Reds, the Phillies, and the minor-league Newark Bears voiced similar sentiments. In the face of Landis' votes, NAPBL President Bramham urged patience:

> I hope all our club owners will allay what concerns they may have until we have had time to give full and clear consideration to the situation which now confronts us . . . We have all been through problems before and have learned there usually is a way to have our troubles righted.

Bramham vowed to continue his efforts, urging that "[t]here is more to be accomplished through conferences than through battles."[17] When asked the reason that he rejected the unanimous minor-league proposals, Landis replied that the "legislation didn't originate in the minors. It originated in the majors."[18] With the joint session complete, "[m]ost of the game's brass hats were on their way homeward before the shades of night fell" on Friday.[19]

Integration

Integration was not a formal topic at the 1939 winter meetings, but an unlikely source brought it to the fore. After several sportswriters had taken up black players' cause during the 1930s, an American Communist Party organization followed suit in 1939. The organization gathered as many as 50,000 signatures for a petition to integrate the major leagues. At some point during the winter meetings, the organization presented the petition to the commissioner. Landis considered himself a "super-patriot," so receiving a petition from the Communist Party may have "further deafen[ed] the commissioner's ears to the burgeoning sounds of integration."[20]

Summary

Just as the 1939 winter meetings lacked player movement, the commissioner's tie-breaking votes in the joint session blocked the rule changes that might have significantly affected the business of baseball. Instead of "revolutionizing" major-minor affiliations, the meeting solidified the status quo. But despite the dire predictions, the effect on the minor leagues was inconclusive. The number of minor-league clubs dipped to just 62 during 1943, but that was at the height of World War II; by 1949 the minors had swelled to their high-water mark of 438 teams in 59 leagues. Perhaps the most significant consequence of the meetings was the trade restriction for the American League champion, which was blamed for hamstringing both the 1940 Yankees and the 1941 Tigers before being dropped for 1942.

SOURCES

In addition to the sources cited in the Notes, the author also consulted:

"18,500,000 Attendance Recorded by Minor Leagues at 1939 Games," *New York Times*, December 5, 1939.

"Athletics Sign Simmons," *New York Times*, December 10, 1939.

"Barrow Criticizes Play-Off Proposal," *New York Times*, November 14, 1939.

"Barrow Urges Change for Intentional Pass," *New York Times*, December 2, 1939.

"Baseball Executives Gather for Meetings," *New York Times*, December 1, 1939.

"Baseball in Brief," *Cincinnati Enquirer*, December 5, 7, and 9, 1939.

"Baseball Trade Winds to Blow Around Major League Clubs," *Milwaukee Journal*, October 12, 1939: 2.

"Bees Trade McFayden to Pirates in Exchange for Swift and Cash," *Meriden* (Connecticut) *Record*, December 9, 1939.

"Carew Tower-Netherland Plaza Hotel," *National Historic Landmarks Program.* tps.cr.nps.gov/nhl/detail.cfm?ResourceId=1849&ResourceType=. Accessed April 20, 2011, and February 1, 2012.

"Csar Landis Swings Ax—Declares 93 Detroit Farmhands Free Agents," *Spokane Spokesman-Review*, January 15, 1940: sports 2.

"Dodgers Acquire Berger, Infielder," *New York Times*, December 27, 1939.

"Dodgers, in Deal With Cubs, Get Mancuso and Kimball for Todd," *New York Times*, December 9, 1939.

Drebinger, John. "American League Bars Champion's Trades With Rival Clubs Except on Waiver," *New York Times*, December 8, 1939.

———. "Bramham to War on Clubs in Minors for Flouting Rules," *New York Times*, December 5, 1939.

———. "MacPhail and Durocher Deadlocked After Long Session on Latter's Contract," *New York Times*, December 4, 1939.

"Expect Miserly Baseball Meet," *Spokane Spokesman-Review*, November 8, 1939.

"Facts, Rumors From Cincinnati Baseball Meets," *Chicago Daily Tribune*, December 5, 7, and 8, 1939.

"Fat Contract Awaits McCoy Soon as He Makes Up His Mind," *Pittsburgh Post-Gazette*, January 29, 1940: sports page 1.

"Fireworks Are Expected at 1939 Winter Session of Major League Owners," *Calgary Herald*, December 2, 1939: 7.

"Frisch Signs Flowers as Pirates' Coach; Other News From the Baseball Meetings," *New York Times*, December 7, 1939.

Frye, John. "Big Changes Coming in Baseball," *Cincinnati Enquirer*, December 8, 1939: 14.

"Hilton Cincinnati Netherland Plaza," *Hilton Hotels & Resorts.* 1.hilton.com/en_US/hi/hotel/CVGNPHF-Hilton-Cincinnati-Netherland-Plaza-Ohio/index.do.

Accessed April 20, 2011, and February 1, 2012.

"Hilton Cincinnati Netherland Plaza," *Historic Hotels of America, National Trust for Historic Preservation.* Histcrichotels.org/hotels-resorts/hilton-cincinnati-netherland-plaza/.

Accessed April 20, 2011, and February 1, 2012.

"History," *Hoy Texas School for the Deaf Tournament*. tsd.state.tx.us/hoyx/history.html.

Accessed May 3, 2011.

Lanctot, Neil. *Negro League Baseball: The Rise and Ruin of a Black Institution* (Philadelphia: University of Pennsylvania Press, 2004).

"Lombardi Wins Oddity Prize for Beauty Nap," *Chicago Tribune*, December 17, 1939: B3.

McGowen, Roscoe. "MacPhail Offers New Inter-League Series Plan," *New York Times*, October 26, 1939.

"Major, Minor Baseball Winter Meeting Starts," *Los Angeles Times*, December 4, 1939: A14.

Morris, Jeff, and Michael Morris. *Haunted Cincinnati and Southwest Ohio* (Charleston, South Carolina: Arcadia Publishing, 2009).

"New Rules Proposed for Minor Leagues," *New York Times*, November 14, 1939.

"Out of the Past." *Chicago Daily Tribune*, December 6, 1939: 35.

Pietrusza, David. *Judge and Jury: The Life and Times of Judge Kenesaw Mountain Landis* (South Bend: Diamond Communications, 1998).

Pitts, Carolyn. "*National Historic Landmark Nomination, Carew Tower-Netherland Plaza Hotel*" (Washington, D.C.: National Parks Service, 1993).

"Rule on Invasions Changed In Minors," *New York Times*, December 7, 1939.

Schwartz, John. "The Sacrifice Fly," *SABR Research Journals Archive*. research.sabr.org/journals/sacrifice-fly. Accessed May 3, 2011.

"Showdown Looms on Farm Issue at Baseball Meetings This Week," *New York Times*, December 3, 1939.

Smith, Lou. "Rest Easily, You Redleg Fans, Bucky And Johnny Sign," *Cincinnati Enquirer*, December 8, 1939: 14.

———. "Sports Sparks," *Cincinnati Enquirer*, December 7 and 8, 1939.

"Stress Technique in Baseball Film," *New York Times*, November 9, 1939.

"Tigers Acquire Bartell," *New York Times*, December 7, 1939.

Vaughan, Irving. "Medwick Will Be Chief Topic at Major Meet," *Chicago Tribune*, November 26, 1939: B8.

———. "Landis Levies $2,500 in Fines on Four Clubs," *Chicago Tribune*, November 30, 1939: 27.

———. "Sox Trade Walker; League Curbs Yankees," *Chicago Tribune*, December 8, 1939: 35.

———. "Landis May Rule Today on Player Deals," *Chicago Tribune*, December 22, 1939: 27.

Wolner, Edward W. "A City-Within-a-City and Skyscrapers Patronage in the 1920's," *Journal of Architectural Education*, XLII, Winter 1989: 10-23.

"Writers Move to Place Gehrig in Hall of Fame," *New York Times*, December 8, 1939.

NOTES

1 Lou Smith, "Reds Hope to Make Deals at Meet Opening Here Monday," *Cincinnati Enquirer*, December 3, 1939: 14.

2 John Drebinger, "Giants and Six Other National League Clubs Bid for Outfielder West of Bees," *New York Times*, December 6, 1939.

3 Lou Smith, "If Giles Can Outtalk Bobby Quinn He May Get Max West," *Cincinnati Enquirer*, December 5, 1939: 16.

4 "1939." *Charlton's Baseball Chronology*. baseballlibrary.com/chronology/byyear.php?year=1939. Accessed May 9, 2011.

5 John Drebinger, "Bees Part With Pitchers Turner and Lanning in Deals With Reds and Pirates," *New York Times*, December 7, 1939.

6 Lou Smith, "Give Us Outfielder or Two and We'll Repeat, Says Giles," *Cincinnati Enquirer*, December 4, 1939: 14.

7 Lou Smith, "Reds Get Jim Turner for Scarsella and Cash," *Cincinnati Enquirer*, December 7, 1939: 15.

8 John Drebinger, "Baseball Chains Face Strict Rule," *New York Times*, December 10, 1939.

9 Irving Vaughan, "Trade Winds Are Soon to Shift to Cincinnati," *Chicago Tribune*, December 3, 1939: B2.

10 "Baseball Chains Score Over Landis," *New York Times*, December 6, 1939.

11 Ibid.

12 Daniel R. Levitt, *Ed Barrow: The Bulldog Who Built the Yankees' First Dynasty* (Lincoln: University of Nebraska Press, 2008), 332.

13 Lou Smith, "Hope for New Outfielder Is Abandoned by Warren Giles," *Cincinnati Enquirer*, December 9, 1939: 13.

14 "Landis Wrecks Efforts to Restrict His Control Over Farm Systems," *Baltimore Sun*, December 9, 1939, 14; George Kirksey, "Steam Roller Steered by Landis," *Cincinnati Enquirer*, December 9, 1939: 12.

15 John Drebinger, "Landis' Vote Decides for American League Policy Curbing Farm Systems," *New York Times*, December 9, 1939.

16 "Hope for New Outfielder Is Abandoned by Warren Giles."

17 "Yankees Discuss Help for Browns," *New York Times*, December 9, 1939.

18 "Steam Roller Steered by Landis."

19 "Hope for New Outfielder is Abandoned by Warren Giles."

20 Talmage Boston, *1939: Baseball's Pivotal Year* (Ottawa: The Summit Publishing Group, 1994), 170.

— 1940 —
LANDIS' FINAL REIGN

By Nick Waddell and Bill Nowlin

THE 1940 MAJOR-LEAGUE WINTER meetings, held at Chicago's Palmer House on December 10 and 11, saw a number of proposals fail to be adopted. Commissioner Kenesaw Mountain Landis voted for the status quo in most instances, though in a couple of notable votes he sided with the National League in one case and the American League in another. In terms of productive work being accomplished, the *New York Times* wrote that "the baseball magnates set a new low"—and they adjourned, "scattered as though some one had droped [sic] a time bomb in their midst."[1]

Convening in Chicago represented a move back to the norm, as the previous year's meeting had been held in Cincinnati (to celebrate baseball's purported 100th anniversary) instead of the usual New York City or Chicago location.

Landis did benefit personally; he was unanimously re-elected as commissioner for four more years, with his term now set to expire on January 12, 1946, at an annual salary of $65,000. Should he have completed this extended term, he would have served a full 25 years as commissioner.[2]

1940 Minor-League Meetings

The National Association's minor-league meetings took place in Atlanta at the Ansley Hotel on December 4-6. The Coca-Cola Company sponsored a banquet at the Piedmont Driving Club on the eve of the conclave. There were 892 registrants for the meetings, with many others also in attendance. Commissioner Landis spoke to those gathered, the first time he had done so in eight years. He talked about the likelihood of war, and alluded to the problems baseball had faced after the conclusion of the First World War, with a call to maintain high ideals and integrity.

The so-called Baltimore Amendment was a hot topic. A variation of the 1939 amendment would allow major-league clubs the ability to assign players to affiliated minor-league clubs. The NA passed again, for the second year in a row, the "legislation that caused controversy at Cincinnati" in 1939.[3] It was expected that the true opposition to the amendment would not be shown until after the meetings and instead it would surface at the minor-league meeting scheduled for January 6, 1941, in Louisville. That meeting was expected to be followed by a joint conference between the major and minor leagues in March. There was general discussion on a number of points but most were referred to an executive committee meeting the following day.

The minor leagues sought more autonomy over their teams and actions; they also wanted to act in concert to help stabilize the minor leagues economically after to a decline of around 33 percent in attendance, although only one league (the four-club, Class-D Arkansas-Missouri League) had been forced to disband, while four new leagues had been formed. J. Walter Morris, president of the East Texas League, proposed a "stabilizing fund" of $151,000 that could be loaned to clubs in need; National Association President W.G. Bramham proposed to up the ante to $250,000.[4]

An indication of the complexity of work being done at National Association headquarters in Durham, North Carolina, may be found in the figure of 14,268 contracts processed by the office, part of a total filing (including option notices, assignments, players released, etc.) of 36,779 transactions.[5]

Hanging over all meetings was the awareness that, as *The Sporting News* editorialized, "the threat of war remains and there is a likelihood of the game losing

THE PALMER HOUSE

The Palmer House hotel on State Street in Chicago, where the 1940 major-league meetings were held, was historic. Potter Palmer was a prominent Chicago businessman. He began as a dry-goods seller in Oneida, New York, and then later Lockport, New York. Palmer fell in love with Chicago on a visit, and opened a dry-goods store in the city in 1852. He made most of his money buying low on cotton and wool before the Civil War. By the time he retired in 1865, Palmer was worth between $3 million and $4 million. He helped found Field, Palmer, and Leiter, which later became Marshall Field and Co.

Marshall Field had introduced Palmer to Bertha Honoré, who was 23 years younger than the 44-year-old Palmer. Palmer and Honoré married in 1870. As a wedding gift, Palmer had his namesake hotel built for his wife. The Chicago Fire of 1871 destroyed the opulent hotel only 13 days after it opened, but Palmer rebuilt it after securing a $1.7 million loan. The hotel reopened on November 8, 1873. Bertha Palmer decorated the Palmer House with French influences to honor her heritage as well as her friendship with Claude Monet.

The Palmer House is also known as the birthplace of the brownie. Bertha wanted a dessert to be served at the Columbian Exposition World Fair in 1893 (the same World's Fair that was haunted by serial killer H.H. Holmes). The Palmer House staff followed Bertha's suggestions of what she wanted to serve, and developed the small chocolate cake-like treat that was easy for ladies to consume at the fair.

"About Our Hotel," http://www.palmerhousehiltonhotel.com/about-our-hotel/

---

some of its players under the national selective service draft."[6]

In general, though, while "some of the past conventions have produced bitter debates—and that of 1939 was no exception—there seems to be no serious issue in the offing that will stir up any acrimonious battles on or outside the convention floor."[7]

That said, it's not as if there weren't some topics up for discussion. For instance, there was a move to limit the commissioner's ability to suspend players "for conduct detrimental to baseball." Feeling that the phrase was "too sweeping," many minor-league representatives sought to change the language to read "for moral turpitude."[8] In all, some 30 amendments to the Major-Minor League Agreement were proposed. Many were custodial, such as the idea of assigning serial numbers to players to better help with record keeping (defeated), a requirement that players take a physical examination (not adopted), and the way in which championships in the various leagues were to be determined (this was left to the individual leagues).[9] The same salary limits were left in place. The agreement was due to expire in mid-January of 1942.

As for draft of players into military service, an initial proposal by the National League would have placed these players on a voluntarily retired list.[10] This proposal was withdrawn. All agreed that the player drafted would be placed on the voluntarily retired list, but agreement on other matters (such as the proposed refund of money paid for such players who had been recently acquired) proved much stickier, and the matter was referred to committee, to be discussed during the joint major-league meetings in Chicago.

Before and during the meetings, the St. Louis Cardinals sold a considerable number of players, a process that had begun in the summer with the trade of Joe Medwick to the Brooklyn Dodgers for four players and cash thought to be $125,000 to $150,000. In separate deals on November 25 and December 3, 4, and 5, the Cards sold or traded (receiving cash as well) infielder Joe Orengo, infielder Stu Martin, catcher Mickey Owen, and right-handed pitcher Bob Bowman. "Sure, we took money in those deals," said Cardinals owner Sam Breadon. "We had to have money. You can't run a big organization like ours on a home gate of 332,000 admissions."[11] The Brooklyn Dodgers were the biggest spenders at the meetings.[12]

Much of the doings at the meetings was reported over WSB radio by Ernie Harwell, with a number of notables (Connie Mack, Ford Frick, Will Harridge, Bill McKechnie, Rogers Hornsby, Joe Cronin, and many more) appearing on the program.

After the meetings concluded, *The Sporting News* praised Atlanta for unprecedented hospitality, but concluded that "no change" was the overall result. "Despite the number of amendments offered, discussed and passed upon, the policy of the National Association remained the same on a majority of important points," the paper said.[13]

Many deals were consummated at the minor-league meetings, both between major-league clubs and by minor-league clubs.[14]

Many of those attending the minor-league meetings traveled directly from Atlanta to Chicago for the major-league meetings. The leagues met separately for two days, then met jointly on the third day.

American League Meeting

The AL named Clark Griffith (Washington), Don Barnes (St. Louis Browns), Connie Mack (Philadelphia A's), and William Briggs (Detroit) to its Board of Directors.

"Yankee Law"

After the Yankees won four consecutive pennants (1936-1939), the American League adopted a "non-trading rule" barring the defending champions from making a trade with any other club in the league except via waivers. Despite his team now being the one forbidden to trade, the president of the 1940 pennant-winning Detroit Tigers, Walter Briggs, voted to uphold the so-called Yankee Law. The Yankees, Browns, and Red Sox were in favor of abolishing the prohibition.

National League Meeting

Ford Frick was re-elected National League president for a four-year term, with a "substantial" but undisclosed raise. Cardinals president Sam Breadon was named vice president and member of the board of directors. Cincinnati president Powel Crosley, Brooklyn president Larry MacPhail, and Philadelphia president Gerry Nugent were also named to the board.

Bill Klem, a 36-year veteran of umpiring, was named umpire-in-chief for the National League, charged with supervising umpires. Klem succeeded Ernie Quigley. Klem would umpire as needed, but was formally replaced on the active umpire roster by former American Association umpire Jocko Conlan.[15]

Joint Meeting

The Baltimore Amendment

In something of a surprise, the so-called Baltimore Amendment was adopted in Chicago, rather than referred to the later meetings. The amendment allowed teams to sign players for the purpose of assigning them to a minor-league club, with two caveats: The assignment must be between affiliated clubs, and all assignment transactions were to be reported to the commissioner.[16]

The amendment was first raised during the 1936 National Association meeting in Montreal. Commissioner Landis insisted that assignment transactions be reported to him and the president of the National Association; failure to do so could result in a fine from $50 to $250. The minor leagues rejected Landis's proposal, claiming that reporting was too detailed, and that violations were not clearly explained.

This amendment was again a point of contention at the 1939 Winter Meeting in Cincinnati. As a result, the commissioner met with representatives from the American League, National League, and minor leagues at Belleair, Florida, in February 1940 to discuss the provisions of an acceptable amendment. The Pony League raised the issue at the National Association convention, which led to the discussion at the 1940 Winter Meetings. *The Sporting News* noted that the adoption of the amendment could lead to an increase in the number of scouts for major-league teams instead of minor-league teams. The adoption of the amendment, in combination with the extension of the commissioner's term in office, was said to embody "a fitting and timely demonstration of Organized Ball's national unity."[17]

Night Games

Another hot topic was the number of night games a team could play. The discussion centered on how many games would be prudent, seven or 14. The National League voted to limit the number to seven, while the American League voted 5-3 to have fewer than seven. Commissioner Landis evened out the league vote, and seven became the maximum. Many teams had reasons for wanting more games. The St. Louis Browns had played 14 night games the previous year, and wanted to do so again, as about 50 percent of their attendance of 240,000 came to those games.[18] The Washington Senators had just installed a lighting system at Griffith Stadium, and the Philadelphia Athletics also saw attendance increased by lights. The National League had maintained a seven-game limit ever since lights were introduced in Cincinnati in 1935. The American League argued that it should be able to dictate the rules for its clubs. The leagues argued for over an hour and a half, until Landis stepped in and sided with the National League.[19]

All-Star Game/Cooperstown Game

During spring training in 1939, the league held a Spring All-Star Game in Tampa, Florida. The league voted to abolish that game for a variety of reasons, mainly the possibility of player injury. Another issue was travel, as not all of the teams trained in Florida. Instead, the league decided to hold an annual exhibition game in Cooperstown, New York, beginning in 1941. The first game would be between Cleveland and Cincinnati. The 1941 All-Star Game, meanwhile, was awarded to Detroit.

Wartime Plans

A national defensive service list was proposed by the National League. If players were called to active military duty, they would be placed on the list, their contracts would remain with their teams, but they would not be counted against a club's player limit. This was adopted in the joint session.[20]

The leagues agreed to continue an annual $20,000 gift to the American Legion for baseball purposes. The league also decided to have further discussions with the defense agencies on how to best support any war efforts. The first suggestion was to donate baseball equipment.[21]

Disabled List

A two-person-maximum 60-day disabled list was created for each team. The Boston Red Sox proposed the idea, which was adopted by the American League. The National League fought against it, until Commissioner Landis sided with the AL. The disabled list was 60 calendar days, except after August 1.

Doubleheaders

Washington owner Clark Griffith proposed a rule banning doubleheaders. This was nothing new; he raised the issue yearly, without support. Griffith sought to abolish doubleheaders "except on the last trip of the current season and then only in the event there is no other available date for the playing of the extra game."[22] The proposal was not adopted, and teams could schedule doubleheaders beginning with the fourth Sunday of the season (except for St. Louis, which was allowed to start them a week earlier).

Hall of Fame

The Baseball Writers' Association of America proposed including certain writers in the Baseball Hall of Fame. This idea was tabled for a future date.

Roster Limits

The National Association submitted two amendments that had been agreed upon at its meeting. One proposed by the Southern Association limited the number of players on a Class A-1 or A roster to 32, which had to be reduced to 18 within 30 days after the season began. The roster could be increased for the last 20 days of the season. This proposal was adopted by the major leagues. The other amendment, proposed by Springfield of the Three-I League, required all players to take a physical paid by the club; any subsequent medical or dental treatment was to be the player's financial responsibility. This amendment was defeated.[23]

One of the more interesting side stories of the meeting was the decision on pitcher Rufus Melton. The Phillies drafted Melton, allegedly to sell him to Brooklyn for $15,000. At issue was whether there was collusion; it was alleged that the Dodgers had given the Phillies $7,500 to draft Melton. Dodgers president Larry McPhail admitted he offered the $15,000 to the Phillies, but would not comment on the $7,500. Landis ruled that Melton would stay with the Phillies for the 1941 season, without any further penalties assessed to either side.[24]

Transactions

The number of transactions involving major leaguers was relatively low, and the names involved were more of the bench-player variety. The biggest trade was a three-team deal: Washington received outfielder Doc Cramer from Boston; Cleveland received outfielder Gee Walker from Washington and catcher Gene Desautels and right-handed pitcher Jim Bagby from the Red Sox; Boston received catcher Frank Pytlak, right-handed pitcher Joe Dobson, and infielder Odell Hale from Cleveland. Cramer would be an everyday player for another five seasons and have limited roles for three more. Walker played five more seasons in Ohio. Desautels had a part-time role for five more seasons, missing the 1944 season after enlisting in the US Marines. Bagby was a workhorse starter for Cleveland for another three seasons. Pytlak became the starting catcher for Boston in 1941, his last as a starter. He served in the US Navy during World War II and played in only 13 games over two seasons after he returned in 1945. Dobson would average 24 starts a year over his next 11 seasons (and would later operate the Winter Haven club in the Florida State League). Hale's last season was 1941.

Brooklyn and Cincinnati swapped infielders, with Pep Young heading to the Reds for Lew Riggs. Riggs was a favorite of Brooklyn president Larry MacPhail, who had twice previously acquired him, first when MacPhail was president of the Columbus Red Birds, and again when he was general manager of the Cincinnati Reds. The New York Giants purchased outfielder Morrie Arnovich from the Reds, and signed six-time All Star and MVP catcher Gabby Hartnett for what became Hartnett's final season. Hartnett had been the Cubs' manager for the previous two-plus seasons, but was let go after the 1940 campaign due to player unrest. Harnett sought a two-year contract from the Red Sox to be a coach. When Boston declined, the Giants entered the picture with a one-year contract as a pinch-hitter and player-coach to be a backup catcher.[25]

The Richmond Colts (Piedmont League) talked with the Giants about being an affiliated club, but the Giants decided to retain their agreement with Clinton (Three-I). The Giants had lost $10,000 the previous year because of Clinton, but agreed to a continuation when the Clinton owners agreed to take on any possible financial losses themselves. Richmond did receive two rookies from the Giants, as well as exhibition games against the parent club.[26]

STRANGE BET

Brooklyn manager Leo "The Lip" Durocher was at it again. Durocher got his nickname because of his mouth, and the 1940 Winter Meetings added to that legend. He was so confident in his team that he offered an open bet to anyone that his Brooklyn pitching staff triumvirate of Hamlin, Wyatt, and Higbe would win more games than the Reds' Derringer, Walters, and Thompson. The Reds trio had helped lead the club to a World Series title the year before, combining for 58 wins, while the Dodgers' trio had only 38. There is no word if anyone took Durocher up on his bet, but had they done so, they would have lost. Brooklyn's pitchers combined for 52 wins, helping the Dodgers to the 1941 pennant, while the Reds pitchers had 37 for their third-place team.

"Winter Book Makes Challedon 3-1 Favorite to Win $100,000 Santa Anna Handicap," *Detroit Free Press*, December 28, 1940: 11.

Conclusion

All in all, editor Edgar Brands of *The Sporting News* concluded, "[E]xcept for a few minor concessions the minors desire, it seems there now is nothing in the way of an amicable understanding over the revision of the Major-Minor Agreement."[27]

NOTES

1 John Drebinger, "Joint Session Action Limits Each Club in Majors to Seven Home Night Games," *New York Times*, December 12, 1940: 38.

2 As it turned out, Landis died on November 25, eight days after being elected to his new seven-year term.

3 Edgar G. Brands, "Minors Refuse to Recede From Fixed Policies," *The Sporting News*, December 12, 1940: 3.

4 Edgar G. Brands, "Bramham Proposes Minors Reserve $250,000 for Stabilizing Fund," *The Sporting News*, December 5, 1940: 2. Apparently a large number of postponements (more than 2,000 games postponed, according to *The Sporting News* issue of November 28) had severely depressed attendance. Distribution of the fund was to be on the basis of "membership and protection fees paid in 1931-40."

5 "14,268 Contracts Filed," *The Sporting News*, December 5, 1940: 2.

6 "Minors' Thirty-Ninth Annual Gathering," *The Sporting News*, November 28, 1940: 4.

7 Ibid.

8 Edgar G. Brands, "Minors Hold Fire on Limiting Landis in Pact Revisions," *The Sporting News*, December 5, 1940: 1.

9 A summary of the amendments appeared in *The Sporting News*, November 21, 1940: 7.

10 "Organized Ball, in Harmony Move, Stands Firm Behind Landis," *The Sporting News*, December 19, 1940: 5.

11 Dick Farrington, "'Had to Get Cash,' Breadon Declares of Big Money Deals," *The Sporting News*, December 12, 1940: 1.

12 Associated Press, "Dodgers Get Catcher Owen of Cards for Two Players and $65,000," *New York Times*, December 5, 1940: 35.

13 "Minors Accept Challenge of the Future," *The Sporting News*, December 12, 1940: 4.

14 The various deals are listed in "Shifting of Players in Deals at Atlanta," *The Sporting News*, December 12, 1940: 7.

15 Reports of the separate league meetings were summarized in *The Sporting News*, December 19, 1940: 5, 8. See also Associated Press, "Landis' Term Extended; Klem Becomes Supervisor," *Christian Science Monitor*, December 11, 1940: 15.

16 "The Game's Own Unity Program," *The Sporting News*, December 19, 1940: 4.

17 Ibid.

18 "Decision on Night Ball Commendable," *The Sporting News*, December 19, 1940: 4.

19 Most of these decisions taken, including the springtime All-Star Game, are summarized in Edgar G. Brands, "Organized Ball, in Harmony Move, Stands Firm Behind Landis," *The Sporting News*, December 19, 1940: 5. See also Associated Press, "Night Games Stay at Seven," *Boston Globe*, December 12, 1940: 21.

20 Organized Ball, in Harmony Move, Stands Firm Behind Landis."

21 "Majors Provide Special Status to Those Drafted Into Army," *The Sporting News*, December 19, 1940: 8.

22 Organized Ball, in Harmony Move, Stands Firm Behind Landis."

23 "Majors Provide Special Status to Those Drafted Into Army."

24 Associated Press, "Landis Disapproves Phillies' Offer of Melton to Dodgers," *Boston Globe*, December 12, 1940: 21. Melton apparently never made it in Organized Baseball.

25 "Player Market Dull," *The Sporting News*, December 19, 1940: 5.

26 "Colts Get Two Players But Fail to Arrange Tie-Up With Giants," *The Sporting News*, December 19, 1940: 5.

27 Edgar G. Brands, "Organized Ball, in Harmony Move, Stands Firm Behind Landis."

1941
WAR AND UNCERTAINTY

By Jeremy Green

Introduction and Context

Minor-League Winter Meeting

THE PROSPECT OF WAR CAST A long shadow over the National Association meeting for 1941. Europe and Asia had been mired in conflict for more than two years by this time, and just days after the meetings concluded, the United States would be forced to enter the second worldwide war of the twentieth century. A peacetime military draft had been in effect since October 1940 and baseball players, typically being in the prime of their lives and generally in good health and good physical condition, were superior material for military service.[1] Indeed, the national emergency had sapped players not only for military service but for work in the burgeoning and well-paying defense industries. On the other hand, the national emergency had effectively ended the Depression, and people returned to ballparks in droves. Attendance at games was generally up, with the minors drawing a reported 15 million fans in 1941, up 3 million from 1940, while the majors, though suffering a decrease of over 30,000 fans, still drew a reported 10 million.[2] It was in this atmosphere that the minor-league magnates and business staff met to conduct business at their 40th annual convention.

The National Association meeting was held in Jacksonville, Florida, from December 3 to 5 at the George Washington Hotel. This was the first time the NABPL had held a winter meeting in Florida, though the state itself was no stranger to baseball; as early as the 1880s, professional teams had been coming to Florida for spring training. Jacksonville, then (and currently) Florida's largest city, supported a city league as early as 1886 and played host to a spring match between the Washington Senators and New York Giants in March of 1888. Jacksonville was the New York Giants' spring training site and was the home base for the Tars, a Class-B Giants affiliate in the South Atlantic League. Jacksonville was reaping the benefits of wartime prosperity with its busy port and a new air base.[3]

In addition to player trades, the minors hoped to use the meetings to deal with player shortages related to the draft and particularly rules that limited the number of veteran players on teams in lower classifications. Several teams also hoped to conclude working agreements with major-league clubs that were expanding their farm systems.

Major-League Winter Meeting

By the time of the major-league meetings, the United States had entered World War II. Japan attacked the American naval and air bases at Pearl Harbor, Hawaii, on December 7, 1941; Congress voted to declare war on Japan the next day. Four days later, at the conclusion of the major-league meetings, Germany and Italy joined their Axis partner in declaring war on the United States.[4]

Though there was some uncertainty as to how the war would affect the availability of players and certain aspects of the game, the magnates felt that based on baseball's continuance through the outbreak of World War I, the 1942 season would go on in spite of the emergency.[5] The expectations of the press and magnates were confirmed when, in a letter to Commissioner Kenesaw Mountain Landis dated January 15, 1942, President Franklin Delano Roosevelt gave professional baseball the "green light" to continue operations.[6]

In addition to the war, the major-league meetings were also hit by illness that struck down their executive staff; Commissioner Landis was going through a bout of pneumonia, while American League President Will Harridge was still recuperating from surgery. To reduce the strain of travel on the two leaders, both of whom lived in the Chicago area, the leagues agreed to move the meetings from New York to the Palmer House hotel in Chicago, from December 9 to 11. President Ford Frick waived the National League's right to call for the meeting to be held in New York, and in return the senior league got dibs on setting the meeting location for 1942 and 1943.[7]

Player Movement

Minor Leagues

A number of trades were conducted at the National Association meetings, despite a manpower shortage that found affiliate and independent clubs focusing mainly on recruiting talent.[8] A total of 286 minor leaguers were swept up in the peacetime draft.[9] Perhaps in other circumstances, the leagues would have been less affected by these losses, but 1940 also saw a drop in reserve players for the first time in six years, a decline in the number of leagues to 41 (from 43), and an increase in the number of ineligible players.[10] Several players had retired to well-paying defense-industry jobs and were unlikely to be lured back to less steady and potentially less lucrative minor-league positions.[11]

In spite of these losses, National Association President William Bramham was confident that 1942 would see defense industries scaling back and more players being released from the military.[12] It would take only days to shatter Bramham's optimism.

Among the arrangements made in Jacksonville, Jack Zeller, general manager of the Detroit Tigers, promised to send an unnamed Detroit pitcher to Toronto.[13] Minneapolis closed a deal with Brooklyn for catcher Angelo Giuliani and pitcher Van Lingle Mungo, both of whom had been assigned to their Montreal affiliate and but would play for the Millers in 1942.

The Milwaukee Brewers got outfielder Woody Jensen on trial from Montreal and almost got outfielder Ron Northey of Williamsport until the Phillies countered with a better offer.[14] Numerous major leaguers were also traded to the minors or sent down to affiliate and independent teams, and in return minor leaguers ascended to "The Show." (See the table in Appendix One for the volume of trading done in Jacksonville, as recounted in *The Sporting News*.)[15]

Changes among major- and minor-league managers and coaches were also announced in Jacksonville. Among them was Mel Ott's appointment as player-manager of the New York Giants, replacing Bill Terry, who was moved into the front office to head the farm system. Team owner Horace Stoneham reported that Ott was fully responsible for trades and the signing of new players. Indeed, Ott had very firm ideas about the players he wanted to acquire, specifically mentioning outfielder-first baseman Johnny Hopp of the Cardinals or, if they couldn't get Hopp, the Cardinals' other first baseman, Johnny Mize. Ott expressed concern over first baseman Babe Young's draft status and preferred Hopp's utility in both the infield and outfield should the team lose Young.[16] Ott wound up getting Mize for right-hander Bill Lohrman, first baseman Johnny McCarthy, and catcher Ken O'Dea, plus cash rumored to be $50,000. Mize would eventually slug his way into the Hall of Fame.[17]

Major Leagues

Detroit was sapped by the loss of key players like first baseman-outfielder Hank Greenberg, who was drafted into the Army, and southpaw pitcher Fred Hutchinson, who was serving in the Navy. With veterans like second baseman Charley Gehringer approaching retirement, the Tigers were desperate for new blood.[18] Players and free agents thus enjoyed the chance to actually weigh offers and accept the best.[19]

But America's entry into the war put the magnates in a cautious mood. While most baseball professionals believed the season would continue, they had not yet received the go-ahead from FDR. So trading was brisk at the Palmer House and a number of major deals were completed.

The Cardinals-Giants trade was the biggest of the meeting. In addition, Ott paid the Cincinnati Reds

$20,000 for third baseman Bill Werber and acquired outfielder Hank Lieber from the Chicago Cubs for pitcher Bob Bowman and an undisclosed amount of cash.[20]

Washington and Boston put together a major deal in which Red Sox pitcher Jack Wilson and outfielder Stan Spence went to the Senators in exchange for pitcher Ken Chase and outfielder John Welaj.[21] (Spence would blossom in D.C., being named to four All-Star squads.) The Senators also dealt with the Tigers, picking up outfielder Bruce Campbell and infielder Frank Croucher and shipping All-Star outfielder Doc Cramer and infielder Johnny Bloodworth to Detroit.[22]

In Jacksonville, rumors had circulated about the Red Sox possibly trading Jimmie Foxx, but by the Chicago meeting those rumors had been squelched. It was announced that he would be kept on as a utility player alongside player-manager Joe Cronin.[23]

In the National League, the Brooklyn Dodgers conducted a number of player transactions. Brooklyn snapped up Pittsburgh infielder Arky Vaughan, a future Hall of Famer, for four players, pitcher Luke Hamlin, catcher Babe Phelps, infielder Pete Coscarart, and outfielder Jimmy Wasdell. The Dodgers also picked up outfielders Don Padgett from the Cardinals and Johnny Rizzo from the Phillies, and sold pitcher Mace Brown to the Red Sox.[24]

Not be outdone by their crosstown rival Giants and Dodgers, the Yankees made some deals. New York traded one of its top prospects, outfielder Tommy Holmes, to the Boston Braves for two players named later, first baseman-outfielder Buddy Hassett and outfielder Gene Moore. With Joe DiMaggio covering center field, Holmes was seen as redundant. The Yanks also traded third baseman Buddy Blair to the Philadelphia Athletics for a former all-American running back, outfielder Eric Tipton, and pitcher Johnny Babich.[25] The Yankees also picked up outfielder Tuck Stainback and shortstop Boyd Perry from Detroit to complete a September deal when the Tigers received Yankee infielder Bill Hitchcock.[26]

The Athletics sent outfielder Wally Moses to the Chicago White Sox for pitcher Jack Hallett and outfielder Mike Kreevich.[27]

The Business Side

Minor Leagues

Little business was on the agenda in Jacksonville. There were no officers to elect and American Association President George Trautman sought a year's postponement of action to renew the National Agreement, which was due to expire on January 12, 1942. Landis had not been well enough to oversee changes to the agreement. The minors considered only six amendments to the current Agreement, to be passed on to the majors for approval.[28]

An amendment championed by Frank D. Lawrence, owner of the Piedmont League's Portsmouth club, proposed that Class-B clubs no longer be required to carry six "required players," defined as those with less than three years of professional baseball experience. Rookies were more liable to be found in the lower minors and to be more likely to be drafted for military service. Lawrence hoped that by allowing smaller clubs more veteran athletes, gaps in manpower could be reduced.[29] The plan was approved in Jacksonville and it was decided to reduce the number of required players from six to four in the B, C, and D classifications.[30]

Another regulation up for review prohibited bonus payments to first-year Class-D players and to free agents below the AA classification. This was seen as especially detrimental and unfair to independent lower-level clubs which, unlike farm clubs, could not have a major affiliate pay a bonus and then option a player to a lower classification.[31] Drafted by the Southern Association, the proposition as written was defeated, then modified to permit bonus payments down to the A-1 classification.[32]

Section 11i of the National Agreement, which covered player reacquisition and terms of optional service, was also amended by the minors. A sore point between Commissioner Landis and the rest of professional baseball, player reacquisition had been debated twice before a temporary compromise was arranged prior to the 1940 season, understood by Landis to be revisited during the next Major-Minor Agreement. Since that agreement had been postponed, the majors and minors had rewritten the language of the section

STARTING TO OFFICIALLY USE THE NOGGIN

In November 1941 the Class-B Interstate League reportedly became the first league in Organized Baseball to require that clubs purchase batting helmets for players.* League President Arthur Ehlers said, "We can't force the players to wear them, but is compulsory for the clubs to buy them."

Lee MacPhail Jr., business manager of Reading, a Brooklyn Dodgers farm club, advanced the proposal. MacPhail's father, Dodgers president Larry MacPhail, responded to a series of players being beaned in 1940 by asking that all Dodgers players wear helmets during spring training.** Batting helmets weren't new at the time; players like Skeeter Newsome wore polo-like caps in 1938 after multiple beanings, including a skull fracture.***

Additionally, teams including Des Moines and Cedar Rapids of the Western League tested helmets in 1937 after events like the beaning of Mickey Cochrane,**** and the conversation continued as Fred Schulte, Joe Moore, Buddy Hassett, and other players also were beaned.*****

Based on the number of beanings in 1938, there was mention that Washington owner Clark Griffith would suggest the idea of skullcaps,****** but the absence of reports on this topic suggests no formal discussion took place.

---

* "A MacPhail Proposal," *New York Times*, November 25, 1941: 34.
** "Plastic Protectors Inside Caps Will Be Worn By Dodger Batters," *New York Times*, March 9, 1941: S1.
*** "York's Injury Revives Demand for Skullcap," *Detroit Free Press*, July 23, 1938: 9; "Yankees Seek Fourth in a Row," *Asbury Park* (New Jersey) *Evening Press*, April 11, 1938: 13.
**** "Players Approve Helmets to Stop 'Bean ball' Harm," *Indianapolis Star*, May 31, 1937: 18.
***** "Schulte 4th Star 'Beaned'," *Oakland Tribune*, June 6, 1937: 13.
****** "York's Injury Revives Demand for Skullcap."

and proposed to make the changes effective immediately. The minors voted unanimously in favor of the amended Section III.[33]

The original 1940 rule and the proposed 1941 revision were repeated verbatim in *The Sporting News* on December 11, 1941, illustrating the changes the minors hoped to make to the original rule:

1940 version: "A player reacquired by the same club or system shall, so far as Rule 11-c is concerned, be credited with having been under minor league optional assignment for the intervening period; provided that, if reacquired by a major league club, that club shall be charged with one season of major league optional service and the balance of the player's minor league service shall be charged as minor league optional service. A player reacquired from a lower club of the same ownership or control shall, for the purposes of this rule, be regarded as reacquired."

1941 proposed revision: "Any assignment of a player's contract to any affiliated club in a lower classification shall, so far as Rule 11-c (referring to optional assignments) is concerned, be considered an optional assignment in determining the player's optional service record. In the event there is more than one such assignment during any one year, that shall count as only one optional assignment against the player's optional service record. The return of a player's contract conditionally assigned by a lower classification club to a higher classification club shall not be considered as an assignment of the player's contract from a higher classification club to a lower classification club. In the case of the player's contract being acquired by a major league club from an affiliated minor league club, the optional assignment of the contract of such a player by the major league club shall be limited to two years."[34]

President Bob Stedler of the Pony League proposed an amendment increasing from 30 days to 45 days the time that would count toward a full year for drafting players.

In response to the number of players called up for military service, the minors also suggested an amendment that would treat players on the National Defense List the same as ineligible or voluntarily retired players.

The final amendment to the agreement involved creating a committee to study a merit-based system for promotion of umpires for all organizations below AA classification.

Bramham, addressing the combined clubs in Jacksonville, relayed a stern message from Commissioner Landis that reminded minor-league clubs to obey laws and meet financial obligations or face stiff penalties if they flouted the laws.

In Jacksonville, a dozen minor-league clubs arranged alliances or ended affiliations with major-league and higher classification minor clubs. The new arrangements were as follows:

Minor Team:	Agreement Arranged:
Augusta, Georgia	Switched from New York Yankees affiliate to independent
Wasau, Wisconsin	Signed with Cleveland Indians
Macon, Georgia	Agreement with Los Angeles, gave Chicago Cubs Class-B outlet
Dayton, Ohio	Brooklyn Dodgers
Baltimore, Maryland	Cleveland Indians
Kingsport, Tennessee	Brooklyn Dodgers
Montgomery, Alabama	Dallas
Bowling Green, Kentucky	Nashville
LaCrosse, Wisconsin	St. Louis Cardinals
Cheyenne, Wyoming	Brooklyn Dodgers
Charleston, South Carolina	New York Giants
Jacksonville, Florida	New York Giants

Major Leagues:

The major leagues had a fuller business agenda than the minors, though the meeting's start date, just 48 hours after the Pearl Harbor attack, saw war concerns move to the forefront. The majors pledged an immediate $25,000 to Army and Navy sports programs and voted to donate the proceeds of the 1942 All-Star Game to the programs. The gate receipts from the previous year had totaled over $100,000.

The majors agreed with the National Association to postpone the new Major-Minor Agreement for one year. But the majors struck down two of the amendments passed by the National Association. There proved to be no middle ground to be found on Section III and the rewritten amendment on player reacquisition, which had passed unanimously in Jacksonville, was voted down by both major leagues in Chicago. The majors also rejected the proposal regarding the extension of days in which a player's draft status would be determined.

The major leagues did concur on the status of players who were drafted for the war. They would be regarded as voluntarily retired, though they would be placed on a separate list. Another alteration the majors considered and approved was a change in dates for the draft meetings and final transfer of players. The date for the annual draft would be moved back to November 1 instead of the evening before the World Series' first game, while the deadline for transfers would be October 1 instead of September 10. It was hoped that the new dates would give teams more time to appraise players and would end the awkwardness of calling up players before the end of the minor leagues' seasons. The minors approved the motion by a mail-in vote.

The majors also considered a motion by Clark Griffith of the Washington Senators and Don Barnes of St. Louis Browns to increase the number of night games at major-league parks. FDR in his Green Light letter would recommend increasing the number of night games, and this change was favored by a majority of the American League magnates, but the National League and Landis were unconvinced and the number of night games remained static for the time being.

In addition to stumping for more night games, Don Barnes came to Chicago with an even more surprising and disruptive idea: moving the long-suffering Browns to Los Angeles. The proposal was rejected unanimously by the magnates and the commissioner, but it did open up the possibility that West Coast baseball would become a reality at some point and that the cities on the Pacific Coast were growing in size and stature relative to the Eastern metropolises.

The onset of may have war added to jitters about such a major shakeup in league cities.[35]

Elections were held at the Palmer House for the vice presidency and board of directors for both leagues. Clark Griffith of Washington and Sam Breadon of the St. Louis Cardinals were re-elected vice presidents of the American and National Leagues respectively. The American League Board was represented by the Chicago White Sox, Cleveland Indians, New York Yankees, and Boston Red Sox, while the National League Board was to be represented by the Chicago Cubs, New York Giants, Pittsburgh Pirates, and Boston Braves.[36]

Several minor rulings were voted on, including:
- Approval of the customary exception to the doubleheader rule that would allow both St. Louis teams to hold doubleheaders after their third Sunday home game. Other clubs had to wait until after the fourth home Sunday game before they could schedule a doubleheader.
- Passage of a rule barring doubleheaders created by pushing back regularly scheduled game to the final series.
- Approval of a rule that if the postponement of a contest requires transfer between cities, a game cannot be called off less than one hour before the game's scheduled start time.
- Rejection of a proposal to create a spring war-charity rookie game.[37]

Summary

Professional baseball faced numerous challenges at the start of World War II, and the national emergency ensured that many of these issues would not be revisited until after the war. Though the sport would be played throughout the war, with the blessings of President Roosevelt and to the betterment of the nation's morale, manpower concerns would continue to dog baseball until 1945. Just as the war would take a toll on the nation, it would have an impact on the nation's game. About 90 percent of professional baseball players would serve in World War II, more than 5,000 in all.[38] Hank Greenberg, Ted Williams, Johnny Mize, and many other players with promising and in some cases potentially legendary careers would see their playing days cut short by military service. The war would not only draw players from the game, but fans as well as attendance dropped by about one million between 1942 and 1943.

Evident in the 1941 meetings was the longstanding strain in the relationship between major- and minor-league baseball. Though there was accord on such items as the National Agreement, the draft, and the status of enlisted ballplayers, the National Association and the major leagues remained at odds over optioned players, bonuses, and efforts at player retention.

The minor-league franchises would prove most vulnerable to the loss of revenue and support during the war, and could expect little to no assistance from the majors, contracting in the first year of the war from 304 teams to 206.[39] The minors were contracting as early as 1941, and proposals like the six amendments recommended to the National Agreement were seen as ways to stanch the losses.

The 1941 Winter Meetings also hinted at changes to come to the game after the war, including an increase in night games, the transfer of franchises to the West Coast, and a contraction and slow decline in the number of minor leagues and teams. All of the above were in the cards for baseball in the coming years.

Appendix One:

Major-league teams are in bold.

Player	Acquiring Team	Selling Team	Terms
Pitcher Earl Overman	Fort Worth	Dallas	Trade: Pitcher Jackie Reid
Outfielder Guy Curtright	St. Paul	Shreveport	Cash/Undisclosed
Infielder Lynn Myers	Toronto	Rochester	Cash/Undisclosed

Catcher Verne Richards	Louisville	Springfield, Mass.	Cash/Undisclosed
Outfielder Tony Gridaltis	Milwaukee	Springfield, Mass.	Cash/Conditional Sale
Catcher Angelo Giuliani	Minneapolis	**Brooklyn Dodgers**	Cash/Undisclosed
Pitch Van Lingle Mungo	Minneapolis	**Brooklyn Dodgers**	Cash/Undisclosed
Outfielder Woody Jensen	Milwaukee	Montreal	On Trial
Infielder Hal Quick	Portsmouth, Va.	Williamsport, Pa.	Trade: Second Baseman Don Curry
Catcher Gus Hixson	Williamsport, Pa.	Wilkes-Barre, Pa.	Cash/Undisclosed
Pitcher Charlie Barrett	**Cincinnati Reds**, transferred to Syracuse, N.Y.	Birmingham	Cash/Undisclosed
Outfielder Kermit Lewis	San Francisco	**Cincinnati Reds**	Transfer
Catcher Ray Mueller	Sacramento	**Pittsburgh Pirates**	Cash/Undisclosed
Outfielder Debs Garms	Sacramento	**Pittsburgh Pirates**	Cash/Undisclosed
Outfielder Walter Harrington	Augusta, Ga.	DeLand, Fla.	Cash/Undisclosed
Outfielder Earl Pugh	Charleston, S.C.	DeLand, Fla.	Cash/Undisclosed
Pitcher Bernard DeForge	Portsmouth, Va.	Birmingham	Cash/Undisclosed
Shortstop Thomas Nelson	Pensacola	Birmingham	Cash/Undisclosed
Pitcher Paul Gehrman	Los Angeles	Birmingham	Cash/Undisclosed
Pitcher Jim Trexler	Little Rock	Buffalo	Cash/Undisclosed
Pitcher Al Fisher	Knoxville	Oklahoma City	Trade: Pitcher Jennings Poindexter and First Baseman Alex Hooks
Outfielder Bud Hafey	Oklahoma City	Memphis	Cash/Undisclosed
Pitcher Sheldon Jones	Jersey City	Oklahoma City	Trade: Outfielder Hershel Martin and Cash
Outfielder Eddie Marleau	Dallas	Oklahoma City	Trade: Pitcher Pat Beasley and Cash
Infielder Pep Young	Columbus, Ohio	Sacramento	Cash/Undisclosed
Pitcher Pete Hader	Memphis	Columbus, Ohio	Cash/Undisclosed
Outfielder Marshall Mauldin	Memphis	Knoxville	Cash/Undisclosed
Pitcher Pete Stine	Augusta, Ga.	Knoxville	Cash/Undisclosed
Catcher Paul Pride	Augusta, Ga.	Knoxville	Cash/Undisclosed
Infielder Russ Bevel	Augusta, Ga.	Knoxville	Cash/Undisclosed
Infielder Frank Metha	Fort Worth	Knoxville	Cash/Undisclosed
Shortstop Frank Scalzi	Sacramento	Knoxville	Trade: Outfielder Arnold Moser

Pitcher Elmer Rummans	Houston	Knoxville	Trade: Pitcher Steve Warchol
Outfielder William Duke	Knoxville	Elmira, N.Y.	Cash/Undisclosed
Third Baseman Ulmont Baker	Knoxville	Concord, N.C.	Cash/Undisclosed
Outfielder Roy Pinkston	Knoxville	Lexington, N.C.	Cash/Undisclosed
Outfielder Elmer Weinschreider	Jamestown, N.Y.	Muskegon	Cash/Undisclosed
Pitcher Lee Sherrill	Memphis	Asheville, N.C.	Cash/Undisclosed
Second Baseman Carl McNabb	Elmira	Hagerstown	Cash/Undisclosed
Pitcher Allyn Stout	Elmira	Atlanta	Cash/Undisclosed
Outfielder Paul Easterling	Elmira	Dallas	Cash/Undisclosed
Shortstop Mickey Burnett	Pocatello	Mobile	Trade: Infielder Mervin Bensmiller
Outfielder Judson Kirke	Pocatello	Mobile	Trade: Infielder Mervin Bensmiller
Outfielder Joe Molina	Pocatello	Johnson City, Tenn.	Cash/Undisclosed
Shortstop Dick Culler	St. Paul	Nashville	Cash/Undisclosed
Outfielder Charles Chute	St. Paul	West Palm Beach	Cash/Undisclosed
Shortstop Elmer Kirchoff	St. Paul	West Palm Beach	Cash/Undisclosed
Pitcher Joe Hatten	Montreal	Minneapolis	Trade: Pitcher Van Lingle Mungo, Catcher Angelo Giuliani
Outfielder Jake Powell and Pitcher Steve Rachunok	Indianapolis	Montreal	Cash/Undisclosed
Second Baseman Billy Adair and Pitcher Bob Ferguson	Memphis	Montgomery	Cash/Undisclosed
Pitcher Walter Brown	Memphis	Salina, Kan.	Cash/Undisclosed
Outfielder Red Reeves	Memphis	Pensacola	Cash/Undisclosed
Pitcher Bill Curlee	Memphis	Sacramento	Cash/Undisclosed
Outfielder Red Treadway	Atlanta	Wilson, N.C.	Cash/Undisclosed
Pitcher Milton Rosenstein	Atlanta	Miami Beach	Cash/Undisclosed
Outfielder Red Ferrell	Atlanta	Springfield, Mass.	Cash/Undisclosed
Outfielder Emil Mailho	Oakland	Atlanta	Cash/Undisclosed
First Baseman Walter Stockhill	Decatur	Greenville, S.C.	Cash/Undisclosed
First Baseman Paul Schoendienst	Shreveport	Clovis	Cash/Undisclosed
Catcher Herb Crompton	Shreveport	Atlanta	Cash/Undisclosed
Pitcher Jess Dobernic	Los Angeles	Milwaukee	Cash/Undisclosed
Pitcher Lee Stine	Portland, Ore.	Los Angeles	Cash/Undisclosed
Outfielder Maximillian F. Earhart	Waycross, Ga.	N/A	Rookie/New Player
Infielder Joe Vitari	Waycross, Ga.	N/A	Rookie/New Player
Outfielder Sherwood Schuerbaum	Macon	Columbus, Ga.	Cash/Undisclosed

Shortstop Thomas Nelson	Macon	Pensacola	Cash/Undisclosed
Infielder Deason Loveless	Macon	Selma	Cash/Undisclosed
Pitcher Kirby Hayes and Pitcher Darren Arden	Macon	Miami	Cash/Undisclosed
Catcher Bob Garbark	Buffalo	Milwaukee	Cash/Undisclosed
Pitcher Clare Bertram	Milwaukee	Tulsa	Trade: Infielder Herb Stroud, Infielder George Fink, and unnamed pitcher
Outfielder Tony Gridaltis	Milwaukee	Lansing	Cash/Undisclosed
Outfielder Bill Norman	Milwaukee	Houston	Cash/Undisclosed
Pitcher Harold Vandenberg	Milwaukee	Syracuse	Cash/Undisclosed
Pitcher Hal Johnson	Fort Worth	El Paso	Cash/Undisclosed
First Baseman Joe Yourkovitch	Montgomery	Fort Worth	Cash/Undisclosed
Catcher Del Friar and Second Baseman Ray Taylor	Savannah	Shreveport	Cash/Undisclosed
Pitcher Onnie Robinson	Augusta, Ga.	Savannah	Cash/Undisclosed
Pitcher Doyle Lade	Savannah	Salina, Kan.	Trade: Pitcher Hugh Klaerner
Pitcher John McPartland	Dallas	Pampa, Tex.	Cash/Undisclosed
Pitcher Clem Hausman	Dallas	Borger, Tex.	Cash/Undisclosed
Outfielder Norman De Weese	Albany, N.Y.	Dallas	Cash/Undisclosed
Third Baseman Dale Case, Pitcher Robert Cash, Outfielder George Galios, Outfielder Birl Horton, Outfielder Joe LaPiana, First Baseman Bob Williams, Infielder William Reyes	Lancaster, Pa.	El Paso	Cash/Undisclosed
Infielder Dale Gill and Outfielder Jaime Rodriguez	Lake Charles, La.	El Paso	Cash/Undisclosed
Pitcher Orlando Rodriguez and Second Baseman Salvador Sparacino	Portsmouth, Va.	El Paso	Cash/Undisclosed
Outfielder Lloyd Warner	**Philadelphia Phillies**	**Cincinnati Reds**	Released by Cincinnati, signed by Phillies
Outfielder Ron Northey	**Philadelphia Phillies**	Williamsport, Pa.	Cash/Undisclosed
Outfielder Mervin Connors	Dallas, TX	Texarkana, TX	Cash/Undisclosed
Pitcher Al Sachen	Dallas	Pensacola	Cash/Undisclosed
Catcher Jim Grilk	Toronto	Sacramento	Cash/Undisclosed

Outfielder Calvin Chapman and Pitcher Buck Marrow	Dallas	Chattanooga	Cash/Undisclosed
Outfielder Royce Watson and Pitcher Hope Beard	Wilmington	Lynchburg	Cash/Undisclosed
Infielder Benny Hassler, Outfielder Joe Mene, Outfielder Marvin Pelton	Wilmington	Selma	Cash/Undisclosed
First Baseman Bob Prichard	Wilmington	Charlotte	Cash/Undisclosed
Catcher Joe Glenn	Oakland	Louisville	Cash/Undisclosed
Infielder Buddy Blair	**Philadelphia Athletics**	Newark	Trade: Pitcher John Babich and Outfielder Eric Tipton
Pitcher Earl Reid	Indianapolis	Newark	Cash/Undisclosed
Pitcher Boots Poffenberger	San Diego	Nashville	Cash/Undisclosed
Outfielder Paul Armstrong	Dallas	Montgomery	Cash/Undisclosed
Shortstop Jim McLeod and Catcher Ted Clawitter	Augusta, Ga.	Montgomery	Cash/Undisclosed
First Baseman Tommy Canavan	Birmingham	Ogden	Cash/Undisclosed
Pitcher Rex Cecil, Pitcher James Morris, Outfielder Keith Frazier	Jackson, Miss.	Stockton	Cash/Undisclosed
Pitcher Eddie Kowalski	Charleston, W.Va.	Saginaw	Cash/Undisclosed
Second Baseman Ray Viers, Third Baseman Cecil Hubbard	Montgomery	Marshall, Tex.	Cash/Undisclosed
Outfielder Bob Price, Pitcher Bill Vandenberg, Utility Player Clarence Benton	Richmond	Marshall, Tex.	Cash/Undisclosed

NOTES

1 Norman Polmar and Thomas B. Allen, *World War II: America at War 1941-1945* (New York: Random House, 1991), 724-725.

2 "Bramham Says 15,000,000 Saw the 1941 Contests – 277 Players Were Inducted – Managers Named, Deals Made," *New York Times,* December 4, 1941: 35; "Big League Crowds Exceeded 10 Million," *New York Times,* October 28, 1941: 30.

3 Frederick G. Lieb. "City, Now Army-Navy Center, Ready to Put On Big Parade of Florida Hospitality for Visitors," *The Sporting News,* November 27, 1941: 1.

4 Polmar and Allen, 10.

5 Edgar G. Brands, "Majors Gird to Carry On During U.S. Emergency; Vote Funds to Give Equipment to Men in Service," *The Sporting News,* December 18, 1941: 7.

6 "Stay in There and Pitch – F.D.R.," *The Sporting News*, January 22, 1942: 1.

7 J.G. Taylor Spink, "Majors May Meet in Chi," *The Sporting News*, November 20, 1941: 1.

8 Edgar G. Brands, "Jax Session Starts Biggest Trade Rush," *The Sporting News,* December 4, 1941: 1.

9 "Bramham Urges Immediate Preparations for 1942," *The Sporting News,* December 4, 1941: 2, 9.

10 "41 Minors Reserve 4,348 Players for 1942, Drop of 172," *The Sporting News,* November 27, 1941: 12.

11 Ibid.

12 "Bramham Urges Immediate Preparations for 1942."

13 Bunny Morganson, "Grimes Goes to Leafs as Part of Buc Tie-Up," *The Sporting News,* December 11, 1941: 1.

14 "Passing Through the Gateway to Florida,." *The Sporting News,* December 11, 1941: 3, 10, 13.

15 "Talent at Premium in Player's Market," *The Sporting News,* December 11, 1941: 3, 11.

16 "Ott Has Full Power as Pilot of Giants," *The Sporting News*, December 11, 1941: 1, 17.

17 Dan Daniel, "Giants Stir N.Y. Fans by Volleys of Cash in Mize and Other Deals," *The Sporting News* December 18, 1941: 1.

18 Sam Greene, "Hank Greenberg May March Right Back Into Army Service," *The Sporting News*, December 11, 1941: 1.

19 "Talent at Premium in Player's Market."

20 Daniel, "Giants Stir."

21 "Caution of Traders Slows Player Mart," *The Sporting News*, December 18, 1941: 7, 11.

22 Sam Greene, "Success of Tigers Transfusion Rests With Bloodworth," *The Sporting News*, December 18, 1941: 1.

23 "Caution of Traders."

24 Daniel, "Giants Stir."

25 "Caution of Traders."

26 Daniel, "Giants Stir."

27 "Caution of Traders."

28 "No Officers to Elect," *The Sporting News*, November 27, 1941: 8.

29 J.G. Taylor Spink, "Independents Fight Talent Monopoly," *The Sporting News*, November 20, 1941: 1, 6.

30 Edgar G. Brands, "Dispute over '11-i' Again Made an Issue," *The Sporting News*, December 11, 1941: 3, 11

31 Spink, "Independents Fight Talent Monopoly."

32 Brands, "Dispute over '11-i' Again Made an Issue."

33 Ibid.

34 Ibid.

35 David Finoli, *For the Good of the Country: World War II Baseball in the Major and Minor Leagues* (Jefferson, North Carolina: McFarland and Company, Inc., 2002), 17.

36 "Majors Gird."

37 Ibid.

38 Steven R. Bullock, *Playing for Their Nation: Baseball and the American Military During World War II* (Lincoln: University of Nebraska Press, 2004), xii; Finoli, *For the Good of the Country*, 309.

39 Finoli, *For the Good of the Country*, 17.

1942
GREEN LIGHT – MATTERS OF MANPOWER AND THE MILITARY

By Frederick C. Bush

Introduction

IN JANUARY 1942, ONE MONTH AFTER the attack on Pearl Harbor had made the United States a combatant in World War II, Commissioner Kenesaw Mountain Landis wrote a letter to President Franklin D. Roosevelt in which he had inquired "whether professional baseball should continue to operate."[1] Roosevelt's famous reply, now known as the "green light letter," stated, "I honestly feel that it would be best for the country to keep baseball going" so that Americans could have access to recreation and respite from their wartime labors.[2] Baseball had thus persevered through the 1942 season. As the December 1942 winter meetings in Chicago approached, however, the sport was facing manpower, transportation, gas, and tire shortages, and there were still a few people— including Cleveland Indians president Alva Bradley—who believed that all play should be suspended for the duration of the war.

Bradley was concerned that fans would heckle ballplayers for playing games rather than serving in the military, and he claimed that he did not want to subject his players to such criticism. A *Sporting News* editorial took Bradley to task for his "apologetic" attitude, asserting, "When a guy isn't in service, his government knows why, and is satisfied," and "A player so yelled at may have a better reason for not being in the Army than the yelling fan has."[3] Bradley, who had said that he would rather close his park than "invite the cries of the wolf pack," eventually had to concede, "I suppose the fact that I received so few replies indicates that there is no strong public opposition to the game under war conditions."[4]

Indeed, support for baseball's continuance during wartime came from all corners. Before the game's magnates descended upon his city, Chicago Mayor Edward J. Kelly wrote a letter of welcome, published in *The Sporting News*, in which he echoed Roosevelt's opinion that baseball provided "an effective and wholesome outlet of recreation during this period of turmoil and strife."[5] *The Sporting News* also published a letter from Private Gerald C. Bohnen of the Army Air Forces, who had played minor-league ball in Clovis (New Mexico) and Duluth (Minnesota) in 1942, who wrote, "As a ball player, I am interested in seeing the game go on. It is a morale builder for the nation in time of war."[6]

Powel Crosley Jr., the president of the Cincinnati Reds, compared baseball's role in the nation's war effort to that of the military's noncombat service units. He summed up baseball's cooperative spirit with wartime restrictions and regulations as he stated his confidence that baseball could continue to be played while asserting, "It must, of course, be secondary to matters directly affecting the war effort, and we must forget profits for the duration."[7]

Baseball's winter meetings normally had the goal of improving the game in order to maximize profits, so the idea of having to forgo them was an unfamiliar one. More significantly, the manpower shortage was creating a scenario in which many minor-league teams would be forced to suspend operations despite their desire to continue to play. As both the major- and minor-league club leaders held their meetings in Chicago, manpower was the issue most vital to all concerned.

Major-League Meetings

The major-league clubs held their meetings first, the American League on December 1 and the National League on December 2 at the Palmer House hotel. The major leagues' joint session on December 3 was held at Judge Landis's hotel of residence, the Ambassador West, to accommodate the commissioner, who was convalescing after a recent operation. Though there were, as always, disagreements about various issues, these were now "subordinated to the welfare of all, so that the game can carry on."[8]

Both disagreement and compromise were in evidence as the loss of players to the military and to defense jobs caused the clubs to examine the player limit. The scope of the losses was brought to the fore by St. Louis Cardinals president Sam Breadon, who reported that since the conclusion of the 1942 baseball season a mere two months earlier, the Cardinals and their minor-league affiliates had lost 67 players to the military.[9] In light of such losses, New York Giants owner Horace Stoneham wanted to increase the player limit from 25 to 27, while New York Yankees president Ed Barrow wanted an increase to 30 (but no fewer than 28) so that the clubs might still have a viable roster once their inevitable losses took place. Philadelphia Athletics owner Connie Mack, on the other hand, proposed a reduction to 21 in the belief that this number of players would be sufficient and that all the clubs would be able to maintain it.

In the end, all attempts at increasing or decreasing the player limit were defeated, and the clubs agreed to keep the same 25-man maximum that had been allowed over the past several seasons.

The major-league clubs were so concerned about their personnel that only one trade took place during the meetings, with the Cincinnati Reds sending shortstop Eddie Joost, pitcher Nate Andrews, and cash to the Boston Braves for shortstop Eddie Miller. There was also one managerial shift, with Steve O'Neill, the former skipper of the Cleveland Indians who had run the Beaumont team in the Texas League in 1942, taking over the Detroit Tigers, who had fired Del Baker after two consecutive sub-.500 seasons following their 1940 World Series appearance. So few potential deals had even been discussed that Branch Rickey, now the president of the Brooklyn Dodgers, made what was humorously called "the most startling announcement of the convention" as he notified the press, "I wish to announce that I have nothing to announce, although I was willing enough to make some deals."[10]

The hardships facing baseball at the moment also led to an agreement to extend the current Major-Minor Agreement to January 12, 1944; it was the second extension granted to the pact, which had expired on January 12, 1942. Though the spirit of cooperation again prevailed via the extension of the agreement, the major leagues voted down the South Atlantic League's proposed amendment to the agreement, which would have frozen the contracts of players who had last appeared with now-disbanded clubs.

The clubs did approve a proposal by Breadon that called for revising the draft rules in regard to payment of the selection fee for players on the National Defense, voluntarily retired, and suspended lists. In the past, clubs had not had to pay the selection fee until the player reported to the team, but they would now have to pay the fee when the player was selected. Teams would have to draft more cautiously as this new rule "plac[ed] the responsibility of the performer reporting, or being available, on the club making the selection."[11]

A brief but controversial episode that occurred during the major leagues' joint session also involved personnel—or rather potential personnel—for major-league ballclubs and also involved one of the more complex aspects of Landis's legacy as commissioner. On December 3, 10 representatives from the Chicago chapter of the CIO (the labor organization whose full name was the Congress of Industrial Organizations) gathered outside the clubs' meeting room at the Ambassador West Hotel and "demanded a hearing in behalf of Negro players, claiming 'discrimination against employment of Negro players by major league clubs.'"[12] The representatives threatened to take the issue before the fair practices board of the union if they were denied a hearing, but Commissioner Landis nevertheless refused them an audience at the meeting.

Landis had already had to deal with baseball's race issue in July, after Dodgers manager Leo Durocher had made reference to a "grapevine understanding"[13] (more commonly referred to as baseball's "gentleman's agreement") that kept blacks out of baseball. Landis met with Durocher, after which the Dodgers skipper claimed he had been misquoted, and Landis subsequently issued the following statement:

> Negroes are not barred from organized baseball by the commissioner and never have been in the 21 years I have served. There is no rule in organized baseball prohibiting their participation and never has been to my knowledge. If Durocher, or if any other manager, or all of them, want to sign one, or twenty-five Negro players, it is all right with me. That is the business of the managers and the club owners. The business of the commissioner is to interpret the rules of baseball, and to enforce them.[14]

In spite of Landis's assertion that black ballplayers were not barred, it would take until April 15, 1947, when baseball was under the auspices of Commissioner Happy Chandler, for Jackie Robinson to break the major leagues' "color barrier" when he took the field at first base for the Brooklyn Dodgers at Ebbets Field.

As for the brief commotion caused by the Chicago CIO members, Terry Kandal, the chairman of the group of 10 and president of Auto Workers Local 719, conceded that they had acted improperly that day but asserted that they would continue to pursue the matter through a formal request with Landis's office.

While the matter of who would actually be able to play baseball as the war continued was of greatest concern, the baseball itself also was addressed at the meetings. Cincinnati Reds general manager Warren Giles had planned to propose at the meetings that the National League ask baseball manufacturers to arm their game with a livelier ball. Hitting and scoring had been on a dramatic decline over the past few years and Giles, propounding an outlook that continues in baseball circles into the twenty-first century that "baseball's chief appeal comes from hitting," was concerned that "unless the decline is checked, the fans are going to lose some of their interest in the game."[15]

During the meetings, there was no discussion of a livelier ball; however, the specifications for the ball still had to be addressed due to wartime materials shortages. A new center for the ball would have to be used, and Landis instructed the two league presidents to reach an agreement at a later date regarding which of two products they would use to replace the cork center that had been used in the past. The alternatives involved either a core of reclaimed rubber or a core that consisted of a smaller cork core that was increased to baseball size by encasing it in reclaimed balata, which was the substance used for golf-ball covers. The latter option was developed by Spalding and was favored by the American League; however, as there was still disagreement between the two leagues, further tests were to be done and the results to be presented to Landis and the two league presidents before a decision was made. In the meantime, it was also agreed that clubs would use their remaining supplies of 1942 balls until they were exhausted.[16]

One additional factor concerning play was the number of night games allowed, which remained at 14 games per team, except for Washington, which was permitted to play 21. Cincinnati determined that it would play only seven night games due to poor attendance at such contests in the 1942 season. Dimout regulations were likely to preclude New York and Brooklyn from holding night games, and it was uncertain whether the Philadelphia Athletics or Phillies would be permitted by the government to play under the electric lights at Shibe Park.

The Phillies had a greater problem to consider than whether or not they would be able to play night games, namely what was to become of the franchise. The Phillies' fate turned out to be another matter that was much discussed without any resolution being reached. Though it was reported that four different propositions were made to Phillies president Gerald Nugent and National League President Ford Frick, none was adopted. Frick emphasized that whatever was eventually decided at a later date, the Phillies would not move to Baltimore or anywhere else, as he declared that "clubs are not moved to other cities anymore."[17]

The final key issue to be addressed at the major-league meetings, which was of vital concern both to baseball and to the US government, was travel. Military transportation needs were now so great that passenger travel by rail could no longer be fully accommodated. Joseph B. Eastman, the government's director of defense transportation, wrote to Commissioner Landis, NL President Frick, and AL President Will Harridge to request that baseball curtail its travel, and he even offered some solutions to the transportation problem.

Eastman first addressed spring training, suggesting that "travel to spring training might be minimized [by] the selection of a training site as near as possible to the permanent headquarters of the team," and that preseason exhibition schedules should be eliminated or "drastically curtailed."[18] Second, he advised that "long duplicate trips must be avoided during the regular season."[19]

Baseball complied with Eastman's request by revamping schedules, eliminating side trips for exhibition games, and allowing two days for travel between certain series, all of which reduced travel by 46,000 mile. Most teams were unwilling to change their spring-training sites, citing commitments already made to those communities, but they did agree to take no more than 30 players to spring training sites in the South instead of up to 50 as they had done in previous years. Washington Senators owner Clark Griffith declared, "We're going to try to skeletonize (travel) in every way possible. … I believe the ODT will have reason to feel pleased the way Organized Ball co-operates."[20]

A team's desire to retain its current training site was apt to become a moot point, however, when after the winter meetings teams that intended to train either in California, Texas, or Florida were advised by Eastman to have alternate locales in mind because the military intended to use campsites in those states. Eastman informed both leagues that they would know whether they could train in any of those three states by February 7, 1943.

As the major-league meetings came to an end, baseball also demonstrated its support for the war effort in other ways. It was agreed that all of the receipts from the July 7, 1943, All-Star Game in Philadelphia would be donated to the Ball and Bat Fund to provide equipment for military personnel; an additional $2,500 from each league and $20,000 from the commissioner's treasury were also given to the fund. Each team also agreed to donate the proceeds from one of its home games to the Army, Navy, or some other war service branch. Baseball also offered its services to the Office of War Information in the preparation of shortwave radio broadcasts for the armed forces abroad.

Minor-League Meetings

In the wake of the major-league meetings, the National Association met in Chicago, the city of the organization's birth in 1901, for the sixth time, on December 4-5. The NA's member clubs obviously faced the same primary issues as the major-league franchises, but the situation was far direr for the cash-strapped minor-league teams, and the likelihood that most teams would be able to operate throughout the course of the war was in doubt.

First and foremost on the agenda was the manpower shortage, although tire and rubber rationing, dimouts, and transportation issues were additional factors working against the continuation of minor-league play. Of the 26 minor leagues that had completed the 1942 season, 24 declared their intentions to play in 1943; however, the shortage of players made it likely that "the number starting next season would be between 12 and 14, with the former figure the most likely."[21]

In spite of the major leagues' defeat of the plan to freeze player contracts, a proposal was made to put the NA on record as being in favor of "freezing of all except active players to the rosters of disbanding clubs," but as was the case with the big-league clubs, the move was voted down.[22] It was decided, however, that the territories of disbanded clubs and leagues could be frozen for the duration of the war and that clubs from disbanded leagues that wished to continue play could temporarily join other leagues "through mutual agreement between the two loops concerned, or with the approval of the president of the National Association."[23] Amid such circumstances, the trade market in the minors—just as had been the case with the major leagues—was understandably stagnant.

The minor leagues were also scrambling to do their part to comply with Eastman's request that baseball reduce its travel. Since it was left up to each league to decide how best to cut down on travel, compliance with the government's request took on various forms. The Inter-State League set an example for other circuits to follow when its president, Arthur Ehlers, announced from league headquarters in Harrisburg, Pennsylvania, that its member clubs would hold spring training at their home fields, believing "that better, or just as good, results will be obtained by staying at home to train."[24] In the South, the Texas League decided that its clubs would make only three road trips in 1943 rather than the usual four, which would save 15,000 travel miles.[25]

The dire financial straits of many franchises led to a bit of intrigue during the December 4 session in the form of an attempted "raid" on the NA's treasury, which would have divided most of the umbrella organization's money between the clubs that finished the 1942 season.[26] The proposition failed, but it resulted in two major concessions: the abolition of the 2 percent fee on player transactions charged by the NA's administration, and permission for cash-strapped clubs to apply for loans that would see them through the war's duration. While the abolition of the transaction fee would provide immediate relief to all clubs, that fee made up the bulk of the NA's revenue, which put the amount of cash that would be available for loans in doubt.

Oddly, in the midst of all the wartime hardships that had to be addressed, there was a second conspiracy—the ouster of the Southern Association's president—that became the major story of the meetings. Major Trammell Scott, who had led the league for the previous four seasons, had angered the owners of both the Little Rock and Memphis franchises during the 1942 season, and Little Rock owner Roy L. Thompson used Scott's delayed arrival in Chicago (yet another point of contention with the league's club owners) as an opportunity to present Billy Evans as a replacement for Trammell.

What made the Southern Association presidential fiasco even more unbelievable was the sheer serendipity of Evans's availability for the job. The former major league umpire and Cleveland Indians general manager was in Chicago because he expected to be named interim president of the American Association while its elected president, George M. Trautman, served in the Army; Trautman, however, resigned his military commission instead and returned to his job as league president. This turn of events suddenly had put Evans, a 32-year baseball man, out of a job when he happened upon Thompson, who then set in motion his plan to supplant Scott. The owners sided with Thompson and, though no election had been scheduled to be held, they voted in Evans as the new president in what was for all intents and purposes a bloodless coup.

The unseating of Scott was an example of how the business of baseball was quite often conducted, which was in an aggressive manner. However, in 1942 this episode was the exception rather than the norm. For the most part, owners of both the major- and minor-league clubs realized that cooperation with one another was necessary if baseball were to persevere through what was becoming the greatest military struggle in the history of mankind.

NOTES

1 Gerald Bazer and Steven Culbertson, "When FDR Said 'Play Ball,'" archives.gov/publications/prologue/2002/spring/greenlight.html, accessed September 30, 2015.

2 Ibid.

3 "Scribbled by Scribes," *The Sporting News*, December 3, 1942: 4.

4 "Bradley Finds Cold Trail in Wolf Hunt," *The Sporting News*, December 3, 1942: 6.

5 "Happy to Play Host," *The Sporting News*, December 3, 1942: 4.

6 "Game a 'Morale-Builder'," *The Sporting News*, December 10, 1942: 3.

7 "Keynote for Chicago Meetings," *The Sporting News*, November 26, 1942: 4.

8 "Chicago to Sound 'Go' Signal for Game," *The Sporting News*, December 3, 1942: 4.

9 "Warming Up at the Palmer House," *The Sporting News*, December 10, 1942: 10.

10 "From Major League Fronts in Chicago," *The Sporting News*, December 10, 1942: 3.

11 Edgar G. Brands, "Mileage Reduced, Service Aid Voted," *The Sporting News*, December 10, 1942: 3.

12 "Majors Arrive at Several Centers of the Ball, but Settle on None," *The Sporting News*, December 10, 1942: 10.

13 David Pietrusza, *Judge and Jury: The Life and Times of Judge Kenesaw Mountain Landis* (South Bend, Indiana: Diamond Communications, 1998), 417.

14 Pietrusza, 418.

15 "Giles Wants Old Zip Put Back Into Ball," *The Sporting News*, November 26, 1942: 3.

16 "Draft Price for Player in Service Due at Once," *The Sporting News*, December 10, 1942: 3.

17 "Athletics to be Hosts to All-Stars July 1," *The Sporting News*, December 10, 1942: 10.

18 "Travel 'Without Waste' Requested of Major Leagues by ODT Director," *The Sporting News*, December 10, 1942: 3.

19 Ibid.

20 "40 Per Cent Slash in Travel, Aim of Majors, Says Griff," *The Sporting News*, December 17, 1942: 1.

21 Edgar G. Brands, "Loans Authorized, Deal Fees Dropped," *The Sporting News*, December 10, 1942: 3. In fact, only 10 leagues began play in 1943, with nine finishing the season; the Twin Ports League disbanded in July.

22 Ibid.

23 Ibid.

24 "Inter-State Clubs Expected to Condition on Home Fields," *The Sporting News*, December 10, 1942: 5.

25 "Texas to Cut Mileage," *The Sporting News*, December 10, 1942: 8.

26 Brands, "Loans Authorized, Deal Fees Dropped."

1943
WAR ON THE HOME FRONT

By Nick Klopsis

Introduction and Context

BASEBALL'S 1943 WINTER MEETINGS were held in New York City from November 29 to December 3. The minor leagues and the major leagues took care of their business at the New Yorker Hotel, marking the first time in 24 years that both the majors and minors sat down together in New York.

The overall theme of the meetings could be summed up in three simple letters: war. World War II efforts continued to hit baseball particularly hard, with many of the game's stars trading in their baseball uniforms for military fatigues. As a result, several major-league clubs were looking for new talent while holding on to the few star players they still had. Meanwhile, the minor leagues were bracing themselves for one of the most heated battles baseball had ever seen — the re-election of National Association President William G. Bramham.

Player Movement

Despite the fact that many teams came into New York looking to replace men who were now serving in the war, player movement was surprisingly slow. Empty trade rumors filled the halls of the New Yorker Hotel, as teams were reluctant to deplete their rosters any further. The possibility that more players could continue to be lost to the military meant that general managers would consider a trade only if they were blown away by an offer.

The main example of this was the trade whirlwind surrounding Cleveland Indians pitcher Jim Bagby. The right-hander had just come off his second consecutive All-Star season, starting a major-league-high 33 games while posting a 17-14 record and a 3.10 ERA. But Bagby was at odds with player-manager Lou Boudreau, stemming from an incident in September in which Boudreau fined Bagby $100 for not taking a warmup run before a night game in Washington. Bagby told reporters that he participated in warmups before Boudreau arrived at the ballpark. Boudreau did not lift the fine, and Bagby demanded to be traded. The Indians did not field any offers for Bagby during the season, with Boudreau saying that he "would rather have a disgruntled winner than a happy loser."[1] But at the outset of the winter meetings, the Indians reversed their stance and began listening to potential trading partners. Cleveland wanted an outfielder in exchange for Bagby, and three teams were rumored to be in the running, the Detroit Tigers, the Chicago White Sox, and the Washington Senators. The Tigers, who were preparing to lose pitcher Tommy Bridges to the draft after the meetings, offered aging All-Star center fielder Doc Cramer, while the White Sox were rumored to be willing to part with either right fielder Wally Moses or center fielder Thurman Tucker.[2] The Senators reportedly offered a package that included outfielder Bob Johnson, right-handed pitcher Bobo Newsom, and shortstop John Sullivan in exchange for Bagby, infielder Russ Peters, and left fielder Jeff Heath. However, the Indians suddenly pulled Bagby off the trading block late in the meetings when their left-handed ace, Al Smith, was reclassified by his local draft board as 1-A. The reclassification meant that Smith was immediately eligible to serve in the military should the government select him. Boudreau said that any deals would have to wait until March, when each team knew where it stood concerning players serving in the military.

The only big-name deal that occurred took place very late in the meetings. The Senators, who failed to get Bagby from the Indians, sold Bob Johnson to the Boston Red Sox about five minutes before the meetings officially closed. The Red Sox, who had bid for Johnson's services in 1942, paid an undisclosed amount of money to Washington. The sale marked the end of the 37-year-old Johnson's disappointing one-year stint with the Senators. Although the outfielder was named to his sixth All-Star team and finished fifth in MVP voting, injury brought about career lows in batting average (.265), home runs (7), and RBIs (63). Despite this, the move was lauded not only by Red Sox owner Tom Yawkey, but also by Senators owner Clark Griffith (ironically, he would later declare the deal to be the worst he ever made), A's skipper Connie Mack (who managed Johnson in Philadelphia), and even Yankees manager Joe McCarthy (who noted that Johnson would greatly benefit from Fenway Park's short left-field wall).

Meanwhile, New York Giants ace Carl Hubbell retired to become the team's new farm-system director. Affectionately nicknamed The Meal Ticket, Hubbell spent his entire 16-season career with the Giants and finished with a 253-154 record, a 2.98 ERA, and 1,677 strikeouts. Hubbell, who was known for his devastating screwball and would be elected to the Hall of Fame a few years later, had previously expressed a desire to stay involved in baseball and mentor younger players once his days on the mound were over.

The Business Side

While player transactions were lukewarm at best, league business exploded on the very first day of the meetings. The minor leagues held the floor at the New Yorker for the first three days, and they wasted no time in providing instant drama. William G. Bramham, the

QUOTES OF IRA LEWIS FROM THE RACE BAN DISCUSSION AT THE 1943 MEETINGS

Ira Lewis spoke as a member of the media and president of the *Pittsburgh Courier*. After the meetings, the *Courier* published some of Lewis's reported statements.*

"It is also quite noteworthy that the largest football crowd to attend any game in America this past season was the game last Saturday in Chicago, between White and Negro high school teams — 85,000 people."

"Then, gentlemen, if your investments are not jeopardized, and it is admitted that colored players will add color to the game, both figuratively and literally, and the question of travel and segregation areas are problems of the players themselves, it looks very much as though the bar against the Negro player had become an outmoded pretense."

"I ask you gentlemen, in the name of the America we all love; in the name of the democracy that we associate with the word America, that you undo this wrong; that you do away with this mean precedent, this gentlemen's understanding and agreement, and let our national pastime be a game for all the boys in America. I hold this to be just and fair and in keeping with the highest American tradition."

After Lewis spoke, Howard Murphy of the *Baltimore Afro-American* noted four recommendations:

1. Immediate steps be taken to accept Negro players into the framework of Organized Baseball.
2. The process for promotion and elevation in baseball be applied without prejudice.
3. Same system for selection of players be used.
4. Joint statement be made by the leagues.

---

* "Publishers Place Case of Negro Players Before Big League Owners," *Pittsburgh Courier*, December 11, 1943: 1.

69-year-old president of the National Association, who was credited with pulling the minor leagues through the Great Depression, was up for re-election, but his bid for another term would not be a cakewalk by any means. If Bramham, already in office for 11 years, wanted to remain president, he would have to go up against threats of secession that would throw the entire structure of baseball into chaos.

The seeds of rebellion began even before the meetings convened in New York. Due to the war, only nine of 25 dues-paying leagues operated during the 1943 season.[3] In addition, Bramham had spoken out earlier in the year against two amendments proposed by the top-level AA leagues (American Association, International League, and Pacific Coast League). One amendment would reformat the voting system to give more voting power to higher leagues, and the other would remove the stipulated prices that higher leagues would have to pay to lower leagues for drafting territorial rights. In response to Bramham's public opposition to the amendments and the lean state of the minor leagues, the International League nominated its president, Frank J. Shaughnessy, to run against Bramham on the first day of the meetings. Upon nomination, Shaughnessy seemed to have a 5-4 majority, thanks to the backing from the three AA leagues, plus the Piedmont League and the Pony League. However, the decision to nominate Shaughnessy was about more than removing Bramham from power; it was also the minor leagues' chance to revolt and become their own independent entity. If Shaughnessy was elected, the minor leagues would not renew the major-minor league agreement that tied the two organizations together, effectively breaking free from the control of Commissioner Kenesaw Mountain Landis.[4] Bramham was faced with a near-certain ouster. In a final effort to remain in power, the president cited Section 34 of the National Association agreement, which allowed the 16 suspended leagues to vote because they had paid dues. What made the ruling especially controversial was the fact that Bramham and the nine active leagues had voted during the season that suspended leagues had no voting rights, which at the time caused an uproar among the 16 currently inactive leagues. Bramham's ruling in New York was a complete reversal of that earlier decision. Thankful for their new lease on life, the reinstated leagues overwhelmingly backed Bramham and he scored a landslide victory and a new five-year term at $25,000 per year. The insurgent leagues cried foul, questioned the legality of the reinstatement, and appealed the decision to Commissioner Landis—the very man whom they were trying to break away from just a day earlier. Landis upheld Bramham's decision, putting a definitive end to the rebellion. Then, on the final day of the three-day minor-league affair, both of the amendments at the heart of the rebellion were vetoed. Bramham closed out the minor-league agenda by lashing out at his opponents, saying that the owners "are sitting on a barrel of TNT and should not try to create discord."[5]

Once the fireworks from the minor leagues died down, the remaining business came and went with little fanfare. Both the American and National Leagues approved a recommendation by the Baseball Writers Association that called for All-Star rosters to be decided via War Bond sale. Every fan who purchased a War Bond between the beginning of the season and June 15 would be able to cast a ballot for the 1944 All-Star Game, which was scheduled for Forbes Field in Pittsburgh. The New York Yankees' proposal to increase roster sizes from 25 to 30 was rejected, while the Senators won the right to have unlimited night games (as opposed to 14 for every other team). In addition, the minor leagues vetoed a proposal from Landis's office that aimed to restrict the use of minor-league parks for exhibition games 10 days after the end of the season. If the amendment had passed, minor-league clubs would be deemed liable if an exhibition game was played at their stadium, and the team would have to pay a fine. The minor-league teams did not want to serve as "play policeman" for Landis, so they turned down the proposal.[6]

A few front-office changes were made as well, with the most notable being the Philadelphia Phillies naming former Yankees left-hander Herb Pennock as their general manager. Known as the Squire of Kennett Square during his Hall of Fame career, Pennock had been serving as the farm director for the Red Sox.

Meanwhile, the Yankees re-signed Joe McCarthy to a three-year deal, ensuring that the skipper who had brought them seven World Series titles and eight American League pennants would be back.

The last day of the meetings brought with it a very interesting case that foreshadowed the future. During the joint American League-National League meeting, Commissioner Landis invited actor and singer Paul Robeson and three black journalists, Ira F. Lewis of the *Pittsburgh Courier*, John Sengstacke of the *Chicago Defender*, and Howard Murphy of the *Baltimore Afro-American,* to plead their case in favor of integration in baseball. It marked the first time a black person had spoken face-to-face with the leaders of Organized Baseball about this topic. Before the four men spoke, Landis read a joint American League-National League statement that said, "There is no rule, formal or informal, or any understanding—unwritten, subterranean or sub-anything—against the hiring of Negro players by the teams of organized baseball."[7] While all four delegates made pleas to the owners about integration, Lewis's speech seemed to be the most intriguing. He drew parallels to other sports and entertainment outlets, noting how it had quickly become commonplace to see black athletes playing college football and black actors on Broadway. Lewis then drew Landis's ire when he directly challenged the commissioner's opening statement by saying, "We believe that there is a tacit understanding, there is a gentlemen's agreement that no Negro players be hired."[8] That assertion silenced the room and seemed to draw the approval of the owners for its sheer boldness. At the conclusion of the meeting, the owners met privately, then returned to tell the four delegates, "Each club is entirely free to employ Negro players to any and all extent it pleases. The matter is solely for each club's decision, without restriction whatsoever."[9]

Summary

The three-day clash at the outset of the 1943 winter meetings helped to solidify the future of the National Association and baseball at large. With the re-election of William G. Bramham to a new five-year term, the sport avoided a scenario in which there would be three separate, independently run associations in direct competition with one another. Also, John Drebinger of the *New York Times* wrote that the minor-league fireworks were "a show that is not likely to make New York regret it is playing host to the national pastime's 'little fellows' for the first time in twenty-four years," hinting at the possibility that the minor leagues would be invited to join the major leagues at future meetings.[10] Because of the war, there was a lack of player movement during the meetings, as teams attempted to figure out exactly who would and would not be serving military duty and decided to hold onto their players. Meanwhile, it would be another two years after the plea by Robeson, Sengstacke, Lewis, and Murphy at the joint meeting that the color barrier was broken.

SOURCES

In addition to the sources cited in the Notes, the author also consulted:

Associated Press. "Minor Leagues Lose Fight to Oust Bramham," *Washington Post*, December 1, 1943: 18.

———. "Pennock Signs as Headman of Phillies," *Los Angeles Times*, December 2, 1943: 12.

———. "Pitcher Says Their Dislike is Mutual," *Washington Post*, January 20, 1944.

———. "Sox Buy Johnson From Washington," *Christian Science Monitor*, December 3, 1943: 8.

———. "Third Day of 'Revolution' At New York," *Christian Science Monitor*, December 1, 1943: 17.

———. "Tigers Re-Engage Manager O'Neill," *New York Times*, November 28, 1943: S6.

Dawson, James P. "Hubbell, Pitching Ace 16 Years, Signs as Giants' Farm Director," *New York Times*, December 1, 1943: 28.

Drebinger, John. "International Backs Shaughnessy to Succeed Bramham as Minor League Czar," *New York Times*, November 30, 1943: 31.

———. "Landis Upholds Bramham Ruling, Crushing Class AA Minor Leagues' Revolt," *New York Times*, December 3, 1943: 29.

———. "Voting Coup Re-elects Bramham, Foils Move in Minors to End Landis Rule," *New York Times*, December 2, 1943: 33.

Feder, Sid (Associated Press). "Fiery Session Is Forecast at Baseball Meet," *Atlanta Constitution*, November 29, 1943: 16.

———. "Heated Debate Promised at This Week's Meetings of Baseball Leagues," *Hartford Courant*, November 28, 1943: C3.

Povich, Shirley. "Bagby, Heath, Peters Eyed by Nat Boss," *Washington Post*, December 2, 1943: 18.

Troy, Jack. "Minor Leagues Retain Bramham as President," *Atlanta Constitution*, December 2, 1943: 13.

Vaughan, Irving. "Open Baseball Season April 18," *Chicago Tribune*, December 3, 1943: 29-30.

Webb, Melville. "Red Sox May Try Johnson at First," *Boston Globe*, December 4, 1943: 5.

NOTES

1 Shirley Povich, "This Morning With Shirley Povich," *Washington Post*, December 1, 1943: 18.

2 According to the *Chicago Tribune*, Boudreau initially showed interest in trading Bagby to the White Sox for outfielder Moose Solters. However, the White Sox sold Solters to Milwaukee. See Irving Vaughan, "White Sox Bid For Bagby, Indians' Pitcher," *Chicago Tribune*, December 2, 1943: 27-28.

3 John Drebinger, "Revolt by Minor Leagues Against Landis Control Looms at Meetings Today," *New York Times*, December 1, 1943: 28. The nine dues-paying minor leagues were the American Association, the International League, the Pacific Coast League, the Eastern League, the Southern Association, the Inter-State League, the Piedmont League, the Appalachian League, and the Pennsylvania-Ontario-New York (Pony) League.

4 Additionally, Jack Cuddy of the *Los Angeles Times* reported that if the minor leagues broke away from the majors, the lower-level B, C, and D leagues would further break away from the newly formed group and form their own "wildcat" organization in boycott of Shaughnessy and the higher leagues. Jack Cuddy, "Minors Reported Pulling Away From Landis Control," *Los Angeles Times*, December 1, 1943: 10.

5 Associated Press, "Smith 1-A, So Indians Might Not Sell Jim Bagby," *Boston Globe*, December 3, 1943: 26.

6 The major leagues had come to an agreement on this amendment a day before the minors vetoed it. However, they decided not to enact it until they had a chance to fine-tune its wording, specifically what would happen if a team was playing in a park that it did not own. Associated Press, "Smith's Reclassification Blocks Jim Bagby Trade," *Christian Science Monitor*, December 3, 1943: 8.

7 David K. Wiggins, "Wendell Smith, the *Pittsburgh Courier-Journal* and the Campaign to Include Blacks in Organized Baseball, 1933-1945," *Journal of Sport History* 10, no. 2 (1983): 21.

8 Ibid.

9 John Drebinger, "Cox Retracts Admissions on Betting, Gets New Hearing Before Landis Today," *New York Times*, December 4, 1943: 17.

10 "Revolt by Minor Leagues Against Landis Control Looms at Meetings Today."

1944
A NEW ERA WITHOUT LANDIS

By Joe Marren

Introduction and Context

AS WORLD WAR II SEEMED TO BE winding down (even though the Battle of the Bulge in Europe was only days away and the Pacific invasions of Iwo Jima and Okinawa were still in the future), recovery from the war was the watchword at the 43rd annual baseball winter meetings. The nation was beginning to think about being at peace again, and the various paths to readjustment were being planned in all walks of life. For baseball, normalcy meant the winter meetings, as the minors and their major-league brethren met in Buffalo's Hotel Statler from December 6 to 8, while the major leaguers convened by themselves in New York City's Hotel New Yorker from December 11 to 13.

But a sense of loss would pervade the normal business routine for the expected 1,000 baseball men at the meetings. It was the first winter meetings since 1920 that was not chaired by Commissioner Kenesaw Mountain Landis, who had died in Chicago on November 25, just days before the meetings. Landis had been chosen to be the first commissioner in 1920 and formally assumed his duties on January 12, 1921. And just as in 1920, Organized Baseball would have to find at least a temporary way to run things until it decided who—or what group—would be in charge. Expediency had to be paramount, as baseball writers reminded the moguls, because the Major-Minor League Agreement was set to expire in January 1945 and the Major League Agreement would end in January 1946, though baseball officials had given a 10-member committee until February 6, 1945, to draft a new major-league pact.

Governance wasn't the only thing penciled on and off various agendas; there was good news and bad news and the same-old news given to minor-league owners and executives at their meeting. The seemingly annual problem of what to do about territorial incursions and even the threat of such incursions by the major leagues was the same-old news that was discussed. The bad news, as might be expected, was financial—1944 expenses were $35,588 more than revenues and, as a result, the National Association of Professional Baseball Leagues was forced to dip into a reserve fund to balance the books. The good news, on the other hand, was that the baseball executives were looking ahead to the end of the war and anticipating a future that would be joyous, even in Mudville. In particular, the meetings in Buffalo had "the greatest optimism"[1] among the minors since before the start of the war, and maybe that's why it was the best-attended meeting since the 1941 confab in Jacksonville.

There were 10 leagues in the Association that year, the same number that started play in 1944 (and one more than '43), and there was talk of two to four more leagues resuming play as the nation hoped to shift from war to peace in the coming spring and summer of 1945.[2] William G. Bramham, president of the Association, believed this indicated not only stability but also the possibility of growth. He reported that although Winston-Salem of the Piedmont League and Jackson of the Southeastern League had suspended play in 1944, the 15 leagues that had suspended active status during the war had renewed their membership and protection fees.[3] So the future of baseball held promise.

Minors Seek Security

The problem with that promise, though, was that it might mean growth—and therefore competition for the minors—by the majors. Such a paradox begs an explanation: Major-league baseball was still predominantly a Northeastern sport in 1944, with St. Louis serving as both the southernmost and westernmost city. The minor-league magnates, worried about postwar territorial incursions into Los Angeles, San Francisco, Baltimore, and Buffalo, proposed 13 amendments to the Major-Minor Agreement. One of the amendments put forth, by Pacific Coast League President Clarence Rowland, would require the major-league team to compensate both the affected minor-league owner and the league itself, as well as give that owner an option to somehow be involved in operating the major-league franchise.[4]

However, the majors didn't take any action on that amendment at their meeting the following week in New York City. Nor did they agree to a hike in draft prices paid for minor-league players. Presidents Rowland, Frank Shaughnessy (International League), and George Trautman (American Association) of the three AA leagues (the highest classification at that time) said in Buffalo that they wanted $10,000 per player instead of the current $7,500 in compensation when a player was drafted. Lower leagues would consequently also be paid one-third more.

The minors also wanted a say in who would rule the baseball world in the wake of Landis's death. But who—or what—would be the boss was a matter of some controversy at the meetings. At first a plan was floated for a triumvirate made up of American League President Will Harridge, National League President Ford Frick, and the late commissioner's secretary, Leslie O'Connor, to run things. This was the way baseball had been structured before the Office of the Commissioner was established, and opposition came from powerful owners and executives including Clark Griffith of the Washington Senators, Horace Stoneham of the New York Giants, Ed Barrow of the New York Yankees, and Branch Rickey of the Brooklyn Dodgers.

The sport was, in fact, being run by Harridge, Frick, and O'Connor at this time. No action was taken during the meetings on a successor to Landis, but what really got the major- and minor-league owners arguing was whether to pick a baseball man for the job or look to an outsider to be the next commissioner. Griffith, Stoneham, and Rickey favored looking outside the sport while Barrow favored promoting from within.[5] As the reasoning went, Griffith felt that someone from outside the sport would guarantee that baseball didn't return to the pre-Landis commission days, when the sport was almost ruined by gamblers and other unsavory elements. Griffith said he wanted someone with a national reputation "who carries the confidence of the public."[6] Others, however, thought that with postwar changes on the horizon, an insider was really needed. Yet another argument was that Landis had wielded too much power and baseball should simply revert to the three-man commission it had utilized before he was hired.[7]

But there was one thing everyone agreed on—at least publicly—and that was the unanimous election of Landis to the Hall of Fame, which took place on December 10, just two weeks after his death. He was the first selection to the Hall since Rogers Hornsby's induction in 1942 and the fifth nonplayer.[8]

Football Competition

Branch Rickey had warned about a football incursion into the baseball season back in 1943, saying that one day football would start as early as Labor Day and run for months. So at the meeting in Buffalo a committee was named to meet with professional football owners to try to work out a solution to what baseball termed the encroachment of pro football into the baseball season. With the anticipated addition of the All-American Football Conference in 1946 to compete with the National Football League, the baseball powers worried that football was taking up September and October dates in their ballparks. In response to the scheduling pressure, the majors passed the Barrow Regulation at their meeting in New York. At that time, many football teams rented the hometown ballpark for their games, and the Barrow Regulation prohibited the major-league club from renting its ballpark to a football team as long as the baseball team had a chance of playing in the World Series. (Remember, there were no league playoffs in baseball at the time. Unless there was a rare tie in the standings, something that had actually not yet occurred, the top team in each league would automatically meet in the World Series in late September or early October.) So the Barrow rule would effectively deny a football team in a major-league city a place to play until mid-October.

Those in baseball thought this was only fair, while football people begged to differ, charging that baseball began its season too early and ended too late. Football owners would think about building their own stadiums, they told reporters.[9] But baseball owners didn't take that threat seriously, the newspapers reported, since the cost of building a stadium would be prohibitive and not economical because it would be used only a handful of times in the football year. Or so went the quaint thinking at the time.

Night Ball

Stadium usage didn't only center around competition with football; there was also the issue of nighttime baseball games; specifically, who would play them and how often. Before the meetings, Griffith said he wanted a blank check to play as many games as possible at night. Others, like Rickey and Barrow, wanted to set a limit on how many night games a team could schedule in a season. The two St. Louis teams, the Cardinals and the Browns, were allowed an unlimited number of night games, except on holidays and Sundays, yet their respective executives said they didn't know if they would take advantage of the ruling that had been handed down by Judge Landis.[10]

There were a host of reasons why night baseball was a topic: No stadiums added lights during the war, so only those with lights in the 1930s were capable of holding night games; electricity was needed for the war effort in industrial cities; municipalities on the Atlantic Ocean tried to keep illumination down so as not to silhouette shipping for German submarines; and, frankly, tradition. St. Louis was one of the cities with stadium lights and it wasn't on an ocean.[11]

The upshot was that each team playing in a stadium equipped with lights was allowed to schedule as many night games as it wished for 1945, though holiday and Sunday games were still required to be played during the day, and the host team was also required to get formal consent from the visitors to play at night.

Manpower Issues

Regardless of when games were played, it was revealed during the meetings that who might be playing them could prove to be an issue in 1945. The Selective Service System wanted to reclassify all men between the ages of 26 and 37 to make more of them eligible for the military draft if they weren't working in an essential industry. While it was widely believed the ruling was put in place to help keep the vital war production factories busy rolling out the needed tanks, guns, ships, and shells, what especially worried baseball men was that the War Department had already told Selective Service it would be needing 60,000 to 80,000 more men in January and February. And that was only part of the whammy: Selective Service officials said that most men under 30 who had been classified 4-F prior to February 1 would be re-examined.[12] As *The Sporting News* pointed out, every major-league team had several 4-F players and that, combined with the War Department's decision to more closely scrutinize who was being discharged, meant fewer athletes might be available to play.[13] Consequently, player deals were at a minimum during the 1944 winter meetings. On the other hand, when the war was over the clubs would have to ponder what to do with their returning vets, so it was decided at the meetings to temporarily increase player limits after the war.

All this uncertainty about who could play, and when, had major-league magnates wondering if the players would at some point try to unionize; there was already a report circulating at the meetings that Pacific Coast League players had begun talking with the Congress of Industrial Organizations (CIO), a federation of unions.

Postwar Planning

As the end of the war seemed to be in sight, the formal disbanding of the Postwar Planning Committee took place in Buffalo, though that didn't mean baseball stopped planning for the future. The owners and executives at the meeting discussed several committee concerns, such as increasing fan interest by realigning several leagues and building better ballparks with lighting and public-address systems. No formal action was taken on these two matters, but two other suggestions were adopted: the re-establishment of a promotions department to deal with the press, and the beginning of a re-examination of the rules and a retraining of umpires with the creation of an Office of Umpire Adviser for the National Association. It was voted to fund the umpire adviser job for two years at a salary of $6,500 per year, although no one was named to the post. Among other duties, the adviser would be expected to work with the leagues to offer preseason clinics, keep tabs on umpire compliments and complaints, and rank umpires by ability at the end of every season. However, the major leagues, in their New York meeting, did not vote to fund the position.

The Postwar Planning Committee had also been charged with looking into the future of baseball and, in some cases, it did not like what it saw. For instance, it thought that high-school baseball was in sharp decline because there were fewer teams and players. According to a report presented at the Buffalo meeting, there were 40 percent fewer student playing baseball than there had been five years before.[14] To try to help reverse that dismal number, Warren Giles, general manager of the Cincinnati Reds, advocated a series of clinics in 15 states, taught by major leaguers. Although the minors voted to set aside $5,000 for the clinics as well as a training film, the majors did not fund that project either.

Leagues and Players

Baseball wasn't giving just high schoolers the cold shoulder; it also apparently wasn't planning on going international. Representatives from the Mexican National Baseball League were in Buffalo in hopes of gaining recognition by the association.

"We have been practically assured of recognition by Bramham, and our six league cities are planning to go in for a complete program, including lights for night games," said L.A. Michaels, vice president of the El Paso Texans.[15] Michaels was in Buffalo for the meeting with Ernest Calderon, director of the Chihuahua team, and Frank Montes, vice president of the Juarez team.

However, no action was taken even though Rogers Hornsby endorsed the idea, and published reports said Bramham had promised league officials a Class-B recognition.[16] (Hornsby was at the meeting in Buffalo in an unsuccessful attempt to buy the minor-league Minneapolis team from owner Mike Kelley.)

The winter meetings were usually Rumor Central for big trades and other player moves, and once in a while some of those rumors actually came true. But trading at the 1944 meetings was scant. Only four deals were worked out, three of them involving the Chicago White Sox:

- The White Sox sent left-handed pitcher Jake Wade (2-4 in 1944; he wound up with a 27-40 career mark) to the New York Yankees for lefty pitcher Johnny Johnson (0-2 in '44; 3-2 lifetime).
- They sent shortstop-second baseman Skeeter Webb to the Detroit Tigers for utility infielder Joe Orengo. Webb retired after the 1948 season with a .219 batting average in 699 games, while Orengo called it a career at the end of 1945, finishing with a .238 batting average in 366 games.
- The White Sox' last trade had outfielder Ed Carnett going to Cleveland for outfielder Oris Hockett. Carnett played in 30 games for the Indians and ended his career in 1945 with a .268 batting average in 158 games. Hockett, who was an All-Star in 1944, also saw 1945 prove to be his last year in the majors, as he finished with a .276 batting average in 551 games.
- In addition, the Cincinnati Reds sent outfielder Tony Criscola to the Pacific Coast League's San Diego Padres. Criscola never made it back to the majors and his final career stats show a .248 batting average in 184 games.
- And finally, it was announced that the 1945 All-Star Game would be held on Tuesday, July 10, in Boston's Fenway Park. Since Fenway Park didn't have lights at the time, it would be the first time since the 1941 game in Detroit that the All-Star Game would be played in daylight.

Consequences

With the death of Landis, a whole new era opened for baseball near the middle of the twentieth century. Just as some baseball owners feared, football would one day grow and come to rival baseball for the nation's entertainment dollars and attention. Much of that had to do with television, of course, which was able to mold football while encountering old-fashioned resistance from baseball.

Buffalo never again hosted the winter meetings. Its place of prominence in the nation's manufacturing heartland declined to an afterthought as many of its industries withered or moved from the Rust Belt to the Sun Belt for a variety of reasons, including climate and a "perfect storm" of economic forces beyond its control.

Baseball was also buffeted by change in the years after the war. It painfully showed the nation how to keep its promises of equality for all as Jackie Robinson joined the boys of summer in their games. Just a generation of players later, as baseball and the nation still struggled with civil rights, free agency helped to open the vaults as players and agents could now negotiate with owners from a position of strength.

Baseball also expanded to the West Coast and into Canada. St. Louis was now the middle ground between the coasts and no longer the metaphorical end of the line with the majors going no farther west or south. But expansion, free agency (and, yes, collusion), and integration were matters for other winter meetings in other cities.

SOURCES

In addition to the references cited in the Notes, the author also consulted the following:

Brands, Edgar G. "Choice of Landis Starts Hall of Fame Speed-Up," *The Sporting News*, December 21, 1944.

———. "Landis' Death Speeds Vital Decisions," *The Sporting News*, December 7, 1944.

———. "Minors Dipped Into Reserves for $35,588 in '44," *The Sporting News*, December 7, 1944.

Burns, Ed. "Sox Slash Home Night Schedule to 14 Contests," *The Sporting News*, December 21, 1944.

Daniel, Dan. "Barrow Joins Opponents of 3-Man Commission," *The Sporting News*, December 7, 1944.

———. "Yanks Land Jake Wade in First Big Move for Big '45," *The Sporting News*, December 14, 1944.

Drebinger, John. "Baseball Pays Tribute to Landis by Picking Him for Hall of Fame," *New York Times*, December 11, 1944.

"Farm Foes Routed by Big Leagues," *The Sporting News*, December 14, 1944.

Hall, Halsey. "Hornsby's Bid Hanging Fire," *The Sporting News*, December 14, 1944.

Hedrick, Sturgis. "Convention Sidelights," *Buffalo Evening News*, December 7, 1944.

Kritzer, Cy. "33⅓% Raise in Draft Prices Approved by Minor Leagues," *Buffalo Evening News*, December 7, 1944.

———. "Minors Set Up $5000 Fund for Schoolboy Baseball Clinic," *Buffalo Evening News*, December 8, 1944.

———. "Rowland, Veeck Lead Minor Leagues' Fight to Curb Majors' Rule," *Buffalo Evening News*, December 5, 1944.

———. "Sale of Minneapolis Team to Hornsby Reported Near," *Buffalo Evening News*, December 6, 1944.

"Landis Named to Hall of Fame," *The Sporting News*, December 14, 1944.

Lieb, Frederick G. "Breadon Dons Ear Muffs for Trade Talkers," *The Sporting News*, December 7, 1944.

Major-Minor Code Faces Revampment," *Washington Post*, December 6, 1944.

"Meetings to Pass on Vital Issues," *The Sporting News*, December 7, 1944.

"Minor Leagues in Buffalo for Annual Meetings," *Christian Science Monitor*, December 5, 1944.

Peterson, Leo H. "2 New Minor Leagues to Start in '45." *Washington Post*, December 7, 1944.

Reichler, Joe (Associated Press). "Majors Threaten to Reject Minors' Draft Price Boost," *Buffalo Evening News*, December 11, 1944.

Stedler, Bob. "Sport Comment," *Buffalo Evening News*, December 5, 6, and 9, 1944.

Wurzer, Tony. "Convention Sidelights," *Buffalo Evening News*, December 8. 1944.

NOTES

1. Edgar G. Brands, "Optimism Reigns at Minors' Confab," *The Sporting News*, December 14, 1944.

2. Baseball representatives heard at the meeting in Buffalo that the Carolina League and North Carolina State League would be revived in 1945. The Quebec-Ontario League was looking to add Quebec City and Three Rivers so it could resume play in 1945. And the Northwest International League was expected to vote for resumption at its annual meeting in January. However, the Mexican League representative in Buffalo did not appear at a meeting to answer questions about player eligibility and other

matters; reporters speculated that it was unlikely the league would have been approved for admission into the National Association of Professional Baseball Leagues.

3 Brands, "Bramham Still Opposes, but Bows to 'Red Inking,'" *The Sporting News*, December 7, 1944.

4 Compensation for drafted players in 1944 was $7,500. The proposed amendment by the Pacific Coast League would double the price paid to the minor-league team to $15,000. Also, in 1944, if a major-league team expanded into a minor-league team's territory, the major club would have to pay the minor club's league $5,000 and a negotiated amount to the affected minor-league team. If the teams couldn't agree on a price, the matter would be decided by the commissioner.

5 Shirley Povich, "Griff Favors Naming a New Czar at Once," *The Sporting News*, December 7, 1941; Brands, "Majors Name Council to Rule Until New Pact," *The Sporting News*, December 14, 1944; Brands, "Majors Reaffirm Policy on One-Man Government," *The Sporting News*, December 21, 1944; Bob Stedler, "Sports Comment," *Buffalo Evening News*, December 11, 1944.

6 "Griff Favors Naming a New Czar at Once."

7 "New Czar's Power Will Be Debated," *Hartford Courant*, December 10, 1944.

8 Landis was selected by the Major League Advisory Committee, which had been set up in August to help get nineteenth century players and others into the Hall, which had inducted its first class in 1936. The committee included Stephen C. Clark, president of the National Baseball Museum in Cooperstown, chairman; Paul S. Kerr, secretary; Connie Mack, owner of the Philadelphia Athletics; Ed Barrow, president of the New York Yankees; Bob Quinn, head of the Boston Braves; Sid Mercer of the *New York Journal-American*; and Mel Webb of the *Boston Globe*. Mack was vacationing in California and sent his vote via telegram.

9 Dan Daniel, "Majors Deny Grid Pros' Charge of 'War,'" *The Sporting News*, December 21, 1944.

10 The question about scheduling night games was brought up by Clark Griffith of the Senators, who wanted no limits placed on the number of night games a team could play. The Philadelphia Phillies wanted 14 night games, but opposed the league office dictating to teams the number of night games they could play. Branch Rickey of the Brooklyn Dodgers and Ed Barrow, president of the New York Yankees, thought seven night games a season were enough for a team. After a joint meeting between the St. Louis Browns and Cardinals in Pittsburgh on July 11, the two teams from St. Louis were given a blank check by Commissioner Landis to schedule as many night games as they pleased; however, reports said they entered the meeting in Buffalo not certain how many night games they would set. Cardinals president Sam Breadon said local needs should allow clubs to set a night schedule. Breadon presented the findings from his survey of night games in St. Louis and found that attendance at continuous night games fell after the middle of July, but he said it still was higher than that of day games during the same period.

11 See baseballhistorian.com/fans_favorites.cfm?hero=922 for information on lights; see baseballhistorian.com/argue.cfm?argue_id=18&search=y for cities along the coast and the U-boat menace; see baseballhistorian.com/american_heroes.cfm?hero=1043 for electricity and the war effort.

12 Not all men who registered for the draft were found to be eligible. A full 30 percent were rejected for physical defects, which included muscular and bone malformations, hearing or circulatory ailments, mental deficiency or disease, hernias, and syphilis.

13 "Majors Deny Grid Pros' Charge of 'War'"; "Stepped-Up Draft Order May Hit Game," *The Sporting News*, December 21, 1944; Brands, "Player Deals Slowed by Manpower Order," *The Sporting News*, December 14, 1944.

14 Brands, "Postwar Planning Urged at Buffalo Convention," *The Sporting News*, December 14, 1944; Cy Kritzer, "Minors Set Up $5,000 Fund for Schoolboy Baseball Clinic," *Buffalo Evening News*, December 8, 1944.

15 "Outlook 'Exceedingly Bright,' Say Mexican Loop Leaders," *Buffalo Evening News*, December 6, 1944.

16 There were six teams in the league when it applied: Chihuahua, El Paso, Juarez, Parral, Torreon, and Saltillo. Published reports said the year-old league had drawn more than 500,000 fans in its inaugural season. El Paso and Juarez had lights for night games.

1945
RESUMING PEACETIME BASEBALL

By Andy Bokser

FOR THE FIRST TIME SINCE 1941, Major-league baseball was able to conduct its winter meetings without having to adjust to World War II, which had decimated rosters and affected the quality of play over the previous four years. After the war ended in August 1945, the commissioner, league presidents, and team owners met in Chicago for three days at the Palmer House, December 10-13.[1] The two leagues had individual meetings on Monday and Tuesday, and a joint meeting with the commissioner on the closing day.[2] At that time the baseball decision-makers were looking forward to a full season with their returning major-league players.

The 1945 Winter Meetings were going to be conducted under the stewardship of the new Major League Baseball Commissioner Albert Benjamin ("Happy") Chandler. The former United States Senator and Governor of Kentucky was selected unanimously on a third ballot of the major-league team owners in early 1945 to replace the first baseball commissioner, Judge Kenesaw Mountain Landis, who died in November 1944.[3]

Commissioner Chandler kept his Senate seat until he assumed his duties as commissioner on November 1, 1945. The new regime was planning to move the commissioner's office from Chicago (where the lease was to expire on December 15, 1945 to Cincinnati.[4] That was approximately one week after Branch Rickey announced that he had signed Jackie Robinson to a contract with the Dodgers' minor-league Montreal Royals. Chandler had supported the game-changing move by the Dodgers.[5]

Delivering a statement at the opening of the meetings was General Jacob L. Devers, the former commander of the North African Theater of Operations and the Sixth Army Group in Europe.[6] He credited baseball with helping to set a standard for the teamwork that had contributed to the Army's success in Europe during the war. General Devers also advised the assemblage that 498 major-league players were still in military service on December 1, but that he expected most of them to be available for the 1946 season.[7]

One of the results of the Winter Meetings was baseball's reaffirming its commitment to protect the returning veterans' jobs in baseball.[8] In addition to preparing for the influx of former players to their rosters, the major leagues needed to resolve a brewing dispute with respect to the number of night games the teams could play in the coming season.

In particular, the St. Louis Browns and Cardinals, along with the Washington Senators (who in 1945 played 41 games under the lights at home),[9] wanted to have carte blanche in determining the number of night games they could schedule.[10] While the National League agreed with affording the individual clubs unrestricted rights to scheduling night games instead of going back to the previous limit of seven games a year, the American League, while willing to let the Senators and the Browns play 33 night games each, wanted to restrict the other teams to no more than 14.

Neither the Chicago Cubs, Detroit Tigers, nor Boston Red Sox had lights. However, the rules did not force a team to accept night games on the road if they had an objection. A major argument raised by those opposed to unlimited night games was that it would spoil the novelty for fans.[11] One of the writers reporting the events of the Winter Meetings voiced the concern that unlimited night games would bar young fans from seeing the game and cause the game to die out. Arthur Daley of the *New York Times* cited the Chicago White Sox as a random example, writing that in 1940 they had an average attendance of about

30,600 for seven night games, but only 11,500 per game for their 22 night games in 1945.[12]

The ultimate decision regarding night games was made when new Commissioner Albert B. "Happy" Chandler agreed with the National League about expanding the teams' rights to schedule night games. The former Kentucky governor, while diplomatically not criticizing either side in the dispute, reportedly was convinced that it would be bad for baseball for there to be differences in the rules between the two major leagues.[13]

Nevertheless, minor differences did exist in the leagues' rules; for instance, the National League permitted a player ejected from the first game of a doubleheader to play in the second game, while the American League did not. In another exercise of his powers to reduce the differences between the two leagues, Chandler did agree to apply to both leagues the National League rule permitting a 30-man roster until June 15, instead of allowing the American League's rule permitting the expanded roster until 31 days after the commencement of the season (around May 15). The owners also passed an amendment banning twilight-night doubleheaders unless caused by postponements.[14]

The owners strongly supported their commissioner over proposed rule amendments sought by the minor leagues to curtail some of his authority. Prior to the major-league winter meeting, Chandler responded to the rumblings from the minor leagues about this, saying, "I will insist on all the prerogatives enjoyed by Judge [Kenesaw] Landis in the running of my office.... If the minors don't like it, they are at liberty to secede from the Union."[15] For example, the minor leagues did not want Chandler to be in charge of organizing and implementing the promotional plan for baseball. Meeting at the Deschler-Wallick Hotel in Columbus, Ohio, December 5 to 7, they also voted 21 to 3 for an amendment stating that the commissioner could not determine that an existing rule was "conduct detrimental to baseball," as his predecessor had done. Chandler stated that despite the vote he still had the inherent authority to determine what was harmful to baseball. By having his power as commissioner reaffirmed at the meeting, the major leagues failed to support the actions of the minor leagues to deprive Chandler of his power over the promotional campaign for baseball. They also approved his ruling that prohibited baseball from signing high-school players until they were out of school for more than one year.[16]

Before the Winter Meetings, the commissioner made it clear that he wanted to take the lead role in organizing the promotional plan for baseball in the coming postwar season. And the major-league owners formally granted him that authority at their meetings.[17] Under the rules then in existence, the minor leagues' attempt to curtail the commissioner's power could succeed only if the major leagues approved the minor leagues' proposed rule changes.[18]

There was one change to the powers and role of the commissioner: Unlike Landis, Chandler did not retain the right to veto league rules that he believed were detrimental to baseball.[19] Nevertheless, while the major leagues did not specifically overrule the minor leagues' vote, they also acknowledged that the commissioner had the authority to determine when a rule or act was harmful to baseball and to block the implementation of such a rule.

However, not all of the minor-leagues' applications were defeated by their major-league counterparts. The latter approved the minors' proposal to create a Triple-A level and elevate the Pacific Coast League, American Association, and International League to that status (from their previous Double-A designation); the Texas League was reborn and, along with the Southern Association, placed at the Double-A level; and the South Atlantic League was also revived and granted the right to operate as a Single-A league.

The major leagues denied the request by the Pacific Coast League to be recognized as a third major league, but in an apparent attempt to soften the rejection, they advised the PCL that the issue would be studied further. Stadium seating capacities were one of the reasons the 16 major-league clubs did not want to expand their membership to include the Pacific Coast League. For instance, the Oakland and Sacramento ballparks could each hold just 11,000 spectators, San Diego was limited to 12,000 and Portland was just a little larger at 12,500. All of these were far smaller than the existing major-league teams.[20] Another reason offered to the PCL was contained in a joint statement by league Presidents Ford Frick (National League) and Will Harridge (American League), which declared that promoting the league to the major-league level would be unfair to players since it would give the Pacific Coast League the privilege of drafting minor-league players, but once they started playing at the major-league level, those teams would not be able to afford to pay those players top major-league salaries.

The president of the Pacific Coast League, Clarence Rowland, reacted to the unfavorable determination, stating that the major leagues were merely delaying the inevitable, and that the people of California, Washington, and Oregon want better than minor-league baseball.[21]

The major leagues also enacted rules that restricted the practice of giving out large signing bonuses. Henceforth, if a player was signed for an annual salary and a bonus exceeding $6,000, the signing team could not send him to the minor leagues unless no other team claimed him on waivers. Moreover, if he was claimed by another team, his team could not withdraw the waivers. And if the "bonus baby" did end up going to the minors after all teams passed on him, he would be subject to the annual player draft. Chandler put teeth into the rule by adding the provision that a major-league team violating the rule would lose the player, be unable to re-sign him for three years, and be fined $2,000. In addition, the individual transgressor for the team would be fined $500.

At the minor-league meetings, National Association President W.G. Bramham also decried the "unbridled payment of bonuses" because it contributed to the financial problems of many teams. Bramham also warned the membership that there was "rampant" gambling in some minor-league parks, the participants were operating "brazenly," and that leagues and teams that failed to take steps to curb it could bring about the "forfeiture of their membership in the National Association." However, he stated that there was no evidence that any players or umpires were involved in the gambling.[22]

In covering the Winter Meetings for *Baseball Magazine*, Dan M. Daniel anticipated discussions and action in Chicago regarding Jackie Robinson's signing with the Brooklyn Dodgers' Montreal minor-league team. However, he reported no discussion or action taken at the time of the Dodgers' potentially game-changing signing.[23]

Trading at the meeting was light. Among the few reported transactions, the Reds sold their longtime first baseman, Frank McCormick, to the Phillies for $40,000; the Red Sox sold infielder Skeeter Newsome to the Phillies and traded left-handed pitcher Vic Johnson and cash to the Indians for right-hander Jim Bagby; and the Giants purchased the contract of pitcher (and sometimes outfielder) Clint Hartung.[24] One reason offered for the lack of player moves was that the teams were unsure of how well the returning veterans would perform in 1946. Cubs' manager Charlie Grimm, for example, said that with six of his nine catchers returning from the service, he wanted to see how they played in the spring before moving any of them.[25]

Discharged from the US Marines as a captain after three years of service, veteran pitching star Ted Lyons turned down the request from the White Sox that he become a coach, as he felt he could still pitch. The White Sox granted his wish.[26] But the right-hander was able to go only 1-4 before retiring as a player in 1946 and succeeding Jimmy Dykes as the White Sox' manager. (Lyons was elected to the Hall of Fame in 1955.)

The meetings broke up with the general consensus that Commissioner Chandler could live up to his nickname of "Happy," since the major-league owners had largely ratified his powers when the minor leagues sought to reduce them. Chandler having been in office only about a year since the death of Landis, it was clear that the major-league owners were going to give him time to grow on the job. Prior to his ouster in 1951, Chandler oversaw the long-overdue integration of major-league baseball, suspended Leo Durocher for "conduct detrimental to baseball," provided money in 1947 for the new players' pension fund, and negotiated lucrative (for the time) television and radio contracts with proceeds from both going into the pension fund.²⁷ The strong support given to Chandler by the National and American Leagues at the 1945 Winter Meetings certainly help set the stage for his positive influences on the national pastime.

NOTES

1. Irving Vaughan, "Coast's Major Demand Faces Ballot Today," *Chicago Tribune*, December 10, 1945.
2. John Drebinger, "Arc-Light Games Leading Problem as Majors Gather," *New York Times*, December 9, 1945.
3. Terry Bohn, "Happy Chandler," *www.sabr.org/node33749*
4. Tom Swope, "Fancy Trim Being Put on New Capitol," *The Sporting News*, November 29, 1945
5. Terry Bohn, "Happy Chandler."
6. britannica.com/biography/Jacob-L-Devers.
7. John Drebinger, "Chandler Blocks Night Game Limit," *New York Times*, December 13, 1945.
8. Ibid.
9. "Griffith States Views," *New York Times*, December 9, 1945.
10. Dan M. Daniel, "Failure to Revive Prewar Restrictions on Night Baseball Featured Major Sessions," *Baseball Magazine*, February 1946.
11. Ibid.
12. Arthur Daley, "Sports of the Times—Short Shots in Sundry Directions," *New York Times* December 14, 1945.
13. Daniel.
14. Drebinger, "Chandler Blocks Night Game Limit."
15. "Chandler to Insist on Majors Giving Him Landis' Authority," *Brooklyn Daily Eagle*, December 10, 1945.
16. Daniel.
17. "Programs for Minors' Convention," *The Sporting News*, December 6, 1945.
18. "Griffith States Views," *New York Times*, December 9, 1945.
19. *Official Baseball 1946*.
20. H.G. Salsinger, Preface, *Major League Baseball 1946* (New York: Whitman Publishing Company, 1946), 4.
21. Drebinger, "Big League Status Is Denied to Coast," *New York Times* December 12, 1945.
22. E.G. Brands, "Franchises at Stake in War on Gambling," *The Sporting News*, December 6, 1945, 2.
23. Daniel.
24. Ibid.
25. Drebinger, "Chandler Defies Threats of Minors," *New York Times* December 10, 1945.
26. "Big League Status Is Denied to Coast."
27. "Baseball History—Albert Benjamin "Happy" Chandler mlb.mlb.com/mlb/history/mlb_history_people.jsp?story=com_bio_2.

1946
TRANQUILITY AND TURBULENCE

By Jerry Nechal

PUNCTUATED BY ENOS SLAUGHTER'S mad dash around the bases in Game Seven of the World Series, the 1946 season saw major-league baseball back on the upswing. Total attendance had climbed to more than 11 million, a 71 percent increase over the previous season. The total also well exceeded the prewar 1941 figure of 9.7 million. Stars like Ted Williams, Joe DiMaggio, and Bob Feller returned from wartime military duty to dazzle their fans. The National League produced a thrilling pennant race between the Brooklyn Dodgers and St. Louis Cardinals, ultimately settled in a playoff. The World Series was an exciting one, going the full seven games. Slaughter scored the deciding run in the eighth inning of the final game on a play that would be talked about for decades to come.

As the major-league owners headed into their December 5-7 Winter Meetings in Los Angeles, harmony seemed to be the prevailing mood. Although they had been apprehensive about Commissioner Happy Chandler when he succeeded the despotic Judge Kenesaw M. Landis in 1945, and there had in fact been some early conflicts between Chandler and the owners, he now seemed to have solidified his standing and support. He was "now regarded far and wide as an able administrator.... Club owners, managers, and players seek his counsel."[1] Commissioner Chandler himself declared, "My prediction is that this will be the best meeting ever."[2]

This upbeat frame of mind seemed prevalent despite that fact that the owners were only a few months removed from two historic controversies that had occurred during the season. In August they had met in Chicago to address player defections to the Mexican League, and the threat of a strike by the Pittsburgh Pirates over collective-bargaining rights. After that meeting, it was rumored that the owners in secret had voted 15 to 1 against Jackie Robinson's entry into the major leagues.[3] Purportedly, a report had been distributed at the meeting that stated, "(T)he use of Negro players would hazard all physical properties of baseball."[4]

However, on the surface, attitudes were upbeat. Chandler optimistically stated, "Naturally we have problems—every business has, but I don't think you will find any serious controversies arising."[5]

In reality, below the surface the 1946 meeting marked the first time that the owners had ever been forced to respond to the organized demands of the players. Negotiating with the players was a new phenomenon for owners who in prior years had for the most part dictated the terms of employment.

Two 1946 events were responsible for this change. Several players had migrated to the new Mexican League, and the threat of further defections loomed over the owners. At the same time, labor lawyer Robert Murphy had attempted to organize the Pirates. Although a vote by Pirates players to unionize had failed and a threat to boycott a game against the New York Giants had dissipated, the owners responded by acknowledging the players as a group, and they negotiated several concessions to major-league players as a whole. These included a guaranteed minimum salary of $5,000, a limitation on pay cuts to a maximum of 25 percent, $25 per week in living expenses during spring training, and the creation of a pension plan. Ralph Kiner from that Pirates team recalled that "It was a matter of money.... The minimum salary was nothing."[6]

At the Winter Meetings, the players continued to make demands that received the attention of the owners. The players complained about the owners' "gentleman's agreement"[7] that allowed them to hoard and keep talent in the minor leagues. Owners had been able to retain players put on waivers. If they were claimed by another team, the owner could revoke the waiver call. A new rule stated that a claiming club got the player on the third call. Another player demand approved at the meetings was a ban on scheduling a doubleheader after a night game. Finally, the owners began to work out the details of the pension plan. The plan was to be funded by each player contributing $250 per year, a sum that would be matched by his owner. Also, and more important in the long term, the proceeds from World Series broadcasting and the All-Star Game would go to the pension plan.[8]

The setting for the meetings was also unique and added to the drama that would play out in the coming days. The 1946 major-league meetings shared the limelight with the minor leagues. In this pre-television era, the minor leagues provided an attractive local offering to baseball-starved fans. Collectively, the minors were a large and thriving business. For the first time in three years, both the major-league owners and the minor-league National Association were meeting at the same time and in the same location. The National Association, the governing body for all professional baseball teams affiliated with major-league baseball through their farm systems, faced two important tasks. The first was the replacement of William G. Bramham, who was retiring after having served 14 years as president. The second was the negotiation of a new agreement with the major leagues.

Known as "The Major of the Minors," Bramham had ruled the National Association since 1932.[9] The former judge had shepherded the minors from bankruptcy and only 11 leagues at the beginning of his reign to a peak of 44 leagues in 1940.[10] At age 72, however, he was dealing with health concerns and had decided to retire. Going into the 1946 meetings, there was speculation about the potential of a bitter fight to replace Bramham, with as many as 12 candidates being mentioned.[11] Nevertheless, George M. Trautman, executive vice president of the Detroit Tigers, emerged as the leading candidate. Initially there was some apprehension about his close connection with the major leagues and the potential of a "dictatorship."[12] In the end, however, opposition dissipated and Trautman was unanimously elected president.

Trautman was a protégé of Branch Rickey, having gained entry into minor-league baseball when The Mahatma made him president of the Columbus Red Birds in 1933. His tenure there was a success and Trautman was subsequently elected president of the American Association in 1935. He had been with the Tigers only one year, and was being groomed as the successor to general manager Jack Zeller. As the president of the National Association, Trautman was given a five-year contract at $25,000 per year.

A new agreement between the Association and the majors had in the past proved itself to be an elusive goal. The existing major-minor contract was now 25 years old (it had been extended numerous times).[13] Previous committees had made recommendations on a new pact, but no action was ever taken due to various objections by one party or the other. Finally, at the 1946 Winter Meetings both sides accepted the recommendations of the current committee. As a compromise, a shorter duration was proposed; the new agreement would last for five years, with options to renew for additional five-year increments. Receiving the most attention was the language granting "veto power" to the minor leagues.[14] The majors appeased the minors by giving them greater autonomy, granting them the right to terminate the major-minor agreement with an affirmative vote of three-fourths of the Association's members.

In the new agreement, language was also changed regarding the power of the commissioner over the minors. Language that had allowed the commissioner to unilaterally rule on items "detrimental" to baseball was removed.[15] In a series of new clauses, these powers were reduced. The new language was similar to what had been adopted at the major-league level after the death of Commissioner Landis and the appointment of Chandler.

Retiring National Association President Bramham did not go quietly into the night, giving a final passionate speech to the Association. He spoke out strongly against the evils of wild spending on bonus money to attract players.[16] Likewise, he vehemently cautioned the audience on the presence of gambling in the minors. "These roaches have become a menace to the game, Bramham declared."[17] He went on to mention the "moral laxity among certain officials, players and fans, public gambling, intimidation of players by thugs … collusion between players and bookmakers …"[18] Commissioner Chandler was quick to respond to Bramham's gambling concerns. "Certainly the public doesn't question the integrity of the game," he said. "We are proud that in the majors last season not a single player, coach, manager, or umpire was under suspicion. However, we will continue to exercise every precaution to merit the confidence and will assist all leagues to that end."[19] Bramham's successor, Trautman, was quick to piggyback on Chandler's response, promising to stamp out gambling in minor-league parks.[20]

On bonuses for players, Bramham asserted that the "scramble for their services had gone far beyond reason and set a pace that the poorer clubs cannot maintain and stay within their incomes."[21] The annual report of the National Association revealed that more than $2 million had been paid to players in the 1946 season. There were also reports of minor-league teams whose attendance had doubled but who still lost money because of bonus payments. The delegates took these concerns under advisement. The new Major-Minor League Agreement established a classification labeled Bonus Players for both the major and minors. The designation was assigned to newly signed players who were paid bonus money above defined amounts. The fixed minimum amount that would trigger a bonus classification ranged from $600 in Class D to $6,000 in the majors. A Bonus Player would retain the label for his career. If he was optioned to a lower classification or playing level, he would be subject to an unrestricted draft.

The Los Angeles meeting location was also significant on a couple of other fronts. It was the first time the major-league and minor-league groups had met in a minor-league city. (The Pacific Coast League was seeking major-league status at the time.)[22] At the same time, the minor leagues, including the PCL, were seeking formal protection against intrusion into their territories by the major leagues.

Approaching the Winter Meetings, PCL officials were adamant in their determination to protect their territory and in becoming a third major league. With the two large markets in Los Angeles and San Francisco, the PCL was also concerned that a major-league owner could move a team there and severely disrupt their league. Within the past year there had been rumors that singer/actor Bing Crosby, a part-owner of the Pirates, would buy a team and move it to the West Coast.[23] Accordingly, just prior to the meetings, Pacific Coast League members adopted a resolution calling for major-league status for the PCL immediately.[24] The resolution was consistent with their efforts in recent years. The majors had also previously appointed a committee to discuss this request. Beyond major-league status, the West Coast league and the rest of the minor-league teams also sought formal veto power against the invasion of their territory.

The Pacific Coast League was again unsuccessful in its demands for major-league status. After listening to the plans of PCL President Clarence Rowland and the advisory committee, the National and American Leagues did not act, but again "took the subject under advisement."[25] However as a concession, it was agreed that in the event of expansion into their territory, the affected minor league would be "entitled to adequate compensation through an arbitration board."[26]

As they still are, the Winter Meetings were of interest to the fans because of the possibility of player trades. Before the 1946 meetings, Branch Rickey had raised expectations in this area. He predicted, "There will be a lot of action. Maybe we will set a record for that kind of activity. … The pot is boiling, and when it steams, you can believe that something is on its way."[27] With five new big-league managers and two new owners, this sentiment did not appear far-fetched.

Nevertheless, Rickey's predictions failed to materialize. Despite some provocative rumors that made it into the press, there were no blockbuster transactions involving prominent players. Perhaps the most significant rumor held that slugger Hank Greenberg would move from the Tigers to the Yankees. The

Tigers, however, were reluctant to let Greenberg go, except on very favorable terms. Detroit owner Walter Briggs reportedly demanded from New York infielder Snuffy Stirnweiss, the 1945 batting champ; catcher Aaron Robinson; and another unnamed player. The Yankees quickly rejected this proposal.[28] In another failed attempt, the Cardinals vetoed an exorbitant offer of $150,000 from the Phillies for outfielder Enos Slaughter.[29]

In the absence of blockbusters, there were a number of deals involving lesser-known younger players and/or older veterans on the decline. Some of the lesser-known players would go on to prominent moments or careers in the big leagues. In what was considered a major swap, the Yankees traded outfielder Hal Peck, left-handed pitcher Gene Bearden, and right-handed hurler Al Gettel to Cleveland for second baseman Ray Mack and catcher Sherm Lollar. Bearden, a previously unheralded knuckleballer, went on to have a career year with the Indians in 1948, posting 20 wins, including the victory in the one-game AL championship playoff game with the Red Sox. Lollar played 17 more years in the majors with the Yankees, Browns, and White Sox, was named to seven All-Star teams, won three Gold Glove awards, and drove in five runs as the White Sox lost to the Dodgers in the 1959 World Series. Pittsburgh obtained outfielder Gene Woodling from Cleveland in exchange for veteran catcher Al Lopez. Future Hall of Famer Lopez was at the tail end of a 19-year playing career, and the 24-year-old Woodling ultimately played 17 years in the majors with seven teams, including five world championship seasons with the Yankees. The Phillies purchased veteran right-handed pitcher Dutch Leonard from Washington, the White Sox bought utilityman Jack Wallaesa from the Phillies, and the Cardinals sold right-handed pitcher Charlie "Red" Barrett to the Boston Braves.

The predictions of consensus and tranquility at the Winter Meetings had prevailed. A new agreement had been reached with the minors. The National Association had selected a new president with minimal discord. The issue of excessive bonus payments had been dealt with. Baseball appeared well positioned for the future. The next 10 years would later be seen by many as baseball's Golden Age.

On the other hand, new or unaddressed issues loomed. At least one significant item was not publicly discussed: In a few months the major leagues would have their first modern black player, with Commissioner Chandler helping to pave the way for that event, to the dismay of several owners. On another front, the issue of West Coast major-league expansion remained unresolved. Finally, for the first time, the players had been dealt with at the bargaining table by the owners. This scenario was an early preview of coming attractions.

NOTES

1. Arch Ward, "In the Wake of the News," *Chicago Tribune*, December 5, 1946: 47.
2. "Chandler Happy California Site of Diamond Meet," *The Sporting News*, December 3, 1946: 6.
3. John Paul Hill. "Commissioner A.B. 'Happy' Chandler and the Integration of Major League Baseball: A Reassessment," *NINE: A Journal of Baseball History and Culture* 19 (1) (Fall 2010): 28-52
4. Ibid.
5. *The Sporting News*, December 3, 1946: 6.
6. Ibid.
7. Dan Daniel, "Players Win New Concessions From Majors," *The Sporting News*, December 11, 1946: 1.
8. "Majors Draft Pension Plan," *The Sporting News*, December 11, 1946: 2.
9. E.V. Mitchell, "Bramham: The Major of the Minors Since '32," *The Sporting News*, December 11, 1946: 7.
10. Ibid.
11. Edgar G. Brands, "Minors Elect Trautman as New Head," *The Sporting News*, December 11, 1946: 3.
12. Ibid.
13. E.G. Brands, "Veto Powers for Minors in New Pact," *The Sporting News*, December 4, 1946: 1.
14. Ibid.
15. "Majors Delay P.C.L. Boost," *Los Angeles Times*, December 11, 1946: 10.
16. Edgar G. Brands, "Wild Spending Threating Minors—Bramham," *The Sporting News*, December 4, 1946: 2.
17. Al Wolf, "Bramham Raps Baseball Gambling," *Los Angeles Times*, December 5, 1946: 10.

18 J.G. Taylor Spink, "Bramham Gambling Warning in 1927 Recalled," *The Sporting News,* December 11, 1946: 2.

19 Arch Ward, "Majors Vote All-Star Game to Cubs' Park," *Chicago Tribune,* December 7, 1946: 21.

20 Ibid.

21 "Wild Spending Threating Minors—Bramham."

22 Edgar G. Brands, "Minors Meeting on West Coast for Third Time," *The Sporting News,* December 4, 1946: 9.

23 Edgar G. Brands, "Coast Loop in Dither Over Invasion by Majors," *The Sporting News,* November 27, 1946: 2.

24 Al Wolf, "P.C.L. Presses for Major Rating," *Los Angeles Times,* December 3, 1946: 6C.

25 "Coast Fails to Gain Major Status," *The Sporting News,* December 11, 1946: 12.

26 Ibid.

27 Dan Daniel, "Pot Boiling for Record Swapping Season," *The Sporting News,* November 27, 1946: 1.

28 John Rosengren, *Hank Greenberg, The Hero of Heroes* (New York: New American Library, 2013), 296.

29 Stan Baumgartner, "Rivals Fearing Phillies, Refuse Tempting Deals," *The Sporting News,* December 11, 1946: 12.

— 1947 —
LATIN AMERICA, LEO THE LIP, AND HIGH SCHOOL HIJINKS

By Gary Levy

THE ANNUAL WINTER MEETINGS OF the National Association ventured to sunny Miami to hold sessions in the McAllister and Columbus hotels from December 3-5, 1947. Major-league representatives stayed at the McAllister, Columbus, or Martinique hotels.[1] The annual joint meetings of the American and National Leagues followed shortly afterward, in frosty New York City, at the luxurious Waldorf-Astoria over December 9-11. Major issues that arose again at both gatherings included the drafting of players out of high school, expanded play in Cuba and Latin America (perhaps the reason for the Miami locale for the National Association meetings?), the possible return of manager Leo Durocher to Brooklyn after a one-year suspension, and continued experimentation with night baseball and baseball on television. Much controversy and disparity was also present across baseball, as many thought that Joe DiMaggio's winning of the American League MVP Award over Ted Williams by one vote (202-201) was a bum deal.[2] Finally, much was made of an end to the career of many longtime stars, including Hank Greenberg, Stan Hack, Mel Harder, Billy Jurges, Thornton Lee, Ernie Lombardi, Joe Medwick, Red Ruffing, and Mel Ott, at the end of the previous 1947 season, all said to be "trading spiked shoes for bedroom slippers."[3]

Regardless of the many issues facing major-league baseball, the two leagues continued to thrive as six of eight teams in the National League (Boston, Brooklyn, Chicago, New York, Pittsburgh, and St. Louis) all set home attendance records and drew over one million fans. (Not far behind were Cincinnati and Philadelphia who both drew about 900,000 home fans.) All told, the National League drew almost 10.4 million, with home and away games involving Brooklyn, which lost to the Yankees in the seven-game 1947 World Series, accounting for over 1.8 million spectators. In fact, only home and away games involving the Phillies failed to draw two million.[4] The American League pulled in almost 9.5 million, with half of the eight teams drawing over one million (Boston, Cleveland, Detroit and New York). Yankee attendance alone exceeded two million. American League attendance might have approached that of the NL if the St. Louis Browns had drawn more than their paltry 320,474.

Not surprisingly, rumors swirled aplenty about the Browns being purchased and moved out of St. Louis, quite possibly to Baltimore or Los Angeles. Robert Rodenberg, owner of the Baltimore Colts of the All-American Football Conference, was originally thought to be in the lead to land the Browns, but a handful of other potential buyers also emerged in the Chicago, Kansas City, and Los Angeles markets. But a sale of the Browns, and their St. Louis ballpark (the somewhat dilapidated Sportsman's Park, which also hosted the National League Cardinals), was far from a straightforward matter. The hope was that the Cardinals would be interested in purchasing the ballpark from the Browns, but movement on that point had been sluggish at best. Most significant was the opposition by Washington Senators owner Clark Griffith, who quipped, "Bob Rodenberg had better read the rules of baseball before talking about bringing a major-league franchise into Baltimore."[5]

The 1947 National Association convention was a record-breaker, with official registrations reaching 1,200 and upward of 400 additional baseball officials, players, and writers attending the Miami meetings.[6] The convention began officially on December 3 with a welcome address from Judge Wayne Allen, president of the International League, as well as Miami Mayor Robert Floyd, and Dr. Rafael Inclan, president of the Cuban Professional League. Inclan spoke about the large expansion of organized baseball in Cuba and his pleasure in becoming associated with the National Association.[7] The annual banquet was held on December 4, and included a greeting from Florida Governor Millard Caldwell. Eastern League President Tommy Richardson served as master of ceremonies and introduced the new St. Louis Cardinals owner, former US Postmaster General Bob Hannegan. The banquet ended with a two-hour spectacular showcasing local talent from Miami's many nightspots.[8]

The convention spanned several days, with plenty of time built in for attendees to enjoy the many attractions of Miami, as well as a trip to Cuba. (Havana was 228 miles from Miami.) Some convention attendees decided to remain in Miami after the meetings to attend the dedication of the new Everglades National Park on December 6.[9] Both newspaper writers and league presidents took up Havana Mayor Nicolas Castellanos on his invitation to visit the island nation during the convention to see the baseball being played there.[10] Upon his return from the island, National Association President George M. Trautman praised the Cuban leagues, their players, and their fans, noting that in Cuba the game was played year-round.[11] Although the Cuban leagues were considered "unclassified affiliates," they had been approved by the National Association to select minor-league players for their rosters with the consent of their teams. During these meetings, the National Association would expand its presence in Latin America by adding unclassified affiliates in Venezuela and Panama, starting in 1948, while Puerto Rico League President Jorge Cordova also actively pursued the same agreement. Mexican Baseball Commissioner Alejandro Aguilar also announced his league's interest in forming an agreement. "Eventually, perhaps, the majors might even establish farm clubs in Latin-American leagues and uncover future Big League prospects among the native talent," *The Sporting News* editorialized.[12]

However, the single most pressing item facing resolution at the meetings was, again, a request by Pacific Coast League President Clarence Rowland that the league be certified for special dual minor/major-league status, thus raising its standing above that of the American Association.[13] The PCL would in turn change its name to Pacific Major League and be under the supervision of major-league baseball, its commissioner, and its executive committee. However, the requested special status would still require the PML to agree to certain minor-league rules and draft practices. For example, the PML would require a player to have six years of service (instead of the current four years) before they would be eligible for the major-league draft, and the selection price would increase from $10,000 to $25,000. In return, the PML would drop its right to draft players from any Triple-A league teams and would agree to pay increased prices to leagues in the lower classifications, and to waive its rights to draft umpires from any classification.[14] The draft of PCL players in the new organization would not go through the National Association; it would be overseen by the commissioner.[15] This was at least the third time that Rowland had attempted to push this type of arrangement forward.[16]

The request was thought by some to be a means of calming some PCL teams and fans (and owners) who had repeatedly requested immediate recognition and transformation to full major-league status, in addition to a fear by some PCL members that certain teams might "go outlaw" if left to their own means. The request detailed a five-year period in which individual PCL teams could transition from minor- into major-league status, unless the entire PCL itself became a major-league division.

On November 30, before the convention began, American Association President Frank C. Lane met with league directors in Miami to mount an opposition group. Lane said that though he couldn't speak officially at that point, "I am strongly of the opinion we will oppose the inconsistency of the Coast League's proposal."[17]

PCL President Rowland's proposal met significant opposition during the convention, but nonetheless awaited a final decision by the American and National Leagues in their December meetings. Toward the end of the National Association convention Rowland was overhead to say, "I don't know whether or not we are going to get the brush [from the major leagues]. I do know that the Pacific Coast League should be a major league right now, but if it isn't so recognized, a lot of kibitzers who think there's going to be an invasion of Los Angeles and San Francisco may as well mute their trumpets. And the same goes for the fellows who are suggesting that the American and National be expanded to include Los Angeles, San Francisco, Oakland, and Hollywood."[18] Before leaving Miami to attend the major-league meetings in New York, Happy Chandler denied that he was going to recommend to major-league owners that the PCL clubs in Los Angeles, San Francisco, Oakland, and Hollywood be reorganized into major-league clubs, but the *San Francisco Examiner* wrote that "Chandler positively will make such a recommendation and it's better than an even money that it will receive the blessing of the American and National leagues."[19]

Meanwhile, Robert L. Finch, director of public relations for the National Association, urged that major building and rehabilitation be done on ballparks throughout the minor leagues. Finch estimated the total property value of the 388 parks in the minors to be more than $54 million. Finch said a survey of minor-league ballparks showed that many were in need of significant repair. "For an institution that is proclaimed to be the national game of the United States of America, this is not too creditable a picture," he said..[20] Unsatisfactory conditions in Triple-A parks included lack of restroom and concession spaces, poor seats, no roofs or ramps, inadequate parking, and insufficiently short left fields. Aging grandstands and locations in industrial and/or poor neighborhoods were also mentioned. According to the survey, Double-A ballparks had many of the same deficiencies, and some were too small and fire hazards. Ballparks in Class A leagues lacked visitor club dressing rooms, inadequate umpire quarters (including no baths), poor restrooms, a lack of public transportation to the ballparks and grandstand posts obstructing fan views. Class B, C, and D ballparks were also cited for poor drainage, excessive mud, light poles on the field, condemned facilities, inadequate drinking facilities, and more.[21] Finch concluded, "It is an axiom that where the best people go the crowd will follow. The best people will not patronize shabby parks for long."

In other business, Minneapolis was approved as the site for the 1948 National Association meetings.[22] Discussion of making batting helmets mandatory also peaked in light of the near-fatal beaning of St. Paul shortstop Bob Ramazzotti. Reporters noted an atypically large number of sporting-goods manufacturers on hand. Wares displayed ranged from bats, mitts, and player equipment to ballpark lights, tarpaulins, and animated scoreboards. Coca-Cola was there handing out key-chain souvenir flashlights.[23]

A player-pension plan for minor-league players similar to that for major leaguers was presented in Miami, but no commitments were made and it remained doubtful that such a plan would ever be approved because of factors such as brief careers, frequent movement, and the relatively low pay of many minor-league players.[24]

Some significant decisions were made, by delegates, in part because of a new arrangement that allowed league presidents, along with two delegates from each club, to be the only parties to vote on official Association matters. The delegates approved a uniform standard for resiliency of the baseball that would go into full effect in 1949. Other regulations approved included a larger player limit for teams in Class B, C, and D leagues, with the aim being better baseball, and an agreement that both players and club officials sign official affidavits on player contracts to avoid any salary shenanigans.[25] Protection and membership fees for the National Association were increased temporarily for the year, from 2 percent to 3 percent for player transactions. All minor-league players were approved to play winter ball after October 31 regardless of length of service to their home club. This rule was intended to make it easier for players to participate in Cuban, Panamanian, Puerto Rican, and Venezuelan league play, all under agreement with the National Association.

Several scoring rule changes were adopted with the aim of greater uniformity in scoring throughout the minor leagues. A December 4 meeting of more than 30 official scorers, statisticians, and writers at the McAllister Hotel led by Bob Hooey, sports editor of the (Columbus) *Ohio State Journal*. Their recommendations included requesting all news wire services to use the same type of box-score form; permitting the official scorer some discretion on plays where a batter is awarded three bases because a fielder throws his glove at a batted ball (should the batter be credited with a single, double, or triple; should the fielder be charged with an error?); changing the rule so that a batter interfered with while running to first base would not be charged with an at-bat; charging the catcher with an error on catcher's-interference plays; listing of each pitcher's complete record in the box score, including runs and earned runs allowed; requiring a starting pitcher to work at least five full innings of a nine-inning game before being eligible for a win; and recommending that a digest of differences between scoring rules in the minors and majors be compiled.[26] In a related move, National Association President Trautman was expected to create a committee of writers and scorekeepers to "serve as a central bureau for clarification of other scoring problems."[27]

The Western League's hope of expanding from its current eight teams failed, with the Topeka club deciding to remain in the Western Association. Kansas City, Kansas, was determined to be ineligible for a team as long as its twin city in Missouri refused to give up its territorial control. The Cedar Rapids, Iowa, team decided to enter the Three-I League rather than join the Western League.[28] It was reported that Trautman's predecessor, Judge William G. Bramham, who had retired at the 1946 convention and had died in July 1947, was reported to have left an estate estimated at $41,663. The National Association voted to provide his widow with a monthly pension of $200. Bramham was the National Association president from 1932 to 1946.[29]

Several player sales and swaps and player personnel decisions involving minor-league teams were made during the meeting, particularly near its conclusion.[30] The first official deal of the convention was the purchase of right-handed pitcher Dick Callahan by the Atlanta Crackers of the Double-A Southern Association from the Triple-A American Association Louisville Colonels.[31] However, the meetings were lacking in deals involving major-league clubs. "Outside of the sales of veteran Pittsburgh first baseman Elbie Fletcher to the Cleveland Indians and Jeff Heath of the St. Louis Browns to the Braves, the player mart at the convention was dull.[32] The New York Giants were interested in southpaw Johnny Vander Meer of the Reds, but could not come to an agreement on which outfielder Cincinnati wanted in return. The Reds were looking to part with shortstop Eddie Miller, particularly to an interested Cubs club, but no deal emerged. However, former major-league catcher (and future major-league manager) Al Lopez, who had been released by the Indians, was hired as player-manager of the American Association's Indianapolis Indians.[33]

As for the major-league meetings, the American and National Leagues held separate sessions in New York City December 9 and 10, and met jointly on the 11th at the Waldorf-Astoria Hotel. The meetings allowed the major-league magnates to meet Robert E. Hannegan, the new owner of the St. Louis Cardinals, and afforded Baltimore Colts owner Bob Rodenberg the opportunity to test the waters on his proposition to purchase the St. Louis Browns.[34] Issues of high priority for the meetings were possible decisions regarding the drafting of high-school, college, and American Legion players. The American League owners gave league President Will Harridge a new 10-year contract. In July their National League brethren had given their president, Ford Frick, a four-year extension. Both league presidents were paid $40,000 annually.[35]

Controversy had arisen before the meetings, resulting in a high-profile tiff between Commissioner Chandler and Chicago White Sox general manager Leslie M. O'Connor (who had served as secretary to Chandler's predecessor, Kenesaw Mountain Landis). The feud came about when the White Sox signed George Zoeterman, a 17-year-old high-school left-hander from Chicago Christian High School to a

1947 contract as a batting-practice pitcher and a player contract for 1948. The contracts had been approved by A.L. President Harridge.

Chandler voided the deal as being in violation of major-league Rule 3 (often called the "high-school rule") and major-minor league Rule 3, which contained provisions dictating signing of high-school players. He also fined the White Sox $500. O'Connor replied defiantly that the high-school rule explicitly applied to students in schools that were members of the National Federation of High Schools. (Zoeterman's school was not.) Chandler replied that the "high-school rule will continue to be enforced as I have explained to you heretofore." To which O'Connor replied, "I am regretfully obliged to inform you that, so far as our club is concerned, we will observe the rule as written and not otherwise."[36]

A furious Chandler announced that the White Sox team was "denied representation under the major-league agreement" until the team complied with his directive. Chandler had essentially suspended the White Sox from all major-league activities, including the November player draft, and participating in any official business, let alone playing the 1948 season.[37] Chandler also acted to remove O'Connor from the Executive Council. American League President Harridge called a "special meeting" of AL club owners for October 31 in Cleveland.

At the meeting the AL owners were ordered by Chandler to name someone to replace O'Connor on the Executive Council.[38] If O'Connor hoped his league would back him, he was disappointed. The AL owners decided unanimously to "keep hands off" Chandler's decision. They also voted to appoint a new member to replace O'Connor on the Executive Council.[39] A disappointed O'Connor remarked that he would have an announcement the next week about his intentions, "But you shouldn't have much trouble guessing the answer."[40]

The next week the White Sox paid the $500 fine and Chandler lifted the suspensions of O'Connor and the White Sox. O'Connor apologized publicly, offered to resign his position (it was declined, though O'Connor did step down a year later), and admitted to behaving stubbornly and not in the best interests of baseball.

Zoeterman became a free agent, and after graduating in January he was eligible to sign with any major-league club except the White Sox. Zoeterman said he was sorry he couldn't play for his hometown White Sox, but that 12 other major-league clubs had made him offers. He signed with the Chicago Cubs, but left baseball after three years in the minors.

This controversy over the high-school rule led to further action regarding the recruitment of amateurs. The American Association of College Baseball Coaches asked that the majors prohibit the signing of college players until their class had graduated, but although the Executive Council had recommended a "hands-off" policy, the majors tabled the proposal, which basically killed it. A separate suggestion that clubs could not recruit American Legion ballplayers was also tabled and left to die.

The New York Giants had been expected to go all out at the major-league meetings to land pitching help, but determined that other teams were trying to exact too high a price for hurlers. For example, Philadelphia was open to trading but the Giants would have had to give up outfielder-pitcher Carl Hartung and infielder Buddy Blattner. Other clubs asked the Giants for untouchable players like first baseman Johnny Mize, to which Giants GM Mel Ott responded, "Nothing doing." Mize had led the NL in 1947 with 51 home runs, 138 RBIs, and 137 runs scored.[41]

The return of a major-league manager to active status following a suspension would ordinarily have been a mundane affair, but nothing about Leo Durocher was ever boring. Durocher's 1947 suspension as Brooklyn manager was based on an "accumulation of unpleasant incidents" alluded to by Commissioner Chandler. Making things more complicated, replacement manager Burt Shotton had directed the team to the National League pennant in 1947, and a seven-game World Series loss to the Yankees.[42] Rickey had hoped to announce Durocher's return as manager in early December, but resistance to that notion had grown from a small group in Brooklyn (likely the Catholic Youth Organization). Father Vincent J.

Powell, diocesan director of the CYO, had just met with Dodgers president Branch Rickey, who likely shared the CYO's attitudes regarding Durocher.[43] Durocher had met several times with Rickey.[44] The final decision was Rickey's to make, and he said he was not sure yet if Durocher would be asked to manage or if he would renew Shotton.[45]

The fan outcry for Durocher's return began shortly after the end of the World Series, but any official announcement about the issue was slow to emerge. Lou Niss, sports editor of the *Brooklyn Eagle*, wrote, "All the evidence points to Branch Rickey's desire to name Durocher. It must be remembered that he didn't fire him. Commissioner Albert Benjamin Chandler did that."[46] The uncertainty likely contributed to a blunder by the National League at its annual managers' dinner, where the manager of the NL team that had won the pennant was to be recognized. The event was quickly canceled once it was realized that the winning manager, Shotton, was perhaps no longer manager.[47]

The Pittsburgh Pirates rebuilt almost their entire infield, replacing everyone but third baseman Frankie Gustine. "The remainder of the inner works will have a definite Brooklyn tinge," with former Dodgers Eddie Stevens at first, Monty Basgall at second, and Stan Rojek at short.[48] As it happened, Danny Murtaugh emerged as the team's everyday second baseman. The Pirates retained only Ralph Kiner in the outfield so more changes were in the works in the Steel City. The Pirates also sent infielders Billy Cox and Gene Mauch and southpaw Preacher Roe to Brooklyn in exchange for All-Star outfielder Dixie Walker (the 1946 MVP runner-up), right-hander Hal Gregg, and lefty Vic Lombardi. Pittsburgh also sent Brooklyn $100,000. In the end, the Pirates added 18 new faces, including manager Bill Meyer, and released, traded, or sold numerous players, including such notables as right-hander Jim Bagby Jr. (released); first baseman-outfielder and future Hall of Famer Hank Greenberg (retired), and outfielder Gene Woodling (sent to minors, where he was eventually purchased by the Yankees and made substantial contributions to their run of five straight World Series triumphs).

Significant controversy surrounded trades involving St Louis Browns infielder Johnny Berardino. Originally, the Browns had traded Berardino to the Senators for infielder Jerry Priddy and $25,000. However, upon hearing of the trade, Bernardino announced he would retire from baseball to pursue an acting career. Commissioner Chandler refused to immediately cancel the deal, merely holding it in abeyance, but then Senators president Clark Griffith asked the Browns to cancel the trade, which they agreed to do, and Washington instead sold Priddy to St. Louis for $25,000.[49] St. Louis proceeded to trade Berardino again, this time to Cleveland, for outfielder-first baseman George Metkovich and $60,000, with the Browns "guaranteeing delivery of the player." Experts noted that, technically, the trade sending Berardino to Washington could not have been voided until the infielder refused to report to Washington and/or had been asked to be placed onto the voluntarily retired list.[50] At least one owner was not pleased by this, stating, "If a player can get himself sold to the club of his choice by alternately retiring and returning to the active list then the player, and not the club, is dictating the deal."[51]

The New York Yankees finally completed a trade, sending outfielder-third baseman Allie Clark to the Indians for right-handed pitcher Red Embree at the end of the meetings. Ironically the Yanks could have secured Embree from the Tribe when they traded second baseman Joe Gordon to Cleveland in 1946, but the Yanks chose another right-hander, Allie Reynolds, instead. For their part, the Yankees had more important concerns at this time, as Joe DiMaggio remained unsigned, and wanted a significant raise from his 1947 salary of $42,500.[52]

Less than three weeks earlier, the Red Sox had made news by sending nine players plus $165,000 to the St. Louis Browns in two separate deals made on consecutive days. In exchange, the Red Sox received two All-Stars, shortstop Vern Stephens and right-handed pitcher Jack Kramer, plus Ellis Kinder, another righty. Now in their bid to return to the World Series, they picked up another former All-Star, outfielder

Stan Spence, from Washington for second baseman Al Kozar and outfielder Leon Culberson.[53]

Baseball continued tweaking and experimenting with television, as well as night baseball. Early in the meetings the St. Louis Browns, whose attendance continued to lag, pushed forward a proposal to allow them unlimited night ball. However, Browns general manager Bill DeWitt quickly withdrew the proposal, presumably after sensing an overwhelming lack of support by other American League owners. Thus, night baseball rules remained the same as before — the Yankees, Tigers, and Red Sox refused to play more than two night games in any road series, and New York's three teams, the Yankees, Giants, and Dodgers, refused to play more than 14 night games a year in their own ballparks.[54]

National League teams showed no such refusals regarding night ball, and seemed quite amenable to unlimited night play. Seemingly a more progressive league, the National League also recognized the potential of televised baseball, and at the meetings the league named a television committee composed of President Ford Frick and owners Phil Wrigley of Chicago, John Quinn of Boston, and Horace Stoneham of New York. "We don't know exactly what to expect from television in the future, but I believe it will be terrific. It is in the same experimental state which radio was some time ago and we discovered that radio improved attendance. I believe we will find that television will have the same healthy effect," Frick said.[55]

NOTES

1. "Lobby Breezes From Miami," *The Sporting News*, December 10, 1947: 21.
2. "Most Valuable Voting Under Fire," *The Sporting News*, December 10, 1947: 12.
3. "Trading Spiked Shoes for Bedroom Slippers," *The Sporting News*, December 19, 1947: 1.
4. "National Rejoices Over Gate Record," *The Sporting News*, December 17, 1947: 6.
5. "L.A. vs. Baltimore in Bids for Browns," *The Sporting News*, December 10, 1947: 1.
6. "1,200 Register for Convention," *The Sporting News*, December 10, 1947: 5.
7. "Minors Adopt Changes in Their Rules," *The Sporting News*, December 10, 1947: 16.
8. "Banquet Highlights Convention," *The Sporting News*, December 10, 1947: 21.
9. "Scenic Views for Motorists," *The Sporting News*, December 3, 1947: 3.
10. "Warm Greeting in Havana for Convention Delegates," *The Sporting News*, December 10, 1947: 7.
11. "Trautman Visits Cuba: Praises O.B. League," *The Sporting News*, December 10, 1947: 7.
12. "Majors Can Aid Latin-American Unity," *The Sporting News*, December 10, 1947: 12.
13. "Coast Ambitions Facing A.A. Veto," *The Sporting News*, November 19, 1947: 6.
14. "Coast to Make Stab for Major Status at Miami," *The Sporting News*, November 19, 1947: 6.
15. "Coast Demands Dual Major-Minor Status," *The Sporting News*, November 19, 1947: 1.
16. "Rowland Goes Home Empty-Handed," *The Sporting News*, December 17, 1947: 12.
17. "Coast Ambitions Facing A.A. Veto."
18. "Rowland Goes Home Empty-Handed."
19. "Chandler Plan to Suggest Ten-Club Majors Denied," *The Sporting News*, December 10, 1947: 10.
20. "Clean Up, Paint Up Parks — Plea to Minors," *The Sporting News*, December 3, 1947: 1.
21. "Bigger and Better Minor Parks Demanded in Report by Finch," *The Sporting News*, December 3, 1947: 2.
22. "Minneapolis to be Host to '48 Minors' Convention," *The Sporting News*, December 10, 1947: 5.
23. "Lobby Breezes From Miami."
24. "Pension Plan for Minors Offered at Miami Confab," *The Sporting News*, December 10, 1947: 5.
25. "New Standards Go Into Effect in '49; Attempt to Abolish Bonus Rule Defeated," *The Sporting News*, December 10, 1947: 5.
26. "Minors Adopt Many Changes in Their Rules," *The Sporting News*, December 10, 1947: 16.
27. "New Study Planned of Rules on Scoring," *The Sporting News*, December 10, 1947: 21.
28. "Western Expansion Plan Dropped for '48 — Johnson," *The Sporting News*, December 10, 1947: 20.
29. "Bramham Estate Inventoried at $41,663," *The Sporting News*, December 17, 1947: 1.
30. "Many Late Deals and Pilot Choices at Minors' Confab," *The Sporting News*, December 17, 1947: 13.
31. "Lobby Breezes From Miami."

32 "Trade Winds Fall to Whisper Among Miami Palm Trees," *The Sporting News*, December 10, 1947: 17.

33 "Lopez Appointed Manager of Indianapolis Indians," *The Sporting News*, December 10, 1947: 17.

34 "Leagues Meet Dec. 9-10, Joint Session on Dec. 11," *The Sporting News*, December 3, 1947: 5.

35 "Harridge Receives New 10-Year Pact," *The Sporting News*, December 17, 1947: 5.

36 "Exchanges by O'Connor and Chandler Revealed," *The Sporting News*, November 5, 1947: 4.

37 Ibid.

38 "Harridge, Who Approved Contracts, Calls Meeting," *The Sporting News*, November 5, 1947: 4.

39 Ed Burns, "$500 Note Ends O'Connor-Chandler Feud," *The Sporting News*, November 12, 1947, 5-6.

40 "O'Connor an 'Able' Arguer, But Failed to Sway League," *The Sporting News*, November 12, 1947: 6.

41 "Giant Hunt for Pitcher Stalls When Rivals Ask Young Stars," *The Sporting News*, December 12, 1947: 13.

42 "The Lip—And His Future," *The Sporting News*, December 17, 1947: 12.

43 J.G. Taylor Spink, "Looping the Loops," *The Sporting News*, November 19, 1947: 6.

44 "Buildup for Lip as Dodger Pilot Gains Speed," *The Sporting News*, November 19, 1947: 1.

45 "Christmas on December 25—But When Dodger Pilot?" *The Sporting News*, November 12, 1947: 2.

46 "Brooklyn Sports Editor Predicts Return of Leo," *The Sporting News*, November 12, 1947: 2.

47 "Managers' Dinner Lost in Dodger Pilot Shuffle," *The Sporting News*, December 17, 1947: 5.

48 "One Title Already Won by Bucs—They're Tops in N.L. Turnover," *The Sporting News*, December 17, 1947: 9.

49 "Possible Precedent Seen in Dealings for Berardino," *The Sporting News*, December 17, 1947, 7.

50 Ibid.

51 "Berardino The Shadow—He's Here, Then There," *The Sporting News*, December 17, 1947: 9.

52 "Stick-to-Finish Harris Obtains Embree at Last," *The Sporting News*, December 17, 1947: 10.

53 "Deals, Hot in Miami, Chilled in Wintry Blasts at New York," *The Sporting News*, December 17, 1947: 7.

54 "Browns' Move to Permit Unlimited Night Ball Fails," *The Sporting News*, December 17, 1947: 5.

55 "N.L. Studies Television and Its Future in Game," *The Sporting News*, December 17, 1947: 5.

1948

CONCERNS AND CONFLICTS REGARDING TELEVISED BALL GROW STRONGER

By Gary Levy

THE NATIONAL ASSOCIATION OF Professional Baseball Leagues, comprising 58 leagues, held its 47th annual Winter Meetings in Minneapolis December 7-11, 1948, to engage in, among other things, its yearly "carnival of buying and selling baseball talent."[1] More than 1,200 people in all, 1,100 of them officially registered delegates, attended.[2] In advance, there was speculation that many substantial trades and exchanges of talent would take place, and that the delegates would discuss the effect of televised games on attendance, along with recommendations from the two major leagues that rules on bonus payments be amended.[3]

The meetings started on a light note, with a luncheon headlining Frank Frisch, now a coach with the New York Giants; Carl Hubbell, the Giants farm director; Billy Evans, Tigers general manager; Casey Stengel, the new manager of the New York Yankees; Bill Meyer, manager of the Pittsburgh Pirates; Lefty Gomez, the former Yankees hurler; Bill Veeck, owner of the 1948 world champion Cleveland Indians); Leo Durocher, the Giants manager; and George I. Trautman, president of the National Association. The event turned out to be a roast of Frisch more than anything else.

Not surprisingly, Durocher and his stories dominated the event. He told of how in 1934 Dizzy Dean had taken it upon himself to replace Spud Davis as a baserunner in the World Series against the Tigers, without manager Frisch's knowledge or permission. Dean was famously hit in the head on the basepath with a throw but nonetheless finished the game and clinched the Series with a large bump on his head. Durocher also told about how Freddy Fitzsimmons had once said something unflattering to umpire Beans Beardon, who asked him what he had said, to which Fitzsimmons snapped, "You've been guessing all afternoon, so guess what I said." Carl Hubbell reminisced about how he was having problems pitching to Rogers Hornsby. After tossing three fastballs inside, as third baseman Frisch had instructed him to do, Hubbell asked again what he should pitch Hornsby. Frisch replied, "You're the pitcher, I'm just a third baseman."[4]

Unlike the other speakers of the day, president Trautman was the only serious orator, urging everyone to help improve interest in baseball as a pastime, rather than simply winning games. He "asked that the sport always be kept above reproach to justify the faith of youngsters and the public."[5]

At the first business meeting of the gathering, Trautman put forth his recommendation that baseball conduct the annual player draft at the winter meetings. His goal, he said, was to make the draft process more efficient. With all the club owners there, "there could be preliminary discussions and investigations of players desired through the draft. ... The whole thing could be accomplished with a minimum of confusion, with as many as 300 or 400 ballplayers changing hands in the matter of a few hours."[6] Attendees approved a recommendation that the 1949 and 1950 meetings be held in Baltimore and Columbus, Ohio, respectively.[7] They also approved a $5,000 pay raise for Trautman, to $30,000, with three years remaining on his contract.[8]

Three International League cities, Baltimore, Jersey City, and Newark, all showed significantly lower attendance in 1948 because of competition from televised major-league games. League President Frank J. Shaughnessy urged that televising of both major- and minor-league night games be barred because of their negative impact on minor-league gates. Shaughnessy maintained that minor-league night-game attendance was being hurt because televising night games was "simply advising the fans seeking and having time for recreation to get it at home without cost."[9] Association President Trautman added, "Up until now, increased attendance has saved our lives," and that generally ticket prices were stable, but that the increasing costs of minor-league operations presented "a very real problem" for minor-league baseball.

Thus, on day three of the convention, 54 minor-league representatives voted unanimously (the other four minor leagues were not in attendance for the vote) to ban radio and TV telecasts beyond 50 miles from the station."[10] The vote was largely symbolic unless the major leagues also voted it down at their coming meetings, for the ban. The major leagues' concern for the health of minor-league baseball may have been overshadowed by the revenue being promised to them by television moguls.[11]

An amendment presented by Atlanta of the Southern Association to eliminate the bonus rule gained only seven votes and failed. A number of other proposals were also voted down, including limiting each major- and minor-league team to one bonus player a year; fixing the bonus level of the majors at $7,500 and the minors at $5,000; alternatively, fixing the bonus level of the majors and the minors at $6,000; allowing teams to option bonus players under certain waiver conditions; and optioning one year of a bonus player without having to ask waivers. The one change made to the bonus rule was to require that the amount of the bonus be made public before the contract was signed, including "such payments as are made to college men to help them with their education."[12]

In early December Boston Braves shortstop Alvin Dark was overwhelmingly voted the major leagues' 1948 Rookie of the Year. Dark got 27 votes, with left-

THE ESTATE THAT RUTH BUILT

One subject of much discussion was the controversy and drama that loomed as two parties readied to fight over the estate of George Herman "Babe" Ruth, who had died on August 16, 1948. Ruth's final will was dated August 9, 1948, and in it he left the majority of his estate of about $400,000 to his wife, Claire, along with his "furnishings, paintings, stockholdings, motorboat, and other 'odds and ends.'"[1] Ruth also specified that upon Claire's death, the George Herman Ruth Foundation was to get 10 percent of what remained in the estate left to her. His two adopted daughters, Dorothy (from his first marriage) and Julia (from his marriage to Claire), would split the other 90 percent. Each daughter was also bequeathed $5,000.

Daughter Dorothy hired a lawyer, asserted that she was the victim of unfair provisions, and did not accept the $5,000 cash bequest. The lawyer, Harrold T. Garrity, said Dorothy had "signed a waiver when the will was probated August 23, agreeing not to contest its terms, but found subsequently that she wasn't being fairly dealt with." Garrity said she had signed the waiver in "haste and grief." Additionally, when the trust fund was originally created in 1927, Dorothy was named Babe's beneficiary. However, in the week before his death, Babe removed Dorothy as beneficiary and replaced her with Claire.

Garrity declared, "The first thing I am going to do is see the widow and try to learn whether she's prepared to make some adjustments in behalf of the girl."

1 William Henderson, "Legal Battle Over Ruth's Estate Threatened by Adopted Daughter," *The Sporting News*, December 15, 1948: 2. All quoted material here comes from Henderson's article.

hander Gene Bearden of Cleveland coming in second with 8 votes and Phillies outfielder Richie Ashburn, Philadelphia Athletics left-hander Lou Brissie, and Red Sox first baseman Bill Goodman tied with three votes each. This was the second Rookie of the Year award; the 1947 winner was Brooklyn's Jackie Robinson. Dark had played a pivotal role in helping the Braves to their first pennant since 1914.[13] (In 1947 and 1948, one major-league Rookie of the Year was named; starting in 1949 a winner was picked for each league.)

Early in the meetings the Chicago Cubs got things moving by acquiring Pittsburgh third baseman Frankie Gustine in exchange for catcher Clyde McCullough. The move was expected to help each team address a weakness. Chicago also sent left-handed pitcher Cliff Chambers to the Pirates in exchange for right-handed pitcher Calvin McLish.[14] Few other trades of note took place.[15]

On December 9 Commissioner A.B. "Happy" Chandler announced that he would lead an inquiry into the Giants' signing of Fred Fitzsimmons as a coach allegedly while he was still a member of the Boston Braves. The case was made a bit more exasperating by the fact that it was somehow associated with Giants manager Durocher, who had been suspended by Chandler in 1947 for conduct detrimental to baseball. "Evidence has been presented to me that the New York ballclub tampered with Fitzsimmons even before the 1948 season ended," Chandler said. "If this is the case, that constitutes a breach of baseball law, and I would not be doing my job if I were to overlook that matter—whether it concerned a club that Leo Durocher is connected with or anyone else's club."[16] The commissioner said it was not the Braves who had filed a complaint, but that was not relevant.[17]

The major leagues held their meetings December 13-15 at the Palmer House in Chicago, and quickly voted down the National Association's proposal to limit radio and TV telecasts of major-league games.[18] On the bonus issue, they deferred any action pending action by a joint committee, to be established by the commissioner, in early 1949.[19] It was reported that most major-league owners favored maintaining the current rules that restricted teams from signing players with significantly large bonus payments, but wanted more vigorous enforcement of the rules. The owners' sentiment was that "the present rule provides too many loopholes for evasion and, in plain words, 'there is a lot of cheating going on, which should be checked.'"[20]

In less controversial matters, American League Vice President Connie Mack and National League Vice President Philip K. Wrigley we re-elected.[21]

The two leagues gave a green light to more night baseball. The Senators and Browns had sought unlimited night games; this was rejected, but the American League owners did agree to permit teams to schedule at least four home night games, instead of the previously allowed two, with every other team without having to get their consent.[22] The National League set the number at five games, led by a strong push by Boston's Braves. The difference was expected to be ironed out in a joint meeting under Chandler the next day. Both leagues banned night ball on Sundays, on a day before a scheduled doubleheader, or on the night of a visiting team's departure for another city.[23] National League owners also voted that no team could refuse fewer than five night games with any other club; American League owners made it four. Commissioner Chandler could have cast a vote to make the two leagues agree on a common number, but he said that was unnecessary since there were no conflict of interests involved.[24]

Gabe Paul, assistant to the president of the Cincinnati Reds, followed up on Trautman's proposal and recommended a dramatic shift in how players would be drafted by minor- and major-league clubs. Unlike the past, when drafts were conducted via mail or telegraph over several weeks in November with the first team filing for a player receiving the player, the new model proposed that the draft order follow the order of finish the previous season, from the worst up, with the draft continuing until the top teams finished selecting. Selections would take place over a two- or three-day period. The proposal had been studied by a committee of minor- and major-league owners and administrators appointed by Trautman, and major-league owners appeared supportive. An official vote on the proposal was set for the 1949 convention.[25]

Hall of Famer Eddie Collins, acting president of the Association of Professional Ball Players of America, told the leagues that the association's fund to help out "aged and indigent" ex-players were running low because of less revenue from All-Star Games. Commissioner Chandler reassured Collins, and American League and National League Presidents Will Harridge and Ford Frick promised to cooperate to maintain the fund when necessary.[26]

George Weiss, general manager of the Yankees, declared that he was ready to deal any player on the roster except for Joe DiMaggio and Tommy Henrich. White Sox general manager Frank Lane was reported to be particularly interested in Yankees third baseman Bill Johnson. Lane was also eyeing St. Louis Browns third baseman Bob Dillinger (as were up to five other teams), and had offered as much as $100,000 for the infielder. Lane was also supposedly after Yankees pitcher Allie Reynolds.[27] The Athletics' Connie Mack supposedly had offered $150,000 in cash along with five players in exchange for Dillinger.[28] Giants manager Leo Durocher was also said to have claimed that any player on this roster was available, including Johnny Mize.[29] Detroit joined the ranks of teams seeking a deal with the White Sox, trying to get White Sox second baseman Cass Michaels.[30]

None of these players changed addresses. Many blamed the lack of trades on mischief-maker Bill Veeck, owner of the 1948 World Series champion Cleveland Indians, who all but admitted that he was acting to prevent his team's strongest rivals from making themselves better via trade. "Every time one of the better clubs in his circuit steps out to make a deal, the dynamic Cleveland owner throws a block with a better offer," one sportswriter wrote.[31] Veeck had offered infielder Johnny Berardino to several teams, including the Yankees, Tigers, and White Sox, but there were no takers. The Giants, meanwhile, tried unsuccessfully to pry lefty Johnny Vander Meer from the Reds for infielder Bill Rigney.[32] Cleveland did sign former Indians catcher and Tigers manager Steve O'Neill to return as a coach in 1949.[33] (O'Neill had been recently fired by the Tigers.)

The Chicago Cubs swung a deal with the Phillies for two right-handed pitchers, knuckleballer Dutch Leonard and Walter Dubiel, in exchange for first baseman Ed Waitkus and right-handed pitcher Hank Borowy. The Indians acquired right-hander Early Wynn and first baseman Mickey Vernon from the Senators for right-handed pitchers Joe Haynes and Ed Klieman and 1948 World Series star first baseman Eddie Robinson.[34] After hearing of the Cleveland trade, Yankees manager Casey Stengel (whose team had traded earlier for pitcher Fred Sanford) lamented, "This is a rugged league. You go to bed winning the pennant and wake up in second place."[35]

The Yankees had been able to acquire St. Louis Browns right-handed pitcher Fred Sanford and catcher Roy Partee for $100,000, catcher Sherm Lollar, and right-handed pitchers Red Embree and Dick Starr. After the trade was concluded, the Browns' DeWitt declared, "There will be no more major transactions by the Browns"— which seemed to close what had been fairly widespread speculation that St. Louis would be trading third baseman Bob Dillinger.[36]

The major leagues finalized business by approving Brooklyn as the location for the 1949 All-Star Game. In what seemed to be an annual occurrence, the Triple-A Pacific Coast League again requested special status that would give them additional protection from their players being drafted and to receive a higher payment for players who were drafted. After listening to the pleas made by PCL President Clarence Rowland, the majors again rejected the request.[37]

The owners later attempted to create an "invasion barrier" to keep major-league teams from popping up on the West Coast without the consent of all major-league members. They declared that "minor leagues or clubs applying for major league classification must assume responsibility for any necessary adjustments of territorial rights of others, must have adequate population, income and park facilities and must establish that operation once the major league status requested is practical and justified."[38] The plan must have worked, because wealthy oilman and politician Edwin Pauley, who had been vying to purchase the St. Louis Browns and move them to LA, said he had given up on the

APPARENT BASEBALL COMMUNICATION ISSUES OF THE 1940S

Happy Chandler wasn't thrilled when he spoke at the minor-league convention banquet. He said, "It is our mission to keep baseball at a high level. If you are going to fire a fellow, tell him about it first. Don't let him read about it in the papers."[1]

Chandler was likely referring to the Detroit front office firing manager Steve O'Neill. O'Neill had been fired, and was notified by a newsman asking for a comment. Said O'Neill, "The least they could do was to let me know before they released the story to the papers." The Tigers indicated that they had sent a letter and a telegram, but neither arrived before the story was released. General manager Billy Evans noted that the decision not to rehire O'Neill was made on a Saturday morning. According to Evans, "At that time, we decided not to release the story until Monday and I immediately sent O'Neill an air mail special letter telling him that he was not to be retained in 1949." Evans continued, "But fearful that the story might leak out if we waited until Monday to officially release it, we later decided to break the story Saturday afternoon. We then sent O'Neill a telegram."

Making the story even more complex was the fact that Evans and O'Neill had a previous relationship in Cleveland. Here is the late-arriving letter sent to O'Neill by Evans.[2]

> Dear Steve:
>
> Knowing that you are much concerned as to your status for the 1949 season, I have been equally concerned about getting the information to you at the earliest possible moment.
>
> The consensus of the Detroit club is that a change in management is desirable. In these days of quick managerial changes your record of six years as manager of the Tigers is definitely out of the ordinary. I am inclined to think that the announcement may come within a day or two, and therefore I am trying to get the rather unhappy message to you before you read about it in the paper. Baseball is like that – a precarious business from an executive standpoint. I speak from experience.
>
> I am sure you know that it is not an easy story for me to tell you. Just prior to the close of the season I expressed to you the uncertainty as to next year's picture.
>
> We have been together under similar circumstances. However, at that time, I was erased from the picture before you were.
>
> I am hopeful that in some manner I can strengthen the club for the 1949 season. Just how it can be done at this time I have no idea because of player scarcity. Yet I realized it is expected I somehow improve the Tigers. That remains to be seen.
>
> It was nice to come back to the big leagues to work with you, since you first served as a big league manager under my direction. I have enjoyed the last two years very much. I do hope that you make a connection that will prove a happy and satisfactory one. Kindest regards.

1 "Chandler Swings at Tiger Tactics," *The News-Journal* (Wilmington, Delaware), December 10, 1948: 28.

2 "Did You Ever Wonder How a Big-league Manager Is Fired?" *Detroit Free Press*, November 8, 1948: 21.

idea. "Too many complications," Pauley said. "It would cost in the millions before you could buy a franchise, then gain Coast League rights to move an American or National League club into their territory."[39]

As expected, Commissioner Chandler met with Giants manager Leo Durocher, team treasurer Edgar Feeley, and new coach Fred Fitzsimmons to discuss the accusation that the Giants had tampered with Fitzsimmons while he was employed by the Boston Braves. Chandler announced that no decision regarding the accusation would be announced until the following month at the earliest.[40] All parties remained relatively silent on the matter; speculation was that Chandler would fine Durocher and Fitzsimmons. Durocher admitted that he had made an "innocent technical mistake" in talking with Fitzsimmons.[41] Apparently, such underhanded activities were not as rare as Chandler thought, as the Browns' Bill DeWitt later asserted that similar types of discussions had in previous years led to at least two of his coaches being signed by other clubs while still in his team's employ. He identified them as Earle Combs and Zack Taylor (signed by the Red Sox and Pirates respectively).[42] Regardless, major-league owners later voted to change the legal status of coaches, by first removing them from the reserve list and then giving them new contracts that would make them free agents once their team's season was over.[43]

The report on 1948 attendance showed that it was up in the American League and down in the National League. American League attendance was 11,150,099, an increase of 1,528,917 from 1947. National League attendance was 9,770,743, a decrease of 617,727. National League teams leading in attendance (adding together home and road figures) were Brooklyn (3,050,523), New York (2,687,599), and Boston (2,665,123).[44] The Pittsburgh Pirates set a new home attendance record of 1,517,021, topping their old record by 178,078. Second behind the Pirates were the New York Giants, who drew 1,459,269 to the Polo Grounds, and the World Series runner-up Boston Braves, with 1,455,439. American League home attendance leaders were the World Series champion Cleveland Indians (2,620,627) followed by the New York Yankees (2,373,901).[45]

The regular disagreements and quarrels among baseball writers and fans surfaced again as Stan Musial was named the National League Most Valuable Player after a season in which he hit .376, batted in 131 runs, and blasted 39 homers. It was his third MVP Award, the others coming in 1943 and 1946. Braves righthander Johnny Sain and infielder Alvin Dark were a distant second and third behind Musial. Somewhat absurdly, some thought that Musial had won in part because he had such a "bad year" in 1947, when he "only" hit for a .312 average, with 95 runs batted in and 19 home runs. On hearing such rumblings, Musial replied, "Maybe you and I have different ideas as to what constitutes a 'bad year.' I hit 312, which ain't hay, and I knocked in only eight fewer runs than I did the year before. I hit more home runs than I ever did in the majors before."[46]

Cleveland player-manager Lou Boudreau was voted the American League MVP by a wide margin after he batted .355 with 106 RBIs and 18 homers. Joe DiMaggio and Ted Williams were second and third respectively.

NOTES

1 "Baseball Talent on Sale This Week at Convention of Minor Leagues," *Hartford Courant,* December 5, 1948: 3.

2 "Major Leaguers 'Cut Up' at Minor Loop Luncheon," *The Sporting News,* December 15, 1948: 6.

3 "Minor Leagues Meet to Trade," *Washington Post,* December 5, 1948: C6.

4 "Major Leaguers 'Cut Up' at Minor Loop Luncheon."

5 Ibid.

6 Carl Lundquist (United Press), "Trautman Urges Big Clearing Plan," *Washington Post,* December 9, 1948: B8. There was no action taken on this proposal.

7 "Baltimore Selected for '49 Conclave," *The Sporting News,* December 15, 1948: 5.

8 "Major League Moguls Move Into Chicago," *Chicago Daily News,* December 11, 1948: A2; "Minor Loop Club Owners Not Worried," *Hartford Courant,* December 11, 1948: 9.

9 "Minors Would Ban Night-Game Video," *New York Times,* December 6, 1948: 33.

10 Ibid.

11 Edgar G. Brands, "Coast's Major Aspirations Dealt New Setback," *The Sporting News,* December 22, 1948: 2.

12 "Baltimore Selected for '49 Conclave," *The Sporting News,* December 15, 1948: 5.

13 John Drebinger, "Alvin Dark, Braves, Named Rookie of Year in Majors," *New York Times,* December 5, 1948: 81.

14 Irving Vaughan, "Cubs Get Gustine; McCullough, Chambers Go," *Chicago Tribune,* December 9, 1948: C1.

15 "Major League Bid Shelved by Pauley," *The Sporting News,* December 22, 1948: 2.

16 "Fred Fitzsimmons Goes Before Chandler Tuesday in 'Tampering' Inquiry," *Boston Globe,* December 10, 1948: 46.

17 "Chandler Denies Making Scapegoat of Durocher," *New York Times,* December 10, 1948: 37.

18 "Majors Vote Down Minors' Broadcast Ban," *Chicago Daily News,* December 14, 1948: B2.

19 Irving Vaughan, "Major Leagues Wind Up their Annual Confab," *Chicago Tribune,* December 15, 1948: C1.

20 "Alvin Dark, Braves, Named Rookie of Year in Majors."

21 John Drebinger, "Yanks Get Sanford, Partee from Braves," *New York Times,* December 14, 1948: 41.

22 Ibid.

23 Ibid.

24 "Major Leagues Wind Up Their Annual Confab."

25 E.G. Brands, "Radical Change Considered for Minors Draft," *The Sporting News,* December 15, 1948: 11.

26 "Major League Moguls Move Into Chicago."

27 Irving Vaughan, "Sox Bid for Yanks' Reynolds, Johnson: Tigers Push to Get Michaels," *Chicago Tribune,* December 8, 1948: C1.

28 John Drebinger, "Minors Seek to Limit Baseball Broadcasts and Telecasts," *New York Times,* December 10, 1948: 37.

29 John Drebinger, "Giants and Yankees in Trading Mood," *New York Times,* December 8, 1948: 45.

30 "Sox Bid for Yanks Reynolds, Johnson: Tigers Push to Get Michaels."

31 "Minors Seek to Limit Baseball Broadcasts and Telecasts."

32 Dan Daniel, "Four-Man Swap by Cubs, Pirates Breaks Ice Jam Holding Up Trade Flow," *The Sporting News,* December 15, 1948: 9.

33 "Minors Seek to Limit Baseball Broadcasts and Telecasts."

34 John Drebinger, "Indians Land Vernon and Wynn While Phils Get Waitkus," *New York Times,* December 15, 1948: 49.

35 "Casey Goes to Bed in First Place, Wakes Up in Second," *The Sporting News,* December 22, 1948: 7.

36 "Yanks Get Sanford, Partee from Braves."

37 "Major Leagues Wind Up Their Annual Confab."

38 "Ex-Player, Ex-Pilot Steve Given Tribe Coaching Role," *The Sporting News,* December 15, 1948: 9.

39 "Coast's Major Aspirations Dealt New Setback."

40 "Major Leagues Wind Up their Annual Confab."

41 "Braves Acquire Pete Reiser in Late Deal With Brooklyn," *Christian Science Monitor,* December 15, 1948: 18.

42 "DeWitt Urges Coach, Scout 'Open Season,'" *The Sporting News,* December 15, 1948: 2.

43 Dan Daniel, "Majors Lift Coaches Off 'Hot Seat,' Fitzsimmons Case Causes Rule Change," *The Sporting News,* December 22, 1948: 6.

44 "N.L.'s '48 Gate 9,770,743, Giving Majors 20,920,842," *The Sporting News,* December 22, 1948: 6.

45 Ibid.

46 Tom Meany, "Says Musial Tops 'Em All," *The Sporting News,* December 15, 1948: 10.

— 1949 —
BONUSES, BARGAINS, AND BROADCASTS

By Jeremy Green

Introduction and Context

Minor-League Winter Meeting

THE 1949 WINTER MEETINGS SAW several firsts for the National Association of Professional Baseball Leagues: the first time a meeting was held in Baltimore, the first time a player draft was held during a meeting, and the first time an incumbent Association president missed a meeting. The meeting itself was held at the Lord Baltimore Hotel from December 5 to 9. Baltimore hoped to use the meeting to promote itself as a future home for a major-league franchise. Having a storied history as an early center of professional baseball and having fielded major-league teams in the late nineteenth/ early twentieth century, Baltimore was enthusiastic about the sport. Attendance for Baltimore's International League team, the Orioles, was impressive and exceeded that of several major league teams.[1] Baltimore Mayor Thomas D'Alessandro expressed the wish of a future big-league franchise for the city in his opening remarks to the convention.[2]

The Baltimore session was one of the largest Winter Meetings to date, it was reported.[3] Orioles business manager Herb Armstrong and owner Jack Dunn received accolades from the local and national press for their handling of the gathering, which brought more than 2,500 baseball professionals representing 59 minor leagues to the city.[4]

The meeting was marred, however, by the absence of the Association president, George Trautman, who was recuperating from ulcer surgery at White Cross Hospital in Columbus, Ohio. Vice President Frank J. Shaughnessy presided over the meeting in Trautman's place.[5]

The National Association meeting was also notable for the extent to which the major leagues dominated affairs in Baltimore. Minor-league clubs voted and acted in accord with their major-league affiliates on the important issues discussed at the convention, such as the Bonus rule.[6]

The impact of television on minor-league attendance, stirred considerable tension and was the object of much discussion at the Baltimore meetings.

Major-League Winter Meeting

The major leagues met at the Commodore Hotel in New York City from December 12 to 14. Like the minor-league meetings, the New York sessions were dominated by discussions of broadcasting, the bonus rule, and the rule for recruiting high-school players, as well as trades. Though there remained many matters to be discussed regarding TV and radio, some of the controversy over broadcast rights for games and player pensions had been largely defused by Commissioner A.B. "Happy" Chandler before the Winter Meetings. Chandler signed a seven-year contract with the Mutual Broadcasting Company and the Gillette Company to broadcast World Series games; baseball received $1,370,000 and earmarked the money for the players' pension fund.[7] The American and National Leagues remained divided on several key issues, such as regulations for night games, playoff tiebreaking protocols, and whether or not to repeal the Bonus rule.[8]

Player Movement

Minor Leagues

In previous years, the minor-league draft had been conducted remotely via mail or telegram; in 1949 for the first time, a draft was conducted at the Baltimore meetings using a system of preferential draws.[9] Starting with Triple-A clubs and continuing down to Class C, teams selected draftees in reverse order of their finish. Thus, league leaders got the last picks. A bulletin board was set up in the hotel to track the order of teams and transactions, and clubs signed 222 players, a record for the time, for a total of $449,050.[10]

Among major transactions, the Chicago Cubs sold relief pitcher Bob Muncrief to their Triple-A Los Angeles club.[11] Another notable deal, the most expensive to date conducted between a Pacific Coast League club and a major-league team involved Harold Saltzman, a right-handed pitcher with the Portland Beavers, who was sold to the Cleveland Indians for $100,000.[12] A University of Oregon graduate, Saltzman had joined Portland at the tail end of the 1948 season as a reliever after being called up from the Salem club. During the Beavers' spring training in 1949, he was coached by former Tigers pitcher Tommy Bridges, and during the season he won 23 games, including four shutouts.[13] (Saltzman was 11-10 for Indians Triple-A farm team San Diego, and then left Organized Baseball.)

Major Leagues

One of the biggest player transactions at the major-league meeting was a trade between the Giants and the Braves in which New York acquired shortstop Alvin Dark and second baseman Eddie Stanky in return for Boston outfielder Willard Marshall, third baseman Sid Gordon, shortstop Buddy Kerr, and pitcher Sam Webb.[14] The Braves did brisk business with other teams in the National League, selling outfielder Marvin Rickert to Pittsburgh for cash and trading pitcher Bill Voiselle to the Cubs for infielder Gene Mauch and cash. Also in the National League, the Cardinals sent outfielder Ron Northey and infielder Lou Klein to the Reds for outfielder Harry Walker.[15]

In the American League a St. Louis Browns third baseman Bob Dillinger and outfielder-first baseman Paul Lehner were traded to the Philadelphia Athletics for outfielder Ray Coleman, infielder Frankie Gustine, infielder Bill DeMars, and outfielder Rocco Ippolitto, plus $100,000 in cash. Philadelphia traded third baseman Hank Majeski to the Chicago White Sox for relief pitcher Ed Kleiman. The Detroit Tigers traded right-hander Lou Kretlow and $100,000 to the Browns for second baseman Gerry Priddy. The Tigers offered $170,000 to the Browns for infielder Connie Berry and outfielder Earl Rapp, but St. Louis declined the offer.[16]

The Business Side

Minor Leagues

The Bonus rule was a key topic at the Baltimore meeting. The rule targeted major-league teams that signed players for bonuses in excess of $4,000, and then sent them to minor-league affiliates. According to the rule, clubs that failed to place a bonus player on the major-league roster for at least two seasons lost their rights to the player.[17]

In a caucus, a majority of minor-league teams voted to end the Bonus rule but fell 13 votes shy of the three-quarters majority needed to strike down the rule.[18] In terms of major-league affiliations, the Cardinals and Reds were among the most ardent supporters of the rule, with the Phillies leading the opposition.[19]

The minors voted in favor of changing the regulations for high-school-age players. Under the new rule, a high-school student could sign with a professional club after the class in which he first entered high school had graduated.[20]

This altered the previous arrangement, in which a player who had either left school early or who did not finish high school on schedule had to wait until his last enrolled class (potentially later than the class in which he started school) graduated to enter Organized Baseball.[21]

One motion defeated by the minors was an amendment that would have given clubs in lower classifications a June 1 deadline to sign players lacking any professional experience for the following season. The minors also voted down several additional amendments, including an unrestricted draft for players with eight to nine years of experience, ending the draft for the Pacific Coast League, allowing 15 days for the recording of contracts and sales, and a proposal from Joe Cronin to move back the deadline for transferring players to 30 days after the season's end for the assignee's club.[22]

The new medium of television further divided the minor leagues, in particular the question of whether they should adopt the same regulations as the majors for broadcasts. Even though only 2.3 percent of all US households owned a television in 1949, a lack of programming meant that the networks used baseball to fill time, and over half the stations covered minor-league games.[23] Eight of the 59 circuits voted against adopting the regulations on the grounds that they would make leagues powerless over their own territories, and that the minors required their own regulations.[24] Indeed, the minors were feeling threatened by the new medium. There was talk of eliminating minor-league franchises anywhere within 50 miles of stations that broadcast major-league games. The New England League, which folded after the 1949 season, blamed its demise on the advent of televised baseball.[25] The vote did allow clubs control over the broadcast of home and away games by stations within their territories, but not those by stations that covered major- and minor-league teams outside the home club's territory and in the opposition's territory.[26]

Several rules regarding the conduct of play were recommended during the Baltimore meetings. Among the changes suggested by the scoring committee were:

1. A unanimous vote to credit a batter with a single when an infielder tossed his glove and it made contact with the ball; the fielder would be charged with an error.

2. In the case of glove contact by an outfielder, the batter would get a single, double, or triple, based on the umpire's judgment, and the fielder would be charged with an error.

3. A batter who bunts with two men on base and fails to advance both runners would no longer be credited with a sacrifice.

4. Any player who allows a runner to reach first base or advance to another base due to interference would be charged with an error. The current rule gave an error only to a catcher who tipped a batter's bat.

5. A player must appear in at least two-thirds of his team's games to qualify for the batting championship.

6. The definition of an earned run was made clearer.

7. Pitching records would now show the number of home runs hit off a pitcher.[27]

The Chicago Cubs acquired a much-needed new minor-league affiliate during the Baltimore meetings with their purchase of Newark's Triple-A club. The Cubs wanted to move their new acquisition to Springfield, Massachusetts, which was lacking a minor-league club after the collapse of the New England League. The Cubs had an affiliation with Los Angeles of the Pacific Coast League, but saw that club as more of an independent team, designed to win games and draw fans, than to suit their developmental purposes.[28]

Also written into the major-minor league rules was recognition for the special status of playing managers by formalizing the minor-league practice that playing managers could not be drafted without their consent.[29]

Finally, the minors selected St. Petersburg, Florida, as the location for their 1950 Winter Meetings.[30]

Major Leagues

The major-league meetings in New York covered much of the same ground as the minor-league meetings and had many of the same concerns. The chief issue in New York, as it had been in Baltimore, was the Bonus rule. While the minors had voted against the rule but did not have the required three-quarters majority, the two major leagues were divided on retaining the Bonus rule, with the National League voting 6 to 2 to retain it while the American League voted 5 to 3 against. This left the deciding vote to Commissioner Chandler, a longtime opponent of the Bonus rule, who cast a vote against it. Chandler was confident that the minor leagues would amend their decision

DEPARTMENT OF JUSTICE MAKES AN ANNOUNCEMENT ABOUT ITS INVESTIGATION OF BROADCASTING AND TELEVISING BASEBALL GAMES

The following is a press release issued by the US Department of Justice on October 27, 1949.[1]

Attorney General J. Howard McGrath today announced that the Department of Justice was suspending further action in its investigation of alleged restraints in the broadcasting and telecasting of major league baseball games until such time as the situation can be evaluated as it will exist under new major league rules recently adopted by baseball. Substantial changes in the major league broadcasting and telecasting rules were adopted by representatives of the two major leagues in an effort to eliminate the causes of complaints which led to the Department's investigation. The Department is informed that these changes are being put into effect immediately.

Herbert A. Bergson, Assistant Attorney General in charge of the Antitrust Division, in commenting on the matter, stated that the investigation which has been in progress by the department was instituted following complaints concerning alleged restrictions imposed by the major leagues upon the play-by-play broadcasting and telecasting of their games. He said that the Department's investigation has been directed toward determining whether unreasonable restraints have been imposed by the major leagues which would deny to radio and television stations reasonable access to the broadcasting and telecasting of the games of major league clubs wherever the individual major league club is itself willing to grant or sell those rights....

Complaints received by the Department of Justice over a period of time were directed principally against a major league rule requiring each major league club to refuse to permit the broadcast or telecast of its own games at any time from a station located within 50 miles of the ball park of another major or minor league baseball club without the consent of the other baseball club. This area was known as the local club's "home territory." The Department was informed that many baseball clubs used this veto power completely to prevent the broadcast in their home territories of baseball games played by other clubs.

Some baseball clubs in the minor leagues required local radio stations to pay them for the privilege of broadcasting games played by other teams. Some clubs granted limited consents to the broadcast of games of other team which, in effect, gave the exclusive right to broadcast all baseball games in the area to a single local radio station, and denied this right to all other sponsors and local stations. Complainants had also asserted that the contract between the commissioner of baseball, the Mutual Broadcasting System, and the sponsor of the world series games denied many people the opportunity to hear these games because no Mutual station happened to be located in their particular areas.

Under the new rule the local club will have no power to object to the broadcasting or telecasting of the major league games of other clubs in its home territory at any other time. The local club will have no power to sell its consent to a broadcast or telecast of the game of another club even within this period. It will not be necessary for a station to pay the local baseball club for the right to broadcast or telecast games played by other clubs. In addition, the Department has been informed that the local major or minor league clubs will no longer be permitted to give a local radio station or sponsor the exclusive right to broadcast the games of other clubs in its home territory, or to designate the station that will broadcast or telecast such game....

Attorney General J. Howard McGrath stated: "Baseball is accurately referred to as the great American game. It is also an important commercial enterprise upon which thousands of Americans depend for their livelihood. Both the fans who desire to hear or see baseball broadcasts or telecasts, and the businessmen engaged directly or indirectly in bringing these broadcasts and telecasts to the public, are entitled to freedom from unreasonable restraints. It is hoped that the changes which have been put into effect as a result of the Department's investigation will have this effect."

1 Dean A. Sullivan, *Late Innings: A Documentary History of Baseball 1945-1972* (Lincoln: University of Nebraska Press, 2002), 43-45; Sullivan's text is obtained from the original source, Subcommittee of the Committee on Interstate and Foreign Commerce, Broadcasting and Televising Baseball Games, 83rd Congress, 1st sess., 1953, 13-15.

to retain the rule in a mail vote.[31] Chandler explained his opposition to the rule in a speech to the assembled major-league magnates:

"The wisdom of the rule has always been questioned by a substantial number of the clubs and provides a temptation to both players and managers to attempt to evade it. Its enforcement has therefore been difficult, and in my opinion the best interests of baseball will be served by its repeal."[32]

As in the Baltimore meeting, the new rule for high-school students was also adopted by the major leagues, this time over Chandler's objection.[33] Also regarding younger players, a request from the NCAA that the leagues pass a rule for college students similar to the one for high-school students that barred scouts from approaching players was voted down.[34] Chandler also struck down a motion that would allow high-school and college coaches to serve as scouts for professional teams. Personally opposed to such an arrangement, Chandler also maintained that the motion was not on the agenda and could not be adopted without unanimous consent.[35]

Of particular importance during the meetings, in particular during second-day sessions, were regulations concerning the broadcast of games on radio and television. The new regulations, which had been arranged between the major leagues and the US Department of Justice, stipulated that teams could authorize broadcasts outside a 50-mile radius of their ballpark at hours when a club in the broadcast area was not playing. As noted in *The Sporting News*:

"The rule stipulates a three and one-half hour period for one game and five and one-half hours for a double-header. During these periods, the Yankees for example, could not authorize a broadcast of a stadium game in, let us say, Buffalo."[36]

Several rules and regulations regarding the conduct of play were also passed in New York. Among the major decisions were:

1. A motion to allow the spitball back in the game was defeated 7 to 1 by the American League. Tigers general manager Billy Evans cast the sole vote in favor. The National League declined to even discuss the matter.[37]

2. Both leagues rejected the adoption of a uniform set of rules for breaking a first-place tie during a pennant race, despite Commissioner Chandler's preference for a consistent method for tiebreaking. The National League would continue to break the tie in a best-of-three series, while and American League would maintain its single-game runoff to decide a winner.[38]

3. Players now had to remain on the disabled list for only 30 days instead of 60.[39]

4. A uniform height of 15 inches above the surrounding field for major-league pitchers' mounds was adopted.[40] Detroit Tigers pitcher Freddie Hutchinson, a member of the American League players committee, was the driving force behind this measure.[41]

Night games and game curfews were also a major point of discussion at the New York meeting and, as with their decision to retain separate systems for tiebreaking, demonstrated a lingering division between the leagues in terms of conduct of games. The National League voted to allow ballpark lights to be turned on when afternoon games, in the event of a tie score or failure to complete nine innings, ran into darkness. The senior league also discarded its 12:50 A.M. curfew, allowing for tie games to continue until one side prevailed regardless of how long the game ran. The only exceptions were in cases where local ordinances applied curfews or limits to a game. The league also restored its suspended-game policy; a game that had to be halted (primarily) due to a curfew would resume the next time the two teams met.[42]

The National League took further steps toward embracing night ball when it voted to restore the twilight doubleheader, which the American League had already allowed. The Cardinals went so far as to make their 1950 home opener against Pittsburgh a night game.[43] This was the first time an opening game would be played under lights.[44]

The American League, in contrast, voted to allow lights for day games only during the final series of season with teams vying for either first, second, third, or fourth place in the standings.[45]

Further business at the meeting saw the election of officials, with the Athletics' Connie Mack being elected to the American League vice presidency and the Browns' William De Witt selected for the Executive Council.[46] In the National League, Phil Wrigley of the Cubs took over the vice presidency, while Frank McKinney of the Pirates was elected to represent the league on the Executive Council. Branch Rickey of the Dodgers, Bob Carpenter of the Phillies, Cincinnati's Warren Giles, and Fred Saigh of the Cardinals were all appointed to the league's Board of Directors.[47]

Commissioner Happy Chandler found much to be happy about in the form of a new seven-year contract and a $15,000 raise, upping his salary to $65,000 a year, effective before the 1950 World Series.[48] Granted during the meetings, the raise was announced by Frank McKinney, spokesman for a five-man committee appointed by the major leagues to oversee the commissioner's contract. McKinney cited Chandler's leadership under "one of the most perplexing periods in the game's annals."[49] (Chandler's happiness would subside after it was discovered that the new contract was illegal under the terms in the current contract. At the 1950 meetings, in fact, the contract issue bubbled up again, and instigated the nonrenewal of Chandler's contract in 1951.)

Comiskey Park in Chicago was chosen as the site for the 1950 All-Star Game, which was to be held on July 11.[50] The *Chicago Tribune* was again granted the rights to conduct the poll to select players for the All-Star Game.[51]

Summary and Close

The meetings of 1949 found baseball to be straddling two eras, and in many ways, they reflected numerous concerns that had been dogging professional baseball since its inception. There were apprehensions over the bonus rule, the draft, player contracts, the rights of the minor leagues, and the old divisiveness between the majors that continued to be manifested in the form of separate approaches to tiebreaking and night games. Commissioner Chandler's attempts to assert himself over these divisions and impose unity and consistency on the leagues met with only mixed success, and in spite of the raise he had been granted, there was unease over his handling of affairs, not the least of which regarded television.

At the same time, 1949 saw a raft of new concerns for professional baseball in the form of broadcast media, especially the perceived threat, as well as potential opportunities, of television. Even as early as 1949, television contracts were lucrative enough to support the player pension fund and perceived as damaging enough to threaten minor-league clubs and, indeed, entire leagues. There were also novel and lasting changes made to the player draft in the minors, and greater influence was exerted by major-league clubs over the affairs of their minor-league affiliates.

NOTES

1 Joseph E. Shaner, "Record of Big Gates No. 1 Sales Argument," *The Sporting News*, December 7, 1949: 3.

2 C.M. Gibbs, "Chicago Stags Defeat Bullets by 84 to 72 at Coliseum: International Meeting Opens Baseball Convention," *Baltimore Sun*, December 8, 1949: 23.

3   Louis M. Hatter, "Minor League Baseball Convention Opens Here Today," *Baltimore Sun*, December 5, 1949: 15.

4   "Minor League Baseball Convention Opens Here Today"; C.M. Gibbs, "Minor League Meeting Ends," *Baltimore Sun*, December 10, 1949: 13.

5   "Minor League Baseball Convention Opens Here Today."

6   "Minors' Fate Rests in Majors' Hands," *The Sporting News*, December 14, 1949: 10.

7   Dan Daniel, "Repeal of the Bonus Rule Expected to Be Chief Issue for Majors," *The Sporting News*, December 7, 1949: 20.

8   John Drebinger, "National League Votes Afternoon Lights, Ends Night-Game Curfew," *New York Times*, December 13, 1949: 47.

9   "First Formal Draft Held by Minors in Baltimore," *The Sporting News*, December 7, 1949: 10.

10 Edgar G. Brands, "Record Total of 222 Players Drafted by Minors," *The Sporting News*, December 14, 1949: 7. A photograph of the bulletin board accompanies the article.

11 Edgar Munzel, "Cubs Seek Higher Polish on Talent in New AAA Unit," *The Sporting News*, December 14, 1949: 2.

12 L.H. Gregory, "Saltzman, Just an Eager Beaver in Spring, now a $100,000 Indian," *The Sporting News*, December 14, 1949: 8. See also Obituary of Harold Saltzman, *The Oregonian (Portland, Oregon)*, January 18, 2011: obits.oregonlive.com/obituaries/oregon/obituary.aspx?n=harold-saltzman&pid=147910977.

13 Ibid.

14 Ken Smith, "Stanky Key to Leo's New Type of Club," *The Sporting News*, December 21, 1949: 1.

15 Dan Daniel, "Dramatic Rush of Trading Closes Meetings," *The Sporting News*, December 21, 1949: 7.

16 Ibid.

17 "Bonus Rule," Baseball-Reference.com, last modified on April 11, 2011, accessed on June 10, 2012, baseball-reference.com/bullpen/Bonus_rule.

18 Edgar G. Brands, "Minors Defeat Bonus Repeal in Hot Fight," *The Sporting News*, December 14, 1949: 5, 6.

19 By classification, the three Triple-A leagues unanimously favored repeal, the two Double-A leagues split their vote, three of the four Class-A leagues voted against repeal, Class B voted 6 to 5 for repeal, Class C voted 8 to 5 against repeal, and Class D voted 16 to 9 in favor. See Brands, "Minors Defeat Bonus Repeal in Hot Fight." This table breaks down voting by league:

Minor Leagues Favoring Repeal of Bonus Rule	Minor Leagues Favoring Retention of Bonus Rule	Minor Leagues Passing/Abstaining
American Association, Big State, Border, Canadian-American, Coastal Plain, Colonial, East Texas, Eastern, Eastern Shore, Far West, Georgia-Alabama, Georgia-Florida, International, Interstate, K-O-M, Kitty, Middle Atlantic, Mountain States, North Atlantic, Pacific Coast, Piedmont, Pony, Rio Grande, Sooner State, Southeastern, Southern Association, Sunset, Tobacco State, Virginia, Western Carolina, Western International, Wisconsin State.	Alabama State, Appalachian, Arizona-Texas, Blue Ridge, Carolina, Central Association, Central, Cotton States, Evangeline, Florida International, Florida State, Georgia State, Mississippi-Ohio Valley, New England, North Carolina State, Northern, Ohio-Indiana, Pioneer, South Atlantic, Texas, Three-I, Tri-State, Western Association, Western League, West Texas-New Mexico.	California League

20 Ibid.

21 "Repeal of Bonus Rule."

22 "Minors Defeat Bonus Repeal in Hot Fight."

23 James R. Walker and Robert V. Bellamy Jr., *Center Field Shot: A History of Baseball on Television* (Lincoln: University of Nebraska Press, 2008), 24.

24 Ibid.

25 Edgar G. Brands. "Game's Map Develops TV 'Shell Holes,'" *The Sporting News*, December 14, 1949: 1.

26 "Minors Defeat Bonus Repeal in Hot Fight."

27 Edgar G. Brands. "Changes in Scoring Rules Suggested by Minor Group," *The Sporting News*, December 14, 1949: 18.

28 "Cubs Seek Higher Polish on Talent in New AAA Unit."

29 "Minors Defeat Bonus Repeal in Hot Fight."

30 "Minors' Convention Ends," *New York Times*, December 10, 1949: 14.

31 Dan Daniel, "Majors Grease the Skids for Bonus Rule," *The Sporting News*, December 21, 1949: 5-8.

32 Ibid.

33 Ibid.

34 Ibid.

35 "Ban on Hiring of School Coaches to Scout Bushes," *The Sporting News*, December 21, 1949: 6.

36 "Majors Grease the Skids for Bonus Rule."
37 Ibid.
38 "National League Votes Afternoon Lights."
39 Daniel. "Majors Grease the Skids for Bonus Rule."
40 Ibid.
41 "National League Votes Afternoon Lights."
42 Ibid.
43 Ibid.
44 "Majors Grease the Skids for Bonus Rule."
45 "National League Votes Afternoon Lights."
46 Ibid.
47 "Majors Grease the Skids for Bonus Rule."
48 Dan Daniel, "Chandler Receives $15,000 Boost, Promise of a New Pact in October," *The Sporting News,* December 21, 1949: 1.
49 Ibid.
50 "National League Votes Afternoon Lights."
51 "Majors Grease the Skids for Bonus Rule."

— 1950 —
THE HAPPY DAGGER

By Nick Klopsis

Introduction and Context

THE 1950 WINTER MEETINGS WERE held in St. Petersburg, Florida, from December 3 to December 13. It was the third time in history that the Sunshine State played host to the winter meetings — they were in Jacksonville in 1941, while Miami was the site in 1947.

At first, it was expected that the meetings would come and go rather quietly. The war between North Korea and South Korea had begun nearly six months earlier and the United States and United Nations were now becoming increasingly involved. The *New York Times* reported at the onset of the meetings that only a handful of teams were open to trades, fearing the loss of their players to a possible World War III.[1] In addition, league business initially appeared to be pretty straightforward, with the only headlining issues being the potential elimination of the oft-criticized bonus rule and the high-school rule. Not too many people in attendance, then, would have predicted that the owners would suddenly turn against Commissioner Albert B. "Happy" Chandler and refuse to extend his contract.

Player Movement

As is customary, the first few days of the meetings brought rumors but no action. Several newspapers had reported that New York Yankees general manager George Weiss and Chicago White Sox general manager Frank Lane were seen talking details of a possible trade involving Chicago first baseman Eddie Robinson. The White Sox were in need of an outfielder and were willing to part with Robinson, a former All-Star who had hit .314 in 119 games on the South Side after being acquired from the Washington Senators at the end of May. The Detroit Tigers were also rumored to be in the running for Robinson, but eventually no deals came to fruition and Robinson stayed put. The lack of early trades was summed up best by Giants manager Leo Durocher, who had 14 infielders on his roster and was looking to trade a few of them. Durocher told John Drebinger of the *New York Times*, "I have been here for three days, ready to listen to anybody with a reasonable proposition. You would think plenty would come to us. ... Yet up to this moment not a single club has come to us with anything resembling an offer for a trade. You can frisk me for the answer."[2]

The first deal of the meetings came over the weekend, when owners and general managers were not formally scheduled to meet. After the Robinson talks fizzled, the White Sox traded right-hander Ray Scarborough and left-hander Bill Wight to the Boston Red Sox for outfielder Al Zarilla and two pitchers, righty Joe Dobson and rookie southpaw Dick Littlefield. For the Red Sox, acquiring Scarborough was a classic case of "if you can't beat 'em, make a trade to get 'em." Scarborough had been a continual thorn in Boston's side, beating the Red Sox in crucial pennant-deciding games in both 1948 and 1949 as a member of the Senators. The Red Sox initially wanted left-hander Billy Pierce in the deal but settled on Wight, who had gone 10-18 with a 3.53 ERA for the White Sox in 1950. Meanwhile, the White Sox filled their need for an outfielder with Zarilla, who hit a career high .325 with Boston in 1950; they also cured a hex of their own by obtaining Dobson, who had gone 14-4 in his career against them.

The Red Sox continued trying to reshape their roster. Toward the end of the meetings, Boston was rumored to be close to purchasing catcher Mike Guerra from the Philadelphia A's. The rumors surrounding Guerra struck a bit of a nerve with Senators manager Bucky Harris, who sought Guerra for reasons other than his catching skills—he wanted him because of his fluency in Spanish. Cuban pitchers Connie Marrero, Sandy Consuegra, Carlos Pascual, Julio Moreno, and Rogelio Martinez all appeared in games for the Senators in 1950, and Harris wanted a backstop "who can make these pitchers understand what I want them to do."[3] Some outlets reported that the Red Sox would then turn around and trade Guerra to the Senators for catcher Al Evans, but such a deal never materialized. Guerra's sale to the Red Sox was finalized five days after the meetings concluded, and he eventually was traded to the Senators for catcher Len Okrie and cash after the start of the 1951 season.

To prepare for the eventual purchase of Guerra, the Red Sox sold catcher Birdie Tebbetts to the Cleveland Indians. The 36-year-old became a source of friction on the Red Sox squad after calling several Boston pitchers "juvenile delinquents" and "moronic malcontents" following their late-season collapse.[4] After hearing the news of the sale, Tebbetts said he would consider retiring to sell insurance full-time, but ultimately decided to stick around for a couple more years before embarking on a second career as a scout, manager, and front-office executive.

The Business Side

By far the big moment of the meetings came when the 16 owners surprisingly voted against renewing Commissioner Happy Chandler's contract. Coming into the meetings, it was widely expected among media members and owners that a new contract would merely be a formality. After all, Pirates owner Frank McKinney, a close friend of Chandler's, had tried to introduce a resolution to renew Chandler's contract during the 1949 winter meetings. However, such a resolution was illegal—as per the commissioner's current contract, Chandler had to be notified at least a year in advance whether or not he would be retained.[5] Chandler had signed a seven-year contract in 1945 after replacing Kenesaw Mountain Landis, so any surprise resolutions (or re-elections) would not be possible in 1949. As such, they had to wait until this year's meetings before they could revisit the issue—his contract officially was set to expire April 15, 1952, so the coming 1951 season would represent the necessary one-year advance notice.

The dominos began to fall late on December 11, when all 16 major-league club owners came together to have a trial vote regarding Chandler's contract. With 12 votes needed for renewal, the vote found nine clubs in support of renewal and seven clubs against.[6] The owners then went into formal session and held the official vote. This time, the vote was split with eight in favor and eight against. When the owners informed Chandler of their vote, the commissioner demanded a revote. The final vote came back with nine in favor and seven against.[7] The final news came as a shock to Chandler, who was visibly shaken the next day at the joint major-league meeting. In his prepared statement, Chandler declared that he would finish the remainder of his term "until the last second."[8] Following this, the owners held a separate closed session in their hotel, where they voted unanimously to "select and elect" a new commissioner as quickly as possible.[9] The owners did not attempt to buy out Chandler's contract, though New York Yankees president Dan Topping said that was what the seven dissenters wanted.[10] Other owners doubted the possibility of forcing Chandler out before his term was up, since it required a unanimous vote of all 16 owners to do so. The league vowed to reopen the issue at meetings to be held in New York in February. (The meetings eventually were held in March.) On the day after the winter meetings' conclusion, the owners voted unanimously to form a committee to search for Chandler's replacement. The committee would be headed by four owners, two from each league: Lou Perini of the Boston Braves, Phil Wrigley of the Chicago Cubs, Del Webb of the New York Yankees, and Ellis Ryan of the Cleveland Indians.[11]

To this day, it is still unclear why the owners, led by Fred Saigh of the Cardinals, Perini of the Braves, and Webb of the Yankees, wanted Chandler out. Some people blamed the way Chandler handled the investigation into Paul Pettit's $100,000 "bonus baby" contract.[12] Others claimed it was lingering resentment stemming from integration in 1947, or because Chandler had insisted on getting a new contract.[13] Still others pointed to Chandler's statement, at the beginning of the meetings in St. Petersburg, that baseball would fold if another world war broke out.[14] Chandler himself thought it was because he voided a deal between the Yankees and the White Sox for outfielder Dick Wakefield.[15] The only owner to comment at the time of the vote was Topping, who vaguely chalked it up to Chandler's entire body of work. "I'd imagine it was an over-all thing," Topping told reporters after the closed-door meeting. "They didn't think he was doing a good job."[16]

Despite the fallout from the Chandler vote, there was still important business to be taken care of at the joint major-league meeting, which took all of about 20 minutes. Shortly after the bombshell announcement about the commissioner, the major leagues also voted to eliminate the bonus rule, which had been the subject of great controversy throughout the previous decade. For months it had been widely expected that the bonus rule would be abolished, with the motion to repeal beginning on October 31. The bonus rule had stated that any player who was signed to a contract greater than $4,000 had to stay on the team's 25-man roster for two years. It was designed to prevent wealthy teams from stockpiling untested talent, but became especially controversial as teams simply kept the "bonus babies" in the majors without giving them very much playing time, even though riding the bench in the majors, rather than perfecting their craft in the minors, was proving to be harmful to most of these young players. In addition, teams had (naturally) found ways around the bonus rule, often by paying players under the table. In the end, the rule was repealed immediately with no other alternatives suggested.[17]

In addition to killing the bonus rule, the major leagues also voted to eliminate the controversial high-school rule. The original rule prohibited teams from talking to high-school players until they had either received their degree or their original class had graduated. This proved to be a detriment to the game as a whole, as colleges would swoop in and offer the high-school athletes a football scholarship. The rule would officially be repealed at the end of the 1951 season.[18] In the meantime, both leagues agreed to create an eight-man committee of both major- and minor-league officials to create a new version of the rule, one that would most likely allow teams to negotiate with high-school players.[19]

Additionally, the major leagues rejected a proposal by the National Association to restrict television and radio broadcasts in minor-league territory. Previously, a major-league game could air in minor-league territory as long as it did not directly conflict with a minor-league home game. However, minor-league attendance continued to drop, as baseball fans chose to stay home and watch major-league stars on television rather than go to the local ballpark to watch ballplayers trying to work their way up to the big leagues. This was most evident with the Jersey City Giants of the Triple-A International League, who were within broadcast range of the Yankees, the New York Giants, and the Brooklyn Dodgers. According to the *Encyclopedia of Minor League Baseball*, Jersey City's attendance fell from 173,000 in 1949 to a paltry 63,000 in 1950, forcing the club to relocate to Ottawa.

The latest proposal was a three-point plan that called for a total ban on broadcasting major-league games at any time on a day when a local minor-league team was scheduled to play, as well as more promotion of minor-league clubs and general curtailment of networks. The minor-league owners made quick work in passing the resolution, and National Association President George M. Trautman presented it to the major leagues. Big-league owners, however, naturally quite content with the revenue they were receiving from their television broadcasts, laughed the proposal off the table. Local television broadcasts brought the 16 major-league owners a total net income of $2.3 million in 1950, and they were not necessarily concerned with how those broadcasts affected the minor leagues.[20]

A few other notable decisions were made over the course of the meetings, though they ended up being overshadowed by Chandler's ouster and the repeal of the bonus and high-school rules. Among them were the American League's decision to allot two days after season's end for any makeup games that could potentially affect the pennant race; the owners' vote to have the 1951 All-Star Game at Briggs Stadium in Detroit in celebration of the city's 250th birthday; Trautman's re-election to a five-year, $35,000-a-year term as president of the National Association; and Ford Frick's re-election to a new four-year, $55,000-a-year term as National League president.[21]

Summary

The surprising decision not to renew Happy Chandler's contract sent a shockwave through baseball, with the effects of the vote continuing well into the season until Chandler finally officially resigned in July of 1951. Meanwhile, the lingering effect of television on minor-league attendance continued to fester. Despite a strong plea from the National Association, the major-league owners brushed the issue off without giving it any thought, and the problem would fester for more than a decade until it became necessary for the majors and minors to completely revamp their relationship.

SOURCES

In addition to the sources cited in the Notes, the author also consulted:

Associated Press. "Major-Minor Committee Approves Dropping of Baseball Bonus Rule," *New York Times*, November 1, 1950: 45.

———. "Ottawa Bids for Jersey City Franchise," *Washington Post*, December 5, 1950: 19-20.

Daley, Arthur. "Sports of the Times: The Word Is Arrogate," *New York Times*, June 11, 1965: 22.

Drebinger, John. "Broadcast 'Evils' Worrying Minors," *New York Times*, December 4, 1950: 44.

———. "Nation's Baseball Officials Gather for Annual Meetings in Florida," *New York Times*, December 3, 1950: S6.

Johnson, Lloyd, and Miles Wolff, editors. *The Encyclopedia of Minor League Baseball* (Durham, North Carolina: Baseball America, 1997).

Povich, Shirley. "Chisox Get Al Zarilla, Dobson and Littlefield," *Washington Post*, December 11, 1950: 11.

Nemec, David, and Saul Wisnia. *100 Years of Baseball* (Lincolnwood, Illinois: Publications International, 2002).

Smith, Ken. "Major Leagues to Continue Radio, Television Broadcasts," *Atlanta Daily World*, December 8, 1950: 6.

"Clubs Doubt They Can Put Chandler Out," *Washington Post*, December 13, 1950: B3.

NOTES

1. John Drebinger of the *New York Times* wrote, "…with all the uncertainty hanging in the air over the foreign situation, the major league clubs have suddenly become fearful lest any move they make will prove to be the wrong one. No one will let go of an old player because no one is certain that by next summer that old hand may not be one of the key members of the club. No one wants to risk trading for a youngster because by tomorrow he may be on his way to a military training base." See "Uncertain World Conditions Halt Baseball Trades," *New York Times*, December 7, 1950: 59.

2. Ibid.

3. John Drebinger, "Chandler Hopes Rise as Several Clubs Waver in Fight to Oust Him," *New York Times*, December 14, 1950: 54.

4. "Tebbetts Reveals Sox Dissension; Blasts 'Juvenile, Moronic' Pitchers," *Boston Globe*, October 3, 1950: 7.

5. John Drebinger, "Majors Fail to Buy Contract of Chief," *New York Times*, December 13, 1950: 61.

6. Ibid.

7. Ibid.

8. Ibid.

9. Ibid.

10. Irving Vaughan, "Majors Vote to Name New Commissioner," *Chicago Tribune*, December 13, 1950: E1.

11. United Press, "Majors Appoint Committee to Find Successor to Chandler," *New York Times*, December 15, 1950: 46.

12. Pettit was a high-school pitching sensation in California. In 1949, still only 17, he was approached by an enterprising movie producer named Frederick Stephani, who wanted to film the life story of an athlete but couldn't afford to sign an established star. Convinced that Pettit eventually would make it big, Stephani signed him to a 10-year personal-services contract for $85,000, then three months later sold that contract to the Pittsburgh Pirates for $100,000. The Cardinals and other teams cried foul, but Chandler's investigation concluded that there had been no wrongdoing. The movie was never made, and Pettit eventually would win just one game in the majors.

13. Associated Press, "Happy Refuses to Quit Post," *Los Angeles Times*, December 13, 1950: C1-2.

14. John Drebinger, "Chandler Out as Baseball Head in '52 as New Contract Is Denied," *New York Times*, December 12, 1950: 1, 48.

15. Lyall Smith, "Onus on the Bonus." *Baseball Digest*, June 1950. books.google.com/books?id=FS4DAAAAMBAJ&printsec=frontcover&source=gbs_ge_summary_r&cad=0#v=onepage&q&f=false. Accessed June 11, 2011.

16. "Majors Vote to Name New Commissioner."

17. John Drebinger, "Minor Leagues Vote to End Bonus Rule and Ease High School Recruiting Ban," *New York Times*, December 8, 1950: 43.

18 Ibid.

19 Ibid.

20 Steven A. Reiss, *Encyclopedia of Major League Baseball Clubs* (Westport, Connecticut: Greenwood Publishing Group, 2006), xxi.

21 See Associated Press, "A.L. Permits 2 Extra Days For Playoffs," *Washington Post*, December 12, 1950: 17-18, and "Minor Leagues Vote to End Bonus Rule and Ease High School Recruiting Ban."

— 1951 —
OPEN CLASSIFICATION

by Steven Bryant

Introduction

AT THE 1951 WINTER MEETINGS, THE major topic of discussion was the future of the minor leagues. Attendance in the minors was down 20 percent in the 1951 season, a total loss of more than 7 million. In another important matter, for the first time in baseball history, rules that set forth the requirements for a minor league to obtain major status were to be presented.

This was Ford C. Frick's first Winter Meeting as commissioner. Frick, who succeeded Albert C. "Happy" Chandler after Chandler's contract was not renewed, would later be criticized for inaction in his career as commissioner,[1] and the first example of his not casting the deciding vote when teams deadlocked on legislation or a policy issue appeared at these sessions.

Open Classification and Requirements for Major Status

The Triple-A Pacific Coast League had been campaigning for years to achieve major-league status, and at a league meeting in August 1951 they announced they would withdraw from the National Association if they continued to be subjected to the major-league draft. With Congress already investigating baseball's antitrust exemption, including a focus on the situation with the PCL, the majors had little choice but to do something to placate the league and the lawmakers.

The minor-league meetings were held December 3 through 7 at the Deshler-Wallick Hotel in Columbus, Ohio. In anticipation, the requirements to be met by any league seeking classification as a major were announced on November 27. Additionally, a new classification between Triple-A and the majors, Open Classification, was created. The new classification would be "designated to facilitate the development of a circuit to the point it would be ready for Major ranking," Frick said.[2] Players on an Open Classification team would be excluded from the draft if they waived their selection rights or had less than five years of service. The draft price for an Open Classification player would be $15,000 instead of the $10,000 price tag on Triple-A players.[3] To achieve Open Classification, a league had to show an aggregate population of 10 million, have an aggregate park capacity of 120,000, and average a paid attendance of 2,250,000 for the preceding five years.[4]

For a league to reach major-league status, Commissioner Frick announced, there were 11 steps:

1. Any group of eight clubs mutually agreeing to all requirements and responsibilities as provided under the proposed regulations must apply to the major-league Executive Council. The eight clubs are responsible for all necessary territorial indemnities and financial obligations.

2. The clubs must present with their application complete data establishing their ability to meet the requirements for advanced status, including a full statement of stock ownership, financial ability, and character, both for the group and its individual members.

3. The proposed league shall show an aggregate population of 15 million in the eight cities.

4. Each club shall have a potential capacity of at least 25,000 in its ballpark.

5. They shall have had an average total paid attendance of 3.5 million over a three-year period preceding the application.

6. They shall provide a balanced schedule of at least 154 games.

THE CELLER HEARINGS

"In my opinion, baseball is now operating in violation of the antitrust laws," said Congressman Emmanuel Celler (D-New York), chairman of the House Judiciary Subcommittee on Monopoly, on May 4, 1951.* The issue of the reserve clause and its legality gained new attention, reportedly because radio and television broadcasts had created aspects of commerce that hadn't existed during the Supreme Court's Federal League case of 1915.**

On July 30, 1951, Ty Cobb—claiming faulty memory—led off the testimonials as the subcommittee began hearings.*** Baseball management types like Commissioner Ford Frick followed Cobb's testimony over the first week. In the second week, ousted Commissioner Happy Chandler offered an interesting take when asked about baseball owners: "Some of the owners never played the game and don't know where first base is. I'm not going to pass on the character of all the fellows who own clubs. But I think there are some owners the sport could do without. I think it's the wrong idea when they insist it's a big business and entitled to be operated as a business instead of a sport."****

Congress paused the hearings until after the World Series, and then heard from the players. Fred Hutchinson, Pee Wee Reese, and Lou Boudreau apparently all testified in favor of the reserve clause, while Danny Gardella's lawyer, Frederic Johnson, spoke against what he deemed an unconstitutional government within a government.*****

After 1,643 pages of testimony and exhibits, and approximately nine months of consideration, in May 1952 the subcommittee decided on no legislative action at that time.****** *******

* "Celler Says Baseball Violates Trust Law, Favors Exemption," *Washington Post*, May 5, 1951: 13.

** "Baseball Before Congress: Committee Wants to Know Whether Sport Should Be Exempt From Anti-Trust Laws," *New York Times*, August 5, 1951: 120.

*** "Baseball Players Are Not 'Peons,' Ty Cobb Tells Washington Hearing," *New York Times*, July 13, 1951: 1.

**** "More Major Leagues Proposed by Chandler in Testimony at Baseball Inquiry," *New York Times*, August 7, 1951: 29.

***** "Reese, Boudreau Agree With View: Hutchinson of Tigers, League Delegate, Wants Players to Vote on Commissioner," *New York Times*, October 20, 1951: 26.

****** "Celler Baseball Report Due," *Washington Post*, May 21, 1952: B17.

****** "House Committee 'Clears' Baseball," *Atlanta Constitution*, May 23, 1952: 32.

---

7. They shall adopt the major-league minimum-salary agreement with no maximum salary limitations.

8. They will become parties to the Major League Agreement and the Major-Minor League Agreement.

9. They will accept the uniform major-league player's contract and agreement.

10. They will join in the players' pension plan or adopt a comparable plan.

11. They shall apply for major-league status at least six months before the meeting at which the application must be considered, and at least 10 months before the opening of the season in which they hope to participate under major-league status.[5]

Since the Open Classification creation was seen as being aimed at the Pacific Coast League—the only league that would truly meet the stated qualifications—a fight was anticipated at the Columbus gathering. To the surprise of many, it did not happen, and the proposal was passed unanimously.[6] International League President Frank Shaughnessy did try to have the proposal amended to give his league and the American Association parity in the draft with the Pacific Coast League, but it was rejected. The minor leagues were not given the opportunity to vote on the regulations to reach major-league status.

When the major-league teams met at the Commodore Hotel in New York City December 8-10, they approved the creation of the Open Classification, and also approved Frick's regulations for a minor league to reach major-league status.[7]

Television/Radio

Attendance in the minor leagues was down for the second straight year. Fifty-nine leagues drew 41,982,335 fans in 1949, and in 1950 attendance fell to 34,735,967 in 58 leagues. In 1951 there were just 50 leagues with a total attendance of 27,625,527, a drop of some 20 percent from 1950 and 34 percent from 1949's highwater mark.[8] Only the Gulf Coast, Provincial, Kitty, and Southwest International Leagues[9] saw an increase in fans over the previous year. With such a sharp drop in attendance, the minors were blaming radio and television broadcasts by the majors in their markets.

In a speech at the National Association meeting, President George Trautman accused the majors of having a selfish attitude on allowing broadcasts in minor-league markets.

Trautman's remarks did not fall on deaf ears; Branch Rickey, on behalf of the Pittsburgh Pirates, pledged that the Pirates would not adopt any broadcasting policy that interfered with the minors.

The president of the Western League, US Senator Edwin C. Johnson of Colorado, presented a resolution that would require major-league clubs to place half of their receipts from airing games in minor-league territories into a fund from which clubs suffering from these broadcasts would be reimbursed. The resolution was unanimously adopted by the minors.[10]

At the majors' meetings in New York, Yankees general manager George Weiss said, "I am convinced something must be done to relieve the radio situation for the minor leagues," and announced that the club would not enter into a contract with either the Mutual or Liberty network's "Game of the Day."[11]

Senator Johnson's proposal for the minors to get a cut of games broadcast into their territories was acknowledged, but drew no further action.

Roster Limits and 24-Hour Recall

The two most contentious issues facing the majors were a proposal for a 24-hour recall rule and a proposed reduction of rosters from 25 players to 23.

The proposal for roster reduction, sponsored by the Boston Braves and the two Philadelphia clubs, would cut roster size from 25 to 23 from mid-May until September 1. The number of players a club could have on option to the minors would be increased from 15 to 17.

Branch Rickey sponsored a proposal to eliminate the 24-hour recall of optioned players from the minors, and bar their recall altogether before the close of the minor-league season. The practice of recalling players from minor-league teams with just a 24-hour notice was long hated by minor-league teams, with National Association President Trautman calling it "an insidious practice."[12]

E.J. "Buzzie" Bavasi, vice president of the Brooklyn Dodgers, spoke out against both proposals, warning that major-league baseball might be seriously harmed if they passed. "If both went through, we would be in tough shape," he declared. "No club could afford one injury of any consequence and be able to present the quality of baseball which is now so pleasing to the fans."[13] With a 23-player limit he felt, each club would most likely give up one pitcher and one fielder, meaning one less relief pitcher and one less pinch-hitter for each game. The Cubs were also soundly against the proposals, feeling that they would hamper the club's rebuilding program.[14]

While the proposal to eliminate the 24-hour recall got a "sound beating," the proposal to reduce roster sizes was deadlocked at 8 to 8, with Commissioner Frick's "no" vote breaking the tie. Frick instituted a policy of refusing to cast a vote that would make any changes when the teams were deadlocked, opting instead for the status quo. While it had been expected that as the former president of the National League, he would vote in favor of the roster reduction (since a majority of National League clubs favored it), he said, "I am not going to cast my tiebreaking vote for new legislation. That, in my opinion, would not be right."[15]

High-School Rule

Both the minors and majors approved a new rule regarding the signing of high-school players. During 1952, clubs would be allowed to contact high-school players at any time, but could not sign them until their high-school eligibility expired. Students who dropped out of high school before their eligibility expired must sit out one year before they could be signed.

Effective in 1953, players would be allowed to be signed at any time, but could not play in Organized Baseball until their original class graduated. A student who left school early could be granted permission to play at any time.

Players' Liaison

For the first time, major-league players won the right to have a liaison person in the commissioner's office. The liaison would be a full-time representative and serve as a clearinghouse for any player problems that might arise. The plan was for a former player or a man who has held an administrative position in baseball to be elected at the 1952 All-Star Game.[16]

Player Transactions

The biggest trade rumor going into the 1951 Winter Meetings was Ted Williams going to the Yankees. While the Red Sox front office and manager Lou Boudreau denied any plans to trade Williams, *The Sporting News* reported that trade would involve Joe DiMaggio (who was mulling retirement and would ultimately make that pronouncement on December 11, the day after the Winter Meetings ended), infielder Jerry Coleman, catcher Charlie Silvera, and one other Yankee to be determined.[17] *The Sporting News* also reported that the Red Sox had received permission from the Yankees to talk with DiMaggio, who told them he was enthusiastic about playing in Fenway Park in the coming season.[18] Adding fuel to the trade rumors, the Red Sox made a trade on November 28, acquiring outfielder Ken Wood and catcher Gus Niarhos from the St. Louis Browns in exchange for catcher Les Moss and outfielder Tom Wright.

When Yankees GM George Weiss was asked during the meetings in Columbus about the possibility of a Williams-DiMaggio trade, he said, "This much I would like to make clear on the Williams situation. Up to this moment I haven't so much as discussed the matter with Joe Cronin or anyone else connected with the Boston club. What is more, I won't if DiMaggio notifies us that he will be back next spring. For in that case we would have no interest in Williams whatsoever. However, should Joe decide to quit, well, I guess you could say we would be interested."[19]

On December 8 Red Sox manager Boudreau called a press conference. While Boston reporters prepared themselves for the news of Williams being traded, Boudreau instead stunned them by stating, "I'm taking Williams off the trading mart. Ted will be my regular left fielder next season. I'm informing all other American League clubs we'll consider no offer, no matter how attractive, for Ted."[20]

In the end, the meetings produced only two deals, both coming on the last day, December 10. The Philadelphia Phillies received right-hander Howie Fox, infielder Connie Ryan, and catcher Smoky Burgess from the Cincinnati Reds for catcher Andy Seminick, first baseman Dick Sisler, infielder Eddie Pellagrini, and left-handed pitcher Niles Jordan. A few hours later the New York Giants sent infielder Eddie Stanky to the St. Louis Cardinals for infielder-outfielder Chuck Diering and left-handed pitcher Max Lanier.

Other Business

The National Association drew a crowd of 1,200 to its annual banquet, on December 6, the largest attendance in the history of the meetings.[21] Minor-league baseball awarded the King of Baseball title for the first time, presenting it to Pacific Coast League President Clarence "Pants" Rowland. The honor, for dedication and service to baseball, has been awarded annually ever since.

This was the 50th National Association convention, and favors to celebrate the golden anniversary included a plate that depicted baseball scenes from 50 years before on the outer edge, with the poem "Casey at the Bat" in the center.[22]

At the major-league meetings, the Philadelphia Phillies were awarded the 1952 All-Star Game. This would be the first time the Phillies would host the midsummer extravaganza, though not the first time the game was held at Shibe Park, as the A's had hosted in 1943. The Phillies had been scheduled to host the 1951 game but bowed out in favor of Detroit, which was celebrating the 250th anniversary of its founding. Though the American League voted to assign the 1953 All-Star Game to Cleveland, Cincinnati would end up hosting in 1953, and Cleveland in 1954.

The major-league clubs considered the possibility of calling for annual eye tests for umpires, and allowing umpires to work while wearing glasses.[23]

NOTES

1 Robert H. Boyle, "Perfect Man For the Job," *Sports Illustrated*, April 9, 1962.

2 Dan Daniel, "'Tough' Requirements for Major Status Listed," *The Sporting News*, December 5, 1951.

3 Edgar G. Brands, "Many Hot Subjects Among Proposals Put Before Minors," *The Sporting News*, December 5, 1951.

4 "Wide Gap Between Open Class and Rating as Major," *The Sporting News*, December 5, 1951.

5 Ibid.

6 Edgar G. Brands, "Minors Pull Watch on 24-Hour Recall Rule," *The Sporting News*, December 12, 1951.

7 "Way Cleared for Coast," *The Sporting News*, December 19, 1951.

8 Clifford Kachline, "Minors' Gate Tobogganed 20 Per Cent in '51," *The Sporting News*, December 5, 1951.

9 The Southwest International League's attendance was higher in 1951 than that of the previous year's Arizona-Texas and Sunset Leagues, from which the league was formed.

10 "Minors Pull Watch on 24-Hour Recall Rule."

11 Dan Daniel, "Yankees Nix 'Game Of Day' For Sticks," *The Sporting News*, December 12, 1951.

12 Edgar G. Brands, "Trautman Hoists Storm Signals, Cites Violation of Salary Limits," *The Sporting News*, December 12, 1951.

13 Joe King, "Cutting Roster to 23 Would End Clutch Pitching, Hitting—Bavasi," *The Sporting News*, December 5, 1951.

14 Edgar Munzel, "Bruins, Rebuilding on Youth, to Oppose Cut in Player Limit," *The Sporting News*, December 5, 1951.

15 Dan Daniel, "Frick Demands Majority for New Laws," *The Sporting News*, December 19, 1951.

16 Tommy Devine, "Players Gain Right to Liaison Man Attached to Commissioner's Office," *The Sporting News*, December 19, 1951.

17 Bob Ajemian, "Lou, Eager to Trade Ted, Seeks Jolter in Exchange," *The Sporting News*, December 5, 1951.

18 Ibid.

19 John Drebinger, "Yanks Interested in Getting Williams From Red Sox if DiMaggio Retires," *New York Times*, December 5, 1951.

20 Bob Ajemian, "No Poaching! Splinter Off Trade Limits," *The Sporting News*, December 19, 1951.

21 Edgar Brands, "25-Year Men Are Honored at Convention Banquet," *The Sporting News*, December 12, 1951.

22 "Gold Convention Favors," *The Sporting News*, December 5, 1951.

23 Dan Daniel, "Big Leagues Echo Economy Keynote of Minors' Confab," *The Sporting News*, December 12, 1951.

— 1952 —
CHANGING DEMOGRAPHICS AND BROADCAST CHALLENGES

By Gregory H. Wolf

DESCRIBED BY EDWARD BURNS OF the *Chicago Tribune* as "one of the most important meetings in baseball history"[1] and "one of the most harmonious sessions"[2] by *New York Times* sportswriter John Drebinger, the 1952 Baseball Winter Meetings took place in Phoenix from December 1 to 7. "Never before, perhaps," wrote *The Sporting News*, "has the agenda of both the National Association and the majors been so tightly packed."[3] More than 1,000 representatives from the minor and major leagues, led by Commissioner Ford Frick, National League President Warren Giles, American League President Will Harridge, and minor leagues President George M. Trautman, convened in the desert city to discuss issues facing baseball and consider at least 29 amendments to the Major-Minor Rules and 17 changes to the National Association Agreement.

To the casual fan, 1952 seemed like another fine year in major-league baseball. The Brooklyn Dodgers, led by Roy Campanella, Jackie Robinson, Duke Snider, and Gil Hodges, won a big-league-best 96 games to secure their third NL pennant since integrating baseball in 1947. Their crosstown rivals in the American League, the New York Yankees, held off the pitching-strong Cleveland Indians in an exciting pennant race to capture their fourth consecutive flag under skipper Casey Stengel. The Bronx Bombers extended their stranglehold on the World Series title, claiming their 18th championship in 31 seasons in dramatic fashion by winning Games Six and Seven of the fall classic at Ebbets Field behind the hurling of Vic Raschi and Allie Reynolds.

Notwithstanding the excitement generated by the World Series, the major and minor leagues were concerned about the financial integrity of the sport. The big leagues were distressed by the continued precipitous decline in attendance. After a record 20,938,388 spectators had passed through the turnstiles in 1948, attendance then dropped in each successive year. The number for 1952 stood at 14,005,094, a decline of more than 1.6 million from the previous year. The situation in the minors was equally grave. In 1949 there were 59 leagues with teams in a record-high 448 cities; by 1952 there were 43 leagues with teams in 324 cities. During that three-year span, attendance dropped from 41 million to 25 million.[4] Given the context of declining attendance throughout Organized Baseball, it is no wonder that many of the amendments and much of the discussion at the winter meetings focused on measures designed to improve the financial well-being of the sport.

Racism: A Brouhaha as the Meeting Convened

Five years after Jackie Robinson integrated baseball with the Brooklyn Dodgers, African-Americans comprised only 2.9 percent of all major leaguers in 1952. They had debuted on only five teams (Dodgers, Indians, St. Louis Browns and Cardinals, and the Boston Braves); in addition, Minnie Miñoso had become the first black Latino player when he debuted with the Chicago White Sox in 1951. On the eve of the winter meetings in Phoenix, Jackie Robinson, speaking on the television program *Youth Wants to Know*, charged the New York Yankees' baseball executives with prejudice and racism. "It seems to me the Yankee front office has used racial prejudice in its dealings with Negro ball players," he said on November 30."[5] Robinson made it clear, however, that he did not think that the players were prejudiced.

Robinson's comments, widely described in media outlets as controversial, caused a brouhaha just as baseball owners and executives were arriving in Phoenix. George Weiss, GM of the Yankees, went on the offensive. "The Yankees are not going to promote a Negro player to the Stadium simply to say that they have such a player," he said unapologetically. "We are not going to bow to pressure groups. And we are not going to bow to Jackie Robinson, either."[6] The charge of racism was not new to the Yankees, who had had pickets outside Yankee Stadium in 1952 demanding that the team sign and promote black players. New York had yet to invite a black player to its spring training. The team's top candidate, Victor Felipe Pelot, whose Puerto Rican origin was masked by the Americanization of his name to Vic Power, was considered by some team scouts as a marginal talent at best even though he was an All-Star with Kansas City in the Triple-A American Association. (He would go on to have a fine big-league career, collecting 1,700 hits and compiling a .284 career batting average, while earning seven Gold Gloves and being named to four All-Star teams.) Three years later, in 1955, Elston Howard became the first black American to don the Yankee pinstripes. According to scholars such as Lee Lowenfish, the integration of baseball was further exacerbated by an emerging quota system throughout the 1950s which limited the number of African-Americans in organizations' farm systems and teams.[7]

Rule 5 Draft

The winter meetings kicked off with the Rule 5 draft on Monday, December 1, marking the first time that the draft took place at the annual winter extravaganza.[8] Major-league teams could draft minor leaguers who were not on a club's 40-man roster for a set price, ranging from $15,000 for the Open Classification Pacific Coast League and $10,000 for the two Triple-A leagues (American Association and International League) to $7,500 for lower leagues. The acquisition price, as well as the stipulation that the drafted player must be added to the new club's 40-man roster, made the draft a risky proposition. At the draft, attended by more than 400 representatives and lasting a brief 22 minutes, only 11 players were chosen, all but one from second-division clubs, in the smallest draft since 1943. The most prominent name was right-handed pitcher Elroy Face, whom Branch Rickey, GM of the Pittsburgh Pirates, selected from Brooklyn's affiliate in the International League, the Montreal Royals. The minor leagues conducted their draft the next day, beginning with the PCL and progressing through lower leagues.

Two Bombshells

On December 3 the meetings were sent into an uproar by proposed amendments that had drastic implications for the major and minor leagues. The Dallas Eagles of the Double-A Texas League, one of the few independently owned minor-league teams, offered what John Drebinger called a plan "that would just about overthrow the entire structure of the farm system in organized baseball."[9] Presented by Prentice Wilson, legal counsel for the Eagles, the amendment sought to set up a committee to review the major-minor league agreement and establish a new pact the following year. According club owner Dick Burnett, the amendment aimed to end the major leagues' control of the minor leagues. "What we want," he said, "is for no one man at one desk to control 500 players," a not-so-subtle reference to clubs like the Dodgers, Cardinals, and Pirates, each of whom fielded at least 15 minor-league teams.[10] Complaints about big-league clubs' "chain gangs" in the minors had been levied for two decades; however, Burnett caused an uproar when he threatened legal action to achieve his goals. When the amendment was defeated 27 to 16, Wilson was undeterred, asserting, "The vote today clearly reveals the domination of the minors by the majors."[11]

Bill Veeck Jr., controversial owner of the St. Louis Browns, offered an equally earth-shattering amendment. Presented on behalf of his affiliate, the San

Antonio Missions, also in the Texas League, Veeck's amendment forbade major-league teams to sign any player without previous professional experience. In essence, only minor-league clubs could sign amateurs while big-league teams would be required to exclusively draft minor-league players. Furthermore, to increase the opportunity for each player to have a shot at the big leagues and keep any team from stockpiling players, every minor-league player would be eligible to be drafted after one year of service. By all accounts, Veeck's amendment took the meetings by surprise and angered many. Members of the National Association of Professional Baseball Leagues, the minors' umbrella organization, voted down the proposal without even discussing it.

Two-League Waiver Rule

Arguably the most important new amendment passed at the winter meetings was the two-league waiver requirement for big-league transactions after the June 15 trading deadline. Under the previous rule, players involved in waiver transactions after the June 15 deadline had to pass through waivers only in the league in which they played before they could be acquired by the highest bidder in the other league. Teams had exploited this loophole for decades, but the recent success of the New York Yankees' acquisitions drew the ire (and jealousy) of owners. Flush with cash, the Yankees had acquired Johnny Mize from the Giants (1949), Johnny Hopp from the Pirates (1950), Johnny Sain from the Braves (1951), and Ewell Blackwell from the Reds (1952) for between $25,000 and 50,000 and well after the trading deadline. Each of those players subsequently played a role on Yankees' pennant winners.

The new rule stipulated that waivers by all teams in both leagues had to be obtained before a team could acquire a player. The original amendment had proposed a new date for the trading deadline (July 15), but the National League protested vehemently; consequently, the June 15 trading deadline remained in place. In addition, waiver claims were prioritized in reverse order of the team's record to give less-competitive teams the first opportunity to acquire a player.[12]

The $4,000 Bonus Baby

The modern farm system that Branch Rickey had developed as GM of the St. Louis Cardinals in the 1920s and 1930s had grown to include to 41 leagues in 1939. After that number dipped during the wartime years, it peaked with 59 leagues in 1949. In an effort to sign players, fill rosters, and stockpile talent, big-league clubs enticed amateur free agents with increasingly large bonuses. The signing of Bobby Brown for a record $60,000 by the New York Yankees in 1946 signaled a breaking point. For organizations not as well-heeled as the Yankees, the search for talent was now becoming an unsustainable, blatantly inequitable practice, so the major and minor leagues enacted an amendment in 1946 creating the "Bonus Player." As Brent P. Kelley explained in his authoritative study on the bonus rule, *Baseball's Biggest Blunder: The Bonus Rule of 1953-1957*, this amendment defined a bonus player based on the amount of money he received to sign a professional contract: more than $6,000 at the big-league level, $4,000 for Triple-A players, and progressively less for the lower levels. The key to this amendment, explained Kelley, was that "players could not be optioned and assigned to a lower classification without irrevocable waivers first being asked," which meant that the team would lose both the player and the money it had given to him. And that player was allowed to spend only one year in the minors before he had to be promoted to the major-league roster.[13] Just four years later, after a widespread perception of cheating and paying undeclared bonuses, the majors and minors rescinded the amendment. The result was foreseeable: teams resumed their practice of paying exorbitant bonuses to high-school players and untried free agents.

Recognizing the need to address reform regarding the practice of paying bonuses, the majors and minors passed a new bonus amendment in 1952. It defined a bonus player in much the same way as the previous rule; however, the new amendment differed by levying heavy fines and penalties to enforce it. Under the new legislation, a bonus player was any free agent receiving more than a $4,000 bonus with the majors or top minor leagues; or $3,000 with a Class-B minor-league team or lower. Despite recognizing that the bonus rule of 1946 was detrimental to players' development by limiting how and when the players could be farmed out, the owners once again decided to insert similar language into the new rule. The bonus baby signed to a major-league contract was required to spend the first two years on the parent club before he could be farmed out; if signed to a minor-league contract, the player could not be moved up or down in the farm system for one year. The commissioner was granted the authority to levy fines of $2,000 or more on clubs and $500 or more on officials who violated the rule, as well as suspend any guilty parties. Baseball clubs, however, still had the right to give free-agent amateurs bonuses as large as they wanted. The new bonus rule failed to deter clubs from paying large bonuses; if anything bonuses increased throughout the decade. At the 1958 winter meetings the stipulation that big-league bonus babies spend two years on the major-league roster was repealed.[14]

High School Signings

The history of baseball is filled with stories about high-school players who signed a professional contract and subsequently debuted in the majors or minors while still of high-school age. The practice of signing high-school athletes prior to graduation reached its apex during World War II when clubs scouted and searched for replacement talent in every possible venue. Joe Nuxhall, who debuted with the Reds as a 15-year-old in 1944, and three 16-year-olds—Rogers McKee, Ralph "Putsy" Caballero, and Carl Scheib—debuted as wartime players.

The major leagues enacted an amendment in 1952 to prohibit the signing of high-school players until their class had graduated, though teams and scouts were permitted to speak to and negotiate with them. Violation of the high-school signing rule could lead to the commissioner declaring the illegally signed player a free agent and levying a fine on the club.[15]

24-Hour Recall and July 31 Date

A sore spot for minor-league teams had been the practice of major-league clubs recalling players they had sent to the minor leagues. Especially troublesome was the practice of assigning a player to the minors on 24-hour recall notice, thereby limiting a minor-league team's ability to plan ahead. Minor-league teams resented losing a player who might be in the middle of a hot streak, or who was an important player during a pennant drive or postseason playoffs; both scenarios could affect the team's attendance and thus the financial bottom line of a minor-league club. This issue also highlighted the growing tension between major-league and minor-league clubs, which over the course of the previous two decades had lost their independence and were attempting to hold on to their last vestiges of autonomy.

According to the new amendment, a major-league player optioned to the minor leagues was required to remain with that club for at least 10 days. Furthermore, he had to be physically fit to play. Any player optioned after July 31 had to remain with the minor-league club until the conclusion of the minor-league season. An exception was granted in the case of an emergency injury on the big-league club which necessitated the immediate recall of a minor leaguer.

Roster Limits

In an amendment that could have had far-reaching consequences on the rosters of major- and minor-league teams, Bill Veeck proposed to reduce midseason major-league rosters from 25 to 23 players.[16] The *New York Times* reported that the proposal would have caused "spirited discussion" had Commissioner Frick permitted action on the floor.[17] It was widely believed that the National League was prepared to vote in favor of the change.[18]

Television, Radio, and Broadcasting Rights

Perhaps the biggest issue facing baseball was television. As with the proliferation of radio broadcasts of baseball games in the 1920s, the major leagues had difficulty determining if televised broadcasts were beneficial or detrimental to attendance. James R. Walker and Robert V. Bellamy have argued in their exhaustive study, *Center Field Shot: A History of Baseball* on Television, that baseball initially had a favorable impression of television's effect on the popularity of the sport.[19] According to Walker and Bellamy, baseball accounted for more than 50 percent of all radio airtime in June and July in 1947. Record attendance throughout the major and minor leagues in 1948 only heightened the positive impression of television broadcasts. *The Sporting News*, on the other hand, voiced its concern about the deleterious effects of televised broadcasts by 1949; by the early 1950s, optimism about television broadcasts of baseball waned as attendance in parks plummeted.

In order to protect minor-league clubs, the major leagues had instituted rules that prohibited broadcasting big-league games within 50 miles of a minor-league park without the club's permission. However, under pressure from the Department of Justice's antitrust commission, that rule was abolished in 1947, drawing the ire of the minor leagues, whose very existence many felt was threatened as attendance fell precipitously over the next five years.

On the eve of the 1952 winter meetings, Fred Saigh, owner of the St. Louis Cardinals, suggested that major-league baseball broadcasts should be banned for one year "to see if TV really is as harmful as we think."[20] It was an opening salvo that gave rise to heated discussion that week in Phoenix.

Despite Saigh's suggestions, major-league clubs were hard-pressed to sign television deals that would guarantee much-needed income in light of the decline in attendance. At the winter meetings, seven of the eight AL clubs signed a groundbreaking two-year reciprocal agreement that guaranteed the visiting team a percentage of the radio and television broadcast revenue. The lone holdout was the St. Louis Browns, whose maverick owner, Bill Veeck Jr., refused to sign any contract that did not guarantee that 50 percent of the revenue would be earmarked for the visiting club. The result was disastrous for the cash-strapped owner, who, according to the *New York Times*, was completely shut out of the television and radio market at home and on the road.[21]

The situation was murkier, and a lot more contentious, in the National League, where a few teams signed separate deals to pay visiting clubs. The St. Louis Cardinals forged agreements with the Chicago Cubs and Cincinnati Reds. However, other teams could continue to broadcast games with opponents even if they had not signed an agreement to do so. Fred Saigh of the Cardinals, for example, threatened a lawsuit against the Boston Braves, whose owner, Lou Perini, claimed that he would continue to televise home games with the Redbirds.

Commissioner Frick stood on the sidelines, going so far as saying, "I cannot see how I could become involved" as teams jockeyed for position with their television deals. "I do not know what our policy should be with regard to television. One thing I can tell you definitely," said Frick. "Neither league can force a member club to accept the telecasting of its games in foreign cities."[22]

The Plight of the Minor Leagues

It was no secret that the minor leagues were hemorrhaging. Attendance had declined more than one-third in just three years. Consequently, the minor leagues looked to their big-league brethren for a lifeline. Major-league teams could negotiate exclusive television deals, but the overwhelming majority of minor-league teams lacked that ability. On December 3 US Senator Edwin Johnson of Colorado, president of the Western League, gave an impassioned 40-minute speech arguing that the minor leagues will "become saturated with television accounts of major-league games with an increasing detrimental impact on baseball."[23] According to the AP, the influential Democrat offered a resolution calling for all money from the broadcasts of major-league games in a minor-league territory to be placed in a trust fund. "Give us a little help," appealed George Trautman, president of the minor leagues, to the majors, "before you destroy us."[24]

"The major leagues fail to recognize the plight that the minor leagues are in," opined syndicated columnist Dan Daniel.[25] Warren Giles, president of the NL, gave credence to those comments by suggesting that the only way the minor leagues could gain sound economic footing was by contracting to 20 leagues. Far from conceding that the encroachment of major-league broadcasts into minor-league markets was detrimental, Giles claimed that there was a shortage of players to field so many teams, many of which lacked the resources to compete and enjoyed only limited support in their communities. Fred Saigh of the Cardinals suggested that small-town newspapers, whose headlines boasted of the major leagues instead of the local minor-league club, were partly responsible for the lack of community support by ignoring baseball in their own backyard.[26]

The major leagues rejected Johnson's proposal, but decided to establish a committee to study the issue. It would join a similar committee made up of representatives from the minor leagues, and present its findings in July 1953.

The minors did retract for the 1953 season. Gone were the Class-B Interstate League, the Class-C Southwestern International League, and four Class-D Leagues, the Coastal Plain, the Kansas-Oklahoma-Missouri (KOM) League, the North Carolina State League, and the Western Carolina League. The latter two merged to form the Tar Heel League. Of the 39 leagues set to play in 1953, the following classifications were represented: Open (1), Triple A (2), Double A (2), Single A (4), Class B (7), Class C (10), and Class D (12), plus the independent Mexican League.

A Fourth Major League?

At the 1951 winter meetings, the Pacific Coast League, one of the three Triple-A leagues along with the International League and the American Association, was elevated to an open classification. Nominally above Triple A, the PCL was considered by many to be on its way to becoming a third major league. When postwar America's shifting demographics brought a population boom to the West Coast, the PCL, with clubs in large metropolitan areas like Los Angeles, San Francisco, San Diego, and Seattle, filled a natural void as big-league clubs remained concentrated east of the Mississippi River save for the two St. Louis teams.

At the advent of the 1952 winter meetings, there was considerable discussion among IL and AA executives about creating another open-classification league which would eventually become the fourth major league. Frank Shaughnessy, president of the IL, suggested that the largest cities in those two circuits, like Kansas City, Milwaukee, Montreal, and Baltimore, could support a new major league, which he predicted could become reality in the next five or six years.[27]

The discussion about a fourth major league, however, gained little traction among NL and AL executives. Instead of focusing on a new league, they focused on legislation making relocation of current big-league teams easier, and also developed a contingency plan for the minor-league team that would be displaced by the relocation.

Prelude to Relocation

No major-league team had relocated since 1903, when the AL Baltimore Orioles moved to New York and became the Highlanders (renamed the Yankees in 1913; and, in reality, this move was not so much a relocation as much as it was a replacement of a team that went out of business). En route to the winter meetings, Dodgers president Walter O'Malley recognized that a franchise shift, either Lou Perini's Boston Braves or Bill Veeck's cash-strapped Browns, was imminent. "I think there is a call to action on our part," he said. "Should an American League club wish to move to a city in which the National League has no franchise, the latter league should have no vote in the matter."[28] Recognizing the need for one of those teams to escape a two-team city, the major leagues ultimately passed legislation that paved the way for the relocation and realignment of franchises. Sportswriter Joe King lauded the liberalization of relocation laws as the "most exciting rule change enacted in baseball in many years."[29] The former rule required majority approval of all eight clubs of the league involved and a majority of clubs in the other circuit to approve a franchise shift; the new rule stipulated that if a big-league club transferred to a city that did not currently have a major-league team, approval was confined only to the league of the relocating team. Furthermore, a majority of five teams in the NL and six teams in the AL was required. If, however, a major-league club wanted to relocate to a city where there was already a big-league team, unanimous consent of all 16 clubs was required.[30]

Major-league executives recognized that Milwaukee, with its new 28,000-seat stadium, was the most likely choice of a team looking to relocate; however, few of those executives could have guessed that it would be happening just three months later. The St. Louis Browns, one of the prime candidates, found themselves in a conundrum. Owner Bill Veeck also owned Sportsman's Park, where both the Browns and Cardinals played. Veeck had voiced his interest in moving to Milwaukee, where he had owned the Milwaukee Brewers of the American Association in the 1940s (an irony because, in 1902, the Milwaukee Brewers relocated to become the St. Louis Browns), but according to *The Sporting News*, he could not make any public remarks about transferring his club until he sold Sportsman's Park.[31]

But the machinations for relocation were already under way. In 1952 the Boston Braves drew a major-league low 281,278, an average of just 3,653 per game, to Braves Field. According to an AP report, the club had lost approximately $600,000.[32] News broke just days before the winter meetings that majority owner Lou Perini had purchased the remaining 40 percent of the team from its minority stockholders. According to author Saul Wisnia, many speculated that it was a prelude to the club's sale or relocation, possibly to Milwaukee, where Perini owned the Triple-A Milwaukee Brewers and had pledged to help the Midwestern town secure a big-league team.[33]

A Conflict in Cleveland

Owners of major-league teams belonged to an exclusive fraternity, and it was big news any time a principal owner sold his shares of a club. In late 1949 insurance magnate Ellis Ryan had led a syndicate in purchasing the Cleveland Indians from Bill Veeck. But in reports published prior to and during the 1952 winter meetings, club president Ryan had apparently lost a power struggle with other principal owners, including GM Hank Greenberg. The source of the conflict, reported the AP, was Ryan's decision to purchase the Indianapolis Indians of the American Association, which lost money, as well as Ryan's demand for more authority in running the Indians. Ryan abruptly left the meetings on December 4 to return to Cleveland to "straighten out the difference of opinion existing on the Tribe's board of directors."[34] Ryan resigned on December 18, paving the way for Myron Wilson to purchase his shares and become president and principal owner.

Trades

Given the amount of business the major and minor leagues conducted, teams had time to complete only three trades. The most significant involved the Detroit Tigers, who sent right-handed pitchers Virgil Trucks and Hal White and outfielder Johnny Groth to the St. Louis Browns for outfielder Bob Nieman, infielder Owen Friend, and utilityman Jay Porter. The Senators and White Sox exchanged pitchers, with Washington giving up right-hander Mike Fornieles and Chicago parting with southpaw Chuck Stobbs. And Pittsburgh traded catcher Clyde McCullough to the Chicago Cubs for right-handed pitcher Dick Manville.

In what would have been the biggest trade, the Boston Braves agreed in principle to send pitcher Warren Spahn to the Brooklyn Dodgers for various combinations of players. According to Al Wolf of the *Los Angeles Times*, the blockbuster fell apart at the last minute.[35] Spahn would go on to win more games than any other left-hander in major league history.

Minor Business

Several additional items deserve mention. The major leagues agreed to increase World Series umpire salaries by $500; regular umpires would now earn $3,000 and alternates $1,500. Up to $50,000 was allocated to support American Legion baseball, and the same amount was authorized to the Association of Professional Ball Players of America, which aided ill or indigent players.[36]

Voting for the MVP Award

The Baseball Writers Association of America (BBWAA) had awarded the MVPs in each league since 1931. Beginning in 1938 a group of 24 sportswriters (three members from each league city) cast votes for the MVP of each league. The method of voting and the corresponding results had periodically given rise to criticism. The selection of Chicago's Hank Sauer as NL MVP reignited calls for reforming the voting procedure. While Sauer led the league with 37 home runs and 121 runs batted, his Cubs had finished fifth in the league, and many felt that the Philadelphia Phillies' ace Robin Roberts deserved the award on the strength of his 28 wins, the most in the NL since Dizzy Dean's 30 in 1934. Roberts finished second in the voting, though he was named major-league player of the year by *The Sporting News*.

Though some selections had been closer since the format change of 1938, such as when Joe DiMaggio beat Ted Williams by one vote in 1947, there had never been a year when only 18 points separated the top three candidates. (Brooklyn's rookie reliever, Joe Black, was the third man.) In response to renewed criticism the BBWAA, in its session at the winter meetings, created a committee to scrutinize the methods and voting system used to select the MVP and Rookie of the Year award winners in each league. Named to the committee were three highly respected writers: Dan Daniel of the *New York World Telegram & Sun*, Ed Burns of the *Chicago Tribune*, and J. Roy Stockton of the *St. Louis Post-Dispatch*.

Baseball Writers Protest

At the end of the weeklong meeting, the Baseball Writers Association of America lodged a complaint against Organized Baseball, whose sessions took place in hotels in Phoenix spread out over at least 14 miles, a considerable distance without adequate public transportation. Representatives from NL clubs met at the historic Adams Hotel, located in downtown Phoenix, while the AL contingent was housed at Philip K. Wrigley's luxurious Arizona Biltmore Hotel on the outskirts of town. Other sessions and conferences took at the Western Ho, the Royal Palms, and the Camelback hotels.

Conclusion

According to most reports, the 1952 winter meetings were one of the busiest and most successful on record. America was changing and baseball was attempting to keep up with those changes, if not stay a step ahead. The new legislation adopted on the two-league waiver rule, the bonus rule, and the banning of the 24-hour recall of players were hailed as major milestones, or as Commissioner Frick suggested, "in the best interests of the public."[37]

SOURCES

In addition to the sources listed in the notes, the author consulted a considerable number of other articles.

NOTES

1. Edward Burns, "Majors Agree on $4,000 Bonus Player Limit; Retain Prep Rule," *Chicago Tribune*, December 7, 1952: B1.
2. John Drebinger, "Majors Adopt Two-League Waivers, End 24-Hour Recall in Options," *New York Times*, December 8, 1952: 36.
3. *The Sporting News*, December 3, 1952, 12.
4. United Press, "Senate Group Votes to Restrict Radio, TV Game Coverage," *Sarasota Herald-Tribune*, June 11, 1953: 12.
5. "Robinson Charges Yankee Race Bias," *New York Times*, December 1, 1952: 31.
6. *The Sporting News*, December 10, 1952: 3.
7. Lee Lowenfish, "The Rise of Baseball's Quota System," *Nine*, Spring 2008.
8. Associated Press, "Major Moguls Draft Only Eleven Minor Leaguers," *Hartford Courant*, December 2, 1952: 15.
9. John Drebinger, "Dallas Threatens Court Action as Move to End Baseball Farm System Fails," *New York Times*, December 5, 1952: 37.
10. Ibid.
11. Ibid.
12. "Majors Adopt Two-League Waivers, End 24-Hour Recall in Options."
13. Brent P. Kelley, *Baseball's Biggest Blunder: The Bonus Rule of 1953-1957* (Lanham, Maryland: Scarecrow, 1996), 4.
14. The following sources were used for this information: "Majors Adopt Two-League Waivers, End 24-Hour Recall in Options," and "Majors Agree on $4,000 Bonus Player Limit; Retain Prep Rule."
15. Ibid.

16. Associated Press, "Baseball Magnates Have Many Important Problems to Solve at Annual Meeting," *Hartford Courant*, November 30, 1952: C4.

17. "Majors Adopt Two-League Waivers, End 24-Hour Recall in Options."

18. Associated Press, "Veeck Would Prohibit Majors Signing Players Without Previous Pro Experience," *Hartford Courant*, December 5, 1952: 18.

19. James R. Walker and Robert V. Bellamy, *Center Field Shot: A History of Baseball on Television* (Lincoln, Nebraska: Bison Books, 2008).

20. Associated Press, "Saigh Suggests Year Blackout of TV for Test," *Chicago Tribune*, November 27, 1952: G4.

21. "Majors Adopt Two-League Waivers, End 24-Hour Recall in Options."

22. *The Sporting News*, December 17, 1952: 1 and 4.

23. "Trautman Urges Majors to Help Minors 'Before You Destroy Us,'" *New York Times*, December 5, 1952: 37.

24. Ibid.

25. *The Sporting News*, December 3, 1952: 3.

26. "Saigh Suggests Year Blackout of TV for Test."

27. Associated Press, "Top Minors Plan for 4 Big Leagues," *New York Times*, November 29, 1952: 21.

28. Roscoe McGowen, "Weiss Seeks Adoption on Yank Bonus Rule Plan," *New York Times*, November 28, 1952: 34.

29. *The Sporting News*, December 17, 1952: 2.

30. "Weiss Seeks Adoption on Yank Bonus Rule Plan"; *The Sporting News*, December 17, 1952: 2.

31. Multiple issues of *The Sporting News*, including December 3, 10, 17, 1952.

32. Associated Press, "Perini Family to Buy All of Braves Stock," *Chicago Tribune*, November 27, 1952: G5.

33. Saul Wisnia, "From Yawkey to Milwaukee: Lou Perini Makes His Move," in Gregory H. Wolf, ed., *Thar's Joy in Braveland. The 1957 Milwaukee Braves* (Phoenix: Society for American Baseball Research), 2014.

34. *The Sporting News*, December 10, 1952: 7.

35. "Major Moguls Draft Only Eleven Minor Leaguers."

36. "Majors Adopt Two-League Waivers, End 24-Hour Recall in Options."

37. Associated Press, "Two-League Waivers Voted; New Bonus Rule Adopted," *Washington Post*, December 8, 1952: 11.

— 1953 —
PENSION COLLISION

By Abigail Miskowiec

Supreme Court Involvement

ON NOVEMBER 9, 1953, A MONTH after the close of the season, the US Supreme Court chimed in on major-league baseball for the second time in history. George Earl Toolson, a longtime pitcher in the New York Yankees farm system, sued the team, claiming the reserve clause violated federal antitrust laws. Toolson had labored at the Triple-A level for four years before the Newark Bears, his team in the 1949 season, folded; as a result, Toolson found himself assigned to the Single-A Binghamton Triplets. Seeing this as a slap in the face, Toolson took to the courts for redress and an opportunity to sign with another club.

The Supreme Court saw fit to entertain this argument against the ongoing practices of the two major leagues; radio, television, and the promise of West Coast baseball had changed the game since a 1922 decision held that interstate travel was an incidental, rather than essential, component of the sport. Furthermore, the court of Oliver Wendell Holmes had found in the 1922 decision that, though the games made money, baseball was legally a sport, not a business, and therefore was not subject to the Sherman Antitrust Act.[1]

In Toolson v. New York Yankees, Inc., the court, under newly appointed Chief Justice Earl Warren, upheld the 1922 decision by a majority of 7 to 2. One major factor in the decision was a 1951 House Judiciary Committee decision not to define baseball as a monopoly. According to the majority decision, "Congress had no intention of including the business of baseball within the scope of the federal antitrust laws."[2] This ruling set the stage for future pension and reserve-clause battles that eventually resulted in the institution of free agency in 1976.

National Association of Professional Baseball Leagues

From November 30 to December 4, the National Association of Professional Baseball Leagues, the minor-league umbrella organization, gathered at the Atlanta Biltmore hotel. Executives discussed challenges facing the minor leagues, and held the annual minor-league draft. The newly relocated Baltimore Orioles (formerly the St. Louis Browns) of the American League held the first pick and looked to get their season off on the right foot.

Contract Disputes and Player Movement

Many thought the Orioles would select outfielder Wally Moon with the first pick in the draft, but Moon had already been signed by the St. Louis Cardinals in 1950 while attending Texas A&M University. Because of the reserve clause, Commissioner Ford Frick had to declare Moon ineligible for the draft. The Orioles then selected second baseman Vinicio "Chico" Garcia, who wound up playing only 39 games in his one year in the majors. Moon, on the other hand, won the 1954 Rookie of the Year award over the likes of Ernie Banks and Hank Aaron.

Not everything went the Cardinals' way during the meetings, however. The team was locked in a contract dispute with the New York Yankees over 17-year-old Ralph Terry. Both teams claimed to have signed the young pitcher; Frick awarded him to the Yankees. Terry's journeyman career, which included two stints in pinstripes, featured appearances in five consecutive World Series (1960-1964). He found both fame and infamy on the championship stage, giving up Bill Mazeroski's walk-off homer in 1960 but winning World Series MVP honors in 1962.

Although rumors flew left and right at the meetings, few trades were made. Several deals revolving around Philadelphia A's right-handed pitcher Harry Byrd were proposed, but he stayed put. The only major deal saw the Cincinnati Reds trading rookie infielder Alex Grammas to St. Louis for right-handed pitcher Jack Crimian. Crimian would not be the only new thing in Cincinnati in the 1954 season; anti-Communist sentiment pushed the club to rebrand itself as the Cincinnati Redlegs until 1959.

Distribution of Cash Flow Causes Trouble

With the increased popularity of television, the minors estimated that they had lost some 19 million spectators in four years because of the broadcast of major-league games into their territories. A 1950 study published by the Radio-Television Manufacturers Association found that 53 percent of fans in Wilmington, Delaware, preferred to watch the Philadelphia major-league clubs on television rather than venture out to see the local Blue Rocks.[3] An article in the *Atlanta Daily World* asserted that television and radio caused "virtually all of the sports' problems—net return on investments; the possibility of admission hikes; and a system of assuring the minors' retention of key talent to keep fan interest."[4] The NAPBL members wanted to band together to protect their cities from the encroachment by the majors. They demanded a share of the revenue from major-league broadcasts, and a ban on broadcasts within 50 miles of any minor-league city without their consent. These measures were approved and helped to save minor-league baseball's flagging attendance rates.

Meanwhile, Frick saw the minor-league meetings as an opportunity to try to settle the pension dispute with the players. The pension system, established by former Commissioner Albert B. "Happy" Chandler, would not expire until 1956, but the players felt dissatisfied with the recently renewed benefits. Talks between Frick and the player representatives, Ralph Kiner of the NL and Allie Reynolds of the AL, had been ongoing throughout the 1953 season. In late August the players hired J. Norman Lewis to act as their legal guide in the matter.[5]

Among the demands of the players were permission to play baseball in the offseason and the elimination of twi-night doubleheaders and doubleheaders the day after night games. Players also wanted the minimum salary raised above $5,000.

Frick invited 16 player representatives, including Reynolds and Kiner, to meet during the NAPBL meetings in Atlanta. The players refused to attend a conference without Lewis, whom the commissioner had barred from the meetings. Frick said, "I had to stand on my inalienable right as commissioner to summon anyone before me I wanted to in the interests of baseball without any outsiders present."[6] As a result, the relationship between players and executives became strained heading into the major leagues' winter meetings.

Major Leagues

The pension issue continued to hang over the major leagues when executives met the following week in New York. The meetings were held on December 7 and 8 in the Commodore Hotel, but in that short time, many issues were resolved.

Major Moves of Players and Teams

As in the minor-league sessions, few deals were made at the major-league meetings. The one major trade involved a future MVP. The Washington Senators traded outfielder Jackie Jensen to the Red Sox for outfielder Tom Umphlett and left-handed pitcher Mickey McDermott. Jensen, who had played only half a season with the Senators, was the American League MVP while playing for the Red Sox in 1958.

The National League had been looking into the possibility of putting a team in Los Angeles. Regarding one possible venue, the LA Coliseum Commission voted 7 to 1 to bar major-league baseball at the Coliseum because of high temperatures on the field, a ban on beer sales, and the conflicting schedules of local teams. The NL agreed that the venue was not a good fit, a policy it would ignore just a few years later.

THE PLAYER PENSION FUND IN 1953

First year in existence	1946
Revised plan rules	1951
First-year player pay-in	$.27 per day
Player pay-in after first year	Increases each year until reaching $2.50 in sixth year. Stays at $2.50 through year 10. After 10th year, drops to $1.50 per day.
Club pay-in	$1.50 per player on roster per day.
Total pay-in guidance	After 10 years, the player and the club will each have paid $2,300.
Annuities payout start date	Begins when player reaches age 50, provided he has accumulated five years of service in the major leagues.
Annuities payout amount	Five years of service = $50 per month Six years of service = $60 per month Seven years of service = $70 per month Eight years of service = $80 per month Nine years of service = $90 per month Ten or more years of service = $100 per month
Additional benefits	Active players protected by $10,600 life insurance policy that can be signed over as a $100-per-month annuity for survivors for the 10 years following the death of the player.
Average pay-in per year	$100,000 by players $125,000 by clubs
Pension fund operational cost	$500,000 – the difference in operational cost and pay-in was made up through television revenue.
Additional fund costs	Basic obligation to provide pensions for players who joined the fund late in their careers and made only one or two payments; those players received credit for previous playing experience (where they hadn't been paying into the fund.) To take care of such cases, the clubs earmarked TV-radio receipts for a special central fund.

Players and the clubs battled over the central fund. Players insisted that broadcasting money belonged to the pension fund. Owners argued that the central fund, where the broadcasting money was kept, existed as a joint bank account for the 16 clubs.

Fund description was detailed in "Players Claim Radio-TV Cash, But League Says They're 'Misled,'" *Des Moines Register*, December 10, 1953: 17; and "Player, Owner Contribute Same Amounts to Pension," *Des Moines Register*, December 10, 1953: 19.

The idea of baseball in the California sun would not die, though. Frank Shaughnessy, president of the International League, proposed expanding the majors into two 12-team leagues and then dividing each league into Eastern and Western divisions. The top four teams in each division would then participate in a best-of-seven postseason playoff. In this case, even if a team ran away with the division title, fans could look forward to the possibility of an upset in the playoffs. Shaughnessy targeted San Francisco, Los Angeles, and Seattle as possible landing spots for teams.[7] The National League relaxed the requirement for relocation; a club owner would need a three-quarters vote of his fellow owners rather than a unanimous one. Thus was the inevitable transition to the West Coast eased.

More than a few notable players inked their first deal during the 1953-54 offseason. A future Rookie of the Year, shortstop Tony Kubek (1957), signed with the New York Yankees. The Brooklyn Dodgers signed two future Hall of Famers, right-hander Don Drysdale and outfielder Roberto Clemente. (The Pittsburgh Pirates would pick up Clemente in the Rule 5 draft the next season.) Pittsburgh nailed down another future Hall of Fame member, second baseman Bill Mazeroski. The Chicago White Sox also got in on the action, signing 1956 Rookie of the Year and future Hall of Fame shortstop Luis Aparicio as a free agent.

Rule Changes

The 1953 meetings featured rule changes that remain to this day. A rather trivial matter, leaving gloves, glasses, and other accouterments on the field between innings, was officially banned. Hank Greenberg, a leading advocate for the change, reasoned, "We don't want games to be decided by accidents or outside interference."[8] For the players, this meant an end to some of their shenanigans, such as using the discarded gloves for target practice or pulling pranks on teammates and opponents alike. According to the *Boston Globe*, Yankees shortstop Phil Rizzuto was a prime target. Red Sox players once sneaked a dead mouse into his glove, and he was routinely plagued by rubber snakes.

Pension Committee

After the tension between the commissioner and player representatives in Atlanta, the players decided not to go to the meetings in New York. Still, the news from the winter meetings mostly concerned the pension plan.

Indians general manager Hank Greenberg (who would be voted into the Hall of Fame in 1956) and Pirates general manager John Galbreath formed a two-man committee to study the effects of ending the pension plan. On the other hand, Babe Dahlgren, a former major leaguer who had presided over the first pension plan meeting in 1947, suggested a "no pension, no play" policy for players.

The executives did vote to make changes to some playing rules, as suggested by the players, including a ban on twi-night doubleheaders and spring night games. The AL banned night games on getaway days if either team had to play the next afternoon, but the NL did not follow suit.

Conclusion

The pension dispute was not settled at the 1953 winter meetings, and the tension carried through the winter and into the baseball season. When the conflict finally ended in 1954, the players formed the Major League Baseball Players Association. The organization became an official labor union in 1966 and is still in existence today.

SOURCES

In addition to the sources mentioned in the notes, the author also consulted:

"Baseball Executives Hail Ruling as Tremendous Victory for National Game," *New York Times*, November 10, 1953: 40.

John Drebinger, "California Cities Prime Prospects," *New York Times*, December 7, 1953: 46.

NOTES

1. Federal Baseball Club of Baltimore v. National League of Professional Baseball Clubs, 259 U.S. 200, 42 S. Ct. 465, 66 L.Ed. 898 (1922).
2. Toolson v. New York Yankees, et al, 346 U.S. 356, 75 S. Ct. 78, 98 L.Ed. 64 (1953).

3   Dean A. Sullivan, ed. *Late Innings: A Documentary History of Baseball, 1945–1972* (Lincoln: University of Nebraska Press, 2002), 47.

4   "Minor League Meet Gets Underway Here," *Atlanta Daily World*, December 1, 1953: 4.

5   United Press, "Baseball Players Hire Own Counsel," *New York Times*, August 22, 1953: 9.

6   John Drebinger, "Baseball Players and Frick at Odds," *New York Times*, December 3, 1953: 2.

7   "Shaughnessy Plan for Two 12-Team Major Leagues Builds Up Clamor," *Ellensburg* (Washington) *Daily Record*, November 6, 1953: 8.

8   Harold Kaese, "New Rule: Players Can No Longer Leave Gloves on Playing Field: How Can They Play Tricks on Pesky?" *Boston Globe*, January 24, 1954: C1.

1954
LOOKING WEST

By Bill Felber

THE 1954 WINTER MEETINGS OPENED on December 6 at New York's Hotel Commodore with an agenda filled with issues that had plagued the sport for years. They included the ongoing decline of the minor leagues, the increasing misalignment of major-league franchises with the national population, and player-management conflicts. Owners left the meeting two days later—a day before the scheduled conclusion—congratulating themselves on concluding their business so efficiently, although in fact they had solved none of those key issues.

There was reason for industrywide concern. Granted, gate attendance had risen by about 11 percent from 1953—15.9 million fans came out in 1954, 1.6 million more than in the previous season. But even the superficial could see how misleading that increase was. Most of it was attributable to the shift of the St. Louis Browns franchise to Baltimore. During their final season in St. Louis, the Browns drew fewer than 300,000 fans; they debuted in Baltimore to more than 1 million. A second big driver was the surprising pennant performance of the New York Giants, who drew 1.15 million to the Polo Grounds, 300,000 more than in 1953.

The more meaningful truth was that half of the 16 major-league teams saw a drop in attendance in 1954. Those suffering franchises included the Philadelphia Athletics, which by the start of the winter meeting had already been sold to Arnold Johnson and transferred to Kansas City. And it was not merely the game's have-nots feeling pain. The Yankees drew about 60,000 fewer fans in 1954, the Dodgers were down about 140,000, and the Red Sox were off some 95,000 from the previous season. In Pittsburgh, a third consecutive last-place finish prompted just 475,494 fans to pay to watch the Pirates, a nearly 17 percent decline from 1953.

Minor-League Meetings

The major-league meeting was preceded by the annual gathering of minor-league executives, a heated weeklong session held from November 28 to December 2 in Houston. With relations between the two levels of professional baseball strained by years of unresolved disagreements over revenue, financial support, television, and compensation levels for player purchases, the Houston session was a necessary and central precursor to New York.

The session's predominant issue—the continued decline of minor-league franchises in general—was exacerbated for the third consecutive season by a big-league franchise shift, this time of the Athletics. Because Kansas City had been an American Association city, that shift left one of the premier minor leagues in search of an eighth member. The problem of the 1955 minor-league realignment was even more acute because the Cardinals wanted to move their top farm team, which had been in Columbus, Ohio, to Omaha, a Western League city that it viewed as a more lucrative market. On November 29 the Yankees sold the rights to Kansas City's Double-A franchise to the owners of the Denver club of the Western League, who announced their intent to join the American Association.

Both by agreement and precedent, the Western League deserved to be compensated for the loss of its two largest territories. But there was no set formula to determine the compensation level. When the Braves' 1953 move to Milwaukee prompted the American Association to invade Toledo, it paid $50,000 in compensation, and the International League paid $48,000 in compensation for the rights to a territory to replace Baltimore a year later. The Cardinals offered the Western League $35,000 for the rights to Omaha, but Western League President Edwin Johnson, a US senator from Colorado, initially demanded $100,000,[1] plus another $150,000 to surrender Western League rights to Kansas City.[2]

With the compensation issue at a stalemate, minor-league President George Trautman appointed a five-member arbitration panel to settle the differences.

The broader issue of the ongoing decline of the business of minor-league baseball remained unresolved. Minor-league attendance, showing a continual pattern of decline since 1949, had fallen another 6 percent in 1954, with paid attendance for 33 leagues (down from 37) at 19,585,819, a total of 1,218,773 fewer than in the previous year. The Class-B Gulf Coast League and Class-D Wisconsin State League were not able to open at all in 1954, while the Class-B Florida International, Class-C Mountain States League, and the Class-D Tar Heel League all disbanded during the summer.

Minor-league executives saw their problem as one of incursion into their territories by major-league teams via television. "The most important issue before the convention is a reasonable solution to the radio-television problem," Trautman said.[3] On November 22 Frank Lawrence, owner of the Portsmouth (Virginia) Merrimacs of the Class-B Piedmont League, filed suit against Commissioner Ford Frick and the 16 major-league clubs, alleging breach of contract for permitting big-league games to be aired within 50 miles of Portsmouth. Lawrence alleged that his club was "damaged by invasion of minor league territory" by the broadcasts.

"Someone asked me if I was trying to put the major leagues out of business," Lawrence said. "I replied that a fair exchange is no robbery. They have been trying to put us out, and they have put half our leagues out of business already."[4] In the action, filed in US District Court in New York City, Lawrence demanded $250,000 in compensation. Howard Green, president of the Texas-based Big State League, introduced a resolution that would have put the minors on record in support of the lawsuit. But the resolution was ruled out of order by Trautman.[5]

Although less litigious, other minor-league owners were equally agitated by the worsening attendance figures. The 33 leagues voted 19 to 14 to terminate the entire major-minor agreement over the TV dispute. Because the resolution required a three-fourths vote for approval, the 19-to-14 majority was insufficient for passage. And even had it passed, the agreement would have remained in force unless also terminated by both major leagues, an outcome considered at the time to be unimaginable. Still, the result had obvious ominous ramifications for any accord between the majors and minors over television.

On more mundane matters, minor-league teams held their annual draft. A total of just 44 players were drafted from lower classifications, costing $132,950, the least draft activity since the end of World War II.[6] By comparison, one year earlier 84 players had been drafted. Among the 44 taken at the 1954 meeting were four who had at one time been on major-league rosters: shortstop James Clarkson, by Los Angeles of the Pacific Coast League from Dallas of the Texas League; first baseman Ed Mickelson, by Portland of the Pacific Coast League from Shreveport of the Texas League; left-handed pitcher Larry Lassalle, by Fort Worth of Texas League from Waco of the Big State League; and right-handed pitcher Lazaro Naranjo, by Hollywood of the Pacific Coast League from Chattanooga of the Southern Association.[7]

Finally, the minors requested that major-league teams reduce rosters from 25 to 23, presumably to infuse more talent into the minor-league system.[8]

Majors' Response

When the major-league meetings opened in New York, club owners made short work of that part of the agenda pertaining to minor-league teams. They approved a new working arrangement by which Class-B teams would get $3,500, Class-C teams $3,000, and Class-D teams $2,500 in exchange for signing working agreements that would let major-league teams select players from their rosters at the end of a season. Previously, lower-level teams had been paid as little as $100 annually for that privilege. The big-league clubs also agreed to underwrite most of the costs of minor-league spring training, including transportation, and to pay part of the minor-league manager's salary.[9]

Major-league executives and close observers were effusive in praise of the owners' farsightedness. Dodgers farm director Fresco Thompson said the changes would cost Brooklyn $30,000 a year but "it will be money well spent, especially so where the money is used for managers."[10] Frick called the new agreement "by far the most important piece of legislation passed at these meetings … the means of survival for many clubs in lower minor-league categories."[11] White Sox GM Frank Lane called it "the greatest thing the major leagues have done for the minors since I've been around baseball.[12]

The Sporting News editorially lauded the deal with the minors, saying it "should dispel much of the erratic thinking which pictures the major league club owner as a heartless bogeyman willing to see the minors in constant and sometimes fatal trouble brought on by his own indifference to their plight."[13]

That was, however, all the minor leagues obtained. On a split vote, major-league owners defeated the proposal to shrink rosters. A majority of National League club owners agreed to do so, but American League owners unanimously rejected the idea, and Frick—tasked with breaking the tie between the leagues—went along with the majority of club owners in opposing a reduction. Then they adopted a rule prohibiting any major-league club from signing a college player who had completed his freshman year until after his class had graduated or until he turned 21. Again fearful of a talent drain, minor-league executives had voted down such a restriction.

There was no disagreement about the minors' appeal against television's incursion into their territory. Team owners took up the question and unanimously squashed it. In doing so, they cited legal uncertainties regarding their ability to restrict telecasts. It was noted that a TV/radio ban had been rescinded a few years earlier when federal officials told magnates it would not stand up to a legal challenge.[14] In addition to the Portsmouth suit, the Liberty Broadcasting Company had already filed a second suit, claiming its freedom to broadcast baseball games was being proscribed by regulations limiting the reach of such telecasts. "These two views are directly contrary, and where does that leave us, the major league owners," said Dodgers owner Walter O'Malley in defending the majors' reticence to act.[15] *The Sporting News* editorially gave minor-league owners little sympathy. "If a change in airways policy would bring the majors in conflict with the laws of the land as interpreted by the Justice Department, the majors hardly could be expected to make such a change," it contended. It characterized other negative impacts on minor-league gates, citing "the automobile, the television set and many other new factors," as social changes which must be accepted."[16]

Pirates general manager Branch Rickey dressed down minor-league executives for their reluctance to recognize that some communities simply wouldn't support minor-league ball. "Radio and television have nothing to do with the merits of the farm system," he said, claiming that the major-league teams were doing plenty to help the minors. "The minors are continually asking for help, but their narrow vision has hindered any progress in solving their problems," he asserted.[17]

The minors, the creator of the farm system said, "must help themselves."[18]

Expansion

American League owners took up a proposal by Indians GM Hank Greenberg to expand to 10 teams for the 1956 season. Greenberg sought creation of a four-member committee to report on the practicality of expansion at the league's 1955 summer meeting.

This was a catch-up step for the AL, given that the National League had already authorized a similar committee, which was to report in February. The chief target of both leagues was no secret: Los Angeles, with close to 2 million residents, headed both leagues' wish lists, while others being mentioned included San Francisco, Seattle, Portland, Minneapolis-St. Paul, Toronto, Montreal, Houston, Dallas, and Indianapolis. Proposed 162-game schedules were reported to have already been drawn up by both leagues.

With the National League already focusing on Los Angeles and San Francisco, published reports suggested that the American League's top targets were probably Minneapolis-St. Paul and Toronto. But there was widespread debate about whether expansion should or would take place. "Geographically it offers too many obstacles," said Yankees owner Del Webb. Instead, he advocated for realignment of the existing 16 franchises into Eastern and Western leagues, the Alleghenies serving as a rough boundary. Webb didn't specify the makeup of the leagues, but logically his idea would have created an "Eastern League" consisting of the Dodgers, Giants, Phillies, Pirates, Red Sox, Yankees, Orioles, and Senators. The "Western League," would have been composed of the Tigers, White Sox, Indians, Athletics, Reds, Braves, Cardinals, and Cubs. "But I'm afraid that would take a bit of doing," Webb added.[19]

Webb said he found no strong sentiment among club owners for more than eight teams. "Some of the magnates believe that a 10-club league would be whittled down to eight by a process of elimination at the turnstiles within a few years," he said.[20]

Cubs owner Phil Wrigley took the lead in arguing the case for expansion. Wrigley, who also owned the Los Angeles Pacific Coast League franchise, had submitted a detailed expansion plan at a secret meeting of NL owners on November 22. That report included such practical details as railroad mileages, transportation costs and a sample schedule.[21] He assured reporters that the major leagues would be in Los Angeles in less than two years. "It's coming awfully fast," Wrigley said.[22]

Lane agreed. "I can't understand why so many people believe a league of that size (10 teams) would be unfeasible," he said. "It would give baseball a much-needed shot in the arm."[23]

For its part, The Sporting News egged on the American League's expansion study. The league, it asserted, could operate indefinitely profitably with its present membership. "But if it did this," it added, "it would close its ears against the counsel of … several cities large enough and eager enough to deserve the best that baseball has to offer. There is, no longer … any doubt that the majors, both of them, will become ten-club leagues."[24]

Even before the opening of the major-league meeting, though, NL President Warren Giles was openly talking down the prospect of expansion. "I satisfied myself at our owners meeting that (owners) feel it would not be practical at this time to move any of their present franchises (or expand)," Giles said.[25] "There just aren't enough good players around to maintain the high standard of play." He said that picture "perhaps will change within five years."

O'Malley said he saw "no immediate expansion to 10 teams," but added that "I personally believe that California will have major-league baseball in the near future … certainly in less than five years."[26]

He added that other areas would also be scrutinized. "You have to recognize that Minneapolis-St. Paul already has voted funds for a ballpark," he said. He noted that Toronto, Montreal, and several Texas cities were also working on proposals. "The major-league club owners will have some very enticing offers to consider soon," he said.

Finally, O'Malley assured fans that the Dodgers would not move to Los Angeles. He did not deny interest in the idea; rather, he said league rules, which require a unanimous vote for a franchise shift, would prevent it. "Horace Stoneham wouldn't let us," he said. "The Giants need us and we need the Giants."

Stoneham was skeptical of the West Coast's readiness to support major-league teams. The problem, he said, wasn't population numbers alone, but the demographics behind those numbers. In his mind, much of the westward migration consisted of skinflint retirees. "I'd like to see some figures on what percentage of Californians are living on pensions or paid-up annuities," Stoneham said. "People in that category live on a tight budget with no provision for buying tickets to ballgames."[27]

At the conclusion of the meeting, Frick waved away intimations of a race between leagues for the potentially rich expansion territories, and particularly for California. "I am sure that before long (the leagues will go into joint session) to take up all the angles and all the problems which would have to be met if they were to increase their membership to ten clubs," he said.[28]

Frick dangled his own idea, the addition of a brother league to the AL and NL. "It is my firm belief," he said, "that the true solution of the need for major expansion lies in the organization of a third league." In 1954, the easiest way to accomplish that would have been to elevate the Pacific Coast League to major-league status; in fact, prior to the 1952 season the PCL's status had been changed from Triple A to "Open" in anticipation of just such a step. Frick predicted that within four years at least four West Coast cities—Los Angeles, San Francisco, Seattle, and Portland—would be ready.[29]

The commissioner added, however, that any initiative for increasing the number of franchises would have to percolate up from the cities; it would not flow down from the existing roster of clubs. "It must be a grassroots enterprise," he said, emanating from "a deep desire of certain cities to move up with the aid of local capital and local determination." Frick said the major leagues "are not on a recruiting campaign."[30]

Player Relations

Allie Reynolds and Ralph Kiner, representatives of a players committee, met with club owners to discuss requests from player representatives for changes to the basic agreement. For the most part, Reynolds and Kiner got nowhere. The owners heard, and then rejected, a request for a 20 percent increase in the minimum salary, from $6,000 to $7,200 per year. They also voted down a player request for permission to deal directly with Caribbean clubs over winter-league contracts instead of being required to go through their teams. Also dispatched were proposals for players to be paid moving expenses when they were traded during spring training, and to alter the March 1 spring-training deadline.[31] Frick said the March 1 rule will be "rigidly enforced."[32]

The owners did agree to three player requests. One was that contracts be issued by January 15 rather than February 1. The second approved of players being served dinner on trains after night games. The third authorized hotel rate compensation when players were housed in private homes during spring training.

The Big Deal

Easily the biggest trade of the winter season unfolded before the meetings started. On November 18 new Baltimore general manager Paul Richards announced that the Orioles had reached agreement with the Yankees on a two-phase swap that by December 1 would grow to encompass 17 players. In its final form, the deal sent right-handed pitchers Don Larsen, Bob Turley, and Mike Blyzka, catcher Darrell Johnson, infielder Billy Hunter, outfielder Jim Fridley, and first baseman Dick Kryhoski to the Yankees in exchange for right-handed pitchers Harry Byrd and Jim McDonald and southpaw Bill Miller, catchers Hal Smith and Gus Triandos, outfielder Gene Woodling, infielders Willie Miranda, Kal Segrist, and Don Leppert, and minor-league outfielder Ted Del Guercio. Larsen, 21, Turley, a 23-year-old flamethrowing 14-game winner in 1954, Woodling, and Triandos were the stars of the deal.

Richards enthusiastically promoted the trade as injecting a badly needed dose of winning Yankee spirit into his Orioles. But others were harsher in their assessment of the new GM's debut deal. "I would have asked as much for Jack Harshman as Richards received for Bob Turley, Don Larsen and Billy Hunter combined," panned White Sox GM Frank Lane. He said the Orioles, a seventh-place team in 1954, their first year in Baltimore, had "traded away the only worthwhile things they had."[33]

A second, less spectacular premeeting deal also set some tongues wagging. On November 16, one day before the Orioles-Yankees trade was announced, Indians GM Greenberg acquired slugging outfielder Ralph Kiner from the Cubs in exchange for right-handed pitcher Sam Jones, outfielder Gale Wade, and $60,000. Kiner, 33, had batted .285 with 22 home runs for the Cubs, and Greenberg thought he would bring power to a Cleveland club which had won 111 games in 1954 but needed to stay ahead of the Yankees. In fact, Kiner batted just .243 in 1955, though he did hit 18 home runs in 321 at-bats for the runner-up, 93-win Indians, and retired after the season.

On November 30 the Cubs announced the sale of outfielder Frankie Baumholtz to the White Sox for $20,000. This deal, however, was later negated by Giles, who said the Cubs had failed to gain league waivers on the former Ohio University star. He was returned to the Cubs, where he batted .289 in 1955 before being sold to the Phillies a year later.

Deals at the Meeting

The presence of Lane and Richards at the meeting ramped up speculation about a feverish round of trades, but that frenzy never really developed.

Lane tried. Despite his panning of the Orioles' roster minus Larsen, Turley, and Hunter, on December 6 he got together with Richards for a seven-player swap that sent infielder Jim Brideweser, right-handed pitcher Bob Chakales, and catcher Clint Courtney from Baltimore to Chicago. In exchange, the Orioles received left-hander Don Ferrarese, right-hander Don Johnson, catcher Matt Batts, and second baseman Freddie Marsh.

That same day Lane traded right-handed pitcher Leo Cristante and first basemen Ferris Fain and Jack Phillips to the Tigers for first baseman Walt Dropo, left-handed pitcher Ted Gray, and outfielder Bob Nieman.

On December 8 the Reds traded right-handed relief pitcher Frank Smith to St. Louis for third baseman Ray Jablonski and right-handed pitcher Gerry Staley. Superficially one-sided in favor of the Reds, the deal was essentially a St. Louis ploy to open up playing time for rookie third baseman Ken Boyer. At Houston in 1954, Boyer had batted .319 with 202 hits, 21 home runs, and 116 RBIs in helping the Buffaloes to the Texas League crown. Described in the press as "another Pie Traynor with a glove," Boyer was also considered a fielding upgrade over Jablonski.[34] None of the actual principals in the deal did much in 1955. Jablonski batted .240 for Cincinnati, Staley went 5-8 in 18 starts for the Reds and Yankees, and Smith was 3-1 in 39 innings of bullpen work for St. Louis. Boyer batted .264 with 18 home runs for the Cardinals, became a seven-time All-Star and was the National League's Most Valuable Player in 1964.

On December 13 the Dodgers, long rumored to be shopping third baseman Billy Cox and left-handed pitcher Preacher Roe, finally sealed the deal. They traded both to Baltimore for minor leaguers John Jancse (a right-handed pitcher), Harry Schwegeman (an infielder), and $50,000. Roe retired, Cox batted just .211 for Baltimore in his final big-league season, and neither of the Dodgers acquisitions ever made it to the majors.

A second deal, with potentially greater impact to the Dodgers, fell through. That proposed trade was reported to have involved Brooklyn's shipment of infielder Jim Gilliam and one of two right-handers — Bob Darnell or Bob Milliken — to the Reds for left-handed pitcher Fred Baczewski, catcher Hobie Landrith, and outfielder Wally Post. There was no public indication how close the deal came to being finalized. Gilliam, of course, became one of the stars of Brooklyn's 1955 World Series victory over the Yankees.

Finally, on December 14 the Giants traded infielder Billy Klaus to the Red Sox for catcher Del Wilber. Klaus batted .283 for Boston at the outset of a nine-season big-league career. Wilber, a 35-year-old veteran part-timer for eight seasons, was assigned to the Giants' Triple-A farm team. Instead he asked for and was granted his release.

The Reds and Phillies both made offers for Dodger star Jackie Robinson, the Phillies also seeking outfielder Carl Furillo and Gilliam. But all talks between Brooklyn and Philadelphia fell through when the Dodgers asked for left-handed pitching star Curt Simmons and catcher Smoky Burgess.

Rules Changes

Club owners approved a new rule prohibiting anyone owning stock in one club from buying stock in another. The rule was aimed at Arnold Johnson, owner of Yankee Stadium at the time he bought the Athletics. Johnson had been forced to sell the stadium as a condition of his purchase of the team.

Giles proposed a new rule declaring that any "official game" stopped "by rain, darkness or for any other reason before nine innings" would be treated as a suspended game, to be completed at a later date. His action was viewed as a response to a mid-September game between the Braves and Dodgers called by rain in the last of the fifth with Brooklyn leading.35 Cost-conscious NL club owners, however, rejected this proposal "almost unanimously" in an undisclosed vote.36

A rules committee chaired by Jim Gallagher of the Cubs presented five changes to the game's rules, all of which were adopted. The committee also included International League President Frank Shaughnessy, Nashville owner Larry Gilbert, Cleveland GM Greenberg, Tigers GM Muddy Ruel, Boston GM Joe Cronin, Dodgers minor-league director Fresco Thompson, PONY League President Vince McNamara, and Phillies executive George Fletcher. These were the changes:

1. A rule was changed to demand that the pitcher deliver the ball within 20 seconds after it has been returned to him. The third-base umpire was directed to monitor this with a stopwatch. Previously, the count had begun when the pitcher took the rubber, and in truth it was hardly ever enforced.
2. The catcher's triangle was removed from behind home plate; instead, the catcher was to be required to remain behind the bat during an intentional base on balls.
3. A technicality regarding the submission of lineup cards was removed. This changed stemmed from an awkward protest that arose during a Buffalo victory over Toronto the previous season. Toronto manager Luke Sewell had written the name of the same player at two positions on his card. The error had not been detected until after the lineups were turned in. The rule was amended to say that in case of such an obvious error, the umpire would have the right to make the change once the error was called to his attention, assuming it was done before the game began.
4. The catcher interference rule was rewritten to give the batter first base and all runners an additional base. Previously, runners had only been permitted to advance on catcher's interference if they were forced.
5. The rules committee also approved the use of laminated bats.37

Major-League Draft

At the major-league draft, held before the meetings began, the following players were taken:

Round 1: Roberto Clemente, outfielder, Montreal Royals, by Pittsburgh Pirates; Art Ceccarelli, left-handed pitcher, Birmingham Barons, by Kansas City Athletics; Jim King, outfielder, Rochester Red Wings, by Chicago Cubs; Bob Kline, infielder, Toronto Maple Leafs, by Washington Senators; Glen Gorbous, outfielder, Montreal Royals, by Cincinnati Redlegs; Ben Flowers, right-handed pitcher, Louisville Colonels, by Detroit Tigers; Joe Trimble, right-handed pitcher, Burlington Pirates, by Boston Red Sox; Roberto Vargas, left-handed pitcher, Indianapolis Indians, by Milwaukee Braves; Mickey Grasso, catcher, Indianapolis Indians, by New York Giants.

Round 2: Bob Spicer, right-handed pitcher, Los Angeles Angels, by Kansas City Athletics; Vicente Amor, right-handed pitcher, Oklahoma City, by Chicago Cubs; Jerry Dean, left-handed pitcher, Buffalo, by Cincinnati Reds

Round 3: Cloyd Boyer, right-handed pitcher, Rochester Red Wings, by Kansas City Athletics.38

Odds and Ends

On December 7 the Yankees announced the signing of Elston Howard as the franchise's first black player. Howard had batted .331 for Toronto in 1954. With the trade of Gene Woodling to Baltimore, Howard was seen as a prospect for left field, as well as at catcher, his natural position.39

American League officials honored Washington's owner Clark Griffith in recognition of his 85th birthday, November 21. At the actual celebration a few weeks earlier, the gifts included an engraved silver bullet presented by television's Lone Ranger. President Eisenhower wired his congratulations, expressing "sincere respect and appreciation for the wonderful contribution you have made, over many years, to our great national sport."⁴⁰

NL owners adopted a new constitution and rules, drawn up by league treasurer Fred Fleig in conjunction with Cubs business manager Jim Gallagher and Milwaukee GM John Quinn. They also replaced the league's board of directors with three club representatives, one each from Brooklyn, Chicago, and Cincinnati.

They also re-elected Giles to another four-year term as league president; his contract was due to expire in 1955.

The retirement of umpire Bill McGowan for health reasons was announced. He had umpired for 30 years, but had been ill for part of 1954. He would succumb to a heart attack just days later.

The Post-mortem

Wrigley left the meeting championing expansion, but also advocating interleague cooperation. "Baseball simply refuses to recognize that we are living in a changing world," he said. "If it doesn't alter its attitude soon … the parade will have passed it by." He cited its hesitation about entering Los Angeles as a case in point. "According to the latest figures I have, Los Angeles since World War II has increased three times the total population of Kansas City. Furthermore, since the war it has had new housing units which equals the total housing units in the city of Detroit."⁴¹

Wrigley was especially critical of his fellow owners' intransigence, finding them unwilling to pull together for the common good. "The American League is against everything the National League wants, and the minor leagues are against everything the majors propose," he said. "And that's tremendously costly to baseball as a whole because industries that pull together in the common interest are invariably the most successful."⁴²

NOTES

1 He later reduced the demand on the Omaha franchise to $60,000. "Minor Leagues Vote Down TV, Radio Baseball," *Chicago Tribune*, December 2, 1954: C4.

2 "Yankees Sell Their Kansas City American Association Franchise," *New York Times*, November 30, 1954: 37.

3 "More Liberal System on Working Agreements Adopted," *The Sporting News*, December 8, 1954: 5.

4 "Lawrence Blasts Majors for Radio-TV Selfishness," *The Sporting News*, December 8, 1954: 5.

5 "Gloomy Future for Minor League Baseball Pointed Up at Houston Meeting," *New York Times*, December 4, 1954: 21.

6 "Minor Clubs Draft Only 44 Players—19 of Them Pitchers," *The Sporting News*, December 8, 1954: 9.

7 Ibid.

8 "Minors Ban Outside Radio, Television," *Los Angeles Times*, December 3, 1954: C1.

9 "Majors Veto Radio-TV curb; Minors Gain Financial Aid," *Chicago Tribune*, December 8, 1954: C1.

10 "Big Leagues Revamp Working Agreement With Minors," *New York Times*, December 8, 1954: 46.

11 "Majors Show They Want to Help," editorial, *The Sporting News*, December 15, 1954: 12.

12 "Lane Hails Hookup Prices as Great Help for the Lower Minors," *The Sporting News*, December 15, 1954: 8.

13 "Majors Show They Want to Help."

14 "Owner of Portsmouth Club Files Suit Against Majors for $250,000," *Hartford Courant*, November 23, 1954: 27.

15 "TV Question Ticklish," *New York Times*, November 28, 1954: S10.

16 "Majors Show They Want to Help."

17 "'Silly' to Say Farm System Is Failing, Declares Rickey," *The Sporting News*, December 15, 1954: 2.

18 Ibid.

19 "Yankees Sign Howard, Then Send Negro Star to Play Winter Ball," *New York Times*, December 8, 1954: 46.

20 Ibid.

21 "White Sox Boss Active at New York Convention: Most Valuable Expansion Talk Sample Schedule," *Christian Science Monitor*, December 7, 1954: 18.

22 "Wrigley Predicts Majors Here Soon," *Los Angeles Times*, November 24, 1954: C1.

23 "Yankees Sign Howard, Then Send Negro Star to Play Winter Ball."

24 "AL to Stop, Look and Listen on Moves," *The Sporting News*, December 15, 1954: 12.

25 "Wrigley Predicts Majors Here Soon."

26 Ibid.

27 Dick Young, "Clubhouse Confidential," *The Sporting News*, December 8, 1954: 16.

28 "Frick Favors Third Major League," *The Sporting News*, December 15, 1954: 10.

29 Ibid.

30 "Third Major Loop Favored by Frick," *The Sporting News,* December 15, 1954: 10.

31 "Majors Veto Radio-TV Curb; Minors Gain Financial Aid."

32 "Big Leagues Revamp Working Agreement With Minors."

33 Dick Young, "Clubhouse Confidential," *The Sporting News,* December 8, 1954: 16.

34 Bob Broeg, "Cards' Trade Puts Kid Boyer On Spot, Along With F. Smith," *The Sporting News,* Dec. 15, 1954: 11.

35 "Rival Major Leagues to Give Expansion Serious Consideration," *Hartford Courant,* December 5, 1954: B4.

36 "Chisox Secure Walt Dropo in Big Deal With Tigers," *Hartford Courant,* December 7, 1954: 15.

37 "New Rule Requires Clocking at Meeting," *The Sporting News,* December 15, 1954: 11.

38 "Major Draft," *The Sporting News,* December 1, 1954: 6.

39 "Yankees Sign Howard, Then Send Negro Star to Play Winter Ball."

40 "Griffith Honored on 85th Birthday," *New York Times,* November 22, 1954.

41 "Study Suburban Parks, Woo Older Fans—Wrigley," *The Sporting News,* December 8, 1954: 2.

42 Ibid.

1955
MAJORS AND MINORS CLASH OVER MONEY

By Dale Voiss

THE 1955 MAJOR-LEAGUE BASEBALL season went pretty much as predicted, except for the climactic event. The New York Yankees won their sixth American League pennant in seven years, but this time they lost the World Series to their crosstown rivals, the Dodgers, who won their only World Series while based in Brooklyn. A pair of catchers, the Dodgers' Roy Campanella and the Yankees' Yogi Berra, captured their leagues' MVP awards.

While the season had been an enjoyable one, there was concern among those who held the future of the game in their hands as the annual Winter Meetings loomed at the end of November. The number one reason? Television. TV was having a growing impact on American culture as a whole, and baseball was no exception. Not surprisingly, TV was also playing a role in the rancor developing between the major leagues and the minor leagues. Baseball Commissioner Ford Frick said before the meetings opened that "the problems of baseball can be summarized under the heading of 'Television and Radio.'"[1]

There was a growing concern among baseball people that television was serving as a distraction to fans, many of whom would rather sit at home and watch television rather than attend games. This problem was made no easier by the continued apprehension among minor-league owners that radio and TV broadcasts of major-league games into their home areas were hurting minor-league attendance, which had declined. (Minor-league attendance had dropped 45 percent since the end of World War II.[2])

There was a lingering animosity between the majors and minors over the broadcasts. In November of 1954 the Portsmouth (Virginia) club in the Class-B Piedmont League had sued the majors for a quarter of a million dollars, claiming that games being broadcast into Portsmouth were hurting the team financially.[3]

As a result, much of the talk at both the minor- and major-league Winter Meetings centered on broadcasting. Things became more contentious when Cincinnati Reds president Gabe Paul referred to minor-league owners as "plain lazy," and blamed falling minor-league attendance on indolence, rather than the broadcast troubles. Some of the minor-league magnates were "just plain lazy," Paul said. He was rebuked by Harold Cooper, general manager of the International League's Columbus (Ohio) club. Cooper claimed that Paul was "the worst offender" on the broadcast issue because Reds games were being broadcast into Columbus.[4] This acrimony continued into the next year and resulted in Paul and Cooper becoming involved in a fistfight at the 1956 meetings.

The four-day minor-league meetings opened at the Deshler-Hilton Hotel in Columbus on November 28, the city which was also the home of minor-league headquarters. Just as the minor-league meetings were opening, Brooklyn Dodgers president Walter O'Malley proposed that the revenue from a proposed televised "game of the week" be split equally between major- and minor-league teams. O'Malley said the arrangement would result in a $1.5 million windfall for the minor leagues and a like amount for the major-league clubs.[5] Minor-league teams were delighted to hear O'Malley's proposal but did not add the item to the meeting's agenda.

Despite O'Malley's efforts, the minors' concerns remained. On November 30 George Trautman, the president of the National Association of Professional Baseball Leagues, the minor-league organization, told the delegates that "baseball men everywhere needed to begin to look at what was best for the game instead of what was best for their individual self-interest."⁶ He also warned the majors that the minors would "shortly be unable to furnish the recruits for major league play" if changes weren't made.⁷ There later was an announcement that the minors would insist on a fair deal when they went to renew the major/minor-league agreement, which was set to expire in January 1957. Ultimately the majors rejected the minor leagues' proposal to limit broadcasts to a team's "home territory."⁸

On December 1, as their meetings were closing, the minor-league owners agreed in executive session to keep the current bonus rule in effect. The rule stated that a player signed for more than $4,000 must be kept on the club's roster for two years. There had been a proposal to allow these players to be sent down to the minors but make them eligible for the annual player draft after one or two seasons.

In another sign of the animosity the minors felt toward the big leagues, they voted to cut the time a returning serviceman could be kept on the roster before being counted against the player limit. The limit had been one year but the minors voted to cut it to 30 days, an action that needed concurrence from the major leagues.

Also discussed at the minor-league meetings was what to do about the Miami situation. Miami had developed into a very lucrative market and two Triple-A leagues, the International and the American Association, desired to locate a franchise there.

A leading player in this discussion was the Milwaukee Braves, who wanted to relocate their Triple-A Toledo franchise to Miami. But the Phillies won the Miami sweepstakes; they were given permission to move their Triple-A team from Syracuse, New York, to Miami, where they became known as the Marlins. (This solution, however, proved to be short-lived. After the 1960 season, the Phillies moved their affiliate back to upstate New York, this time to Buffalo.)

FRICK'S GROUNDWORK FOR FORMULATING A POLICY ON RADIO AND TELEVISION

"We talked with the Department of Justice and proposed a test case which would have given baseball ground rules to follow in dissemination of games by radio and television. We said: 'Why don't we pass a rule which we think is reasonable and fair and [the Justice Department] will sue us immediately and get an injunction that will stop the rule from operating and thus avoid any possibility of triple damage suits by individual stations. Then, by mutual agreement, whoever loses will carry the case to the Supreme Court for a final decision.'"*

---

* "Justice Dept. Turns Down a Majors' Offer," *Carroll Daily Times Herald*, December 6, 1955: 2.

There was also a suggestion by International League President Frank Shaughnessy that the league begin to schedule games with teams from the American Association. Shaughnessy said baseball should try new things to entice fans to come to games.

Commissioner Frick had suggested to the US Department of Justice that baseball be allowed to draw up its own broadcasting rules. On November 25 the Justice Department declined to endorse the proposal, saying that localities could not be deprived of the radio and television broadcasts.⁹

A nationwide survey of 20,000 people taken on behalf of major-league baseball showed that fans wanted a game that was played at a faster pace. They also wanted to have better parking at the ballpark and lower concession prices, and indicated a growing interest in the game. Nevertheless, baseball felt it was losing its share of the entertainment dollar because although the game was growing in popularity it wasn't seeing increased revenue from that growth. Frick, believing that the fans' complaints needed to be addressed, encouraged a discussion on how to improve overall baseball revenue. It was becoming harder to draw fans now that so many of them had television in their homes.[10]

The major-league meetings began December 5 at the Palmer House in Chicago with the American and National Leagues meeting in separate sessions for two days before going into joint session.

The American League immediately addressed the problem of slow games. The average game in 1955 was 2 hours and 31 minutes, the longest in the game's history. AL President Will Harridge asked the owners to come up with some ideas to speed up games.[11]

Two significant on-field rules were passed at the meetings. In an effort to address concerns over the speed of the game, the American League announced that it had adopted a rule allowing only one visit to the mound by a manager, coach, or other nonplayer while the same pitcher was pitching. A second such trip would result in the removal of the pitcher. (Visits by catchers or other players would not be affected.)[12]

The NL did not adopt the rule, but did pass one that required all hitters to wear batting helmets.[13]

As the meetings were closing, the major-league magnates said they were willing to work with minor-league leaders in striking a new major/minor-league agreement, but they rejected two proposed amendments from the minors. They voted down the idea that the majors ban broadcasts into the home area of minor-league teams. (The Justice Department had already warned baseball that this would be illegal.) Also, they declined to ratify the minors' proposal to lower from one year to 30 days a returning serviceman's exemption from counting on the player limit.[14]

In the player acquisition side of the meetings, on November 29 the Rule 5 player draft was held in Columbus. It was just the third time both the major-league and minor-league player drafts were held on the same day. Ten players, eight of them pitchers, were taken by major-league clubs. The most significant draftee was former New York Giants star outfielder-first baseman (and future Hall of Famer) Monte Irvin, whom the Chicago Cubs selected from the Giants' Minneapolis farm team.

On the 30th the Detroit Tigers acquired right-handed pitcher Virgil Trucks from the White Sox for reserve outfielder John Phillips. The 38-year-old Trucks had spent his first 12 seasons with Detroit before being dealt to the St Louis Browns in a six-player trade in December of 1952. Six months later he was swapped again, to the White Sox.

In other player news, right-handed pitcher Hal Jeffcoat announced he would retire from baseball after being traded by the Cubs to the Reds. Jeffcoat, who had spent the first eight years of his career with the Cubs, later changed his mind and reported to the Reds, where he pitched through the 1959 season.

The Cubs traded third baseman Randy Jackson and right-hander Don Elston to Brooklyn for three players. One of the three, outfielder Moose Moryn, became an All-Star in Chicago, reaching double digits in home runs for four straight years. Third baseman Don Hoak went on to have excellent seasons in Cincinnati and Pittsburgh, while controversial right-hander Russ Meyer proved to be almost at the end of the line.

In a sad note, while the major-league meetings were being held, the announcement came that the great Honus Wagner had passed. Wagner died in Pennsylvania at the age of 81. Many words were spent talking about the life of the Hall of Fame shortstop.

The 1955 Winter Meetings were essentially about the broadcasting problem. With television making deeper inroads into American life, baseball needed to find a way to make it work to the financial benefit of all parties.

NOTES

1 Dan Daniel, "Frick Suggests Policy Shaping Role for Office," *The Sporting News*, November 23, 1955.

2 Edward Prell, "Majors Seek New Radio-TV Plan," *Chicago Tribune*, December 6, 1955: C3.

3 Clifford Kachline, "Dallas Still Pushes Burnett's Buttons on Majors Domination," *The Sporting News*, November 30, 1955.

4 Earl Lawson, "Clubs Depend Too Much on Majors' Help," *The Sporting News*, November 30, 1955.

5 "O'Malley Has Plan for Minors," *Washington Post and Times Herald*, November 30, 1955.

6 "Majors Warned That Minors May Be Unable to Supply Talent," *Hartford Courant*, December 1, 1955: 23.

7 Ibid.

8 Irving Vaughn, Majors Veto Suggestions by Players," *Chicago Tribune*, December 7, 1955: C1.

9 John Drebinger, "Baseball Plan to Get Government Ruling on Radio, TV Curbs Hits Snag," *New York Times*, December 6, 1955: 48.

10 United Press, "Frick Wants Fans' Peeves Considered in Order to Get Entertainment $ Share," *Hartford Courant*, December 6, 1955: 15.

11 Ibid.

12 Harold Kaese, "Fenway Games Slowest in League, but Rival Managers to Blame," *Boston Globe*, December 7, 1955: 26.

13 Ibid.

14 Vaughn.

1956
A LOVE-FEST

By Jim Wohlenhaus

THE 1956 WINTER MEETINGS OF THE two major leagues were scheduled to be held December 10-12, 1956 at the Palmer House in Chicago.

As was customary, the minor leagues met before the major leagues, and in 1956 the National Association Winter Meetings were held in Jacksonville, Florida, from December 3 to 6 at the George Washington Hotel. Out of that conclave came proposals that affected the major leagues at their meetings. Many of the same people attended both meetings, so since most of the minors' proposals were accepted, it could be said afterward that the minors were having a love-fest with the major leagues. At least in December of 1956.

The Minor Leagues' Winter Meetings

In a preview of the minor-league meetings, Clifford Kachline wrote in *The Sporting News* that there were few "hot potato" issues before the minors' convention.[1] Kachline laid out the areas that would be under discussion:

- A proposal by the Austin club of the Double-A Texas League for the radio and television broadcast of a major-league "Game of the Day," with the majors and minors splitting the proceeds. Understandably, the proposal was expected to be doomed.
- Four amendments to the major/minor-league agreement related to the bonus rule, either to eliminate it entirely or to substitute a draft of first-year players. This, too, was expected to be defeated, given general satisfaction with the existing rule, though an alternate plan, allowing major-league clubs to select up to three players, was given a 50/50 chance of passing.
- An amendment requiring big-league teams to cut down to three players above the limit by Opening Day was thought to have some chance of passage. This would help minor-league clubs operate closer to full strength, rather than have to wait for a later cutdown date by the majors.
- The Pacific Coast League might expect to lose some of the privileges of separate "open class" status previously accorded it, Kachline wrote.

About all that came of any kind of broadcast discussion was a fistfight between general managers Gabe Paul of the Cincinnati Redlegs and Harold Cooper of the Columbus Jets of the Triple-A International League. Cooper believed that Paul was not cooperating and was beaming Cincinnati games into the Columbus area. When Paul spotted Cooper at the session, he snapped at him, "You're a damned liar, going around saying those things about me."

"You can't call me a liar," Cooper shouted back and swung a left that grazed Paul's shoulder.

The two men scuffled until other delegates separated them. Eventually, the two combatants dropped the issue.[2]

As for the bonus situation, the discussions centered on the requirement that a player given more than $4,000 for signing his first contract would be considered a bonus player and must be retained on the big league club roster for two years.

The amendments consisted of a proposal by the Detroit Tigers to eliminate all bonus regulations. As a substitute measure, the Chicago White Sox and Cincinnati Redlegs proposed the establishment of a draft of first-year players.

As anticipated, most major-league organizations were satisfied to stick with the present rule and all four proposals were defeated.

The matter of Opening Day major-league rosters was arguably the most important issue discussed at the meeting of the minor leagues. The owners felt that getting the better players at the very beginning of their season would help them immensely at the gate, instead of having to wait to see who might come their way later. Some said it was hard to get people to buy tickets by promoting the fact that better players were coming.

Although many trades were said to be in the works, only one deal took place during the minor-league meetings. The Tigers sent right-handed pitchers Ned Garver and Virgil Trucks, southpaw Gene Host, and first baseman Wayne Belardi, plus $20,000, to the Kansas City Athletics for infielder Jim Finigan, right-handers Jack Crimian and Bill Harrington, and first baseman Eddie Robinson. Edward Prell of the *Chicago Tribune* wrote that the trade "was dominated by tired, high salaried ball players."[3]

The major-league and minor-league drafts were held in that order. There was grumbling that this could be the smallest major-league draft ever. This was attributed to a lack of capable players and the fact that major-league teams were "hiding" their best players on teams in the Open Classification Pacific Coast League. Nine players were drafted; 10 had been selected in 1955 and 13 in 1954. The 1956 draftees were:

Ed Blake (right-handed pitcher), by Kansas City from Toronto (independent).

Jerry Lynch (outfielder), by Cincinnati from Hollywood (a Pittsburgh farm team).

Lloyd Merritt (right-handed pitcher), by St. Louis from Richmond (Yankees).

Cal Neeman (catcher), by Chicago Cubs from Denver (Yankees).

Tom Patton (catcher), by Baltimore from Omaha (St. Louis).

Bob G. Smith (left-handed pitcher), by St. Louis from San Francisco (Red Sox).

Jack Spring (left-handed pitcher), by Boston from Miami (Philadelphia).

Norm Larker (first baseman-outfielder), by Chicago White Sox from Montreal (Brooklyn).

Gil Coan (outfielder), by Detroit from Minneapolis (New York Giants).

Eleven players were taken in the minor-league draft:

Chuck Essegian (outfielder), by St. Louis from Sacramento (independent).

Marion Fricano (right-handed pitcher), by Cincinnati from Memphis (White Sox).

Bill Froats (left-handed pitcher), by New York Giants from Memphis (White Sox).

Roger McCardell (catcher), by New York Giants from Jacksonville (Milwaukee).

Eddie Phillips (infielder-outfielder), by Detroit from Omaha (St. Louis).

Leo Posada (outfielder), by Kansas City from Corpus Christi (Milwaukee).

Daryl Robertson (infielder), by Milwaukee from St. Cloud (New York Giants).

Bob Thorpe (outfielder), by Detroit from Wichita (Milwaukee).

Charlie White (catcher-third baseman), by Baltimore from Wichita (Milwaukee).

Ed White (outfielder), by New York Giants from Memphis (White Sox).

Maury Wills (shortstop), by Cincinnati from Pueblo (Brooklyn).

In another development, college spokesmen appeared before the minor-league convention and urged adoption of a rule to protect college athletes from professional scouts. The major leagues had a ban against signing college players during their freshman or sophomore year The minor leagues had no such ban. Nothing came of this.

The minor-league delegates voted to change their organization's name from the National Association of Professional Baseball Leagues to the National Association of Baseball.[4] They also agreed to drop the term "minor league" from all literature.[5] The major/minor-league agreement was rechristened the "professional baseball agreement."[6] The Mexican League, citing the fact that there were professional baseball teams in Canada, Cuba, and Mexico, in addition to those in the United States, suggested that the name be changed to the International Association, but nothing came of that, either.[7]

Two other proposals were passed. One was to lower, from one year to 30 days, the time when a returning serviceman does not count on the player roster. (The proposal had been vetoed by the major leagues the year before.) The other was for the consolidation of the minor and major leagues' winter meetings.

The Major Leagues' Winter Meetings

The major-league meetings took place in Chicago. It was scheduled for December 10-12, but the delegates finished their business early and adjourned after only two days.

On December 10 the American and National Leagues met separately to take care of business pertaining to their respective leagues. Among other things, the American League re-elected President Will Harridge to a 10-year term.

The junior circuit also amended its constitution to provide for a two-out-of-three playoff in the event of a first-place tie—the same as in the National League. Previously, AL rules called for a one-game playoff, as had occurred in 1948.

In the major leagues, visiting teams receive a share of gate receipts, and the National League owners rejected a request by the Cincinnati club that the share be raised to 40 cents on all admissions over 91 cents. There was agreement in another area, however—postponed games that had to be played after a team's last visit to a city should be played off in that city, if at all possible, if they had a bearing on the championship.

Other than that, not much happened in the league meetings, and the joint major-league meeting took place on December 11, with Commissioner Ford Frick presiding.

At the joint session the majors:

Adopted a 28-player roster limit by Opening Day, affirming the proposal from the minor leagues.

- Rescinded the rule banning the signing of a college player from the start of his sophomore year until his class has graduated or he has turned 21. In this action the major leagues acceded to the policy of the minors, who refused to accept any restriction on the signing of college players.
- Agreed to hold the Winter Meetings in the same city with the National Association, with the meetings to be held in a minor-league city in odd-numbered years and a major-league city in even-numbered years.
- Rejected, for the second time in four years, Cleveland general manager Hank Greenberg's proposal for interleague play.[8] Greenberg's proposal was strongly resisted by his own American League.[9]
- With air travel by teams increasing, one of the more important discussions by the major leagues concerned "disaster plans."[10] The owners recognized the need for a plan that could be put into effect quickly should a team be wiped out in a plane crash. If this happened, they agreed, the seven other clubs in the affected team's league would submit lists of 10 players apiece, with the victim of the catastrophe being permitted to select three from each club. The American League proposed a price of $50,000 for the first player, $75,000 for the second player, and $100,000 for the third taken from a club. Each league named a three-man group to work out details.

Two trades were consummated on the last day. The New York Yankees traded catcher Charlie Silvera, a player to be named, and cash to the Chicago Cubs for another player to be named later (it turned out to be catcher Harry Chiti). The Cubs then traded catcher Hobie Landrith, left-handed pitcher Jim Davis, right-handed pitcher Sam Jones, and utilityman Eddie Miksis to the St. Louis Cardinals for right-handed pitcher Tom Poholsky, left-handed pitcher Jackie Collum, catcher Ray Katt, and minor-league infielder Wally Lammers.

SOURCES

In addition to the sources mentioned in the Notes, the author consulted Retrosheet.org and the following articles:

Bailey, Mercer. "Minors Ask Majors to Cut Squads," *Washington Post and Times Herald,* December 7, 1956.

Daniel, Dan. "Another Minor League Convention," *The Sporting News,* December 5, 1956.

Drebinger, John. "Giants, Eager for Trades, Press for Thomas of Pirates," *New York Times*, December 5, 1956.

———. "Change in Majors' Player-Limit Rule Looms as Minors Open Convention; Early Roster Cut to 28 Is Favored," *New York Times*, December 6, 1956.

———. "Player Limit, Interleague Games Top Issues on Majors' Agenda," *New York Times*, December 9, 1956.

———. "Giants, Dodgers Still Seek Deals," *New York Times*, December 13, 1956.

———. "Major League Owners Lift All Restrictions on Signing of College Players," *New York Times*, December 12, 1956.

Kachline, Clifford. "Surprise Resolution Hails Majors for Financial Help," *The Sporting News*, December 12, 1956.

Munzel, Edgar. "Majors Bury College Rule, Coaches Howl," *The Sporting News*, December 19, 1956.

———. "Players' Pool to Be Set Up by Each Loop," *The Sporting news*, December 26, 1956.

———. "Provides 40 More Players by Mid-April," *The Sporting News*, December 19, 1956.

Prell, Edward. "Deals Simmer as Big League Chiefs Meet," *Chicago Tribune*, December 9, 1956.

Reichler, Joe (Associated Press). "Tigers Get Robinson, Finigan in 8-Man Deal," *Washington Post and Times Herald*, December 4, 1956.

———. "Majors Rescind College Rule," *Washington Post and Times Herald*, December 12, 1956.

Reidenbaugh, Lowell. "Majors Pick Only Nine in Draft Downtrend," *The Sporting News*, December 12, 1956.

"Baseball Men Angry Over Lack of Talent," *Los Angeles Times*, December 3, 1956.

"Cincinnati, Columbus Officials End Dispute," *Los Angeles Times*, December 5, 1956.

"Colleges Urge Minor League Baseball to Adopt Protective Signing Rule," *Hartford Courant*, December 5, 1956.

"Frick Backs Minor League Proposal," *Harford Courant*, December 7, 1956.

"Majors Rescind College Player Rule," *Hartford Courant*, December 12, 1956.

"Minor Leaguer Socks Reds Gabe Paul as Fist Fight Marks Baseball Parley," *Hartford Courant*, December 4, 1956.

"Minor Leagues Fight Changes in Bonus Plan," *Boston Globe*, December 7, 1956.

"Minors Seek Earlier Date for Cutdown," *Christian Science Monitor*, December 6, 1956.

"Minors Vote Early Cuts by Majors," *Los Angeles Times*, December 7, 1956.

"Re-Election for Ten Years, A.L.'s Tribute to Harridge," *The Sporting News*, December 19, 1956.

"Tigers, A's Make Eight-Player Deal," *Los Angeles Times*, December 4, 1956.

"Trade Rumors Dominate Minor League Meetings," *Christian Science Monitor*, December 5, 1956.

"Trade Rumors Persist as Minor Meetings End," *Christian Science Monitor*, December 7, 1956.

"TV Dispute Overcome by Majors," *Hartford Courant*, December 5, 1956.

NOTES

1. Clifford Kachline, "Few Hot-Potato Issues Before Minors' Confab," *The Sporting News*, December 5, 1956: 2.

2. United Press, "Fight Enlivens Baseball Meeting," *Boston Globe*, December 4, 1946: 23. See also Tom Swope, "Gabe's Tropical Souvenirs Include Mexico Farm Club," *The Sporting News*, December 12, 1956: 6.

3. Edward Prell, "Big Leaguers Arrive for 3 Day Meeting," *Chicago Tribune*, December 8, 1956: B2.

4. United Press, "Minors Have New Name," *New York Times*, December 15, 1956: 67.

5. Clifford Kachline, "Aid Plan Makes Game One Happy Family," *The Sporting News*, December 12, 1956: 15.

6. "Minors Have New Name."

7. Ibid.

8. Harold Kaese, "Radical Inter-League Play Scheme Has Good Points ... And Weak Ones," *Boston Globe*, December 11, 1956: 14.

9. Greenberg's plan called for each team to play four games against every team in the opposite league, with the contests to count in the regular 154-game schedule. J.G. Taylor Spink, *Baseball Guide and Record Book 1957* (St. Louis: Charles C. Spink & Son, 1957), 110.

10. Edgar Munzel, "Major Leagues Shape Disaster Plan,'" *The Sporting News*, December 26, 1956: 1.

1957

SUNDAY NIGHT FIGHT

By Mike Lynch

THE 1957 BASEBALL WINTER Meetings, held in Colorado Springs, Colorado, from December 2 to 7, had many issues on the table—the relocation of the Brooklyn Dodgers and New York Giants to Los Angeles and San Francisco, respectively; remuneration to and realignment of the Pacific Coast League; major-league television rights in minor-league territories; minor-league draft and bonus rules; an appeal to the Baseball Writers Association of America (BBWAA) to adopt an open ballot when voting for awards; and even a pay-per-view television plan.

Although the move of the Dodgers and Giants to California had a major impact on the National and Pacific Coast Leagues, *The Sporting News* gave top billing to the open-ballot debate in its coverage of the meetings. In a close vote by the BBWAA, New York Yankees center fielder Mickey Mantle edged Boston Red Sox left fielder Ted Williams for the American League Most Valuable Player Award, 233 votes to 209.

Red Sox owner Tom Yawkey issued a public statement calling two of the 24 voters "incompetent and unqualified to vote" after they listed Williams 9th and 10th on their ballots.[1] Scribe Joe Cashman of the *Boston Daily Record* blamed the snub on personal animosity between the writers and the temperamental slugger. It was that animosity that cost Williams at least two previous MVP awards (and arguably a third.)[2]

Some suggested that voters should be forced to make their ballots public to hold them accountable for their selections. Others, like J. Roy Stockton, sports editor of the *St. Louis Post-Dispatch*, proposed to let the players decide who was most valuable to their respective teams, then allow a five-man committee to make the final decision.[3]

The argument for the 38-year-old Williams was that he had won his fifth batting title with a .388 average, the highest in the major leagues since he hit .406 in 1941.[4] Besides, some pointed out, he also had four more home runs than Mantle. The argument against him was equally prudent, though. "Without his bat, Williams is just another ball player," insisted Joe Williams of the *New York World-Telegram & Sun*,[5] although, to be fair, the Red Sox left fielder committed only one error in 125 games and posted a career-best .995 fielding percentage.

The argument for Mantle was that he was a five-tool player who won games with his "bat, glove, throwing arm and leg speed," and who played through injuries to help the Yankees win their 23rd pennant. Some thought utility infielder Gil McDougald was the Yankees' most valuable player, but Joe Williams balked at the notion. "More than any other member of the team, Mantle put the Yankees in the World's Series. ..."[6]

Despite the outrage, the BBWAA voted to keep their balloting secret to avoid "favorite-son pressure from home-town fans who understandably often are prejudiced in a player's behalf."[7] The writers were also concerned with "timidity or outside influences that might cause an MVP voter to vote provincially rather than nationally."[8] They also voted down a proposal to limit the ballot to only five choices rather than 10, and redefined the guidelines that determined a player's rookie status.[9]

The Sporting News also focused on the Dodgers and Giants, and what Dan Daniel called "one of the most astonishing financial situations in the history of major league ball."[10] The teams agreed to pay $900,000 to the Pacific Coast League over three years as compensation for the PCL losing its two largest markets. And the

Dodgers would have to pay $100,000 in both 1958 and '59 for the unexpired lease on Ebbets Field in Brooklyn. Not to mention having to build a new ballpark in Los Angeles, estimated at $10 million.

The Dodgers purchased Los Angeles' Wrigley Field, the PCL's Los Angeles Angels and their territorial rights, and the Fort Worth Cats of the Texas League on February 21, 1957, for $3 million.[11] They transferred Wrigley Field to the City of Los Angeles in exchange for 300 acres in Chavez Ravine where they wanted to build their stadium,[12] but until then their plan was to add seats to Wrigley, which had a capacity of only 20,457. Instead they ended up playing in the Los Angeles Coliseum, a massive football stadium that needed to be renovated to make it viable for baseball. The Dodgers also agreed to pay Los Angeles $30,000 a year for 20 years to support a recreation center next to Dodger Stadium.[13]

The Giants, on the other hand, already had a stadium waiting for them in San Francisco, albeit one with a tiny capacity. Seals Stadium, home of the PCL's San Francisco Seals and Mission Reds, held only 18,500 spectators and, even with renovations that added seats, had a capacity of 22,900 when the Giants debuted on April 15, 1958. They'd spend only two years there before moving to Candlestick Park in 1960.

The 54-year-old Pacific Coast League was turned on its head and only five of the eight teams remained intact—Portland, Sacramento, San Diego, Seattle, and Vancouver—while the Hollywood Stars, Los Angeles Angels, and San Francisco Seals searched for new cities to play in. "The rips have been stitched," wrote Bob Stevens in *The Sporting News*, "but the success of the mend depends upon the hemstitchers' ability to back up their claims and promises with thread that won't suddenly disintegrate."[14]

The Seals, a Red Sox affiliate, went 101-67 under manager Joe Gordon and copped the league championship in 1957. And they boasted the league's batting champ (second baseman Ken Aspromonte) and wins leader (left-hander Leo Kiely). The Stars finished third with a record of 94-74 and featured three PCL All-Stars in third baseman Jim Baumer, catcher Bill Hall, and right-hander George Witt. The Angels finished sixth at 80-88, but had slugging first baseman Steve Bilko, who had consecutive seasons of 55 and 56 home runs in 1956 and '57, respectively, and was the "most popular player in L.A. history in any sport up to the time the big leagues got [there]."[15]

But the three franchises were moved—the Seals went to Phoenix under Giants management and adopted the big-league club's name; the Angels moved to Spokane, Washington, and remained Dodgers property, but played as the Indians; and the Stars moved to Salt Lake City and adopted the name Bees, a Salt Lake staple in the old PCL, Utah-Idaho League, and Pioneer League.[16] Bob Cobb, a West Coast restaurant owner who had purchased the Stars in 1938 and built a ballpark with investments from Hollywood legends including Cecil B. DeMille, Bing Crosby, Gary Cooper, and Gene Autry, took a financial beating, selling the team for an estimated $145,000, far less than his asking price.[17]

The first day of the baseball meetings, held at the Antlers Hotel in Colorado Springs on December 2, featured the Rule 5 draft, with the Cleveland Indians landing outfielder Gary Geiger, who would go on to have a solid if undistinguished 12-year career, mostly with the Red Sox, and the Chicago Cubs netting infielder Tony Taylor, a future All-Star who spent 19 years in the majors, 15 of them with the Philadelphia Phillies.

But the most pressing issue was the minor leagues' fight against major-league teams that wanted to televise their games into minor-league territory on Sunday night. International League President Frank "Shag" Shaughnessy insisted that Sunday TV would be a "death blow" to the minors, and said he was ready and willing to take legal and congressional action.[18] The International League's board of directors authorized Shaughnessy to seek legal counsel and gave him permission to use as much of the circuit's $350,000 treasury as necessary.[19]

Not only did Shaughnessy have the support of the American Association, Pacific Coast League, and Texas League, but from Commissioner Ford Frick as well. "Believe me," Frick said, "if it were up to me, I'd issue an order at once, barring the Sunday telecasts. But my hands are tied."[20] Shaughnessy even went so far as to ask Congressman Emanuel Celler, a Democrat from New York and chairman of the House Judiciary Committee, to reopen its antitrust investigation of baseball from the previous summer.[21]

"The minor league complaint," wrote the *New York Times*, "is that the glamour of major league baseball, for free on television, has taken the luster off their games, cut deeply into their gate receipts and threatens them with ruin."[22] Celler called the plan "the height of folly" and claimed the majors would be "eating their young" if they televised Sunday games in minor-league territories.[23] National Association President George M. Trautman gave an impromptu speech to the newly formed Minor League Baseball Writers' Organization in which he stated, "There is an unfortunate cleavage between the majors and the minors … and yet we attempt to live in the same house."[24] Eventually, however, the majors won out.

While CBS was corralling Sunday telecasts, the International Telemeter Corporation of Los Angeles came up with a more forward-thinking plan designed to get baseball to think further into the future. Paul McNamara, the company's vice president, told convention delegates that a "pay-as-you-see" television plan could gross as much as $25 million in future World Series revenue.[25] McNamara demonstrated a closed circuit "pay-TV" model that had been in development for nine years and had drawn interest from 110 potential franchise owners. *The Sporting News* wrote that several major-league clubs, including the Dodgers and Giants, had explored the idea of a pay-per-view option rather than giving away its product on free TV.[26]

December 3 saw a sizable deal made at the major-league level when the Chicago White Sox sent future Hall of Fame outfielder Larry Doby, along with left-handed pitcher Jack Harshman, right-handed pitcher Russ Heman, and first baseman-outfielder Jim Marshall, to the Baltimore Orioles for outfielder Tito Francona, a future All-Star, former batting champ Billy Goodman, and right-handed pitcher Ray Moore. Although Doby had enjoyed another good year in Chicago, the fans had booed him during the season because his numbers weren't up to par and White Sox management felt they couldn't go into 1958 with a player the fans were so down on.[27]

The minor-league draft was also held that day but the only player of note who was drafted was former Brooklyn Dodgers wunderkind Karl Spooner, who had struck out 27 batters in his first two major-league starts, both complete-game victories, in 1954, only to see his career sputter afterward under the weight of a sore left arm. He appeared in 29 games with the Dodgers in 1955, but appeared in only 17 minor-league games in 1956-1957 before being selected by the St. Louis Cardinals in the '57 draft. (Spooner would pitch in 11 games for two Cardinal affiliates in 1958 and then retire from baseball.)

December 4 saw the trade of another future Hall of Famer when the Indians shipped veteran hurler Early Wynn and All-Star outfielder Al Smith to the White Sox for All-Star outfielder Minnie Miñoso and infielder Fred Hatfield. "I'm the happiest guy in the Broadmoor Hotel," said new Indians manager Bobby Bragan when he heard that Miñoso was coming to Cleveland. "If I had to name the six or eight most exciting players in baseball, Miñoso would be one of them. And from what I understand about the Cleveland picture, he's the type of player we need."[28]

Wynn forced his way out of Cleveland by writing a column in *The Sporting News* that expressed his frustration about rumors that he'd be dealt. "Just a week ago I was saying I wish they'd either trade me or cut out the conversation," wrote the righty hurler.[29] New Indians general manager Frank Lane got the message loud and clear and sent Wynn packing, but there was no animosity between the two. In fact, Wynn called Lane his favorite general manager and Lane kidded Wynn about using his "favorite medium" to make his point.[30]

Another deal, made on December 5, had major implications on baseball history—the Cincinnati Reds sent outfielders Curt Flood and Joe Taylor to the St. Louis Cardinals for pitchers Willard Schmidt, Marty Kutyna, and Ted Wieand. The three right-handers Cincinnati acquired won only six games for the Reds and every one of them came from Schmidt, while Flood helped the Cardinals win two World Series, won six Gold Gloves, and was named to three NL All-Star teams in his 15-year career.

A more controversial deal was consummated between the Chicago Cubs and Milwaukee Braves when the Cubs sent right-handed pitcher Bob Rush, fellow righty Don Kaiser, and outfielder Eddie Haas to the Braves for left-handed pitcher Taylor Phillips and catcher Sammy Taylor. Opponents of the deal, most of whom were National League general managers, felt the acquisition of Rush all but guaranteed another pennant for the Braves, who were defending NL champions. "What did [the Braves] use on those poor Cubs, a shotgun?" asked bewildered Phillies GM Roy Hamey.[31]

Rush was a two-time All-Star who had enjoyed his best season in 1952, when he went 17-13 with a 2.70 ERA for the Cubs, but was only 6-16 with a 4.38 ERA in 1957, and after 10 years in the majors was only 110-140 with a 3.71 ERA in 339 games. Still, men like Phillies manager Mayo Smith, Giants vice president Chub Feeney, and manager Bill Rigney, and Dodgers vice president Buzzie Bavasi were apoplectic that the Cubs would give up so much to the defending champ for so little in return.[32]

On December 6 the Phillies traded veteran southpaw Harvey Haddix to Cincinnati for slugging outfielder Wally Post in what was deemed an even swap.

Several other issues were voted on during the convention, two of which passed by substantial majority votes. A draft of four-year players was adopted and the bonus rule was repealed. Any player reserved by an Open Classification (Pacific Coast League), Triple-A or Double-A team, who had been in Organized Baseball for four years, was now subject to an unrestricted draft. Single-A players had to have only three years in Organized Baseball to be subject to the draft, and lower classifications required only two years.[33]

The bonus rule, which had been devised to curtail the wealthiest teams from signing and hoarding the best talent, had been used off and on since 1947. In its latest version it stated that any player who was paid or promised more than $6,000 must remain on a major-league roster for two years before he could be sent down to the minors. A player who signed a $4,000 contract with a minor-league club was also considered a bonus player and subject to an unrestricted draft before he could be sent to another team.[34]

"In killing the bonus rule for the second time in five years, the game has again thrown open the gates to unrestricted bidding for untested young talent," wrote *The Sporting News*.[35]

Other issues that were resolved included an amendment by the Scoring Rules Committee that allowed a scorer to change a call pending a check with players and umpires on the field. It was also suggested that direct phone lines be installed in as many major- and minor-league fields as possible so scorers could quickly and easily contact players and umpires.[36]

NOTES

1. *The Sporting News*, December 4, 1957: 14.
2. Ibid. In 1941 Williams finished second to Joe DiMaggio in MVP balloting despite hitting .406 and leading the league in several offensive categories, while DiMaggio led in only two. But the latter played for a pennant winner and had enjoyed a historic 56-game hitting streak. In 1942 Williams was head and shoulders above MVP winner Joe Gordon at the plate, but Gordon played second base for a pennant winner, while Williams's Red Sox finished nine games behind the Yankees. In 1947 Williams was the best hitter in the AL but lost to DiMaggio again by a single vote. Some voters were claimed to have listed Williams at the end of their ballots. But to be fair, others left DiMaggio off their ballots completely.
3. *The Sporting News*, December 4, 1957: 13.
4. Among players 38 or older with at least 500 plate appearances, Williams's .388 average is the highest ever.
5. *The Sporting News*, December 4, 1957: 14.
6. Ibid. Although nobody knew what Wins Above Replacement (WAR) or Win Shares (WS) were in 1957 because they hadn't been "invented" yet, the writers got the vote right and it's not really close. Mantle led the AL in both categories with 11.3 and 50.5, respectively, while Williams came in second in both with 9.7 and 35.5, respectively. In fact, going back to 1901, Mantle's Win Shares in 1957 rank 10th all-time through 2015. Williams's aren't even in the top 100.
7. *The Sporting News*, December 11, 1957: 1.
8. Ibid.
9. *The Sporting News*, December 11, 1957: 2; On October 7, 1957, the BBWAA voted to ban a player from Rookie of the Year voting if 1) he was on a major-league roster when the 25-player rule was in effect from May 15 to September 1; 2) he had more than 75 at-bats in any previous season in the majors; 3) he had pitched more

than 45 innings in any previous season in the majors. During the Winter Meetings the writers increased the at-bats limit to 90 and defined the roster status as no more than 45 days, so as not to punish a player who was merely riding the bench and not gaining experience.

10 *The Sporting News*, December 11, 1957: 1.
11 sabr.org/bioproj/park/3912a666.
12 Dodger Stadium opened on April 10, 1962, and cost $23 million to build.
13 *The Sporting News*, December 11, 1957: 6.
14 *The Sporting News*, December 11, 1957: 13.
15 baseball-reference.com/bullpen/Steve_Bilko.
16 Salt Lake City's baseball history dates back to 1901. The city's teams were known as the Elders and Skyscrapers before becoming the Bees in 1915.
17 *The Sporting News*, December 11, 1957: 1, 6.
18 *The Sporting News*, December 11, 1957, 5.
19 Ibid.
20 Ibid.
21 Ibid.
22 *New York Times*, January 16, 1958; Congress chose to do nothing about major-league baseball airing a Sunday "game of the week" and CBS began airing games in 1958.
23 *The Sporting News*, December 11, 1957: 5.
24 *The Sporting News*, December 11, 1957: 16.
25 *The Sporting News*, December 11, 1957: 9.
26 Ibid. Telemeter's plan included a coin-operated box that connected to any television set and would unscramble a signal when the proper amount of money was deposited. It was first tested in Palm Springs, California, in 1953 and for $1.25 box owners could watch *Forever Female*, a movie starring William Holden and Ginger Rogers. Though it was ahead of its time, Telemeter never got off the ground, serving only 5,800 households at its peak. The company signed a deal with the National Hockey League's Toronto Maple Leafs and the Canadian Football League's Toronto Argonauts in 1961, but discontinued the experiment in 1965.
27 *The Sporting News*, December 11, 1957: 4; Doby hit only 14 home runs, his lowest output since his rookie season in 1948, but his OPS+ of 127 was actually better than the 126 he had posted in 1956, when he hit 24 homers and drove in 102 runs.
28 *The Sporting News*, December 11, 1957: 3.
29 *The Sporting News*, December 11, 1957: 4.
30 Ibid.
31 *The Sporting News*, December 11, 1957: 22.
32 Ibid. Rush had a solid season for the Braves in 1958, going 10-6 with a 3.42 ERA in 147⅓ innings, but he lost his lone World Series start, and won only 7 games for them after that and was sold to the Chicago White Sox in June 1960. Kaiser never pitched for the Braves and was out of the majors at 22; Haas was great for the Braves in a 1958 cup of coffee, but suffered a compound fracture of his ankle during spring training in 1959 and spent the whole year on the disabled list. He returned in 1960 and hit his only major-league home run, but played sparingly and was out of the majors, as a player, at age 25, resurfacing in 1985 as the Atlanta Braves' manager for much of the season. Phillips was a complete bust, going 8-17 with a 5.44 ERA for the Cubs, Phillies, and White Sox from 1958 to 1963, while Taylor had one decent year with the Cubs, batting .269 with 13 homers and 43 RBIs in 1959 on his way to an undistinguished six-year career spent primarily as a backup catcher.
33 Selection prices were set at $25,000 if a player was drafted by a major-league team; $15,000 by the PCL; $12,000 by Triple A, and on down to $1,000 if a player was drafted by a Class-C club.
34 *The Sporting News*, December 11, 1957: 15.
35 Ibid.
36 *The Sporting News*, December 11, 1957: 16.

CONTRIBUTORS

MARSHALL ADESMAN has been a member of SABR for some 40 years. A former minor league General Manager and Business Manager, he also spent twenty years working at Duke University, and is the co-author (with Chris Holaday) of *The 25 Greatest Baseball Teams of the 20th Century (Ranked)*, published by McFarland and Company in 2009. Now retired, he is devoting much of his time to writing about baseball, which includes serving as an Associate Editor for this book, and to catching up on all the reading he couldn't do while he was a working stiff.

RICHARD BOGOVICH is the author of *Kid Nichols: A Biography of the Hall of Fame Pitcher* and *The Who: A Who's Who*, both published by McFarland & Co. Most recently he wrote a chapter on Jorge Comellas of the Cubs for *Who's on First: Replacement Players in World War II*, after having contributed to *Inventing Baseball: The 100 Greatest Games of the Nineteenth Century*. He resides in Rochester, Minnesota.

ANDY BOKSER has been a member of SABR since 1983. When he is not spending time with his wife and three children or watching baseball games, he runs his solo law practice in Brooklyn, New York.

STEVEN BRYANT attended Peru State College and University of California - San Diego and has a BS in business. A member of SABR since 2004, his baseball interests include Japanese baseball, ballparks, and minor league baseball. He currently works in the insurance industry and spends his free time introducing his son to baseball, and feeling guilty about making him a Padres fan.

FREDERICK C. (RICK) BUSH, his wife Michelle, and their three sons Michael, Andrew, and Daniel live in northwest Houston. He has taught both English and German and is currently an English professor at Wharton County Junior College in Sugar Land. Though he is an avid fan of the hometown Astros, his youth has left him with an abiding affinity for the Texas Rangers and Pittsburgh Pirates as well. He has contributed articles to SABR's BioProject and Games Project sites and has written contributions for upcoming SABR books about the 1986 Boston Red Sox, 1979 Pittsburgh Pirates, Milwaukee's County Stadium, and the Montreal Expos. Currently he is serving as an associate editor, photo editor, and contributing writer for a SABR book about the Houston Astrodome.

BILL FELBER is a retired newspaper editor and the author of seven books, six of them on baseball. He was the editor of the SABR publication, *Inventing Baseball*. He was recipient of the 2007 Sporting News-SABR Baseball Research Award. A contributing writer for The National Pastime Museum website, Felber has been a SABR member since 1982. He lives in Manhattan, Kansas.

ERIC FROST is a neonatal intensive care nurse in Houston. He is a graduate of Excelsior College and Texas A&M University. A lifelong Astros fan, Eric is intrigued by the ways that off-the-field events continue to influence baseball. Several years ago, he served two separate stints as a baseball umpire. To the relief of several high-school baseball coaches, Eric's umpiring career was brief, but the experience left him with an appreciation for baseball rules and a special interest in the game's behind-the-scenes roles.

AIMEE GONZALEZ holds a B.A. in Political Science/International Relations from the University of Miami and an M.A. in International Relations from New York University. She is currently a web consultant for small businesses and is working on her doctorate in Learning Technologies at the U of MN. No matter where she lives, she will always be a Twins fan. She can be contacted at agco610@gmail.com.

JEREMY GREEN is Public Services Librarian at Carroll Community College in Westminster, Maryland. He has a Masters of Library and Information Science from the University of Michigan. A Detroiter by birth, he currently resides in Baltimore and follows the Tigers as best as he can from a distance.

PAUL HENSLER received his Master's degree in History from Trinity College in Hartford, Connecticut, and is a member of the Society for American Baseball Research, as well as the Phi Alpha Theta National History Honor Society. The author of *The American League in Transition, 1965-1975: How Competition Thrived When the Yankees Didn't* (McFarland, 2013) as well as several essays on baseball published by SABR and *NINE: A Journal of Baseball History and Culture*, he has also lectured on baseball in the 1960s and made presentations at the Cooperstown Symposium on Baseball and American Culture. For more information, please visit www.paulhensler.com.

CHRIS JONES is an attorney at Anthony & Middlebrook, P.C., where his practice focuses on church and nonprofit law. He is a lifelong baseball fan and a member of SABR since 2015. The highlight of his playing days was being drafted by the Toronto Blue Jays in the 2001 amateur draft. He resides in the Dallas/Fort Worth area with his wife and four children.

STEPHEN R. KEENEY is a lifelong Reds fan and a SABR member since 2015. He graduated from Miami University in 2010 with degrees in History and International Studies, and from Northern Kentucky University's Chase College of Law in 2013. After passing the bar exam he moved from his hometown of Cincinnati to Dayton, Ohio, where he works as a union staff representative and lives with his wife, Christine.

NICK KLOPSIS is a New York-based sports journalist. His work has appeared in various print and online outlets, including *Newsday*, ACCInsider.com, the *New York Daily News*, amNewYork, and Fameology.net. He has covered major- and minor-league baseball, college football, the NFL, the Winter Olympics, mixed martial arts, and various high school sports during his short career. Nick graduated from New York University in 2011 with a bachelor's degree in Journalism and Economics. His interest in covering the Winter Meetings stems from his desire to highlight their long-standing impact on the current baseball landscape. Nick can be reached at nicholas.klopsis@gmail.com.

TED LEAVENGOOD is a SABR member and the author of three books, including *Ted Williams and the Washington Senators*, and *Clark Griffith, the Old Fox of Washington Baseball*. He is managing editor and regular contributor to the historical baseball site, Seamheads.com, and has been a frequent contributor elsewhere, including MASN Sports. Before retirement, he worked as an urban planner for the U.S. Department of Housing and Urban Development, Fairfax County, Virginia, and the City of Atlanta. He lives in Chevy Chase, Maryland, with his wife.

BOB LEMOINE holds three masters degrees but doesn't know what to actually do with them, so he returned to his first real passion: baseball history and the Red Sox. When he is not working as a high school and public librarian (okay, one degree was actually Library Information Science), he spends a ridiculous amount of time researching old newspapers and books in writing baseball biographies and game summaries for SABR, which he joined in 2013. He has a terrible tendency of rarely saying "no" to a project, as he imagines all the new research out there to do. When he does eat, sleep, and do laundry, he does them in Rochester, New Hampshire.

R. J. LESCH works as a business analyst, when he can spare the time from being a husband, stepfather, White Sox fan, and sabre fencer. He now lives in Carlisle, Pennsylvania. He studied mathematics and works with complex information systems, so naturally his baseball research interests involve ballplayers in vaudeville and the intricacies of Deadball-Era league politics. New to step-fatherhood, he is making up for lost time by taking online courses in "embarrassing dad jokes" and "boyfriend interrogation tactics."

LEN LEVIN, a SABR member since 1977, has been the copyeditor for many SABR publications. A resident of Providence, Rhode Island, he is a retired newspaper editor and adjunct journalism instructor. When he isn't busy editing for SABR, he works part-time editing the opinions of the Rhode Island Supreme Court.

GARY LEVY grew up in the suburbs of Cleveland, Ohio but now lives just outside Baltimore, Maryland. He is a committed, lifelong Cleveland Indians fan, who joined SABR in 2008. He hopes to witness a World Series championship for the Tribe before he leaves this Earth, but is not counting on it. These chapters are his first foray into baseball writing, but otherwise he has published broadly as a Developmental Psychology Professor and an Associate Provost of Budget and Planning (now at Towson University). His favorite Indians players, to date, include Nap Lajoie, Tris Speaker, Earl Averill, Hal Trosky, Al Rosen, Sandy Alomar, Kenny Lofton, and Francisco Lindor.

JASON C. LONG is a tax and real estate attorney with Steinhardt Pesick & Cohen, P.C., in Birmingham, Michigan. A former judicial clerk at the Michigan Supreme Court, he is an honors graduate of Oakland University and the University of Detroit Mercy School of Law, and attended the University of Michigan Ross School of Business. Mr. Long has published articles and chapters concerning tax and real estate legal topics, but this is his first foray into writing about baseball. A lifelong Detroit Tigers fan, Mr. Long finds the business of baseball almost as fascinating as the play on the field.

MIKE LYNCH was born in Boston in the year of Yastrzemski and has been a diehard Red Sox fan ever since. A member of SABR since 2004, he lives in West Roxbury, Massachusetts. His first book, *Harry Frazee, Ban Johnson and the Feud That Nearly Destroyed the American League*, was published in 2008 and was named a finalist for the 2009 Larry Ritter Award in addition to being nominated for the Seymour Medal. He's also written, *It Ain't So: A Might-Have-Been History of the White Sox in 1919 and Beyond* and *Baseball's Untold History: Volume I—The People*, and his work has been featured in SABR books about the 1912 Boston Red Sox and 1914 Boston Braves.

JOE MARREN is a professor and chair of the Communication Department at SUNY Buffalo State. He was an award-winning reporter and/or editor for 18 years prior to starting his academic career in 2002.

CHRIS MATTHEWS is a writer for *Fortune Magazine*, where he covers real estate, macroeconomics, and public policy.

ABIGAIL MISKOWIEC holds a BFA in Acting and a BA in Journalism from New York University, as well as an MA in Theatre Education from Emerson College. She currently teaches English in her hometown of Charleston, West Virginia.

JERRY NECHAL is a retired administrator at Wayne State University, who resides in Sylvan Lake, Michigan. He has previously written for the *Baseball Research Journal* and completed several Detroit Tiger biographies for the SABR Bio Project. In addition to SABR, he is also a member of the Mayo Smith Society. Other interests include architecture, theater, listening to live music, hiking, and mountain biking. He continues to long for a bleacher seat in old Tiger Stadium.

BILL NOWLIN found out he had an aptitude for business when he and two friends founded the Rounder Records music label. Though totally unaware of the meaning of the word "invoice" at the time (despite being a college professor), he and his partners somehow built a very successful company that has lasted over four decades. In the middle 1990s, he began to devote time again to his childhood passion of baseball, and with Jim Prime wrote *Ted Williams: A Tribute*. That was so much fun, he hasn't stopped since, now having written or edited, usually in collaboration with others, more than 50 books, mostly on baseball but also on music and history.

JIM OVERMYER is the author of two books on Negro League baseball, *Queen of the Negro Leagues, Effa Manley and the Newark Eagles*, and *Black Ball and the Boardwalk: The Bacharach Giants of Atlantic City, 1916-1929*, and has contributed to several others. He is an editor of *Black Ball*, the annual journal of black baseball history, and was a member of the National Baseball Hall of Fame special committee in 2006 that elected 17 black baseball figures to Hall membership.

DENNIS PAJOT is retired and living in Milwaukee, Wisconsin. His research hobby is Milwaukee baseball of the 19th Century and the Deadball Era. He has authored two books on baseball: *The Rise of Milwaukee Baseball—The Cream City from Midwestern Outpost to the Major Leagues, 1859-1901* and *Baseball's Heartland War, 1902-1903—The Western League and American Association Vie for Turf, Players and Profits*, both published by McFarland & Company, Inc.

JACOB POMRENKE is the Director of Editorial Content for the Society for American Baseball Research. He is also the editor of *Scandal on the South Side: The 1919 Chicago White Sox*, published in 2015, and chairman of SABR's Black Sox Scandal Research Committee. He lives in Scottsdale, Arizona, with his wife, Tracy Greer, and their cats, Nixey Callahan and Bones Ely.

SILVIO SANSANO is a secondary school history teacher, a graduate in History and Political Science from the University of Toronto. Silvio spent three years as a sports journalist for the Varsity Newspaper at the University of Toronto. Silvio currently has his own online blog on the Varsity website, called "The Extra Inning," which strictly focuses on topics and discussions around Major League Baseball (http://thevarsity.ca/blogs/3412). His interest spans across many areas in the game, from the business side of baseball to the scouting and player development of young players. Silvio is a passionate baseball fan and a student of the game and hopes to travel to Japan soon to observe Japanese baseball culture.

ZAK SCHMOLL is a former Major League Baseball Featured Columnist at Bleacher Report. He graduated from the University of Vermont in 2013 with a double major in Business Administration and Statistics. In his free time, he plays power soccer, the fastest growing sport in the world for power wheelchair users.

TRAVIS STERN teaches theatre history and dramatic literature as an Assistant Professor in the Department of Theatre Arts at Bradley University in Peoria, Illinois. He received his PhD in Theatre from the University of Illinois at Urbana-Champaign where he wrote his dissertation on the theatrical activity of four Hall of Fame players around the turn of the Twentieth Century.

ELY SUSSMAN was fortunate to spend much of his early childhood at ticker tape parades, cheering on the New York Yankees during their 1990s dynasty. His introduction to baseball came through his fanatic father, and the Society for American Baseball Research has further fueled his obsession. After transplanting to South Florida, he received his B.S. in Broadcast Journalism and Mathematics from the University of Miami. He's now happily employed with the market's ABC television affiliate, the "One & Only" WPLG Local 10. Feel free to connect with him at MrElyminator@gmail.com.

DALE VOISS is a 56-year-old Wisconsin native and longtime Brewer fan who has written several biographies for the SABR BioProject. He currently lives in Madison, Wisconsin.

NICK WADDELL is a Wayne State University graduate in chemical engineering, but more importantly he is a lifelong Detroit Tigers fan. Currently, he resides in Chicago, and proudly wears his Old English "D" whenever he can.

STEVE WEINGARDEN has co-led the SABR Business of Baseball Committee since late 2009. He is an industrial-organizational psychologist. His work involves the fields of learning, talent management, organizational culture, and organizational development. He also has studied the effects of executive leadership and succession on MLB team performance. Previously, Steve worked in the radio industry as a newscaster, producer, and sports talk show host. Once, on the Tiger Stadium infield, Ernie Harwell invited Steve to call him on his home phone number. Steve has received communications awards, published in academic outlets and with professional associations. He learns something new every day.

JIM WOHLENHAUS is retired and now has more time to devote to baseball history. He doesn't have a specific interest, except prior to 1961. He listens to games still, but does not follow them on television as the productions are too "Hollywood." In 1961, Jim was batboy for the Denver Bears, the AAA American Association team of the Detroit Tigers. The best player on that team was probably Dick McAuliffe. He has been a Retrosheet volunteer off and on for years and was the first MLB datacaster covering the Colorado Rockies.

A lifelong Pirates fan, **GREGORY H. WOLF** was born in Pittsburgh, but now resides in the Chicagoland area with his wife, Margaret, and daughter, Gabriela. A Professor of German Studies and holder of the Dennis and Jean Bauman Endowed Chair in the Humanities at North Central College in Naperville, Illinois, he edited the following SABR books: *Thar's Joy in Braveland. The 1957 Milwaukee Braves* (2014), *Winning on the North Side: The 1929 Chicago Cubs* (2015), and *A Pennant for the Twins Cities: The 1965 Minnesota Twins* (2015). He is currently working on a project about the Houston Astrodome and co-editing a book with Bill Nowlin on the 1979 Pittsburgh Pirates.

SABR BioProject Team Books

In 2002, the Society for American Baseball Research launched an effort to write and publish biographies of every player, manager, and individual who has made a contribution to baseball. Over the past decade, the BioProject Committee has produced over 6,000 biographical articles. Many have been part of efforts to create theme- or team-oriented books, spearheaded by chapters or other committees of SABR.

THE 1986 BOSTON RED SOX:
THERE WAS MORE THAN GAME SIX

One of a two-book series on the rivals that met in the 1986 World Series, the Boston Red Sox and the New York Mets, including biographies of every player, coach, broadcaster, and other important figures in the top organizations in baseball that year. .
Edited by Leslie Heaphy and Bill Nowlin
$19.95 paperback (ISBN 978-1-943816-19-4)
$9.99 ebook (ISBN 978-1-943816-18-7)
8.5"X11", 420 pages, over 200 photos

THE 1986 NEW YORK METS:
THERE WAS MORE THAN GAME SIX

The other book in the "rivalry" set from the 1986 World Series. This book re-tells the story of that year's classic World Series and this is the story of each of the players, coaches, managers, and broadcasters, their lives in baseball and the way the 1986 season fit into their lives.
Edited by Leslie Heaphy and Bill Nowlin
$19.95 paperback (ISBN 978-1-943816-13-2)
$9.99 ebook (ISBN 978-1-943816-12-5)
8.5"X11", 392 pages, over 100 photos

SCANDAL ON THE SOUTH SIDE:
THE 1919 CHICAGO WHITE SOX

The Black Sox Scandal isn't the only story worth telling about the 1919 Chicago White Sox. The team roster included three future Hall of Famers, a 20-year-old spitballer who would win 300 games in the minors, and even a batboy who later became a celebrity with the "Murderers' Row" New York Yankees. All of their stories are included in Scandal on the South Side with a timeline of the 1919 season.
Edited by Jacob Pomrenke
$19.95 paperback (ISBN 978-1-933599-95-3)
$9.99 ebook (ISBN 978-1-933599-94-6)
8.5"x11", 324 pages, 55 historic photos

WINNING ON THE NORTH SIDE
THE 1929 CHICAGO CUBS

Celebrate the 1929 Chicago Cubs, one of the most exciting teams in baseball history. Future Hall of Famers Hack Wilson, '29 NL MVP Rogers Hornsby, and Kiki Cuyler, along with Riggs Stephenson formed one of the most potent quartets in baseball history. The magical season came to an ignominious end in the World Series and helped craft the future "lovable loser" image of the team.
Edited by Gregory H. Wolf
$19.95 paperback (ISBN 978-1-933599-89-2)
$9.99 ebook (ISBN 978-1-933599-88-5)
8.5"x11", 314 pages, 59 photos

DETROIT THE UNCONQUERABLE:
THE 1935 WORLD CHAMPION TIGERS

Biographies of every player, coach, and broadcaster involved with the 1935 World Champion Detroit Tigers baseball team, written by members of the Society for American Baseball Research. Also includes a season in review and other articles about the 1935 team. Hank Greenberg, Mickey Cochrane, Charlie Gehringer, Schoolboy Rowe, and more.
Edited by Scott Ferkovich
$19.95 paperback (ISBN 9978-1-933599-78-6)
$9.99 ebook (ISBN 978-1-933599-79-3)
8.5"X11", 230 pages, 52 photos

THE TEAM THAT TIME WON'T FORGET:
THE 1951 NEW YORK GIANTS

Because of Bobby Thomson's dramatic "Shot Heard 'Round the World" in the bottom of the ninth of the decisive playoff game against the Brooklyn Dodgers, the team will forever be in baseball public's consciousness. Includes a foreword by Giants outfielder Monte Irvin.
Edited by Bill Nowlin and C. Paul Rogers III
$19.95 paperback (ISBN 978-1-933599-99-1)
$9.99 ebook (ISBN 978-1-933599-98-4)
8.5"X11", 282 pages, 47 photos

A PENNANT FOR THE TWIN CITIES:
THE 1965 MINNESOTA TWINS

This volume celebrates the 1965 Minnesota Twins, who captured the American League pennant in just their fifth season in the Twin Cities. Led by an All-Star cast, from Harmon Killebrew, Tony Oliva, Zoilo Versalles, and Mudcat Grant to Bob Allison, Jim Kaat, Earl Battey, and Jim Perry, the Twins won 102 games, but bowed to the Los Angeles Dodgers and Sandy Koufax in Game Seven
Edited by Gregory H. Wolf
$19.95 paperback (ISBN 978-1-943816-09-5)
$9.99 ebook (ISBN 978-1-943816-08-8)
8.5"X11", 405 pages, over 80 photos

MUSTACHES AND MAYHEM: CHARLIE O'S THREE TIME CHAMPIONS:
THE OAKLAND ATHLETICS: 1972-74

The Oakland Athletics captured major league baseball's crown each year from 1972 through 1974. Led by future Hall of Famers Reggie Jackson, Catfish Hunter and Rollie Fingers, the Athletics were a largely homegrown group who came of age together. Biographies of every player, coach, manager, and broadcaster (and mascot) from 1972 through 1974 are included, along with season recaps.
Edited by Chip Greene
$29.95 paperback (ISBN 978-1-943816-07-1)
$9.99 ebook (ISBN 978-1-943816-06-4)
8.5"X11", 600 pages, almost 100 photos

SABR Members can purchase each book at a significant discount (often 50% off) and receive the ebook edtions free as a member benefit. Each book is available in a trade paperback edition as well as ebooks suitable for reading on a home computer or Nook, Kindle, or iPad/tablet.
To learn more about becoming a member of SABR, visit the website: sabr.org/join

The SABR Digital Library

The Society for American Baseball Research, the top baseball research organization in the world, disseminates some of the best in baseball history, analysis, and biography through our publishing programs. The SABR Digital Library contains a mix of books old and new, and focuses on a tandem program of paperback and ebook publication, making these materials widely available for both on digital devices and as traditional printed books.

Greatest Games Books

TIGERS BY THE TALE:
GREAT GAMES AT MICHIGAN AND TRUMBULL
For over 100 years, Michigan and Trumbull was the scene of some of the most exciting baseball ever. This book portrays 50 classic games at the corner, spanning the earliest days of Bennett Park until Tiger Stadium's final closing act. From Ty Cobb to Mickey Cochrane, Hank Greenberg to Al Kaline, and Willie Horton to Alan Trammell.
Edited by Scott Ferkovich
$12.95 paperback (ISBN 978-1-943816-21-7)
$6.99 ebook (ISBN 978-1-943816-20-0)
8.5"x11", 160 pages, 22 photos

FROM THE BRAVES TO THE BREWERS: GREAT GAMES AND HISTORY AT MILWAUKEE'S COUNTY STADIUM
The National Pastime provides in-depth articles focused on the geographic region where the national SABR convention is taking place annually. The SABR 45 convention took place in Chicago, and here are 45 articles on baseball in and around the bat-and-ball crazed Windy City: 25 that appeared in the souvenir book of the convention plus another 20 articles available in ebook only.
Edited by Gregory H. Wolf
$19.95 paperback (ISBN 978-1-943816-23-1)
$9.99 ebook (ISBN 978-1-943816-22-4)
8.5"X11", 290 pages, 58 photos

BRAVES FIELD:
MEMORABLE MOMENTS AT BOSTON'S LOST DIAMOND
From its opening on August 18, 1915, to the sudden departure of the Boston Braves to Milwaukee before the 1953 baseball season, Braves Field was home to Boston's National League baseball club and also hosted many other events: from NFL football to championship boxing. The most memorable moments to occur in Braves Field history are portrayed here.
Edited by Bill Nowlin and Bob Brady
$19.95 paperback (ISBN 978-1-933599-93-9)
$9.99 ebook (ISBN 978-1-933599-92-2)
8.5"X11", 282 pages, 182 photos

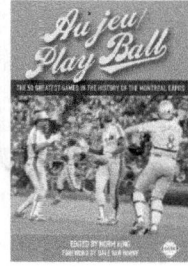

AU JEU/PLAY BALL: THE 50 GREATEST GAMES IN THE HISTORY OF THE MONTREAL EXPOS
The 50 greatest games in Montreal Expos history. The games described here recount the exploits of the many great players who wore Expos uniforms over the years—Bill Stoneman, Gary Carter, Andre Dawson, Steve Rogers, Pedro Martinez, from the earliest days of the franchise, to the glory years of 1979-1981, the what-might-have-been years of the early 1990s, and the sad, final days.and others.
Edited by Norm King
$12.95 paperback (ISBN 978-1-943816-15-6)
$5.99 ebook (ISBN978-1-943816-14-9)
8.5"x11", 162 pages, 50 photos

Original SABR Research

CALLING THE GAME:
BASEBALL BROADCASTING FROM 1920 TO THE PRESENT
An exhaustive, meticulously researched history of bringing the national pastime out of the ballparks and into living rooms via the airwaves. Every play-by-play announcer, color commentator, and ex-ballplayer, every broadcast deal, radio station, and TV network. Plus a foreword by "Voice of the Chicago Cubs" Pat Hughes, and an afterword by Jacques Doucet, the "Voice of the Montreal Expos" 1972-2004.
by Stuart Shea
$24.95 paperback (ISBN 978-1-933599-40-3)
$9.99 ebook (ISBN 978-1-933599-41-0)
7"X10", 712 pages, 40 photos

BioProject Books

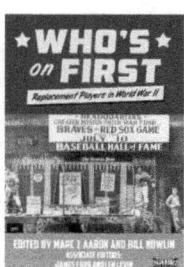

WHO'S ON FIRST:
REPLACEMENT PLAYERS IN WORLD WAR II
During World War II, 533 players made the major league debuts. More than 60% of the players in the 1941 Opening Day lineups departed for the service and were replaced by first-timers and oldsters. Hod Lisenbee was 46. POW Bert Shepard had an artificial leg, and Pete Gray had only one arm. The 1944 St. Louis Browns had 13 players classified 4-F. These are their stories.
Edited by Marc Z Aaron and Bill Nowlin
$19.95 paperback (ISBN 978-1-933599-91-5)
$9.99 ebook (ISBN 978-1-933599-90-8)
8.5"X11", 422 pages, 67 photos

VAN LINGLE MUNGO:
THE MAN, THE SONG, THE PLAYERS
40 baseball players with intriguing names have been named in renditions of Dave Frishberg's classic 1969 song, Van Lingle Mungo. This book presents biographies of all 40 players and additional information about one of the greatest baseball novelty songs of all time.
Edited by Bill Nowlin
$19.95 paperback (ISBN 978-1-933599-76-2)
$9.99 ebook (ISBN 978-1-933599-77-9)
8.5"X11", 278 pages, 46 photos

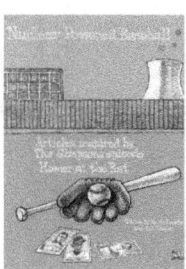

NUCLEAR POWERED BASEBALL
Nuclear Powered Baseball tells the stories of each player—past and present—featured in the classic Simpsons episode "Homer at the Bat." Wade Boggs, Ken Griffey Jr., Ozzie Smith, Nap Lajoie, Don Mattingly, and many more. We've also included a few very entertaining takes on the now-famous episode from prominent baseball writers Jonah Keri, Joe Posnanski, Erik Malinowski, and Bradley Woodrum.
Edited by Emily Hawks and Bill Nowlin
$19.95 paperback (ISBN 978-1-943816-11-8)
$9.99 ebook (ISBN 978-1-943816-10-1)
8.5"X11", 250 pages

SABR Members can purchase each book at a significant discount (often 50% off) and receive the ebook edtions free as a member benefit. Each book is available in a trade paperback edition as well as ebooks suitable for reading on a home computer or Nook, Kindle, or iPad/tablet.
To learn more about becoming a member of SABR, visit the website: sabr.org/join

Society for American Baseball Research

Cronkite School at ASU
555 N. Central Ave. #416, Phoenix, AZ 85004
602.496.1460 (phone)
SABR.org

Become a SABR member today!

If you're interested in baseball — writing about it, reading about it, talking about it — there's a place for you in the Society for American Baseball Research. Our members include everyone from academics to professional sportswriters to amateur historians and statisticians to students and casual fans who enjoy reading about baseball and occasionally gathering with other members to talk baseball. What unites all SABR members is an interest in the game and joy in learning more about it.

SABR membership is open to any baseball fan; we offer 1-year and 3-year memberships. Here's a list of some of the key benefits you'll receive as a SABR member:

- Receive two editions (spring and fall) of the *Baseball Research Journal*, our flagship publication
- Receive expanded e-book edition of *The National Pastime*, our annual convention journal
- 8-10 new e-books published by the SABR Digital Library, all FREE to members
- "This Week in SABR" e-newsletter, sent to members every Friday
- Join dozens of research committees, from Statistical Analysis to Women in Baseball.
- Join one of 70 regional chapters in the U.S., Canada, Latin America, and abroad
- Participate in online discussion groups
- Ask and answer baseball research questions on the SABR-L e-mail listserv
- Complete archives of *The Sporting News* dating back to 1886 and other research resources
- Promote your research in "This Week in SABR"
- Diamond Dollars Case Competition
- Yoseloff Scholarships

- Discounts on SABR national conferences, including the SABR National Convention, the SABR Analytics Conference, Jerry Malloy Negro League Conference, Frederick Ivor-Campbell 19th Century Conference
- Publish your research in peer-reviewed SABR journals
- Collaborate with SABR researchers and experts
- Contribute to Baseball Biography Project or the SABR Games Project
- List your new book in the SABR Bookshelf
- Lead a SABR research committee or chapter
- Networking opportunities at SABR Analytics Conference
- Meet baseball authors and historians at SABR events and chapter meetings
- 50% discounts on paperback versions of SABR e-books
- 20% discount on MLB.TV and MiLB.TV subscriptions
- Discounts with other partners in the baseball community
- SABR research awards

We hope you'll join the most passionate international community of baseball fans at SABR! Check us out online at SABR.org/join.

SABR MEMBERSHIP FORM

	Annual	3-year	Senior	3-yr Sr.	Under 30
U.S.:	☐ $65	☐ $175	☐ $45	☐ $129	☐ $45
Canada/Mexico:	☐ $75	☐ $205	☐ $55	☐ $159	☐ $55
Overseas:	☐ $84	☐ $232	☐ $64	☐ $186	☐ $55

Add a Family Member: $15 each family member at same address (list names on back)
Senior: 65 or older before 12/31 of the current year
All dues amounts in U.S. dollars or equivalent

Participate in Our Donor Program!

Support the preservation of baseball research. Designate your gift toward:
☐ General Fund ☐ Endowment Fund ☐ Research Resources ☐ _____
☐ I want to maximize the impact of my gift; do not send any donor premiums
☐ I would like this gift to remain anonymous.

Note: Any donation not designated will be placed in the General Fund.
SABR is a 501 (c) (3) not-for-profit organization & donations are tax-deductible to the extent allowed by law.

Name _____

E-mail* _____

Address _____

City _____ ST _____ ZIP _____

Phone _____ Birthday _____

* Your e-mail address on file ensures you will receive the most recent SABR news.

Dues $_____

Donation $_____

Amount Enclosed $_____

Do you work for a matching grant corporation? Call (602) 496-1460 for details.

If you wish to pay by credit card, please contact the SABR office at (602) 496-1460 or visit the SABR Store online at SABR.org/join. We accept Visa, Mastercard & Discover.

Do you wish to receive the *Baseball Research Journal* electronically?: ☐ Yes ☐ No
Our e-books are available in PDF, Kindle, or EPUB (iBooks, iPad, Nook) formats.

Mail to: SABR, Cronkite School at ASU, 555 N. Central Ave. #416, Phoenix, AZ 85004

www.ingramcontent.com/pod-product-compliance
Lightning Source LLC
Chambersburg PA
CBHW081343080526
44588CB00016B/2359